ZAGAT SURVEY

Back in 1979, we never imagined that an idea born during a wine-fueled dinner with friends would take us on an adventure that's lasted three decades – and counting.

The idea – that the collective opinions of avid consumers can be more accurate than the judgments of an individual critic – led to a hobby involving friends rating NYC restaurants. And that hobby grew into Zagat Survey, which today has over 350,000 participants worldwide weighing in on everything from airlines, bars, dining and golf to hotels, movies, shopping, tourist attractions and more.

By giving consumers a voice, we – and our surveyors – had unwittingly joined a revolution whose concepts (user-generated content, social networking) were largely unknown 30 years ago. However, those concepts caught fire with the rise of the Internet and have since transformed not only restaurant criticism but also virtually every aspect of the media, and we feel lucky to have been at the start of it all.

As we celebrate Zagat's 30th year, we'd like to thank everyone who has participated in our surveys. We've enjoyed hearing and sharing your frank opinions and look forward to doing so for many years to come. As we always say, our guides and online content are really "yours."

We'd also like to express our gratitude by supporting **Action Against Hunger,** an organization that works to meet the needs of the hungry in over 40 countries. To find out more, visit www.zagat.com/action.

Nina and Tim Zagat

ZAGAT®
CELEBRATING 30 YEARS

New York City
Nightlife
2009/10

EDITOR
Curt Gathje

Published and distributed by
Zagat Survey, LLC
4 Columbus Circle
New York, NY 10019
T: 212.977.6000
E: nynightlife@zagat.com
www.zagat.com

ACKNOWLEDGMENTS

We thank Caren Weiner Campbell, Leigh Crandall, Jonathan Durbin, Jeremiah Furr, Nathan Lacy, Nancy Lambert, Scott Laughlin, Julie Mehta, Bernard Onken, Mary Phillips-Sandy, Joanna Prisco, Brian Rattiner, Laura Siciliano-Rosen, Brendan Spiegel, Rachel Syme, Martin Tyrrell and Steve Weinstein, as well as the following members of our staff: Christina Livadiotis (assistant editor), Brian Albert, Sean Beachell, Maryanne Bertollo, Jane Chang, Sandy Cheng, Reni Chin, Larry Cohn, Bill Corsello, Carol Diuguid, Alison Flick, Jeff Freier, Andrew Gelardi, Michelle Golden, Justin Hartung, Karen Hudes, Roy Jacob, Garth Johnston, Ashunta Joseph, Cynthia Kilian, Natalie Lebert, Mike Liao, Dave Makulec, Andre Pilette, Kimberly Rosado, Becky Ruthenburg, Jacqueline Wasilczyk, Sharon Yates, Anna Zappia and Kyle Zolner.

The reviews in this guide are based on public opinion surveys. The ratings reflect the average scores given by the survey participants who voted on each establishment. The text is based on quotes from, or paraphrasings of, the surveyors' comments. Phone numbers, addresses and other factual data were correct to the best of our knowledge when published in this guide.

Our guides are printed using environmentally preferable inks containing 20%, by weight, renewable resources on papers sourced from well-managed forests. Deluxe editions are covered with Skivertex Recover® Double containing a minimum of 30% post-consumer waste fiber.

SUSTAINABLE FORESTRY INITIATIVE

Certified Chain of Custody
Promoting Sustainable Forest Management
www.sfiprogram.org

PWC-SFICOC-260

ENVIROINK™

The Inks used to print the body of this publication contain a minimum of 20%, by weight, renewable resources.

Contents

Ratings & Symbols

	Zagat Top Spot	Name	Symbols		Zagat Ratings			
					APPEAL	DECOR	SERVICE	COST

| Area,
Address &
Contact | 🅉 Tim & Nina's ⌀ | ▽ 23 | 5 | 9 | $5 |

W 50s | 4 Columbus Circle (8th Ave.) | 1/A/B/C/D to 59th St./ Columbus Circle | 212-977-6000 | www.zagat.com

Review,
surveyor
comments
in quotes

Open from sunrise to sunset, seven days a week, this "deep dive" bar with a bathroom and phone booth across the street looks like a cross between the Waldorf and a LES tattoo parlor; however, "dirt-cheap" prices, a "free-flowing tap and unlimited pretzels" draw "spaced-out crowds" of "multi-pierced patrons"; P.S. don't trip on any of the customers on the way out.

Ratings   **Appeal, Decor** and **Service** are rated on the Zagat 0 to 30 scale.

0 – 9	poor to fair
10 – 15	fair to good
16 – 19	good to very good
20 – 25	very good to excellent
26 – 30	extraordinary to perfection
▽	low response	less reliable

Cost   Our surveyors' estimated price of a typical single drink. For unrated **newcomers** or **write-ins,** the price range is shown as follows:

| I | below $7 | E | $11 to $14 |
| M | $7 to $10 | VE | $15 or more |

Symbols   🅉   highest ratings, popularity and importance
⌀   no credit cards accepted

About This Survey

This **2009/10 New York City Nightlife Survey** is an update reflecting significant developments since our last Survey was published. It covers 1,315 bars, clubs and lounges in the five boroughs, including 111 important additions. We've also indicated new addresses, phone numbers and other major alterations, and surveyed recent arrivals as well as last year's unrated properties to bring this guide up to the minute. In the spirit of the subject matter, we've also tried to make this a fun read.

WHO PARTICIPATED: Input from 6,121 enthusiasts forms the basis for the ratings and reviews in this guide (their comments are shown in quotation marks within the reviews). Collectively they bring an annual total of roughly 641,000 nights' worth of experience to this Survey. We sincerely thank these participants – this book is really "theirs."

HELPFUL LISTS: Our top lists and indexes can help you find exactly the right place for any occasion. See Key Newcomers (page 9), Most Popular (page 10), Top Ratings (pages 12–19) and the 98 handy indexes starting on page 224.

COMPANION GUIDES: In addition to covering nightlife, we also publish New York City restaurant, entertaining and shopping guides and maps, as well as guides to the surrounding suburban areas.

ABOUT ZAGAT: This marks our 30th year reporting on the shared experiences of consumers like you. What started in 1979 as a hobby has come a long way. Today we have over 350,000 surveyors and now cover airlines, bars, dining, entertaining, fast food, golf, hotels, movies, music, resorts, shopping, spas, theater and tourist attractions in over 100 countries.

INTERACTIVE: Up-to-the-minute news about openings plus menus, photos and more are free on **ZAGAT.com** and the award-winning **ZAGAT.mobi** (for web-enabled mobile devices). They make it possible to contact thousands of places with just one click.

BE A SURVEYOR: We invite you to join any of our surveys at **ZAGAT.com.** There you can share your experiences with thousands of others year-round. In exchange for doing so, you'll receive a free copy of the resulting guide when published.

AVAILABILITY: Zagat guides are available in all major bookstores as well as on **ZAGAT.com.** You can also access our content when on the go via **ZAGAT.mobi** and **ZAGAT TO GO** (for smartphones).

FEEDBACK: To improve this guide, we invite your comments about any aspect of our performance. Tell us if we missed a deserving bar or got something wrong. Just contact us at **nynightlife@zagat.com.**

New York, NY
June 17, 2009

Nina and Tim Zagat

What's New

It was a year of mixed messages for NYC nightlife. The sagging economy suggested that nightlife would stumble like every other business, and indeed 56% of our surveyors reported they were going out less than usual. Yet our openings-vs.-closings tally was strictly business as usual: 111 notable newcomers (compared with 122 last year) and only 66 closings (vs. 83 last time out). About the only thing that seemed certain was the decline of bottle service, that symbol of hedge-fund excess. Nowadays most clubs are hedging their bets, acknowledging that $400 bottles of booze are "available" but rarely required for admittance.

UP AND DOWN AND UP: If 2008 was a stellar year for rooftops, in 2009 the place to be was underground, perhaps reflecting a bunker mentality in leaner times. New basement lairs included **BEast, Bijoux, Cabin Down Below, Chloe, Macao Trading Co., RDV, 675 Bar** and **Southside,** all smallish spots with varying degrees of exclusivity. But the rooftop isn't done yet, with brand-new aeries at **Above Allen, Eden, Empire Hotel Rooftop, Hudson Terrace, mad46** and **Ravel Rooftop.**

HOT BLOCKS: The Lower East Side's Allen Street had a banner year, with five newcomers: **Above Allen, Diamond's Wine Bar, Shang Bar, Sorella** and **White Slab Palace.** A former meatpacking area in Harlem became a different kind of meatpacking scene when an old freight house at 135th Street and 12th Avenue was transformed into three happening lounge/eateries: **Body, Covo** and **Talay.** That other, more renowned Meatpacking District, long written off by trendsetters as passé, had something of a comeback with the openings of **Bijoux, The Griffin, RDV, 675 Bar, Standard Hotel Living Room** and a spin-off of **SEA.** On the flip side of the coin, the coldest block of the year was Chelsea's once-buzzing West 24th Street, where the **Cutting Room, Gypsy Tea** and **Madison** all shuttered.

NINETY-NINE BOTTLES OF BEER ON THE WALL: While the wine bar craze reached its apex last year with a record 22 debuts, its blue-collar brother, the beer bar, was building up steam. Newcomers offering extensive lists of esoteric suds included **East Village Tavern, The Gibson, Lillie's, Pony Bar** and **Stag's Head.** Still, the wine-bar phenomenon was far from finished, with a wave of fresh arrivals: **Balon, Brookvin, City Winery, Clo, Desnuda, Diamond's Wine Bar, Nectar, Pierre Loti, Sorella, Sweet & Lowdown, Vino, Vino 313** and **Vintage Irving.**

A SCENE GROWS IN BROOKLYN: Brooklyn burgeoned with a bunch of appealing new arrivals: Boerum Hill welcomed **Building on Bond,** Carroll Gardens showcased **Chestnut Bar** and **Prime Meats,** and Cobble Hill hosted **Char No. 4** and **Clover Club** (voted the year's best newcomer). Elsewhere, **Belleville Lounge, Brookvin, Cabana Bar** and **249 Bar** gave Park Slope some pizzazz, while Williamsburg rolled out **Brooklyn Bowl, Mother's, Public Assembly** and **The Richardson.**

Menus, photos, voting and more - free at ZAGAT.com

COCKTAIL ARTS: Expertly mixed, stirringly priced cocktails were served at seven new temples of mixology: **Apothéke, Clover Club, Macao Trading Co., Madam Geneva, Mayahuel, Prime Meats** and **Raines Law Room;** Sasha Petraske, whose **Milk and Honey** popularized the genre in 2000, added to his empire with **Dutch Kills** and **White Star.** Even so, many are skeptical: 51% of surveyors said that mixology was simply "an excuse to charge more for drinks."

TENPINS REVIVAL: Two new state-of-the-art bowling alleys rolled into town, jazzed up with 21st-century touches: **Brooklyn Bowl** also includes a 600-seat performance space and food by Blue Ribbon, while **Lucky Strike Lanes** offers (optional) bottle service plus a private lounge equipped with its own bar and four lanes. Meanwhile, Leisure Time Bowl in Port Authority got an overhaul and a new name, **Frames.**

GOODBYE, BABY, AND AMEN: It was last call for two nightlife legends, **Lotus** and **Scores,** now residing in that big nightclub in the sky. Other closings of note included **G Spa & Lounge, Grace, Hog Pit, Kanvas, KingSize, Le Figaro Cafe, Level V, The Plumm, Red Rock West, Rififi, Rise, Rubyfruit, Socialista** and **Spotlight Live.** (For our entire list, see page 270).

RANDOM NOTES: **Beekman Bar and Books** opened with a legal indoor smoking room, the first in the city since the tobacco ban went into effect in 2003; still, illegal smoking was considered a badge of edginess at select hip boîtes around town . . . "Secret bars," a staple of NY nightlife since Prohibition, snuck onto the scene with the hush-hush openings of **Cabin Down Below,** hidden under an East Village pizzeria, and **Bleecker Heights Tavern,** hanging over a Five Guys burger joint . . . Manhattan's prime dive-bar boulevard, the shabby stretch of Ninth Avenue behind Port Authority, welcomed two appropriately grungy arrivals, **Blue Ruin** and **508 Sports Lounge;** at the same time, dive-bar patron saint Tracy Westmoreland (founder of the notorious Siberia) decamped to Prospect Heights to open a new venture, **The Manhattans;** whether it will become a destination is anyone's guess, given its out-of-the-way address . . . Absinthe enjoyed a fleeting reign as the spirit du jour, but its popularity seemed greater among trend writers than actual patrons; similarly, batch bourbon and hand-cut ice cubes enjoyed brief vogues . . . Finally, some stats: 10% of surveyors say that NYC nightlife is "making a comeback," 67% dub it the "same as it ever was" and 23% feel it's "declining"; the LES was voted the city's hottest neighborhood, and the Meatpacking District rated the most overrated; as for music, 30% preferred DJs, 29% live music, 18% jukeboxes and 23% said silence was golden.

New York, NY
June 17, 2009

Curt Gathje

KEY NEWCOMERS

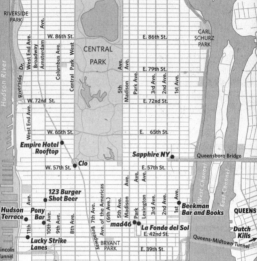

Key Newcomers

Our editors' take on the year's top arrivals. See page 269 for a full list.

See page 269 for a full list.

Above Allen	La Fonda del Sol
Apothéke	Le Poisson Rouge
BEast	Lillie's
Beekman Bar and Books	Lucky Strike Lanes
Bell House	Macao Trading Co.
Bijoux	Madam Geneva
Brooklyn Bowl	mad46
Brookvin	Manhattans
Cabin Down Below	Mayahuel
Char No. 4	Mr. West
Chloe	123 Burger Shot Beer
Clo	Pony Bar
Clover Club	Prime Meats
Delicatessen	Raines Law Room
Desnuda	RDV
Dutch Kills	Santos Party House
Eldridge	Sapphire NY
Ella	SideBar
Empire Hotel Rooftop	675 Bar
Gates	Southside
Globe	Van Diemens
Greenhouse	White Slab Palace
Griffin	White Star
Hudson Terrace	Wilfie & Nell

The year to come shows plenty of potential with such intriguing projects in the works as **Simyone,** a reworking of Lotus, the club that jump-started the Meatpacking District phenomenon; **Avenue,** a new West Chelsea lounge from Noah Tepperberg and Jason Strauss, the masterminds behind **Marquee** and **Tao**; **Warren 77,** a vintage sports-themed bar from NY Ranger Sean Avery and **Beatrice Inn** proprietor Matt Abramcyk; **Cellar Cocktail Lounge,** a posh hideaway in TriBeCa's new Smyth Hotel; and two beer gardens, **Der Schwarze Koelner** in Fort Greene and **Studio Square,** an 18,000-sq.-ft. colossus scheduled to open in Long Island City.

Most Popular – Manhattan

1 Pastis	26 Pravda
2 Buddha Bar	27 Cain Luxe
3 Balthazar	28 Dos Caminos
4 Spice Market*	29 Calle Ocho
5 Blue Water Grill	30 Marquee
6 Brother Jimmy's	31 Son Cubano
7 Hudson Hotel	32 Four Seasons Hotel Bar
8 230 Fifth	33 Ulysses*
9 Asia de Cuba	34 Blue Note
10 Tao	35 W Union Square*
11 Divine Bar	36 Blue Fin
12 Campbell Apartment	37 APT
13 Union Square Cafe	38 Angel's Share
14 Stanton Social	39 Boat Basin Cafe
15 Buddakan	40 Houston's*
16 Flatiron Lounge	41 SushiSamba*
17 Pegu Club	42 Duvet
18 Plunge*	43 Park
19 Bungalow 8	44 Brandy Library
20 Ginger Man	45 One*
21 Gramercy Tavern	46 Coffee Shop
22 Rosa Mexicano	47 King Cole Bar
23 Bar Veloce	48 Employees Only
24 d.b.a.	49 Gotham Bar & Grill*
25 Heartland Brewery	50 McSorley's

Most Popular – Brooklyn

1 d.b.a. Brooklyn	11 Wicked Monk*
2 Waterfront Ale House	12 Floyd, NY
3 Union Hall	13 Brooklyn Social
4 SEA	14 Delia's Lounge
5 Blue Ribbon Brooklyn	15 200 Fifth*
6 Joya	16 Brooklyn Brewery
7 Gate	17 Peggy O'Neill's*
8 Total Wine Bar	18 Pete's Candy Store*
9 Barcade	19 Moe's
10 Southpaw*	20 Brooklyn Inn

* Indicates a tie with place above

Most Visited

BY GENDER

FEMALE
1. Stanton Social
2. Aspen
3. Duvet*
4. Brother Jimmy's
5. Heartland Brewery
6. Libation
7. Blue Water Grill
8. Pastis
9. Spice Market
10. Rosa Mexicano

MALE
1. Brother Jimmy's
2. Heartland Brewery
3. Oak Bar
4. Spice Market
5. Aspen
6. Blue Water Grill*
7. Algonquin
8. Balthazar
9. Duvet
10. Hudson Hotel*

BY AGE

TWENTIES
1. Libation
2. Duvet
3. Brother Jimmy's
4. PS 450
5. 230 Fifth
6. Aspen
7. Home*
8. Stanton Social
9. Heartland Brewery
10. Marquee

THIRTIES
1. Brother Jimmy's
2. Stanton Social
3. Spice Market
4. Heartland Brewery
5. Aspen
6. Duvet
7. Pastis
8. Hudson Hotel
9. Blue Water Grill
10. Buddha Bar

FORTIES
1. Algonquin
2. Heartland Brewery
3. Pastis
4. Oak Bar
5. Blue Water Grill
6. Rosa Mexicano*
7. Balthazar
8. Empire Hotel Rooftop
9. Aspen
10. Nobu 57*

FIFTIES
1. Oak Bar
2. Rainbow Grill
3. Algonquin
4. Heartland Brewery
5. Union Square Cafe*
6. Zinc Bar
7. B. B. King Blues
8. Blue Water Grill
9. Balthazar
10. Blue Note
11. Tavern on the Green*

Top Appeal Ratings

Excludes places with low votes, unless indicated by a ▽.

28 King Cole Bar	Salon de Ning*
27 Otheroom	Grape & Grain
Sakagura	Von*
Stonehome	Boathouse
Daniel	'disiac*
Milk and Honey	Four Seasons Bar
PDT	21 Club*
Brooklyn Inn	Freemans
Bemelmans	Nublu
26 Louis 649	25 Brooklyn Social
Angel's Share	Clover Club*
Cafe Carlyle	Total Wine Bar
Rayuela	Pegu Club
One if by Land	Dizzy's Club
Little Branch	Jade Bar
Gramercy Tavern	Champagne Bar/Plaza
Kemia Bar	Campbell Apartment
Cávo	Vol de Nuit
Jazz Standard*	SEA
Room*	La Lanterna

BY CATEGORY

AFTER WORK/UPTOWN

27 Bemelmans
24 Shalel Lounge
 Boat Basin
23 Calle Ocho
22 Rosa Mexicano
18 Merchants, NY

AFTER WORK/MIDTOWN

28 King Cole Bar
26 Four Seasons Bar
 21 Club
25 Campbell Apartment
 Nobu 57
24 Oak Bar

AFTER WORK/DOWNTOWN

24 Church Lounge
23 City Hall
22 Ulysses
 Sequoia
21 Walker's
19 Southwest NY

ART BARS

26 Nublu
25 Box

23 Supreme Trading
 Bowery Poetry
21 KGB
 Nuyorican Poets*

BEER SPECIALISTS

27 Otheroom
26 Room
25 Vol de Nuit
 Bohemian Hall
 Mug's Ale
24 Spuyten Duyvil

BOWLING ALLEYS

24 Gutter▽
22 Bowlmor Lanes
 Lucky Strike Lanes
20 Harlem Lanes
19 300 New York

CABARETS

26 Cafe Carlyle
25 Box
 Oak Room
 Joe's Pub
24 Don't Tell Mama
23 Feinstein's/Regency

COCKTAIL EXPERTS

- 27 Milk and Honey
  - PDT
  - Bemelmans
- 26 Angel's Share
  - Little Branch
  - Freemans

COFFEEHOUSES

- 22 Grey Dog's
  - Cafe Lalo
  - Cafe Gitane
- 21 Arlo & Esme
  - Edgar's Cafe
  - Caffe Dante

COMEDY CLUBS

- 23 Comedy Cellar
- 21 Carolines
- 19 Gotham Comedy
- 18 Eastville Comedy
  - Stand-Up NY
- 17 New York Comedy

DANCE CLUBS

- 25 Touch
- 23 Cielo
- 21 Swing 46
  - Santos Party House
- 20 Aura
  - Kiss & Fly

DIVES

- 25 Jimmy's Corner
- 22 55 Bar
  - Great Lakes
  - Sophie's
  - 169 Bar
- 21 Otto's Shrunken

EUROS

- 25 Grand Bar
  - Bungalow 8
  - Balthazar
- 24 Asia de Cuba
  - Tao
  - Cain Luxe

FRAT HOUSE

- 22 Half Pint
- 21 Molly Pitcher's
  - Stout
- 20 123 Burger Shot
  - Genesis
  - Tonic East

GAY

- 24 Therapy
- 23 Vlada
- 22 Eagle
  - Easternbloc
  - xes lounge
  - Townhouse

HOOKAHS

- 23 Cloister Cafe
- 22 Kush
- 21 Babel Lounge
  - Karma
- 18 Katra
  - Moomia Lounge

HOTEL BARS

- 28 King Cole Bar
- 27 Bemelmans
- 26 Salon de Ning
- 25 Jade Bar
  - Champagne Bar/Plaza
  - Country Champ. Lounge

IRISH

- 24 Wilfie & Nell
- 23 George Keeley's
  - McSorley's
- 22 Molly's
  - Dublin 6
  - Swift

JAZZ CLUBS

- 26 Jazz Standard
- 25 Dizzy's Club
- 24 Village Vanguard
  - Smalls
- 23 Birdland
  - Blue Note*

LATIN

- 24 Ñ
- 23 Calle Ocho
  - Sala
  - Flor de Sol
  - Son Cubano
  - Ideya

LESBIAN

- 20 Cubby Hole
- 18 Henrietta Hudson
- 16 Ginger's

MATURE CROWDS

- 28 King Cole Bar
- 27 Daniel
  - Bemelmans

26 Cafe Carlyle
Four Seasons Bar
21 Club

MEAT MARKETS
25 Touch
230 Fifth
Grand Bar
Plunge
24 Tao
Cain Luxe

MUSIC CLUBS
26 Nublu
25 Joe's Pub
24 Union Hall
Bowery Ballroom
23 Beacon Theatre
Rockwood Music

NEWCOMERS
25 Clover Club
Madam Geneva
Macao Trading Co.
24 Empire Hotel Rooftop
Char No. 4
Wilfie & Nell

PIANO BARS
24 Don't Tell Mama
23 Brandy's
22 Townhouse
Marie's Crisis
21 Ella
Uncle Charlie's

POOL HALLS
21 Slate
19 Tropical 128▽
Fat Cat
18 Pressure
17 Amsterdam Billiards
15 Soho Billiards

PUNK BARS
21 Manitoba's
20 Don Hill's
19 Duff's▽
Mars Bar
18 Ding Dong Lounge▽
Trash▽

QUIET CONVERSATION
28 Black Mountain Wine▽
King Cole Bar

27 Bemelmans
Otheroom
Milk and Honey
PDT

ROOFTOPS
26 Salon de Ning
25 230 Fifth
Plunge
24 Bookmarks
Empire Hotel Rooftop
Ava Lounge

RUSSIAN
24 Pravda
21 Russian Vodka Rm.
Rasputin
KGB
20 Russian Samovar
Anyway Cafe

SPEAKEASY-STYLE
27 Milk and Honey
PDT
26 Little Branch
Freemans
25 Brooklyn Social
Death & Co

SPORTS BARS
21 40/40
Molly Pitcher's
SideBar
Lansdowne Road
20 Kinsale Tavern
Bar 108

STRIP CLUBS
22 Hustler Club
21 Sapphire NY
Ten's
20 Rick's Cabaret
18 Pussycat Lounge
Corio

WINE BARS
27 Stonehome
26 Grape & Grain
Von*
25 Total Wine Bar
In Vino
24 La Bateau Ivre

BY LOCATION

CHELSEA

25	Morimoto
	230 Fifth
	Bungalow 8
24	Buddakan
	Cain Luxe
	Bar Veloce

EAST 40s

27	Sakagura
25	Campbell Apartment
24	Bookmarks
	Top of the Tower
23	Whiskey Blue
	World Bar

EAST 50s

28	King Cole Bar
26	Four Seasons Bar
25	Four Seasons Hotel Bar
24	Le Bateau Ivre
	Vero
	Tao

EAST 60s

27	Daniel
25	Regency Hotel Bar
24	Club Macanudo
	Plaza Athénée
23	Feinstein's/Regency
22	Accademia di Vino

EAST 70s

27	Bemelmans
26	Cafe Carlyle
	Boathouse
24	Vero
	Sake Hana
21	Baraonda

EAST 80s

23	Brandy's
	Uptown Lounge
	Bar @ Etats-Unis
22	Auction House
	Cavatappo Wine
	Gaf Bar

EAST 90s

22	Biddy's
20	Kinsale Tavern
19	Blondies
17	Brother Jimmy's
13	Big Easy
	Bar East▽

EAST VILLAGE

27	PDT
26	Louis 649
	Angel's Share
	Grape & Grain
	Nublu
25	Death & Co
	In Vino*

FINANCIAL DISTRICT

24	Bridge Cafe
22	Ulysses
21	Trinity Place
20	P.J. Clarke's
19	SouthWest NY
18	Pussycat Lounge

FLATIRON/UNION SQUARE

26	Gramercy Tavern
25	Flatiron Lounge
	Eleven Madison Pk.
24	Union Square Cafe
	Tabla
23	Blue Water Grill

GARMENT DISTRICT

21	Keens Steak
	Stout
20	Rick's Cabaret
	HK Lounge
	Hammerstein Ballroom
	Mr. Black

GRAMERCY PARK

25	Jade Bar
24	Bar Jamón
23	Rose Bar
22	3Steps
	Japonais
	Molly's

GREENWICH VILLAGE

26	One if by Land
25	Vol de Nuit
	La Lanterna
	Gotham B&G
	Otto
24	Dove

LITTLE ITALY

24	La Esquina
	Obivia
23	GoldBar
	Xicala
20	Onieal's Grand St.
19	Randolph

LOWER EAST SIDE

27 Milk and Honey
26 Rayuela
  Freemans
25 Box
  Allen & Delancey
  Stanton Social

MEATPACKING DISTRICT

25 Tenjune
  Plunge
24 Spice Market
  Ono
  Buddha Bar
  Pastis

MURRAY HILL

26 Jazz Standard
25 Country Champ. Lounge
24 Asia de Cuba
  'inoteca
  I Trulli Enoteca
  Pine Tree Lodge

NOHO

26 Von
25 Madam Geneva
24 Temple Bar
  Bond Street
23 Chinatown Brasserie
  Sala

NOLITA

24 Public
  Bar Veloce
  Pravda
23 Eight Mile Creek
  Peasant*
22 Shebeen

SOHO

26 Room
25 Pegu Club
  Sway
  Blue Ribbon
  Grand Bar
  Balthazar

TRIBECA

25 Macao Trading Co.
  Brandy Library
24 Megu
  anotheroom
  Church Lounge
  Petrarca Vino

WEST 40s

26 Kemia Bar
25 Jimmy's Corner
  Oak Room
24 View Lounge
  Don't Tell Mama
  Rainbow Grill

WEST 50s

26 Salon de Ning
  'disiac
  21 Club
25 Champagne Bar/Plaza
  Touch
  Modern

WEST 60s

25 Dizzy's Club
24 Café des Artistes
  Empire Hotel Rooftop
23 Bar Masa
  MO Bar
  Stone Rose

WEST 70s

24 Shalel Lounge
  Boat Basin
23 Beacon Theatre
22 Bin 71
21 Dive 75
  Wine & Roses

WEST 80s

23 Calle Ocho
  George Keeley's
22 Cafe Lalo
21 Prohibition
  Edgar's Cafe
20 Dead Poet

WEST 90s & UP

23 Nectar
  Minton's
22 Smoke
  67 Orange Street
  Body
21 River Room

WEST VILLAGE

27 Otheroom
26 Little Branch
24 Village Vanguard
  Smalls
  Wilfie & Nell
  Employees Only

BRONX

- 21 An Béal Bocht
- 17 Yankee Tavern
- 16 Hard Rock Cafe
- 12 Stan's▽

BROOKLYN: CARROLL GARDENS/BOERUM HILL/COBBLE HILL

- 27 Brooklyn Inn
- 25 Brooklyn Social
-    Clover Club*
- 24 Char No. 4
-    B61
-    Joya

BROOKLYN: FORT GREENE

- 27 Stonehome
- 22 Moe's
- 19 Hideout
-    Frank's Cocktail
- 17 Five Spot▽

BROOKLYN: HEIGHTS/DUMBO

- 24 Superfine
- 22 Floyd, NY
- 21 Rebar
- 20 Water St. Bar
-    Waterfront Ale Hse.
- 14 Eamonn's

BROOKLYN: PARK SLOPE

- 25 Total Wine Bar
-    Barbès
- 24 Union Hall
- 23 Blue Ribbon Bklyn.
-    Buttermilk
- 22 Great Lakes

BROOKLYN: WILLIAMSBURG

- 25 SEA
-    Mug's Ale
- 24 Hotel Delmano
-    Spuyten Duyvil
-    Barcade
- 23 Pete's Candy Store

QUEENS: ASTORIA/L.I.C.

- 26 Cávo
- 25 Bohemian Hall
-    L.I.C. Bar
- 22 Water Taxi Beach
-    Hell Gate Social
-    Vino di Vino

STATEN ISLAND

- 23 Killmeyer's
- 20 Cargo Café
- 19 Martini Red
- 17 Beer Garden
-    Muddy Cup▽
-    L'Amour

Top Decor

29	Megu	Tabla*
28	Daniel	Morimoto
27	SEA	Chinatown Brasserie
	Tao	Champagne Bar/Plaza
	Buddakan	Modern
	Rayuela	Pegu Club
	Kemia Bar	

		25	Therapy
	King Cole Bar		Eleven Madison Pk.
	Cávo		Le Cirque
	Campbell Apartment		Clover Club
	Bemelmans		Hudson Hotel
	Spice Market		Oak Room

			Union Hall
26	One if by Land		Asia de Cuba
	Brandy Library		Gramercy Tavern
	Buddha Bar		Ono
	Public		Ritz-Carlton
	In Vino		Café des Artistes
	Macao Trading Co.		EN Shochu Bar
	Grand Bar		Plaza Athénée
	Rose Bar*		

OLD NEW YORK

Bill's Gay Nineties	McSorley's
Campbell Apartment	Oak Bar
Ear Inn	Old Town Bar
Globe	Pete's Tavern
Keens Steak	P.J. Clarke's (East Side)
Landmark Tavern	United Palace
Lenox Lounge	White Horse

OUTDOORS

Boathouse	Hudson Terrace
Bookmarks	Ono
Cávo	Park
Delancey	Rink Bar
5 Ninth	230 Fifth

ROMANCE

Allen & Delancey	Le Colonial
Apothéke	Milk and Honey
Auction House	Pegu Club
Bookmarks	Shalel Lounge
Dove	Spice Market
La Lanterna	Temple Bar

VIEWS

Above Allen	Plunge
Ava Lounge	Rare View
Boat Basin	Ravel Rooftop
Chelsea Brewing	River Room
Highbar	Salon de Ning
Metropolitan Museum	230 Fifth

Top Service

27 Daniel

26 Gramercy Tavern
Milk and Honey
King Cole Bar
One if by Land
Grape & Grain

25 21 Club
Gotham B&G*
Wogies*
Bemelmans
Total Wine Bar*
Ritz-Carlton Star Lounge
Four Seasons Hotel Bar
Gaf Bar*

24 Trinity Pub*
Four Seasons Bar
Oak Room
Plaza Athénée
Clover Club
Angel's Share
Barbès
Biddy's*
Louis 649*
Union Square Cafe
Eleven Madison Pk.
Brandy Library

Little Branch
Carnegie Club
Keens Steak*
Stonehome*
Champagne Bar/Plaza
Killmeyer's
PDT
Sakagura
Cafe Carlyle
L.I.C. Bar
Bar Masa
Tabla*
Blue Ribbon
8th St. Winecellar
I Trulli Enoteca

23 Last Exit
Blue Ribbon Bklyn.
In Vino
Gilt
Vero*
Brooklyn Social
Hideaway
Char No. 4
B61
Mug's Ale*

NIGHTLIFE
DIRECTORY

| | APPEAL | DECOR | SERVICE | COST |

Abbey, The
`21` `12` `21` `$7`

Williamsburg | 536 Driggs Ave. (bet. N. 7th & 8th Sts.) | Brooklyn | L to Bedford Ave. | 718-599-4400

A "blessedly unpretentious" sanctuary for "less sceney" sorts, this Williamsburg "nook" is a "standard" boozer where "cheap drinks" are served with "no attitude" and both the jukebox and the "video games rock"; it's "nothing thrilling", but "hipsters are actually tolerable" here.

Abbey Pub
`19` `15` `20` `$7`

W 100s | 237 W. 105th St. (bet. Amsterdam Ave. & B'way) | 1 to 103rd St. | 212-222-8713

"Get away from the scenesters and frat boys" at this "divey" UWS "hangout" where the "easy vibe" encourages both scruffy "locals" and a "plethora of Columbia" scholars to pull up a pew; "perfectly ordinary" in the best sense, it's "been there forever" and is "good for the nabe."

Abilene
`20` `15` `19` `$7`

Carroll Gardens | 442 Court St. (3rd Pl.) | Brooklyn | F/G to Carroll St. | 718-522-6900 | www.abilenebarbrooklyn.com

This "neighborhoody" Carroll Gardens watering hole is a "go-to" for "chilled-out locals" and a "great place to get to know the zillions of new people moving into the area"; amenities include "ice-breaking board games", "consistent Brooklyn people-watching" and "good tunes."

NEW Above Allen
`22` `21` `17` `$14`

LES | Thompson LES Hotel | 190 Allen St., 7th fl. (Houston St.) | F/V to Lower East Side/2nd Ave. | 212-460-5300 | www.thompsonles.com

Swanky cocktailing lands on Allen Street via this new seventh-floor terrace jutting off the Thompson LES Hotel, where a "cool", glassed-in greenhouse equipped with a retractable roof offers panoramic downtown vistas; expect pricey pops, nibbles via the in-house restaurant, Shang, and an iffy door policy – though it's meant to be private (members and hotel guests only), it seems more likely that admission will depend on supply and demand.

Z Accademia di Vino
`22` `22` `20` `$15`

E 60s | 1081 Third Ave. (bet. 63rd & 64th Sts.) | 4/5/6/N/R/W to 59th St./Lexington Ave. | 212-888-6333 | www.accademiadivino.com

There's "finally a hit" at this revolving-door Upper Eastsider, an "attractive" space that's been reinvented as an enoteca/trattoria/pizzeria, featuring a "superb wine list" of mostly Italian labels decanted at two separate bars; despite a "few kinks" servicewise, there's "lots of action" for "geriatric and young" types alike at this "much needed" spot.

Ace Bar
`21` `17` `17` `$7`

E Village | 531 E. Fifth St. (bet. Aves. A & B) | L to 1st Ave. | 212-979-8476 | www.acebar.com

Like a "Chuck E. Cheese for the not-so-grown-up", this East Villager offers everything from Skee-Ball to video games plus "cheap brews" in an ample space resembling "your cool friend's basement"; throw in a "rad" collection of "old-school lunchboxes" and it saves everyone from "preppies" to "frat boys" the fare to "Coney Island."

	APPEAL	DECOR	SERVICE	COST

Ace of Clubs ⊠

| | 19 | 13 | 18 | $10 |

NoHo | 9 Great Jones St. (Lafayette St.) | 6 to Bleecker St. | 212-677-6963 | www.aceofclubsnyc.com

Sited beneath NoHo's Acme Bar & Grill, this performance space has "music and booze" in spades given its "great live" bills of indie-rock upstarts; the down 'n' dirty digs are "surprisingly decent" for a show, but frill-seekers draw "a dead man's hand."

Aces & Eights

| | 15 | 14 | 17 | $7 |

E 80s | 1683 First Ave. (87th St.) | 4/5/6 to 86th St. | 212-860-4020
NEW **E Village** | 34 Ave. A (bet. 3rd & 4th Sts.) | F/V to Lower East Side/ 2nd Ave. | 212-353-2237
www.acesandeightsnyc.com

"Frat" types "relive college" at this "rowdy" UES outpost, done up as a "dingy" gunslinger's saloon with "saddle" seats at the bar, pool downstairs and "professional-grade" beer pong tables; most reckon the crowd's "typical", but it's "cheap enough" for horsing around; N.B. the new East Village outpost (in the Mo Pitkin's space) opened post-Survey.

Against the Grain

| | ▽ 22 | 18 | 23 | $9 |

E Village | 620 E. Sixth St. (bet. Aves. B & C) | F/V to Lower East Side/ 2nd Ave. | 212-358-7065

Spun off from Grape and Grain, the wine bar next door, this "beer-focused" East Villager pours a "great selection" of exotic brews along with a limited selection of vinos; the "understated" space may be slightly bigger than a shoebox with a communal table parked in the middle, but what it lacks in size it makes up for in conviviality.

Agozar!

| | 18 | 15 | 19 | $11 |

NoHo | 324 Bowery (Bleecker St.) | 6 to Bleecker St. | 212-677-6773 | www.agozarnyc.com

"If you love mojitos", the "yummy" variety at this NoHo Cuban bar/ restaurant just plain "rocks" abetted by margaritas, sangria and "delicious small plates"; the brick-lined space is "small" but "festive", and an "everyday happy hour" keeps things "totally affordable."

Algonquin Blue Bar

| | 23 | 22 | 22 | $14 |

W 40s | Algonquin Hotel | 59 W. 44th St. (bet. 5th & 6th Aves.) | 7/B/D/F/V to 42nd St./Bryant Park | 212-840-6800

Algonquin Lobby Lounge

W 40s | Algonquin Hotel | 59 W. 44th St. (bet. 5th & 6th Aves.) | 7/B/D/F/V to 42nd St./Bryant Park | 212-840-6800
www.algonquinhotel.com

The "cultured" atmosphere is "infectious" at these Theater District "legends", once "home to the literary Round Table" and always "worth visiting" when you're in the mood to "feel like Nick and Nora"; the Blue Bar is perfect for a "quietly elegant assignation", while the "staid", "wood-paneled" Lobby Lounge is a great place to meet and greet pre- or post-show.

Alibi

| | 17 | 16 | 18 | $10 |

G Village | 116 MacDougal St. (bet. Bleecker & W. 3rd Sts.) | A/B/C/ D/E/F/V to W. 4th St. | 212-254-9996 | www.alibiny.com

"Hip" cats "never feel out of place" at this "li'l lounge" in the Village where "fierce drinks" and serious DJ sets provide every excuse for "chilling out"; since the hideaway locale keeps it off most most-wanted lists, it typically "doesn't get too crowded."

Allen & Delancey
25 | 24 | 21 | $14

LES | 115 Allen St. (Delancey St.) | F/J/M/Z to Delancey/Essex Sts. | 212-253-5400 | www.allenanddelancey.net

Relive the "romance" of "old New York" at this "beautiful" bar fronting a "high-end" LES restaurant, an "arty, haute" hideaway outfitted with "exposed brick, dark wood" and the "most flattering" lighting in town; maybe it's "not a hot spot", but for an "upscale" interlude, it's "tremendously appealing."

Alligator Lounge ⊖
20 | 13 | 18 | $8

Williamsburg | 600 Metropolitan Ave. (Lorimer St.) | Brooklyn | G/L to Metropolitan Ave./Lorimer St. | 718-599-4440

Alligator Greenpoint ⊖

NEW **Greenpoint** | 113 Franklin St. (Greenpoint Ave.) | Brooklyn | G to Greenpoint Ave. | 718-383-6000

"Starving hipsters" snap up the "personal pizzas" served gratis with every drink at this "dive-ish" Williamsburg bar, also favored for pool and low-rent "lounging in the back"; ok, "Grimaldi's it's not", but it's cooler than a "soup kitchen" if you're "trying to save a buck" – "who can argue?"; N.B. the new Greenpoint sibling (in the old Lost & Found space) opened post-Survey.

Alphabet Lounge
18 | 13 | 17 | $8

E Village | 104 Ave. C (bet. 6th & 7th Sts.) | L to 1st Ave. | 212-780-0202 | www.alphabetnyc.com

Your "favorite '80s music rules" at this "far East Village" bar where "young" revelers congregate under the disco ball to soak up the "raucous party atmosphere" and suck down "reasonably priced drinks"; lookswise, it's "nothing special", but there's "enough room" for a "dance-off" or just "being silly with the girls."

American Trash
13 | 10 | 16 | $7

E 70s | 1471 First Ave. (bet. 76th & 77th Sts.) | 6 to 77th St. | 212-988-9008

The "no-nonsense authenticity" speaks for itself at this Upper East Side "urban biker" bar, a "lived-in" dump featuring "trailer-park" mementos, "tattooed" staffers and "metal-lovers'" mood music; it's an excuse to don your "trashiest" duds and "get loaded" with the "freaks of the world", so if that doesn't appeal, "keep walking."

Amsterdam Billiards/Union Square
17 | 14 | 17 | $11

E Village | 110 E. 11th St. (4th Ave.) | 4/5/6/L/N/Q/R/W to 14th St./Union Sq. | 212-995-0333 | www.amsterdambilliards.com

Transplanted from the UWS to the Union Square area, this East Village felt forum is "spacious" enough to provide "tables for everyone" from novices to "real pool sharks" in tidy digs enhanced with "cocktail waitress" service; for "serious billiards" action, it's pretty dam "comfy", though "high prices" could be a sticking point.

NEW Amsterdam 106
19 | 18 | 19 | $9

W 100s | 938 Amsterdam Ave. (106th St.) | 1 to 103rd St. | 212-280-8070 | www.divebarnyc.com

Enjoy a "hard-to-find beer" at this "cool" new "haven" near Columbia, a "friendly" grad-student "hang" featuring spiffed-up surroundings, a stunning ceiling and a "great selection" of craft drafts; it's fast becoming a "favorite" of locals who admit there "aren't too many choices up here."

An Béal Bocht 21 | 17 | 20 | $6

Bronx | 445 W. 238th St. (bet. Greystone & Waldo Aves.) | 1 to 238th St. | 718-884-7127 | www.anbealbochtcafe.com

A "sure bet" for the "boys and girls from Manhattan College", this "lively" Riverdale pub offers "fast" service, "great prices" and "lots of Irish" cred; admirers also raise a "pint of Guinness" to the live Celtic music, and thanks to a redo, there's now "more space" ("I'm moving in").

Anchor, The 18 | 15 | 16 | $12

SoHo | 310 Spring St. (bet. Greenwich & Hudson Sts.) | 1 to Houston St. | 212-463-7406 | www.theanchornyc.com

The "J.Crew" crew washes up at this "trendy dive bar" in West SoHo, a "grungier version of Sway across the street" that's decked out in downscale "marine decor"; brace yourself for "hordes" of "sweaty stowaways" psyched for "unpretentious" partying and "dancing with sailors", even if saltier sorts see an "amateurish" scene.

Angels & Kings 19 | 16 | 17 | $9
(aka AK-47)

E Village | 500 E. 11th St. (bet. Aves. A & B) | L to 1st Ave. | 212-254-4090 | www.angelsandkings.com

The "vibe is rock 'n' roll" at this ruby-hued East Village bar/lounge that's appropriately owned by "Fall Out Boy's Pete Wentz" and some other "young celebrity rockers"; although ultimately "nothing special", at least it's "hip without being obnoxious" about it; N.B. 'Starlette Sundays', a weekly sapphic shindig, is still going strong here.

⤷ Angel's Share 26 | 23 | 24 | $12

E Village | 8 Stuyvesant St., 2nd fl. (9th St. & 3rd Ave.) | 6 to Astor Pl. | 212-777-5415

"Drink is revered" at this "swank" East Village "den" tucked "upstairs off a sushi place" that's a "temple" of "precision" mixology, with "superlative cocktails" and a "hush-hush" ambiance made to share with "your one and only"; just know to "follow the rules" – no standing, loud talking or parties of more than four – and "be prepared to wait."

Angry Wade's 14 | 10 | 16 | $7

Cobble Hill | 222 Smith St. (Butler St.) | Brooklyn | F/G to Bergen St. | 718-488-7253

This sports-oriented joint is a rare "hangout" on the Smith Street strip that's "low-key" enough to "watch a game", shoot some stick or "warm up" by the fireplace; foes fume the "crowd can be tough", but 'hoodies who "keep going back" shrug "take it or leave it."

Annex, The 22 | 14 | 16 | $9

LES | 152 Orchard St. (bet. Rivington & Stanton Sts.) | F/J/M/Z to Delancey/Essex Sts. | 212-673-3410 | www.theannexnyc.com

"Alternative types" and "Sid Vicious" disciples pull on their "skinny jeans" and head for this "too-cool" Lower East Side bar/performance space that hosts "great" live bands along with DJs with a taste for "awesome Brit rock"; the bi-level setup is way basic and "loud", and the "raw vibe" is definitely "not for poseurs."

	APPEAL	DECOR	SERVICE	COST

Annie Moore's
16 14 19 $9

E 40s | 50 E. 43rd St. (bet. Madison & Vanderbilt Aves.) | 4/5/6/7/S to 42nd St./Grand Central | 212-986-7826

"When in transit", commuters train their sights on this "basic" Irish tavern hard by Grand Central, secure that they won't miss the "ride home" (the schedules scroll on screens above the bar); since "it's all about the convenience", it couldn't be any more "jammed after work."

anotheroom
24 20 22 $10

TriBeCa | 249 W. Broadway (bet. Beach & N. Moore Sts.) | 1 to Franklin St. | 212-226-1418 | www.theroomsbeerandwine.com

"Very intimate" given its shadowy interior and "tiny" size, this candle-lit TriBeCan is a "hip" but "attitude-free" haven for "post-30s" with a yen for a "quiet" glass of wine or "exotic beer" (hard liquor isn't served); "if you can grab a seat", it's "secluded" enough to really "get to know a date."

Antarctica
17 11 19 $9

SoHo | 287 Hudson St. (Spring St.) | C/E to Spring St. | 212-352-1666 | www.antarcticabar.com

Its Way West SoHo address is "really off" the map, but this "down 'n' dirty" bar draws a "varied" clientele with "drinks in pint glasses" served up "fast and cheap"; the "low-rent" style is polarizing, but you'll "fit in" (and drink free) if your name matches the moniker of the night.

Antik
18 19 17 $12

NoHo | 356 Bowery (bet. 4th & Great Jones Sts.) | 6 to Astor Pl. | 212-388-1655 | www.antiknyc.com

"Catering to models and too-cool types", this "small", "table-service" lounge perched above King's Cross in NoHo hosts the usual "singles" antics in "brothel"-esque digs bedecked with chandeliers and velvety banquettes; it "can be a fun spot", but skeptics who've "seen better" say there's "no reason for such a tough door."

Anyway Cafe
20 17 18 $11

E Village | 34 E. Second St. (bet. Bowery & 2nd Ave.) | F/V to Lower East Side/ 2nd Ave. | 212-533-3412
Manhattan Beach | 111 Oriental Blvd. (West End Ave.) | Brooklyn | B/Q to Brighton Beach | 718-648-3906
Sheepshead Bay | 1602 Gravesend Neck Rd. (16th St.) | Brooklyn | Q to Neck Rd. | 718-934-5988
www.anywaycafe.com

Students of "Russian culture" are hard-pressed to find a "wider selection" of "delicious, often dangerous" vodka infusions than at this "cozy" East Village cafe and its brace of Brooklyn offshoots; otherwise, expect "dim" lighting and "friendly" vibeskis jazzed up with "live music."

Apartment 138
19 18 18 $9

Cobble Hill | 138 Smith St. (bet. Bergen & Dean Sts.) | Brooklyn | F/G to Bergen St. | 718-858-0556

Youthful "singles" in residence at this "quaint" Cobble Hill bar/eatery say it's worth checking out for a casual "chat" or a quaff "out back in the garden"; add "pretty good" food and a "functional game room" with foosball, pool and "Pac-Man", and many are ready to move in.

	APPEAL	DECOR	SERVICE	COST

☑ NEW Apothéke
| | 23 | 23 | 21 | $15 |

Chinatown | 9 Doyers St. (Bowery) | 4/5/6/J/M/N/R/Q/W to Canal St. |
212-406-0400 | www.apothekenyc.com

Hidden in an obscure "Chinatown back alley", this "dark", "sexy"
lounge plays up its apothecary theme with "mad scientist" staffers in
"white lab coats" dispensing "specialty elixirs" from a bar chock-full of
pharmaceutical paraphernalia; the encyclopedic drink selection (including their take on the spirit du jour, absinthe) helps distract from
the "wallet-burning" prices and unnecessarily "harsh doormen."

APT
| | 21 | 23 | 16 | $13 |

Meatpacking | 419 W. 13th St. (bet. 9th Ave. & Washington St.) | A/C/E/L
to 14th St./8th Ave. | 212-414-4245 | www.aptwebsite.com

"Can I live here?" ask scenemakers at this "old-guard" double-decker
Meatpacking lounge, a "dark, classy" suite of rooms (complete with
"bed and study") done up "like a page out of *Wallpaper*"; the "bumping" downstairs bar features aptly "relevant" DJs and the mixed crowd
includes "Uptown, Downtown and Euro" occupants, but it's "not the
best-kept secret" – and the "strict door" means you "never know if
you'll get in."

Ara Wine Bar
| | 22 | 21 | 20 | $11 |

Meatpacking | 24 Ninth Ave. (bet. 13th & 14th Sts.) | A/C/E/L to 14th St./
8th Ave. | 212-242-8642 | www.arawinebar.com

Get "mellow in the midst" of the Meatpacking madness at this
"cute wine bar", a "low-key" option to "consort with friends" before
hitting the "next hot spot"; with its choice vintages, "reasonable"
costs and "haremlike back room", it's no surprise the "intimate" space
"fills up fast."

Arctica
| | 18 | 18 | 18 | $10 |

Murray Hill | 384 Third Ave. (bet. 27th & 28th Sts.) | 6 to 28th St. |
212-725-4477 | www.arcticabar.com

Murray Hill denizens chill in "slightly more upscale" style at this
"spacious" venue that goes with the floe with a polar exploration
theme; foes shrug it's just "another Third Avenue bar", but fans say
the "not expensive" pricing and "date-worthy fireplace" distinguish it
from the pack.

Arlene's Grocery
| | 20 | 11 | 15 | $7 |

LES | 95 Stanton St. (bet. Ludlow & Orchard Sts.) | F/V to Lower East Side/
2nd Ave. | 212-995-1652 | www.arlenesgrocery.net

Grab some "indie" glory at this "gritty" LES showcase for "young B-list
bands" providing "lots of entertainment" on the "cheap" for "raucous"
audiences; yes, it's "a total dive", but "Monday night karaoke" with live-
musician backing lets all comers "fulfill their dreams of rock stardom."

Arlo & Esme
| | 21 | 20 | 17 | $10 |

E Village | 42 E. First St. (bet. 1st & 2nd Aves.) | F/V to Lower East Side/
2nd Ave. | 212-777-5617

Cafe by day, this bi-level East Villager morphs into a "rowdy" after-
dark destination as a "younger", "far-from-glitterati" crowd convenes
in the "quaint" upstairs bar or the "mazelike series" of "chill grottos"
in the basement; its "late-night party" rep makes for a house so
"packed" that wags tag it the "capital of Sardine-ia."

	APPEAL	DECOR	SERVICE	COST

Aroma
▽ 25 | 21 | 26 | $14

NoHo | 36 E. Fourth St. (bet. Bowery & Lafayette St.) | 6 to Astor Pl. | 212-375-0100 | www.aromanyc.com

Those who sniff out this "quaint" NoHo wine bar call it a "charming little find" where the owners "greet you with warmth" and a "keen knowledge" of their list of Italian labels (plus "delicious" nibbles on the side); there "aren't a lot of seats", but it's "great for a date" if you can "find a spot."

Art Bar
20 | 17 | 17 | $9

W Village | 52 Eighth Ave. (bet. Horatio & Jane Sts.) | A/C/E/L to 14th St./8th Ave. | 212-727-0244 | www.merchantsny.com

A longtime Village "go-to", this "lively" bar is a "conversation-friendly" spot to appraise the "cool" crowd and maybe bid for "someone new"; don't miss the "rendezvous in the back", a "loungey hideout" with paintings, a "central fireplace" and "comfy couches."

Arthur's Tavern ⊅
22 | 14 | 17 | $9

W Village | 57 Grove St. (bet. Bleecker St. & 7th Ave. S.) | 1 to Christopher St. | 212-675-6879 | www.arthurstavernnyc.com

It's still a "grand ol' time" at this vintage Village jazz bar, a slightly "stale" space where the "classic" bebop, Dixieland and blues acts deliver the "nitty gritty" with "no cover charge"; it really "packs them in", "but stay for a while" and you'll leave with "a smile on your face."

⊡ Asia de Cuba
24 | 25 | 20 | $15

Murray Hill | Morgans Hotel | 237 Madison Ave. (bet. 37th & 38th Sts.) | 6 to 33rd St. | 212-726-7755 | www.chinagrillmgt.com

"Always cool" and "swankier than swank", this habitually "hopping" Murray Hill eatery boasts a "small bar area" that's "still a scene" comprised of "well-heeled" "pretty people" hobnobbing amid "dreamy white decor"; both the "steamy vibe" and "fabulous cocktails" are "buzz-worthy", and though "you'll pay the price", all that "eye candy is free."

Aspen
21 | 22 | 18 | $13

Flatiron | 30 W. 22nd St. (bet. 5th & 6th Aves.) | F/V to 23rd St. | 212-645-5040 | www.aspen-nyc.com

Aspen Social Club

NEW **W 50s** | Stay Hotel | 157 W. 47th St. (bet. 6th & 7th Aves.) | N/R/W to 49th St. | 212-221-7200 | www.aspensocialclub.com

The "closest to the slopes you'll get" in the Flatiron, this smooth bar/eatery flaunts a "modernist ski lodge" motif (with pine woodwork, a "fire pit" and "Lucite taxidermy") that lures a "late 20s" crowd in from the cold; the "classy cabin" atmosphere and "strong drinks" set heads "aspenning", though a frosty few find it "too popular" and "expensive"; N.B. the same sexy formula has been replicated at the new Times Square satellite.

Athens Café
17 | 16 | 14 | $11

Astoria | 32-07 30th Ave. (bet. 32nd & 33rd Sts.) | Queens | N/W to 30th Ave. | 718-626-2164

"Heart-of-Astoria" cafe where "locals line up" for their "famous frappes" ("like coffee on crack") or the harder stuff; pluses include "outdoor seating" and "big screens" for "*futbol*", though some thunder like Zeus at the "inattentive" service.

	APPEAL	DECOR	SERVICE	COST

NEW At Vermilion

	-	-	-	E

E 40s | 480 Lexington Ave. (46th St.) | 4/5/6/7/S to 42nd St./Grand Central | 212-871-6600 | www.thevermilionrestaurant.com

This airy new bar/lounge/restaurant in the old Django digs offers local desk jockeys liquid relief before catching a train at nearby Grand Central; the minimalist, white-on-white design has a corporate feel (reinforced by the fluorescent lighting over the bar) that matches its corporate crowd and expense account–worthy price tags.

Auction House

	22	23	19	$10

E 80s | 300 E. 89th St. (bet. 1st & 2nd Aves.) | 4/5/6 to 86th St. | 212-427-4458

When Upper Eastsiders "don't want to pound beers", the area's scarce "non-frat" options include this "baroque" lounge, reminiscent of an "intimate art museum" with "plush" velvet seating, "Gothic paintings" and "deep burgundy" trimming; all that "antique" chic makes this "oasis" a "grown-up" destination in a neighborhood that "needs a few more."

Aura

	20	20	18	$16

Flatiron | 5 E. 19th St. (bet. B'way & 5th Ave.) | 4/5/6/L/N/Q/R/W to 14th St./Union Sq. | 212-671-1981 | www.auranyc.com

A "hopping" spot on a "smaller" scale, this Flatiron lounge projects an aura of efficiency as it bundles two "well-appointed" levels – including a VIP balcony and downstairs dance floor – into its compact quarters; it's short of mesmerizing, but "local types" can count on a "solid time."

Australian, The

	20	18	21	$10

Garment District | 20 W. 38th St. (bet. 5th & 6th Aves.) | 7/B/D/F/V to 42nd St./Bryant Park | 212-869-8601 | www.theaustraliannyc.com

Down Under comes to Midtown at this "authentic Oz bar" in the Garment District, a "publike" joint featuring "friendly Australian bartenders" pulling pints; whether "after work" or to just "watch the footy", it's a "refreshing change of pace" akin to "being back in Sydney."

Automatic Slim's

	17	11	15	$8

W Village | 733 Washington St. (Bank St.) | A/C/E/L to 14th St./8th Ave. | 212-645-8660

"Prepsters" and "bachelorettes" automatically fill this "no-frills" West Village "party" bar, a "rowdy" outpost blasting a "terrific '80s/'90s" soundtrack; sure, the "very tight" quarters are "packed" with "homogeneous" "striped-shirts", but it's still a "guilty pleasure" for many.

Ava Lounge

	24	24	18	$12

W 50s | Dream Hotel | 210 W. 55th St., 14th fl. (bet. B'way & 7th Ave.) | N/Q/R/W to 57th St./7th Ave. | 212-956-7020 | www.avaloungenyc.com

"Upscale business" types dub this "small yet sophisticated" Midtown "aerie" the "sleekest" of retreats, merging a "mod" penthouse lounge with a "super" roof deck commanding "awesome views" down Broadway; patrons "pay a premium" in both bucks and "attitude", but it's a safe bet they "won't be bothered by meatheads."

Babel Lounge

	21	18	18	$11

E Village | 131 Ave. C (8th St.) | L to 1st Ave. | 212-505-3468

Have an "authentic" Arabian night at this "cute" Alphabet City Mideasterner where "Moroccan drinks", "hookah pipes" and belly dancing complement the DJ's "pleasing mix" of "international" tracks; boosters babble it's a "real treat", and when the close quarters get "cramped", the patio is a handy way to "escape the heat."

☑ Bacaro

21 | 22 | 19 | $15

Chinatown | 136 Division St. (bet. Ludlow & Orchard Sts.) | F to E. B'way | 212-941-5060

Channeling a "classic Venetian wine bar" in Chinatown, this "charming" offshoot of Peasant is a "rustic jewel" furnished with a marble bartop, "cozy farm tables" and a brick-lined basement grotto that's simply "first date perfection"; it's usually "busy" with "lotsa hotties" sampling "nice" Italian vinos, so waits come with the territory.

Back Fence

17 | 11 | 17 | $7

G Village | 155 Bleecker St. (Thompson St.) | A/B/C/D/E/F/V to W. 4th St. | 212-475-9221 | www.thebackfenceonline.com

"Cover bands" bring back "classic rock" to the Village at this veteran barroom, a "rugged throwback" with "cheap brew" on tap and "sawdust" and "spent peanut shells" underfoot; its "a little grimy" and "NYU infested", but if you're in the mood for "trashed sing-alongs", a "good time" awaits.

Back Forty

22 | 18 | 21 | $11

E Village | 190 Ave. B (bet. 11th & 12th Sts.) | L to 1st Ave. | 212-388-1990 | www.backfortynyc.com

Backed for its "comfortable", rusticated style, this East Village bar/bistro (and Savoy sibling) plies "30-ish" sorts with "interesting beers" and "lovely wine options" that "marry well" with "farm-to-table" bites like its "lauded" burger; it lays on the "low-key charm" for a "reasonable price", though for many the "food's the real draw" here.

Back Page

18 | 13 | 16 | $7

E 80s | 1472 Third Ave. (bet. 83rd & 84th Sts.) | 4/5/6 to 86th St. | 212-570-5800

This Upper East Side sports bar wins "major points" for its "mind-blowing" "TV-to-person ratio" married to a space "large" enough for fans to "watch the big game from every angle"; otherwise it's "very typical", though if "wings are your thing" theirs flutter above the rest.

Back Room

23 | 23 | 19 | $10

LES | 102 Norfolk St. (bet. Delancey & Rivington Sts.) | F/J/M/Z to Delancey/Essex Sts. | 212-228-5098.

Accessed down a "dark alley", this Lower East Side "faux speakeasy" radiates "Prohibition" chic with its "low-lit", "1920s library" look, abetted by cocktails in "china cups", brown-bagged beers and a VIP room hidden behind a bookcase; although it's "alluring" as all get-out, insiders who hoped to keep it a "semi-secret" say the "gimmick wears thin" now that it's been "found out."

Baker Street

18 | 16 | 20 | $8

E 60s | 1152 First Ave. (63rd St.) | F to Lexington Ave./63rd St. | 212-688-9663 | www.bakerstreetnyc.com

Once the TGI Friday's "where they filmed *Cocktail*", this "sports-oriented" East Side Irish pub is now a "simple local spot" to "catch a game" or scarf down some "decent" vittles; most detect "nothing special", but barmen with "total recall" help ensure that it's "always alive."

| | APPEAL | DECOR | SERVICE | COST |

NEW Balon
E 80s | 245 E. 81st St. (bet. 2nd & 3rd Aves.) | 6 to 77th St |
646-641-2282

| - | - | - | E |

The wine bar gets a classy spin at this upscale UES venue that's more open and airy than the genre norm; the vino list, heavy on Spanish and Italian vintages, is on the pricey side and can be paired with the usual small-plate nibbles.

Ⓩ Balthazar

| 25 | 23 | 21 | $15 |

SoHo | 80 Spring St. (bet. B'way & Crosby St.) | 6 to Spring St. | 212-965-1414 | www.balthazarny.com

The "closest thing to Paris this side of the pond", this SoHo brasserie remains "abuzz" with "clamorous" throngs – everyone from "models to tourists" – who show up for the "top-notch" service and "amazing" (if "costly") tipples; as the "gold standard" for "people-watching" and "celeb-hunting", it's still "delivering the goods" with the "exceptional" panache that's made this one a "classic."

BAMcafé

| ▽ 21 | 24 | 16 | $11 |

Downtown Bklyn | Brooklyn Academy of Music | 30 Lafayette Ave. (bet. Ashland Pl. & St. Felix St.) | Brooklyn | 2/3/4/5/B/D/M/N/Q/R to Atlantic Ave. | 718-636-4100 | www.bam.org

The "right place" for a "pre-show" pop at the Brooklyn Academy of Music, this "quirky" cafe draws a crowd that's "as diverse as the U.N.", despite being on the "pricier" side; weekend music performances keep it "culturally significant", but "check their calendar" since the schedule and hours of operation are flexible.

B&S NY
(aka Boots & Saddles)

| ▽ 14 | 13 | 16 | $8 |

W Village | 76 Christopher St. (bet. Bleecker St. & 7th Ave. S.) | 1 to Christopher St. | 212-633-1986 | www.bootsnsaddle.com

Still hanging in there, this circa-1974 gay bar (originally known as Boots & Saddles but quickly nicknamed Bras & Girdles) is a relic from back in the day when Christopher Street was the epicenter of NYC gay life; now it's been somewhat spiffed up, but despite "great go-go boys" and beer blasts, it strikes most as "tired out."

Banjo Jim's

| 21 | 14 | 20 | $6 |

E Village | 700 E. Ninth St. (Ave. C) | L to 1st Ave. | 212-777-0869 | www.banjojims.com

Hear the "real America" at this Alphabet City "hole-in-the-wall", an "old-school joint" that hosts a "wonderful" nightly hoedown with free "live entertainment" ranging from "folk rock" to "banjos and bluegrass"; a "great beer selection" for "cheap" provides plenty of twang for the buck.

Baraonda

| 21 | 19 | 16 | $12 |

E 70s | 1439 Second Ave. (75th St.) | 6 to 77th St. | 212-288-8555 | www.baraondany.com

Practice your "fake accent" at this "vibrant" Upper East Side "Eurotrash headquarters", a "highly social" bar/eatery where the "slinky-shirted" "get wild" with "late-night tabletop dancing" on Wednesdays and Sundays; just be prepared for "'tude", and "bring the earplugs" for those "thumping" decibels.

	APPEAL	DECOR	SERVICE	COST

Bar @ Etats-Unis
| | 23 | 18 | 22 | $14 |

E 80s | 247 E. 81st St. (bet. 2nd & 3rd Aves.) | 4/5/6 to 86th St. | 212-396-9928 | www.etatsunisrestaurant.com

Though "so tiny" it's "easy to overlook", this cozy UES wine bar (parked across the street from its mother ship eatery) is a "winner" for "creative cocktails" and "well-chosen" vinos poured by the glass; just "get there early" – seats are "hard to come by."

Baraza ⌀
| | 22 | 18 | 18 | $8 |

E Village | 133 Ave. C (bet. 8th & 9th Sts.) | L to 1st Ave. | 212-539-0811 | www.barazany.com

With the deckhands at this "tiny" East Villager spinning "pumping" Latin sounds, it only takes a couple of "great caipirinhas" and mojitos before the "whole place gyrates"; the "pleasant, unpretentious" clientele is a plus since on "crowded" nights that's who you'll be "bumping into."

Barbès
| | 25 | 21 | 24 | $8 |

Park Slope | 376 Ninth St. (6th Ave.) | Brooklyn | F to 7th Ave. | 347-422-0248 | www.barbesbrooklyn.com

The "music du jour" is the "main draw" at this "small" Park Sloper that hosts a "really diverse" live lineup along with "movie screenings" in its back room; those hanging out in the front applaud their "friendly next-stool neighbors" and *très extraordinaire* bartenders.

Barcade
| | 24 | 17 | 20 | $7 |

Williamsburg | 388 Union Ave. (bet. Ainslie & Powers Sts.) | Brooklyn | G/L to Metropolitan Ave./Lorimer St. | 718-302-6464 | www.barcadebrooklyn.com

A "real blast" for "'80s arcade" veterans, this "warehouselike" Williamsburg playground boasts a "gold mine" of "vintage video games" matched by a "wide array" of "phenomenal microbrews" on tap; it's short on frills, but the "über-fun" concept still "scores high."

Bar Carrera
| | 23 | 20 | 21 | $13 |

E Village | 175 Second Ave. (bet. 11th & 12th Sts.) | 6 to Astor Pl. | 212-375-1555

NEW **G Village** | 146 W. Houston St. (MacDougal St.) | 1/2/3 to Houston St. | 212-253-9500
www.barcarrera.com

"Cute" with a Spanish accent, this East Village wine bar and its new Village spin-off are simpatico spots to "hang out" and sample an "extensive" list of Iberian vintages while grazing on "tempting" tapas; the "small, narrow" setups make it easier to turn up the "romantic" heat.

Barcelona Bar
| | 21 | 17 | 19 | $10 |

W 50s | 923 Eighth Ave. (bet. 54th & 55th Sts.) | C/E to 50th St. | 212-245-3212 | www.barcelonabarnyc.com

Though it's a "simple" setup, this Hell's Kitchen bar is worth checking out given its "endless variety of shots" that can be accessorized with "props" to give each of them a theme; if you don't mind long, narrow quarters and "young crowds", the "good times" here are worth a shot.

☑ Bar Centrale
| | ▽ 29 | 25 | 25 | $15 |

W 40s | 326 W. 46th St., 2nd fl. (bet. 8th & 9th Aves.) | A/C/E to 42nd St./Port Authority | 212-581-3130

"More exclusive" than the usual "Broadway hideaway", this "civilized" lounge near Restaurant Row redoubt Joe Allen is the "real deal" for theatrical "celeb-spotting" in "chic" digs staffed by "chipper" troupers serving "expensive drinks" and "stylish comfort food"; too bad it's "not a secret anymore", so "unless you're a somebody", reservations are advised.

Barcibo Enoteca

22 | 21 | 22 | $14

W 60s | 2020 Broadway (69th St.) | 1 to 66th St. | 212-595-2805 | www.barciboenoteca.com

"Another Upper West Side winner" from the Bin 71 boys, this "lively" Lincoln Center–area wine bar boasts a "focused" Italian list, "friendly" servers and a "sophisticated" following; granted, the "dimly lit" digs offer "no elbow room whatsoever", but what's "tight" to some is "cozy" to others.

Bar Coastal

14 | 11 | 17 | $8

E 70s | 1495 First Ave. (78th St.) | 6 to 77th St. | 212-288-6635 | www.barcoastal.com

"Low-maintenance meatheads" in "shorts and sandals" coast into this "typical" Upper East Side sports bar to down "fairly priced" suds and atomic wings; predictably, the "guys always outnumber the girls", but these dudes don't care – "they're more interested in the game."

Bar East

▽ 13 | 12 | 18 | $6

E 90s | 1733 First Ave. (90th St.) | 4/5/6 to 86th St. | 212-876-0203 | www.bareast.com

This "laid-back" Irish pub deep in Yorkville is just "what you'd expect", but at least they try with "prompt" service and "cheap-as-hell" drink specials; add darts, pool and live bands (in The Underscore basement space) and it can be "fun with the right crowd."

Bar 89

22 | 24 | 19 | $12

SoHo | 89 Mercer St. (bet. Broome & Spring Sts.) | N/R/W to Prince St. | 212-274-0989 | www.bar89.com

An "attitude-free oasis" that's "trendy" but "never over the top", this "sleek" SoHo lounge is most "remarkable" for its "high-tech bathrooms" equipped with "see-through" doors that "magically fog up" when locked ("trust 'em"); the "soaring" design, "social" staffers and "potent cocktails" are all "most appealing" – and it's "priced accordingly."

Bar 515

15 | 15 | 15 | $9

Murray Hill | 515 Third Ave. (bet. 34th & 35th Sts.) | 6 to 33rd St. | 212-532-3300 | www.bar515.com

Like "too many bars on that stretch" of Third Avenue, this "sporty" Murray Hill hang recalls "wild college nights" with its "loud" "frat brats" and "drunk B&Ters" ("is 515 an area code in Jersey?"); then again, "if you're 22, this might be your scene" thanks to the "popular" drink specials and "huge projection screens."

Barfly

16 | 12 | 16 | $8

Gramercy | 244 Third Ave. (20th St.) | 6 to 23rd St. | 212-473-9660 | www.barflyny.com

"Sports and beers it is" at this "bare-bones" Gramercy jock joint, a "neighborhood" fly-by equipped with the "typical" plethora of TVs plus darts and pool; maybe it's just a "spruced-up dive" that "lacks a cool crowd", but the "well-priced" pours "keep locals happy."

	APPEAL	DECOR	SERVICE	COST

Bar 44

21 | 21 | 19 | $14

W 40s | Royalton Hotel | 44 W. 44th St. (bet. 5th & 6th Aves.) | 7/B/D/F/V to 42nd St./Bryant Park | 212-944-8844 | www.royaltonhotel.com
Lobbyists confirm this "revamped" version of the Royalton Hotel's ground-floor bar "still impresses" with a "snazzy" teak-toned setting including a "roaring fireplace" that makes you "wish the drinks would last longer"; "über-chic but also über-expensive", it's "pure class" for some, an "aging prom queen" to others.

Bar 41

19 | 18 | 19 | $11

W 40s | Hotel 41 at Times Sq. | 206 W. 41st St. (bet. 7th & 8th Aves.) | 1/2/3/ 7/N/Q/R/S/W to 42nd St./Times Sq. | 212-703-8600 | www.hotel41.com
"Meet an accountant" or a tourist at this "hidden" Theater District hotel bar, an "Ernst & Young hangout" that also draws Port Authority spillover; for everyone else, it's a snug "after-work" enclave with "good service" that's just the thing when you "actually want to have a conversation."

Bar 4

▽ 20 | 17 | 23 | $9

Park Slope | 444 Seventh Ave. (15th St.) | Brooklyn | F to 7th Ave. | 718-832-9800
Park Slope's singletons consider this "small" bar/lounge a good enough "neighborhood place" for a "casual night" out, albeit one with flavored martinis and DJs to sweeten the 4-mula; given the "dark", candlelit ambiance and "reasonable prices", there's no excuse not to bring a "date."

Bar Great Harry

▽ 20 | 14 | 21 | $7

Carroll Gardens | 280 Smith St. (Sackett St.) | Brooklyn | F/G to Carroll St. | 718-222-1103 | www.bargreatharry.com
Forget the plain, "run-of-the-mill" interior: this Smith Street dive bar sports a very serious list of craft beers that's regularly rotated and includes many hard-to-find brands; otherwise, it's a "basic", just-folks pub "in a neighborhood where nothing is basic anymore."

Bar Italia

20 | 20 | 19 | $14

E 70s | 1477 Second Ave. (77th St.) | 6 to 77th St. | 212-249-5300
"Cool but casual", this UES wine bar is a "nicely appointed" enoteca where the "authentic Italian vibe" is abetted by 40 labels by the glass and a "primarily Euro crowd"; the pace may seem slow, but the "relaxing" mood is a "welcome change" from the fratty fun houses nearby.

Bar Jamón

24 | 20 | 21 | $14

Gramercy | 125 E. 17th St. (Irving Pl.) | 4/5/6/L/N/Q/R/W to 14th St./ Union Sq. | 212-253-2773 | www.barjamonnyc.com
They "really know their Spanish wines" at this "teeny" Gramercy tapas-and-vino specialist, an annex of next-door neighbor Casa Mono that plies an "excellent list" of labels and nibbles in a "jammed" "communal" space; consensus says it's "too popular", so "don't expect any privacy" but do expect a "major wait" to get in.

Bar Masa

23 | 24 | 24 | $18

W 60s | Time Warner Ctr. | 10 Columbus Circle, 4th fl. (60th St.) | 1/A/B/C/D to 59th St./Columbus Circle | 212-823-9800 | www.masanyc.com
You won't find the masses at this "swanky" sanctum in the Time Warner Center's premium-priced restaurant Masa, where they're "se-

rious about their cocktails" and sakes if you're serious about shelling out some yen; it's the "ideal" of understated class, and a midpriced Masa menu seals the deal.

Bar Nine
15 | 13 | 16 | $8

W 50s | 807 Ninth Ave. (bet. 53rd & 54th Sts.) | C/E to 50th St. | 212-399-9336 | www.barnine.com

A "low-key alternative" in Hell's Kitchen, this "dark", roomy bar/lounge offers slackers the opportunity to chill on the "worn", "comfy couches" in back; otherwise, it's very "ordinary", but the tapsters "treat you well" and "live music" keeps the mood upbeat.

Bar None
11 | 9 | 14 | $8

E Village | 98 Third Ave. (bet. 12th & 13th Sts.) | L to 3rd Ave. | 212-777-6663 | www.barnonenyc.com

The "second home" of "NYU miscreants", this East Village "frat house" facsimile is a "meatfest to the max" with "grimy" digs and an "unbeatable late happy hour"; expect lots of New Orleans Saints fans, plus some random post-grads who "don't know they're too old" for this.

Bar on A
17 | 14 | 16 | $9

E Village | 170 Ave. A (11th St.) | L to 1st Ave. | 212-353-8231

"Hide from the world" behind velvet curtains at this "cool", casual East Villager, a "neighborhood go-to" for low-stress lounging; spoilers suggest the "typical" scene has "seen better days", but its "sexy" side is enhanced by eye-catching burlesque every Sunday.

NEW Bar 108
20 | 20 | 20 | $12

G Village | 108 W. Houston St. (Thompson St.) | 1 to Houston St. | 212-505-2015 | www.bar108nyc.com

One part lounge, one part sports bar, this "cozy" new Village watering hole is a "cool" step up from the rowdy college bars nearby, lit by both candlelight and plasma screens; a marble bartop, floor-to-ceiling windows and tile floors bring some charm to the otherwise standard setup.

Barracuda ⊅
19 | 14 | 18 | $9

Chelsea | 275 W. 22nd St. (bet. 7th & 8th Aves.) | C/E to 23rd St. | 212-645-8613

"High-energy yet lowbrow", this "trashy" Chelsea gay bar is a "tried-and-true standby" where "all types" cruise by for "boozy" mingling; the "dark", "denlike" space is "showing its age", but "ever-evolving decor" and "periodic drag shows" help "keep it fresh."

Barrage
20 | 18 | 21 | $8

W 40s | 401 W. 47th St. (bet. 9th & 10th Aves.) | C/E to 50th St. | 212-586-9390

This Hell's Kitchen gay bar gets no flak from the "pretty boys" lured by its "loungelike", DJ-driven style and "surprisingly unpretentious" atmosphere; the servers keep "on top of things", and the 11 PM-midnight drink deals are a surefire way to "go to bed happy."

Barramundi
∇ 19 | 16 | 19 | $8

LES | 67 Clinton St. (bet. Rivington & Stanton Sts.) | F/J/M/Z to Delancey/Essex Sts. | 212-529-6999 | www.barramundiny.com

"You can still smell the cedar" at this Lower East Side bar's latest incarnation, a "dark" haunt that gets its classic looks from "polished

	APPEAL	DECOR	SERVICE	COST

"wood", "loungey" banquettes and "quirky" curios on display; the "chill" regulars are mostly "approachable", and given the "middle-of-nowhere" address, it's "seldom overcrowded."

Barrio Chino

∇ 22 | 16 | 18 | $10

LES | 253 Broome St. (bet. Ludlow & Orchard Sts.) | B/D to Grand St. | 212-228-6710 | www.barriochinonyc.com

The "superb tequila selection" is a "gold mine" for margarita mavens at this Lower East Side "find", an "offbeat" choice for "fresh, creative" drinks in a cantina setting with crossover Chinese accents; throw in "homemade" Mexican late-night eats, and it's no wonder that the "little" room is often "packed."

Barrow Street Ale House

18 | 13 | 17 | $7

G Village | 15 Barrow St. (bet. W. 4th St. & 7th Ave. S.) | 1 to Christopher St. | 212-691-6127 | www.barrowstreetalehouse.com

Most Villagers "can't figure out" if this old-timer is "one of a dying breed" of downscale saloons or just a "total frat bar"; it supplies "cheap brews" "without attitude", so you can either "take in a game" or meet up for "low-key" conversation – at least until it's "swamped with college kids."

Bar 6

23 | 20 | 19 | $11

G Village | 502 Sixth Ave. (bet. 12th & 13th Sts.) | 1/2/3/L to 14th St./ 7th Ave. | 212-691-1363

Once a red-hot prospect, this French-Moroccan Village "bistro with a bar" still hosts a "jovial" crowd in "comfy" quarters with a sense of "sass and fun" ("wear a beret"); with its "tried-and-true" rep intact, the space is "a little too small" for the weekend "crowds."

Bar Tabac

22 | 20 | 17 | $9

Cobble Hill | 128 Smith St. (Dean St.) | Brooklyn | F/G to Bergen St. | 718-923-0918 | www.bartabacny.com

"Oui oui", this "faux Frenchie" bar/bistro in Cobble Hill attracts both "poseurs", "expats" and locals to its "cute" quarters, and becomes a "hoppin'", "spill-onto-the-sidewalk" scene come summer; maybe the service is "blasé", but those starving for a "slice of Paris" simply "love this place."

Bartini's Lounge

17 | 16 | 17 | $13

Forest Hills | 1 Station Sq. (71st Ave.) | Queens | E/F/G/R/V to Forest Hills/ 71st Ave. | 718-896-5445 | www.bartinislounge.com

Mixing over "600 types of martinis", this cushy Forest Hills basement is a "lounging and partying" locus for both "locals" and those laid over at the nearby "LIRR station"; but stirred-up critics claim it's an "overpriced" lair for "wannabe Manhattanites" with a "less-than-classic feel."

⌧ Bar Veloce

24 | 21 | 22 | $12

Chelsea | 176 Seventh Ave. (bet. 20th & 21st Sts.) | 1 to 23rd St. | 212-629-5300

E Village | 175 Second Ave. (bet. 11th & 12th Sts.) | L to 3rd Ave. | 212-260-3200

⌧ Veloce Club

NoLita | 17 Cleveland Pl. (Spring St.) | 6 to Spring St. | 212-966-7334 www.barveloce.com

"Stylish" but "never pretentious", these "all-Italian" enotecas are "bustling" with cork dorks engaged in "wine-infused" repartee thanks

to an "amazing" by-the-glass selection poured by "dressed-up" oenol-
ogists; both the "micro-size" East Villager and its roomier Chelsea
spin-off have all the "sophistication" one could want, while the NoLita
offshoot has a more loungelike feel.

Bateaux New York

▽ 22 | 18 | 17 | $17

Chelsea | Chelsea Piers | Piers 61 & 62 (Hudson River & W. 23rd St.) |
C/E to 23rd St. | 212-352-2022 | www.bateauxnewyork.com
Ship out from Chelsea Piers for a three-hour tour with dinner, dancing
and swinging live entertainment on this glass-walled cruise boat; all
hands agree it's a matchless "experience" for its large-as-life skyline
views, particularly at sunset.

Bayard's Ale House

17 | 14 | 17 | $11

W Village | 533 Hudson St. (Charles St.) | A/C/E/L to 14th St./8th Ave. |
212-989-0313 | www.bayardsalehouse.com
Though "not fancy", this West Villager brings the old Sazerac House
space "back to life" as a "neighborhood hangout" where the pints are
"cheerfully dispensed" and the "laid-back attitude" remains intact;
with "lots of choices" on tap and "decent bar food", it just might become a "staple" again.

Bayard's Blue Bar

▽ 19 | 20 | 21 | $14

Financial District | 1 Hanover Sq. (bet. Pearl & Stone Sts.) | 2/3 to Wall St. |
212-514-9454 | www.bayards.com
"After a hard day" of trading, Wall Street blue bloods convene at this
"classy" bar in the India House, where the "quiet" refinement suggests
a time-capsule version of "old New York"; though it's predictably "expensive", unwinding here is the kind of "wonderful" experience that
money *can* buy; N.B. closed on weekends.

BB&R

▽ 18 | 16 | 18 | $10

E 80s | 1720 Second Ave. (bet. 89th & 90th Sts.) | 4/5/6 to 86th St. |
212-987-5555 | www.bbrnyc.com
The unabbreviated name ("Blonde, Brunette and a Redhead") may
lure the "frat boys", but this clean-cut sports bar is one of the Upper
East Side's "calmer" places to let your hair down; besides the game-
tuned plasma screens, it features a "great area" in back for shooting
pool and a "photo booth" if you need a "reason to smile."

B Bar

18 | 18 | 14 | $10

NoHo | 40 E. Fourth St. (bet. Bowery & Lafayette St.) | 6 to Astor Pl. |
212-475-2220 | www.bbarandgrill.com
Though "no longer" in its '90s prime, this "big" NoHo bar/lounge is still
worth a visit to watch "freshly minted yuppies" engage in "low-key
schmoozing"; when it gets "too crowded", the "wonderful" patio's a
"saving grace" – and the gay party Beige bodes "fun on Tuesday nights."

B. B. King Blues Club

21 | 18 | 17 | $13

W 40s | 237 W. 42nd St. (bet. 7th & 8th Aves.) | 1/2/3/7/N/Q/R/S/W
to 42nd St./Times Sq. | 212-997-4555 | www.bbkingblues.com
Catch "name acts" "up close and personal" at this Times Square music
venue where the "quality" lineups and "excellent sound system" atone
for the "very commercial" feel; off-notes include "tourists", "tight"
seating and "blah" food that's "priced to give you the blues", but go
"just for the show" – the "talent it brings in" is "worth it."

	APPEAL	DECOR	SERVICE	COST

Beacon Theatre

23 | **-** | **14** | **$11**

W 70s | 2124 Broadway (bet. 74th & 75th Sts.) | 1/2/3 to 72nd St. | 212-465-6500 | www.beacontheatre.com

An Upper West Side beacon of "rock 'n' roll hoochie-coo", this "landmark" live music venue brings some of the "best acts" to town in an "easy-in-easy-out" midsize hall; granted, the bars are "makeshift" and the drinks are on the "pricey" side, but no one minds so long as it keeps delivering such "incredible shows" – and it's been recently renovated to its former glory.

NEW BEast

21 | **21** | **21** | **$11**

(aka Bar East)

LES | 171 E. Broadway, downstairs (bet. Jefferson & Rutgers Sts.) | F to E. B'way | 212-228-3100 | www.broadwayeast.com

"Every night's a hipster convention" at this arty new "basement-level bar" parked on the LES/Chinatown border beneath green eatery Broadway East (no surprise, it specializes in organic/eco-friendly wines and cocktails); the "tiny", brick-walled space gets way "crowded" at prime times, maybe because of its reputation as a "make-out" den.

☑ Beatrice Inn

21 | **17** | **16** | **$15**

W Village | 285 W. 12th St. (W. 4th St.) | A/C/E/L to 14th St./8th Ave. | 212-243-4626

It's "harder to get into than Fort Knox", but this semi-private, "über-exclusive" Village "lair" is the latest hot spot to "see, bea seen" and party with "kool kids" and "beautiful young Hollywood" folk in a shabby-chic warren of "cozy rooms"; it's "no dice" unless you're one of the "lucky few" on the guest list, so most say "don't bother."

Beauty Bar

19 | **21** | **16** | **$9**

E Village | 231 E. 14th St. (bet. 2nd & 3rd Aves.) | L to 3rd Ave. | 212-539-1389 | www.beautybar.com

Enjoy a "martini and a manicure" at this "high-concept" East Village bar, a "retro beauty salon" replica where patrons ranging from "hipsters" to "debutantes" can "get a buzz on" perched "under a '50s perm helmet"; fans call it "kitsch forever and a day", though aesthetes suggest this "funky" den could use a "makeover."

Becky's

18 | **13** | **19** | **$7**

E 60s | 1156 First Ave. (bet. 63rd & 64th Sts.) | F to Lexington Ave./63rd St. | 212-317-8929

"Bring your accent" to this "no-nonsense" East Side sports bar with a "casual" U.K. fan base, soccer and rugby matches playing on the "many TVs" and "not many girls in sight"; brew connoisseurs say the import-heavy tap selection helps to redeem the "dingy" digs.

NEW Beekman Bar and Books

23 | **23** | **20** | **$14**

E 50s | 889 First Ave. (50th St.) | 6 to 51st St./Lexington Ave. | 212-758-6600 | www.barandbooks.net

The latest edition in the "classy" cigar-bar franchise, this Eastsider stays on the same page with an "opulent", ultra-"clubby" space staffed by an "attentive" crew dispensing "fancy drinks" and stogies (though "smokers are segregated to a separate room"); for swells unfazed by the "premium" pricing, it's a "smart" spot for a "sophisticated" rendezvous.

Beer Bar at Cafe Centro

<table>
<tr><td></td><td>APPEAL</td><td>DECOR</td><td>SERVICE</td><td>COST</td></tr>
<tr><td></td><td>17</td><td>13</td><td>14</td><td>$10</td></tr>
</table>

E 40s | 200 Park Ave. (45th St. & Vanderbilt Ave.) | 4/5/6/7/S to 42nd St./ Grand Central | 212-818-1222 | www.cafecentrony.com

Have a "cold one" before "getting back to Westchester" at this "corporate commuter" "hot spot" atop Grand Central Station; the bar inside is always "convenient", but the scene really takes off in the summer when the "outdoor area" below the Park Avenue overpass is "jam-packed" with "rambunctious" folks psyched for some "fresh air"; N.B. a renovation is not yet reflected in the Decor score.

Beer Garden

`17` `13` `16` `$8`

Staten Island | 1883 Victory Blvd. (Mountainview Ave.) | 718-876-8900

There's no "actual garden", but that doesn't bother the "scrappy blue-collar" regulars of this Staten Island sports bar who show up to reap "good value" from the "healthy" suds selection; locals make "the hike" to catch "live bands", though the weekend crowds can be "out of control."

NEW Beer Island ∅

`23` `18` `21` `$10`

Coney Island | 3070 Stillwell Ave. (bet. Coney Island Boardwalk & Surf Ave.) | Brooklyn | D/F/N/Q to Coney Island/Stillwell Ave. | no phone | www.beerislandconeyisland.com

Only in NY would someone truck in sand to Coney Island, but that's exactly what's happened at this vast alfresco suds dispenser west of the boardwalk with a "fun" beach party vibe and a sea of tables and umbrellas; Southampton it ain't, but it does offer chicken and BBQ vendors as well as a stellar view of Friday night's weekly fireworks show.

Beer Table

▽ `24` `19` `22` `$11`

Park Slope | 427B Seventh Ave. (bet. 14th & 15th Sts.) | Brooklyn | F to 7th Ave. | 718-965-1196 | www.beertable.com

This "great" Park Sloper pours a "really nice" selection of rare and esoteric beers – including a number of daily changing tap brews – offered along with impeccably sourced cheeses and charcuterie at pleasingly reasonable prices; no surprise, the long communal tables lining the "small", brick-lined space fill up fast.

NEW Belleville Lounge

`-` `-` `-` `M`

Park Slope | 332 Fifth St. (5th Ave.) | Brooklyn | F/M/R to 4th Ave./9th St. | 718-832-9777 | www.bellevillebistro.com

An adjunct to the popular Park Slope French bistro, this new lounge has an appropriately Gallic air, with a bar imported from Paris and vintage knickknacks on display; high ceilings and a skylight lend an airy feel, while a tiny stage is available for performance-minded types.

Z NEW Bell House

`22` `23` `23` `$11`

Gowanus | 149 Seventh St. (bet. 2nd & 3rd Aves.) | Brooklyn | F/M/R to 4th Ave./9th St. | 718-643-6510 | www.thebellhouseny.com

"Live music" lovers give this "huge new" Union Hall sibling in Gowanus a ringing endorsement for its "cool" combo of a "bar up front" and a warehouse-size rear performance area; despite the "out-of-the-way" location, it's becoming a "mecca" for "late 20s" types anticipating "many a good show."

	APPEAL	DECOR	SERVICE	COST

Belmont Lounge
16 | 16 | 17 | $9

Gramercy | 117 E. 15th St. (bet. Irving Pl. & Park Ave. S.) | 4/5/6/L/N/Q/R/W to 14th St./Union Sq. | 212-533-0009

Expect "no models but no grunge either" at this "low-key" Gramercy lounge, an "appealing" hideaway for a "basic drink"; it's a good place to get "cozy" in the rear DJ den or the heated patio, but be ready to "battle" the "big, bad" brood bound for The Fillmore.

Bembe ⊄
23 | 20 | 18 | $8

Williamsburg | 81 S. Sixth St. (Berry St.) | Brooklyn | L to Bedford Ave. | 718-387-5389 | www.bembe.us

After some "cravable" tropical drinks, even introverts can't "resist bustin' a move" at this "steamy" Williamsburg lounge where "pumping" island music backed by live "drum circles" fuels "hormone-charged" revelry till the wee hours; fans stake out a spot in the "sardinelike" scene and show 'em "what your mama gave ya."

⚡ Bemelmans Bar
27 | 27 | 25 | $17

E 70s | Carlyle Hotel | 35 E. 76th St. (Madison Ave.) | 6 to 77th St. | 212-744-1600 | www.thecarlyle.com

"Quintessential UES mojo" lives on at this hotel bar "legend", a "top-class" tribute to the "plush" life complete with murals by *Madeline* creator Ludwig Bemelmans and the "sounds of a live piano"; the "pro" staff tends to an "older, richer" clientele, so "cash in a bond and enjoy."

B Flat
22 | 19 | 21 | $12

TriBeCa | 277 Church St., downstairs (bet. Franklin & White Sts.) | 1 to Franklin St. | 212-219-2970 | www.bflat.info

There's "nothing flat" about this "high-end", "low-key" Angel's Share spin-off in TriBeCa, a "swanky" "subterranean escape" where the "doting staff" prides itself on "expertly made" cocktails with "delectable" Far Eastern twists; though the "dark" setting may be too "bare"-bones for aesthetes, "sophisticated" sorts still give it an "A-plus."

Biddy's Pub
22 | 14 | 24 | $6

E 90s | 301 E. 91st St. (bet. 1st & 2nd Aves.) | 4/5/6 to 86th St. | 212-534-4785

Itty-biddy and "overlooked by many", this UES pub is a "pretension-free" zone overseen by "Irish barkeeps" who are among the most "charming guys on the planet"; an ultra-"snug" hideaway for "cheap" pints with your mates, it's also "more mature" than most in this 'hood.

Big Bar ⊄
19 | 15 | 19 | $8

E Village | 75 E. Seventh St. (bet. 1st & 2nd Aves.) | 6 to Astor Pl. | 212-777-6969

"Big it's not" unless you count the super-sized "personality" of this "cute" East Village "drop-by", a "cozy" spot where "friendly" staffers cue up DJ sets and dispense "reasonably priced drinks"; with nary a "B&T to be seen", it proves that "small packages" do deliver "good things."

Big Easy
13 | 11 | 14 | $7

E 90s | 1768 Second Ave. (bet. 92nd & 93rd Sts.) | 4/5/6 to 86th St. | 212-348-0879 | www.bigeasynyc.com

"If you're seriously missing college", party down "New Orleans"–style at this Upper East Side theme bar, a "sleazy" slice of "frat life" complete with budget suds, "beer pong" and "rowdy debauchery"; while critics contend it's an "overcrowded" roomful of "overgrown" grads, others "don't really remember much" about it.

Big Nose Kate's
14 | **11** | **16** | **$12**

Staten Island | 2484 Arthur Kill Rd. (St. Luke's Pl.) | 718-227-3282
A "real trip to get to" but decidedly "different", this "converted church" on Staten Island's south shore is an "Old West saloon" mock-up where the "long bar" is dependably "active" with "noisy" varmints; but skeptics sniff it's a "grungy" "biker blast" with "ditzy" service and a snoutful of "attitude."

NEW Bijoux
23 | **22** | **18** | **$17**

Meatpacking | 55 Gansevoort St., downstairs (bet. Greenwich & Washington Sts.) | A/C/E/L to 14th St./8th Ave. | 212-255-8555 | www.bijouxlounge.com
Well-"hidden" behind a signless door, this "exclusive" underground lounge beneath the Meatpacking District's Merkato 55 is catnip for "hip 'n' trendy" types willing to "offer up their first born" to prowl its shadowy, chandeliered chambers; but even those able to drop megabucks to "party like a celeb" wonder if it's "worth all the hype."

Bill's Gay Nineties
20 | **15** | **21** | **$11**

E 50s | 57 E. 54th St. (bet. Madison & Park Aves.) | E/V to 5th Ave./53rd St. | 212-355-0243 | www.billsnyc.com
"Step into a time warp" at this "atmospheric" Midtown taproom, a '20s-era survivor that's "one of the few" to retain its "old-school" speakeasy looks via vintage portraits of pugilists and racehorses; its "loyal following" is far from gay, but they still maintain the nightly piano bar is "always a good time."

Billymark's West ⊄
15 | **8** | **17** | **$9**

Chelsea | 332 Ninth Ave. (29th St.) | A/C/E to 34th St./Penn Station | 212-629-0118 | www.billymarkswest.com
"Long live the dive bar!" is the rallying cry at this "cheap" West Chelsea "hole-in-the-wall" where darts, pool, video games and "dumpy characters" are the hallmarks of low-rent "perfection"; if you're in the mood for "drinking a lot" and "singing along" with the juke, billy right up.

Bin No. 220
21 | **19** | **20** | **$13**

Seaport | 220 Front St. (bet. Beekman St. & Peck Slip) | 2/3/4/5/A/C/J/M/Z to Fulton St./B'way/Nassau | 212-374-9463 | www.binno220.com
Don't expect "ale-swigging fishermen" at this "lovely little" South Street Seaport wine bar, an "upscale alternative" "hidden away" on "tourist"-trod turf that pours "excellent" Italian vinos, including 70 selections by the glass; the "cozy" premises are popular with "youngish Wall Street" sorts who don't mind shelling out for the "cool" vibe.

Bin 71
22 | **19** | **19** | **$12**

W 70s | 237 Columbus Ave. (71st St.) | 1/2/3 to 72nd St. | 212-362-5446 | www.bin71.com
This "cozy bin" of a wine bar is "tightly packed" with "chatty" Upper Westsiders hoping to "score a sliver" of space for some "quality" sipping matched with "appetizing nibbles"; the "casual" mood and "know-a-lot" staff are distinct pluses, but "good luck" finding foot room, "much less a seat."

Birdland
23 | 19 | 18 | $14

W 40s | 315 W. 44th St. (bet. 8th & 9th Aves.) | A/C/E to 42nd St./
Port Authority | 212-581-3080 | www.birdlandjazz.com

Some of the "best" names in "swingin' jazz" land onstage at this "comfortable" Theater District supper club, a "convenient" pick for natives and "out-of-towners" alike; "any table" provides a "decent view", but to avoid "expensive" outlays, the less-well-off may be better off barside.

Bitter End
19 | 12 | 15 | $10

G Village | 147 Bleecker St. (bet. La Guardia Pl. & Thompson St.) | A/B/C/D/E/F/V to W. 4th St. | 212-673-7030 | www.bitterend.com

"Renowned" for its role in "launching careers", from Bob Dylan to the Indigo Girls, this "landmark" Village music club safeguards "nostalgia" for "true music lovers'" in "unassuming" (ok, "collegiate") digs; it proudly preserves its "'60s grunge" vibe while enduring as a forum for current "up-and-coming artists."

Black & White
19 | 14 | 18 | $7

E Village | 86 E. 10th St. (bet. 3rd & 4th Aves.) | 6 to Astor Pl. | 212-253-0246

Whether you're "indie, punk or prep", this East Village rocker bar aims to please with "awesome" DJs spinning "all the classic" toonz in a "low-key" but "just-hip-enough" setting; alright, it's not far from a "dive", but the "young" regulars prefer to consider it a "neighborhood joint gone wild."

Black Bear Lodge
17 | 17 | 18 | $6

Gramercy | 274 Third Ave. (bet. 21st & 22nd Sts.) | 6 to 23rd St. | 212-253-2178 | www.bblnyc.com

"Come in from the cold" and drink "for cheap" at this "cabinlike" Gramercy "hang" where the "tacky lodge" look and "back fireplace" bring to mind the slopes "in Vermont . . . or something"; it "fits the bill" for a "night out with the boys", but "if you're over 30, you'll feel old" here.

Black Betty
19 | 17 | 18 | $7

Williamsburg | 366 Metropolitan Ave. (Havemeyer St.) | Brooklyn | G/L to Metropolitan Ave./Lorimer St. | 718-599-0243 | www.blackbetty.net

An "international crowd" is betting on a "late-night party scene" at this Mideastern bar/eatery in Williamsburg, where the DJing and dancing are so "amazing" that few fret that the seraglio decor is getting "ragged around the edges"; if the indoors overheats, the "backyard" is a welcome retreat.

Black Door
20 | 16 | 19 | $9

Chelsea | 127 W. 26th St. (bet. 6th & 7th Aves.) | 1 to 28th St. | 212-645-0215

Refreshingly "nontrendy", Park Bar's larger Chelsea sibling is a "reliable local" for "upscale postgrads" who claim the "dim lighting", vintage vibe and "affordable" prices "get you in a drinking mood"; it's an "easy" stop for "after-work" unwinding, and the "secret back room" is "fabulous for parties."

BlackFinn
17 | 15 | 17 | $8

E 50s | 218 E. 53rd St. (bet. 2nd & 3rd Aves.) | E/V to Lexington Ave./53rd St. | 212-355-6607 | www.blackfinnnyc.com

"Hordes" of "ex-frat boys" keep comin' back to this East Midtown sports bar, a "typical" setup outfitted with "flat-screens galore" (plus "mini-TVs in every booth"); for "hard" partying with "no pretension", the "happy-hour" specials will have you convinced you're "still in college."

🄱 Black Mountain Wine House ∇ 28 | 24 | 25 | $13

Carroll Gardens | 415 Union St. (Hoyt St.) | Brooklyn | F/G to Carroll St. | 718-522-4340 | www.blackmountainwinehouse.com

Farmhouse chic comes to Carroll Gardens via this rustic wine bar, a "cozy" spot (incongruously named after a Led Zeppelin tune) complete with a "fab fireplace", mismatched furniture and a tiny front patio equipped with Adirondack chairs; the vino list highlights small producers from around the globe matched with "tasty" small-plates bites.

Black Rabbit - | - | - | I

Greenpoint | 91 Greenpoint Ave. (bet. Franklin St. & Manhattan Ave.) | Brooklyn | G to Greenpoint Ave. | 718-349-1595 | www.blackrabbitbar.com

At this Greenpoint barroom, the carrots on a stick include a cozy fireplace, a picnic table–equipped back patio and booths tucked away behind saloon-style doors; a small-bites menu complements the sizable selection of classic cocktails and tap brew on offer, while bingo, trivia and game nights keep hip types hopping.

Black Sheep 15 | 11 | 19 | $7

Murray Hill | 583 Third Ave. (bet. 38th & 39th Sts.) | 4/5/6/7/S to 42nd St./Grand Central | 212-599-3476 | www.blacksheepnyc.com

It's "often overlooked", but Murray Hill "locals" easily find their way to this "average" Irish pub, knowing they won't be fleeced; some snub the "hit-or-miss crowd", but sheepish supporters say it's "actually a decent place" – so long as you "bring the party with you."

Blackstone's ∇ 17 | 15 | 17 | $7

E 50s | 245 E. 55th St. (bet. 2nd & 3rd Aves.) | E/V to Lexington Ave./53rd St. | 212-355-4474 | www.blackstonesbarnyc.com

For "after-work" elbow-bending with ample elbow room, this immense Midtown Irish joint includes a main bar for sports viewing, tables for a "game of pool" and an "appealing back room" with atrium-style "glass walls" and a stone fireplace; blending "a college bar with a pub", it should satisfy fans of both.

Blarney Stone 14 | 9 | 17 | $8

Chelsea | 340 Ninth Ave. (bet. 29th & 30th Sts.) | A/C/E to 34th St./Penn Station | 212-502-4656
E 40s | 710 Third Ave. (bet. 44th & 45th Sts.) | 4/5/6/7/S to 42nd St./Grand Central | 212-490-0457
Financial District | 11 Trinity Pl. (Morris St.) | 1/R/W to Rector St. | 212-269-4988
Financial District | 121 Fulton St. (bet. Nassau & William Sts.) | 2/3/4/5/A/C/J/M/Z to Fulton St./B'way/Nassau | 212-267-4042
Garment District | 410 Eighth Ave. (bet. 30th & 31st Sts.) | A/C/E to 34th St./Penn Station | 212-594-5100
W 40s | 307 W. 47th St. (bet. 8th & 9th Aves.) | C/E to 50th St. | 212-245-3438

"If you've got nowhere else to go", these "old-school", ultra-"basic" Irish pubs await with "cheap" fluids, "steam-table" grub and "rough-around-the-edges" decor; doubters deem its "creepy" crowd too "depressing", but those who recognize a "real man's kind of joint" salute the "last of a dying breed."

| | APPEAL | DECOR | SERVICE | COST |

NEW Bleecker Heights Tavern
| | - | - | - | M |

W Village | 296 Bleecker St., 2nd fl. (7th Ave. S.) | 1 to Christopher St. | 212-675-6157

Brought to you by the owners of Blackstone's, this new West Villager operates from the standard sports bar playbook, with the usual brick walls, plasma screens, cheap brews and rowdy crowds; what distinguishes it from the pack, however, is its hidden, second-floor perch, accessed only by a staircase inside the ground-floor tenant, a Five Guys burger joint – which conveniently supplies the grub as well.

Bleecker Street Bar
| | 18 | 12 | 18 | $7 |

NoHo | 56-58 Bleecker St. (bet. B'way & Lafayette St.) | 6 to Bleecker St. | 212-334-0244 | www.bleeckerstreetbarnyc.com

It's "nothing fancy", but pool, darts, "decent tunes" and taps that "flow at a good price" ensure there's "no shortage of things to do" at this NoHo "standby"; the "brown-wood" decor and "random" clientele come with the territory, but it's still "not bad" for a "college kids' watering hole."

Blender Theater
| | 19 | 15 | 16 | $13 |

Murray Hill | 127 E. 23rd St. (bet. Lexington & Park Aves.) | 6 to 23rd St. | 212-777-6800 | www.blendertheater.com

Catch your "fave indie band" at this "nice-size" Murray Hill music hall that mixes it up with a "wide assortment" of acts presented in a "converted movie theater" setting affording "good views" from both reserved seating and stagefront standing room; its bars vend "basic" booze for "stiff" tabs, but given the swell entertainment, it's a "great" blend.

Bleu Evolution
| | 19 | 20 | 17 | $10 |

Washington Heights | 808 W. 187th St. (bet. Ft. Washington & Pinehurst Aves.) | A to 190th St. | 212-928-6006 | www.bleuevolutionnyc.com

When Washington Heights dwellers yearn to "feel more downtown than uptown", this "eclectic" bar/eatery is a "mellow getaway" set in "colorful" digs stocked with "kitschy" antiques and augmented by a patio; a few are blue over the "spotty service", but for "cool vibes" it doesn't have "much competition" in these parts.

Blind Pig
| | 19 | 16 | 20 | $8 |

E Village | 233 E. 14th St. (bet. 2nd & 3rd Aves.) | L to 3rd Ave. | 212-209-1573 | www.blindpignyc.com

HDTVs tuned to "sporting events" practically "serve as lighting" at this "down-to-earth" East Village "joint" that "keeps guys happy" with "inexpensive" pops and "'90s" toonz; it's "harmless" enough for an "after-work" snort, though skeptics say the "typical frat" scene is a boar.

Z Blind Tiger Ale House
| | 20 | 15 | 19 | $8 |

G Village | 281 Bleecker St. (Jones St.) | 1 to Christopher St. | 212-462-4682 | www.blindtigeralehouse.com

"Beer geeks" welcome back this "veritable hops heaven", now "reincarnated" in a Bleecker Street address that "stays true" to the original's "serious" suds selection and "no-frills charm" (even if it's now "too close to NYU"); it still earns its stripes with a "dizzying array" of "gourmet" microbrews, but be prepared to "bust through the crowd" to get them.

	APPEAL	DECOR	SERVICE	COST

Blondies
19 | 13 | 20 | $8

E 90s | 1770 Second Ave. (bet. 92nd & 93rd Sts.) | 6 to 96th St. | 212-410-3300
W 70s | 212 W. 79th St. (bet. Amsterdam Ave. & B'way) | 1 to 79th St. | 212-362-4360
www.blondiessports.com

"Game-day nirvanas", these "pure sports bars" don't disappoint "avid" fans who turn up for the "cold brew priced right", "killer" Buffalo wings and, of course, "more TVs than customers"; so round up your "college buds" for some "yelling" and "fight songs", but go before the "big game" kicks off or else "it'll be impossible to find room."

Blue and Gold Tavern ⊖
18 | 9 | 17 | $5

E Village | 79 E. Seventh St. (bet. 1st & 2nd Aves.) | 6 to Astor Pl. | 212-473-8918

"Get wrecked on a budget" at this "dive-iest" of East Villagers, beloved for its "super-cheap" booze, "jukebox greatness" and "sticky", "time-stood-still" premises; just be prepared to "push your way through" the "older drinkers", "students on the prowl" and "obnoxious frat types" who move in on weekends.

Blue Donkey Bar
18 | 15 | 20 | $12

W 80s | 489 Amsterdam Ave. (bet. 83rd & 84th Sts.) | 1 to 86th St. | 212-496-0777 | www.homersworldfamous.com

Young Upper Westsiders burro down at this "small" "local" bar to "catch a happy hour" or recreate with pool, arcade games and "air hockey in the back"; snacks from Homer's malt shop next door help make it an "up-and-comer", though a few hold out for "more atmosphere."

Blue Fin
23 | 23 | 20 | $14

W 40s | W Times Square Hotel | 1567 Broadway (47th St.) | N/R/W to 49th St. | 212-918-1400 | www.brguestrestaurants.com

Like a "fish out of water" in the "heart of Times Square", Steve Hanson's "high-energy" seafood swanketeria boasts a "glass-encased" main-floor bar with a "voyeuristic view of the tourists" on the street plus a "sleek" upstairs room with "cool live jazz"; add in "top-shelf drinks" and "swift" service, and this "really chic" spot is "worth the hefty price tag."

⏸ Blue Note
23 | 17 | 17 | $15

G Village | 131 W. Third St. (bet. MacDougal St. & 6th Ave.) | A/B/C/D/E/F/V to W. 4th St. | 212-475-8592 | www.bluenote.net

See "world-class jazz" masters so "up-close" you'll "be ducking the trombone" at this "famous" Village music club where the "definitive" lineups keep the "funky" space jammed with cognoscenti and "tourists" alike; "stuck-up" service and "exorbitant" prices elicit some "blue notes", but when you're "five feet away from legends", the rest is "incidental."

Blue Owl
23 | 22 | 19 | $11

E Village | 196 Second Ave. (bet. 12th & 13th Sts.) | L to 1st Ave. | 212-505-2583

"Cocktails are the focus" at this East Village underground lounge where "personable bartenders" mix "unique creations" in speakeasy-esque quarters adjoined by a "super-secret", password-for-entree private room; it adds "a touch of class" to a street that's "in need of some", so its "slightly older" crowd doesn't give a hoot that it's "pricey."

Blue Ribbon

25 | 19 | 24 | $14

SoHo | 97 Sullivan St. (bet. Prince & Spring Sts.) | C/E to Spring St. | 212-274-0404 | www.blueribbonrestaurants.com

Insiders prize the "authentic Downtown vibe" at this "busy" SoHo eatery where the "small" bar is "crowded with diners" hunkering down over oysters and sampling the "extensive wine list" until a table opens up; it's also a "celebrated late-night hangout" where "all the chefs" and restaurant workers wind up to wind down.

Blue Ribbon Brooklyn

23 | 21 | 23 | $13

Park Slope | 280 Fifth Ave. (bet. 1st St. & Garfield Pl.) | Brooklyn | M/R to Union St. | 718-840-0404 | www.blueribbonrestaurants.com

A "breath of fresh air" for "upscale" Park Slopers, this satellite of the SoHo stalwart combines the "classiest" of atmospheres with "unpretentious service" and a "Brooklyn neighborhood feel"; an "easy place to chill" over oysters and wine, it "never fails" to make you "feel like you're in Manhattan" – especially when the check arrives.

Blue Ribbon Downing Street Bar

23 | 22 | 22 | $14

G Village | 34 Downing St. (bet. Bedford & Varick Sts.) | 1 to Houston St. | 212-691-0404 | www.blueribbonrestaurants.com

As "delightful" as "all things Blue Ribbon" are, this "beauty" of a wine bar (sited across from the like-named Village bakery) is staffed by "wise men" purveying a "finer grade of spirits and vino" in a "smart shoebox" of a space; true-blue fans tolerate the "cramped" quarters, knowing the Bromberg clan "won't let you down."

Blue Ribbon Sushi Bar & Grill

22 | 21 | 22 | $15

W 50s | 6 Columbus Hotel | 308 W. 58th St. (bet. 8th & 9th Aves.) | 1/A/B/C/D to 59th St./Columbus Circle | 212-397-0404 | www.blueribbonrestaurants.com

A fresh after-work "hideaway" for Midtown tipplers, this "upscale" bar adjunct to Blue Ribbon Sushi "in the heart of Columbus Circle" adheres to its Japanese theme with a pared-down design and a drinks list incorporating shochu and green tea salt; despite little street presence, it's already been discovered, so expect a tight fit at prime times.

NEW Blue Ruin ⬁

- | - | - | I

Garment District | 540 Ninth Ave. (bet. 39th & 40th Sts.) | A/C/E to 42nd St./Port Authority | no phone

It's all about the cheap hooch at this new dive bar parked on the back side of Port Authority; it has a lot to live down to given its pedigree (fka Bellevue Bar, fka Why Not?), but seems up to the task with trashy barmaids, ragtag decor, a pool table and one very loud jukebox.

Blue Seats

16 | 19 | 15 | $12

LES | 157 Ludlow St. (bet. Rivington & Stanton Sts.) | F/V to Lower East Side/2nd Ave. | 212-614-3033 | www.theblueseatsnyc.com

"Watch a game" – or watch *all* the games" – at this LES "sports fans' heaven", a "high-end", streamlined venue fielding "more plasma screens than you can imagine" and "fantastic booth seats" with personal tubes; but razzers see red at the booths' "ridiculous" hourly minimums and call the upscale concept "out of place in this 'hood."

	APPEAL	DECOR	SERVICE	COST

Blue Smoke

	21	18	21	$12

Murray Hill | 116 E. 27th St. (bet. Lexington Ave. & Park Ave. S.) | 6 to
28th St. | 212-447-7733 | www.bluesmoke.com

"Roll up your sleeves" for "booze, brews and barbecue" at Danny
Meyer's Murray Hill smokehouse, a "winner" for its "festive energy"
and "satisfying Southern feel"; some reckon the BBQ "feast" is the "attraction" here, but the bar's frequently "three deep", and catching
"cool" live combos in the basement club, the Jazz Standard, is
a "major" draw.

☑ Blue Water Grill

	23	24	21	$14

Union Sq | 31 Union Sq. W. (16th St.) | 4/5/6/L/N/Q/R/W to 14th St./
Union Sq. | 212-675-9500 | www.brguestrestaurants.com

The "wow factor" endures at Steve Hanson's Union Square seafood
stronghold, a former "bank building" that emanates "class on all
fronts" as "top-notch" staffers oversee a "vaulted" main-floor bar
populated by "chatty professionals"; add outside seating on the "ve-
randa" plus live "jazz in the cellar", and anyone "ready to shell out
some cash" is in for a "whale of a time."

Boat

	20	13	21	$6

Boerum Hill | 175 Smith St. (bet. Warren & Wyckoff Sts.) | Brooklyn |
F/G to Bergen St. | 718-254-0607

Hiply "mellow without the L train attitude", this Boerum Hill bar is
where "indie rockers" drink "cheap" and feed "one of the best jukeboxes" around; aye, it's a "very dingy" vessel, but the "friendly" service and "heavy pours" keep "all hands on deck."

☑ Boat Basin Cafe

	24	16	13	$9

W 70s | W. 79th St. (Hudson River) | 1 to 79th St. | 212-496-5542 |
www.boatbasincafe.com

Occupying some of the Upper West Side's "best real estate", this seasonal alfresco dock for "socializing Hamptons castoffs" boasts a
"million-dollar view" and "gorgeous summer sunsets" over the
Hudson; it's "a pain to get home" from and the "mass appeal"
may cause "dizzying waits", but the uniquely "scenic" setup makes it
all "worthwhile."

☑ Boathouse

	26	23	18	$13

E 70s | Central Park | Central Park Lake, enter on E. 72nd St.
(Central Park Dr. N.) | 6 to 68th St. | 212-517-2233 |
www.thecentralparkboathouse.com

"What a setting!" exclaim spectators at this "picturesque" indoor/
outdoor venue "surrounded by Central Park", a "classy" lakeside
venue where "watching the gondolas go by" makes for an instant "va-
cation"; the seasonal open-air bar is "blissful in the summer", and the
"romantic" possibilities "won't let you or your date down."

Bob

	19	14	17	$9

LES | 235 Eldridge St. (bet. Houston & Stanton Sts.) | F/V to Lower East Side/
2nd Ave. | 212-529-1807

"Hip-hop lovers" are bound to bob up at this "box-sized" Lower East
Side bar where "awesome DJs" hit the decks to spin the "best selection"
of beats; it's a consistently "kicking" time, though the "crammed"
space gets "pretty hot and sweaty" – "just like in music videos."

| | APPEAL | DECOR | SERVICE | COST |

☑ Bobo

22 | 23 | 20 | $15

W Village | 181 W. 10th St. (7th Ave. S.) | 1 to Christopher St. |
212-488-2626 | www.bobonyc.com

"Tucked away" in a "charming" Village townhouse, this elegantly antiqued bar in a "super" eatery oozes the kind of Continental "cool" that's a third-date deal-sealer; indeed, the "intimate" setting and "crisp service" can be so "romantic", no one will notice if you "skip the food."

NEW Body

22 | 19 | 16 | $14

Harlem | 701 W. 135th St. (12th Ave.) | 1 to 137th St./City College |
212-694-1416 | www.bodynewyorkcity.com

One of the anchors of the burgeoning club row on West Harlem's 12th Avenue, this "cool" new lounge/eatery is a 7,000-sq.-ft., tri-level colossus that "turns into a club" on weekend nights; though "salsa and hip-hop nights" bring in droves of "fun"-seekers, cynics say "it's not about how you feel but how you look" here.

Bogart's

14 | 14 | 16 | $11

Murray Hill | 99 Park Ave. S. (39th St.) | 4/5/6/7/S to 42nd St./
Grand Central | 212-922-9244 | www.bogartsonpark.com

Of all the gin joints in the world, Murray Hill's young "suits" turn up at this one "after work" since it's so "convenient" given the lack of options in the 'hood; it's "nothing special", but "management consultants" in a "back-to-college" mood make it their "headquarters."

Bohemian Hall

25 | 14 | 16 | $8

Astoria | 29-19 24th Ave. (31st St.) | Queens | N/W to Astoria Blvd. |
718-274-4925 | www.bohemianhall.com

Enjoy the "fresh air" and "bohemian bonhomie" at Astoria's "premier beer garden", a "huge" outdoor expanse where "merry mobs" of "families", "yuppies" and "unkempt hipsters" stake out "picnic table–style" seats to put away suds by the pitcher; its "popularity" produces "intense waits on line", so "if you don't have fun" here, there's "no hope left."

Boiler Room ⊄

17 | 9 | 19 | $7

E Village | 86 E. Fourth St. (bet. 1st & 2nd Aves.) | F/V to Lower East Side/
2nd Ave. | 212-254-7536 | www.boilerroomnyc.com

"Not your typical gay bar", this "raunchy" East Village "dive" is a chance to blow off steam with "friendly" chaps who are "ready to party"; still, some say it "used to be fun", but these days feels "kind of lame."

Bond Street

24 | 23 | 19 | $14

NoHo | 6 Bond St. (bet. B'way & Lafayette St.) | 6 to Bleecker St. |
212-777-2500

Bond with some chic "young things" at this "handsome" NoHo "hot spot", split into an enduringly "trendy" downstairs lounge made for "chilling" over "must-have" martinis and an upstairs sushi restaurant that's a "fantastic nosh"; either way, you'll "impress your date", but be ready for hyper pricing and "hipper-than-thou" attitude.

Bongo

18 | 19 | 20 | $14

Chelsea | 299 10th Ave. (bet. 27th & 28th Sts.) | C/E to 23rd St. |
212-947-3654 | www.bongonyc.com

This far West Chelsea bar/eatery "time-warped back a few decades" to hit the "perfect spot" with its retro furnishings, a tasteful ensemble straight from the "set of *That '70s Show*"; otherwise it drums up support with "honest drinks", oyster-centric chow and a "cool vibe" that "the few and special" will surely take to.

| | 24 | 22 | 20 | $13 |

Bookmarks

E 40s | Library Hotel | 299 Madison Ave., 14th fl. (41st St.) | 7/B/D/F/V to 42nd St./Bryant Park | 212-983-4500 | www.hospitalityholdings.com
Reminiscent of the (imaginary) "rooftop of your own Manhattan apartment", this "oasis above the Midtown fray" is a "fashionable" alfresco space crowning a "hip boutique hotel", with a slim slate patio, garden furniture and a winter solarium; golly, it's "expensive", but the "tight quarters" are still thronged with "Euro tourists" and other "cosmopolitan" types.

| | 17 | 14 | 20 | $9 |

Boss Tweed's Saloon

LES | 115 Essex St. (bet. Delancey & Rivington Sts.) | F/J/M/Z to Delancey/Essex Sts. | 212-475-9997 | www.bosstweeds.com
A "regular pub" with "down 'n' dirty" Irish vibes, this Lower Eastsider persuades "college" types to turn out with an "extended" happy hour and extras including a patio and pool table; but those opposed consider a "filled-to-the-gills" "frat bar" the "least cool" place to be.

| | ▽ 15 | 12 | 18 | $7 |

Botanica

NoLita | 47 E. Houston St. (bet. Mott & Mulberry Sts.) | 6 to Bleecker St. | 212-343-7251
With its "eclectically decorated" digs, copacetic service and "low" cost, this NoLita basement is "everything you'd ever want in a dive bar"; it "brings you back" to a time before "rampant gentrification" with a "great happy hour" that helps customers get "hammered well into the night."

| | 22 | 21 | 21 | $15 |

Bottega del Vino

E 50s | 7 E. 59th St. (bet. 5th & Madison Aves.) | 4/5/6/N/R/W to 59th St./Lexington Ave. | 212-223-3028 | www.bottegadelvinonyc.com
A "magnet" for "Euros and Euro wannabes", this "beautiful" Midtown restaurant (descended from the Veronese original) uncorks an "enviable variety" of "superb" vintages in its froufrou front wine bar; staffed by a "top-notch" team, it's "expensive" but "worth every penny" when you need an "escape to Italy."

| | 20 | 18 | 17 | $14 |

Boucarou

E Village | 64 E. First St. (bet. 1st & 2nd Aves.) | F/V to Lower East Side/2nd Ave. | 212-529-3262 | www.boucaroulounge.com
Plan on "staying to party" as this "roomy" East Village restaurant transforms itself nightly into a "crowded" lounge with beaucoup banquettes, "interesting cocktails" and "on-point" DJs; so even if jaded go-getters see a "so-so" scene and somewhat "bored" service, "for the layperson it will do just fine."

| | 19 | 16 | 17 | $11 |

Bounce

E 70s | 1403 Second Ave. (73rd St.) | 6 to 77th St. | 212-535-2183

Bounce Deuce

E Village | 103 Second Ave. (6th St.) | F/V to Lower East Side/2nd Ave. | 212-533-6700
www.bounceny.com
"There aren't many like" these sports bar/lounges where "more than enough flat-screens" air "all games all the time" and the

"Cosmo crowd" roots for the designer drinks and "sleek" surroundings; it's made for "more mature" jocks, though traditionalists gripe it's "not a club, so lower the music."

Bourbon St.

15	11	16	$7

W 70s | 407 Amsterdam Ave. (bet. 79th & 80th Sts.) | 1 to 79th St. | 212-721-1332 | www.bourbonstreetnyc.com

"Get your New Orleans on" at this "cheap 'n' easy" Upper Westsider, a "post-collegiate pub crawl" point with all the "beer specials", "frat-boy wannabes" and "chicks dancing on the bar" that you can stand; though dismissed by some as "cheese city", the "packed house" suggests it's a "helluva lot more fun than it should be."

NEW Bourbon Street B&G

20	19	20	$9

W 40s | 346 W. 46th St. (bet. 8th & 9th Aves.) | A/C/E to 42nd St./Port Authority | 212-245-2030 | www.bourbonny.com

"They've got the New Orleans look down" at this Restaurant Row bar/eatery, a "spacious", Big Easy-themed duplex that's "worth hitting up" for a "post-work/pre-theater" pop; though "not a packed social scene", it's a "decent" enough drop-by despite a distinct "frat" following.

Bourgeois Pig

24	19	20	$12

E Village | 111 E. Seventh St. (bet. Ave. A & 1st Ave.) | L to 1st Ave. | 212-475-2246

"Ooh-la-la", this East Village boîte channels a "European drawing room" with "bohemian accoutrements" like mirrors, a chandelier and "grandma's-living-room" couches setting the scene for a bougie lineup of "wonderful wines" and French nibbles; the bigger digs may be "slightly scruffy", but with "a date who's paying" it's an "enjoyable rendezvous."

Bowery Ballroom

24	17	16	$9

LES | 6 Delancey St. (bet. Bowery & Chrystie St.) | F/V to Lower East Side/2nd Ave. | 212-533-2111 | www.boweryballroom.com

Those who "choose to rock" tout this Lower Eastsider as the "ideal music venue" for catching "top indie bands" in a "medium-small" hall boasting "awesome sound", "unobstructed" views and "cool vintage" looks; "bars upstairs and down" dispense somewhat "watery drinks", but the show is what "it's all about" here, so fans have "no complaints."

Bowery Electric

21	17	19	$11

E Village | 327 Bowery (2nd St.) | B/D/F/V to B'way/Lafayette St. | 212-228-0228 | www.theboweryelectric.com

Cranking up the voltage on the "oh-so-hot Bowery", this "way cool" bar/lounge gives the "tight jeans" set an outlet to hear "awesome DJs" spinning rock 'n' roll in a "long", "dim" space; if the current electricity's "not over the top", word is it shows "lots of potential" and "you'll never have to wait to get in."

Z Bowery Hotel Bar

23	23	19	$14

E Village | Bowery Hotel | 355 Bowery (bet. 2nd & 3rd Sts.) | F/V to Lower East Side/2nd Ave. | 212-505-1300 | www.theboweryhotel.com

Confirming "the Bowery's makeover" with a dose of vintage "New York glam", this "quiet", "oh-so-swanky" lobby bar revives the "robber baron" era with enough "taxidermy", Persian carpets and "dark wood" to make its "privileged" patrons "feel like Astors"; just beware that it's technically "for guests only" and the hotel "rooms may be cheaper than the drinks."

| | APPEAL | DECOR | SERVICE | COST |

Bowery Poetry Club
NoHo | 308 Bowery (bet. Bleecker & Houston Sts.) | F/V to Lower East Side/
2nd Ave. | 212-614-0505 | www.bowerypoetry.com

23 | 19 | 22 | $7

A "throwback" to "beatnik joints" past, this NoHo art space gives "poets and other performers" a forum to present "the new and the now"
while literati "drink, relax" and enjoy "something different"; who
knows, the "infusion of culture and counterculture" may even make
you "feel young and hip" again.

Bowery Wine Company
E Village | 13 E. First St. (bet. Bowery & 2nd Ave.) | F/V to Lower East Side/
2nd Ave. | 212-614-0800 | www.bowerywineco.com

20 | 18 | 20 | $12

Bowery "winos" are redefined at this roomy vino specialist that offers
"elite" East Villagers a "decent" array of wines and "tasty treats"
served by a "helpful" crew; snipers suggest the venue "lacks pizzazz"
("feels like an airport bar"), but the condo crowd is crazy about
the "outdoor seating."

Bowlmor Lanes
G Village | 110 University Pl., 3rd fl. (bet. 12th & 13th Sts.) | 4/5/
6/L/N/Q/R/W to 14th St./Union Sq. | 212-255-8188 |
www.bowlmor.com

22 | 17 | 14 | $11

If that "jones to bowl" strikes, this "retro" Village alley is pimped out
with "nightclublike" lights and music plus a full bar where "ultracool"
players circulate; the booze, "per-frame" fee and "shoe rental" can get
"pricey", but these are the "liveliest" lanes around, and when you're
ready to roll "there aren't too many others" to pin hopes on.

⊠ Box, The
LES | 189 Chrystie St. (bet. Rivington & Stanton Sts.) | B/D to Grand St. |
212-982-9301 | www.theboxnyc.com

25 | 23 | 19 | $18

"Expect the wild and the unexpected" at this "steamy", late-night LES
supper club, a "Victorianish" cabaret where "naughty" performers engage in "vaudeville" acts, "over-the-top burlesque" and overall "debauchery" suggesting the "decline of Western civilization"; be
prepared to "throw money to the wind", and since it's one of the "hottest" scenes around, "good luck getting in."

Boxcar Lounge
E Village | 168 Ave. B (bet. 10th & 11th Sts.) | L to 1st Ave. | 212-473-2830 |
www.boxcarlounge.com

18 | 15 | 17 | $8

It's hardly as "big as a boxcar", but this East Villager's railroad space
is an "enjoyably petite" retreat where regulars who engineer some
room feel "at home" enjoying a "happy hour that lasts forever" (from
4 to 10 PM on Sundays); if it's "too crowded", just make tracks for the
"patio in back."

Branch
E 50s | 226 E. 54th St. (bet. 2nd & 3rd Aves.) | E/V to Lexington Ave./
53rd St. | 212-688-5577 | www.branchny.com

17 | 18 | 15 | $12

Quite "swanky for Midtown", this weekends-only club suits the
suits with "boutiquelike" looks and a sizable split-level space providing "lots of room to dance"; it's also "not a pain to get in",
though foes whack it as "too expensive" and "pretentious" given
the "lackluster crowd."

	APPEAL	DECOR	SERVICE	COST

ⓩ Brandy Library
TriBeCa | 25 N. Moore St. (bet. Hudson & Varick Sts.) | 1 to Franklin St. | 212-226-5545 | www.brandylibrary.com — **25** | **26** | **24** | **$14**

Check out the "perfect dram" at this "top-shelf" TriBeCa "temple of libation" that keeps "serious drinkers" in "fine spirits" with its "jaw-dropping selection"; channeling a "wood-paneled gentleman's club" with "bookshelves" stocked with bottles and "sophisticated" sommeliers, it appeals to "older" finance types who don't flinch at the "eye-popping tabs."

Brandy's Piano Bar
E 80s | 235 E. 84th St. (bet. 2nd & 3rd Aves.) | 4/5/6 to 86th St. | 212-744-4949 | www.brandysnyc.com — **23** | **14** | **20** | **$10**

Whether you're coming from "Broadway" or "Nebraska", you'll want to "bust out a tune" at this Upper East Side piano bar where the "witty" staff hosts "fabulous" songfests and open-mike nights; it's a "blast" "even if you're not gay", but the "teeny" room "fills up fast", so insiders "arrive early."

Brasserie 8½
W 50s | 9 W. 57th St. (bet. 5th & 6th Aves.) | F to 57th St. | 212-829-0812 | www.brasserie812.com — **21** | **22** | **21** | **$13**

"Posh but not stuck up", this sunken Midtown lounge/restaurant has enough "comfy" "upper-class" élan to win over a "date" or a "client" – "if you can stand the prices"; the "swanky", "'60s-throwback" design features an "epic winding staircase" that will "wow upon first sight" but makes for "intimidating" entrances and tricky "navigating" once you've had a few.

Brass Monkey
Meatpacking | 55 Little W. 12th St. (bet. 10th Ave. & Washington St.) | A/C/E/L to 14th St./8th Ave. | 212-675-6686 | www.brassmonkeybar.com — **19** | **15** | **18** | **$9**

A "normal bar" that "sticks out" in the Meatpacking District's "club-hopping" jungle, this "no-attitude" duplex is a "refreshing" exception that vends "cheaper" hooch to "unfancy" folk (it's "not full of trendy-wendies"); even though there's lots of room, when the "boisterous" "party animals" swing by it can get "too tight to maneuver"; N.B. there's also a breezy roofdeck space.

Brazen Head
Boerum Hill | 228 Atlantic Ave. (bet. Boerum Pl. & Court St.) | Brooklyn | F/G to Bergen St. | 718-488-0430 | www.brazenheadbrooklyn.com — **20** | **13** | **21** | **$6**

The "phenomenal tap list" makes this Boerum Hill "neighborhood bar" an "HQ" for "beer geeks", construction workers" and "Brooklyn Law students"; if there's "nothing particularly cool" going on, it's worth heading over for "friendly conversation" and that "patio in the back."

Bridge Cafe
Financial District | 279 Water St. (Dover St.) | 4/5/6/J/M/Z to Brooklyn Bridge/City Hall | 212-227-3344 | www.eatgoodinny.com — **24** | **19** | **23** | **$10**

Nestled under the Brooklyn Bridge lies this Financial District landmark, a "wooden" tavern serving the sauce since 1794 down among the "girders"; "history buffs" may imagine they're "walking into another century", though the "government and business types" hanging out here are right "up to date."

Broadway Dive

W 100s | 2662 Broadway (bet. 101st & 102nd Sts.) | 1 to 103rd St. | 212-865-2662 | www.divebarnyc.com

APPEAL	DECOR	SERVICE	COST
15	12	18	$7

No kidding, it's strictly "down 'n' dirty", but this "aptly named" UWS fixture is "still going strong" as a "local crowd" – everyone from "college kids" to "lone men" – gets nice and "relaxed" over budget bevvies; while "not a first date place", it's handy "in a pinch" for "watching the Mets and drinking a cold one."

Brooklyn Ale House

Williamsburg | 103 Berry St. (N. 8th St.) | Brooklyn | L to Bedford Ave. | 718-302-9811 | www.brooklynalehouse.net

APPEAL	DECOR	SERVICE	COST
▽ 18	14	21	$6

Among the "last remaining" Billyburg bars with a "true neighborhood vibe", this slacker "haven" houses an ample assortment of "beers on tap" plus a "pool table in the back"; the "nice bartenders save the day" at a place that's both "dog-friendly" and "a little dog-eared."

NEW Brooklyn Bowl

Williamsburg | 61 Wythe Ave. (bet. 11th & 12th Sts.) | Brooklyn | G to Nassau Ave. | 718-963-3369 | www.brooklynbowl.com

APPEAL	DECOR	SERVICE	COST
-	-	-	M

Taking bowling to a new level, this 23,000-sq.-ft. Williamsburg juggernaut offers a live performance space and food from Blue Ribbon in addition to 16 state-of-the-art lanes; set in a former ironworks warehouse, it's adjacent to Brooklyn Brewery (which is supplying some of the suds) – and just a couple of blocks from The Gutter, the nabe's other pinhead palace.

Brooklyn Brewery

Williamsburg | 79 N. 11th St. (bet. Berry St. & Wythe Ave.) | Brooklyn | L to Bedford Ave. | 718-486-7422 | www.brooklynbrewery.com

APPEAL	DECOR	SERVICE	COST
23	15	20	$7

The beer's produced "on the spot" and tapped at "rock-bottom prices" at this Williamsburg brewery that provides a chance to sample the "freshest" suds during its "limited hours" (Friday nights and Saturday afternoons only); there's also a tour available, but most go to snag "a picnic table" in the "warehouse" space and mingle with the "raucous community."

☑ Brooklyn Inn ⌀

Boerum Hill | 148 Hoyt St. (Bergen St.) | Brooklyn | F/G to Bergen St. | 718-522-2525

APPEAL	DECOR	SERVICE	COST
27	24	21	$6

"Old-world Brooklyn" is "charmingly" preserved at this "beautiful" Boerum Hill saloon where the "amazing carved wooden bar" recalls an "era past", while the "rocking jukebox" and "relaxed vibe" are totally contemporary; it "feels like home" to local habitués, which may explain why they "can be a little territorial."

☑ Brooklyn Social ⌀

Carroll Gardens | 335 Smith St. (bet. Carroll & President Sts.) | Brooklyn | F/G to Carroll St. | 718-858-7758

APPEAL	DECOR	SERVICE	COST
25	23	23	$8

"Old school and hip" merge at this Carroll Gardens "standout", once a Sicilian social club and now an "elegant" preserve of "speakeasy charm" where "super-chill bartenders" ply an "inventive repertoire" of specialty cocktails; the "tin ceiling" and "classic jazz" confer a "cool backdrop" for the socializing "hordes in skinny jeans", but there's "no attitude" here, *capisce*?

	APPEAL	DECOR	SERVICE	COST

NEW Brookvin

▽ 22 | 17 | 21 | $13

Park Slope | 381 Seventh Ave. (bet. 11th & 12th Sts.) | Brooklyn | F to 7th Ave. | 718-768-9463 | www.brookvin.com

From the owner of Park Slope's Big Nose Full Body vino shop across the street comes this "cozy" wine bar, whose "unusual" selection of vintages is matched with locavore-friendly small plates (the house-cured charcuterie is a must); "knowledgeable" staffers, a "no-pretenses" air and a lovely back garden add to its allure.

Broome Street Bar

16 | 13 | 16 | $8

SoHo | 363 W. Broadway (Broome St.) | C/E to Spring St. | 212-925-2086

"Lighten up" at this "low-key" SoHo refuge, a brush with "'60s" mellowdom, where the "solid beer selection" makes for "great daytime drinking" with "spot-on" burgers on the side; the "no-frills" interior "hasn't changed in decades", but like the longtime clientele, it's "aged well."

☒ Brother Jimmy's BBQ

17 | 13 | 16 | $8

E 70s | 1485 Second Ave. (bet. 77th & 78th Sts.) | 6 to 77th St. | 212-288-0999

E 90s | 1644 Third Ave. (92nd St.) | 6 to 96th St. | 212-426-2020

Garment District | 416 Eighth Ave. (31st St.) | A/C/E to 34th St./Penn Station | 212-967-7603

NEW Murray Hill | 181 Lexington Ave. (31st St.) | 6 to 33rd St. | 212-779-7427

W 80s | 428 Amsterdam Ave. (bet. 80th & 81st Sts.) | B/C to 81st St. | 212-501-7515

www.brotherjimmys.com

"Yee-haw!", these "Deep South" themers are a "frat-tastic flashback" to "college days" populated by "red state expats" in "baseball caps and khakis" getting trashed on "PBRs" and "fishbowls of sugary swamp drinks"; sure, they're "immature", but with "ACC sports action", "rockin' '80s" tunes and waitresses "cuter than the Hooters girls", "how can they be bad?"

Bryant Park Grill/Cafe

22 | 20 | 18 | $12

W 40s | 25 W. 40th St. (behind NY Public Library) | 7/B/D/F/V to 42nd St./Bryant Park | 212-840-6500 | www.arkrestaurants.com

A "favorite" with "after-work suits" on "summer evenings", this "yuppie central" locus in Bryant Park is a "key outdoor" hunting ground where "largely single" hopefuls "scope the scene" sipping high-priced libations; they get so crowded that it's "tough to get service", though the indoor grill is a calmer "oasis" that's equally "attractive."

B-Side

▽ 17 | 12 | 20 | $6

E Village | 204 Ave. B (bet. 12th & 13th Sts.) | L to 1st Ave. | 212-475-4600

"Low-key" sorts sidle into this "easygoing" East Village "dive" to imbibe "on the cheap", notably that "shot-and-a-beer special" guaranteed to "make your eyes water"; but aside from the "great jukebox" and "pool table", the atmosphere charts about as high as "your buddy's place."

B61 ♻

24 | 18 | 23 | $7

Carroll Gardens | 187 Columbia St. (Degraw St.) | Brooklyn | F/G to Carroll St. | 718-643-5400 | www.almarestaurant.com

"Named after a bus line", this Carroll Gardens bar is a local stop for underserved neighbors "hungry for places" featuring "excellent" drinks, a "good jukebox" and a free game of pool; the "warm" staff and

	APPEAL	DECOR	SERVICE	COST

Manhattan views from the front windows may move you to stay for a bite "upstairs at Alma."

Bua

21 | 20 | 19 | $8

E Village | 122 St. Marks Pl. (bet. Ave. A & 1st Ave.) | 6 to Astor Pl. | 212-979-6276 | www.buany.com

Like a "stepped-up" Irish pub, this East Village bar/lounge is a low-lit "chill spot" enhanced by "exposed brick", shuttered windows and "friendly lads behind the bar"; the "young" crowd can make for a "full house at times", but the sidewalk seating helps ease the "squeeze."

Bubble Lounge

22 | 20 | 19 | $14

TriBeCa | 228 W. Broadway (bet. Franklin & White Sts.) | 1 to Franklin St. | 212-431-3433 | www.bubblelounge.com

"Wall Streeters" and "couples" out for a "sophisticated tryst" surface at this "plush" TriBeCa champagne lounge, a "sexy", "long-on-style" enclave of "faded opulence" that still delivers some "fizz"; but the "high-maintenance" tabs are "annoying" unless "your rich uncle is paying", and the trendsetters popped out "15 minutes ago."

Buceo 95

▽ 21 | 21 | 21 | $12

W 90s | 201 W. 95th St. (bet. Amsterdam Ave. & B'way) | 1/2/3 to 96th St. | 212-662-7010 | www.buceo95.com

The owners of the UWS Dive Bar go upscale with this "lovely" wine bar featuring high ceilings, a marble bartop and a tavern-esque vibe; a refined selection of mostly European wines is offered by the quartino or by the bottle, while the open kitchenette supplies "eclectic" tapas items.

☒ Buddakan

24 | 27 | 21 | $16

Chelsea | 75 Ninth Ave. (16th St.) | A/C/E/L to 14th St./8th Ave. | 212-989-6699 | www.buddakannyc.com

A "grand space with even grander expectations", this Chelsea Market Asian "wonderland" is the "ultimate hot spot" for a "beautiful" crowd that keeps the "exotic" ground-floor lounge "happening"; "snooty service" and "hefty" tabs come with the territory, but after a gawp at the "sumptuous" space (especially its "monumental" main dining room), all agree the "sights are worth the price."

Buddha Bar

24 | 26 | 19 | $15

Meatpacking | 25 Little W. 12th St. (bet. 9th Ave. & Washington St.) | A/C/E/L to 14th St./8th Ave. | 212-647-7314 | www.buddhabarnyc.com

If you can't "get to Paris to see the original", this swank bar/restaurant brings its "'wow' factor" to the Meatpacking District on a "huge" scale, spreading "Asian flair" over a "magnificent" space with a colossal "Buddha as the centerpiece" and a "fab" soundtrack; with a "red-rope crowd" fanning the "souped"-up scene, it can be "tough" to access, but sure to send those "willing to shell out" the bucks into "nirvana."

NEW Building on Bond

- | - | - | M

Boerum Hill | 112 Bond St. (Pacific St.) | Brooklyn | C/G to Hoyt-Schermerhorn | 347-853-8687

Coffee shop by day, bar/eatery by night, this split personality Boerum Hill venue boasts a round-the-clock low-key vibe that's made it a neighborhood hit; it's furnished in an artfully distressed style (think unfinished wood, exposed pipes) by the design team responsible for places like Suba and The Box.

	APPEAL	DECOR	SERVICE	COST

Bull and Bear
21 | 19 | 21 | $15

E 40s | Waldorf-Astoria | 570 Lexington Ave. (49th St.) | 6 to 51st St./
Lexington Ave. | 212-872-4900 | www.bullandbearsteakhouse.com
The "fat cats" bear down on this "old-school" "standby" in the Waldorf,
a "men's-clubbish" lair that's like a "wood-and-leather" annex of the
"Stock Exchange" (there's even an in-house ticker); the "generous
pours" may help you "clinch a deal", but "bring a client and expense it."

Bull McCabe's
17 | 11 | 17 | $6

E Village | 29 St. Marks Pl. (bet. 2nd & 3rd Aves.) | 6 to Astor Pl. |
212-982-9895 | www.ryansnyc.com
This "epitome" of no-bull East Village grunge unites "guys in black
leather" and "NYU" slummers in "dark" quarters equipped with a pool
table, dartboard and "rocking" juke; sure, "cheap drinks are the draw",
but what other dive has a "downed plane" in its backyard garden?

Bull's Head Tavern
18 | 13 | 18 | $8

Gramercy | 295 Third Ave. (bet. 22nd & 23rd Sts.) | 6 to 23rd St. |
212-685-2589
"Don't bother dressing up" for this "laid-back" Gramercy hangout, a
"divey" destination where "mostly male" "post-collegians" head to
"relax and play pool"; for "only five bucks", Thursday night's "cover
band" provides "'90s nostalgists with a reliably "jamming" time.

Bungalow 8
25 | 23 | 18 | $16

Chelsea | 515 W. 27th St. (bet. 10th & 11th Aves.) | C/E to 23rd St. |
212-629-3333
Catch "celebs in their natural habitat" at scenestress Amy Sacco's "im-
possibly chic" West Chelsea lounge, a longtime stronghold of "relentless
buzz", where "Paris, Lindsay and company" hold court amid the banquettes and "palm trees"; once a "hot ticket", some say its glory days are
over although "making it past the velvet rope" can still be a challenge.

Burp Castle
18 | 16 | 18 | $9

E Village | 41 E. Seventh St. (bet. 2nd & 3rd Aves.) | 6 to Astor Pl. |
212-982-4576
Make it a "quiet night out" at this East Village beer specialist with a
vast variety of brews (stressing "fabulous Belgians"), Gregorian
"chants" on the soundtrack and monastic house rules to "shush" any
loud chatter; there's much "worth savoring" if you hold suds holy,
though these days purists "miss the bartenders' monk outfits."

Bushwick Country Club
∇ 18 | 18 | 20 | $7

Williamsburg | 618 Grand St. (Leonard St.) | Brooklyn | L to Grand St. |
718-388-2114 | www.bushwickcountryclub.com
Find out if you're "hip enough to be white trash" at this Williamsburg
bar where the "kitschy" gimmicks include a "photo booth" and a
"funny-looking", six-hole "miniature golf course in back"; more con-
ventionally, it also boasts "cheap drinks" and a "sweet" staff.

Butter
22 | 24 | 20 | $15

E Village | 415 Lafayette St. (bet. Astor Pl. & E. 4th St.) | 6 to Astor Pl. |
212-253-2828 | www.butterrestaurant.com
If you're "cool enough to get by the bouncer", spread out with the
"high rollers" and enjoy some "celebrity spotting" in this "woodsy"

East Village eatery's "sexy" downstairs lounge; it draws some mighty tasty "eye candy", and even skeptics concede the "famous Monday night" parties are as "trendy" as they come.

Buttermilk Bar

23 | 15 | 20 | $7

Park Slope | 577 Fifth Ave. (16th St.) | Brooklyn | M/R to Prospect Ave. | 718-788-6297

According to the "cool crowd" currently "gentrifying" South Park Slope, this "dark" bar "churns out great drinks" for low dough and throws in "hipster perks" like "old board games", pinball and an "excellent jukebox"; add occasional live "country music" and there's more than enough "good stuff" to "keep you entertained."

NEW Cabana Bar

22 | 20 | 20 | $11

Park Slope | 648 President St. (5th Ave.) | Brooklyn | M/R to Union St. | 718-399-2161 | www.playafoods.com

Park Slope's closet beach bums welcome this newcomer flanking the Latino eatery Playa, a "cute cabana hut" where "sunny" servers at the frond-fringed "tiki bar" dispense tropical tipples; fitted out with a palm tree, driftwood and an ocean-spray mural, it's stirring up waves of "good vibes."

Cabanas

22 | 23 | 17 | $13

Chelsea | Maritime Hotel | 88 Ninth Ave., rooftop (enter at 16th or 17th Sts.) | A/C/E/L to 14th St./8th Ave. | 212-835-5537 | www.themaritimehotel.com

For your "summer enjoyment", these two "spacious" deck lounges at the Maritime Hotel are "going strong", providing "Miami-esque" alfresco allure and the "right attitude (but not too much)"; it's sometimes "tough to get in" and service can be "sketchy", but boosters soothed by "cool breezes" and cold mojitos shrug "so what?"

NEW Cabin Down Below

- | - | - | M

E Village | 110 Ave. A, downstairs (bet. 6th & 7th Sts.) | L to 1st Ave. | no phone

'Secret' barrooms are a NYC tradition dating back to Prohibition, and the latest is this tiny unmarked space below an East Village pizzeria; furnished like a cozy den with wood paneling, bookshelves and a fireplace, it plays eclectic music, draws a hip (and sometimes famous) crowd and serves no-frills drinks (i.e. no fancy-schmancy specialty cocktails); N.B. there's also a small patio for nicotine fiends.

Cafe Bar

▽ 22 | 19 | 18 | $11

Astoria | 32-90 36th St. (34th Ave.) | Queens | G/R/V to Steinway St. | 718-204-5273

Cafe by day and "hip" bar by night, this Astoria "art" enclave is a "must hangout" for anyone craving a "Williamsburg-esque" experience on local turf; the "cute", "kitschy" room is reliably "hoppin'" but "never packed", and though "you may need to hunt down" service, at least it's always "relaxed."

Z Cafe Carlyle

26 | 24 | 24 | $18

E 70s | Carlyle Hotel | 35 E. 76th St. (Madison Ave.) | 6 to 77th St. | 212-744-1600 | www.thecarlyle.com

Break out "your good duds" for a trip to this "stylish cabaret" in the Carlyle Hotel, "one of the classiest spots" in town thanks to a "yesteryear aura" mixed with "slightly louche charm" that's likely to kindle "romance"; "alas, Bobby Short is gone", but its "well-established talent" still entertains the "older", "well-heeled" attendees who can afford the price of admission.

Café Charbon
23 | 22 | 20 | $10

LES | 168-170 Orchard St. (Stanton St.) | F/V to Lower East Side/2nd Ave. | 212-420-7520

With its faux French facade and an interior "studded with Gallicana", this Lower East Side bar/eatery is an "attractive" charbon copy of a "Paris cafe", though purists are reminded of the "France pavilion at Epcot"; either way, "informed" barkeeps who "mix an unbelievable cocktail" are the real deal here.

Café des Artistes/The Parlor
24 | 25 | 23 | $15

W 60s | 1 W. 67th St. (bet. Columbus Ave. & CPW) | 1 to 66th St. | 212-877-3500 | www.cafenyc.com

For a "special one-on-one get-together", the "excellent lounge" at this "first-class" restaurant near Lincoln Center is a "sophisticated", "old-school" charmer where the "gracious" service and "posh" ambiance are bound to fan any "romantic" flames; it's "not for the immature" or the unsophisticated, but everyone else will "feel like (and pay) a million bucks."

Cafe Deville/Bar Bleu
21 | 18 | 19 | $11

E Village | 103 Third Ave. (13th St.) | L to 3rd Ave. | 212-477-4500 | www.cafedevillenyc.com

This très français East Villager sports a "spacious bar" in the ground-floor restaurant and a "cool little" blue-lit lounge downstairs; incentives include "reasonably priced" pops and an "awesome happy hour" that will up the "sex appeal" if you're here to "hang with a date."

Cafe Gitane ⇔
22 | 18 | 15 | $9

NoLita | 242 Mott St. (bet. Houston & Prince Sts.) | 6 to Spring St. | 212-334-9552

"See and be seen" with a "cosmopolitan" crew at this "stylish" NoLita cafe that's perpetually "filled to the gills" with "Eurotrash" and "trust fund kids" ("don't these people have jobs?"); it's "so pretentious" that you can't help but "love it", but also so "small" that you can count on a "wait every time."

Cafe Lalo ⇔
22 | 19 | 15 | $11

W 80s | 201 W. 83rd St. (bet. Amsterdam Ave. & B'way) | 1 to 86th St. | 212-496-6031 | www.cafelalo.com

Experience "chic(k) cafe" society at this "upbeat" Upper West Side coffee bar, a well-known *You've Got Mail* set lauded for its "fabulous desserts" and "yummy drinks"; despite "ditzy service" and "tightly packed tables" that "make coach class look generous", the "charm" holds up if you arrive at "off-peak times" and "hit the ATM first" ("it's cash only").

Cafe Noir
22 | 17 | 17 | $10

SoHo | 32 Grand St. (Thompson St.) | A/C/E to Canal St. | 212-431-7910 | www.cafenoirny.com

Study "international relations" at this "energetic" SoHo cafe, a "Euro haunt" where the "dim lighting and ceiling fans" lend a noirish mood; it's "cheerful" and "chic without the velvet rope", and it works either for a "first drink" or to "finish off the night."

	APPEAL	DECOR	SERVICE	COST

Cafe Notte
| | 21 | 20 | 20 | $14 |

E 80s | 1626 Second Ave. (bet. 84th & 85th Sts.) | 4/5/6 to 86th St. | 212-288-5203 | www.nottewinebar.com

While a tad more "gentrified" than "its predecessor, Dt.Ut", this "neighborhood-friendly" cafe/wine bar is still "easygoing" enough for a "date" or "grown-up conversation" over a largely Italian list of vinos; with "romantic" candlelight, lots of "comfortable" couches and occasional live music, it "shows promise" despite the "high price point."

Cafeteria
| | 19 | 17 | 16 | $13 |

Chelsea | 119 Seventh Ave. (17th St.) | 1 to 18th St. | 212-414-1717 | www.cafeteriagroup.com

Chelsea's "pretty people" take "24-hour comfort" in this "busy staple", a "favorite alternative to late-night diners" thanks to its "groovy" canteen look, "kicking" music and "hotshot" clientele; it's also "dependable" for "yummy snacking" after "a night of sin", though some bemoan "snitty service" from staffers out of an "Abercrombie & Fitch catalog."

Cafe Wha?
| | 21 | 13 | 16 | $10 |

G Village | 115 MacDougal St., downstairs (bet. Bleecker & W. 3rd Sts.) | A/B/C/D/E/F/V to W. 4th St. | 212-254-3706 | www.cafewha.com

This "high-energy" Village music venue is set in a "bare-bones" "old basement" where the "outrageously good house band" rouses the crowd to "dance and sing in the aisles"; but snoots who call it a "pricey" outing "made for tourists" and "drunken bachelorettes" shrug "whatever . . ."

Caffe Dante ⊄
| | 21 | 16 | 18 | $10 |

G Village | 79-81 MacDougal St. (bet. Bleecker & Houston Sts.) | 1 to Houston St. | 212-982-5275 | www.caffe-dante.com

A Village "mainstay", this "authentic" Italian coffeehouse offers espresso and "fantastic desserts"; the atmosphere's "rushed" and the decor "slightly disheveled", but a "pit stop" is always "worthwhile."

Caffe Reggio ⊄
| | 20 | 18 | 16 | $9 |

G Village | 119 MacDougal St. (bet. Bleecker & W. 3rd Sts.) | A/B/C/D/E/F/V to W. 4th St. | 212-475-9557 | www.caffereggio.com

It's all about the "history" at this "quaint", '20s-era "Village staple", an "old-style Italian cafe" where the "antique furniture" and paintings make for a "cozy" backdrop for a "cappuccino-and-pastry" break; no alcohol is served, so primo "people-watching" provides the buzz.

▣ Cain Luxe
| | 24 | 24 | 19 | $16 |

Chelsea | 544 W. 27th St. (bet. 10th & 11th Aves.) | 1 to 28th St. | 212-947-8000 | www.cainnyc.com

"A-listers" shake their booties to a "jungle beat" at this West Chelsea "club phenomenon" that resembles a "wild African" game lodge and is frequented by tribes of "celebs", "rain-thin models" and "well-dressed" dudes blowing their cash on "exorbitant bottles"; brace yourself for an "impossible door" – "exclusivity is what it's all about."

Cake Shop
| | 20 | 18 | 19 | $8 |

LES | 152 Ludlow St. (bet. Rivington & Stanton Sts.) | F/J/M/Z to Delancey/Essex Sts. | 212-253-0036 | www.cake-shop.com

Like a "lifestyle boutique" for the "socially askew", this "novel" Lower Eastsider is layered into a "cafe/record store on the ground floor" and a "rock venue" downstairs where the "coolest" new bands are bolstered by "great sound" and "reasonably priced booze"; its popularity has some lamenting "so many hipsters, so little space."

Calico Jack's Cantina

E 40s | 800 Second Ave. (bet. 42nd & 43rd Sts.) | 4/5/6/7/S to 42nd St./Grand Central | 212-557-4300 | www.calicojacksnyc.com

"Frat" central near Grand Central, this Midtown Mexican is "squished after work" with "post-college" office drones who arrive jacked to "get down and dirty"; though "loud" and "kinda cheesy", it "really kicks" "if you want to relive your early 20s."

☑ Calle Ocho

W 80s | 446 Columbus Ave. (bet. 81st & 82nd Sts.) | B/C to 81st St. | 212-873-5025 | www.calleochonyc.com

There's "Latin flair" to spare at this "energetic" Nuevo Latino lounge/eatery where the "upscale" UWS "mingle" is fueled by "dangerous" mojitos, "festive" music and staffers who "take good care of you"; it's also a *fantastico* date place" despite the "crowded" conditions, indicating that the area "could use more" like it.

Camp

Boerum Hill | 179 Smith St. (bet. Warren & Wyckoff Sts.) | Brooklyn | F/G to Bergen St. | 718-852-8086

Scout out this "cozy" Boerum Hill bar for an assortment of "campy" trappings, e.g. "taxidermy", a "fireplace" and a "treats" menu starring "s'mores"; it's an "all-liquored-up" way to replay your "fondest memories" of summer, though the resident "hip" kids in attendance suggest there's no "escape from the city."

☑ Campbell Apartment

E 40s | Grand Central Terminal | 15 Vanderbilt Ave. (bet. 42nd & 43rd Sts.) | 4/5/6/7/S to 42nd St./Grand Central | 212-953-0409 | www.hospitalityholdings.com

An "atmospheric throwback" inside Grand Central, this former "railroad magnate's" office is now a paradigm of "old-world glamour", where "well-heeled" types sink into cushy sofas and fork over "wads of cash" for "classy cocktails"; its "not-so-secret" status makes it worth postponing till the "rush-hour crowd dies down" – and "don't wear sneakers" since the "dress code" is strict.

Canal Room

TriBeCa | 285 W. Broadway (Canal St.) | A/C/E to Canal St. | 212-941-8100 | www.canalroomlive.com

Catch a "cool band" in a "good-looking" room at this TriBeCa music venue where DJs and live performers preside over a sleek "redesigned performance space"; the once-sizzling scene might "think it's trendier than it is", but even critics concede it "often has great acts" onstage.

Canyon Road

E 70s | 1470 First Ave. (bet. 76th & 77th Sts.) | 6 to 77th St. | 212-734-1600 | www.arkrestaurants.com

Those "awesome margaritas" make for "mighty happy" trails at this "Southwestern-themed" canteen, a "busy, busy" "after-work escape" for "young" Yorkville yahoos "looking to hook up"; it's "not the biggest bar", but with "munchies" and "solid" scenery, it draws "many first dates."

	APPEAL	DECOR	SERVICE	COST

Cargo Café

20 | 17 | 21 | $8

Staten Island | 120 Bay St. (Richmond Terr.) | 718-876-0539 |
www.cargocafe.com
"Take a ferry ride and stay awhile" at this stalwart Staten Island bar/
eatery, a "dependable local" for "neo-bohemians" sharing down time
and a few beers in decidedly funky digs festooned with oddball art; insiders hail it as "one of the only cool" joints on "The Rock", though it's
"best when there's live music."

Carnegie Club

24 | 23 | 24 | $16

W 50s | 156 W. 56th St. (bet. 6th & 7th Aves.) | N/Q/R/W to 57th St./
7th Ave. | 212-957-9676 | www.hospitalityholdings.com
Bedecked with bookcases and "retro wood paneling", this "comfortably clubby" class act near Carnegie Hall is "one of the last"
few smokers' sanctuaries since it's legal to "enjoy a cigar" in its
mezzanine lounge; sure, "it'll cost ya", but music lovers console
themselves with a live lineup that includes a "Sinatra cover act
on Saturday nights."

Carolines

21 | 16 | 17 | $13

W 40s | 1626 Broadway (bet. 49th & 50th Sts.) | N/R/W to 49th St. |
212-757-4100 | www.carolines.com
Something "really funny" is going on at this renowned Times Square
comedy club, a "top-notch" mecca of mirth where everyone from
"great names" to "worthy new" wits works the room; if the "expensive" covers and "two-drink minimum" aren't as "laughable", it's still
"worth it" to catch "some of the best" talent in the biz.

NEW Casa La Femme

- | - | - | E

W Village | 140 Charles St. (bet. Greenwich & Washington Sts.) | 1 to
Christopher St. | 212-505-0005 | www.casalafemmeny.com
A quiet stretch of Charles Street is home to this third incarnation
of the infamous canoodlers' corner that's now pitched its tents in
the far West Village; while the curtained booths, belly dancer and
overall Ali-Baba-meets-Prada vibe are mostly confined to the restaurant proper, the more sedate bar area allows ample room to relax with
a pricey cocktail.

Casimir

21 | 20 | 16 | $10

E Village | 103 Ave. B (bet. 6th & 7th Sts.) | F/V to Lower East Side/
2nd Ave. | 212-358-9683 | www.casimirrestaurant.com
Authentically "French in style", this "dark, sexy" Alphabet City bistro/
lounge has its own "see-and-be-seen" allure "if you can put up with"
the "Euro" attitude; it's considered a "winner" in spite of the "easily
stressed" service, and when the "intimate" room gets too "crowded",
a "great" garden awaits out back.

NEW Catch-22

20 | 20 | 19 | $13

Flatiron | 4 W. 22nd St. (bet. 5th & 6th Aves.) | N/R/W to 23rd St. |
212-675-0607 | www.catch22nyc.com
With a nod to its WWII-novel namesake, this new Flatiron bar/lounge
(occupying the former Prey digs) vaguely channels a '40s "army/navy"
officer's club replete with wood-paneled quarters and random military
paraphernalia; most salute the "cool" concept, though there "is a
catch": it's "pricey."

	APPEAL	DECOR	SERVICE	COST

Cavatappo Grill
NEW **E 80s** | 1712 First Ave. (bet. 88th & 89th Sts.) | 4/5/6 to 86th St. |
212-987-9260
| | 22 | 19 | 20 | $11 |

Cavatappo Wine Bar
E 80s | 1728 Second Ave. (89th St.) | 4/5/6 to 86th St. | 212-426-0919
NEW **Murray Hill** | 347 Third Ave. (bet. 25th & 26th Sts.) | 6 to 23rd St. |
212-448-1919
www.cavatappo.com

Though only the "size of a shoebox", these "quaint" East Side wine
bars are "worth checking out" for their "excellent" stock (including a
super "selection of reds") decanted by "friendly" folks who freely "offer advice"; "seating is tight", though, so be careful your date doesn't
end up "on someone else's lap."

☑ Cávo
| | 26 | 27 | 20 | $13 |

Astoria | 42-18 31st Ave. (bet. 42nd & 43rd Sts.) | Queens | G/R/V to
Steinway St. | 718-721-1001 | www.cavoastoria.com
Among the "best scenes in Queens", this "stylish" Astoria bar/
restaurant channels "South Beach" via "Mykonos" as its "hot young"
crowd gathers to "party, party, party" into the "wee hours"; the big,
"beautiful" back garden is such an "energetic" singles magnet that
even "Manhattan coolistas" admit it's "worthy of a trip."

Cellar Bar
| | 22 | 23 | 16 | $13 |

W 40s | Bryant Park Hotel | 40 W. 40th St., downstairs (bet. 5th & 6th Aves.) |
7/B/D/F/V to 42nd St./Bryant Park | 212-642-2211 |
www.bryantparkhotel.com
Given the "flattering candlelight", it's no surprise that "good-looking
people abound" in this "ooh-la-la" bar/lounge in the Bryant Park
Hotel; the vaulted ceiling lends the subterranean space a "cool", "cavernous feel", and the specialty cocktails, "heavy beats" and steep tabs
all help "if you want to impress."

Central
| | 19 | 18 | 17 | $10 |

Astoria | 20-30 Steinway St. (bet. 20th Ave. & 20th Rd.) | Queens | G/R/V to
Steinway St. | 718-726-1600 | www.centrallounge.com
Astoria's "solid" outpost of clubland, this massive lounge/restaurant
is par-tay central for the "sexy" "young" locals hitting the dance floor
or recharging in the "nice outdoor garden"; it's "low-key" on school
nights, but the "packed" weekends (when "you need to be buttered up
just to move") are definitely a "great time."

Central Bar
| | 19 | 16 | 16 | $8 |

E Village | 109 E. Ninth St. (bet. 3rd & 4th Aves.) | 6 to Astor Pl. |
212-529-5333 | www.centralbarnyc.com
A "prepster epicenter", this East Village Irish pub is a "spacious" place to
do some "low-maintenance" "sports watching" "without getting a beer
spilled on your J.Crew" duds; and with "weekend DJs" in the house, the
"lounge upstairs" becomes a "sardine-esque" "NYU pickup scene."

Centro Vinoteca
| | 21 | 22 | 19 | $13 |

W Village | 74 Seventh Ave. S. (Barrow St.) | 1 to Christopher St. |
212-367-7470 | www.centrovinoteca.com
"Relaxed without sacrificing sophistication", the curvy, ground-floor bar
at this of-the-moment Village eatery "fills up fast" with a "young" crowd

| | APPEAL | DECOR | SERVICE | COST |

savoring its "heavy pours", "yummy snacks" and "courteous" staffers; it's "lively" and "loud", so be prepared to vie with diners for a barstool.

Champagne Bar at the Plaza
25 | 26 | 24 | $19

W 50s | Plaza Hotel | 768 Fifth Ave. (59th St.) | N/R/W to 5th Ave./59th St. | 212-546-5309 | www.theplaza.com

Set opposite the registration desk of the "legendary Plaza Hotel", this "swanky" lobby lounge is a "special-occasion" treat with bonus "upscale" people-watching on the side; though "old-money" types blithely whip out their "black Amex" cards to settle the tab ("crisis, what crisis?"), most analysts can't rationalize the "ridiculous" pricing.

Channel 4
13 | 10 | 19 | $8

W 40s | 58 W. 48th St. (bet. 5th & 6th Aves.) | B/D/F/V to 47-50th Sts./ Rockefeller Ctr. | 212-819-0095

Happy hour is prime time at this "adequate" Rock Center Irish pub staffed by "friendly bartenders" who "know all about their regular customers" – namely, the NBC Studios employees and other Midtowners who stop into the double-decker digs for an "afterwork" pop; a mural of network celebs on the lower level underscores the TV motif.

NEW Char No. 4
24 | 23 | 23 | $12

Cobble Hill | 196 Smith St. (bet. Baltic & Warren Sts.) | Brooklyn | F/G to Bergen St. | 718-643-2106 | www.charno4.com

A charming new "mecca for bourbon lovers", this "classy" Smith Street bar/Southern restaurant stocks an "incredible selection" of international whiskeys poured by "willing and able" barkeeps in a "modern", amber-hued setting; lovers of premium hooch also note that the dandied-up barbecue menu makes for "perfect pairings."

Cheap Shots ⊘
19 | 8 | 18 | $5

E Village | 140 First Ave. (bet. 9th St. & St. Marks Pl.) | 6 to Astor Pl. | 212-254-6631

"The name tells it all" – with three-dollar shots and frequent specials served up by "old pros", this East Villager entices a "fratlike clientele" planning to "get ripped on a budget"; sure, the room's "dingy" and the floor "sticky", but pool, darts and air hockey "pack 'em in" regardless.

Chelsea Brewing Co.
18 | 15 | 17 | $10

Chelsea | Chelsea Piers | Pier 59 (Hudson River & W. 18th St.) | A/C/E/L to 14th St./8th Ave. | 212-336-6440 | www.chelseabrewingco.com

"Wonderful" waterfront seating and an array of "quality" quaffs make this Chelsea Piers microbrewery a "worthwhile" place to drink and "watch the boats" ply the Hudson on a summer evening; come wintertime, however, folks find the scene "drab" and admit they "wouldn't go out of their way to get there – and it *is* out of the way."

Cherry Tavern ⊘
14 | 6 | 15 | $5

E Village | 441 E. Sixth St. (bet. Ave. A & 1st Ave.) | F/V to Lower East Side/ 2nd Ave. | 212-777-1448

Tipplers "on a mission to get drunk" talk up the five-dollar "tequila-and-Tecate special" at this "small", "old-school" East Villager, also known for its "fun jukebox", video games and pool table; "supercrowded" conditions "late night" prove the "funky" digs don't deter young habitués.

	APPEAL	DECOR	SERVICE	COST

Cherry Tree
▽ 16 | 18 | 19 | $6

Park Slope | 65 Fourth Ave. (bet. Bergen St. & St. Marks Pl.) | Brooklyn | 2/3/4/5/B/D/M/N/Q/R to Atlantic Ave. | 718-399-1353 | www.cherrytreebarnyc.com

A tree grows in Brooklyn – on the ground floor of a Park Slope hostel – bearing fruit for the few folks who have found it; they cite the "charming" spot's "friendly staffers", "lively" brick-walled bar and "gorgeous" outdoor courtyard (complete with a fireplace) suitable for "trading stories with traveling Aussies and Brits."

NEW Chestnut Bar
▽ 22 | 22 | 21 | $11

Carroll Gardens | 271 Smith St. (bet. Degraw & Sackett Sts.) | Brooklyn | F/G to Carroll St. | 718-243-0049 | www.chestnutonsmith.com

A new adjunct to the "established" Carroll Gardens eatery, this "rustic" barroom not only serves as a waiting room for the restaurant but is also an "atmospheric" destination in itself, with brick walls, salvaged wood and rows of antique bottles serving as decor; its U-shaped bartop is already a magnet for laid-back locals.

Chez Josephine
22 | 23 | 20 | $13

W 40s | 414 W. 42nd St. (bet. 9th & 10th Aves.) | A/C/E to 42nd St./ Port Authority | 212-594-1925 | www.chezjosephine.com

An homage to "Josephine Baker's Paris", this "swanky" yet "sweet" Theater District bar/restaurant "always feels like a party", thanks to live piano music nightly, "great cocktails" and the ministrations of "gracious" owner Jean-Claude, the chanteuse's adoptive son; it's also popular for "post-show" nightcaps.

Chibi's Sake Bar
▽ 23 | 19 | 23 | $11

NoLita | 238 Mott St. (bet. Prince & Spring Sts.) | 6 to Spring St. | 212-274-0054 | www.chibisbar.com

"Almost as cute" as its namesake (the owner's "lazy" French bulldog), this "cozy" NoLita sake bar staffed by "ridiculously nice" folks has respondents wishing they could "stay for hours" to savor "after-dinner saketinis" and Japanese bites; despite free mushroom dumplings some nights, wallet-watchers still warn that Chibi "ain't cheap."

Chill Lounge
▽ 17 | 17 | 18 | $10

Murray Hill | 329 Lexington Ave. (39th St.) | 4/5/6/7/S to 42nd St./ Grand Central | 212-682-8288 | www.chilloungenyc.com

Surveyors split on this Murray Hill bar/lounge: fans find its "diverse after-work crowd", "comfortable seating" and happy-hour half-price deals plenty cool, while critics give its exposed-brick-and-leather look a more chilly reception ("seems like a room in someone's basement").

China 1
19 | 21 | 16 | $10

E Village | 50 Ave. B (bet. 3rd & 4th Sts.) | F/V to Lower East Side/2nd Ave. | 212-375-0665 | www.china1nyc.com

The street-level bar at this East Village Chinese restaurant may be "fun and festive", but the Sino scene can get downright "sinful" as you descend into its subterranean lounge, a "sexy", "mazelike" affair where "trendy" types mingle, dance and "flirt" on antique opium-smokers' bedsteads; celebrants say it's a "great place to have a party."

Chinatown Brasserie
23 | 26 | 20 | $12

NoHo | 380 Lafayette St. (Great Jones St.) | 6 to Astor Pl. | 212-533-7000 | www.chinatownbrasserie.com

Name notwithstanding, this "high-end" spot is actually in NoHo, occupying the space that was once Time Cafe; it's now "beautifully" redesigned in streamlined chinoiserie style and boasts a "large, undiscovered" Koi Room in the basement (complete with a pond, natch); the "spacious bar area" attracts an eclectic crowd.

NEW Chloe
22 | 20 | 17 | $13

LES | 81 Ludlow St., downstairs (bet. Broome & Delancey Sts.) | F/J/M/Z to Delancey/Essex Sts. | 212-677-0067 | www.chloe81.com

"Extreme exclusivity at the door" has cool cats buzzing that this subterranean LES lounge is "giving Beatrice Inn a run for its money" as the hippest boîte in town; ok, there's nothing special about the "snooty" staff and "minimal decor" (a "white-subway-tiled" "homage to Parisian bistros"), but the crush of "models" and folks sporting "nerd glasses" are a dead giveaway that the "secret is out."

Choice
∇ 21 | 19 | 19 | $11

Murray Hill | 380 Third Ave. (bet. 27th & 28th Sts.) | 6 to 28th St. | 212-779-1380 | www.choicekitchennyc.com

This Murray Hill venue aims to be an "after-work spot" for a "professional 20s crowd", offering "great specials" throughout its extended happy hours, plus "decent wine" and live jazz on Tuesdays; weekend DJs make dancing, "hanging and people-watching" here an attractive choice.

Chow Bar
18 | 20 | 18 | $11

W Village | 230 W. Fourth St. (10th St.) | 1 to Christopher St. | 212-633-2212

"Worth a stop" for a "girls' night out" or to "show out-of-towners a good time", this "sexy" West Village corner spot has a "retro" Eastern feel, 10 sakes by the glass and Pan-Asian chow to match; just don't expect "a lot of wiggle room" at the "crowded bar", though.

Church Lounge
24 | 23 | 20 | $14

TriBeCa | Tribeca Grand Hotel | 2 Sixth Ave. (White St.) | A/C/E to Canal St. | 212-519-6600 | www.tribecagrand.com

"Trendy but friendly", this "swanky" lounge in the Tribeca Grand Hotel's "cavernous atrium" is a "posh" place to "meet Wall Streeters", "clients from out of town" or film-industry pals over pricey cocktails; still, a few cutting-edgers claim it's now "more touristy than anything else."

Cibar
22 | 22 | 20 | $12

Gramercy | Inn at Irving Pl. | 56 Irving Pl. (bet. 17th & 18th Sts.) | 4/5/6/L/N/Q/R/W to 14th St./Union Sq. | 212-460-5656 | www.cibarlounge.com

"Twentysomething" professionals "say sí" to this bar in a Gramercy townhouse, a "sophisticated" hideaway replete with "generous" specialty martinis, fireplaces and a "cute" bamboo-accented patio; indeed, "the only problem with this place is that too many people know about it."

Cielo
23 | 21 | 18 | $14

Meatpacking | 18 Little W. 12th St. (bet. 9th Ave. & Washington St.) | A/C/E/L to 14th St./8th Ave. | 212-645-5700 | www.cieloclub.com

With a "futuristic" setting that includes a sunken blue "dancing pit", this "intimate" Meatpacking disco brings in "awesome international

DJs" whose "Euro trance and house music" creates "transcendence despite the crush of bodies"; if the "eclectic" crowd is perhaps "less chic than it used to be", don't blame "pompous" bouncers who enforce a stringent "velvet-rope policy."

Cipriani Downtown

24 | 22 | 20 | $17

SoHo | 376 W. Broadway (bet. Broome & Spring Sts.) | C/E to Spring St. | 212-343-0999 | www.cipriani.com

"Uptown and Downtown merge" at this "elegant" SoHo "celeb magnet" where you're likely to bump into "Sean Combs, Donald Trump", "Wall Street men" and "Euro-chic" models being served signature Bellinis by "knowing staffers"; "prices are high, but so is the appeal" for stargazers, though others gripe that "any normal person" just gets "attitude, attitude, attitude."

Circa Tabac

∇ 21 | 17 | 22 | $12

SoHo | 32 Watts St. (bet. 6th Ave. & Thompson St.) | A/C/E to Canal St. | 212-941-1781 | www.circatabac.com

"Smoke 'em if you got 'em – because you can" at this SoHo "secret", one of NYC's few indoor venues exempt from the tobacco ban; if you ain't got 'em, the "cozy" spot sells 150 brands of cigars and cigarettes to accompany its "fabulous martinis"; P.S. a "good ventilation system" helps appease non-puffers.

Citibar

18 | 17 | 20 | $12

E 70s | 1446 First Ave. (bet. 75th & 76th Sts.) | 6 to 77th St. | 212-772-1734 | www.citibarnyc.com

You can "bank on" the "no-frills neighborhood" atmosphere at this "remote" Yorkville saloon, a "low-key hideout" for "sports revelers" and pool sharks where the "drinks are potent" and the staff actually "smiles at you"; it works for the "post-college crowd", even if sophistocrats yawn "don't go out of your way."

NEW Citrine

21 | 21 | 20 | $14

Flatiron | 59 W. 21st St., 2nd fl. (bet. 5th & 6th Aves.) | N/R/W to 23rd St. | 212-727-7775 | www.citrinenyc.com

Flatiron "'it' party" people cite this second-story "Snitch replacement" as a "new hot spot" that substitutes "swanky" lounge airs and "sleek, modern" looks for its precursor's rocker grunge decor; though currently "buzzing with social creatures" and bottle buyers braving the "tough door", some yawn it's a "here-one-minute, gone-the-next" sort of joint.

Citrus Bar & Grill

20 | 19 | 18 | $12

W 70s | 320 Amsterdam Ave. (75th St.) | 1/2/3 to 72nd St. | 212-595-0500 | www.citrusnyc.com

"Kick-your-teeth-in margaritas" concocted from a selection of 100-plus tequilas ap-peel to the twentysomething followers (who "come early and stay late") of this tangerine-hued Upper West Side Latin-Asian restaurant; add in "great music" and a "relaxing" vibe, and it almost "feels like a club" – except for the fact that "you can actually hear people talk."

City Hall

23 | 24 | 22 | $12

TriBeCa | 131 Duane St. (bet. Church St. & W. B'way) | 1/2/3 to Chambers St. | 212-227-7777 | www.cityhallnyc.com

Would-be Boss Tweeds and other "suit"-wearers caucus at this "great big" showplace in a "prime" TriBeCa location not far from its namesake;

surveyors say the "posh" bar's "traditional" furnishings, "warm" service and "terrific drinks" combine to create a "classic" Gotham ambiance – with luck, you may even rub (and bend) elbows with Hizzoner himself.

ℤ NEW City Winery   23 | 22 | 22 | $14

SoHo | 155 Varick St. (Vandam St.) | C/E to Spring St. | 212-608-0555 | www.citywinery.com

"Bringing Napa to NY", this "cavernous" new SoHo wine bar–cum-performance venue is an "oenophile's oenophind" thanks to its "wonderful selection" of vinos (plus small plates for pairing); not incidentally, it also features "adult"-oriented live music, but given the "hangar"-like dimensions, a few wish it were "more intimate"; P.S. amateur vintners can arrange to "make your own wine by the barrel."

Clandestino   ▽ 19 | 16 | 23 | $10

LES | 35 Canal St. (bet. Essex & Ludlow Sts.) | F to E. B'way | 212-475-5505 | www.clandestinonyc.com

"Far from the maddening crowds", this pleasantly "unassuming" LES watering hole at the "remote" eastern end of Canal Street is as much a secret as its name suggests; the few "locals" who've found it confide the "relaxed vibe" and shabby-chic decor are as much a draw as the choice draft beers and secluded garden.

Cleopatra's Needle   18 | 12 | 17 | $11

W 90s | 2485 Broadway (bet. 92nd & 93rd Sts.) | 1/2/3 to 96th St. | 212-769-6969 | www.cleopatrasneedleny.com

"Excellent live jazz every night" entices "young student couples" and "baby-boomer beboppers" alike to this "lively" Upper West Side "institution" made even more "appealing" by its "no-cover, no-attitude" policy; given the music, though, this "cool hang" isn't particularly conducive to a "real conversation."

NEW Clo   22 | 18 | 20 | $16

W 60s | 10 Columbus Circle, 4th fl. (60th St.) | 1/A/B/C/D to 59th St./ Columbus Circle | 212-823-9898 | www.clowines.com

Oenophilia goes "futuristic" at the Time Warner Center's "fresh" new "self-serve" wine kiosk that allows patrons to customize an "awesome" by-the-glass lineup via a "high-tech" touch-screen, then fill their glasses from automatic dispensers using prepaid credit cards; but given the "efficiency" and "pricey", two-ounce pours, it's easy to end up with a "hangover and a big credit card bill."

Cloister Cafe   23 | 23 | 15 | $9

E Village | 238 E. Ninth St. (bet. 2nd & 3rd Aves.) | 6 to Astor Pl. | 212-777-9128

At this longtime retreat (since 1977) on a busy East Village block, the lure is a spacious, "romantic" garden with towering trees creating the illusion of seclusion; however, the faux-monastic, stained glass-enhanced interior is "less charming", ditto the so-so service; N.B. heaters allow year-round courtyard seating.

ℤ NEW Clover Club   25 | 25 | 24 | $13

Cobble Hill | 210 Smith St. (bet. Baltic & Butler Sts.) | Brooklyn | F/G to Bergen St. | 718-855-7939 | www.cloverclubny.com

Cocktail connoisseurs are in clover at this Smith Street "faux speakeasy" where mixology queen Julie Reiner (Flatiron Lounge) offers a list of "delicious, potent" drinks, stressing gin-based concoctions and old-school punches served in cut-glass bowls; the "Roaring Twenties" decor is "gorgeous" – even if the retro thing may be "getting old" – but it's all the "effort put in" here that "justifies the pricey tabs."

Club Macanudo

24	24	23	$13

E 60s | 26 E. 63rd St. (bet. Madison & Park Aves.) | 4/5/6/N/R/W to 59th St./Lexington Ave. | 212-752-8200 | www.clubmacanudo.com
A handsome "haven" of "leather chairs and big cigars", this "high-testosterone" East Side haunt – one of the few NYC venues where "you can still legally smoke" – gets "jammed" with stogie-chomping "martini-and-scotch drinkers" there to "entertain clients" or just "unwind"; regulars recommend "a jacket, a reservation and plenty of cash."

Cock, The ⊄

18	7	12	$8

E Village | 29 Second Ave. (bet. 1st & 2nd Sts.) | F/V to Lower East Side/2nd Ave. | no phone
The "name says it all" at this "skanky", "raunchy" East Village gay dive known for "fierce music", lewd go-go dancers and overall "slutty squalor"; a hard-core few disses the "prefab decadence", but most couldn't care less since this homoerotic hotbed "can't be beat" for "no-questions-asked hook-ups."

Coffee Shop

18	15	13	$11

Union Sq | 29 Union Sq. W. (16th St.) | 4/5/6/L/N/Q/R/W to 14th St./Union Sq. | 212-243-7969
Though infamous for "aloof", "sluggish service" from a staff of "wannabe models", this "retro" Union Square "diner-cum-bar" remains a "staple for anyone under 30" ("before or after your one-night stand"); the boîte really gets "bumping after hours" as "trendies" arrive for their helpings of "fabulousness" and "late-night french fries."

Coliseum Bar

∇ 11	9	17	$7

W 50s | 312 W. 58th St. (bet. 8th & 9th Aves.) | 1/A/B/C/D to 59th St./Columbus Circle | 212-977-3523 | www.thecoliseumpub.com
This Columbus Circle pub opposite the Time Warner Center is an "after-work" standby for corporate "colleagues" and "Fordham Law" students; a revamp left the place "bright and clean", bad news for longtimers who "liked it better" before "it lost its dive appeal."

Columbus 72

∇ 15	17	17	$14

W 70s | 246A Columbus Ave. (bet. 71st & 72nd Sts.) | 1 to 79th St. | 212-769-1492 | www.columbus72.com
Upper Westsiders get their groove back at this behemoth danceteria where each of the four "spacious" rooms blasts the beats of a different genre, including hip-hop, classic rock and techno; club honchos hope "nice VIP seating" and theme nights will lure locals, though doubters discern "better options" Downtown; N.B. the Copacabana, temporarily homeless, hosts a Tuesday night party here.

Comedy Cellar

23	13	16	$10

G Village | 117 MacDougal St. (bet. Bleecker & W. 3rd Sts.) | A/B/C/D/E/F/V to W. 4th St. | 212-254-3480 | www.comedycellar.com
"Always a pick-me-upper", this subterranean Village grin bin has chuckleheads claiming it's got the "best ratio of hysterical-to-bombing comedians" around; a few kvetch about "closer-than-need-be

quarters" and that two-drink minimum, but "surprise celebrity" visits by Chris Rock and other SNL alums turn most frowns upside down.

Comic Strip

17 | 11 | 14 | $15

E 80s | 1568 Second Ave. (bet. 81st & 82nd Sts.) | 6 to 77th St. | 212-861-9386 | www.comicstriplive.com

Since 1975, this "classic" UES standup spot has launched the careers of dozens of household names (Sandler, Seinfeld, Reiser, Garofalo); fans salute the "solid laughs" and "hope they keep up their standards", but foes feel the "program has degraded" from yuk to yuck ("one out of every four jokes is funny"), even if the "entertainment is better than" the "absurdly pricey" booze.

Comix

∇ 23 | 21 | 21 | $10

Chelsea | 353 W. 14th St. (bet. 8th & 9th Aves.) | A/C/E/L to 14th St./8th Ave. | 212-524-2500 | www.comixny.com

Fans are "psyched" about this "chichi" Chelsea venue, a 5,000-sq.-ft. spot that "offers much more" than comedy (i.e. "surprisingly" high-end New American eats), plus half-off happy hours and ambitious programming like the *American Idol*-esque stand-up competition; a few purists are dubious, saying "an 'upscale' comedy club is just not funny", but boosters say "ya gotta believe."

☒ Commerce

22 | 20 | 19 | $14

W Village | 50 Commerce St. (Barrow St.) | 1 to Christopher St. | 212-524-2301 | www.commercerestaurant.com

Although it's "tucked away" on "one of the tiniest" West Village streets, the bar of this chic eatery is usually "filled to the brim" with upmarket types trading "loud" and "lively" banter over "inventive" signature cocktails; the historic "row house" lodgings are adorned with "quaint" fixtures and a '30s-style mural, but most maintain the "crowd itself is the highlight."

Common Ground

19 | 17 | 20 | $7

E Village | 206 Ave. A (bet. 12th & 13th Sts.) | L to 1st Ave. | 212-228-6231 | www.commongroundnyc.com

A "mixed crowd of locals" finds common ground at this "relaxed", bookish East Village pub, "playing Boggle and Connect Four" over a pint or unwinding on "slightly stained velvet couches"; the bartenders somehow manage to be both "hot and friendly", so even if some shrug "nothing special", at least it's "seldom annoying."

Commonwealth

19 | 14 | 21 | $6

Park Slope | 497 Fifth Ave. (12th St.) | Brooklyn | F/M/R to 4th Ave./9th St. | 718-768-2040

This bar in Park Slope may be "dim" and somewhat "vanilla", but its "thirtysomething" clientele appreciates the "attentive" staffers who "accommodate their needs"; other "enticements to daily drinking" include a "great jukebox", Scrabble contests and, during balmy weather, a "fairly large" back garden.

Company

20 | 15 | 22 | $7

E Village | 242 E. 10th St. (bet. 1st & 2nd Aves.) | L to 1st Ave. | 212-420-7101

At this "tiny" East Village neighborhood joint, Company policy dictates you "knock back a few with your best friends" under the supervision of "great bartenders" and assiduous DJs; later, invest a little time and take stock of the "local artwork" on display amid the vaguely retro environs.

Connolly's Pub
| 18 | 15 | 20 | $9 |

E 40s | 14 E. 47th St. (bet. 5th & Madison Aves.) | E/V to 5th Ave./53rd St. | 212-867-3767

E 40s | 150 E. 47th St. (bet. Lexington & 3rd Aves.) | 6 to 51st St./ Lexington Ave. | 212-692-9342

W 40s | 121 W. 45th St. (bet. B'way & 6th Ave.) | 1/2/3/7/N/Q/R/ S/W to 42nd St./Times Sq. | 212-597-5126

W 50s | 43 W. 54th St. (bet. 5th & 6th Aves.) | E/V to 5th Ave./53rd St. | 212-489-0271

www.connollyspubandrestaurant.com

Ok, so this four-leafed cluster of Irish pubs "looks and feels like a franchise", but the Midtowners swarming all its locations at happy hour don't mind, citing pluses like "bebrogued bartenders" and "casual" vibes; N.B. the 45th Street branch is home to the band Black 47 on weekends.

Continental ⊄
| ∇ 16 | 10 | 14 | $7 |

E Village | 25 Third Ave. (bet. 9th St. & St. Marks Pl.) | 6 to Astor Pl. | 212-529-6924 | www.continentalnyc.com

It "still serves cheap drinks", but this gritty "East Village staple" no longer books live bands, relying instead on HDTV and a jukebox; fans fear it will "bite the dust like CBGB's" - "where will the punk rockers go?"

Corio
| 18 | 17 | 16 | $11 |

SoHo | 337 W. Broadway (Grand St.) | A/C/E to Canal St. | 212-966-3901 | www.corionyc.com

"Something different" for SoHo, this double-decker "pad" is known for its "quality" burlesque shows staged in a "cozy" upstairs lounge that's gussied up "bordello"-style (it's named for the celebrated stripper Ann Corio); curiosity-seekers say the red-"hot" talent makes for a tit-illating way to "relax with a special someone."

Cornelia Street Cafe
| 23 | 17 | 19 | $11 |

G Village | 29 Cornelia St. (bet. Bleecker & W. 4th Sts.) | 1 to Christopher St. | 212-989-9319 | www.corneliastreetcafe.com

"Still superior" to many rivals, this "mellow" Village "standby" re-mains a "charming" venue for dinner and more; its slightly "tight" basement cabaret hosts an eclectic mix of "high art" entertainment ("excellent" folk and jazz, poetry readings and even puppetry), while sidewalk tables are "perfect for sharing some wine" while taking in the passing parade.

Corner Bistro ⊄
| 22 | 11 | 17 | $7 |

W Village | 331 W. Fourth St. (Jane St.) | A/C/E/L to 14th St./8th Ave. | 212-242-9502

"Cheap McSorley drafts" and "nonpareil" burgers the "size of your head" - all served till the wee hours, "when it seems most urgent to have one" - keep this "crowded", "salt-of-the-earth" Villager a "post-nightlife" magnet for young types; seating is sparse, so prepare to "cram into a booth with 40 of your closest friends" or, more likely, join the queue "invariably snaking through" the "noisy" taproom.

Cornichon

▽ 21 | 15 | 16 | $11

Williamsburg | 251 Grand St. (bet. Driggs Ave. & Roebling St.) | Brooklyn | L to Bedford Ave. | 718-599-3840 | www.cafecornichon.com

While Williamsburg has its share of Italian wine specialists, this "quiet" Grand Street boîte focuses on French vintages, offering a petite but thoughtful selection from Graves to Margaux, accompanied by the usual nibbles; expect an "atmospheric", candlelit setting with whitewashed brick walls lined with bottles – and a lot of "pickle jokes" thanks to its "sour gherkin" name.

Country Champagne Lounge

25 | 23 | 21 | $16

(aka Champagne Bar at Country)

Murray Hill | Carlton Hotel | 90 Madison Ave., 2nd fl. (29th St.) | 6 to 28th St. | 212-889-7100 | www.countryinnewyork.com

There's lots of sparkle and very little whine among surveyors who've sampled this "romantic" – and "expensive" – mezzanine bar in Murray Hill's revamped Carlton Hotel; given the "unique champagne cocktails" and clubby milieu, some may feel they've been "transported" to "conservative" territory, but if it's too much of a "class act" for you, there are two livelier bars one flight below.

NEW Country Club

19 | 19 | 18 | $14

W Village | 248 W. 14th St. (bet. 7th & 8th Aves.) | A/C/E/L to 14th St./ 8th Ave. | 212-367-0822 | www.countryclubny.com

"Young" preps imitate their "Westchester"-bound elders at this split-level West Village lounge that's outfitted like a Waspy jockey club, sporting dark paneling, hound's-tooth prints and a "dance floor where everyone lets loose"; the signature "Bellinis are a must", though elitists who expected a truly upper-crust enclave moan "would that it were."

NEW Covo

▽ 25 | 22 | 22 | $12

Harlem | 701 W. 135th St. (12th Ave.) | 1 to 137th St./City College | 212-234-9573 | www.covony.com

Set one floor above a popular West Harlem trattoria, this laid-back lounge has a "boudoir-esque" feel that's "perfect for drinks" before or after dinner; occasional live jazz and blues performances add to the mellow vibe, disturbed occasionally by the "loud club next door."

Cowgirl

18 | 18 | 18 | $10

W Village | 519 Hudson St. (10th St.) | 1 to Christopher St. | 212-633-1133 | www.cowgirlnyc.com

Margarita rustlers mosey on over to this "campy" West Village chuck wagon where the "drinks are strong", the crowd is "open-minded" and the "cheesy Western" decor and "Grand Ole Opry tunes" evoke a "private party in a Texas ranch house"; serious drinkers stymied by "slow" service say "pitchers are the way to go here."

Coyote Ugly

13 | 12 | 14 | $8

E Village | 153 First Ave. (9th St.) | L to 1st Ave. | 212-477-4431 | www.coyoteuglysaloon.com

Sure, "beer is for sale here" but the real draw of this East Village "strip club lite" is the "busty" staffers who dole out shots and "writhe on the bar"; a "novelty about 15 years ago" before Hollywood came calling, it's now mostly "tourists" – locals sigh "once is enough."

	APPEAL	DECOR	SERVICE	COST

Crash Mansion

| | 15 | 17 | 16 | $10 |

LES | 199 Bowery (Spring St.) | J/M/Z to Bowery | 212-982-0740 | www.crashmansion.com

Crash partyers who groove on this "huge", "modern" nightspot beneath a Bowery eatery "hope it can stay hot" and praise its eclectic live music roster; still, some critics carp the complex "tries to be too many things" and calls the end result "unremarkable."

Creek and the Cave

| | ▽ 19 | 18 | 21 | $11 |

LIC | 10-93 Jackson Ave. (bet. 11th St. & 49th Ave.) | Queens | 7 to Vernon Blvd./Jackson Ave. | 718-706-8783 | www.thecreekandthecave.com

Much given to "theme parties" and a varied slate of live performance, this arty, "laid-back" space can be an apt "destination after visiting nearby PS 1"; it boasts a bar, lounge and billiard room, and the Long Island City locale ensures it's "not yet spoiled by tourists."

Crocodile Lounge

| | 19 | 12 | 21 | $7 |

E Village | 325 E. 14th St. (bet. 1st & 2nd Aves.) | L to 1st Ave. | 212-477-7747

"Free pizza with every beer" – "need we say more?" – is the hook at this "laid-back", subterranean East Village reptile (a sibling of Williamsburg's Alligator Lounge) where "satisfied customers" cite "friendly bartenders", "affordable drinks" and "super-fun" Skee-Ball in the back; P.S. "tall claustrophobes" warn of "low ceilings."

Croton Reservoir Tavern

| | 17 | 16 | 20 | $9 |

W 40s | 108 W. 40th St. (bet. B'way & 6th Ave.) | 1/2/3/7/N/Q/R/S/W to 42nd St./Times Sq. | 212-997-6835 | www.crotonreservoirtavern.com

"If it's where the water comes from, you might as well get the liquor and mixers here too" crack fans of this brick-and-leather Midtown taproom named after the former reservoir that made way for Bryant Park; a commuter-friendly location between Grand Central and Port Authority is the primary reason it gets "lively after 5 PM."

Croxley Ales

| | 20 | 16 | 16 | $7 |

E Village | 28 Ave. B (bet. 2nd & 3rd Sts.) | F/V to Lower East Side/2nd Ave. | 212-253-6140 | www.croxley.com

Once a filling station, this "easygoing" indoor/outdoor sports bar in the East Village features an "impressive international menu" of more than 100 beers, "cheap wings" and plenty of "big-screen TVs" ("you'll have no problem finding your game"); "slow" service is the main gripe.

Cubby Hole ⌷

| | 20 | 18 | 18 | $8 |

W Village | 281 W. 12th St. (W. 4th St.) | A/C/E/L to 14th St./8th Ave. | 212-243-9041 | www.cubbyholebar.com

On a West Village intersection that's raised its hip quotient with the arrivals of Cafe Cluny and Beatrice Inn, this "friendly neighborhood lesbian bar" ("heteros welcome") retains its "fabulously tacky" decorations "dangling from the ceiling" and its equally "colorful" clientele; "be ready to fight the crowds" on weekends, when the girls can get "raucous."

Cub Room

| | 19 | 18 | 18 | $12 |

SoHo | 131 Sullivan St. (Prince St.) | C/E to Spring St. | 212-677-4100 | www.cubroom.com

Set on a scenic SoHo corner, this streamlined lounge remains a "sure bet" for "investment bankers" and other animals prowling for after-work drinks; denizens dub it "cozy" and "classy", while doubters are bearish, citing "bland" ambiance, "meat-market" vibes and variable service ("oh-so-friendly" vs. "supercilious").

Cupping Room Café

| | 18 | 16 | 16 | $10 |

SoHo | 359 W. Broadway (bet. Broome & Grand Sts.) | C/E to Spring St. | 212-925-2898 | www.cuppingroomcafe.com
The bar at this "cozy" SoHo cafe remains a "standby" for quiet conversation, "good booze" and a "neighborhood" crowd, while happy-hour specials and occasional live music make the mood "lively"; but high-energy types who find the scene too "staid" suggest "wait six hours" and come for breakfast the "morning after."

Daddy-O

| | 21 | 17 | 23 | $9 |

G Village | 44 Bedford St. (Leroy St.) | 1 to Houston St. | 212-414-8884
"Refreshingly attentive" bartenders deliver "well-mixed cocktails" and "make you feel like you're somebody" at this Greenwich Village "find", a "candlelit" crowd-pleaser proffering a wide selection of single-malts and tequilas, "funky" music and "classic bar food" (don't miss those "incredible tater tots"); on school nights, it's a "quiet date place."

Daddy's

| | 19 | 14 | 18 | $6 |

Williamsburg | 437 Graham Ave. (bet. Frost & Richardson Sts.) | Brooklyn | L to Graham Ave. | 718-609-6388
"Kinda rockabilly" in a stripped-down sort of way, this East Williamsburg rec room attracts "hipsters" for "laid-back" loitering indoors and out via extended happy hours, a spacious back patio and the house specialty drink, the Margaveza; critics cite "inattentive bartenders" and wish it felt more "welcoming."

Dakota Roadhouse ⊄

| | ▽ 15 | 10 | 17 | $8 |

Financial District | 43 Park Pl. (bet. Church St. & W. B'way) | 2/3/A/C/E to Park Pl. | 212-962-9800 | www.dakotaroadhouse.com
"Quirky", faux-redneck decor supplies the "charm" at this Financial District honky-tonk where guys in ties come to "relax without the trendy wannabes"; "cheap drinks" and "fried food" supply the energy for watching sports on the "flat-screens" and playing pool, darts and foosball.

Daltons

| | 16 | 13 | 18 | $9 |

W 40s | 611 Ninth Ave. (bet. 43rd & 44th Sts.) | A/C/E to 42nd St./Port Authority | 212-245-5511 | www.daltonsnyc.com
"During game time" this "standard" neighborhood pub near Port Authority turns into an "upscale sports bar" where "voluble football fans" "toss back a few", yell at the (numerous) TVs and snack on some of the "best wings on the West Side"; if ultimately "pretty generic", at least this watering hole is "cleaner than most."

Dangerfield's

| | 16 | 12 | 14 | $13 |

E 60s | 1118 First Ave. (61st St.) | 4/5/6/N/R/W to 59th St./Lexington Ave. | 212-593-1650 | www.dangerfields.com
Like its namesake, this once-"legendary" comedy club gets less and less respect, though some still applaud the presence of sporadic "lively" talent; hecklers jeer that the hefty drink prices, unimpressive service and "run-down" digs are "no joke."

	APPEAL	DECOR	SERVICE	COST

☑ Daniel
27 | **28** | **27** | **$19**

E 60s | 60 E. 65th St. (bet. Madison & Park Aves.) | 6 to 68th St. | 212-288-0033 | www.danielnyc.com

Whether they're "proposing" or just wanting to "make any occasion memorable", "foodies and winies" love this plush, "swank" lounge adjoining Daniel Boulud's flagship Upper East Side restaurant, where "smiling employees" deliver "simply perfect" service; the prices "aren't for the faint of heart", but those with the financial fortitude find evenings here "wonderful in every way."

Danny and Eddie's
14 | **11** | **18** | **$8**

E 80s | 1643 First Ave. (bet. 85th & 86th Sts.) | 4/5/6 to 86th St. | 212-396-2090 | www.dannyandeddies.com

"Basic if slightly run-down", this "out-of-the-way" Yorkville "dive" caters to "friendly barflies" with a pool table and tapsters who "couldn't be nicer"; thanks to karaoke nights and a "great backyard", it's building a rep as a "local" hang.

Dark Room
18 | **13** | **16** | **$9**

LES | 165 Ludlow St. (bet. Houston & Stanton Sts.) | F/V to Lower East Side/ 2nd Ave. | 212-353-0536

Despite – or perhaps because of – its "dim" "dungeon" atmosphere, this subterranean Lower Eastsider has developed a "diverse crowd" of "hipsters", "striped-shirt guys and the women who love them", all "ready to party" ("be prepared to sweat on strangers"); naysayers call the overall feel of "making out in your parents' basement" a negative.

Dave & Buster's
21 | **17** | **17** | **$10**

W 40s | 234 W. 42nd St., 3rd fl. (bet. 7th & 8th Aves.) | A/C/E to 42nd St./ Port Authority | 646-495-2015 | www.daveandbusters.com

"One chain that fits in nicely" in Times Square, this massive arcade (aka "Chuck E. Cheese for grown-ups") appeals to "thirtysomethings" who like to play "games of chance" with a "joystick in one hand and a beer in the other"; ok, the "blinking, flashing, noisy" scene is "not sophisticated", but "we all have to let our inner child out now and then."

David Copperfield's
17 | **14** | **19** | **$9**

E 70s | 1394 York Ave. (74th St.) | 6 to 77th St. | 212-734-6152 | www.davidcopperfields.com

"Frat boys, med students, old folks" and beer-lovers frequent this "low-key" Yorkville hops "haven" where "knowledgeable staffers" oversee a "superior selection" of international brews; maybe there's "no magic" at this "out-of-the-way" pub, but most agree it's "worth a try."

☑ d.b.a.
22 | **16** | **18** | **$8**

E Village | 41 First Ave. (bet. 2nd & 3rd Sts.) | F/V to Lower East Side/ 2nd Ave. | 212-475-5097

☑ d.b.a. Brooklyn

NEW **Williamsburg** | 113 N. Seventh St. (bet. Berry St. & Wythe Ave.) | Brooklyn | L to Bedford Ave. | 718-218-6006
www.drinkgoodstuff.com

The name "should stand for 'Darn Best Ales'" declare devotees of this "always packed" East Village "beer-and-scotch drinkers' utopia" where the "intelligently chosen", rotating inventory is augmented by semi-regular tastings; the weatherproofed back garden remains "ideal" for "afternoon conversation", but cynics nix the "pretentious" service and "frightening" restrooms; N.B. the Williamsburg branch opened post-Survey.

Dead Poet
20 | 18 | 22 | $7

W 80s | 450 Amsterdam Ave. (bet. 81st & 82nd Sts.) | B/C to 81st St. | 212-595-5670 | www.thedeadpoet.com

Bardflies in search of a Wilde time line up at this UWS "hideaway" where "genuinely friendly" barkeeps mix signature cocktails with names like the Walt Whitman and the Emily Dickinson; still, what's "cozy" to some is just plain "teeny-tiny" to others, though "what it lacks in space, it makes up for in charm."

☒ Death & Co
25 | 23 | 22 | $14

E Village | 433 E. Sixth St. (bet. Ave. A & 1st Ave.) | 6 to Astor Pl. | 212-388-0882 | www.deathandcompany.com

Devotees of "drink couture" "die and go to heaven" at this "hip" East Village speakeasy where the emphasis on the art of "inventive mixology" yields "old-world cocktails with modern twists"; the "neo-Goth" interior reeks of "funereal chic", and the "well-regulated crowd" (thanks to a "no-standing" rule) keeps the "feeling of exclusivity intact" – though the "premium" prices are a killer.

Decibel
24 | 17 | 19 | $11

E Village | 240 E. Ninth St. (bet. 2nd & 3rd Aves.) | 6 to Astor Pl. | 212-979-2733 | www.sakebardecibel.com

Still on sound footing, this small East Village sake/soju "grotto" keeps its buzz with a "stunning selection" of "perfect" rice wines "generously" poured by a "knowledgeable staff" and accompanied by "Japanese nibbles"; the basement setting – picture a "Tokyo dive bar" with "graffiti and high-tech toilets" – can be "loud when packed."

Delancey, The
20 | 21 | 17 | $9

LES | 168 Delancey St. (bet. Attorney & Clinton Sts.) | F/J/M/Z to Delancey/Essex Sts. | 212-254-9920 | www.thedelancey.com

"It's all about the all-year-long roof deck" at this LES triplex where the "leafy" alfresco scene comes complete with a view of the Williamsburg Bridge off-ramp; the basement cabaret and main floor barroom have such "different vibes" that you can "go barhopping without leaving the building", but for best results, "bring your own crowd."

Delia's Lounge
22 | 23 | 21 | $11

Bay Ridge | 9224 Third Ave. (93rd St.) | Brooklyn | R to 95th St. | 718-745-7999 | www.deliaslounge.com

Fourteen types of martinis ("need I say more?") entice a "young crowd" to this "low-key" Bay Ridge lair, a "romantic date spot" with a fireplace that's so "cozy" it "feels like a party" in "someone's living room"; "great service" includes valets who make parking "nightmares" go away ("$10 is enough" for them to "keep you right in front").

☒☒☒ Delicatessen
19 | 20 | 17 | $13

SoHo | 54 Prince St. (Lafayette St.) | N/R/W to Prince St. | 212-226-0211 | www.delicatessennyc.com

"Feel the hipsterdom" at this "major" SoHo "social" scene from the Cafeteria crew, a double-decker, glass-walled bar/eatery that includes a sunken lounge and an unexpected underground barroom; though "creative drinks" and a "prime" location draw hordes of "shiny, happy" twentysomethings, holdouts still grouse "get over yourself."

Del Posto

23 | 24 | 23 | $18

Chelsea | 85 10th Ave. (16th St.) | A/C/E/L to 14th St./8th Ave. | 212-497-8090 | www.delposto.com

"Big and bold" describes the room and the flavors at this "soaring", "grandiose" Batali/Bastianich showplace in West Chelsea where "bankers and lawyers" bump up against "hip NYers and the food crowd"; in the bar, "expert" mixologists and "excellent" Italian wines pacify patrons during the "inevitable wait" for a table; P.S. put those "celebratory drinks on a corporate card" if possible.

Den, The

▽ 21 | 19 | 17 | $10

Harlem | 2150 Fifth Ave. (bet. 131st & 132nd Sts.) | 2/3 to 135th St. | 212-234-3045 | www.thedenharlem.com

"Hidden on the ground floor" of a Harlem townhouse, this "sleek" albeit "small" lounge specializes in "strong drinks" with "outrageous monikers" (Marion Berry Mojito, Kung Fu Grip) accompanied by an updated soul food menu; libations are "pricey" and a cover charge is levied whenever there's music (Wednesday through Saturday), but apparently few are deterred: it's "entirely too crowded."

Desmond's Tavern

11 | 7 | 16 | $7

Murray Hill | 433 Park Ave. S. (bet. 29th & 30th Sts.) | 6 to 33rd St. | 212-684-9472 | www.desmondstavern.com

There's "no need to dress up" before showing up at this "grungy" Murray Hill pub, a "perfect place" to "get hammered" on "cheap beers" poured by "crusty old bartenders"; though the "drinks are cold, the food's hot" and the prices "reasonable", "don't come looking for atmosphere."

NEW Desnuda

23 | 20 | 23 | $13

E Village | 122 E. Seventh St. (bet. Ave. A & 1st Ave.) | 6 to Astor Pl. | 212-254-3515 | www.desnudany.com

The former Bourgeois Pig digs are the site of this new East Village wine bar that's a "cozy" nexus for local imbibing albeit a bit short on seats; the narrow, low-lit space is more "theatrical" than the neighborhood norm thanks to the judicious use of copper, marble and mahogany, and the bar snacks, heavy on the ceviche, more ambitious too.

Dewey's Flatiron

14 | 12 | 17 | $8

Flatiron | 210 Fifth Ave. (bet. 25th & 26th Sts.) | N/R/W to 23rd St. | 212-696-2337 | www.deweysflatiron.com

Come quitting time, former "frat boys and sorority girls" gravitate to this "big, boisterous" Flatiron tavern "with 1,000 of their closest buddies"; since the "hot bartenders" are "ever ready with the shots", it's "ok for a swift pint after work", though foes dis the "dingy" decor.

NEW Diamond's Wine Bar

22 | 21 | 22 | $12

LES | 188 Allen St. (bet. Houston & Stanton Sts.) | F/V to Lower East Side/2nd Ave. | 646-861-2195

If "wine is the new martini in NYC", this new LES vino vendor is the latest in the "onslaught of wine-centered bars", brought to you by the owner of the VIP strip club (hence the leggy waitresses who'll uncork your bottle); the narrow sliver of a setting is "ok" spacewise, but a "great" bottle selection helps to distract.

| | APPEAL | DECOR | SERVICE | COST |

Diner, The
| | 19 | 16 | 18 | $12 |

Meatpacking | 44 Ninth Ave. (14th St.) | A/C/E/L to 14th St./8th Ave. |
212-627-2230 | www.thedinernyc.com

Probably the "only diner in town with a velvet rope", this Meatpacking
bar/canteen features grub served by "wannabe actors" amid
'50s-style interiors so "minimalist", they're almost "kitschy"; some
drink here "to avoid the crowds" elsewhere, but more find it "a place
to sober up" – even when it's "head-thumpingly" noisy.

Ding Dong Lounge
| | ▽ 18 | 16 | 19 | $6 |

W 100s | 929 Columbus Ave. (bet. 105th & 106th Sts.) | 1 to 103rd St. |
212-663-2600 | www.dingdonglounge.com

Pleased punks consider this Morningside Heights joint "as slummy as
any East Village spot", and that's a compliment from hard-core regulars
who value its "old-school music cred", "cheap drinks" and "dark, loud"
digs; indeed, the only nonauthentic feature is the "clean bathroom."

☑ 'disiac
| | 26 | 23 | 23 | $9 |

W 50s | 402 W. 54th St. (bet. 9th & 10th Aves.) | C/E to 50th St. |
212-586-9880 | www.disiacloungenyc.com

"If you can find" this Moroccan-style "oasis" hidden on a Hell's Kitchen
side street, "you won't want to leave", given its "exclusive" feel and
"take-you-away-from-it-all" garden patio; the bartenders "mix excellent drinks" and "great sangria" to go with a light, small-plates menu.

Dive Bar
| | 18 | 13 | 19 | $9 |

W 90s | 732 Amsterdam Ave. (bet. 95th & 96th Sts.) | 1/2/3 to 96th St. |
212-749-4358 | www.divebarnyc.com

"True to its name", this "unpretentious" UWS joint is a "classic hangout" with "multiple TVs", "solid pub grub" and "smiling" staffers who
proffer "cheap pitchers" of beer and an "excellent selection" of single-
malts; just "don't expect too much" in the way of decor.

Dive 75
| | 21 | 13 | 20 | $8 |

W 70s | 101 W. 75th St. (bet. Amsterdam & Columbus Aves.) | 1/2/3
to 72nd St. | 212-362-7518 | www.divebarnyc.com

"Losing at Connect Four after five drinks never gets old" at this "come-
as-you-are" Upper Westsider known for its "board games", "cold
brews" and "cool", calming fish tank; the place is "cozy" on "rainy
Sunday afternoons" and "crazy crowded on weekend nights", but
whenever you show up, "BYO food."

Divine Bar
| | 22 | 21 | 19 | $12 |

W 50s | 236 W. 54th St. (bet. B'way & 8th Ave.) | C/E to 50th St. |
212-265-9463 | www.vino-versity.com

The vino is "divine" at this Theater District wine bar that's favored
by "daters in their 20s" for its "romantic" prospects, with a "long
bartop" and cordial staffers serving up "enormous martinis" and
"imaginative, affordable" tastings.

☑ Dizzy's Club Coca-Cola
| | 25 | 24 | 21 | $14 |

W 60s | Time Warner Ctr. | 10 Columbus Circle, 5th fl. (60th St.) | 1/A/
B/C/D to 59th St./Columbus Circle | 212-258-9595 | www.jalc.org

"World-class" live jazz, "beautiful acoustics" and "spectacular views"
of Central Park combine to put this "intimate" yet "comfortable" berth

of the cool at the Time Warner Center miles ahead of other venues; ok, it's "expensive", but "choose the right gig and you're golden" (the "after-hours $10 deal" is an "incredible bargain").

Doc Holliday's

15	9	17	$5

E Village | 141 Ave. A (9th St.) | L to 1st Ave. | 212-979-0312
"Redneck meets hipster" at this "down-home" East Village roadhouse where an "awesome" country-western jukebox inspires regulars to "turn on some Hank" and "two-step around the pool table"; "unbeatable" beer prices and a "friendly staff" make this saloon a "standby" for many, though some say "even if you like grungy, this is pushing it."

Doc Watson's

17	14	18	$8

E 70s | 1490 Second Ave. (bet. 77th & 78th Sts.) | 6 to 77th St. | 212-988-5300 | www.docwatsons.com
Neither the Southern folkie nor Sherlock Holmes' sidekick has anything to do with this "nothing-fancy" UES Irish pub, a "casual" place for locals to "sip Guinness", "mingle" with "some of Ireland's finest transplants" or amuse themselves with tube sports and arcade games.

D.O.C. Wine Bar ⊘

▽ 25	23	23	$10

Williamsburg | 83 N. Seventh St. (Wythe Ave.) | Brooklyn | L to Bedford Ave. | 718-963-1925 | www.docwinebar.com
Oenophiles oendorse this "quaint", "bodega-size" Billyburger where the "lovely" wines (over 20 by the glass, 100 by the bottle) include "lesser known Italians" paired with "savory panini", salumi and "wonderful" cheeses; "friendly, outgoing service" and sidewalk tables are added pluses.

Domaine Bar a Vins

▽ 21	17	21	$12

LIC | 50-04 Vernon Blvd. (50th Ave.) | Queens | 7 to Vernon Blvd./Jackson Ave. | 718-784-2350 | www.domainewinebar.com
Ever-gentrifying Long Island City joins the wine bar craze with the arrival of this "intimate" boîte (a "sign of things to come") brought to you by the owner of nearby Tournesol and offering over 40 vinos by the glass; a zinc bar, vintage light fixtures and occasional live jazz add to its European ambiance.

Don Hill's

20	8	13	$9

SoHo | 511 Greenwich St. (Spring St.) | C/E to Spring St. | 212-219-2850 | www.donhills.com
A "throwback" to the "days of punk, glam and Goth", this SoHo stalwart may be "Manhattan's least-sceney club", drawing an "alternative crowd" for "fab bands new and old" and such random spectacles as amateur female Jell-O wrestling; foes fret over "expensive drinks" and "steep" covers for such a "sketchy" joint, but most maintain the place is a Hill of a "lot of fun."

NEW Donnybrook

▽ 19	18	21	$9

LES | 35 Clinton St. (Stanton St.) | F/J/M/Z to Delancey/Essex Sts. | 212-228-7733 | www.donnybrooknyc.com
"Homey" and "low key", this new LES Irish bar belies its name (meaning 'brawl') with a casual, publike interior equipped with a "long marble bartop", "lots of exposed brick" and a couple of "flat-screens" showing sports; "friendly" tapsters round out its traditional charms.

Menus, photos, voting and more – free at ZAGAT.com

	APPEAL	DECOR	SERVICE	COST

Donovan's ∌

| 20 | 16 | 21 | $9 |

Bayside | 214-16 41st Ave. (Bell Blvd.) | Queens | LIRR to Bayside | 718-423-5178
Woodside | 57-24 Roosevelt Ave. (58th St.) | Queens | 7 to Woodside/61st St. | 718-429-9339

A "bit of Ireland in Queens", these "old-school" Bayside/Woodside pubs provide the "traditional atmosphere" and "excellent" beer the neighbors are looking for – not to mention some of the "best Irish coffee this side of Derry" and "ridiculously good burgers"; N.B. cash only.

Don't Tell Mama

| 24 | 16 | 22 | $11 |

W 40s | 343 W. 46th St. (bet. 8th & 9th Aves.) | A/C/E to 42nd St./Port Authority | 212-757-0788 | www.donttellmamanyc.com

Do "tell mama" (she'll want "to come as well") about this "low-pressure" cabaret/sing-along spot on Restaurant Row, where "hilarious" servers "belt out show tunes" and "Broadway hopefuls" "practice their audition songs" on an open mike; ok, the vibe may be "hokey" and the shtick "canned", but it's an "absolute blast if you're with the right people" – so "grab your favorite tourist and go."

D'Or

| 21 | 23 | 19 | $15 |

W 50s | Dream Hotel | 204 W. 55th St. (bet. B'way & 7th Ave.) | N/Q/R/W to 57th St./7th Ave. | 212-245-1234 | www.amalia-nyc.com

Midtown flaunts its "swankiest side" at this "atmospheric" underground lounge, a former horse stable transformed into a "bat cave"-like series of rooms; sure, the "smokin'" scene is out of d'ordinary, but the "name is appropriate – you'll need lots of gold" to settle the tab.

Dorrian's Red Hand

| 16 | 12 | 16 | $8 |

E 80s | 1616 Second Ave. (84th St.) | 4/5/6 to 86th St. | 212-772-6660 | www.dorrians.com

"Keep your collar up and your morals down" when hitting this "basic" yet "timeless" UES "prep mecca" where "Biff and Muffy's kids" in their "best Waspy duds" gather for "drunken dancing" and "singing to classic rock"; outsiders gripe "beware if you're not blond or blazer-clad."

Dos Caminos

| 22 | 21 | 19 | $13 |

E 50s | 825 Third Ave. (50th St.) | E/V to Lexington Ave./53rd St. | 212-336-5400
Murray Hill | 373 Park Ave. S. (bet. 26th & 27th Sts.) | 6 to 28th St. | 212-294-1000
SoHo | 475 W. Broadway (Houston St.) | 1 to Houston St. | 212-277-4300
www.brguestrestaurants.com

"Potent" margaritas in "every flavor of the rainbow", an "extensive tequila list" and "excellent guacamole" attract amigos to this high-end Mexican chainlet where bartenders have "mixing down to a science"; in summer, "great outdoor patios" are a hot commodity, though "standing room only" bar conditions indoors have some opting to "shake their maracas elsewhere."

Double Down Saloon ∌

| 17 | 11 | 17 | $8 |

E Village | 14 Ave. A (bet. Houston & 2nd Sts.) | F/V to Lower East Side/2nd Ave. | 212-982-0543 | www.doubledownsaloon.com

A "spot-on reproduction of the Vegas original", this "colorful" East Villager has the "dive" thing down pat with a "punk jukebox", "stained pool table" and an "authentic stench"; its "loud, boorish" crowd is easier to take after a couple of "delicious bacon martinis", the house specialty.

☑ Dove, The
24 | 24 | 21 | $10

G Village | 228 Thompson St. (bet. Bleecker & W. 3rd Sts.) | A/B/C/D/E/F/V to W. 4th St. | 212-254-1435

An "underground bar" in the "NYU district" that's "not an underground scene", this "cross between a '20s speakeasy and a tearoom" is a "living room" away from home for "intellectual" types who enjoy "conversation"; "lush" sofas, candles and "muted" music set a "romantic hideaway" mood, lubricated by "creative" cocktails.

Down the Hatch
16 | 10 | 16 | $7

G Village | 179 W. Fourth St. (bet. 6th Ave. & 7th Ave. S.) | A/B/C/D/E/F/V to W. 4th St. | 212-627-9747 | www.nycbestbar.com

Relive "your *Animal House* days" at this "raucous" "basement hangout" near NYU, where "sweaty men" watch sports, "guzzle cheap beer" and down the hatchlings (those "out-of-this-world" chicken wings); ok, it's "small and stuffy" with "sticky floors" and an apparent "age limit of 22", but at least it's "unpretentious."

Downtown Bar & Grill
18 | 16 | 18 | $10

Cobble Hill | 160 Court St. (bet. Amity & Pacific Sts.) | Brooklyn | F/G to Bergen St. | 718-625-2835

With a "mind-blowing assortment" of 900-plus bottled brews and a "rotating draft selection", this Cobble Hill mughouse is a no-brainer for the choosiest "beer lovers"; sure, the rather spare surroundings could be "cozier", but plasma screens tuned to sports provide some distraction.

Draft Barn
- | - | - | M

NEW Gowanus | 530 Third Ave. (bet. 12th & 13th Sts.) | Brooklyn | F/M/R to 4th Ave./9th St. | 718-768-0515

Gravesend | 317 Ave. X (W. 1st St.) | Brooklyn | F to Ave. X | 718-285-2356

The barn doors are open at this laid-back Gowanus newcomer serving over 200 types of brew to locals and greater-borough hopsheads; outfitted like a classic draft house with plenty of stone and wood, it's roomy enough for large groups, featuring a German-accented bar menu that soaks up the suds nicely – especially those beer croutons; N.B. it's a spin-off of a sibling in Gravesend.

Dram Shop
- | - | - | M

Park Slope | 339 Ninth St. (bet. 5th & 6th Aves.) | Brooklyn | F/M/R to 4th Ave./9th St. | 718-788-1444

From the minds behind Angry Wade's, this big Park Sloper comes equipped with a long wooden bar, huge booths and a back patio; there's plenty of entertainment on hand – shuffleboard, pool, board games – all made merrier by an ample selection of tap brew, whiskey and bourbon.

Drom
21 | 19 | 19 | $13

E Village | 85 Ave. A (bet. 5th & 6th Sts.) | F/V to Lower East Side/2nd Ave. | 212-777-1157 | www.dromnyc.com

"Larger than it seems from the outside", this sprawling world music venue/restaurant/lounge salutes gypsy culture, offering eclectic food and drink in the East Village space once home to Opaline; its talent roster is equally global, showcasing everything from Turkish pop stars to Japanese koto masters to bossa nova bands.

	APPEAL	DECOR	SERVICE	COST

Drop Off Service

20 | 16 | 19 | $7

E Village | 211 Ave. A (bet. 13th & 14th Sts.) | L to 1st Ave. | 212-260-2914

Having substituted one kind of suds for another, this erstwhile Laundromat now offers a "huge variety of beers" to a load of "twenty-somethings" who cycle through here regularly "to meet and be met"; with wood paneling and "plenty of room" for "mingling", this "low-key" East Villager is a "great" "middle-of-the-road" option.

Druids

▽ 19 | 15 | 19 | $9

W 50s | 736 10th Ave. (bet. 50th & 51st Sts.) | C/E to 50th St. | 212-307-6410

If not as mystically transcendent as its name implies, this "charming" Irish bar/restaurant in an "out-of-the-way" part of Hell's Kitchen is still "worthwhile" thanks to its "hidden back garden", "friendly bar staff" and "eclectic clientele"; indeed, for a "post-theater drink", it's "worth the trek once in a while."

NEW DTOX

18 | 18 | 17 | $13

E Village | 31 Second Ave. (bet. 2nd & 3rd Sts.) | F/V to Lower East Side/ 2nd Ave. | 212-777-0774

Literally separating The Urge from The Cock, this new East Village gay bar flaunts a moody, ice-blue color scheme, though some report "there's a difference between intimate and just too dark"; though a "step up" from its next-door neighbors, it somehow "doesn't seem to attract as many patrons."

Dublin House

16 | 12 | 17 | $6

W 70s | 225 W. 79th St. (bet. Amsterdam Ave. & B'way) | 1 to 79th St. | 212-874-9528

"Get your Eire on" at this "old-school" UWS boozeteria that "doesn't pretend to be anything" but a "dive"; the bartenders may be "less genial than efficient", but they execute a "damn fine pour of Guinness", and the "grubby" digs look "better blurry" – an effect "easily achieved" here.

Dublin 6

22 | 19 | 22 | $8

W Village | 575 Hudson St. (bet. Bank & W. 11th Sts.) | A/C/E/L to 14th St./8th Ave. | 646-638-2900 | www.dublin6nyc.com

The prospect of "cozy drinks" by a "perfect fireplace" in winter or a "leisurely glass of wine" at a sidewalk table in summer guarantee year-round appeal at this Village Celtic bar; a "relaxed yet smart" vibe and "warm" service from "helpful" barkeeps are additional "treats."

Duff's ⊘

▽ 19 | 14 | 24 | $6

Williamsburg | 28 N. Third St. (Kent Ave.) | Brooklyn | L to Bedford Ave. | no phone | www.duffsbrooklyn.com

"True metalheads" are galvanized by the "over-the-top" horror/biker paraphernalia festooning this "interestingly trashy" (if slightly "scary") Williamsburg haunt; it's "always good for a beer" and the resident badasses are "generally friendly", but be warned: "they'll kick you out if you request ABBA on the jukebox."

Dugout, The

16 | 8 | 18 | $7

W Village | 185 Christopher St. (bet. Washington & West Sts.) | 1 to Christopher St. | 212-242-9113 | www.thedugoutny.net

Gay dudes "not in the mood" for "preening" like the "furry", "sweaty bears" who "relax" and "swill beer" at this "roomy" West Village den;

the confines may be "seedy", but no one cares since the scene provides so many "gents of a certain age and girth" the chance to find a new honey.

Duke's
∇ | 18 | 12 | 21 | $8

E Village | 129 Ave. C (bet. 8th & 9th Sts.) | L to 1st Ave. | 212-982-5563
Covering all the criteria for a "great neighborhood bar", this Alphabet City dive offers the requisite "cold beer", jukebox, pool table and "friendly people", with a small, secluded patio out back as a bonus.

Duke's
18 | 16 | 17 | $9

Gramercy | 99 E. 19th St. (Park Ave. S.) | 6 to 23rd St. | 212-260-2922
Murray Hill | 560 Third Ave. (37th St.) | 4/5/6/7/S to 42nd St./ Grand Central | 212-949-5400
www.dukesnyc.com
"Frat-boy central meets Baton Rouge trailer park" at these "rowdy", "tacky" roadhouses, whose denizens "go for the PBR and stay for the BBQ"; "waitresses in low-rise jeans", "Duke-aritas in mason jars" and college football on "lots of big screens" outweigh the "spotty" service.

Duplex, The
19 | 14 | 19 | $9

G Village | 61 Christopher St. (7th Ave. S.) | 1 to Christopher St. | 212-255-5438 | www.theduplex.com
For more than 50 years, this storied "hetero-friendly gay bar" has been staging cabaret and comedy shows as well as sing-alongs with "seriously good" piano players who belt out show tunes and deliver "bad jokes"; the "strong drinks" keep everyone well-lubricated, and besides, "where else can you hear Joan Rivers for this price?"

Dusk
21 | 17 | 23 | $8

Chelsea | 147 W. 24th St. (bet. 6th & 7th Aves.) | F/V to 23rd St. | 212-924-4490 | www.dusklounge.com
"Is it a bar or is it a lounge?" – this Chelsea "hole-in-the-wall" expresses its "identity issues" by combining brick-walled decor with a pool table and Monday karaoke nights; further entertainment can be found in the "interesting" loos where "one-way mirrors" look out into the taproom.

NEW Dutch Kills ⌿
- | - | - | M

LIC | 27-24 Jackson Ave. (Dutch Kills St.) | Queens | E/G/R/V to Queens Plaza | 718-383-2724 | www.dutchkillsbar.com
Mixology maestro Sasha Petraske branches out to LIC via this long-in-the-making watering hole, a dark, narrow saloon channeling *Gangs of New York* with high ceilings, mahogany wainscoting, tile floors and a sawdust-strewn back room offering occasional live music; granted, the setting is random (an industrial zone several blocks from Queensboro Plaza), but the cocktails are classic, the pricing moderate and the proprietor's attention to detail – think hand-cut ice – just what you'd expect.

Duvet
20 | 23 | 16 | $13

Flatiron | 45 W. 21st St. (bet. 5th & 6th Aves.) | F/V to 23rd St. | 212-989-2121 | www.duvetny.com
"Finally bed that special someone" at this "ethereal" yet "posh" Flatiron nightspot featuring a clutch of "low-slung" king-sizers that act as tables and couches; the setup sounds "interesting" and "romantic" to fans, but foes find it "tacky" and "uncomfortable" ("nowhere to set

| | APPEAL | DECOR | SERVICE | COST |

your overpriced drink"), and rip the "ridiculous" door policies enforced by "obnoxious bouncers."

Dylan Prime

<u>23</u> <u>23</u> <u>22</u> **$13**

TriBeCa | 62 Laight St. (Greenwich St.) | 1 to Canal St. | 212-334-4783 | www.dylanprime.com

A "stylish" yet "energetic" space with "dark wood, dim lights" and a "jam-packed" bar, this TriBeCa meatery feels like a "lounge that happens to be a steakhouse"; it's a "great place for a date" or for businessmen to "bring clients", and such a "favorite" that surveyors will even "navigate the Holland Tunnel traffic to get there."

Eagle, The ⊅

<u>22</u> <u>13</u> <u>19</u> **$7**

Chelsea | 554 W. 28th St. (bet. 10th & 11th Aves.) | C/E to 23rd St. | 646-473-1866 | www.eaglenyc.com

"You can't find more machismo" in Chelsea than at this "trashy, trampy" tavern where "rough-and-tumble" "daddies, bears" and assorted leathermen are on the "prowl"; though hard-core types detect a "watered-down" scene ("S&M = stand and model"), nobody can resist the "friendly" Sunday afternoon beer blasts on the roof deck.

Eamonn's

<u>14</u> <u>13</u> <u>18</u> **$12**

Brooklyn Heights | 174 Montague St. (Clinton St.) | Brooklyn | 2/3/4/ 5/M/N/R/W to Borough Hall | 718-596-4969 | www.eamonns.net

"Politicians and state officials" caucus at this "good ol' Irish pub" near Brooklyn's Borough Hall, a "friendly social venue" that's also a "corporate hangout" at happy hour; drink prices may be "absurd" but with lots of "space" and later hours "than most other places in the Heights", most district voters consider it a viable candidate.

Ear Inn

<u>21</u> <u>15</u> <u>18</u> **$7**

SoHo | 326 Spring St. (bet. Greenwich & Washington Sts.) | 1 to Houston St. | 212-226-9060 | www.earinn.com

Sure, it's "older than dirt" (the building's from 1817), but this historic SoHo watering hole decked out with "authentic relics from bygone eras" may be the "most comfortable bar in the city"; thanks to an "eclectic crew of bartenders" pouring "excellent Guinness on tap", this "landmark destination" is "easygoing" enough to make it "worth the walk west."

East End Tavern

<u>16</u> <u>14</u> <u>19</u> **$9**

E 80s | 1589 First Ave. (bet. 82nd & 83rd Sts.) | 4/5/6 to 86th St. | 212-249-5960 | www.eastendtavernnyc.com

Ok, "you can go to nicer places", but this Yorkville "neighborhood" pub fits the bill for "mid-20s" post-collegians out to "drink at a moderate price" while eyeballing "plenty of flat-screens" (including "mini-TVs" at each booth); still, some report this "typical" Irish joint is "underused", maybe because "if you've seen one, you've seen them all."

Easternbloc ⊅

<u>22</u> <u>17</u> <u>19</u> **$7**

E Village | 505 E. Sixth St. (bet. Aves. A & B) | 6 to Astor Pl. | 212-777-2555 | www.easternblocnyc.com

"Hot bartenders and cool patrons" work all the engels at this gay bloc party in the East Village, a revolutionary revamp of the former Wonderbar into a "post-Soviet" lounge with up-to-the-minute "go-go boys"; dissidents declare the "decor's trying a little too hard", but collaborators claim this "cozy" "chat-up" spot is quite *commie il faut*.

	APPEAL	DECOR	SERVICE	COST

East of Eighth
Chelsea | 254 W. 23rd St. (bet. 7th & 8th Aves.) | C/E to 23rd St. | 212-352-0075 | www.eastofeighthny.com

19 | 17 | 18 | $10

"Straight, gay, who cares?" – this "comfortable" Chelsea duplex features two bars where you can clink wine glasses with "neighborhood eccentrics" and revel in occasional "drag entertainment"; frosting the cake, a "fabulous garden" out back can "make you forget you're in Manhattan" altogether.

East River
Williamsburg | 97 S. Sixth St. (bet. Bedford Ave. & Berry St.) | Brooklyn | J/M/Z to Marcy Ave. | 718-302-0511 | www.eastriverbar.com

▽ 20 | 20 | 23 | $10

This "big" repurposed paint factory – still sporting its original brick and ceiling beams – now offers booze and beers at "excellent prices" to local Williamsburgers who dig its "dumpy" aesthetic; there's also an outdoor space resembling a "used car lot" that's a magnet for "summer drinkers", BYO BBQ grill-outs and indie film screenings.

East Side Company Bar
LES | 49 Essex St. (Grand St.) | F/J/M/Z to Delancey/Essex Sts. | 212-614-7408

24 | 20 | 21 | $11

Another "speakeasy venture" from mega-mixologist Sasha Petraske (Milk and Honey), this "less exclusive" LES hideout is the kind of place "you could easily pass" without noticing; inside, the long, narrow space recalls a "very chic subway car" where "unmatched" bartenders use "fresh ingredients" to concoct "creative cocktails"; unsurprisingly, the pace is "slow" but the "heavenly" highballs are "worth the wait."

NEW East Village Tavern
E Village | 158 Ave. C (10th St.) | L to 1st Ave. | 212-253-8400 | www.eastvillagetavernnyc.com

19 | 15 | 18 | $10

Outwardly it's only a "small" "local hangout", but this new East Villager aims to please with an "amazing beer selection" featuring rotating craft brews on tap and hand-pumped cask ale, all at "decent prices"; downsides include a plain, bare-brick setting and a following that's "a bit fratty."

NEW EastVille Comedy Club
E Village | 85 E. Fourth St. (2nd Ave.) | F/V to Lower East Side/2nd Ave. | 212-260-2445 | www.eastvillecomedy.com

18 | 13 | 18 | $10

Catch "first-rate" jesters both known and "up-and-coming" as they polish their stand-up routines at this East Village ha-ha hacienda, an ultra-"casual" room with bare-bones appointments and a "no-attitude vibe"; even though the material "doesn't always work", it's usually "fun anyway."

NEW Eden
W 40s | 268 W. 47th St. (8th Ave.) | N/R/W to 49th St. | 212-398-2188 | www.edennyc.net

19 | 18 | 16 | $13

Further evidence of the Theater District's nightlife renaissance, this revamped rooftop (fka Jade Terrace) may lack sweeping city vistas, but its open-to-the-sky atrium design does offer ample drinking-by-starlight opportunities; it draws a "pretty good crowd" after work thanks to some hard-working party promoters.

	APPEAL	DECOR	SERVICE	COST

Edgar's Cafe ⊄
21 | 17 | 17 | $10

W 80s | 255 W. 84th St. (bet. B'way & West End Ave.) | 1 to 86th St. | 212-496-6126

"Beat the crowds at Cafe Lalo" by opting for this UWS competitor, a "civilized" and slightly "more romantic" place to "meet and talk" late-night over "delicious desserts" and a glass of wine; service can be "rushed", but interiors designed to honor its namesake Edgar Allan Poe keep loyal literature lovers ravin'.

Edge, The
19 | 15 | 18 | $11

E Village | 95 E. Third St. (bet. 1st & 2nd Aves.) | F/V to Lower East Side/2nd Ave. | 212-477-2940

"It is what it is" could be the motto of this "low-key" East Village "hangout", a brick-walled boozer that makes up for its "lack of atmosphere" with "all kinds of entertainment" (dartboards, a pool table, Connect Four); though far from cutting-edge, it's worth a stop when you just want to veg.

1849
17 | 15 | 17 | $7

G Village | 183 Bleecker St. (bet. MacDougal & Sullivan Sts.) | A/B/C/D/E/F/V to W. 4th St. | 212-505-3200 | www.1849nyc.com

Pioneering it ain't, but this "Gold Rush–themed" Village saloon offers a place to "kick back" over suds, "a burger and a game" if nothing else pans out; just "beware" that the "cheap drinks" and "cheesy Old West" trappings may spur a "stampede" of "NYUsters" and "tourists" out to stake their claims.

8th St. Winecellar
23 | 21 | 24 | $12

G Village | 28 W. Eighth St., downstairs (bet. 5th & 6th Aves.) | A/B/C/D/E/F/V to W. 4th St. | 212-260-9463 | www.8thstwinecellar.com

"Hidden" amid Eighth Street's "cheesy shoe shops", this Village vino specialist is a "stress-free" underground retreat vending a "fantastic selection of wines" augmented by "tasty snackables"; the "friendly" staff and "manageable" tabs are just the ticket for a "semi-quiet evening", but "come early or you'll have no seat."

Eight Mile Creek
23 | 18 | 22 | $9

NoLita | 240 Mulberry St., downstairs (bet. Prince & Spring Sts.) | 6 to Spring St. | 212-431-4635 | www.eightmilecreek.com

"Awesome Aussies" with "adorable accents" abound at this "truly authentic" Down Under bar in NoLita – aptly located in a basement – where "expats watch cricket" and snack on regional delicacies; "scintillating service" and a "welcoming" atmosphere make many "never want to leave."

NEW Eldridge, The
22 | 19 | 16 | $16

LES | 247 Eldridge St. (bet. E. Houston & Stanton Sts.) | F/V to Lower East Side/2nd Ave. | 212-505-7600 | www.theeldridge.com

Notorious long before it opened, this "tiny" LES lounge was loudly promoted as a "hard-to-get-into" nightclub; outside, there's a faux used-bookshop facade designed to throw uncool cats off the scent, but inside it's all very slick with a wall of champagne bottles and gold flakes garnishing everything from the drinks to the floorboards; still, given the "pretentious" mood, "rude" service and "expensive" tabs, many feel there's "more hype than fun" to be had here.

Element

▽ 22 | 24 | 19 | $12

LES | 225 E. Houston St. (Essex St.) | F/V to Lower East Side/2nd Ave. | 212-254-2200 | www.elementny.com

The Lower East Side's very own dance palace, this "spacious" triplex is set in the former Provident Loan Society bank building; the "great layout" includes a street-level dance floor, a mezzanine catwalk overlooking the action and a "cool-looking" downstairs lounge (the former vault) that's been reconfigured with wraparound banquettes and semiprivate nooks.

Elettaria

24 | 24 | 22 | $13

G Village | 33 W. Eighth St. (bet. 5th & 6th Aves.) | A/B/C/D/E/F/V to W. 4th St. | 212-677-3833 | www.elettarianyc.com

A "surprise on a shoe-store street", this "trendy" Village eatery features a "wraparound" bartop that buzzes with "hip" downtowners and "spoony couples" hobnobbing over "original" "couture cocktails"; a swell refurb of a "low-ceilinged" former retail space, it's so "warm and inviting" you may "never want to leave the bar when your table's ready."

Eleven Madison Park

25 | 25 | 24 | $14

Flatiron | 11 Madison Ave. (24th St.) | 6 to 23rd St. | 212-889-0905 | www.elevenmadisonpark.com

At Danny Meyer's "divine" Madison Square Park destination, "expertly made cocktails", "fantastic bar snacks" and "white-glove service" underscore the setting's "civilized" "1940s NYC feel"; though the "minuscule" corner lounge may provide "less a bar scene than a waiting-for-your-table scene", patrons who are "trying to impress" will do so with ease.

11th St. Bar

▽ 21 | 14 | 22 | $8

E Village | 510 E. 11th St. (bet. Aves. A & B) | L to 1st Ave. | 212-982-3929 | www.11thstbar.com

"Terrific for gatherings" thanks to "big wooden tables" and a well-equipped back room, this "divey" East Village Irish pub hosts everything from "poetry readings" to Celtic bands; the rest of the time, a "relaxed" vibe and "friendly" proprietors make this "quiet neighborhood bar" "feel like home."

NEW Ella

21 | 21 | 20 | $12

E Village | 9 Ave. A (bet. 1st & 2nd Sts.) | F/V to Lower East Side/2nd Ave. | 212-777-2230 | www.ellalounge.com

Named in honor of songbird Ella Fitzgerald, this retro-chic East Village duplex is done up in 1940s nightclub style with an "overwhelmingly red" color scheme and drinks named after Joan Crawford flicks; jazzy live acts in the basement piano lounge make for a "smooth" scene that "tries a little harder than most", even if the crowd is "more Justin Timberlake than Humphrey Bogart."

NEW El Morocco

20 | 20 | 19 | $12

Harlem | 3534 Broadway (145th St.) | 1 to 145th St. | 212-939-0909 | www.elmoroccconyc.com

Inspired by "lost but not forgotten nights" at the same-named celeb playground of yesteryear, this Harlem nightclub comes in "Latin Quarter–like" guise with its trademark zebra-stripe upholstery modernized with industrial light and sound; when you're ready to rumba, beats from merengue to hip-hop ensure the dance floor is "usually full."

	APPEAL	DECOR	SERVICE	COST

El Quinto Pino

| 20 | 18 | 20 | $13 |

Chelsea | 401 W. 24th St. (bet. 9th & 10th Aves.) | C/E to 23rd St. | 212-206-6900

"Cute 'n' cozy", this "teeny-tiny" Chelsea tapas bar makes the most of its pint-size dimensions by serving an "authentic" repertoire of "fab" Spanish vinos and "excellent" munchables; the "limited seating" can be "a bit awkward", but it's usually "just crowded enough" to close the gap with a "date."

El Rio Grande

| 19 | 15 | 17 | $10 |

Murray Hill | 160 E. 38th St. (bet. Lexington & 3rd Aves.) | 4/5/6/7/S to 42nd St./Grand Central | 212-867-0922 | www.arkrestaurants.com

Large yet "crowded", this Murray Hill cantina is the rio thing for "twenty-somethings" drawn to its "excellent outdoor patio" for imbibing, snacking and "mingling"; amigos warn that after "more than two" of the "fall-on-your-face margaritas" "someone will have to take you home" – an outcome some at this "hookup" haven may have intended all along.

NEW Elsa

| 21 | 20 | 23 | $11 |

E Village | 217 E. Third St. (bet. Aves. B & C) | F/V to Lower East Side/2nd Ave. | 917-882-7395

"Hidden behind a tailor shop", this "cozy", "candlelit" East Village newcomer (fka The Hanger) is a back-room homage to yesteryear frock star Elsa Schiaparelli; it's "romantic" in a "bohemian" way, with "friendly" servers, designer drinks and an antique sewing machine that's been transformed into a beer tap.

Emmett O'Lunney's
(fka Harmony View)

| ▽ 16 | 14 | 21 | $8 |

W 50s | 210 W. 50th St. (B'way) | 1 to 50th St. | 212-957-5100 | www.harmonyview.com

Featuring hard-to-miss neon out front, this "cavernous" Theater District Irish pub is a "boxy", split-level taproom lined with indoor neon signage of a more vintage variety; expect "friendly" staffers and a busy "after-work scene" made up of local desk jockeys, heavy on publishing types (Hachette is right across the street).

Empire Hotel Lobby Bar

| 19 | 18 | 18 | $13 |

W 60s | Empire Hotel | 44 W. 63rd St. (bet. B'way & Columbus Ave.) | 1 to 66th St. | 212-265-7400 | www.empirehotelnyc.com

Back on the scene following a "fabulous redo", this "sexy respite" in the Lincoln Center-area hotel is an "attention-getting" enclave with soaring ceilings, a "soothing" soundtrack and "comfy seating" for high-maintenance tipplers; of course, it's predictably "pricey", but worth it for the "pizzazz" factor alone.

Z NEW Empire Hotel Rooftop

| 24 | 23 | 18 | $14 |

W 60s | Empire Hotel | 44 W. 63rd St., 12th fl. (bet. B'way & Columbus Ave.) | 1 to 66th St. | 212-956-3313 | www.chinagrillmgt.com/empireNY

The "suits" get "sceney" at this "posh", "year-round rooftop" overlooking Lincoln Center, a "stylish oasis" boasting an enclosed lounge, twin terraces with "striking views" and "red neon" illumination courtesy of the "huge Empire Hotel sign"; there's "plenty of space" for the "throngs" "on the hunt", but "look sharp" and "be prepared to shell out" for the privilege.

	APPEAL	DECOR	SERVICE	COST

☑ Employees Only

24 | 22 | 22 | $13

W Village | 510 Hudson St. (bet. Christopher & W. 10th Sts.) | 1 to Christopher St. | 212-242-3021 | www.employeesonlynyc.com

It "feels like 1929" at this "slightly mysterious", speakeasy-esque Villager with a concealed entrance (behind a tarot-card reader) to help "keep the riffraff out"; look for "dapper bartenders" whipping up "perfect old-school cocktails" for a "swinging" crowd, though "service suffers" when the "cozy" confines get "panic-inducingly crowded."

Enid's

▽ 19 | 20 | 18 | $8

Greenpoint | 560 Manhattan Ave. (Driggs Ave.) | Brooklyn | L to Bedford Ave. | 718-349-3859 | www.enids.net

"Williamsburg spillovers" splash down in this quirky, spacious Greenpoint bar that's not exactly a "destination" but still handy for a "quick" quaff and a game of pinball "if you're passing by"; critics complain of one "classic" problem here: "all attitude, no service."

EN Shochu Bar

22 | 25 | 19 | $13

W Village | 435 Hudson St. (Leroy St.) | 1 to Houston St. | 212-647-9196 | www.enjb.com

Enraptured endorsers of this "hip" West Village "oasis" applaud the "amazing" array of sakes and sojus by the glass and the "inventive" cocktail list served in a "stunning" space that's a "mix of Japanese and Western" aesthetics; "incredible" housemade tofu and "delicious small plates" entice many to stay for dinner.

Epistrophy ⇗

21 | 21 | 17 | $10

NoLita | 200 Mott St. (bet. Kenmare & Spring Sts.) | 6 to Spring St. | 212-966-0904 | www.epistrophycafe.com

A "delightful" alternative, this "low-key" NoLita enoteca is a "welcoming" locale for "grabbing a glass of wine", getting a "small bite to eat" and taking in some "occasional jazz"; service is "friendly" but occasionally "as erratic as a Thelonious Monk solo."

Epstein's Bar ⇗

14 | 10 | 14 | $9

LES | 82 Stanton St. (Allen St.) | F/V to Lower East Side/2nd Ave. | 212-477-2232 | www.epsteinsbarnyc.com

This LES "joint" aims to "keep it simple" with "DIY" interiors, "dim lighting", basic service and "decent burgers" ("can't beat the two-for-one deal on Sundays"); critics of this "nondescript watering hole" say it has "no decor", "no theme", "no atmosphere" and conclude "no draw."

Escuelita

17 | 10 | 14 | $11

Garment District | 301 W. 39th St. (bet. 8th & 9th Aves.) | A/C/E to 42nd St./Port Authority | 212-631-0588 | www.enyclub.com

Happy campers "let loose" at this Garment District gay drag club where boys will be girls and "everything is ok"; on weekends, "fierce" divas deliver "gut-splitting" performances, between which "go-go" guys and "hot butch" types twist and shout to Latin and house music.

ESPN Zone

18 | 19 | 15 | $11

W 40s | 1472 Broadway (42nd St.) | 1/2/3/7/N/Q/R/S/W to 42nd St./ Times Sq. | 212-921-3776 | www.espnzone.com

Times Square's "beer-fueled sports mecca" delights diehards with "more TVs than you can count" and "amazing" video games to keep everyone "entertained during halftime"; foes find this testosterzone "touristy", "overhyped and overpriced", but for fanatics – especially during playoffs – it's "pure fun with no pretenses."

Essex

	APPEAL	DECOR	SERVICE	COST
	20	19	18	$11

LES | 120 Essex St. (Rivington St.) | F/J/M/Z to Delancey/Essex Sts. | 212-533-9616 | www.essexnyc.com

"Interesting" multiculti finger food, happy-hour specials and "plenty of room" make this high-ceilinged LES lounge/eatery a neighborhood standby that's particularly "excellent for groups" if you can "snag the semiprivate area" on the mezzanine; hard-core night rangers take sustenance – and a little hair of the dog – at the weekend brunch.

Essex Ale House

	APPEAL	DECOR	SERVICE	COST
	20	17	20	$12

LES | 179 Essex St. (bet. Houston & Stanton Sts.) | F/V to Lower East Side/2nd Ave. | no phone

When you're "tired of all the lounges", this "friendly" Lower East Side brewpub is a "casual" gathering spot offering "decent beers on tap" and an impressive assortment of select bottles; though "not a great place to bring a date", its deep inventory lends some "serious drinker cachet."

Europa

	APPEAL	DECOR	SERVICE	COST
	▽ 17	15	16	$12

Greenpoint | 98 Meserole Ave. (bet. Lorimer St. & Manhattan Ave.) | Brooklyn | G to Greenpoint Ave. | 718-383-2322 | www.europaclub.com

Alternative rockers and footloose Slavs convene at this Greenpoint club–cum–music venue where "energizing" sets from "eclectic" live bands are interspersed with DJs spinning "sizzling dance music" into the wee hours; ironic types add that its resemblance to an Eastern bloc disco has a "distinct charm."

NEW Evolve

	APPEAL	DECOR	SERVICE	COST
	▽ 22	20	21	$13

E 50s | 221 E. 58th St. (bet. 2nd & 3rd Aves.) | 4/5/6/N/R/W to 59th St./Lexington Ave. | 212-355-3395

East Midtown's former O.W. space has evolved into this rechristened gay bar that looks much the same as before, right down to its goes-on-forever bartop; the new twist is a more 'straight-friendly' scene, abetted by weekend party promoters bringing in younger, livelier types.

Excelsior ⊄

	APPEAL	DECOR	SERVICE	COST
	19	18	22	$10

Park Slope | 390 Fifth Ave. (bet. 6th & 7th Sts.) | Brooklyn | F/M/R to 4th Ave./9th St. | 718-832-1599 | www.excelsiorbrooklyn.com

As a "no-attitude" neighborhood gay bar, this Park Slope pioneer provides "decent drinks" via an "extremely friendly staff" plus a bonus patio; the setting is frill-free and the few regulars "do not a happening crowd make", but if you're looking for action in these parts, this is your "only option."

Faces & Names

	APPEAL	DECOR	SERVICE	COST
	18	15	19	$8

W 50s | 159 W. 54th St. (bet. 6th & 7th Aves.) | C/E to 50th St. | 212-586-9311 | www.facesandnames.com

Slightly "classier" than a pub, this "convenient" Midtown taproom satisfies "late-20s, early-30s" types seeking to unwind after work with help from bartenders who make everyone "feel comfortable"; given its hotel-heavy neighborhood, look for an "out-of-town" contingent as well.

| | APPEAL | DECOR | SERVICE | COST |

Failte
▽ 17 | 12 | 19 | $6

Murray Hill | 531 Second Ave. (bet. 29th & 30th Sts.) | 6 to 28th St. | 212-725-9440 | www.failtenyc.com
A "better-than-average" crowd of Celts and their cronies hangs out at this "pleasant" Murray Hill Irish pub, a "welcome outpost" amid a "wasteland of frat-boy sports lounges"; the barkeeps are "friendly" and the vibe "relaxed", but timid tipplers should be prepared for "raucous behavior from time to time."

Fanelli's Cafe
18 | 14 | 18 | $8

SoHo | 94 Prince St. (Mercer St.) | N/R/W to Prince St. | 212-226-9412
Improbably juxtaposed between the "yuppie emporia", this "perfect old-school" bar and grill remains a "refreshing" yet "poignant" relic of pre-gentrification SoHo, with "classic" tile-and-tintype decor and drinks that come with "no sticker shock" and "no attitude"; the only downside is that it's "crowded day and night" – "you can't ever count on getting a seat."

Fashion 40
▽ 18 | 19 | 18 | $11

W 40s | 202 W. 40th St. (7th Ave.) | A/C/E to 42nd St./Port Authority | 212-221-3628 | www.fashion40lounge.com
Comparatively "swanky" for its block, this "modern" bar on the Garment District/Times Square border solicits "hip" Parsons fashionistas and Port Authority commuters by offering "well-made drinks", weekend DJs and "cocktail girls" decked out in the "sexiest dresses imaginable."

Fat Baby
19 | 16 | 17 | $9

LES | 112 Rivington St. (bet. Essex & Ludlow Sts.) | F/V to Lower East Side/ 2nd Ave. | 212-533-1888 | www.fatbabynyc.com
"Always jammed", this "cool" LES hot spot hosts an "eclectic" roster of "obscure NYC rock acts" in its "seedy basement" while "accommodating the masses" upstairs in a glossy lounge with "plush couches", turntablists and a long, polished bar; the "lively yet low-key" crowd (think "banking analysts who think of themselves as arty hipsters") may or may not be from the neighborhood.

Fat Black Pussycat
17 | 16 | 16 | $9

G Village | 130 W. Third St. (bet. MacDougal St. & 6th Ave.) | A/B/C/D/ E/F/V to W. 4th St. | 212-533-4790 | www.thefatblackpussycat.com
Nine lives or not, this Village cat's got "multiple personalities" – "dive pub" in front, dim "lounge behind the curtain" in back – rendering it suitable for "any mood"; "cheap drinks" and a "multitude of beers" make the "loud music", "small bathrooms" and "raucous" crowds bearable.

Fat Cat
19 | 15 | 16 | $9

W Village | 75 Christopher St. (bet. Bleecker St. & 7th Ave. S.) | 1 to Christopher St. | 212-675-6056 | www.fatcatjazz.com
So "down to earth" it's in the basement, this "no-frills" Village combo of pool room and "live jazz" forum has an "eclectic mix of patrons" either shooting stick or digging "old-school" sounds nightly; a sibling of the legendary Smalls, it "brings in great talent" while simultaneously providing space for a "Ping-Pong death match."

	APPEAL	DECOR	SERVICE	COST

Feinstein's at Loews Regency

| 23 | 23 | 22 | $17 |

E 60s | Loews Regency Hotel | 540 Park Ave. (61st St.) | 4/5/6/N/R/W to 59th St./Lexington Ave. | 212-339-4095 | www.feinsteinsattheregency.com

Cabaret is "only as good as the entertainers" and this "timeless" UES venue (overseen by owner-performer Michael Feinstein) is up to the challenge with its slate of "sophisticated" performers; "fabulous martinis" and "personalized service" enhance the "comfortable" setting, so its "old-money", "60+" clientele doesn't mind the "extremely pricey" tabs; N.B. jacket suggested.

Felice

| 22 | 21 | 19 | $14 |

E 60s | 1166 First Ave. (64th St.) | F to Lexington Ave./63rd St. | 212-593-2223 | www.felicewinebar.com

Joining the ever-growing Upper East Side wine bar trend, this "quaint", "Village-esque" venue draws an "eager" crowd that's "not too young" with its "cozy" rusticity, "romantic candlelight" and "savory" Italian vinos; it's a felicitous "scene", especially for those "too lazy to go Downtown."

Fiddlesticks

| 18 | 14 | 15 | $7 |

G Village | 54-58 Greenwich Ave. (bet. 6th Ave. & 7th Ave. S.) | 1/2/3/L to 14th St./7th Ave. | 212-463-0516 | www.fiddlestickspub.com

"Spacious" and "unpretentious" – a combo that's "hard to find in Greenwich Village" – this bar/restaurant comes across with "unbeatable" happy-hour deals in a "warm" setting; though "you have to fight to get a drink" on weekends when the "rowdy twentysomethings" invade, sidewalk picnic tables offer some relief as well as "awesome people-watching."

55 Bar ⊟

| 22 | 14 | 18 | $9 |

G Village | 55 Christopher St. (bet. 6th Ave. & 7th Ave. S.) | 1 to Christopher St. | 212-929-9883 | www.55bar.com

A "real dive" with lotsa "heart", this 1919-vintage Village basement boasts a "long history" as a "local jazz bar" where live jamsters groove nightly for a low-dough cover; between the "friendly older" regulars and curious newcomers, it's liable to be a "rowdy" session.

Fillmore, The

| 22 | 12 | 12 | $8 |

Gramercy | 17 Irving Pl. (15th St.) | 4/5/6/L/N/Q/R/W to 14th St./Union Sq. | 212-777-6817 | www.irvingplaza.com

"One of the better live music venues" around, this "medium-sized" Gramercy concert hall may have changed its name but still showcases everyone from "fresh bands" to "national acts" in a "high-energy" space channeling a "high school gym"; while there's "plenty of canned beer to go around", there's no seating, a word to the wise for those "too old to stand for three hours."

Finnegans Wake

| 15 | 12 | 20 | $8 |

E 70s | 1361 First Ave. (73rd St.) | 6 to 77th St. | 212-737-3664

"Irish tales" delivered "with a lilt and a twinkle of the eye" are on tap at this "standard" Yorkville saloon, a "friendly" place to "have a pint" and some "best-value" pub grub; still, foes fret the digs and denizens are "about as boring as the book" ("if you have an AARP card, you'll fit in").

| | APPEAL | DECOR | SERVICE | COST |

Finnerty's
∇ 10 | 8 | 15 | $6

E Village | 221 Second Ave. (bet. 13th & 14th Sts.) | L to 1st Ave. |
212-677-2655

"Originally on Third Avenue", this relocated East Village dive is not
"what it used to be" – it's now roomier and a tad more upscale – but it
continues to supply "cheap beer", darts, a jukebox and a pool table to
a "starving college student" clientele.

Firefly
19 | 18 | 19 | $11

NoLita | 54 Spring St. (bet. Lafayette & Mulberry Sts.) | 6 to Spring St. |
212-966-8716 | www.fireflynyc.com

Jocks show up at this NoLita sports bar for the "plethora of projection
screens" that make it a "pretty sweet" option for big game–watching; it
may be "too frat-tastic" and rather "out of place in the neighborhood",
but at least it soaks up "the overflow" from the nearby Spring Lounge.

Firehouse
16 | 14 | 18 | $7

W 80s | 522 Columbus Ave. (bet. 85th & 86th Sts.) | 1 to 86th St. |
212-787-3473 | www.firehousenyc.com

The "just-out-of-college" crowd likes this "solid" UWS "staple", a
"convenient" place to "grab a beer, a table on the sidewalk" and some
"killer wings"; despite decor that "pays homage to the Fire Department",
wet blankets feel there are "better options in the neighborhood."

First Edition
15 | 13 | 17 | $11

Bayside | 41-06 Bell Blvd. (41st Ave.) | Queens | LIRR to Bayside |
718-428-8522

"One of the better sports bars in the area", this Bayside vet lures locals
who love "watching their favorite" teams on a "head-spinning" number
of TV screens; a comparatively "upscale" interior adds appeal for "single
women" facing a "clientele that's 90% men" – "both a pro and a con."

Fitzgerald's Pub
∇ 16 | 16 | 20 | $7

Murray Hill | 336 Third Ave. (bet. 24th & 25th Sts.) | 6 to 23rd St. |
212-679-6931 | www.fitzgeraldspubnyc.net

If not the most "original" concept, this Murray Hill Irish pub is nevertheless an "easygoing place to catch up with an old friend", "listen to '80s
songs on the jukebox" or follow a game on the tubes; bartenders who
"consider you a regular" after one visit are known for their "buybacks."

5 Ninth
23 | 23 | 20 | $15

Meatpacking | 5 Ninth Ave. (bet. Gansevoort & Little W. 12th Sts.) |
A/C/E/L to 14th St./8th Ave. | 212-929-9460 | www.5ninth.com

The "feel of exclusivity" earns a "high five" for this "classy"
Meatpacking number, an "impressive", triple-tiered brownstone remade into an "unexpectedly charming" "hardwood hideaway" for a
"low-key chat" over "imaginative" house drinks; when the "small"
ground-floor bar gets too "lively" for comfort, the "cool factor" extends to the "beautiful garden" and "intimate" upstairs dining area.

NEW 508 Sports Lounge
- | - | - | I

Garment District | 508 Ninth Ave. (bet. 38th & 39th Sts.) | A/C/E to
42nd St./Port Authority | 212-594-5541

The raggedy stretch of Ninth Avenue behind Port Authority – the dive
bar capital of Manhattan – now has a new sports bar; set in the former

Door Lounge digs, it's retained much of its predecessor's decor (Moroccan lanterns, anyone?) but has added three flat-screens and a pool table; nevertheless, it's the dollar draft beers that keep it hopping.

Five Spot ▽ 17 | 13 | 17 | $10

Fort Greene | 459 Myrtle Ave. (Washington Ave.) | Brooklyn | G to Clinton/Washington Aves. | 718-852-0202 | www.fivespotsoulfood.com

Brooklynites take five at this Fort Greene spot, a soul food supper club that spotlights "up-and-coming R&B, hip-hop and world-music artists" while also offering open turntable nights and monthly fashion shows; even if drinks and food get mixed reviews, fans who "come for the music" give it a high five.

Flannery's Bar 18 | 12 | 22 | $7

Chelsea | 205 W. 14th St. (7th Ave.) | 1/2/3/L to 14th St./7th Ave. | 212-229-2122 | www.flannerysny.com

The "barman is actually Irish" (and just may "do a shot with you") at this Emerald Isle pub on a busy Chelsea corner where locals come to "relax during the week and party on the weekends"; though it's "no-frills", with dartboards and sports on the tube, "very strong drinks" compensate.

Flashdancers 18 | 14 | 17 | $15

W 50s | 1674 Broadway (bet. 52nd & 53rd Sts.) | 1 to 50th St. | 212-315-5107 | www.flashdancersnyc.com

A "cavalcade of Stars, Tiffanys" and other "hot" strippers shake their moneymakers at this West Midtown jiggle joint where connoisseurs report the "talent is better than in the past"; "expect to drop a load" of cash on "$10 beers and $20 covers", but that's of little concern to customers "here for one reason and one reason only": all that "flesh."

☒ Flatiron Lounge 25 | 24 | 23 | $12

Flatiron | 37 W. 19th St. (bet. 5th & 6th Aves.) | 1 to 18th St. | 212-727-7741 | www.flatironlounge.com

This "civilized throwback" to the "Roaring Twenties" provides a "rare opportunity" for "haute drinking" in the Flatiron thanks to a team of "talented" mixologists concocting "classic", "old-school" cocktails; its "dressy" young professional following is unfazed by the "pricey" tabs: "they've earned the right to charge this much for a drink."

Flight 151 15 | 13 | 17 | $8

Chelsea | 151 Eighth Ave. (bet. 17th & 18th Sts.) | A/C/E/L to 14th St./8th Ave. | 212-229-1868

Bedecked in vintage "aviator decor", this Chelsea pub draws a "straight crowd" of frequent fliers high on its "down-to-earth" vibe and "decent munchies"; a few find it too "gimmicky" (e.g. lavatories where a "pilot's voice makes humorous fake announcements"), yet the fact that there's always "room at the bar" guarantees smooth landings.

Flor de Sol 23 | 21 | 20 | $13

TriBeCa | 361 Greenwich St. (bet. Franklin & Harrison Sts.) | 1 to Franklin St. | 212-366-1640 | www.flordesolnyc.com

Spanish musicians and flamenco dancers provide the flor show at this "happening" TriBeCa tapas hall that also supplies "delicious" snacks and "fantastic sangria"; the candlelit, cushioned interior is "not too fancy" but emits a "sensual" vibe that's "ideal for a date" – even if the bar's "limited space" means they may "get bumped" a bit.

Floyd, NY

APPEAL	DECOR	SERVICE	COST
22	19	20	$7

Brooklyn Heights | 131 Atlantic Ave. (bet. Clinton & Henry Sts.) | Brooklyn | F/G to Bergen St. | 718-858-5810 | www.floydny.com

"Bocce ball is the name of the game" at this "festive" Atlantic Avenue spot most celebrated for its "indoor red-clay court" (and most maligned for its "long sign-up sheet"); cheap "canned" brews, "cozy" living-room decor and a "dog-friendly vibe" bring in the "usual hipsters" along with some "hot Brooklyn law students."

Flûte

APPEAL	DECOR	SERVICE	COST
22	21	20	$14

Flatiron | 40 E. 20th St. (bet. B'way & Park Ave. S.) | 6 to 23rd St. | 212-529-7870

W 50s | 205 W. 54th St. (bet. B'way & 7th Ave.) | N/Q/R/W to 57th St./7th Ave. | 212-265-5169

www.flutebar.com

"Bubbly, bubbly everywhere and oh so much to drink" could be the motto of this "swanky" twosome offering an "unrivaled champagne selection" as well as an "extensive" cocktail list; the smallish Midtown original (a former speakeasy) abounds with "dark, intimate" corners that are "cozy for couples, awkward for others", while the high-ceilinged Flatiron outpost is twice as large; either way, "be prepared to spend."

Fontana's

APPEAL	DECOR	SERVICE	COST
19	20	19	$9

LES | 105 Eldridge St. (bet. Broome & Grand Sts.) | B/D to Grand St. | 212-334-6740 | www.fontanasnyc.com

A "gigantic" refuge in a "condensed city", this Lower Eastsider entices the huddled masses to its "grunge bohemian" digs where you can swill cocktails in the faux-swanky ground floor, "rock out to live bands" downstairs or "make out with the DJ" "up in the balcony"; though the dubious "can't see any reason" to show up, fans believe it's a "budding classic."

Forbidden City

APPEAL	DECOR	SERVICE	COST
19	18	21	$11

E Village | 212 Ave. A (bet. 13th & 14th Sts.) | L to 1st Ave. | 212-598-0500 | www.forbiddennyc.com

"Hip-hop meets Asia" at this "very chill" East Village enclave that's "part bar, part nightclub" and staffed by bartenders who "attend to your needs" before you "even have to ask"; granted, the drinks may be "pricey", but there's no cover for the live music and DJs – plus you can "walk right in."

40c

APPEAL	DECOR	SERVICE	COST
▽ 18	16	19	$11

E Village | 40 Ave. C (bet. 3rd & 4th Sts.) | F/J/M/Z to Delancey/Essex Sts. | 212-466-0800

Bringing some swank to Avenue C, this airy East Village lounge emits a 1940s noir vibe via dim lights and crimson leather booths; the curtained-off niche in the back with a keyhole-shaped entryway (that formerly housed a pool table) has been remade into a space perfect for private parties.

40/40

APPEAL	DECOR	SERVICE	COST
21	21	17	$15

Flatiron | 6 W. 25th St. (bet. B'way & 6th Ave.) | N/R/W to 23rd St. | 212-832-4040 | www.the4040club.com

"If you've got game", "wear the right gear" and spectate "in style" at this Flatiron "hip-hop sports bar", a "swank", "spacious" testament to the "platinum" taste of co-owner Jay-Z (i.e. a gazillion flat-screens,

| | APPEAL | DECOR | SERVICE | COST |

"swinging lounge chairs" and a cognac lounge upstairs); prices are "sky high", but it's "crazy packed" with "bling"-bedecked playas anyway 'cause Hova "knows what works."

49 Grove
18 | 17 | 16 | $11

W Village | 49 Grove St. (Bleecker St.) | 1 to Christopher St. | 212-727-1100 | www.49grovenyc.com

"See and be seen – if you can make out a face" – at this "cavelike" "underground" Village club with low ceilings overhead, "carpeting" underfoot and "decent music" in the air for the "twentysomethings" typically "packed in"; supporters sense "chic", though antis cite an "uptight" staff and "iffy" scene that "tries to be trendy" but delivers "nothing new."

Forum
18 | 18 | 17 | $12

E Village | 127 Fourth Ave. (bet. 12th & 13th Sts.) | 4/5/6/L/N/Q/R/W to 14th St./Union Sq. | 212-505-0360

"Post-college" patricians keep this "lively" bar/lounge near Union Square "jam-packed" on weekends as they toss back "uncomplicated" drinks and shake it to "pop and hip-hop"; though the door's "easy", the scenery is "pretty generic" and "anyone over 24 may feel out of place."

Four-Faced Liar
18 | 13 | 20 | $7

G Village | 165 W. Fourth St. (bet. 6th Ave. & 7th Ave. S.) | A/B/C/D/E/F/V to W. 4th St. | 212-366-0608 | www.thefour-facedliar.com

"Outstanding" bartenders "remember what you drink" at this "authentic" Village pub that aims to be an "Irish *Cheers*"; though "post-frat" carousers occasionally "overrun" the joint, poetry readings and board games add some diversity.

☒ Four Seasons Bar
26 | 25 | 24 | $17

E 50s | 99 E. 52nd St. (Park Ave.) | 6 to 51st St./Lexington Ave. | 212-754-9494 | www.fourseasonsrestaurant.com

There's "fabulous people-watching" in store at this "sophisticated" Midtown "power bar" attached to the restaurant's famed Grill Room, where "superb" staffers treat guests "like royalty" (which, in some cases, they are); otherwise, it's a "money-is-no-object" scene for "older" movers and shakers, all "dressed to the nines" and all engaged in "hushed conversations."

☒ Four Seasons Hotel Bar
25 | 25 | 25 | $18

E 50s | Four Seasons Hotel | 57 E. 57th St. (bet. Madison & Park Aves.) | 4/5/6/N/R/W to 59th St./Lexington Ave. | 212-758-5757 | www.fourseasons.com

Following a revamp to make room for L'Atelier de Joël Robuchon, this Midtown hotel bar remains as "stunning" as ever and draws the same "mature" clientele: "ladies with Hermès bags", their "sugar daddies" and "schmoozing" dealmakers; look for "incredible" martinis, "high-end bar snacks" and "impeccable" service, but to truly fit in, "wear a suit" and "bring your black Amex."

Fourth Avenue Pub
18 | 12 | 19 | $10

Park Slope | 76 Fourth Ave. (Bergen St.) | Brooklyn | D/M/N/R to Pacific St. | 718-643-2273

"If all you want to do is drink", this ultra-"unpretentious" bar in the West Park Slope "wasteland" satisfies "serious" suds sippers with its intriguing drafts, "free popcorn" and "generous" happy hour; a "bare-bones" joint with an "expansive back yard", it's a "throwback" to bygone Brooklyn.

4₂0

15	13	14	$9

W 80s | 420 Amsterdam Ave. (80th St.) | 1 to 79th St. | 212-579-8450 | www.420barandlounge.com

A "neighborhood alternative to all the frat bars", this Upper Westsider pools a "not-too-crazy" "Gen-X hangout" up top with a "comfy" basement "party space" to dive into "if you're in the mood to dance"; but spoilers spout about a "ho-hum" crowd that slows the flow.

Frames
(fka Leisure Time Bowl)

-	-	-	E

W 40s | 625 Eighth Ave., 2nd fl. (42nd St.) | A/C/E to 42nd St./Port Authority | 212-268-6909

Idlers "hanging out at Port Authority" are jazzed by the renovation of this "old-school" pin palace (fka Leisure Time Bowl) into a state-of-the-art venue that will include a new restaurant and nightclub; it's "not cheap" – though you can "reserve online for discounts" – but let's face it, "where else can you bowl in a bus terminal?"

Frank's Cocktail Lounge ⊄

19	15	19	$9

Fort Greene | 660 Fulton St. (bet. Lafayette Ave. & S. Elliott Pl.) | Brooklyn | G to Fulton St. | 718-625-9339 | www.frankscocktaillounge.com

Fort Greene fans rely on this "nothing-fancy" "neighborhood fixture" (since 1974), a "lively" "old-school charmer with some new-school blood"; an "eclectic" mix of locals and hipsters "checks its attitude and inhibitions at the door", claiming that an "exuberant Friday night" here can redeem a "bad week."

Freddy's Bar & Backroom ⊄

▽ 18	9	17	$6

Prospect Heights | 485 Dean St. (6th Ave.) | Brooklyn | 2/3 to Bergen St. | 718-622-7035 | www.freddysbackroom.com

There's more than meets the eye at this "no-frills" "vintage dive" in Prospect Heights where "decent local bands", aspiring comics and opera singers take their turns at the mike and video artists and painters display their works on the walls; fans who like what they see say "you can judge a book by its cover here."

⦿ Freemans

26	22	19	$12

LES | Freeman Alley (off Rivington St., bet. Bowery & Chrystie St.) | B/D to Grand St. | 212-420-0012 | www.freemansrestaurant.com

"Hidden" in a "strange alley" off Rivington Street, this "unmarked" LES restaurant-cum-hipster magnet "now has two bars" (handy since there's "always a wait" for a table); it's decorated in a "speakeasy"-meets-"Elks"-lodge style with lots of "taxidermy", though a few say it "has more self-importance than the usual secret hideaway."

⦿ Frying Pan

-	-	-	M

Chelsea | Pier 66 Maritime (26th St. & West Side Hwy.) | C/E to 23rd St. | 212-989-6363 | www.pier66maritime.com

Now moored on Chelsea's Pier 66, this beloved lightship-cum-party site is a vast alfresco venue that includes a tiki bar vending drinks and pub grub; though it closes relatively early (1 AM), sunset views, Ping-Pong and foosball tables, and a no-hassles vibe still make it a destination.

	APPEAL	DECOR	SERVICE	COST

Full Shilling
	18	17	19	$7

Financial District | 160 Pearl St. (bet. Pine & Wall Sts.) | 2/3 to Wall St. | 212-422-3855

"After a hard day working the market", Financial District types mingle at this "relaxed" taproom with a "gentlemen's club feel" (pretty woodwork" and 116-year-old bar "imported from Ireland"); the staffers' Celtic accents supply some authenticity, and the pub grub's "decent" too.

g ⊘
	20	21	17	$10

Chelsea | 225 W. 19th St. (bet. 7th & 8th Aves.) | 1 to 18th St. | 212-929-1085 | www.glounge.com

"One-night-stand" central for Chelsea boys, this still-"trendy" gay salon "sizzles with energy" as "glamour-puss" types cruise its "circular bar"; even if the "hot-as-a-blowtorch" bartenders "aren't hired for their ability to make a drink" ("attitude straight up is the house specialty"), there are enough patrons "looking for trouble" to distract.

Gaf Bar
	22	17	25	$6

E 80s | 1715 First Ave. (89th St.) | 4/5/6 to 86th St. | 212-427-6482
W 40s | 401 W. 48th St. (bet. 9th & 10th Aves.) | C/E to 50th St. | 212-262-2883

Like a "second living room", these Irish siblings draw in "local folk" for "quiet drinks and a chat"; "competitive darts", video games and "friendly bartenders" with "real heart" keep the trade brisk.

⚡ Galapagos
	-	-	-	M

Dumbo | 16 Main St. (Water St.) | Brooklyn | F to York St. | 718-222-8500 | www.galapagosartspace.com

Following a rent hike at its erstwhile Williamsburg home, this avant-garde performance space has relocated to Dumbo's Main Street and doubled its size in the process; the eclectic bill of acts in store has got nothing on the dramatic space, featuring a large stage opposite rows of half moon–shaped banquettes suspended over a floor of water.

GalleryBar
	19	20	17	$10

LES | 120 Orchard St. (bet. Delancey & Rivington Sts.) | F/J/M/Z to Delancey/Essex Sts. | 212-529-2266 | www.gallerybarnyc.com

A daytime gallery with "rotating art on the walls", this "cool" Lower Eastsider segues into an "unpretentious" nightspot with a "chill atmosphere" upstairs and DJs in its subterranean lounge; it may be a tad "mainstream", but it still gets pretty "hot and sweaty on a weekend."

Gallo Nero
	21	21	23	$12

W 40s | 404 W. 44th St. (bet. 9th & 10th Aves.) | A/C/E to 42nd St./Port Authority | 212-265-6660 | www.gallonerony.com

At 500 strong, the list of vinos is "almost too long" at this "small" but serious wine bar tucked into a "cute" Hell's Kitchen trattoria; "helpful" stewards decant 45 options by the glass and locals say it's "like going to Italy for the cost of a glass of wine."

Galway Hooker
	18	16	18	$9

Murray Hill | 7 E. 36th St. (bet. 5th & Madison Aves.) | 6 to 33rd St. | 212-725-2353 | www.galwayhookernyc.com

An "Irish pub on steroids", this "ginormous" Murray Hill "megabar" draws "big crowds" who show up to suck down "Jaeger bombs", play pool or darts, or just gaze at its "many flat-screens"; the name refers to an Irish sailboat, contrary to what most in this "sausagefest" think.

Garage

21 | 20 | 21 | $11

G Village | 99 Seventh Ave. S. (bet. Barrow & Grove Sts.) | 1 to Christopher St. | 212-645-0600 | www.garagerest.com

Live jazz "without a cover" or minimum is the hook at this "friendly" eatery that began life as an automobile garage in the 1920s and is now a "high-ceilinged" affair with an "enormous" bar; though some find it "pretty standard" stuff, the central Village location and "do-your-own-thing" mood lead many to park here.

Gaslight

17 | 16 | 16 | $11

Meatpacking | 400 W. 14th St. (9th Ave.) | A/C/E/L to 14th St./8th Ave. | 212-807-8444

G2

Meatpacking | 39 Ninth Ave. (bet. 13th & 14th Sts.) | A/C/E/L to 14th St./ 8th Ave. | 212-807-8444
www.gaslightnyc.com

A "nice breather from the Meatpacking District's high-and-mighty scene", this unassuming "backup plan" may be "not as swanky" as its neighbors but sure is a heck of a lot more "affordable"; since it's usually "way too crowded", insiders slip into G2, its lesser-known next-door sibling.

Gate, The

22 | 16 | 20 | $6

Park Slope | 321 Fifth Ave. (3rd St.) | Brooklyn | M/R to Union St. | 718-768-4329

This "popular" Park Slope taproom is a "beer lover's paradise" drawing "upbeat", "free-thinking" folk with "tons of draft microbrews on a constant rotation"; while the interior is a "bit seedy", its "perfect" corner patio "rivals the Gowanus Yacht Club for outdoor enjoyment."

🆕 Gates, The

- | - | - | VE

Chelsea | 290 Eighth Ave. (bet. 24th & 25th Sts.) | C/E to 23rd St. | 212-206-8646 | wwww.thegatesnyc.com

This Chelsea space has housed everything from a louche gay bar (Rome) to a swanky restaurant (Biltmore Room), and now it's morphed into a chichi lounge that's open to all for after-work drinks, but decidedly more selective later in the evening; the opulent decor – much of it salvaged from the old Biltmore Hotel – includes marble, brass and polished wood galore, plus a padded cell-phone booth perfect for drunk dialing.

Gatsby's

13 | 11 | 15 | $8

NoLita | 53 Spring St. (bet. Lafayette & Mulberry Sts.) | 6 to Spring St. | 212-334-4430 | www.gatsbysnyc.com

"Adequate for a pint", this "nothing-special" NoLita Irish bar gets the "cheap drinks" and sports TV thing right, but its "frat-house smell" and "poor service" lead many to "leave it for the B&T crowd."

Geisha

22 | 23 | 19 | $14

E 60s | 33 E. 61st St. (bet. Madison & Park Aves.) | 4/5/6/N/R/W to 59th St./Lexington Ave. | 212-813-1113 | www.geisharestaurant.com

"Still popular with the Euro set", this UES "semi-Japanese" restaurant lures "hot suits" and "thin blonds" to its sleek ground-floor lounge done up in a "cool" David Rockwell design; sure, "service can be spotty" and the pops "costly", but there's enough "high energy" in the place to keep things "lively" here.

Genesis | 20 | 18 | 20 | $9 |

E 80s | 1708 Second Ave. (bet. 88th & 89th Sts.) | 4/5/6 to 86th St. | 212-348-5500 | www.genesisbar.com

"Meet the locals" at this "neighborhood" Yorkville sports bar, a "standard"-issue venue offering "flat-screens" galore, "comfy booths" and "great" Irish pub grub; while a few say it "lacks character", at least the "friendly staff's accents" are amusing.

George Keeley's | 23 | 16 | 22 | $7 |

W 80s | 485 Amsterdam Ave. (bet. 83rd & 84th Sts.) | 1 to 86th St. | 212-873-0251 | www.georgekeeley.com

"Well-chosen" tap brews, "cask ale on draft" and "knowledgeable", "no-attitude" bartenders can lead to "day drinking" at this "above-average" UWS Irish pub also known for the "Premiership soccer" matches broadcast on "lots of TVs"; P.S. if you want to get snug with someone special, "there are plenty of nooks to get lost" in here.

NEW Gibson, The | – | – | – | M |

Williamsburg | 108 Bedford Ave. (N. 11th St.) | Brooklyn | L to Bedford Ave. | 718-387-6296

Though the name suggests a cocktail focus, this new Williamsburg watering hole near McCarren Park is more about scotches and local craft brews than it is about chilling or muddling; set slightly north of Bedford Street's main pub-crawl in the former Triple Crown digs, it's more casual and low-key than its raucous predecessor.

Gilt | 21 | 24 | 23 | $18 |

E 50s | NY Palace Hotel | 455 Madison Ave. (bet. 50th & 51st Sts.) | E/V to 5th Ave./53rd St. | 212-891-8100 | www.giltnewyork.com

An "old-world" setting (Midtown's Villard Mansion in the Palace Hotel) gets a "modern" spin via a purple pod sculpture at this "beautiful" bar set in the "old Le Cirque space"; maybe the prices verge on "outrageous", but that doesn't faze its well-heeled, "grown-up" following who report that this "quiet" enclave is ideal when "you need to be heard."

Z Ginger Man | 22 | 18 | 18 | $8 |

Murray Hill | 11 E. 36th St. (bet. 5th & Madison Aves.) | B/D/F/N/Q/R/V/W to 34th St./Herald Sq. | 212-532-3740 | www.gingerman-ny.com

With a "bazillion beers" on tap and a "gazillion bottles", this "dignified" Murray Hill malt "mecca" draws herds of hopsheads after work, when it's "standing room only" and often "hard to get a drink" (it's "less crowded" on weekends); expect a "professional", "wall-to-wall-wingtips" crowd with a "great guy-to-girl ratio – if you're a girl."

Ginger's ⌀ | 16 | 15 | 19 | $8 |

Park Slope | 363 Fifth Ave. (bet. 5th & 6th Sts.) | Brooklyn | F/M/R to 4th Ave./9th St. | 718-788-0924

"Like a comfortable old chair", this "low-key" Park Slope lesbian hang draws lotsa "girls, girls, girls" with its "friendly neighborhood" vibe and "everyday drink specials"; it's "not a place for a night of dancing", more a "sit-and-chat" scene.

	APPEAL	DECOR	SERVICE	COST

Gin Mill
16 | **13** | **17** | **$7**

W 80s | 442 Amsterdam Ave. (bet. 81st & 82nd Sts.) | 1 to 79th St. | 212-580-9080 | www.nycbestbar.com

"Right-out-of-college" types who "miss the sticky floors" of their youth congregate at this "active" Upper West Side "dive" where "cheap drinks" and a "meat-market" mentality persuade you to "party your ass off like a frat boy"; it's also the "ultimate sports bar for Florida Gators fans", who catch all the action on its 18 flat-screens.

Glass
20 | **22** | **19** | **$12**

Chelsea | 287 10th Ave. (bet. 26th & 27th Sts.) | C/E to 23rd St. | 212-904-1580 | www.glassloungenyc.com

"Whitewashed and futuristic", this West Chelsea lounge sports "cool spaceship" design right down to a rear "escape hatch" leading to a backyard bamboo patio; best known for the two-way mirrors in its "unisex" loos (beware, "people on the street can see your every move"), it's also a serviceable Plan B for those "not in the mood to stand in line at Marquee" next door.

NEW Globe, The
19 | **19** | **20** | **$11**

Gramercy | 158 E. 23rd St. (bet. Lexington & 3rd Aves.) | 6 to 3rd St. | 212-477-6161

"Get away from the hipsters" at this roomy new Gramercy tavern set in a "fully restored", circa-1880 barroom where the dark, tin-ceilinged digs retain an "old-world feel"; "casual" but "not icky and sticky", it's a natural for laid-back types thirsty for a "perfectly poured pint."

Z GoldBar
23 | **24** | **19** | **$16**

Little Italy | 389 Broome St. (bet. Centre Market Pl. & Mulberry St.) | 6 to Spring St. | 212-274-1568 | www.goldbarnewyork.com

"Midas must have been present" at the conception of this "jaw-dropping" Little Italy lounge, an "opulent", "over-the-top" den festooned with chandeliers, gilded ceilings and walls studded with "gold-encrusted skulls"; the door is as "highly guarded" as the "U.S. Mint", admitting only the "famous" and the "glamorously grungy", but if you do get in make sure to have "your accountant on speed-dial" when the bill arrives.

Gonzalez y Gonzalez
18 | **16** | **16** | **$12**

NoHo | 625 Broadway (bet. Bleecker & Houston Sts.) | 6 to Bleecker St. | 212-473-8787 | www.arkrestaurants.com

The "neon sombrero outside" suggests the "over-the-top" shenanigans within this NoHo joint featuring one of the longest bars in town plus dancing to live salsa music; the "chile-pepper-lights" decor thrills "tourists", "suburbanites" and random "NYU students", all packed in like "sardines", all reporting a "fun enough" time.

Z Gotham Bar & Grill
25 | **25** | **25** | **$15**

G Village | 12 E. 12th St. (bet. 5th Ave. & University Pl.) | 4/5/6/L/N/Q/R/W to 14th St./Union Sq. | 212-620-4020 | www.gothambarandgrill.com

"Impress business associates" or just "indulge yourself" at this "fancy-schmancy" Villager, a "classic since the day it opened" more than 20 years ago; sure, it's "more 'grill' than 'bar'", and you might need "Daddy Warbucks" to settle the "pricey" bill, but when it comes to "upscale perfection", "it doesn't get any better" than this; P.S. the "food ain't bad either."

	APPEAL	DECOR	SERVICE	COST

Gotham Comedy Club

19 | 13 | 16 | $13

Chelsea | 208 W. 23rd St. (bet. 7th & 8th Aves.) | 1 to 23rd St. | 212-367-9000 | www.gothamcomedyclub.com

Now that's it's moved to a "cavernous", 10,000-sq.-ft. setting, this Chelsea comedy club has retained its "solid" talent, though some say the digs are "a bit too clean" and "commercial" for the genre; be aware that costs still "add up quickly" thanks to that "ridiculously pricey" two-drink minimum.

Gottino

22 | 22 | 22 | $15

G Village | 52 Greenwich Ave. (bet. Charles & Perry Sts.) | 1/2/3/L to 14th St./7th Ave. | 212-633-2590 | www.ilovegottino.com

"Rustic" yet "civilized", this "terrific" Village wine bar features a "wonderful" Italian vino selection poured "with a smile" by "professional" staffers in a room resembling a "relaxed" patch of Tuscany; it's already drawing "convivial crowds", so go early, since "seats are few and far between."

Gowanus Yacht Club ⊅

23 | 15 | 14 | $5

Carroll Gardens | 323 Smith St. (President St.) | Brooklyn | F/G to Carroll St. | 718-246-1321

A "playfully sarcastic name" lends "hipster" cred to this seasonal Carroll Gardens beer garden, but seafarers say it's the "super-cheap" brews that hook the weekend "crowds" planning to "get drunk on a budget"; a "surly staff" and "pseudo-nautical" decor add to the "low-rent charm."

Grace Hotel Bar
(fka QT Hotel Bar)

18 | 20 | 19 | $12

W 40s | QT Hotel | 125 W. 45th St. (bet. 6th & 7th Aves.) | 1/2/3/7/N/Q/R/S/W to 42nd St./Times Sq. | 212-354-2323

"Giving new meaning to the term 'watering hole'", this "hip" Times Square hotel bar abuts the in-house swimming pool, lending a "steamy LA" vibe to the proceedings; it's just the thing for a secret tryst since it remains "relatively undiscovered", provided you don't mind "bland" decor and the faint "smell of chlorine"; N.B. check out the loos.

☑ Gramercy Tavern

26 | 25 | 26 | $15

Flatiron | 42 E. 20th St. (bet. B'way & Park Ave. S.) | 6 to 23rd St. | 212-477-0777 | www.gramercytavern.com

"When you've outgrown the younger bars of the Flatiron", there's always this "classy" Danny Meyer outpost, a "civilized yet convivial" meeting place for "mature" types seeking "cream-of-the-crop" drinking and dining; true, it may be "more about food than nightlife" (with a bar area that's "filled with diners waiting to eat"), but tipplers say just soaking in the "atmosphere" is worth it.

Grand Bar

25 | 26 | 23 | $14

SoHo | SoHo Grand Hotel | 310 W. Broadway, 2nd fl. (bet. Canal & Grand Sts.) | A/C/E to Canal St. | 212-965-3000 | www.sohogrand.com

As "très chic" as ever, this "swanky" hotel bar/lounge is "still happening" for "beautiful" locals as well as "older, upscale" out-of-towners; parked on the second floor of the SoHo Grand in "spacious", meandering digs, it's just the thing for a perfect "French martini" – but "don't volunteer to pick up the tab unless you're flush."

	APPEAL	DECOR	SERVICE	COST

Grand Café
21 | 20 | 20 | $10

Astoria | 37-01 30th Ave. (37th St.) | Queens | N/W to 30th Ave. | 718-545-1494 | www.grandcafelounge.com

"Very much a scene" in Astoria, this Greek grandstander is a baklava cafe by day turned bar by night, drawing a "youngish, good-looking" clientele with "stylish" decor right out of a "South Beach hotel lobby"; throw in "friendly service" and "outdoor seating" for "people-watching", and locals ask "why bridge and tunnel it?"

Grape and Grain
26 | 21 | 26 | $12

E Village | 620 E. Sixth St. (bet. Aves. B & C) | F/V to Lower East Side/ 2nd Ave. | 212-420-0002

This "intimate", brick-lined East Village wine bar decants a "varied, reasonably priced" vino lineup matched with "lovely" apps in "waaay laid-back" digs; though a "cool date place", the quarters can get "cramped", so the "chill local crowd" whispers "let's keep it a secret."

Grassroots Tavern ⊅
19 | 10 | 17 | $6

E Village | 20 St. Marks Pl. (bet. 2nd & 3rd Aves.) | 6 to Astor Pl. | 212-475-9443

"Putting the 'dive' in 'dive bar'", this "old reliable" East Villager has been on the scene since 1975 and offers a "great jukebox" as well as "cheap" suds; diehards say it's as good a place as any to "bide your time."

Great Lakes
22 | 15 | 20 | $6

Park Slope | 284 Fifth Ave. (1st St.) | Brooklyn | M/R to Union St. | 718-499-3710

"Informal and unassuming", this small Park Slope dive can get "tight" when the "killer", "indie rock"–stocked jukebox gets cranking; crowd-wise, it's a "regulars bar – which is great if you're a regular."

NEW Greenhouse
21 | 21 | 17 | $15

SoHo | 150 Varick St. (Vandam St.) | C/E to Spring St. | 212-807-7000 | www.greenhouseusa.com

"Eco-friendly" clubbing debuts at this "green" SoHo duplex, a "super-packed" danceteria built with "recycled materials", "lit by LED lights" and adorned with "plants on the ceiling"; it's favored by "high-energy" night owls glugging all-natural vodka and "trying to bust a move", though jaded sorts yawn it's "overhyped" and "overpriced."

Greenwich Treehouse
19 | 14 | 17 | $10

W Village | 46 Greenwich Ave., 2nd fl. (bet. Charles & Perry Sts.) | 1/2/3/L to 14th St./7th Ave. | 212-675-0395 | www.greenwichtreehouse.com

This second-floor Villager offers a standard lineup of assorted hooch as well as occasional "Wii bowling"; otherwise, the "quiet, clique-y" regulars provide "limited" excitement, but it's still a "comfortable place to hang" without going out on a limb.

Grey Dog's Coffee
22 | 18 | 19 | $8

G Village | 33 Carmine St. (bet. Bedford & Bleecker Sts.) | A/B/C/D/ E/F/V to W. 4th St. | 212-462-0041

G Village | 90 University Pl. (bet. 11th & 12th Sts.) | 4/5/6/L/N/Q/R/ W to 14th St./Union Sq. | 212-414-4739 www.thegreydog.com

"Sort of like Central Perk but with alcohol" (i.e. beer and wine), these "quintessential" Village cafes are "nice evening hangouts" for "locals",

"NYU" types and "golden retriever owners"; given the "relaxed atmo-spheres", they work with "friends, as well as with a date."

NEW Griffin, The
`- | - | - | VE`

Meatpacking | 50 Gansevoort St. (bet. Greenwich & Washington Sts.) | A/C/E/L to 14th St./8th Ave. | 212-255-6676

The Meatpacking District keeps on keeping on with the arrival of this new club that harkens back to the neighborhood's glory days with elaborate chandeliers, velvet banquettes, a VIP balcony and even bot-tle service (it's set in the former PM space, after all); its major conces-sion to modern times, however, is a lounge area serving cocktails starting at 5:30 PM daily.

Gstaad
`17 | 19 | 17 | $11`

Chelsea | 43 W. 26th St. (bet. B'way & 6th Ave.) | F/V to 23rd St. | 212-683-1440 | www.gstaadnyc.com

"If you can't get to the slopes", try this "spacious", "Scandinavian-sleek" Chelsea bar with a "minimalist" "ski lodge" look (the "only thing missing is the St. Bernard with the cask"); streaming "video footage of skiers" projected on a "giant" screen embellishes the "cool" mood, which is somewhat undercut by "service that leaves something to be desired."

Guest House
`19 | 17 | 16 | $13`

Chelsea | 542 W. 27th St. (bet. 10th & 11th Aves.) | C/E to 23rd St. | 212-273-3700 | www.homeguesthouse.com

Home's "next-door companion", this "high-energy" lounge on West Chelsea's Bottle Service Row treats "well-heeled" guests to "sophisti-cated" surroundings (long leather couches, banks of candles, or-nate wallpaper) along with DJs blasting "kick-ass techno and trance"; foes find it "second-tier luxe" and the crowd "hit-or-miss", while homebodies admit it "may not be the most exclusive club" but is still "fun regardless."

Gutter, The
`▽ 24 | 20 | 18 | $9`

Greenpoint | 200 N. 14th St. (Berry St.) | Brooklyn | G to Nassau Ave. | 718-387-3585 | www.thegutterbrooklyn.com

A "bar-and-bowling-alley" combo, this Greenpoint joint combines eight "old-school" lanes with an equally "retro" taproom vending "cheap, well-selected" brews; it's "aptly named", what with the down-scale vibe, but low rollers swear a "great time is had by all."

GYM Sportsbar
`19 | 14 | 19 | $8`

Chelsea | 167 Eighth Ave. (bet. 18th & 19th Sts.) | A/C/E/L to 14th St./8th Ave. | 212-337-2439 | www.gymsportsbar.com

A "welcome contrast to the fauxhawked clientele of most gay estab-lishments", this Chelsea sports bar is set in a "bare-bones" space that's "more butch than g but not as dingy as the Eagle"; it lures "good-looking but not model-pretty" types – "that's the appeal" – but even if the guy you're cruising is a "closeted jock", there's no question "what team he's on."

Hairy Monk
`17 | 13 | 21 | $7`

Murray Hill | 337 Third Ave. (25th St.) | 6 to 23rd St. | 212-532-2929 | www.thehairymonknyc.com

The "name may not be appealing", but the "retro signage", "plasma screens" and Irish waitresses keep this "standard" Murray Hill sports pub active, particularly during "Sunday afternoon football" season; the crowd's a "little bit older than the rest of the Third Avenue scene" and loaded with "fans of Boston sports and big-hair '80s rock."

Half King

19 | 15 | 19 | $8

Chelsea | 505 W. 23rd St. (10th Ave.) | C/E to 23rd St. | 212-462-4300 | www.thehalfking.com

A "low-key alternative to the hipper-than-hip" alternatives in West Chelsea, this "simple" Irish pub–cum–"literati" salon draws "interesting" folk with weekly book readings, rotating photography exhibits and "late-night hipster cruising" opportunities; it's spread out over "lots of different rooms", but that "nice backyard" garden is the real crowd-pleaser.

Half Pint

22 | 17 | 20 | $11

G Village | 76 W. Third St. (Thompson St.) | A/B/C/D/E/F/V to W. 4th St. | 212-260-1088 | www.thehalfpintnyc.com

With an "amazing" selection of suds (including 100-plus by the bottle), this West Village "local pub" is a bona fide "favorite" despite the ultra-no-frills setting; the "enthusiastic staff" and "easy" mood aren't half bad, but brace yourself for plenty of "NYUers on the weekends."

Hammerstein Ballroom

20 | 13 | 14 | $11

Garment District | 311 W. 34th St. (bet. 8th & 9th Aves.) | A/C/E to 34th St./Penn Station | 212-279-7740 | www.mcstudios.com

Showcasing some of the "top names from many musical genres", this Garment District concert hall originally opened in 1906 as an opera house; foes disparage its "slow bartenders", "poor drink selection" and "not-pretty" setting (that's in definite "need of an update"), but admit it gets the most important thing right: the "acoustics rock."

Hangar Bar ⊄

▽ 13 | 12 | 15 | $8

W Village | 115 Christopher St. (bet. Bleecker & Hudson Sts.) | 1 to Christopher St. | 212-627-2044

This "strictly low-rent" gay watering hole parked on the West Village's "historic Christopher Street corridor" is usually "cruisy, busy and loud", even though some say it feels like a "Jersey bar"; the "mixed race" clientele is its "primary appeal."

Hank's Saloon ⊄

▽ 20 | 9 | 18 | $5

Boerum Hill | 46 Third Ave. (Atlantic Ave.) | Brooklyn | 2/3/4/5/B/D/M/N/Q/R to Atlantic Ave. | 718-625-8003

"Walking the edge of sanity", this "been-there-for-ages" Boerum Hill bar is "more authentic dive than hipster faux dive" with the "career drunks" usually outnumbering the "slummers"; it's trying to reinvent itself with "live music" on weekends, so even if it's "not good on looks", it's certainly "high on character."

Happy Ending

19 | 18 | 16 | $10

LES | 302 Broome St. (Forsyth St.) | J/M/Z to Bowery | 212-334-9676 | www.happyendinglounge.com

The "risqué name" alludes to this Lower Eastsider's former life as an "Asian massage parlor", but today it's a bi-level lounge with "converted steam room" alcoves and waist-high showerheads (they've also kept the original "awning out front"); a "sketchy neighborhood" and "rude" service are downsides, but ultimately most find this "pickup joint" to be "wonderfully creepy."

	APPEAL	DECOR	SERVICE	COST

Harbour Lights

| 21 | 20 | 17 | $13 |

Seaport | Pier 17 | South Street Seaport, 3rd fl. (bet. Fulton & South Sts.) | 2/3/4/5/A/C/J/M/Z to Fulton St./B'way/Nassau | 212-227-2800 | www.harbourlts.com

Like the name says, this South Street Seaport bar/restaurant is all about its "beautiful views" of the harbor and the Brooklyn Bridge; it's made for "sitting outside on a nice summer's evening with your sweetie" and sipping "after-dinner drinks", but be prepared for "costly" tabs.

Hard Rock Cafe

| 16 | 21 | 14 | $11 |

W 40s | 1501 Broadway (43rd St.) | 1/2/3/7/N/Q/R/S/W to 42nd St./Times Sq. | 212-343-3355

NEW **Bronx** | 1 E. 161st St. (River Ave.) | 4/B/D to 161st St./Yankee Staduim | 646-977-8888

www.hardrock.com

A Times Square satellite of the "worldwide tourist trap", this rock 'n' roll-themed bar/eatery is "just like the other locations": "busy", "loud" and "hectic" – "earplugs, anyone?"; still, "teens" hankering to see "Madonna's bustier" and other music "memorabilia" think it's "cool", and it's always "fun watching the out-of-towners"; N.B. the new Yankee Stadium outlet opened post-Survey.

Harefield Road ⊅

| ▽ 20 | 22 | 23 | $7 |

Williamsburg | 769 Metropolitan Ave. (bet. Graham Ave. & Humboldt St.) | Brooklyn | L to Graham Ave. | 718-388-6870

"A bit less trendy" than the typical Billyburg hang, this wood plank-lined "neighborhood pub" is a "laid-back" detour "without hipster attitude" on an "otherwise lonely" stretch; its "killer beer selection" (some 20 on tap) is "lovingly poured", though the mood is too "subdued" for some.

Harlem Lanes

| 20 | 20 | 18 | $11 |

Harlem | 2116 Adam Clayton Powell Jr. Blvd., 3rd fl. (126th St.) | A/B/C/D to 125th St. | 212-678-2695 | www.harlemlanes.com

One of the "only bowling" options north of Port Authority, this Harlem alley features 24 lanes as well as a "flat-screen"-heavy sports bar/arcade complex; the lower level is designed for families, while upstairs is more "club"-like, providing "nice interludes between strikes and spares."

NEW Haven

| 18 | 20 | 17 | $14 |

E 50s | 244 E. 51st St. (bet. 2nd & 3rd Aves.) | 6/E/V to 51st-53rd Sts./Lexington Ave. | 212-906-9066 | www.havennewyork.com

"When you want a proper cocktail" in Turtle Bay, this new "upscale" duplex is a "much-needed" haven catering to the "suit" set with top-shelf pours and a "warm", "comfortable" setting channeling a damask-lined drawing room; it's a "nice change" for the area, despite "hefty" prices, "disjointed" service and an overall "lack of scene."

NEW HeadQuarters

| - | - | - | VE |

Garment District | 552 W. 38th St. (bet. 10th & 11th Aves.) | A/C/E to 42nd St./Port Authority | 212-967-4646 | www.hqnewyork.com

Ok, it's "not a first date spot" – but this Garment District strip club is a "classy" enough joint to "get wasted" and "have a blast" while "admiring the finer bits of a woman"; "anyone can be treated like a king" here, but bring along a king's ransom for the privilege.

Heartland Brewery
16 15 17 $9

Garment District | Empire State Bldg. | 350 Fifth Ave. (34th St.) | B/D/F/N/Q/R/V/W to 34th St./Herald Sq. | 212-563-3433
Seaport | 93 South St. (Fulton St.) | 2/3/4/5/A/C/J/M/Z to Fulton St./B'way/Nassau | 646-572-2337
Union Sq | 35 Union Sq. W. (bet. 16th & 17th Sts.) | 4/5/6/L/N/Q/R/W to 14th St./Union Sq. | 212-645-3400
W 40s | 127 W. 43rd St. (bet. B'way & 6th Ave.) | 1/2/3/7/N/Q/R/S/W to 42nd St./Times Sq. | 646-366-0235
W 50s | 1285 Sixth Ave. (51st St.) | B/D/F/V to 47-50th Sts./Rockefeller Ctr. | 212-582-8244
www.heartlandbrewery.com
"People out to enjoy themselves" like this popular (albeit "touristy") brewpub chain for its "seasonal ales" and "affordability"; but downsides include "rough-around-the-edges" service and "generic, corporate" atmospheres with decor that's a "manufactured effort at charm."

Heathers
▽ 19 17 23 $9

E Village | 506 E. 13th St. (bet. Aves. A & B) | L to 1st Ave. | 212-254-0979
A former after-hours club has morphed into this "unpretentious" barroom that's "tucked away" on an East Village side street; "telepathic hipsters" bent on "being ahead of the cool curve" made it a "scenester clubhouse" overnight, and advocates say it gets "even better as the night wears on."

Heights Bar & Grill
18 14 16 $8

W 100s | 2867 Broadway, 2nd fl. (bet. 111th & 112th Sts.) | 1 to Cathedral Pkwy./110th St. | 212-866-7035
"Always packed (because it's tiny)", this Morningside Heights bar and grill draws "enthusiastic Columbia crowds" with its "good party vibe" and "great margarita happy hour"; but the true "saving grace" is its "second-to-none" roof deck that's a terrific "retreat in the summer."

Hell Gate Social
22 19 21 $9

Astoria | 12-21 Astoria Blvd. (bet. 12th & 14th Sts.) | Queens | N/W to Astoria Blvd. | 718-204-8313 | www.hellgatesocial.com
There's typically "something interesting going on" at this art-filled Astoria bar where "relaxed" socializing, indie film screenings, DJ sets and "cool live music" ensure the action is "not too bad" for the boroughs; still, it's a "best-kept secret" among "locals" since "public transportation is not very close."

Henrietta Hudson
18 14 16 $9

W Village | 438 Hudson St. (Morton St.) | 1 to Christopher St. | 212-924-3347 | www.henriettahudson.com
Dubbed a "local delight" by the grrrls who gravitate to it, this West Village lesbian bar brings in "diverse" groups of "twentysomethings" and "barely legal" beauties looking to "get their dance on"; some say the staff's too "cliquish" and the cover's too "high", but ultimately, girlfriend, it's "still very popular."

Hideaway, The
22 18 23 $12

TriBeCa | 185 Duane St. (Greenwich St.) | 1/2/3 to Chambers St. | 212-334-5775 | www.thehideawaynyc.com
More dapper than the name suggests, this "out-of-the-way" TriBeCa "gem" manages to come off as "low-key and upscale at the same

time"; given the "cool staff" and "fantastic" lineup of wines, beers and munchables, handicappers see this one "rising fast."

Hideout, The
19 | 20 | 19 | $12

Fort Greene | 266 Adelphi St. (bet. DeKalb & Willoughby Aves.) | Brooklyn | G to Clinton/Washington Aves. | 718-855-3010

Hidden away in a former garage, this "small", signless Fort Greene sanctum of mixology features "friendly" barfolk slinging smart cocktails in "cool", "dark" digs that "leave the fussiness to Manhattan"; the premium price tags may be "out of place" in this neighborhood, yet insiders still beg "don't let the secret out."

Hi-Fi
21 | 14 | 18 | $6

E Village | 169 Ave. A (bet. 10th & 11th Sts.) | L to 1st Ave. | 212-420-8392 | www.hifi169.com

It's "all about the jukebox" at this "casual" East Village "hipster heaven" where the "comprehensive, all-inclusive" playlist includes "music that hasn't even been released yet"; otherwise, it's a "big open space" with a "very college" following that's "free of pretense" – and decor.

Highbar
21 | 21 | 17 | $15

W 40s | 251 W. 48th St., 16th fl. (bet. B'way & 8th Ave.) | C/E to 50th St. | 212-229-0010 | www.highbar-nyc.com

Radiating "beach chic", this Hell's Kitchen "rooftop aerie" lures "bankers, marketing girls" and "stick-thin models" into its "fashionable", Miami-esque indoor lounge and "cabana"-equipped terrace boasting "great sunset views"; despite "extravagant" tabs, a "snooty staff" and a "rickety elevator" ride up, it's definitely "worth it" on a "warm summer evening."

Highline Ballroom
21 | 17 | 18 | $12

Chelsea | 431 W. 16th St. (bet. 9th & 10th Aves.) | A/C/E/L to 14th St./8th Ave. | 212-414-5994 | www.highlineballroom.com

Quite the "hub of hip" performances, this "spiffy" West Chelsea music hall is an "intimate yet not claustrophobic" venue (capacity 700) with "clean sightlines", state-of-the-art sound and an "eclectic lineup of classic and contemporary" acts; "plenty of bars", table seating and a "balcony overlooking the action" explain the "high prices."

Hi-Life
17 | 14 | 19 | $9

E 70s | 1503 Second Ave. (bet. 78th & 79th Sts.) | 6 to 77th St. | 212-628-5433
W 80s | 477 Amsterdam Ave. (83rd St.) | 1 to 86th St. | 212-787-7199
www.hi-life.com

"Don't let the outside fool you" – these retro-looking Uptown bar/eateries may sport vintage neon, but inside their cocktails-and-sushi offerings are very contemporary indeed; they're definitely "laid-back" – some say "forgotten" – and "perfect if you just graduated from college."

NEW Hill, The
17 | 17 | 18 | $10

Murray Hill | 416 Third Ave. (bet. 29th & 30th Sts.) | 6 to 28th St. | 212-741-0646 | www.thehillny.com

The split-level Murray Hill space formerly known as Dip is now a "sports bar/lounge combo" that adds couches and candles to the standard "flat-screen" playbook; while it's "decent" enough and "still serves fondue", nonfans cry foul at another "frat"-infested, "cookie-cutter bar" in this "ridiculous part of town."

	APPEAL	DECOR	SERVICE	COST

Hiro
22 | 25 | 17 | $13

Chelsea | Maritime Hotel | 371 W. 16th St. (9th Ave.) | A/C/E/L to 14th St./8th Ave. | 212-727-0212 | www.hiroballroom.com
"Cavernous" and "ultradark", this multilevel number in the Maritime Hotel draws a "hot crowd" into its "paper-lanterned", taste-of-Tokyo lounge and adjoining downstairs ballroom; "to-die-for" sake cocktails and "high-flying, Cirque du Soleil"–esque acrobats compensate for the "nonexistent service" and "pretentious" door.

HK Lounge
20 | 21 | 18 | $11

Garment District | 405 W. 39th St. (9th Ave.) | A/C/E to 42nd St./ Port Authority | 646-354-9062 | www.hkhellskitchen.com
A "trendy place" in a "weird location" behind Port Authority, this slick bi-level venue lures a "cute", "decidedly gay" crowd with an "airy" space equipped with "upscale" extras like an "amazing" loftlike lounge under a retractable roof; it's "on the pricey side", but fans of "pumping music" and "tasty cocktails" keep it "packed on weekends."

Hog Pit
17 | 11 | 17 | $9

NEW **Chelsea** | 37B W. 26th St. (bet. B'way & 6th Ave.) | N/R/W to 28th St. | 212-213-4871 | www.hogpit.com
Wallow in "beer, BBQ and broads" at this newly resurrected redneck dive, now settled in a "bigger, cleaner" Chelsea pen but still appealing to "men's men" (and "horny frat boys") with "cheap" hooch and "scantily clad" tapstresses; maybe it's "not as funky as the original", but when you're "low on cash" it's still a "hoot and holler."

Hogs & Heifers ⊄
16 | 10 | 13 | $8

Meatpacking | 859 Washington St. (13th St.) | A/C/E/L to 14th St./ 8th Ave. | 212-929-0655 | www.hogsandheifers.com
"Good for scaring out-of-towners", this Meatpacking roadhouse "train wreck" is proudly "non-PC in a PC world" with "sloppy drunks", "bachelorettes" and "wannabe bad boys" slugging back PBRs and eye-balling the "thousands of bras" dangling behind the bar; there's usu-ally "too many hogs" and not enough heifers, so first-timers feel there's "no need for an encore."

Holiday Cocktail Lounge ⊄
18 | 8 | 14 | $5

E Village | 75 St. Marks Pl. (bet. 1st & 2nd Aves.) | 6 to Astor Pl. | 212-777-9637
An East Village "dive bar hall-of-famer", this circa-1945 "real hole-in-the-wall" is a "great survivor" with "scary" decor, "unfriendly" bar-keeps and a certain je ne sais quoi ("what is that smell?"); still, if you fancy "getting drunk for cheap with a bunch of old men, this is the place" to do it.

Home
21 | 20 | 17 | $13

Chelsea | 532 W. 27th St. (bet. 10th & 11th Aves.) | 1 to 28th St. | 212-273-3700 | www.homeguesthouse.com
"Home sweet home" if you "love a scene" (and "look the part"), this West Chelsea bottle service joint draws some hot housemates when it's not serving as a "refugee camp for Bungalow 8 rejects"; the black leather couches and red-lit brick walls make for a "sexy" habitat, but be prepared to "shell out" and brace yourself for "door drama" – unless you "have a beautiful girl on your arm."

	APPEAL	DECOR	SERVICE	COST

Home Sweet Home
19 | 17 | 16 | $9

LES | 131 Chrystie St., downstairs (bet. Broome & Delancey Sts.) | J/M/Z to Bowery | 212-226-5708

Be it ever so humble, this "subterranean" Lower Eastsider supplies "funky tunes" and "relatively cheap drinks" in a space channeling "your grandfather's old basement", complete with "wacky taxidermy", "oddball artifacts" and beat-up couches for "late-night smooching"; though it's "not for everyone", "total hipsters" say it sure "feels like home."

Honey
19 | 17 | 18 | $11

Chelsea | 243 W. 14th St. (bet. 7th & 8th Aves.) | A/C/E/L to 14th St./ 8th Ave. | 212-741-0646 | www.honeyny.com

Parked on an unexpected block, this "mellow" Chelsea lounge offers a slinky alternative to 14th Street's taquerias with its mood lighting (read: very dim) and spare design (read: brick and votives); its "moderately pricey" pops can be imbibed publicly at one of the sidewalk tables or more privately in the long, rabbit hole interior.

Hook and Ladder
13 | 10 | 18 | $7

Murray Hill | 611 Second Ave. (bet. 33rd & 34th Sts.) | 6 to 33rd St. | 212-213-5034

"Have some fun the old college way" at this Murray Hill firefighting-themed saloon that's a magnet for "medical students", "beer pong fanatics" and "tons of frat boys"; the "all-you-can-drink specials" and "spacious patio" compensate for the "shabby decor" and "suspect crowd."

Hooters
15 | 11 | 17 | $10

W 50s | 211 W. 56th St. (bet. B'way & 8th Ave.) | N/Q/R/W to 57th St./ 7th Ave. | 212-581-5656 | www.originalhooters.com

"Who cares about the drinks?" – it's the "Hooters girls' attributes" that draw "leering men" to this Midtown outpost of the national chain; some boobs titter this "sexist dinosaur" is getting a "bit played out", but supporters say "if you have a vivid imagination, it's more cost effective than a strip club."

Hop Devil Grill
18 | 12 | 17 | $8

E Village | 129 St. Marks Pl. (bet. Ave. A & 1st Ave.) | L to 1st Ave. | 212-533-4468 | www.hopdevil.com

A "bodacious list" of beers "from 'round the globe" is the hook at this East Villager that stocks both "fresh microbrews" and imported bottles (with an adjunct specializing in Belgian suds); on the downside are "soulless" digs and service that hops from "knowledgeable" to "clueless."

NEW Hose, The
- | - | - | M

E Village | 225 Ave. B, 2nd fl. (13th St.) | L to 1st Ave. | 212-979-8506 | www.thehosenyc.com

The Alphabet City space formerly known as Uncle Ming's has been lightly renovated into this "sleazy" new gay bar with a down-low feel, starting with its unmarked front door and hidden, second-floor perch; there's not much going on in the decor department, but the touchy-feely young crowd provides lotsa ambiance.

	APPEAL	DECOR	SERVICE	COST

☑ Hotel Delmano
24 | 25 | 23 | $13

Williamsburg | 82 Berry St. (9th St.) | Brooklyn | L to Bedford Ave. | 718-387-1945

Proof that "Williamsburg is growing up", this "luscious" "old-world" barroom occupies lovingly antiqued quarters where expert mixologists concoct "decadent" specialty drinks for a patently "hip" clientele; "getting in may be a problem", but if "you can foot the bill" it's arguably the "classiest, most romantic" billet in the 'burg.

NEW Houndstooth Pub
19 | 18 | 20 | $11

Garment District | 520 Eighth Ave. (37th St.) | A/C/E to 34th St./ Penn Station | 212-643-0034 | www.houndstoothpub.com

A new "alternative to the commuter bars" in the "Penn Station radius", this bi-level sibling of Stitch is a "large", "unpretentious" joint with a "friendly" team manning the taps; it's an "easy" option for "after-work" pre-train tippling, and fangfully "not too crowded – yet."

House of Brews
19 | 15 | 22 | $8

W 40s | 363 W. 46th St. (bet. 8th & 9th Aves.) | 1/2/3/7/N/Q/R/S/W to 42nd St./Times Sq. | 212-245-0551

W 50s | 302 W. 51st St. (bet. 8th & 9th Aves.) | C/E to 50th St. | 212-541-7080

www.houseofbrewsny.com

There's "lots of space to get lost in" at this Hell's Kitchen duo vending a "mouthwatering selection" of international brews, but best known for their gimmicky "beer bongs" (96 ounces of suds served in an appropriately shaped glass); the bi-level 51st Street branch is "bigger" than its Restaurant Row sire, though some say both have a "slightly generic feel."

Houston's
20 | 19 | 19 | $12

E 50s | Citicorp Bldg. | 153 E. 53rd St. (enter at 54th St. & 3rd Ave.) | F/V to Lexington Ave./53rd St. | 212-888-3828

Murray Hill | 378 Park Ave. S. (27th St.) | 6 to 28th St. | 212-689-1090 www.houstons.com

"As hip as a chain can be", these "dark 'n' sexy" bar/eateries draw a "clean-cut", "bustling corporate crowd" and those who like to "rub up against all those suits"; despite rather "expensive" pricing, it's so "happening" after work you'd "think they were giving the drinks away."

Huckleberry Bar
22 | 20 | 23 | $11

Williamsburg | 588 Grand St. (bet. Leonard & Lorimer Sts.) | Brooklyn | L to Lorimer St. | 718-218-8555 | www.huckleberrybar.com

An alternative to the typical East Billyburg dives, this "refined" haven is a "calm", "mellow" nexus where "friendly" barmen display their "knowledge of cocktails" "without snobbery"; it's "pricey" to locals (but a "good value if you're from Manhattan"), while the "relaxing" back garden has universal appeal.

Hudson Bar and Books
21 | 22 | 23 | $13

W Village | 636 Hudson St. (Horatio St.) | A/C/E/L to 14th St./8th Ave. | 212-229-2642 | www.barandbooks.net

"Enjoy a first-class smoke" with your whiskey – it's legal at this Village cigar bar that channels a "boys' club" with dark wood and "impeccable service"; sure, it's "expensive" and you'll "walk out smelling like an ashtray", but there's no question that this "impressive" joint also reeks of "class."

	APPEAL	DECOR	SERVICE	COST

Hudson Hotel Bar
| 24 | 25 | 18 | $14 |

W 50s | Hudson Hotel | 356 W. 58th St. (bet. 8th & 9th Aves.) | 1/A/B/C/D to 59th St./Columbus Circle | 212-554-6000

Hudson Hotel Library

W 50s | Hudson Hotel | 356 W. 58th St. (bet. 8th & 9th Aves.) | 1/A/B/C/D to 59th St./Columbus Circle | 212-554-6000

Hudson Hotel Sky Terrace

NEW **W 50s** | Hudson Hotel | 356 W. 58th St., 15th fl. (bet. 8th & 9th Aves.) | 1/A/B/C/D to 59th St./Columbus Circle | 212-554-6000 www.hudsonhotel.com

"Still cool", this "glam" hotel bar near Columbus Circle set in a "wacky", futuristic space (with a "glowing floor" right out of *2001: A Space Odyssey*") is where "pretty people go to get hammered" on "drain-your-bank-account" cocktails; those seeking a "less noisy" scene head for the Library, an equally "stylish" if "smaller sanctuary" fitted out with a "purple pool table" and "hundreds of books", or the 15th-floor outdoor terrace.

NEW Hudson Terrace
| 23 | 23 | 18 | $15 |

W 40s | 621 W. 46th St. (bet. 11 & 12) | C/E to 50th St. | 212-315-9400 | www.hudsonterracenyc.com

So "out of the way" it's "practically in the Hudson", this "unusual" Hell's Kitchen duplex includes a chandeliered bar/lounge, a walled outdoor terrace and an all-seasons rooftop space boasting "heated floors in the winter" and "misters in the summer"; ok, there's "not much of a view" and the pricing is decidedly "pre-crash", but overall it's one "stunning venue."

Hugs
| ▽ 17 | 11 | 17 | $8 |

Williamsburg | 108 N. Sixth St. (bet. Berry St. & Wythe Ave.) | Brooklyn | L to Bedford Ave. | 718-599-5959

Not as sappy as its name might suggest, this "fun" bar on Williamsburg's North Sixth Street strip features shiny, squared-off banquettes and underground DJ sets; Skee-Ball and a photo booth add enough quirky appeal to guarantee that it's "packed to the rafters on weekends."

Hustler Club
| 22 | 21 | 22 | $14 |

W 50s | 641 W. 51st St. (12th Ave.) | C/E to 50th St. | 212-247-2460 | www.hustlerny.com

Spread out over an entire city block in Way West Hell's Kitchen, this mammary mecca is a "hot" mix of "quality" strippers, "neon lights" and ultrapricey cocktails; of course, no one's "really there for the drinks" anyway, so sit back with the "high rollers" and "bachelor party" attendees and "enjoy the scenery."

Ideya
| 23 | 17 | 23 | $10 |

SoHo | 349 W. Broadway (bet. Broome & Grand Sts.) | C/E to Spring St. | 212-625-1441 | www.ideya.net

"It's all about the rum" at this SoHo slice of the Caribbean that's renowned for mixing some of the "best mojitos in Nuevo York" (though you'll "feel them in the morning"); the overall "fun Latin vibe" makes for "enjoyable" times, and if it's "not as hot" as it used to be, the staff sure is.

Iggy's

	APPEAL	DECOR	SERVICE	COST
	17	11	19	$7

E 70s | 1452 Second Ave. (bet. 75th & 76th Sts.) | 6 to 77th St. | 212-327-3043
LES | 132 Ludlow St. (Rivington St.) | F/J/M/Z to Delancey/Essex Sts. | 212-529-2731
www.iggysnewyork.com

"Cheap" pops and "enthusiastic bartenders" lead to some "serious drinking" at this "unpretentious" Irish "dive" duo; the Uptown outpost (with a "makeover paint job") is a "karaoke addict's" paradise, while Downtown draws "David Lee Roth" and other "old-timers" who stop by to "revisit what the LES used to be."

Iguana

	APPEAL	DECOR	SERVICE	COST
	18	19	19	$11

W 50s | 240 W. 54th St. (bet. B'way & 8th Ave.) | C/E to 50th St. | 212-765-5454 | www.Iguananyc.com

"Still bringing 'em in", this Southwestern bar/restaurant in Midtown is best known for its "hopping downstairs" dance floor that draws folks "from all walks of life", including random "lizards looking for action"; "blow-your-mind margaritas" distract from the overall "suburban mall" vibe.

Il Posto Accanto

	APPEAL	DECOR	SERVICE	COST
	24	21	20	$13

E Village | 190 E. Second St. (bet. Aves. A & B) | F/V to Lower East Side/2nd Ave. | 212-228-3562

"Perfect for a date", this "great little wine bar" adjunct to the East Village restaurant Il Bagatto is a "best-kept secret" for "quiet conversation" in "intimate" environs; an "amazing list" of Italian vinos pairs well with the "tasty antipasto" on offer, and as a bonus, the staff's "extremely knowledgeable."

NEW Imperial, The

	APPEAL	DECOR	SERVICE	COST
	18	17	17	$15

Flatiron | 17 W. 19th St. (bet. 5th & 6th Aves.) | L to 6th Ave. | 212-352-2001 | www.theimperialnyc.com

The revolving-door Flatiron spot variously known as Spy, Discothèque and Go-Go has been reinvented yet again, this time as a "pretty good" nightclub-cum-art gallery, with artwork of varying quality serving as decor; that aside, you can expect the usual "B&T"-bottles-and-promoters scene that's defined this space through all its incarnations.

Inc

	APPEAL	DECOR	SERVICE	COST
	∇ 22	22	20	$14

W 40s | Time Hotel | 224 W. 49th St., 2nd fl. (bet. B'way & 8th Ave.) | C/E to 50th St. | 212-320-2984 | www.incloungenyc.com

Newly revamped but as swanky as ever, this chic boîte in the Theater District's Time Hotel has the same luxurious vibe as its earlier incarnations (La Gazelle, O2, Time Lounge); the pops remain just as pricey too, ditto the intimate, secluded air that makes it a natural for fans of quiet conversation or illicit rendezvousing.

Indochine

	APPEAL	DECOR	SERVICE	COST
	20	19	19	$13

E Village | 430 Lafayette St. (bet. Astor Pl. & E. 4th St.) | 6 to Astor Pl. | 212-505-5111 | www.indochinenyc.com

"No matter how many years go by", this circa-1984 French-Vietnamese bar/eatery near the Public Theater hangs in there by doing what it does best: serving "exotic" drinks done "just right" in a "tropical" setting; nevertheless, there's debate about the decor ("ultrachic" vs. "tired") and the crowd ("models" or *Blue Man Group* tourists").

	APPEAL	DECOR	SERVICE	COST

Z 'inoteca

| 24 | 20 | 21 | $12 |

LES | 98 Rivington St. (Ludlow St.) | F/J/M/Z to Delancey/Essex Sts. | 212-614-0473

NEW Murray Hill | Marcel Hotel | 323 Third Ave. (24th St.) | 6 to 23rd St. | 212-683-3035

www.inotecanyc.com

An "extraordinary" Italian wine list paired with "yummy tapas" makes for "amazing" imbibing at this "chill" LES vino venue that's the big brother of the West Village's 'ino; no kidding, it can be a real "mad house" ("expect to wait no matter what"), but somehow the "plenty knowledgeable" staff "handles everything with grace", so whether you're a "novice" or a "wine geek", this place "rocks" – and "they serve till 3 AM"; N.B. the new Murray Hill spin-off repeats the winning formula and ups the ante with a full liquor bar.

International Bar

| - | - | - | I |

E Village | 120½ First Ave. (bet. 7th St. & St. Marks Pl.) | 6 to Astor Pl. | 212-777-1643

The space (and the patrons) may be tight, but the pops are cheap at this old-school East Village dive bar, a longtime neighborhood fixture revived after a hiatus; look for a come-as-you-are crowd swilling $4 well drinks and rocking out to an eclectic, well-curated jukebox.

In Vino

| 25 | 26 | 23 | $11 |

E Village | 215 E. Fourth St. (bet. Aves. A & B) | F/V to Lower East Side/2nd Ave. | 212-539-1011 | www.invino-ny.com

"In vino es veritas" could be the motto of this "down-to-earth" East Village wine bar that stays "true to its roots" with an interesting list of bottles culled "from throughout Italia"; a cozy, "candlelit" setting and "expert" service seal the deal on this enoteca's undeniable "appeal."

Iona ⌘

| ∇ 21 | 20 | 22 | $6 |

Williamsburg | 180 Grand St. (bet. Bedford & Driggs Aves.) | Brooklyn | L to Bedford Ave. | 718-384-5008

"Guinness" on tap, "soccer" on the big screen and "hospitable" barkeeps with authentic "accents" make this Williamsburg hangout feel "just like an Irish bar should"; its rear garden (complete with a Ping-Pong table) is one of the nicest "outdoor spaces this side of the pond."

Iridium

| 21 | 17 | 19 | $15 |

W 50s | 1650 Broadway, downstairs (bet. 50th & 51st Sts.) | 1 to 50th St. | 212-582-2121 | www.iridiumjazzclub.com

"Surprisingly hip for an otherwise dull area", this "intimate" Theater District jazz club swings on Monday nights when the "legendary" Les Paul takes the stage; the rest of the week it hosts similarly "terrific" talent, though "pricey" covers and "expensive drink minimums" lead some to speculate that this "Village Vanguard wannabe" is just "out to make a buck."

Irish Rogue

| 19 | 15 | 19 | $9 |

W 40s | 356 W. 44th St. (bet. 8th & 9th Aves.) | A/C/E to 42nd St./Port Authority | 212-445-0131 | www.theirishrogue.com

A "typical" take on the traditional Irish pub, this Hell's Kitchen bar boasts a roomy main floor lined with "lots of TVs" for sports fans as well as "generic" couches upstairs for "after-work" roguery; while some say "character is lacking", regulars report the "sweet bartenders" add "a bit of charm" – they'll flirt with you no matter how ugly you are."

I Tre Merli
20 | 19 | 20 | $11

SoHo | 463 W. Broadway (bet. Houston & Prince Sts.) | C/E to Spring St. | 212-254-8699
W Village | 183 W. 10th St. (W. 4th St.) | 1 to Christopher St. | 212-929-2221
www.itremerli.com

Granted, it's "not as hot as it was years ago", but the loftlike SoHo branch of this Italian bar/restaurant duo is still prime territory for scoping "all the goodies walking along" West Broadway; its smaller Village sibling is a more "simple" affair with the same "friendly" service.

I Trulli Enoteca
24 | 21 | 24 | $14

Murray Hill | 122 E. 27th St. (bet. Lexington Ave. & Park Ave. S.) | 6 to 28th St. | 212-481-7372 | www.itrulli.com

Oenophiles are trulli enthusiastic about this "stylish" Murray Hill wine bar for its "exciting, unusual" Italian vintages, "excellent tastings" and "knowledgeable" staffers who take care of you without "hovering"; ok, it's "not cheap", and given the "older crowd" it's "not much of a scene" either, but some say it's "ideal for a first date."

Jack Russell's
19 | 17 | 19 | $8

E 80s | 1591 Second Ave. (bet. 82nd & 83rd Sts.) | 4/5/6 to 86th St. | 212-472-2800

The "unreal" number of flat-screens at this "large" Upper East Side sports bar "can be overwhelming" (there are even "TVs in each booth"), but that's what makes it an "awesome game-day" destination; yet despite pool, video games and a "nice beer selection", non-fans growl it's "not extremely exciting."

Jack the Horse Tavern
▽ 22 | 19 | 21 | $11

Brooklyn Heights | 66 Hicks St. (Cranberry St.) | Brooklyn | A/C to High St. | 718-852-5084 | www.jackthehorse.com

A "lovely addition" to Brooklyn Heights, this quaint tavern emits an "easygoing" "neighborhood" vibe that's reflected in its "appealing" decor; while the bar area is "not large", the "welcoming" staff is big-hearted, serving "expertly mixed drinks" and a well-parsed list of brews.

Jade Bar
25 | 24 | 21 | $17

Gramercy | Gramercy Park Hotel | 2 Lexington Ave. (21st St.) | 6 to 23rd St. | 212-920-3300 | www.gramercyparkhotel.com

Goodbye Philippe Starck: Ian Schrager's renovated Gramercy Park Hotel has been done up in haute bohemian style by painter Julian Schnabel, and this "intimate" barroom juxtaposes luxe velvet curtains with avant-garde details like a raw wood-beamed ceiling and big works of "stunning modern art"; no surprise, the pops are poured at "premium" prices, and if you want to walk in, come early – reservations are required after 9 PM.

Jadis
22 | 21 | 22 | $10

LES | 42 Rivington St. (bet. Eldridge & Forsyth Sts.) | F/V to Lower East Side/2nd Ave. | 212-254-1675 | www.jadisnyc.com

"Under the radar" on the Lower East Side, this "inviting" wine bar uncorks a "brilliant" Francocentric selection in a "sexy" cellar lined with "exposed brick" and racks of bottles; a "fab staff" and petite but "comfy" setting have local vinophiles claiming it as their "private hangout."

Jake's Dilemma
16 | 12 | 17 | $7

W 80s | 430 Amsterdam Ave. (bet. 80th & 81st Sts.) | 1 to 79th St. | 212-580-0556 | www.nycbestbar.com

"Bluto Blutarsky" types play "beer pong and foosball" at this "gregarious" Upper West Side "dive" where the "only dilemma is whether to get sauced or not"; "cheap" tabs fuel a "college pickup scene" that can be "outrageously fun" – "if you don't mind crowds."

Jake's Saloon
18 | 15 | 22 | $8

Chelsea | 202 Ninth Ave. (bet. 22nd & 23rd Sts.) | C/E to 23rd St. | 212-366-5110

Chelsea | 206 W. 23rd St. (bet. 7th & 8th Aves.) | 1 to 23rd St. | 212-337-3100

W 50s | 875 10th Ave. (57th St.) | 1/A/B/C/D to 59th St./Columbus Circle | 212-333-3100

www.jakessaloon-nyc.com

Hell's Kitchen locals, "John Jay College students" and even "Katie Couric" (from the nearby "CBS studio") turn up at this "friendly" Irish pub for its "cheap" drinks and "old-school" aura; the newer Chelsea outposts are more "spacious" and "not usually overcrowded."

❷ JakeWalk, The
21 | 17 | 21 | $11

Carroll Gardens | 282 Smith St. (Sackett St.) | Brooklyn | F/G to Carroll St. | 347-599-0294 | www.thejakewalk.com

"Low-key" in a "very Brooklyn" way, this "speakeasy-style" Smith Streeter is a "warm" hideaway operated by "nice folks" who keep everything jake with a smart selection of whiskeys, by-the-glass vinos and "lethal" vintage cocktails; although "a bit pricey" for the area, it's already considered a "neighborhood standard."

Jameson's Pub
16 | 14 | 19 | $8

E 50s | 975 Second Ave. (bet. 51st & 52nd Sts.) | 6 to 51st St./Lexington Ave. | 212-980-4465 | www.jamesonsny.com

A "good jukebox" is about the only frill at this "old-fashioned" Midtown pub, but patrons insist they're "completely at home" thanks to "friendly Irish bartenders" who almost "make alcoholism an attractive prospect"; "honest grub" and "reasonable prices" seal the deal.

Japonais
22 | 23 | 19 | $13

Gramercy | 111 E. 18th St. (bet. Irving Pl. & Park Ave. S.) | 4/5/6/ L/N/Q/R/W to 14th St./Union Sq. | 212-260-2020 | www.japonaisnewyork.com

"Very posh" surroundings make a "swanky outfit" and "mega-high heels" de rigueur at this Union Square–area bar/restaurant cloned from the ballyhooed Chicago original; its "elegant" upstairs lounge is a good perch for "fashionable young professionals" hoping that some "hip older gentleman will send over a bottle of Burgundy."

❷ Jazz Standard
26 | 20 | 22 | $15

Murray Hill | 116 E. 27th St., downstairs (bet. Lexington Ave. & Park Ave. S.) | 6 to 28th St. | 212-576-2232 | www.jazzstandard.com

"Heaven" for "knowledgeable" jazz lovers, this "civilized" subterranean Murray Hill club is known for its "solid" performers, "excellent sightlines" and "great" ribs prepared by its upstairs sibling, Blue

Smoke; there's "more room" at the bar after a renovation, but it's still so "dark" that "you won't notice the barbecue sauce on your shirt."

Jekyll & Hyde

17 | 21 | 15 | $12

G Village | 91 Seventh Ave. S. (bet. Barrow & W. 4th Sts.) | 1 to Christopher St. | 212-989-7701 | www.jekyllpub.com

"Haunted house" decor and "hidden bathrooms" are the "gimmicks" at this "kitschy" Village taproom mainly patronized for its "great beer selection"; otherwise, the "shtick" is a bit too "Disney-esque" for most, who suggest leaving it to "tourists" and the "dreaded NYU crowd."

Jeremy's Ale House

16 | 9 | 17 | $6

Financial District | 228 Front St. (bet. Beekman St. & Peck Slip) | 2/3/4/5/A/C/J/M/Z to Fulton St./B'way/Nassau | 212-964-3537 | www.jeremysalehouse.com

"Thirty-two oz. beers in Styrofoam cups" for "cheap" says it all about this "friendly" Financial District "dive" that attracts everyone from "firefighters" to "future yuppies"; regulars report it's "lost some appeal" following a relocation to "smaller" digs, but it still remains one of the "best bangs for the buck in the whole city."

Jimmy's Corner

25 | 16 | 23 | $6

W 40s | 140 W. 44th St. (bet. B'way & 6th Ave.) | 1/2/3/7/N/Q/R/S/W to 42nd St./Times Sq. | 212-221-9510

"So close, yet so far away from the Times Square hoopla", this "authentic dive" is a "tribute to boxing" festooned with pugilist "memorabilia" and owned by former prizefighter Jimmy Glenn; oozing "retro cool", it's a "long way from the sterile chain joints" in the area and "still good, even after the smoking ban."

Jimmy's No. 43

∇ 22 | 18 | 22 | $8

E Village | 43 E. Seventh St., downstairs (bet. 2nd & 3rd Aves.) | 6 to Astor Pl. | 212-982-3006 | www.jimmysno43.com

A "step above for a bar that sits below" street level, this "atmospheric" East Village basement has a "cozy, caverny" feel and is a "good place for conversation or a date"; it specializes in "handcrafted beer" paired with "excellent" small plates, and the back room (complete with a stage) is "perfect for private parties."

Joe Allen

20 | 17 | 20 | $12

W 40s | 326 W. 46th St. (bet. 8th & 9th Aves.) | A/C/E to 42nd St./Port Authority | 212-581-6464 | www.joeallenrestaurant.com

"Bring your playbill" or your headshot to this Restaurant Row "showbiz hangout", a "perennial theater bar"/eatery that "hasn't changed" much in its 44 years; the crowd's a blend of "Broadway diehards" and "out-of-towners" who show up hoping to "see someone famous."

Joe's Bar ⌺

20 | 15 | 20 | $8

E Village | 520 E. Sixth St. (bet. Aves. A & B) | L to 1st Ave. | 212-473-9093

Though "a bit barren", this "always friendly, always cheap" East Villager is a "perennial" favorite for swilling brew, shooting stick or channeling "Johnny Cash" on the "killer country juke"; staffed by folks "without other aspirations", it's a "standby" where those who "don't expect much" "won't be disappointed."

Joe's Pub

25	22	18	$11

E Village | Public Theater | 425 Lafayette St. (bet. Astor Pl. & E. 4th St.) | 6 to Astor Pl. | 212-539-8778 | www.joespub.com

Everyone from "top names" to wannabes takes the stage at this "grown-up" cabaret adjunct to the Public Theater, a "sophisticated" venue whose "small" dimensions make for "intimate" interactions between the audience and the entertainers; the "arty" talent is an eclectic group with a decidedly "downtown" feel, with the only drawbacks being "uptown prices" and a "rushed turnover between shows."

Johnny Foxes

16	14	18	$9

E 80s | 1546 Second Ave. (bet. 80th & 81st Sts.) | 6 to 77th St. | 212-472-9193 | www.johnnyfoxesnyc.com

"Pretty much a clone" of other UES "frat bars", this Irish sports pub is a "decent spot" to meet up, pound beers and "get a little nuts on weekends"; maybe it's "unexceptional", but it's handy "for an all-day session."

Johnny's Bar

20	12	20	$7

W Village | 90 Greenwich Ave. (bet. 12th & 13th Sts.) | A/C/E/L to 14th St./8th Ave. | 212-741-5279

Whether you're a "cute blond or an aging queen", "all are welcome" at this West Village dive where an "eclectic local crowd" assembles for "no-frills" lubrication; the "anything-goes" vibe makes it easy to "stay later than you want" – hey, "cheap drinks are hard to find nowadays."

Johnny Utah's

20	19	17	$11

W 50s | 25 W. 51st St., downstairs (bet. 5th & 6th Aves.) | B/D/F/V to 47-50th Sts./Rockefeller Ctr. | 212-265-8824 | www.johnnyutahs.com

"Urban cowboys" fortify themselves with "liquid courage" then mount the "mechanical bull" at this "boisterous" Rock Center saloon, an underground Wild West themer that puts out an "after-work cattle call" for the "junior lawyer crowd"; for a "different night out", it supplies some "'whoa' factor", though snobs say the horseplay is "oh-so-tacky."

John Street Bar & Grill

16	10	17	$7

Financial District | 17 John St. (bet. B'way & Nassau St.) | 2/3/4/5/A/C/J/M/Z to Fulton St./B'way/Nassau | 212-349-3278 | www.johnstreet.com

The "market fluctuates", but this Financial District "dive" holds tight with a "grassroots" crowd of "bikers", "construction workers" and random Wall Street "professionals"; maybe the "hole-in-the-wall" decor verges on "dungeon"-like, but it's "cheap", unaffected and open late, a rarity in a "neighborhood that closes early."

Joshua Tree

15	13	16	$8

Murray Hill | 513 Third Ave. (bet. 34th & 35th Sts.) | 6 to 33rd St. | 212-689-0058

W 40s | 366 W. 46th St. (bet. 8th & 9th Aves.) | A/C/E to 42nd St./Port Authority | 212-489-1920 | www.joshuatreebarnyc.com

"Freshen up on your George Michael lyrics" or "sing along to Pat Benatar" at these "'80s party" bars where music videos alternate on the flat-screens with sports; no surprise, they're "frat houses on weekends" with "drunken sorority girls" flirting with out-of-work "investment bankers" while trying to avoid their "previous hookups" in the crowd.

	APPEAL	DECOR	SERVICE	COST

Josie Wood's
14 | 11 | 17 | $6

G Village | 11 Waverly Pl., downstairs (bet. Greene & Mercer Sts.) | N/R/W to 8th St. | 212-228-6806 | www.josiewoods.com

"NYU kids" turn up in force at this "typical college rathskeller" in the Village, a "dark" den with "decent beers on tap" and "serviceable" grub; its "underground" location means there's "limited cell phone reception", but on the bright side, that means there's "no ringing to distract" from watching the game or "perusing the honeys."

Joya ∉
23 | 20 | 21 | $9

Cobble Hill | 215 Court St. (Warren St.) | Brooklyn | F/G to Bergen St. | 718-222-3484

"Small and cozy" and "loud and packed", this "sexy" Cobble Hill Thai may be "overrun by hipsters, but no one can blame them" what with the "strong drinks", "tasty food", "stellar DJs" and "cheap-as-hell" tabs; seasoned regulars say it's "one-stop" shopping for both "creating and nursing hangovers."

Jules
23 | 20 | 15 | $13

E Village | 65 St. Marks Pl. (bet. 1st & 2nd Aves.) | 6 to Astor Pl. | 212-477-5560 | www.julesbistro.com

It "feels like Paris" at this atmospheric East Village bistro best remembered for hosting "live jazz every night" for no cover; though it may be "better for dinner than the bar scene", the amber-lit, vaguely "deco" interior is a "charming" respite for a "nice glass of wine."

Julius ∉
12 | 9 | 17 | $9

G Village | 159 W. 10th St. (Waverly Pl.) | 1 to Christopher St. | 212-243-1928

As the "oldest game in town" – both chronology- and clientelewise – this "granddaddy of NY gay bars" provides a somewhat "seedy" "glimpse of Village lore" as well as "comparatively inexpensive" swill and a "decent burger"; though this "wrinkle room" has the staying power of the "Eveready Bunny", young types feel "no need to stop by."

Kabin
▽ 16 | 13 | 17 | $7

E Village | 92 Second Ave. (bet. 5th & 6th Sts.) | F/V to Lower East Side/2nd Ave. | 212-254-0204

Like a mullet that's business in the front and party in the back, this "isn't-sure-what-it-is" East Villager features a "bar up front", "relaxed pool-table" scene in the middle and a "wannabe lounge" in the rear; the "not-too-fancy" decor is a "trailer park" take on a ski lodge, but "cheap drinks" and a "good location" keep an "eclectic mix of people" coming.

K & M Bar ∉
– | – | – | M

Williamsburg | 225 N. Eighth St. (Roebling St.) | Brooklyn | L to Bedford Ave. | 718-388-3088

A former pierogi shop has been subtly transformed into this Williamsburg watering hole that looks like its been there forever with an ancient tile floor, tin ceiling and tufted booths (the norm for old-school, film noir-ish drinking in these parts); the unusual selection of international brews is more modern, while the bar menu features – what else? – pierogi, steamed or fried.

	APPEAL	DECOR	SERVICE	COST

Karaoke One 7

21 | 15 | 19 | $13

Flatiron | 29 W. 17th St. (bet. 5th & 6th Aves.) | 4/5/6/L/N/Q/R/W to 14th St./Union Sq. | 212-675-3527 | www.karaoke17.com

"Check your shame at the door" and "belt one out" at this "rockin'" Flatiron karaoke joint, a chance to "live out your *American Idol* fantasies" in the "loud" front bar or in one of the "pricey private rooms"; the "extensive" song selection highlights "recent tunes", and it's always fun watching people "making fools of themselves."

Karma

21 | 18 | 18 | $8

E Village | 51 First Ave. (bet. 3rd & 4th Sts.) | F/V to Lower East Side/ 2nd Ave. | 212-677-3160 | www.karmanyc.com

Those who "still like a smoke with their drink" light up legally at this East Village "hookah den" where an "accommodating" staff will bring you a house water pipe and flavored tobacco, or let you puff from your own pack; it may be "too dark to judge the decor", but the vibe is "cozy" and there are bonus "deep beats in the basement."

Katra

18 | 21 | 17 | $12

LES | 217 Bowery (bet. Prince & Rivington Sts.) | B/D to Grand St. | 212-473-3113 | www.katranyc.com

Hidden in the Bowery's "kitchen supply district", this Moroccan themer (fka Mission) is a stylish, "split-level" lounge/restaurant bedecked with hookahs, latticed nooks and "cushy", pillow-strewn banquettes; there's a "bit of a scene" on weekend nights of the "bridge-and-tunnel" variety.

Katwalk

16 | 14 | 15 | $10

Garment District | 2 W. 35th St. (bet. 5th & 6th Aves.) | B/D/F/N/Q/ R/V/W to 34th St./Herald Sq. | 212-594-9343 | www.katwalknyc.com

"Decent" "without being pretentious", this "middle-of-nowhere" Garment District lounge draws "some sort of a crowd" for "after-work happy hour", but is essentially a "guy's bar" thanks to the sporting events broadcast on its many flat-screens; the upstairs balcony may be "nice and cozy", but the overall word is "nothing spectacular."

Keens Steakhouse

21 | 23 | 24 | $13

Garment District | 72 W. 36th St. (bet. 5th & 6th Aves.) | B/D/F/N/ Q/R/V/W to 34th St./Herald Sq. | 212-947-3636 | www.keens.com

An "olde standby" in the Garment District, this "historic", circa-1885 steakhouse is renowned for its "fascinating collection" of clay pipes hanging from the ceiling, "smoked by everyone from Buffalo Bill to Teddy Roosevelt"; its separate "wood-and-candlelit" barroom draws a mostly male clientele with an "excellent selection" of "expense account"–worthy single-malts.

Kemia Bar

26 | 27 | 20 | $11

W 40s | 630 Ninth Ave., downstairs (enter on 44th St.) | A/C/E to 42nd St./Port Authority | 212-582-3200 | www.kemiabarny.com

"Candles, flower petals and killer cocktails converge" at this "atmospheric" underground lounge, the "best-kept secret in Hell's Kitchen" due to a rather hidden location beneath the French eatery Marseille; it's an "exotic", "Moroccan-style scene" with "low seating" and low lighting, and particularly "great after-theater" when the "Broadway gypsies and swing players" show up.

| | APPEAL | DECOR | SERVICE | COST |

Kenny's Castaways

14 | **10** | **14** | **$8**

G Village | 157 Bleecker St. (bet. Sullivan & Thompson Sts.) | A/B/C/D/E/F/V to W. 4th St. | 212-979-9762 | www.kennyscastaways.net

This 42-year-old Village music venue, "famed" for the groups that played there in the "'60s and '70s", still showcases "some undiscovered good acts" as well as "tribute bands" (and "crazy tribute band groupies"); but its "dumpy" looks and "cramped stage" leave many castaways sighing "nothing special."

Kettle of Fish

21 | **16** | **20** | **$8**

G Village | 59 Christopher St. (bet. 7th Ave. S. & Waverly Pl.) | 1 to Christopher St. | 212-414-2278 | www.kettleoffishnyc.com

There's "lots of room for lounging" at this "friendly" Village watering hole, plus "darts or board games" if you want to keep busy; it's "*the* place to be on Sunday night if you love the Packers*" (the owners hail from Wisconsin), and even though there's "no kitchen", you can always "have food delivered."

Keybar

23 | **22** | **21** | **$8**

E Village | 432 E. 13th St. (bet. Ave. A & 1st Ave.) | L to 1st Ave. | 212-478-3021 | www.keybar.com

"Small" but "sexy", this red-lit East Village lounge is a "wintertime must" because of its "wood-burning fireplace" but "cozy" all year long thanks to an extended happy hour and "über-hyper tasty martinis"; though way "past its hidden-secret heyday", it carries on with fun-loving regulars fueled by the bar's "famed Rolo shots."

KGB Bar

21 | **17** | **18** | **$7**

E Village | 85 E. Fourth St., 2nd fl. (bet. 2nd & 3rd Aves.) | F/V to Lower East Side/2nd Ave. | 212-505-3360 | www.kgbbar.com

"Drinks and readings" coexist peacefully at this "small" East Village theme bar with an "off-the-grid", "cool Kremlin" vibe (it looks like a "living room" crossed with a "Soviet-era Moscow pub"); accessed by a "narrow stairwell", it lures a "strange but fun" mix of "intelligentsia" types and showcases the work of "lots of writers" and poets.

Killmeyer's Old Bavaria Inn

23 | **22** | **24** | **$11**

Staten Island | 4254 Arthur Kill Rd. (Sharrotts Rd.) | 718-984-1202 | www.killmeyers.com

"Schnitzel" and suds are the draws at this "kitschy", "moose head"-adorned Deutschlander in Staten Island where "older" dudes in "lederhosen" pass the time "ogling the *frauleins*" in its "ultimate biergarten"; while the bartenders may resist mixing "complicated girlie drinks", no one cares given one of the "biggest beer selections" around.

ⓩ King Cole Bar

28 | **27** | **26** | **$16**

E 50s | St. Regis Hotel | 2 E. 55th St. (5th Ave.) | E/V to 5th Ave./53rd St. | 212-339-6721 | www.starwood.com

The "diamonds-and-furs" set gets all "dressed up" for cocktails at this ultra-"civilized" Midtown hotel bar that's arguably the "swankiest in the city", from the precise mix of the "signature Bloody Mary" to its "fabulous" focal point, the Maxfield Parrish mural; in short, it reeks of "sophistication", so if the "high-society" vibe "doesn't wow you, the price of a drink will."

	APPEAL	DECOR	SERVICE	COST

Kings Cross
22 | 18 | 21 | $12

NoHo | 356 Bowery, downstairs (bet. 4th & Great Jones Sts.) | 6 to Astor Pl. | 212-388-1655

A "bit of old England" buried in an unmarked basement, this "little" Bowery pub offers a "decent beer selection" for laddies in the mood to "hang with friends"; while hardly fit for a king, at least it's "anti-pretentious" – and that's a "tough thing to be in this neighborhood."

King's Head Tavern
14 | 13 | 16 | $7

E Village | 222 E. 14th St. (bet. 2nd & 3rd Aves.) | L to 3rd Ave. | 212-473-6590 | www.kingsheadtavern.com

"NYU kids" and the "after-work" desk jockeys chug "strong drinks that make you want to stay forever" at this "low-key" East Village barroom set in a vast, medieval-style space; maybe it's "nothing that hasn't been done before", but devotees think "they do it right."

Kingswood
23 | 23 | 19 | $13

G Village | 121 W. 10th St. (bet. Greenwich & 6th Aves.) | 1 to Christopher St. | 212-645-0018 | www.kingswoodnyc.com

There's plenty of "Aussie flavor" at this "always-lively" Village gastro-pub, a "beautiful" eatery garnished with "gorgeous lighting" that has "fashion-forward thirtysomethings" flocking to its "groovy bar"; aye, it's "pricey and sceney", but "if you can find room" it's "a winner, mate"; N.B. a downstairs DJ lounge now ups the late-night ante.

Kinsale Tavern
20 | 16 | 21 | $7

E 90s | 1672 Third Ave. (bet. 93rd & 94th Sts.) | 6 to 96th St. | 212-348-4370 | www.kinsale.com

"Authentic to its core", this "solid" UES pub pleases its "real-people" crowd with "rugby on the TV" and "plenty of quality beers on tap"; icing the cake, the "cheerful" bartenders are "quick with conversation" and "proud supporters of the old Irish tradition, the 'buyback.'"

Kiss & Fly
20 | 21 | 17 | $16

Meatpacking | 409 W. 13th St. (bet. 9th Ave. & Washington St.) | A/C/E/L to 14th St./8th Ave. | 212-255-1933 | www.kissandflyclub.com

"Beautiful people" breathe easy at this "hot" Meatpacking District club (fka Aer) that brings on "techno" beats, "strobe lights" and "high rollers" partying under "Roman Coliseum" arches and "Michelangelo-inspired" ceiling art; critics kiss it off as a "Eurotrash stomping ground", but many see "potential" behind the "expectedly tough door."

Klimat
18 | 16 | 19 | $10

E Village | 77 E. Seventh St. (1st Ave.) | 6 to Astor Pl. | 212-777-1112

Eastern bloc beers and wine found nowhere else in town turn up for "good prices" at this funky barroom with a Polish accent; the "garage"-like decor is strictly East Village – "picnic table" seating, homemade light fixtures – ditto the unpretentious mood.

K Lounge
▽ 20 | 24 | 18 | $12

(aka Kama Sutra Lounge)

W 50s | 30 W. 52nd St., 2nd fl. (bet. 5th & 6th Aves.) | B/D/F/V to 47-50th Sts./Rockefeller Ctr. | 212-265-6665

Midtown gets a "lusty" spin via this *Kama Sutra*-themed lounge that "lives up to its name" with "sensual" Indian decor right out of a "harem"; "exotic music" and "lots of cushions" round out the "Bollywood"-esque experience, though some k-vetch it's "too quiet" and the cocktails "way overpriced."

NEW Knave
▽ 22 | 24 | 22 | $12

W 50s | Le Parker Meridien | 118 W. 57th St. (bet. 6th & 7th Aves.) | N/Q/R/W to 57th St./7th Ave. | 212-245-5000

Fashioned out of a former passageway in Midtown's Parker Meridien hotel, this new lounge serves coffee and pastries in the AM, then switches to cocktails and wine after dark; though the space exudes a vaguely medieval vibe (thanks to a vaulted ceiling, heavy curtains and mammoth chandeliers), free WiFi and "high-end" prices supply the modern flourishes.

Kush
22 | 23 | 17 | $11

LES | 191 Chrystie St. (bet. Rivington & Stanton Sts.) | F/V to Lower East Side/2nd Ave. | 212-677-7328 | www.kushlounge.com

Now relocated to "expanded" Lower East Side digs next door to The Box, this "mysterious Moroccan" is a "sensual" spot for digging global DJs while "smoking some hookah"; though it's a bit "pricey", romeos report the "Indiana Jones" vibe and kushioned "private" niches are "atmospheric aphrodisiacs."

Label
▽ 17 | 16 | 18 | $11

LES | 174 Rivington St. (bet. Attorney & Clinton Sts.) | F/V to Lower East Side/2nd Ave. | 212-228-9600 | www.labellounge.com

Ever-happening Rivington Street's latest comer is this modest bar, an "intimate", dimly lit affair with a gritty speakeasy vibe; a serious DJ booth spinning "deep" underground tunes from the self-described 'non-commercial end of the electronic music spectrum' keeps it fresh, while the bar snacks ("homemade empanadas") allude to the neighborhood's funky past.

La Bottega
21 | 20 | 16 | $12

Chelsea | Maritime Hotel | 88 Ninth Ave. (16th St.) | A/C/E/L to 14th St./8th Ave. | 212-243-8400 | www.themaritimehotel.com

This "bustling" bar/eatery is always a "reliable" spot to "people-watch" (read: "meet girls") and due to its prime West Chelsea address, a "perfect location to start or end the night"; come summertime, there's also a vast, "Riviera"-esque outdoor patio, but be prepared to "wait on yourself or wait forever" for service.

La Caverna
18 | 22 | 16 | $9

LES | 122-124 Rivington St., downstairs (bet. Essex & Norfolk Sts.) | F/J/M/Z to Delancey/Essex Sts. | 212-475-2126 | www.lacavernanyc.com

"Decorated like a cave" ("don't bump your head on the stalactites"), this "gimmicky" LES bar may look a bit "cheesy", but spelunkers insist its "reasonable" tabs, "good music" and "young crowd" are worth exploring; foes sum it up succinctly: "pure tackiness."

Z La Esquina
24 | 22 | 18 | $12

Little Italy | 106 Kenmare St. (bet. Cleveland Pl. & Lafayette St.) | 6 to Spring St. | 646-613-7100 | www.esquinanyc.com

A "cool kids' version of a speakeasy", this "sexy" underground cantina/tequila bar in Little Italy is accessed via a "secret entrance" through the employees-only door of a "hole-in-the-wall" taqueria;

though "everyone knows about it" now, the "authentic cuisine", "hip dungeon" decor and "hot social scene" make it "extremely special" – no wonder reservations are practically "unattainable."

NEW La Fonda del Sol
| – | – | – | E |

E 40s | MetLife Bldg. | 200 Park Ave. (enter at 44th St. & Vanderbilt Ave.) | 4/5/6/7/S to 42nd St./Grand Central | 212-867-6767 | www.patinagroup.com

Grand Central's latest after-work destination, this new lounge/eatery is named after a renowned Manhattan restaurant that was considered the hippest thing in town back in 1961; today, designer Adam Tihany reinterprets its mod decor, chef Josh DeChellis is doing the small plates and the signature cocktails are strong (and priced for the strong of wallet); N.B. ignore the official address: the entrance is closest to 44th Street and Vanderbilt Avenue.

Lakeside Lounge
| 19 | 10 | 15 | $7 |

E Village | 162 Ave. B (bet. 10th & 11th Sts.) | L to 1st Ave. | 212-529-8463 | www.lakesidelounge.com

"Grungy and fun", this "no-frills, throw-back-a-drink" dive is a "relic of the East Village before strollers and Starbucks"; hipsters on "cheap dates" crowd in for the "terrific jukebox", "uncensored photo booth" and "solid local rock 'n' roll acts" wailing in the back – just "stay to the front if you want to hear yourself think."

La Lanterna Next Door
| 25 | 23 | 19 | $11 |

G Village | 131 MacDougal St. (bet. W. 3rd & 4th Sts.) | A/B/C/D/E/F/V to W. 4th St. | 212-529-5945 | www.lalanternacaffe.com

Prepare to feel "extremely romantic" at this "yet-to-be-discovered" Village boîte that's a "charming" adjunct to the restaurant La Lanterna di Vittorio; oozing a "Frank Sinatra" vibe with a "fireplace", "dim lights" and nightly "live jazz", it's a "nontrendy" option guaranteed to "transport you away from the hustle and bustle."

La Linea
| 18 | 14 | 17 | $8 |

E Village | 15 First Ave. (bet. 1st & 2nd Sts.) | F/V to Lower East Side/2nd Ave. | 212-777-1571 | www.lalinealounge.com

With its "neighborhood" lounge lineage and "half-price happy hour", this East Village "staple" is a reliable respite for "close-quarters" communion; the "run-of-the-mill" looks and only "competent" bartenders may be nothing special, but it's still "worth an occasional visit."

L'Amour
| 17 | 15 | 17 | $19 |

Staten Island | 2354 Arthur Kill Rd. (Engert St.) | 718-605-3900

Following a "relocation" of the Bay Ridge original, this old-school live rock venue has Staten Island "locals" banging their heads to everything from hardcore to hair metal in suitably sketchy style; some snipe it's a "ridiculous 1989 throwback", but fans "wouldn't have it any other way."

Landmark Tavern
| 21 | 19 | 20 | $9 |

W 40s | 626 11th Ave. (46th St.) | A/C/E to 42nd St./Port Authority | 212-247-2562 | www.thelandmarktavern.org

Fortunately, the "charm survived the remodeling" at this born-again "blast from the past" on the far West Side, a "historic" 1868 Irish pub (supposedly "haunted" upstairs) whose "homey", "olde-time" interior

| | APPEAL | DECOR | SERVICE | COST |

"should be on every guided tour of NYC"; it's certainly "worth the trek" despite being "damned difficult to catch a cab home."

Lansdowne Road
21 | 18 | 20 | $8

W 40s | 599 10th Ave. (bet. 43rd & 44th Sts.) | A/C/E to 42nd St./ Port Authority | 212-239-8020 | www.lansdowneroadnyc.com
"Everyone gets involved in the games" at this "airy" Irish sports pub in Hell's Kitchen with "plenty of televisions" and an ice rail along the bar so you needn't "worry about your drink getting warm"; those downe with "pool, darts" and "friendly" service will "want to hit this road."

Larry Lawrence
▽ 28 | 26 | 24 | $9

Williamsburg | 295 Grand St. (bet. Havemeyer & Roebling Sts.) | Brooklyn | L to Bedford Ave. | 718-218-7866 | www.larrylawrencebar.com
This "never-too-crowded" Williamsburg bar radiates "mystique", starting with its "unmarked", "speakeasy-style" front door and narrow hallway entrance; but inside the "vast", double-height space is a "candlelit" room that's one part "exposed brick", one part "warm" wood, plus an "unusual", "fishbowl"-esque outdoor smoking mezzanine.

Last Exit
20 | 15 | 23 | $7

Cobble Hill | 136 Atlantic Ave. (bet. Clinton & Henry Sts.) | Brooklyn | 2/3/4/ 5/M/N/R/W to Borough Hall | 718-222-9198 | www.lastexitbar.com
Cobble Hill's "first hipster bar" sports a "funky living room–ish setting" with "interesting" artwork on the walls and a "low-key" vibe in the air; a "cool" back garden and occasional "dorktastic trivia" contests lead loyalists to label it "one of the best on Atlantic" Avenue.

Latitude
17 | 17 | 17 | $9

W 40s | 783 Eighth Ave. (bet. 47th & 48th Sts.) | C/E to 50th St. | 212-245-3034 | www.latitudebarnyc.com
At quitting time, "30-ish" "corporate" folk flock to this multilevel Theater District "wonder", a "loud" meet market stocked with plasma screens, pool tables and two upstairs lounges; it adds up to a "lively" time on "otherwise tourist-trap" turf, even if foes mutter "don't go out of your way."

Laugh Lounge
▽ 16 | 15 | 14 | $9

LES | 151 Essex St. (bet. Rivington & Stanton Sts.) | F/J/M/Z to Delancey/ Essex Sts. | 212-614-2500 | www.laughloungenyc.com
The only "comedy lounge on the LES", this double-decker house of mirth offers stand-up on its "cozy" lower level and a posh lounge above; maybe the drinks are "overpriced", but it's "worth it if the comics are good."

Lava Gina
23 | 19 | 23 | $10

E Village | 116 Ave. C (bet. 7th & 8th Sts.) | L to 1st Ave. | 212-477-9319 | www.lavagina.com
It's worth the trek to the far East Village to "chill" at this "very dark" bar/ lounge best known for its "ultradanceable" world music soundtrack; despite the "ha-ha" name (and appropriately "V-shaped" bartop), it "fulfills its niche perfectly", though it can be "hit-or-miss" crowdwise.

NEW Lavish Lounge
- | - | - | M

Astoria | 34-01 36th Ave. (34th St.) | Queens | N/W to 36th Ave. | 718-361-0022 | www.lavishloungeny.com
A lively surprise in a lackluster part of Southern Astoria, this gay lounge sports hodgepodge decor (wood-slat walls, vintage chandeliers, ex-

posed ducts) that matches the jumble of twinks, mature men and lady-friends that habituates it; go-go boys crowd atop the bar when drag star Mimi Imfurst isn't entertaining, while a banquette-flanked side room offers a mellower spot to sit and sip the moderately priced drinks.

Lea
19 | 19 | 16 | $12

E 40s | Helmsley Bldg. | 230 Park Ave. (East Walkway, bet. 45th & 46th Sts.) | 4/5/6/7/S to 42nd St./Grand Central | 212-922-1546 | www.leanyc.com
"Off the beaten path" hidden in the Helmsley Building's East Walkway, this "loungey" bar is a "win-win" situation for desk jockeys given its "cute waitresses" and "not-too-loud" acoustics; close proximity to Grand Central lends commuter appeal (you can easily "stumble down to your track"), but only on weekdays – it's closed weekends.

Le Bateau Ivre
24 | 20 | 19 | $13

E 50s | The Pod Hotel | 230 E. 51st St. (bet. 2nd & 3rd Aves.) | 6 to 51st St./Lexington Ave. | 212-583-0579 | www.lebateauivrenyc.com
For "Paris in the middle of New York", drop by this "great little" Midtown wine bar that draws in "Francophiles" (and "native speakers") with a "wide selection" of French labels; though there's debate about the cost – "pricey" vs. "fairly reasonable" – there's no doubt that they've got the "authenticity" thing down pat.

Le Cirque Wine Lounge
24 | 25 | 22 | $18

E 50s | One Beacon Court | 151 E. 58th St. (bet. Lexington & 3rd Aves.) | 4/5/6/N/R/W to 59th St./Lexington Ave. | 212-644-0202 | www.lecirque.com
Now reincarnated in East Midtown's Bloomberg Tower, this ever-"chic" French restaurant keeps its "well-deserved reputation" intact with this wine lounge that's perfect for "feeling swanky" while sipping a nice little red among other "elite" types; no kidding, it's "very expensive", but watching the sommeliers ascend the room's soaring wine storage tower provides some distraction.

Le Colonial
21 | 22 | 20 | $13

E 50s | 149 E. 57th St. (bet. Lexington & 3rd Aves.) | 4/5/6/N/R/W to 59th St./Lexington Ave. | 212-752-0808 | www.lecolonialnyc.com
Imagine you're a "plantation manager in a bar in 1920s Indochina" to get the drift of this transporting Midtown restaurant where the "super-sexy" second-floor lounge attracts "beautiful" types with a yen for "glam drinks" and "exotic atmosphere"; it's the "perfect place for a torrid affair", even if picky drinkers think it has "seen better days."

Lederhosen
21 | 16 | 20 | $8

W Village | 39 Grove St. (Bleecker St.) | 1 to Christopher St. | 212-206-7691 | www.lederhosennyc.com
Hoist a stein and "say 'ja'" to the "*wunderbar*" lineup of German brews at this Village brauhaus, a "laid-back" source of "schnitzel and suds"; ok, it's "hardly authentic" with its "Ikea furniture" and "tacky landscape mural", but it does pass muster as a "poor man's Zum Schneider."

LelaBar
▽ 25 | 20 | 25 | $12

W Village | 422 Hudson St. (Leroy St.) | 1 to Houston St. | 212-206-0594 | www.lelabar.com
A "quiet" stretch of Hudson Street is home to this "intimate" West Village wine bar purveying an "excellent selection" of global vinos paired with the usual cheese and charcuterie; the minimalist room

is dominated by a big "oval bartop" that's usually frequented by local oenophiles.

ⓩ Lenox Lounge

21 | 17 | 19 | $13

Harlem | 288 Lenox Ave. (125th St.) | 2/3 to 125th St. | 212-427-0253 | www.lenoxlounge.com

As "old-school as old-school can get", this circa-1939 "art deco" jazz club is a real "back-in-time" trip to the days when Billie Holiday and John Coltrane graced the stage of its back performance space, the Zebra Room; the "upbeat" vibe and "excellent" performers compensate for the "pricey drinks."

NEW Le Poisson Rouge

22 | 19 | 18 | $11

G Village | 158 Bleecker St., downstairs (bet. Sullivan & Thompson Sts.) | A/B/C/D/E/F/V to W. 4th St. | 212-796-0741 | www.lepoissonrouge.com

Living up to the "bohemian past" of the Village Gate (its "legendary" precursor), this subterranean Village music venue prides itself on a "diverse" list of "creative bookings", from indie to global acts and beyond; a "funky" lounge area adjoins the midsize performance space, where a "perfect sound system" promises a "loud night out."

Le Royale

▽ 16 | 16 | 19 | $13

W Village | 21 Seventh Ave. S. (Leroy St.) | 1 to Houston St. | 212-463-0700 | www.leroyaleclub.com

Seventh Avenue South is home to this "trendy" dance club that's been given a Pop Art–style refurb but still retains the music-driven, DJ-focused spirit of its former incarnation, Luke & Leroy; the layout is the same as before: a downstairs bar/lounge topped by a second story, let-it-all-hang-out dance floor.

Levee, The

19 | 17 | 21 | $7

Williamsburg | 212 Berry St. (N. 3rd St.) | Brooklyn | L to Bedford Ave. | 718-218-8787 | www.theleveenyc.com

Run by "friendly" Texans, this funky Williamsburg watering hole is a "non-hipster hang in the heart of hipster heaven" where everything from "interesting" microbrews to "beer and whiskey combos" comes at "great prices"; "board games galore" and trashy snacks like "Frito pies" are bonuses.

Lexington Bar and Books

21 | 21 | 21 | $12

E 70s | 1020 Lexington Ave. (73rd St.) | 6 to 77th St. | 212-717-3902 | www.barandbooks.net

"Older", "gentrified" types frequent this "posh whiskey-and-cigar bar" on the Upper East Side, a "classy", "expensive" joint with a jackets-suggested dress code; lined in "dark mahogany" and staffed by waitresses in "aggressive red dresses", it's best known as one of the few places in town where "you can legally smoke" indoors.

Le Zie 2000

22 | 18 | 21 | $13

Chelsea | 172 Seventh Ave. (bet. 20th & 21st Sts.) | 1 to 18th St. | 212-206-8686 | www.lezie.com

Insiders zero in on the "cozy" separate bar area of this Chelsea trattoria, a "lively hideaway" where "talented" mixologists concoct "killer" cocktails and decant "excellent" wines by the glass; "classy but not stuffy", this former "best-kept secret" is common knowledge now, so be ready to "rub elbows" with an eclectic crowd.

	APPEAL	DECOR	SERVICE	COST

Libation

18 | 18 | 16 | $10

LES | 137 Ludlow St. (bet. Rivington & Stanton Sts.) | F/V to Lower East Side/ 2nd Ave. | 212-529-2153 | www.libationnyc.com

"Downtown hipsters and Uptown sophisticates" get up close and personal at this "chic" triple-decker that's a controversial "example of the gentrification of the Lower East Side"; it's "lost a bit of its fun now that everyone knows about it" (hence the "long lines"), but despite the "enormous" dimensions it can still get "very packed depending on the night."

Library

20 | 18 | 20 | $7

E Village | 7 Ave. A (bet. Houston & 2nd Sts.) | F/V to Lower East Side/ 2nd Ave. | 212-375-1352

"Things tend to get a little out of control" at this "noisy", "no-frills" bar thanks to its "blistering punk rock jukebox" (the "loudest in the East Village") combined with "crazy" B movies projected on the back wall; more civilized touches include "bookshelf" decor and good "bang-for-the-buck" drink deals.

L.I.C. Bar

25 | 23 | 24 | $8

LIC | 45-58 Vernon Blvd. (46th Ave.) | Queens | 7 to Vernon Blvd./ Jackson Ave. | 718-786-5400 | www.longislandcitybar.com

"Kinda like" its counterpart the Pencil Factory, this LIC saloon "close to P.S. 1" skews "old-school" with tin ceilings, rugged "woodwork" and a dozen tap brews at "good prices"; its beer garden is "ideal for summer", but despite the "lovable personality", there's "not a huge clientele yet."

NEW Lillie's

- | - | - | M

Flatiron | 13 E. 17th St. (bet. B'way & 5th Ave.) | 4/5/6/L/N/Q/R/W to 14th St./Union Sq. | 212-337-1970 | www.lilliesnyc.com

Honoring 19th-century 'it' girl Lillie Langtry, this airy new Irish pub in the Flatiron exudes a distinct Victorian glow thanks to an antique marble bar, mammoth gold-leafed columns and enough chandeliers to give Versailles a run for its money; up-to-date touches include sports on the tube and an encyclopedic variety of beer and whiskey.

Lion's Head Tavern

15 | 10 | 19 | $7

W 100s | 995 Amsterdam Ave. (109th St.) | 1 to Cathedral Pkwy./110th St. | 212-866-1030

"Locals and grad students" lionize this Columbia-area sports bar for its "cheap, cheap, cheap" wings and beer, overlooking the "dingy", "old-time" surroundings that occur "when men are allowed to decorate on their own"; it's "not exactly a pickup joint", but definitely a "rowdy good time" on game day.

Lips

20 | 19 | 19 | $11

W Village | 2 Bank St. (Greenwich Ave.) | 1/2/3/L to 14th St./7th Ave. | 212-675-7710 | www.lipsnyc.com

"Bring your sense of humor and a camera" to this "hysterical" Village cabaret where "aim-to-please drag queens" lip sync on stage when they're not slinging "delicious" cocktails; ok, it's a tad "long in the tooth" and some say it's a "Disneyland" take on crossdressing ("all that's missing is a tour bus outside"), but it can be "fun" for a "bachelorette party."

	APPEAL	DECOR	SERVICE	COST

Lit

19 | **15** | **17** | **$7**

E Village | 93 Second Ave. (bet. 5th & 6th Sts.) | 6 to Astor Pl. | 212-777-7987 | www.litloungenyc.com

"Hipster central in the East Village", this double-decker "rock 'n' roll lounge bar" draws "tattooed" types with "midpriced" drinks, an art gallery in the back and a "sweaty", "cave"-like basement where "small bands" perform; it may be a "hole", but it's usually "packed to the gills" on weekends with folks "grooving" to the "hot" sounds – "music is the highlight here."

⚡ Little Branch ⊄

26 | **18** | **24** | **$13**

W Village | 20 Seventh Ave. S. (Leroy St.) | 1 to Christopher St. | 212-929-4360 | www.littlebranch.net

Milk and Honey's master of mixology, Sasha Petraske, branches out with this "suave" subterranean Village "hideaway" "tucked behind a nondescript door" and accessed down a "steep stairwell"; inside the noir-ish den, the big attractions are "stellar cocktails made with precision" from "high-end ingredients", and despite debate about the vibe – "1920s speakeasy" vs. "grandma's musty basement" – most hope it "can be kept a quiet secret."

Live Bait

15 | **11** | **16** | **$9**

Flatiron | 14 E. 23rd St. (bet. 5th & Madison Aves.) | N/R/W to 23rd St. | 212-353-2400

"Kitschy bayou decor" sets the relaxed, "Down South" mood at this "mellow" Flatiron dive, a "funky replica" of a fish shack that "keeps on keeping on" with "cold beer and comfort food"; foes fret it's "not quite like it used to be in the '90s – now it's just a "slight step up from a college frat house" with "lots of bait, but no fish."

Living Room ⊄

22 | **17** | **19** | **$9**

LES | 154 Ludlow St. (bet. Rivington & Stanton Sts.) | F/V to Lower East Side/2nd Ave. | 212-533-7235 | www.livingroomny.com

A "fun, cozy place" that looks like a cross between a "coffeehouse" and "your parents' den from the '70s", this Lower East Side music venue mainly showcases "up-and-coming acoustic acts"; since it's "all about the music and nothing else", you can expect a "fantastic" sound system and little attitude.

Living Room Lounge

22 | **18** | **19** | **$11**

Sunset Park | 245 23rd St. (5th Ave.) | Brooklyn | M/R to 25th St. | 718-499-1505

There's "always something going on" at this Sunset Park bar/lounge, host to "good-time" entertainment like karaoke, live bands, open mike and burlesque artists; "cavernous" premises with "comfy" thrift-store couches and "mood lighting" provide ample drinking room, so only the "location leaves a lot to be desired."

Local

16 | **13** | **16** | **$8**

Garment District | 1 Penn Plaza (33rd St., bet. 7th & 8th Aves.) | A/C/E to 34th St./Penn Station | 212-629-7070 | www.localcafenyc.com

"Twentysomething" "frat boy" types engage in the usual "happy-hour" antics at this Garment District barroom best known for its "cool rooftop" deck; look for "sloshed commuters" and plenty of "amazing Penn Station people-watching"; N.B. the East Midtown original has shuttered.

Local 138
19 | 14 | 18 | $9

LES | 138 Ludlow St. (bet. Rivington & Stanton Sts.) | F/J/M/Z to Delancey/Essex Sts. | 212-477-0280

One of the Lower East Side's "few laid-back" locals, this "Irish drinking bar" is a "relatively cheap" refuge with "interesting tap beers" and a brace of semiprivate "window tables" in front; it's a favored "fallback" since the scene's "pretty chilled out."

NEW Local 269
- | - | - | M

LES | 269 E. Houston St. (Suffolk St.) | F/V to Lower East Side/2nd Ave. | 212-228-9874

Funky is the word for this new LES barroom that was last known as Vasmay Lounge (and before that, Meow Mix); the digs are as divey as ever – ditto the come-as-you-are crowd – but this time around there's occasional live music and a very long happy hour (from 2 to 9 PM) to take your mind off your troubles.

Lodge
▽ 18 | 24 | 16 | $9

Williamsburg | 318 Grand St. (Havemeyer St.) | Brooklyn | L to Grand St. | 718-486-9400 | www.lodgenyc.com

Breezy by summer, cozy by winter, this slick Adirondack-themed bar/eatery holds down the fort on a "revitalized" Williamsburg corner with creative cocktails served in a "rustic", "antler-chandeliered" lounge; now if only they can get the "service to match the atmosphere."

Loki Lounge
17 | 14 | 16 | $7

Park Slope | 304 Fifth Ave. (2nd St.) | Brooklyn | M/R to Union St. | 718-965-9600 | www.lokilounge.com

"Something for everyone" could be the motto of this "low-key" Park Sloper fitted out with a pool table, "eclectic jukebox" and "every type of bar game" imaginable, plus a "couch"-strewn lounge and back garden; though the straight-out-of-"Goodwill" decor lays an egg, "reasonable prices" make it more palatable.

Lolita
19 | 18 | 16 | $7

LES | 266 Broome St. (bet. Allen & Orchard Sts.) | F/J/M/Z to Delancey/Essex Sts. | 212-966-7223 | www.lolitabar.net

"Down-to-earth" hipsters populate this off-the-radar Lower East Side bar that's a "refreshing break from the scene" and offers a back room as well as a basement lounge stocked with thrift-shop furniture; "not-bad art" on the walls from "local artists" adds to the creative vibe.

L'Orange Bleue
21 | 20 | 16 | $10

SoHo | 430 Broome St. (Crosby St.) | N/R/W to Prince St. | 212-226-4999 | www.lorangebleue.com

"Birthday and bachelorette" celebrants collide at this "lively" SoHo French-Moroccan known for its "convivial" Monday night belly dancing and overall "loud", "crowded" conditions; too bad about the "slooow service" – some say the "bartender drinks more than the customers."

Loreley
21 | 16 | 19 | $8

LES | 7 Rivington St. (bet. Bowery & Chrystie St.) | J/M/Z to Bowery | 212-253-7077 | www.loreleynyc.com

Experience Rivington-on-the-Rhine at this Lower East Side "bratwurst-and-beer" dispenser vending an "awesome" selection of brews from the Cologne region in workmanlike digs that "don't resort to kitsch"; an outdoor biergarten is the "reason to come in the summer."

Louis 649

26 | 21 | 24 | $9

E Village | 649 E. Ninth St. (bet. Aves. B & C) | L to 1st Ave. | 212-673-1190 | www.louis649.com

East Village hepcats unwind at this "no-cover" "neighborhood jazz joint" featuring "great live" jamsters nightly accompanied by "courteous" barkeeps and "interesting" wines by the glass; it's the kind of "hole-in-the-wall" that "only locals know about", and definitely "worth the trek."

Lounge 47

20 | 20 | 21 | $11

LIC | 47-10 Vernon Blvd. (bet. 47th Ave. & 47th Rd.) | Queens | 7 to Vernon Blvd./Jackson Ave. | 718-937-2044

Not quite trendy but "not a bad start" either, this "down-to-earth" LIC hangout has more than enough "cool", casual character for a "relaxed drink with friends"; regulars dig its '70s retro furniture, but make a beeline for the "fantastic" back garden in clement weather.

Love

∇ 20 | 19 | 17 | $12

G Village | 179 MacDougal St. (8th St.) | A/B/C/D/E/F/V to W. 4th St. | 212-477-5683 | www.musicislove.net

Like a "very '70s" happening hidden in a "dark" Village basement, this weekend club hosts DJs, live bands and all-night dancing amid black-light psychedelia, mirror balls and a bar that "looks like a cave"; though an "interesting experience" with a "great sound system", the less love-struck lament it's "NYU-ish" and "overpriced."

LQ

21 | 22 | 19 | $12

(aka Latin Quarter)

E 40s | Radisson Lexington Hotel | 511 Lexington Ave. (bet. 47th & 48th Sts.) | 6 to 51st St./Lexington Ave. | 212-593-7575 | www.lqny.com

Living up to its name – the initials are short for "Latin Quarter" – this East Midtown club offers a "huge", "great-looking" space that includes a "sunken dance floor" to practice your "salsa and merengue" moves; despite a few patrons "with no sense of fashion" and "always a line" at the door, folks are "ready to have a good time" here and it shows.

Luca Bar ⇗

21 | 22 | 17 | $9

E Village | 119 St. Marks Pl. (bet. Ave. A & 1st Ave.) | L to 1st Ave. | 212-254-1511

Luca Lounge ⇗

E Village | 222 Ave. B (bet. 13th & 14th Sts.) | L to 1st Ave. | 212-674-9400 | www.lucaloungenyc.com

A "chill" spot to "meet friends or throw a party", this East Village barroom features a "cozy" setting and "service on the slow side"; its larger Avenue B sibling, Luca Lounge, closed for some time for renovations, is now back in business.

Lucky Jack's

20 | 17 | 21 | $8

LES | 129 Orchard St. (bet. Delancey & Rivington Sts.) | F/J/M/Z to Delancey/Essex Sts. | 212-477-6555 | www.luckyjacksnyc.com

Belly up to a "really long" bar that practically "stretches from Orchard to Allen streets" at this "classic" LES Irish pub, a "down-to-earth" joint with absolutely "no pretension"; throw in a pool table and a "nice lounge downstairs", and few are tempted to use the "exits on both ends."

| | APPEAL | DECOR | SERVICE | COST |

Lucky's Eleven
- | - | - | E

Little Italy | 173 Mott St. (bet. Broome & Grand Sts.) | B/D to Grand St. | 212-966-9293

From model/nightlife promoter Emma Cleary comes this long-in-the-making underground den in the former Double Happiness space; though not yet open at press time, it will feature the same meandering layout, refreshed with a new bar and wraparound banquettes, as well as a selective door policy that might make entry a challenge.

☑NEW Lucky Strike Lanes
21 | 19 | 17 | $13

W 40s | 624-660 W. 42nd St. (bet. 11th & 12th Aves.) | A/C/E to 42nd St./Port Authority | 646-829-0170 | www.bowlluckystrike.com

A "swanky way to get your bowl on", this LA-based chain rolls out "luxe" lanes in the "no-man's-land" of Way West Hell's Kitchen, upgrading the typical formula with bottle service, a dress code and huge projection screens over the pins; granted, it's "not cheap", but then again, this is "not your typical bowling alley."

Lucky 13 Saloon ⊟
17 | 16 | 21 | $6

Park Slope | 273 13th St. (bet. 5th & 6th Aves.) | Brooklyn | F/M/R to 4th Ave./9th St. | 718-499-7553 | www.lucky13saloon.com

"Punk and heavy metal are alive and kicking" at this Park Slope "dive" where "crazy characters" compare their ink, "rock out" with the hardcore jukebox and grok the band posters on display; somewhat "scary" to squares, it's a bona fide "walk on the Gothy side."

Lucy's ⊟
▽ 19 | 10 | 17 | $7

E Village | 135 Ave. A (bet. 9th St. & St. Marks Pl.) | 6 to Astor Pl. | 212-673-3824

"Named for the proprietor and head barkeep", this East Villager is a "real-deal dive" where you can find Lucy herself "making strong, cheap drinks with a smile"; pool tables, video games and a funky jukebox draw an eclectic, "friendly crowd."

Luke's Bar & Grill ⊟
19 | 14 | 21 | $10

E 70s | 1394 Third Ave. (bet. 79th & 80th Sts.) | 6 to 77th St. | 212-249-7070 | www.lukesbarandgrill.com

"Easygoing" and "accommodating", this "normal" UES bar and grill may have "no hooks", but there's "no snootiness" in the air either; a vaguely "suburban quality" keeps its Waspy "neighborhood crowd" content, despite moans about the "cash-only" policy.

Lunasa
▽ 22 | 20 | 23 | $6

E Village | 126 First Ave. (bet. 7th St. & St. Marks Pl.) | L to 1st Ave. | 212-228-8580 | www.lunasabar.com

"Genuine Irish bartenders", pleasing "happy-hour" specials and an overall "good buzz" draw a "local" following to this East Village taproom that "doesn't try to be something it isn't"; a "nice" garden out back cinches the deal.

☑NEW Macao Trading Co.
25 | 26 | 21 | $14

TriBeCa | 311 Church St. (bet. Lispenard & Walker Sts.) | 1/2/3 to Chambers St. | 212-431-8750 | www.macaonyc.com

Secreted in the basement of a "packed" new TriBeCa eatery, this sexy little lounge vends "creative cocktails" shaken by "Employees Only alums" along with an array of Chinese-Portuguese tidbits; if the tiny space gets too tight, the main bar upstairs supplies the same "expensive" drinks and 1940s Macao atmosphere, but more elbow room.

MacDougal Street Ale House | 18 | 14 | 17 | $8 |

G Village | 122 MacDougal St. (bet. Bleecker & W. 3rd Sts.) | A/B/C/D/E/F/V to W. 4th St. | 212-254-0006

A "nice little hideaway" tucked into a corner of touristy Greenwich Village, this "frat boy hangout" offers the usual cheap suds as well as a jukebox and nonstop sports on the tube; it's a "great place to just be yourself" and reenact your college years.

NEW mad46 | 21 | 21 | 17 | $14 |

E 40s | Roosevelt Hotel | 45 E. 45th St. (enter on 46th St., bet. Madison & Vanderbilt Aves.) | 4/5/6/7/S to 42nd St./Grand Central | 212-885-6095 | www.mad46.com

A seasonal "stomping ground" atop the Roosevelt Hotel near Grand Central Station, this block-long rooftop is a "convenient escape" for "Midtown professionals" who need to "let off steam"; even though the pops are "expensive", the service "slow" and the cityscape views just "ok", it's "often packed" after work; N.B. a new indoor lounge space is handy when the weather's not so hot.

Madame X | 20 | 19 | 18 | $10 |

G Village | 94 W. Houston St. (bet. La Guardia Pl. & Thompson St.) | A/B/C/D/E/F/V to W. 4th St. | 212-539-0808 | www.madamex.com

Decorated like a "red-light district" "vampire's brothel", this crimson-drenched "loungey lounge" on the Village/SoHo border oozes a "sexy", "naughty" vibe with "antique couches galore" and "lots of nooks" made for "getting busy"; an "unusual" back garden is a good place to cool down and "have a smoke" when things get too steamy inside.

Z NEW Madam Geneva | 25 | 22 | 23 | $14 |

NoHo | 4 Bleecker St. (Bowery) | 6 to Bleecker St. | 212-254-0350 | www.madamgeneva-nyc.com

Its moniker is old-time slang for 'gin', and this "original" back-room bar adjacent to NoHo's Double Crown restaurant lives up to it with an "amazing" list of "unique" gin-based cocktails, some topped with a dollop of jam; the AvroKO-designed room is done in a vaguely British Raj style, and though applauded as a "new favorite", many wish it were "a bit bigger."

Mad River | 14 | 12 | 16 | $8 |

E 80s | 1442 Third Ave. (bet. 81st & 82nd Sts.) | 4/5/6 to 86th St. | 212-988-1832 | www.madrivergrille.com

"College boys, boys, boys" populate this "sausage-heavy" "crazy party bar" in Yorkville where you can "let all your inhibitions go" and "have a blast" "bumping and grinding with sweaty strangers"; alright, the "drinks are nothing special" and the overall mood is "juvenile", but to "get drunk and forget your worries", look no further.

Maggie's Place | 20 | 19 | 22 | $9 |

E 40s | 21 E. 47th St. (bet. 5th & Madison Aves.) | B/D/F/V to 47-50th Sts./Rockefeller Ctr. | 212-753-5757 | www.maggiesnyc.com

Given its "proximity to Grand Central Terminal North", this "commuter bar" gets "progressively more crowded as the workweek wears on" with "tourists" and "trolling married guys"; "there's little to distin-guish the place" from the "typical Midtown Irish bar", save for its "staff of Ireland's finest."

Magician ⌐

	16	12	20	$6

LES | 118 Rivington St. (Essex St.) | F/J/M/Z to Delancey/Essex Sts. | 212-673-7851

There's "minimal" decor at this "blank-canvas", no-tricks LES bar-room, but that doesn't faze the "hipsters" who barrel in for "strong" pops at "cheap" tabs (particularly during the "midnight happy hour"); since it's a magnet for local bloggers, you can always "get tomorrow's blog entries here tonight."

Maker's

	▽ 13	10	17	$8

Murray Hill | 405 Third Ave. (bet. 28th & 29th Sts.) | 6 to 28th St. | 212-779-0306 | www.makersbar.com

Part of the Murray Hill bar crawl, this "local" stop works for a "no-frills" drink, even if a "makeover removed some of the 'dive' but also a lot of the charm"; like many of its neighbors, it draws plenty of "drunken frat boys during happy hour", particularly the "overflow" from Tonic East next door.

Malachy's

	14	9	18	$7

W 70s | 103 W. 72nd St. (bet. B'way & Columbus Ave.) | 1/2/3 to 72nd St. | 212-874-4268

An "old-fashioned", "Mickey Rourke" type of joint, this UWS Irish "dive" is populated by "authentic barflies" and Juilliard students; your feet may "stick to the floor" (and the "fried clams will stick to your ribs"), but "if you need an ego boost", "compare yourself with anyone else around."

Mama's Bar

	22	16	20	$7

E Village | 34 Ave. B (3rd St.) | F/V to Lower East Side/2nd Ave. | 212-777-5729 | www.mamasfoodshop.com

An "antidote to the theme-parking of the East Village", this "no-nonsense" spot "makes you feel at home" – assuming your abode's a "grungy" amalgam of distressed concrete and flea-market furniture; its "relaxing atmosphere", "infused vodkas" and eats from Mama's Food Shop next door draw a crowd that "doesn't take itself too seriously."

NEW Manhattans, The

	-	-	-	I

Prospect Heights | 769 Washington Ave. (bet. Grand Ave. & Sterling Pl.) | Brooklyn | 2/3 to Eastern Pkwy. | 917-349-8922

Provocateur Tracy Westmoreland, owner of the fabled Siberia, brings his sketchy take on nightlife to Prospect Heights via this new dive where bottom-shelf booze, tag-sale decor and dirt-cheap deals come with the territory; the only wild card is whether his core following – blotto journos and those who love to drink with them – are up for the schlep to Brooklyn.

Manitoba's

	21	23	23	$5

E Village | 99 Ave. B (bet. 6th & 7th Sts.) | F/V to Lower East Side/2nd Ave. | 212-982-2511 | www.manitobas.com

"Just right for the neighborhood", this "real-deal" East Village bar-room is owned (and occasionally manned) by Dictators front man

'Handsome Dick' Manitoba, the "king of men"; there's "no trendy garbage" at this "hard-core biker hangout" – just "cheap beer", "vintage rock photos" and "Blondie and the Ramones" on its "cool" jukebox.

Mannahatta

NoHo | 310 Bowery (1st St.) | 6 to Bleecker St. | 212-477-1979 | www.mannahatta.us

Ok, it's "not as big or exciting" as its previous incarnation up the street, but this Bowery "post-college" magnet is still manna for "rowdy" "under-25" types who "pack in" to the front bar and "happening" DJ lounge in back; critics nix the "lowbrow crowd" and "lack of character", but admit it's an "easy door."

Mantra

E 50s | 986 Second Ave. (bet. 52nd & 53rd Sts.) | 6 to 51st St./Lexington Ave. | 212-813-1595 | www.mantra986.com

An island of "Meatpacking attitude" in a "sea of frat bars", this bi-level Midtowner gives "20s-to-30s singles" a "cool" destination once they're past the "picky" door; its "clubby appeal" combines minimal lines, flashy fixtures and "thumping music", but "beware of B&Ters."

Margarita Murphy's

Murray Hill | 591 Third Ave. (bet. 38th & 39th Sts.) | 4/5/6/7/S to 42nd St./Grand Central | 212-684-4421

Supposedly an "Irish-Mexican" medley, this Murray Hill "local bar" proves most appealing to Greeks fresh from frat row looking for "after-work" guzzles and "warm service" for "reasonable" tabs; maybe the hybrid notion's weak, but the margaritas are "strong", so "does it matter?"

Marie's Crisis ⊄

W Village | 59 Grove St. (bet. Bleecker St. & 7th Ave. S.) | 1 to Christopher St. | 212-243-9323

"Submerge yourself in show tunes" at this mostly gay West Village piano bar, a "dumpy" "rumpus room" that's an "absolute howl" thanks to the sing-along-happy crowd, a mix of "real divas", "Broadway geeks" and "hen parties"; no problem if you "don't know the words" – there's a "roomful of queens more than happy to shout them all in your ear."

⊠ Marquee

Chelsea | 289 10th Ave. (bet. 26th & 27th Sts.) | C/E to 23rd St. | 646-473-0202 | www.marqueeny.com

Sure, it's "been around awhile" and may be "a little more democratic" than before, but most report this West Chelsea club still provides the expected "door drama" unless you are "knockout gorgeous", "know somebody or, better yet, *are* somebody"; no surprise, it's "best during the week", the "most fun is in the VIP room" and, as for the service, "models might look good but they suck at waitressing."

Mars Bar ⊄

E Village | 25 E. First St. (2nd Ave.) | F/V to Lower East Side/2nd Ave. | no phone

The "roaches wave hello" when you enter what could be the "most disgusting bar in the city", this East Village "dinosaur" where the "crud on the walls" and "graffiti on the ceiling" keep the "happy drunks" inside entertained; it's a good place to "work through an existential crisis", so long as you "wear boots" and "don't use the bathroom."

	APPEAL	DECOR	SERVICE	COST

Marshall Stack
22 | 18 | 22 | $7

LES | 66 Rivington St. (Allen St.) | F/V to Lower East Side/2nd Ave. |
212-228-4667 | www.themarshallstack.com

"Not trashy" but "not sceney" either, this "tin-ceilinged" LES rock 'n' roll
joint may be named for a bank of stage amps but keeps the dial on "mellow" for "laid-back" types with an "array of beers" and "eclectic wines";
it marshals "lots of character", and the "classic jukebox" is way "hot."

Martini Red ⊄
19 | 14 | 18 | $8

Staten Island | 372 Van Duzer St. (Beach St.) | 718-442-0660 |
www.martini-red.com

A "good mix of music" courtesy of open-mike auteurs, DJs and live
bands of all stripes makes this Staten Island "attempt at bohemia" a
handy "hangout" in a land of limited options; just be ready for thrift-
store trappings and a crimson-walled, garishly "grungy" space.

Mason Dixon
17 | 16 | 16 | $8

LES | 133 Essex St. (bet. Rivington & Stanton Sts.) | F/J/M/Z to Delancey/
Essex Sts. | 212-260-4100 | www.masondixonnyc.com

A "touch of Texas" on the LES, this rough-hewn saloon is a "Southern-
fried" "post-college rodeo" complete with a "pen in the back" where easy
riders mount its "mechanical bull"; yup, it's "kind of cheesy", but "kick
back and have a Lone Star" and you'll see why it "draws them in."

Matchless ⊄
21 | 17 | 20 | $9

Greenpoint | 557 Manhattan Ave. (Driggs Ave.) | Brooklyn | G to
Nassau Ave. | 718-383-5333 | www.barmatchless.com

Way "less hipster" than Enid's across the street, this "regular bar" in
Greenpoint set in a converted auto-parts store is a "no-worries" haunt
known for "reasonably priced" microbrews and "live music"; for "neighborhood" denizens seeking "low-key" quaffing, it's a perfect match.

Max Fish ⊄
17 | 17 | 16 | $7

LES | 178 Ludlow St. (bet. Houston & Stanton Sts.) | F/V to Lower East Side/
2nd Ave. | 212-529-3959 | www.maxfish.com

A "favorite" since 1989, this funky "original" has "survived the gentrification" of the Lower East Side and "hasn't changed a bit"; sure, it's
"still too bright" and the crowd's as "eclectic" as ever (think "art
school alumni", "preppies", "trust-fund kiddies"), though it seems to
be getting "younger and younger" every day.

NEW Mayahuel
- | - | - | M

E Village | 304 E. Sixth St. (2nd Ave.) | 6 to Astor Pl. | no phone

Tequila gets the star treatment at this new cocktail bar duplex set on
the East Village's Curry Row; though the design is a bit schizophrenic –
the coolly chic street level is reminiscent of La Esquina, while the
crimson-lit second floor is more Madame X – the well crafted cocktails (from a Death & Co alum) are right on the money.

M Bar
20 | 18 | 20 | $13

W 40s | Mansfield Hotel | 12 W. 44th St. (bet. 5th & 6th Aves.) | 7/B/D/
F/V to 42nd St./Bryant Park | 212-277-8888 | www.mansfieldhotel.com

The Mansfield Hotel's "swanky", "old-school" bar is a hush-hush
"hideout" for "upscale" Midtown types with a "fancy library" feel that
includes a domed skylight; "excellent" albeit "costly" drinks and "un-

obtrusive" background music make it an m-peccable spot for a "quiet" tot that's guaranteed to "impress a date."

McAleer's Pub
15 | 10 | 16 | $6

W 80s | 425 Amsterdam Ave. (bet. 80th & 81st Sts.) | 1 to 79th St. | 212-362-7867 | www.mcaleerspub.com

This "dark" UWS Irish "dive" has "been there forever" and is "not a bad option when the other places on the Amsterdam strip are over-crowded"; the decor may be "down 'n' dirty" and the service so-so, "but that's part of the charm" – along with the "low prices."

McCormack's
19 | 16 | 22 | $7

Murray Hill | 365 Third Ave. (26th St.) | 6 to 28th St. | 212-683-0911 | www.mccormacks.net

"Watch English soccer" and "international rugby games" at this "Irish-all-the-way" Murray Hill pub that has upgraded its viewing capabili-ties, adding four plasma screens; otherwise, it's a fairly "predictable" Guinness dispenser with a fair number of "old men" in attendance.

McCoy's Bar
17 | 14 | 19 | $9

W 50s | 768 Ninth Ave. (bet. 51st & 52nd Sts.) | C/E to 50th St. | 212-957-8055 | www.mccoysnyc.com

"Make it through the recession" at this Hell's Kitchen Irish "joint", an "old-school holdout" where a "very local" clientele "kicks back" over "inexpensive" hooch and takes in sports on multiple tubes; "typical" to some, it's a bona fide "hometown" bar to others.

McFadden's
15 | 13 | 15 | $8

E 40s | 800 Second Ave. (42nd St.) | 4/5/6/7/S to 42nd St./Grand Central | 212-986-1515 | www.mcfaddens42.com

"Life is one big frat party" at this Midtown Irish pub that can get "packed tighter than a woman's suitcase" with the crowds "overflowing onto the sidewalk"; it's such a "total meat market" that you "needn't bother re-moving your wedding ring", but "watch out or you'll get trampled."

McGee's
∇ 15 | 13 | 20 | $8

W 50s | 240 W. 55th St. (bet. B'way & 8th Ave.) | 1/A/B/C/D to 59th St./Columbus Circle | 212-957-3536

"Just another Irish pub", this Midtowner is "perfect pre- or post-theater" and "enough off the beaten path that the tourists don't know about it"; the tri-level space is warmed by a fireplace.

McSorley's ⊄
23 | 16 | 17 | $6

E Village | 15 E. Seventh St. (bet. 2nd & 3rd Aves.) | 6 to Astor Pl. | 212-254-2570 | www.mcsorleysnewyork.com

"History covers every inch" of this "sawdust-floored" East Villager, on the scene since 1854 and the "prototype of every bar that pretends to have been open forever"; there are "only two beers to choose from" here – "light or dark" – and the "gruff", "drink-up-or-get-out" barkeeps "put up with no guff", but the "atmosphere makes up for everything."

McSwiggan's
12 | 8 | 16 | $7

Gramercy | 393 Second Ave. (bet. 22nd & 23rd Sts.) | 6 to 23rd St. | 212-683-3180

Although "freshly scrubbed", this "old shack" in Gramercy Park still strikes most as a "dive" with the requisite "cheap drinks" and Irish barmen; it transforms itself daily from an "old-man's bar in the afternoon" to a "college-kid hangout in the evening."

Megu
24 | 29 | 23 | $15

(aka M Lounge at Megu)

TriBeCa | 62 Thomas St. (bet. Church St. & W. B'way) | 1/2/3 to Chambers St. | 212-964-7777 | www.megunyc.com

"Everything's impressive – including the bill" – at this ultra-"slick" TriBeCan featuring a "high-tech" mezzanine bar that offers the opportunity to "look down at the ice Buddha sculpture without having to pay the sky-high dinner prices"; it also proffers a "fabulous" list of sakes, though imbibers "wish it got a larger crowd."

Mehanata
19 | 16 | 16 | $11

LES | 113 Ludlow St. (bet. Delancey & Rivington Sts.) | F/J/M/Z to Delancey/Essex Sts. | 212-625-0981 | www.mehanata.com

This "trashy Bulgarian" bar brings two floors of "high-energy" Slavic scenery to the LES, complete with a "tiki bar", live "Balkan music" and "sweaty disco" action on the "large dance floor"; maybe "there are cooler places", but its "motley" admirers claim it has "its own special appeal."

Merc Bar
23 | 21 | 20 | $12

SoHo | 151 Mercer St. (bet. Houston & Prince Sts.) | N/R/W to Prince St. | 212-966-2727 | www.mercbar.com

Go "Downtown and feel Upstate" at this "dark" SoHo "classic", done up in a "Rustic Swank" style with "tall ceilings" and "cozy ski lodge" decor; "one of the city's first lounges", it's a "well-kept local secret" with "no hassle to enter", so there's "no need to camp outside to get in."

Mercer Bar
23 | 21 | 19 | $14

SoHo | Mercer Hotel | 99 Prince St. (Mercer St.) | N/R/W to Prince St. | 212-966-5454 | www.jean-georges.com

"Interesting, attractive people" toy with "strong" cocktails at this "classy" SoHo hotel bar that's a bit "past its peak", though no one's informed the "standoff-ish staff" (except perhaps "Russell Crowe"); however, it usually delivers a "solid performance" enlivened by the off-chance that you'll actually "glimpse a celebrity."

Merchants, N.Y.
18 | 18 | 18 | $11

Chelsea | 112 Seventh Ave. (bet. 16th & 17th Sts.) | 1 to 18th St. | 212-366-7267

E 60s | 1125 First Ave. (62nd St.) | 4/5/6/N/R/W to 59th St./Lexington Ave. | 212-832-1551

Financial District | 90 Washington St. (Rector St.) | 1/R/W to Rector St. | 212-363-6000

www.merchantsny.com

Relax and "nurse an affordable drink" at these "upscale" bar/restaurants that draw "decent crowds" with their "loungey feel" and "no-attitude" attitude; sure, there's "not much action" to be had and wags tag them "Manhattan's answer to Bennigan's", but nicotine fiends like First Avenue's "great cigar bar" where indoor inhaling is legal.

Mercury Bar
16 | 14 | 16 | $10

Murray Hill | 493 Third Ave. (bet. 33rd & 34th Sts.) | 6 to 33rd St. | 212-683-2645
W 40s | 659 Ninth Ave. (46th St.) | C/E to 50th St. | 212-262-7755
www.mercurybarnyc.com

"Drunk suits" chase "super-toasted" skirts at the Murray Hill branch of this sports bar duo that's "indistinguishable from all the rest on that stretch of Third Avenue"; "if you'd like to be able to hear anyone speak", try the "more laid-back" Hell's Kitchen edition.

Mercury Lounge
20 | 13 | 15 | $8

LES | 217 E. Houston St. (bet. Essex & Ludlow Sts.) | F/V to Lower East Side/2nd Ave. | 212-260-4700 | www.mercuryloungenyc.com

Hear music the "way it's supposed to be heard" at this "intimate" (read: "small") Lower Eastsider where "up-and-coming bands" start out "before they graduate to the Bowery Ballroom"; patrons agree the "divey", narrow bar area is "always crowded", but split on the sound system: "top-rate" vs. "stinks."

Merkato 55
22 | 22 | 18 | $15

Meatpacking | 55 Gansevoort St. (bet. Greenwich & Washington Sts.) | A/C/E/L to 14th St./8th Ave. | 212-255-8555 | www.merkato55nyc.com

Late night, the bar at this "upscale African restaurant" in the Meatpacking District serves "inventive", "high-priced" cocktails accompanied by "exotic" small plates, but "at the moment", it's best known for its Saturday brunch, a "loud" and "crazy" "complete party scene" that's sort of "like brunching at Studio 54" with a "predictable" "Eurotrash" crowd.

Metro 53
16 | 15 | 17 | $8

E 50s | 307 E. 53rd St. (bet. 1st & 2nd Aves.) | E/V to Lexington Ave./53rd St. | 212-838-0007 | www.metro53.com

This "average" East Side bar tries to stand out from the pack with a "cavernous", bi-level setting and an "abundance of TVs" broadcasting sports; still, its "mainstream" following calls it "hit-or-miss": it's either "Siberia" or "so crowded that the whole room has to shift if you want to move."

Metro Grill Roof Garden
20 | 14 | 15 | $15

Garment District | Metro Hotel | 45 W. 35th St. (bet. 5th & 6th Aves.) | B/D/F/N/Q/R/V/W to 34th St./Herald Sq. | 212-279-3535 | www.hotelmetronyc.com

"Get away from the local grime" at this "surprise" seasonal rooftop crowning a Garment District hotel, a roomy if "plain" setup "overlooking the nearby Empire State Building"; it gives low-maintenance types somewhere to meet "after work", though the unimpressed protest it's "a little too shabby" for the "pricey" tabs.

Metropolitan ⊄
∇ 19 | 13 | 18 | $6

Williamsburg | 559 Lorimer St. (bet. Devoe St. & Metropolitan Ave.) | Brooklyn | G/L to Metropolitan Ave./Lorimer St. | 718-599-4444

Although known as a "gay hipster" haunt, this Williamsburg "neighborhood" barroom also draws heteros to its "campy cool" quarters done up like an "old general store" (enhanced by "two fireplaces" and a "patio as big as all Brooklyn"); better still, there's "plenty of standing room", the mood's "friendly" and the "bartenders don't skimp on the drinks."

Metropolitan Museum Roof Garden   26 | 24 | 14 | $12

E 80s | Metropolitan Museum of Art | 1000 Fifth Ave. (bet. 81st & 82nd Sts.) | 4/5/6 to 86th St. | 212-879-5500

"Unbelievable views" of the skyline and Central Park are the draws at this seasonal rooftop atop the Metropolitan Museum that's only open late (late being 8:30 PM) on Fridays and Saturdays; despite "looong lines", "not enough service" and "expensive" drinks served in "plastic cups", this "wonderful escape" is a chance to experience "NY at its finest."

Metropolitan Room   20 | 19 | 17 | $14

Flatiron | 34 W. 22nd St. (bet. 5th & 6th Aves.) | F/V to 23rd St. | 212-206-0440 | www.metropolitanroom.com

Presenting "civilized entertainment" for both the "over-45 set" and the "iPod generation", this "sophisticated" Flatiron cabaret provides the chance to "hear legends alongside up-and-coming stars" in an "intimate" room; despite some "poor views" from the sidelines, it's "nice to be so close" to the talent – "and they make a mean martini."

Michael Jordan's The Steak House NYC   20 | 20 | 18 | $14

E 40s | Grand Central Terminal | West Balcony (42nd St. & Vanderbilt Ave.) | 4/5/6/7/S to 42nd St./Grand Central | 212-655-2300 | www.theglaziergroup.com

Folks "waiting for Metro North" or "looking to meet a married man" settle in at this "high-end commuter hangout" on a mezzanine overlooking Grand Central Concourse; the "strong pours" and "knockout view" of all the "hustle-bustle" compensate for the "overpricing" – indeed, some find it "hard to leave to catch the train."

Mickey Mantle's   18 | 19 | 17 | $11

W 50s | 42 Central Park S. (bet. 5th & 6th Aves.) | N/R/W to 5th Ave./59th St. | 212-688-7777 | www.mickeymantles.com

"If you like baseball stuff", this "cheerful" sports bar-cum-No. 7 shrine on Central Park South bats out "ok" food and drink in a "Disneyland"-esque, "memorabilia"-laden setting; though athletic supporters say this "tourist" magnet is a "steady hit", they admit it's "not a hall-of-famer."

Milady's   13 | 6 | 14 | $6

SoHo | 160 Prince St. (Thompson St.) | N/R/W to Prince St. | 212-226-9340

"One of the few hold-out neighborhood dives" in "trendy" SoHo, this "untrendy" barroom with "no atmosphere to speak of" is refreshingly "low-key"; still, foes feel "other than the cheap beer", there's "no reason" to show up given the abundance of "other options" to choose from.

☑ Milk and Honey ⌀   27 | 22 | 26 | $15

LES | 134 Eldridge St. (bet. Broome & Delancey Sts.) | J/M/Z to Bowery | 718-308-6881 | www.milkandhoneynyc.com

"Hard to find" and even "harder to get into", this "hush-hush" Lower Eastsider is a "speakeasy in the best sense", accessed only by reserving a booth in advance (the once-secret phone number has been made public); the payoff is "superb cocktails" mixed by "hard-working" bartenders, and though it's "becoming less exclusive", "professional drinkers" report this is "still a very special place" indeed.

miniBar

                                                          ∇ | 20 | 17 | 21 | $7 |

Carroll Gardens | 482 Court St. (bet. 4th & Luquer Sts.) | Brooklyn | F/G to Carroll St. | 718-569-2321 | www.minibarbrooklyn.com

"They aren't kidding about the 'mini' part", but this Carroll Gardens "neighborhood spot" packs maximum personality into its "tiny" dimensions with respectable by-the-glass wines, a "tasty" bourbon selection and "super-friendly" service.

Minton's

                                                          | 23 | 19 | 17 | $12 |

Harlem | 208 W. 118th St. (bet. Adam Clayton Powell Jr. Blvd. & St. Nicholas Ave.) | 2/3 to 116th St. | 212-864-8346 | www.uptownatmintons.com

A "slice of history" from back in the day, this revival of the "classic" Harlem club where cats like Miles, Bird and Diz first began to bop is once again a mecca for "genuine jazz" with nightly shows from "excellent", tradition-minded talents; the room's unfortunately been stripped of its original detail, but the vintage neon sign out front is intact.

MO Bar

                                                          | 23 | 24 | 20 | $17 |

W 60s | Mandarin Oriental Hotel | 80 Columbus Circle, 35th fl. (60th St.) | 1/A/B/C/D to 59th St./Columbus Circle | 212-805-8800 | www.mandarinoriental.com

There's "lots of glitz" in store at this "tiny but beautiful" hotel bar in Columbus Circle's Mandarin Oriental where "businessmen", "out-of-towners" and "couples on first dates" show up for stiff drinks at "stiff prices"; since the windows overlook the "offices next door", insiders suggest the adjoining lobby lounge where seating is limited but the Central Park views are "spectacular."

Mocca

                                                          ∇ | 21 | 20 | 21 | $11 |

TriBeCa | 78 Reade St. (Church St.) | 1/2/3 to Chambers St. | 212-233-7570 | www.moccalounge.com

Coffeehouse by day, lounge by night, this "small" but "upscale" TriBeCan is just the ticket when you "can't quite decide what you want"; large windows and a "pleasant" contemporary look make it a natural for after-work drinks spiced up by "good people-watching."

Moda Outdoors

                                                          | 20 | 16 | 15 | $11 |

W 50s | Flatotel | 135 W. 52nd St. (bet. 6th & 7th Aves.) | B/D/F/V to 47-50th Sts./Rockefeller Ctr. | 212-887-9880 | www.flatotel.com

Even "suits" can have "fun in the summer" thanks to this seasonal hotel bar set in a Midtown atrium walkway, a "convenient place to gather" for an "after-work" recharge as the "pedestrians breeze past"; the "fresh air" is "always appreciated", though the "lively" crowd subsides as evening drinkers switch to commuter mode.

☑ Modern, The

                                                          | 25 | 26 | 21 | $15 |

W 50s | MoMA | 9 W. 53rd St. (bet. 5th & 6th Aves.) | E/V to 5th Ave./53rd St. | 212-333-1220 | www.themodernnyc.com

A "hot spot with cool written all over it", this "crisp, clean" barroom "where style is everything" adjoins Danny Meyer's "swanky" MoMA restaurant; it "lives up to the hype" with "interesting" drinks, "excellent" service and "terrific" nibbles, so even though it's decidedly "expensive", "if you're lucky enough to get a seat at the bar, *don't move.*"

	APPEAL	DECOR	SERVICE	COST

Moe's ✏

Fort Greene | 80 Lafayette Ave. (S. Portland Ave.) | Brooklyn | C to
Lafayette Ave. | 718-797-9536

22 | 20 | 20 | $9

An "incredibly diverse" cross section of Fort Greene's "entire neighborhood demographic" (notably "hipsters of every shape, size and
color") keeps this "cool" joint "mad packed late-night"; mixing the
warmth of *Cheers* with the "irony of *The Simpsons*", it's also a dandy
"warm-up before hitting the city."

Molly Pitcher's Ale House

E 80s | 1641 Second Ave. (85th St.) | 4/5/6 to 86th St. | 212-249-3068 |
www.mollysalehouseny.com

21 | 19 | 21 | $7

The "hours tend to slip away with mystifying speed" at this
"Americanized Irish" sports bar on the Upper East Side that routinely
manages to "bring in a crowd"; formerly Fitzpatrick's, it's been "renovated" into something very "clean", though the adjoining snug has
more of a "pub feel."

Molly's

Gramercy | 287 Third Ave. (bet. 22nd & 23rd Sts.) | 6 to 23rd St. |
212-889-3361 | www.mollysshebeen.com

22 | 19 | 22 | $8

"Like being back in the old country", this "ultimate" Gramercy Irish
pub features "sawdust on the floor", "toasty" logs on the fire and
"sweet" sons of Erin behind the bar (who've "been there for years");
proudly "old-fashioned", it also pours one of the "best pints of
Guinness in the city."

Monday Room

NoLita | 210 Elizabeth St. (bet. Prince & Spring Sts.) | 6 to Spring St. |
212-343-7011 | www.themondayroom.com

▽ 24 | 26 | 26 | $14

A "superb wine bar" – minus the bar – this "intimate" enclave of
old-school style hidden in the NoLita eatery Public provides "comfortable" leather seating and a "super-fun" staff decanting an "outstanding" 60-label list; the small plates on offer are equally
"scrumptious", and the "totally relaxed" vibe works well "any day
of the week."

M1-5 Bar

TriBeCa | 52 Walker St. (bet. B'way & Church St.) | 1 to Canal St. |
212-965-1701 | www.m1-5.com

17 | 15 | 17 | $10

High ceilings and "tons of space" lend this "warehousey" TriBeCa bar
a "loft atmosphere" as its "mature" regulars assemble to shoot stick
or catch a flick on the projection screen; on the other hand, it's way
"out of the way" ("where the heck am I?") and there's "not a lot going
on" most nights.

☒ Monkey Bar

E 50s | Elysée Hotel | 60 E. 54th St. (bet. Madison & Park Aves.) | E/V
to Lexington Ave./53rd St. | 212-308-2950

- | - | - | E

Now owned by *Vanity Fair* editor Graydon Carter, this "glamorous"
Midtown hotel bar is as "classic" as ever, "right out of an episode of
Mad Men" with its beloved simian murals intact; after work, it's quite
the "lively" scene for younger types, while later in the evening, "older,
sophisticated" sorts move in and "go bananas" over the "tradition"
and "appropriately overpriced" pops.

Monkey Town

▽ 21 | 24 | 21 | $8

Williamsburg | 58 N. Third St. (bet. Kent & Wythe Aves.) | Brooklyn | L to Bedford Ave. | 718-384-1369 | www.monkeytownhq.com

Video art is the name of the game at this "novel" Williamsburg eatery/ performance space where the festively decorated front dining room is overshadowed by a spectacular back area fitted out on all four walls with mammoth screens; the programming ranges from the "indie" to the mainstream, though its "bathroom soundscapes" are pointedly avant-garde.

Monster, The ⊘

16 | 13 | 14 | $11

G Village | 80 Grove St. (bet. Waverly Pl. & W. 4th St.) | 1 to Christopher St. | 212-924-3558 | www.manhattan-monster.com

The "'70s don't seem to have ever ended" at this bi-level "blast from the past", one of the "last holdouts from the Village's gay golden age"; upstairs, "show-tune queens" belt out the Judy Garland songbook at the piano, while below some "seriously retro dance music" keeps the crowd of tourists and "neighborhood regulars" hopping.

Moomia Lounge

18 | 17 | 18 | $14

Little Italy | 157 Lafayette St. (bet. Grand & Howard Sts.) | 4/5/6/J/ M/N/R/Q/W to Canal St. | 212-219-4006 | www.moomianyc.com

"Major hieroglyphics" on the walls meet "techno music" on the speakers at this Egyptian-themed Little Italy duplex, a place to party Nile-style with decor that "looks like the inside of a pyramid" (complete with a sarcophagus-equipped downstairs VIP room); flavored hookahs, belly dancers and a many-martini'd menu give you your mummy's worth.

Moonshine ⊘

▽ 19 | 16 | 23 | $5

Red Hook | 317 Columbia St. (bet. Hamilton Ave. & Woodhull St.) | Brooklyn | F/G to Smith/9th Sts. | 718-852-8057 | www.brooklynmoonshine.com

Locals in the Red Hook backwoods take a shine to this "faux white-trash" joint boasting the requisite "great bourbon selection" (chased with "cheap canned brews"), "country classics" on the juke and a summer "beer garden"; if the whereabouts is a "transportation black hole", that's to be expected for a "diamond in the rough."

Moran's Chelsea

19 | 18 | 22 | $12

Chelsea | 146 10th Ave. (19th St.) | C/E to 23rd St. | 212-627-3030 | www.moranschelsea.com

Ok, it's "out of the way", but this longtime Chelsea Gaelic steakhouse is worth a trip for its "beautiful" setting in a circa-1834 building; regulars drop by to "warm up in front of the fire" and bend an elbow at the ancient cherry wood bar, vowing that this "great standby" is "always going to be there."

Morgans Bar

22 | 22 | 19 | $14

Murray Hill | Morgans Hotel | 237 Madison Ave. (bet. 37th & 38th Sts.) | 6 to 33rd St. | 212-726-7600 | www.morganshotelgroup.com

For "secluded canoodling", this "secret rendezvous" in a "dimly lit" Murray Hill hotel basement is just the ticket, lined with "candles" and "squishy sofas", and "never too crowded"; since it's "off most radar screens" these days, the crowd's mainly comprised of "after-dinner" revelers from Asia de Cuba next door.

	APPEAL	DECOR	SERVICE	COST

Morimoto

25 | 26 | 23 | $17

Chelsea | 88 10th Ave. (bet. 15th & 16th Sts.) | A/C/E/L to 14th St./ 8th Ave. | 212-989-8883 | www.morimotonyc.com

One "swanky" West Chelsea joint, this Japanese juggernaut from Iron Chef Masaharu Morimoto extends its "sleek" style to a "minimalist" downstairs lounge, done in concrete and plasticine with a translucent bar, stacked-bottle walls and "must-see toilets"; the "high-tech" atmosphere matched with "expertly mixed" cocktails and "divine" sakes is dizzyingly "amazing", and priced accordingly.

Morrell Wine Bar

24 | 20 | 20 | $15

W 40s | 1 Rockefeller Plaza (49th St., bet. 5th & 6th Aves.) | B/D/F/V to 47-50th Sts./Rockefeller Ctr. | 212-262-7700 | www.morrellwinebar.com

Don't mind the "tourist-crazed location" in Rockefeller Center (and the "hard-to-find" seating): this "oenophile's delight" offers an "amazing by-the-glass selection" and is particularly worthwhile if you can nab one of the "few outside tables"; if the pricing seems "higher than necessary", the same bottles are cheaper at the retail shop next door.

NEW Mother's

▽ 19 | 18 | 20 | $10

Williamsburg | 347 Graham Ave. (bet. Conselyea St. & Metropolitan Ave.) | Brooklyn | L to Graham Ave. | 718-384-7778

"Another bar in Williamsburg", this no-frills newcomer (the sister of Daddy's down the street) offers a "decent" selection of beer and wine for locals with "limited budgets"; a nonworking fireplace and wall of antique mirrors serve as decor, while a standard-issue back patio is pleasant during warm weather.

Moto ⊟

▽ 24 | 27 | 19 | $9

Williamsburg | 394 Broadway (Hooper St.) | Brooklyn | J/M to Hewes St. | 718-599-6895 | www.circa1938.com

"Cool" is the motto of this "great-looking" bar/eatery in the Williamsburg "hinterland", a noirish niche with flaking walls, hardwood seating and a slate-top bar vending choice beers and wines; "great live jazz" boosts the "hip" factor, but given that it's been "discovered", it can be a "tight squeeze."

Motor City ⊟

18 | 20 | 17 | $6

LES | 127 Ludlow St. (bet. Delancey & Rivington Sts.) | F/J/M/Z to Delancey/Essex Sts. | 212-358-1595 | www.motorcitybar.com

For "rock 'n' roll the right way", check out this "solid" LES salute to "old-school" Detroit that attracts a "hard-core" crowd; the "DJ does a decent job" spinning yesteryear's "punk hits", while the "truck-stop" decor is "run-down" yet somehow "semi-charming."

Mr. Black ⊟

20 | 15 | 14 | $12

Garment District | 251 W. 30th St. (bet. 7th & 8th Aves.) | A/C/E to 34th St./Penn Station | 212-695-2747 | www.mrblacknyc.com

Transplanted yet again, this 3.0 take on the gay dance den is now camping out in the Rebel space in the Garment District; although the scene is "not like the NoHo original", it's still "packed to the gills", the music is as "fantastic" as ever and the crowd the same mix of "pretty boys" and "small-time Logo celebs"; N.B. get out your handkerchiefs: the infamous cocktail waiter The Ass has retired.

Mr. Dennehy's
20 | 14 | 20 | $7

G Village | 63 Carmine St. (bet. Bedford St. & 7th Ave. S.) | A/B/C/D/
E/F/V to W. 4th St. | 212-414-1223 | www.mrdennehys.com
This "typical" Irish pub may be "hidden" in the West Village but
has a "Midtown feel" thanks to "plenty of TVs" beaming "sporting
events" and "warm" barkeeps tapping the "usual pint faves"; some
say "pedestrian", but at least it's "never too crowded" and there are
"no tourists" about.

NEW Mr. West
20 | 17 | 17 | $14

Chelsea | 559 W. 22nd St. (bet. 10th & 11th Aves.) | C/E to 23rd St. |
212-414-8700 | www.mrwestlounge.com
Behind its "black box" exterior, this "intimate" West Chelsea lounge
impresses with a "sexy new design" featuring "unique lighting" and
"cozy" banquettes embroidering a "tiny" dance floor; it brings the
"models-and-bottles" scene down to a "manageable" size, but be prepared for a "difficult door" and top-tier tabs.

Z NEW M2
20 | 21 | 17 | $15

Chelsea | 530 W. 28th St. (bet. 10th & 11th Aves.) | C/E to 23rd St. |
212-629-9000 | www.m2ultralounge.com
The "T. rex" of ultra-lounges, this "cavernous" South Beach import set
in West Chelsea's "old Crobar" space offers a "great open layout" furnished with a super-sized fireplace, circular chandeliers, book-lined
walls and private skyboxes; be prepared to "spend a pretty penny",
and given the "huge" dimensions, "exclusivity isn't really an option" –
particularly on the "B&T-to-the-max" weekends.

Muddy Cup ⊄
∇ 17 | 18 | 20 | $9

Staten Island | 388 Van Duzer St. (Beach St.) | 718-818-8100
Though it may be "Staten Island's antonym to Starbucks", this
"small, relaxing" take on a "'60s coffeehouse" is actually an outpost of the statewide chain; nevertheless, there's a "variety of entertainment" that includes "open-mike" nights, poetry readings
and the like.

Mug's Ale House
25 | 12 | 23 | $5

Williamsburg | 125 Bedford Ave. (N. 10th St.) | Brooklyn | L to Bedford Ave. |
718-486-8232 | www.mugsalehouse.com
A "classic old-school boozer", this "top-notch" Williamsburg ale-
house pours a "wide array of premium suds" in "unpretentious"
(i.e. "kinda divey") digs; despite a "considerable blue-collar" following and a "not-good male-to-female ratio", there are plenty of
hipsters on tap due to those "dirt-cheap prices" and "surprisingly
good" pub grub.

Murphy & Gonzalez
17 | 16 | 19 | $10

G Village | 21 Waverly Pl. (Greene St.) | N/R/W to 8th St. | 212-529-1500 |
www.murphy-gonzalez.com
Smack in the "heart of NYU central", this Irish-Mexican hybrid is
home to "football-loving frat boys" and "gum-chewing girls" hankering for affordable tipples accompanied by "sports galore on the
wide-screens"; overlook the "silly" "identity crisis" – an "Irish pub
with nachos?" – and it's "serviceable" enough when you "want
to avoid crowds."

	APPEAL	DECOR	SERVICE	COST

Music Hall of Williamsburg
▽ 22 | 13 | 17 | $10

Williamsburg | 66 N. Sixth St. (bet. Kent & Wythe Aves.) | Brooklyn | L to Bedford Ave. | 718-486-5400 | www.musichallofwilliamsburg.com
Mingle with the "cool" cats and scope out "up-and-coming acts" at this Billyburg music venue (fka Northsix), a multilevel, "standing-room" affair with an industrial look tempered with "postmodern flair"; its three bars include a "roomy" downstairs, but hipsters here for the talent shrug "drinking is optional."

Mustang Grill
16 | 14 | 16 | $9

E 80s | 1633 Second Ave. (85th St.) | 4/5/6 to 86th St. | 212-744-9194 | www.mustanggrill.com
A "decent variety of tequila" ensures there's "always a party" in progress at this UES Southwesterner where the "festive" mood extends to "passageways to rooms and lounges you didn't realize were there"; still, foes fret about "not much atmosphere" and a staff "too busy to help you."

Mustang Harry's
17 | 16 | 18 | $10

Chelsea | 352 Seventh Ave. (bet. 29th & 30th Sts.) | 1/2/3 to 34th St./ Penn Station | 212-268-8930 | www.mustangharrys.com
"Beer guzzling frat boys", "trolling married guys" and random "jersey wearers" populate this "decent" Irish bar whose claim to fame is its close proximity to Penn Station and the Garden; sure, it may have a "suburban", "cookie-cutter" vibe, but that doesn't keep it from being "packed" "pre-concert, pre-game and pre-train."

Mustang Sally's
17 | 15 | 19 | $9

Chelsea | 324 Seventh Ave. (bet. 28th & 29th Sts.) | 1/2/3 to 34th St./ Penn Station | 212-695-3806 | www.mustangsallysny.com
Despite the "chain feel" and "no distinguishing characteristics", this funky Irish bar in the "dry area" around MSG and Penn Station draws a jumble of FIT students, sports fans and "Long Island railroaders"; on big game nights, "expect a crowd" and a "noisy" "rock 'n' roll" sound level.

Ñ ⊭
24 | 18 | 21 | $10

SoHo | 33 Crosby St. (bet. Broome & Grand Sts.) | 6 to Spring St. | 212-219-8856
Ok, it's "a bit dark", but "dark is better" at this "cavelike" wine-and-tapas dispenser since it helps disguise how "tiny" and "narrow" this SoHo "sardine case" really is; "delicious" small plates and sangria that's "as good as you'll find anywhere" keep the crowd "enthusiastic."

Naked Lunch
19 | 12 | 14 | $10

SoHo | 17 Thompson St. (bet. Canal & Grand Sts.) | A/C/E to Canal St. | 212-343-0828 | www.nakedlunchnyc.com
"Young" types "break it down" to "old-school '80s classics" at this "way too crowded" spot that could be the "frattiest bar in SoHo"; despite "no room" on the dance floor, "only one bathroom" and a constant "battle to get a drink", it still packs 'em in.

Nancy Whiskey Pub
17 | 9 | 19 | $7

TriBeCa | 1 Lispenard St. (W. B'way) | 1 to Canal St. | 212-226-9943 | www.nancywhiskeypub.com
"Firemen and cops" rub shoulders with "boho" types at this 42-year-old TriBeCa tavern, a "local dive" that really "smells like a bar" with

shuffleboard and "cheap beer" as the main attractions; as the ratings indicate, there's "not much decor" – but "who needs flash when all you want to do is get hammered?"

National Underground

▽ 23 | 18 | 20 | $12

LES | 159 E. Houston St. (bet. Allen & Eldridge Sts.) | F/V to Lower East Side/2nd Ave. | 212-475-0611

The former Martignetti Liquors digs have been made over into this LES "rock 'n' roll bar"/music club with a "divey" feel; the double-decker setup showcases acoustic acts upstairs and electric sets below, but no matter where you wind up, the tabs are moderate and the mood modest.

NEW Nectar

23 | 22 | 20 | $12

Harlem | 2235 Frederick Douglass Blvd. (bet. 120th & 121st Sts.) | A/B/C/D to 125th St. | 212-961-9622 | www.nectarwinenyc.com

"Just what Harlem needed", this "upscale wine bar" (spun off from next-door vino shop Harlem Vintage) pairs an "eclectic" by-the-glass list with "yummy" apps in a "groovy" contemporary setting; with its "mellow atmosphere" and occasional "jazzy" entertainment, it's an "easy" fit for "grown-ups."

Nevada Smith's

16 | 11 | 15 | $7

E Village | 74 Third Ave. (bet. 11th & 12th Sts.) | L to 3rd Ave. | 212-982-2591 | www.nevadasmiths.net

"Attention soccer fans": this East Village "dive" could be the city's "best footy bar", televising nearly "every game from Europe" starting with matches that begin at "7 AM"; after dark, it's just another "every-day sports bar" with the usual "NYU undergrads" and "sticky floors."

New York Comedy Club

18 | 14 | 16 | $15

Murray Hill | 241 E. 24th St. (bet. 2nd & 3rd Aves.) | 6 to 23rd St. | 212-696-5233 | www.newyorkcomedyclub.com

Helping you maintain your "NY sense of humor", this Murray Hill laugh factory features "quality local talent" and occasional major leaguers yukking it up in a "dive bar" setting; if hecklers aren't amused by the "so-so comedy", "cramped" seats and "pushy staff", at least the "drinks are strong enough" to trigger a few giggles.

Niagara & Lei Bar

19 | 14 | 18 | $7

E Village | 112 Ave. A (7th St.) | L to 1st Ave. | 212-420-9517 | www.niagarabar.com

A random "mess of the usual East Villagers" populates this fre-netic venue where "punks" share pints with "bankers" in the "crowded" bar; downstairs in the tiki lounge, "sweaty bodies" "bust a move" alongside go-go dancers, while "model wannabes monopolize the photo booth."

Night Hotel Bar

▽ 18 | 16 | 17 | $13

W 40s | Night Hotel | 132 W. 45th St. (bet. 6th & 7th Aves.) | B/D/F/V to 47-50th Sts./Rockefeller Ctr. | 212-835-9600 | www.nighthotelny.com

Decidedly "not as mainstream" as other Times Square options, this "intimate" bar/lounge in an *echt* Goth hotel is "done all in black" and caters to big spenders with "highly priced" tipples; it works well pre- or post-theater, and though typically "a little empty", that's "not nec-essarily a bad thing."

| | APPEAL | DECOR | SERVICE | COST |

Nikki Midtown
21 | 24 | 19 | $13

E 50s | 151 E. 50th St., 3rd fl. (bet. Lexington & 3rd Aves.) | 6 to 51st St./
Lexington Ave. | 212-753-1144 | www.nikkimidtown.com

The "beachside" club empire stretching from St. Barths to Sardinia brings "Miami to Midtown" via this "sexy" lounge featuring "dancing on tables", "dining in beds" and "half-naked waitresses sauntering about" in an "all-white, pillow-filled" interior; even though prices are "over the top" and the crowd more "suits" than "St. Tropez", some call it the "best thing to happen to this area since the Waldorf-Astoria."

925 Café & Cocktails
19 | 16 | 19 | $9

E 40s | 800 Second Ave. (42nd St.) | 4/5/6/7/S to 42nd St./Grand Central |
212-661-9125 | www.925nyc.com

A "welcome contrast to its neighboring frat bars" (McFadden's and Calico Jack's), this "good option for adults" near Tudor City offers "dim lighting" and low decibels geared toward a more "upscale" crowd; the only downside lies in the "breathing-room" department – the space reserved for customers is "barely wider than the bar itself."

99 Below
19 | 19 | 21 | $11

G Village | 99 MacDougal St., downstairs (bet. Bleecker &
W. 3rd Sts.) | A/B/C/D/E/F/V to W. 4th St. | 212-387-8292 |
www.99belownyc.com

Name checking its address and "below-street-level" location, this "cozy" Irish pub in the heart of MacDougal Street's frat row is a boxy, wood-lined number with the obligatory tap brews and greasy grub; pricing reflects NYU-size wallets.

Ninth Avenue Saloon ⊄
20 | 14 | 21 | $8

W 40s | 656 Ninth Ave. (46th St.) | C/E to 50th St. | 212-307-1503

Plain as its name, this "mellow" Hell's Kitchen gay bar is a "throw-back" tavern for a "mixed-age crowd" that "drinks beer and eyes each other" in "seedy" quarters; "cheap" pops and sporadic drag shows add incentive, though snoots sneer it's the kind of "dive" you'd find in "Topeka."

Nobu 57
25 | 24 | 22 | $16

W 50s | 40 W. 57th St. (bet. 5th & 6th Aves.) | F to 57th St. | 212-757-3000 |
www.noburestaurants.com

"Living up to the reputation of the original" outpost, this "knockout" Midtown Japanese is "trendy and understated at the same time", re-plete with an "airy" ground-floor bar that's bigger and "livelier than its TriBeCa counterpart" yet shares the same "extravagant design" and "great sake menu"; crowdwise, look for the usual power peeps "dressed to the nines", and as for the pricing, be ready to "wave your expense account around."

No Idea
17 | 9 | 18 | $7

Flatiron | 30 E. 20th St. (bet. B'way & Park Ave. S.) | 4/5/6/L/N/Q/R/W
to 14th St./Union Sq. | 212-777-0100 | www.noideabar.com

"Fresh college grads just off the train from Hoboken" head for this "popular" Flatiron "dive" best known for its "gargantuan mixed drinks" served in "pint glasses" (leaving some with "no idea who they hooked up with" the following morning); P.S. if your name matches their 'name of the day', "you drink for free."

	APPEAL	DECOR	SERVICE	COST

Nokia Theatre

21 | 19 | 17 | $11

W 40s | 1515 Broadway (44th St.) | 1/2/3/7/N/Q/R/S/W to 42nd St./ Times Sq. | 212-930-1950 | www.nokiatheatrenyc.com

"Very nicely done", this midsize Times Square music venue set in the former Astor Plaza movie house showcases "top-quality" talent in a "civilized" theater setup complete with "comfy stadium seating" and three bars; the "totally commercialized" approach subtracts some cred, but having the "floors actually clean" is a "pretty decent" trade-off.

No Malice Palace

19 | 16 | 16 | $8

E Village | 197 E. Third St. (bet. Aves. A & B) | F/V to Lower East Side/ 2nd Ave. | 212-254-9184 | www.nomalice.com

So "dark" that everyone "always looks good", this "true-to-the-neighborhood" East Villager is where "mellow locals" converge to enjoy the plush sofas, outdoor patio and overall "easygoing" mood; on weekends, however, it's more "hit-or-miss" when things "get out of hand."

Novecento

21 | 19 | 19 | $13

SoHo | 343 W. Broadway (bet. Broome & Grand Sts.) | C/E to Spring St. | 212-925-4706 | www.novecentogroup.com

For a "relaxed Buenos Aires vibe", this classy-but-cozy SoHo steakhouse is a prime place to take in some jazz or even "watch Argentine soccer"; things get hotter upstairs at the Malbec Lounge where the small dance floor draws "gorgeous" types writhing to Euro-heavy DJ sets.

Nowhere ⊄

▽ 18 | 10 | 22 | $6

E Village | 322 E. 14th St. (bet. 1st & 2nd Aves.) | L to 1st Ave. | 212-477-4744

There's a "mixed scene" going on at this "run-of-the-mill" East Village "hole-in-the-wall" that caters to both gays and lesbians; the "middle-of-nowhere" address means it's "not a destination", but it's "fun if passing by", especially if you're into "arty hipster" types.

Nublu ⊄

26 | 18 | 18 | $10

E Village | 62 Ave. C (bet. 4th & 5th Sts.) | F/V to Lower East Side/2nd Ave. | no phone | www.nublu.net

"Diverse" crowds keep things interesting at this "spunky", "offbeat" Alphabet City lounge, a midsize spot with "quirky", bachelor-pad looks and a "nice back patio"; "lively" musicians and "talented" DJs play everything from "funk and hip-hop to dance and world music", but no matter what's on the agenda, it usually "feels real" here.

Nurse Bettie

19 | 18 | 18 | $10

LES | 106 Norfolk St. (bet. Delancey & Rivington Sts.) | F/J/M/Z to Delancey/Essex Sts. | 917-434-9072 | www.nursebettieles.com

A tribute to '50s fetish model Bettie Page, this "casual" LES "nook" enjoys "street cred" with "slumming yuppies" and "actual dirty hipsters" nursing "creative" house cocktails in a "kitschy cool" den adorned with pinup art; the "dorm room"-size space can be "packed" or "action-free", depending on the night.

Nuyorican Poets Cafe ⊄

21 | 15 | 18 | $7

E Village | 236 E. Third St. (bet. Aves. B & C) | F/V to Lower East Side/ 2nd Ave. | 212-505-8183 | www.nuyorican.org

Its "incredible" Friday night poetry slams may be legendary, but this "entertaining" East Village cafe also stages "progressive" theater, live jazz, stand-up comedy and fierce MC battles; now in its 35th year, this once-underground haunt hasn't lost its "inclusive" cultural spirit, or thankfully, the "cheap beer."

☑ Oak Bar

APPEAL	DECOR	SERVICE	COST
24	25	23	$17

W 50s | Plaza Hotel | 10 Central Park S. (bet. 5th & 6th Aves.) | N/R/W to 5th Ave./59th St. | 212-758-7777 | www.oakroomny.com
"Olde New York" lives on at this circa-1945 "original" in the Plaza Hotel, back on the scene following a "classy" renovation; the service is "old school", the Everett Shinn murals "perfection", the buffed-up oak woodwork still "smells of Cary Grant" and yes, the price of a couple of cocktails may require "dipping into the money set aside for your kids' education."

☑ Oak Room

APPEAL	DECOR	SERVICE	COST
25	25	24	$16

W 40s | Algonquin Hotel | 59 W. 44th St. (bet. 5th & 6th Aves.) | 7/B/D/F/V to 42nd St./Bryant Park | 212-840-6800 | www.algonquinhotel.com
"Toast the upper crust" at this "refined", "old-fashioned" cabaret in Midtown's Algonquin Hotel, where the mood's "elegant" and the "first-rate" performers usually "sing old jazz and wear a gown"; sure, it's "conservative", the room's an "awkward shape" and it's "expensive", but fans "go for the history" – and the "not-to-be-missed Andrea Marcovicci."

Obivia

APPEAL	DECOR	SERVICE	COST
24	24	22	$12

Little Italy | 201 Lafayette St. (Kenmare St.) | 6 to Spring St. | 212-226-4904 | www.obivia.com
A "hot place to go" in suddenly happening Little Italy, this "hip", "Moroccan-themed" bar/lounge is best known for its "schlocky", "old-school pornos" on the "plasma screens" that make for "great conversation starters"; "sexy cocktails" and "comfy couches" make it a natural when you want to "get cozy with a date."

O'Connell's

APPEAL	DECOR	SERVICE	COST
16	11	17	$8

W 100s | 2794 Broadway (108th St.) | 1 to Cathedral Pkwy./110th St. | 212-678-9738
The "former Cannon's Pub" sticks to its guns as a "garden-variety Irish" joint near Columbia, serving as a "barfly hangout during the day" that yields later on to "neighborhood jocks" who "come to watch sports"; regulars deem it "dingy" but doable unless it's "mobbed" with "annoying" collegians.

O'Connor's ⊠

APPEAL	DECOR	SERVICE	COST
∇ 22	11	23	$5

Park Slope | 39 Fifth Ave. (bet. Bergen & Dean Sts.) | Brooklyn | 2/3 to Bergen St. | 718-783-9721
"Grubby looks" don't faze the alcoholic "old men" and "budget-minded hipsters" who patronize this circa-1930 Park Slope "dive" where a "great staff" pours "cheap", "no-frills" drinks; romeos report it's a "good place to have an affair" – it's "so dark no one will notice your wedding ring."

Odeon

APPEAL	DECOR	SERVICE	COST
20	18	18	$13

TriBeCa | 145 W. Broadway (bet. Duane & Thomas Sts.) | 1/2/3 to Chambers St. | 212-233-0507 | www.theodeonrestaurant.com
"Quintessential" is the word on this "perennial" TriBeCan that's "stood the test of time and for good reason", mainly that "hip but low-key" vibe; maybe the "bar scene isn't as good as the restaurant", but its

"classic" French bistro decor, "knowledgeable staff" and "busy feel" keep tipplers stopping by "year after year" – "if only the walls could talk."

Off the Wagon

| 17 | 11 | 15 | $6 |

G Village | 109 MacDougal St. (bet. Bleecker & W. 3rd Sts.) | A/B/C/D/E/F/V to W. 4th St. | 212-533-4487 | www.nycbestbar.com

"Relive college with a round of beer pong" at this NYU-area sports bar that's a total "sausagefest" with "cheap" pitchers and stellar "hook-up" possibilities; "loud and crowded" most nights with a "falling-down, can't-see-straight" crowd, it's as "fratty as can be – but that's not always bad."

O'Flaherty's Ale House

| 18 | 17 | 19 | $8 |

W 40s | 334-336 W. 46th St. (bet. 8th & 9th Aves.) | A/C/E to 42nd St./Port Authority | 212-581-9366 | www.oflahertysnyc.com

Exuding a "very Irish pub feel", this Restaurant Row bar draws a random mix of tourists, locals and after-work suits to its book-lined, "librarylike" digs, and is a particular "St. Paddy's Day favorite"; a "cool" back garden and cozy fireplace seal the deal.

O'Flanagan's

| 15 | 12 | 19 | $8 |

E 60s | 1215 First Ave. (bet. 65th & 66th Sts.) | 6 to 68th St. | 212-439-0660 | www.oflanagans.com

"Catering to the hospital crowd that works blocks away", this UES "Irish dive" provides a variety of distractions including a pool table, "decent cover bands" and sports on "lots of TVs"; thanks to the "friendly" barkeeps, however, the most popular pastime here is "swilling beer."

☑ Old Town Bar

| 21 | 16 | 17 | $8 |

Flatiron | 45 E. 18th St. (bet. B'way & Park Ave. S.) | 4/5/6/L/N/Q/R/W to 14th St./Union Sq. | 212-529-6732 | www.oldtownbar.com

Expect "no fuss, no glamour and no attitude" at this "old NY" Flatiron saloon where little has changed since its 1892 opening, with the "long wooden bar", "hammered tin ceiling", "neat dumbwaiter" and overall "nitty-gritty" feel intact; it's a place "for drinkers, not scenesters", hence the "refreshing no-cell-phones policy."

Oliver's Bar & Grill

| 17 | 16 | 19 | $12 |

G Village | 190 W. Fourth St. (Barrow St.) | 1 to Christopher St. | 212-647-0500 | www.oliversbarandgrill.com

If you miss Boxers, about the "only difference is the name" at its successor, this "typical" Village saloon with "big windows", a "digital jukebox" and "decent prices"; it's "easy to grab a table" and "hang with friends", though the "touristy" milieu means it's "not a destination."

O'Lunney's

| 21 | 19 | 23 | $9 |

W 40s | 145 W. 45th St. (bet. B'way & 6th Ave.) | 1/2/3/7/N/Q/R/S/W to 42nd St./Times Sq. | 212-840-6688 | www.olunneys.com

This "upscale"-ish Irish pub has been popular "after work" and "pre-theater" for years, given its "right-off-Times-Square" address; "friendly" barkeeps pouring perfect pints of Guinness keep regulars regular.

One

| 22 | 22 | 19 | $13 |

Meatpacking | 1 Little W. 12th St. (9th Ave.) | A/C/E/L to 14th St./8th Ave. | 212-255-9717 | www.theonerestaurants.com

"Less pretentious than its neighbors", this stylishly "dark" Meatpacking spot lures "young, well-dressed" types to its "crowded" ground-floor bar/eatery or the equally "happening" downstairs lounge; while the scene varies from "decent" to "exciting" and the door policy from "easy" to "pretty strict", pricing is definitely on the "posh" side, so you might want to "stick to domestic beer."

O'Neals'
20 | 18 | 21 | $13

W 60s | 49 W. 64th St. (bet. B'way & CPW) | 1 to 66th St. | 212-787-4663 | www.onealsny.com

"Location, location, location" is the name of the game at this "perennial" Irish tavern (since 1964) that's "right across from Lincoln Center"; since it's a natural "before the ballet", there are "crowds before performance time", so regulars pop up post-curtain to soak up the "great pub atmosphere" and banter with the "just-off-the-boat" barkeeps.

One & One
18 | 14 | 18 | $7

E Village | 76 E. First St. (1st Ave.) | F/V to Lower East Side/2nd Ave. | 212-598-9126

Given an enviable corner location at the "heart of everything" in the East Village, this "big" Irish pub is a "comfortable" enough stop featuring 16 beers on tap, sports (usually soccer) on the tube and a sleek basement lounge; ultimately, its "watching-the-world-go-by" sidewalk seats draw the most applause.

151
21 | 17 | 21 | $8

LES | 151 Rivington St., downstairs (bet. Clinton & Suffolk Sts.) | F/J/M/Z to Delancey/Essex Sts. | 212-228-4139

Expect "no nonsense and no pretense" at this "hidden" Lower East Side basement featuring rock DJs and dated bric-a-brac with all the shabby charm of a "comfortable mobile home"; it draws a mix of "hipster wannabes" and "low-key" loungers who hope they "won't be seen" here.

One if by Land, Two if by Sea
26 | 26 | 26 | $15

G Village | 17 Barrow St. (bet. 7th Ave. S. & W. 4th St.) | A/B/C/D/E/F/V to W. 4th St. | 212-228-0822 | www.oneifbyland.com

Famed as *the* "pop-the-question" destination, this "special-occasion" Villager is set in a "fancy-pants" restoration of "Aaron Burr's carriage house", with dueling fireplaces and a pianist in the bar area; the "grand atmosphere" may appeal to more mature audiences, but it's so "romantic" that younger types want to "skip dinner" and go straight to dessert; N.B. be aware that the tab could be more expensive than the ring.

119 Bar ⊉
16 | 9 | 15 | $8

Gramercy | 119 E. 15th St. (bet. Irving Pl. & Park Ave. S.) | 4/5/6/L/N/Q/R/W to 14th St./Union Sq. | 212-777-6158

"Rockers and bikers" rub shoulders with "college" kids psyched for shows at The Fillmore at this Gramercy "dive" where "cheap and grungy" vibes plus "great tunes" equal a "good time all around"; then again, it's "kind of a hole" and "snarky pool mavens" seem to corner the table on cue.

☑ 1 Oak
22 | 20 | 18 | $16

Chelsea | 453 W. 17th St. (bet. 9th & 10th Aves.) | A/C/E/L to 14th St./8th Ave. | 212-242-1111 | www.1oaknyc.com

"Models, celebs and social climbers" are stoked for the "more intimate" lounging of yesteryear at this "much-hyped" West Chelsea club that justifies its name ("stands for 'one of a kind'") with "fancy" quarters, "high energy" and "precision exclusion"; it's a "great night on the town" – provided you're ready to deal with one of the "hardest doors in NYC."

105 Riv
22 | 21 | 18 | $13

LES | The Hotel on Rivington | 105 Rivington St. (bet. Essex & Ludlow Sts.) | F/J/M/Z to Delancey/Essex Sts. | 212-475-2600 | www.hotelonrivington.com

"Young, almost beautiful" types who "can't find the Meatpacking District" line up at this "intimate", "stylish" lounge hidden beside a LES boutique hotel to lap up "innovative cocktails" and "take advantage of the stripper pole"; the "door's tough for a reason", but holdouts huff it's "too pretentious" for the area.

169 Bar
22 | 18 | 19 | $10

LES | 169 E. Broadway (Rutgers St.) | F to E. B'way | 212-473-8866 | www.169barnyc.com

A "holdover from the old LES days", this "local hole-in-the-wall" keeps it "close to real" with its "easygoing" attitude and "not-bad prices"; an "eclectic" lineup of "minor musical acts" kicks in some Crescent City sounds, but go-getters still grumble it's "not memorable enough."

124 Rabbit Club ⌷
▽ 24 | 17 | 23 | $11

G Village | 124 MacDougal St. (bet. Bleecker & W. 3rd Sts.) | A/B/C/D/E/F/V to W. 4th St. | 212-254-0575

"Hidden in the heart of frat-boy row", this "subterranean" MacDougal Street dive features a buzzer-equipped "secret entrance" that leads to a "dark", "narrow" beer bar that's hare-alded for its "knowledgeable" staff and "well-chosen array" of bottled imports; but "now that the rabbit's out of the hat", it's "a little too cozy", unless you cotton to crowds.

🆕 123 Burger Shot Beer
20 | 16 | 18 | $8

W 50s | 738 10th Ave. (bet. 50th & 51st Sts.) | C/E to 50th St. | 212-315-0123 | www.123burgershotbeer.com

"Get messy for cheap" at this Way West Hell's Kitchen sports bar where the "recession-proof" "gimmick" – "dollar sliders, $2 shots and $3 beers" – incites Ft. Lauderdale-style "shenanigans" among "younger" folk; party animals who don't mind the "packed" premises can have a "boozy good time" and still "afford the much-needed cab back home."

Onieal's Grand Street
20 | 19 | 20 | $11

Little Italy | 174 Grand St. (bet. Centre & Mulberry Sts.) | B/D to Grand St. | 212-941-9119 | www.onieals.com

This former '30s speakeasy may "no longer be a hidden gem" – in fact it's a stop on the *Sex and the City* tour – but still exudes a "low-key", "time-gone-by" vibe with its tin ceiling and venetian blinds; "impeccable cocktails" and an "unpretentious" air draw "well-dressed Uptown" types to its off-the-beaten-path Little Italy address, which can be "either very empty or very packed."

Ono
24 | 25 | 20 | $16

Meatpacking | Gansevoort Hotel | 18 Ninth Ave. (enter on 13th St.) | A/C/E/L to 14th St./8th Ave. | 212-660-6766 | www.chinagrillmgt.com

The Meatpacking District's Gansevoort Hotel is home to this "showy" Asian bar/restaurant where a "super-trendy" crowd angles for seats in the "chic", tearoom-esque interior or (even better) the "marvelous outdoor" Garden of Ono; granted, it may be "mad expensive", but the "breathtaking atmosphere" is just the ticket when you "want to throw a few back and feel classy while doing it."

Opal

17 | 15 | 16 | $10

E 50s | 251 E. 52nd St. (2nd Ave.) | 6 to 51st St./Lexington Ave. | 212-593-4321 | www.opalbar.com

"Neighborhood frat boys who miss college" pack this "popular" Midtown bar, an "old reliable" now on its "third remodel"; the "upbeat", "energetic" crowd digs the "model barmaids" and "back dance floor", though a few say it's "not what it once was" – there "aren't as many drunk girls as there used to be" for starters.

Opia

22 | 23 | 20 | $12

E 50s | Renaissance Hotel 57 | 130 E. 57th St., 2nd fl. (bet. Lexington & Park Aves.) | 4/5/6/N/R/W to 59th St./Lexington Ave. | 212-688-3939 | www.opiarestaurant.com

Local suits meet up for "corporate cocktails" alongside "hip-looking Europeans" at this "classy", "not-often-crowded" bar/lounge "hidden" on the second floor of Midtown's Hotel 57; some find it "reasonably trendy", others say it's a "bit passé" (which makes it "more attractive" to folks looking to "escape the paparazzi").

❷ Otheroom ⊘

27 | 21 | 23 | $10

W Village | 143 Perry St. (bet. Greenwich & Washington Sts.) | 1 to Christopher St. | 212-645-9758 | www.theotheroom.com

"Sweet and sexy", this "tiny", "out-of-the-way" West Villager works well for a "romantic rendezvous or serious heart-to-heart", given its "dimly lit" digs, "soul-warming music" and "bartenders who really know their stuff"; it "only serves beer and wine" and "doesn't take credit cards", but fans still "want to keep it a secret" – too bad "it's *really* been discovered."

Otto

25 | 23 | 22 | $12

G Village | 1 Fifth Ave. (enter on 8th St.) | N/R/W to 8th St. | 212-995-9559 | www.ottopizzeria.com

"Enter a novice, exit a wine expert" at Mario Batali's Village pizzeria/ enoteca where a huge, all-Italian list of 500-plus bottles can "keep you reading for hours" (the "well-versed staff" will offer "friendly guidance"); the front bar area, "modeled on a train station", is appropriately "loud" and usually "standing room only" ("don't wear stilettos"), though the overall vibe is "warm", "lightly sprinkled with cool."

Otto's Shrunken Head ⊘

21 | 18 | 16 | $8

E Village | 538 E. 14th St. (bet. Aves. A & B) | L to 1st Ave. | 212-228-2240 | www.ottosshrunkenhead.com

"Tiki fantasy meets garage rock" at this random East Village dive where "tacky Polynesian decor" collides with a tattooed hard-rock crowd; it "takes kitsch to a whole new level" with a "metal DJ" in the front bar and live bands in the back room, and after a couple of frozen "sugary drinks", no one cares that "this place doesn't make sense."

Overlook Lounge

17 | 15 | 20 | $8

E 40s | 225 E. 44th St. (bet. 2nd & 3rd Aves.) | 4/5/6/7/S to 42nd St./ Grand Central | 212-682-7266 | www.overlooknyc.com

An "odd location" keeps it "inconspicuous", but this "casual" barroom near Grand Central is a "local favorite" for "winding down" with barkeeps who "know your name"; the "ton of TVs" for sports, vintage cartoon "artwork" in the rear and a "spacious" second-floor patio make this one worth looking over.

Pacha

20 | 20 | 16 | $13

W 40s | 618 W. 46th St. (bet. 11th & 12th Aves.) | A/C/E to 42nd St./ Port Authority | 212-209-7500 | www.pachanyc.com

"Straight from Ibiza" comes this "fly" clubzilla, an outpost of the international dance club chain that naturally draws the "old Sound Factory crowd" since it occupies the same "infamous" Hell's Kitchen building; expect a "cavernous", four-story setup with "plenty of dark little corners", big-name DJs and "half-naked" go-go gals showering inside glassed-in stalls; downsides include "rude service" and really "long waits at the coat check."

Pacific Standard

▽ 21 | 20 | 21 | $8

Boerum Hill | 82 Fourth Ave. (bet. Bergen St. & St. Marks Pl.) | Brooklyn | 2/3/4/5/B/D/M/N/Q/R to Atlantic Ave. | 718-858-1951 | www.pacificstandardbrooklyn.com

Bringing a taste of the West Coast to Boerum Hill, this taproom serves a "fantastic" rotating selection of Pacific Northwest microbrews In Its spacious front bar or in a "cozy" back room fitted out with couches and a lending library; a rewards program for frequent drinkers offers prizes ranging from private keg parties to BAM memberships.

Paddy Reilly's Music Bar

20 | 17 | 18 | $7

Murray Hill | 519 Second Ave. (bet. 28th & 29th Sts.) | 6 to 28th St. | 212-686-1210

"Friendly barmaids" see to the customers while "foot-stomping Irish bands" – "complete with fiddles" – play up a storm at this Murray Hill tavern that's best known for its all-Guinness tap selection; maybe the "cozy" interior's "a little worn", but that only "adds to its charm."

Palio Bar

22 | 24 | 21 | $15

W 50s | Equitable Center Arcade | 151 W. 51st St. (bet. 6th & 7th Aves.) | B/D/F/V to 47-50th Sts./Rockefeller Ctr. | 212-399-9400 | www.pianoduenyc.net

Back after a hiatus, this "upscale" Midtown boîte returns to the scene with artist Sandro Chia's famed wraparound mural intact; there's plenty of "snob appeal" in the air (starting with its "black Amex" pricing), but even though it's "perfect pre-theater", a somewhat hidden location on a midblock breezeway means it's usually quiet.

Paramount Bar

23 | 23 | 19 | $13

W 40s | Paramount Hotel | 235 W. 46th St. (bet. B'way & 8th Ave.) | A/C/E to 42nd St./Port Authority | 212-413-1010

Paramount Library Bar

W 40s | Paramount Hotel | 235 W. 46th St., 2nd fl. (bet. B'way & 8th Ave.) | A/C/E to 42nd St./Port Authority | 212-764-5500 www.nycparamount.com

"Tourists mix with locals" in the "chic", ground-floor watering hole of this "hip" Theater District hotel where you get "a lot of flash" so long as you're willing to spend "a lot of cash"; the upstairs Library Bar is more subdued, with "comfy couches" and atrium views of the comings and goings in the lobby, but just as "expensive."

| | APPEAL | DECOR | SERVICE | COST |

Paris, The
▽ 19 | 15 | 21 | $10

Seaport | 119 South St. (Peck Slip) | 2/3/4/5/A/C/J/M/Z to Fulton St./B'way/Nassau | 212-240-9797 | www.theparistavern.com

So well "hidden in the South Street Seaport area" that it attracts "more locals than tourists", this circa-1873 taproom is a "good hangout" even if no one knows "what the name is supposed to imply" – it's an Irish joint, "not French"; maybe it's "lost some color since the Fulton Fish Market closed", but at least "the smell is gone" now.

Park, The
21 | 23 | 16 | $12

Chelsea | 118 10th Ave. (bet. 17th & 18th Sts.) | A/C/E/L to 14th St./8th Ave. | 212-352-3313 | www.theparknyc.com

There's a "room for each of your multiple personalities" at this "multi-level", "mansionlike" West Chelsea spot that includes a "tree-lined" bar/restaurant, "hot tub"–equipped roof deck and "beautiful outdoor patio" that's a "smoker's delight"; though it "used to be *the* place" to be seen, there's "no door drama" anymore, resulting in a very "mixed crowd."

Park Bar
21 | 19 | 19 | $10

Flatiron | 15 E. 15th St. (bet. 5th Ave. & Union Sq. W.) | 4/5/6/L/N/Q/R/W to 14th St./Union Sq. | 212-367-9085

"Cool and dark with no attitude", this "tiny" bar off Union Square has a "scholarly feel" with its tin ceiling and vintage woodwork, echoed by "old-school trained" bartenders who know their way around the "premium booze"; sure, it can get "too close for comfort" at prime times, but when it's crowded "people tend to mix and mingle with strangers."

Park Blue
22 | 20 | 22 | $12

W 50s | 158 W. 58th St. (bet. 6th & 7th Aves.) | N/Q/R/W to 57th St./7th Ave. | 212-247-2727 | www.parkbluenyc.com

Set on a quiet Midtown block, this midnight blue lounge features a "fab selection of wines by the half bottle" accompanied by an "excellent" selection of small plates; despite "slight overpricing", it attracts a late-night "restaurant worker" contingent from the Time Warner Center.

Parkside Lounge
18 | 12 | 20 | $7

LES | 317 E. Houston St. (Attorney St.) | F/V to Lower East Side/2nd Ave. | 212-673-6270

"Definitely not next to a park" but "still pouring after all these years", this circa-1955 LES tavern is one "fun, sloppy" haven for "hipsters who want to hang out at an old-man bar" even though the "old men have fled"; it's a "low-key" experience except when there's "live music."

Park Slope Ale House
18 | 15 | 20 | $7

Park Slope | 356 Sixth Ave. (5th St.) | Brooklyn | F to 7th Ave. | 718-788-1756

A "nice selection" of draft beers, fairly priced, is the draw at this "cozy" spot in Park Slope, an old-school tavern enhanced by a pool table, rear patio and "service with a smile"; the "neighborhood" vibe alone makes some "almost want to move to Brooklyn."

Parlour, The
17 | 14 | 18 | $8

W 80s | 250 W. 86th St. (bet. B'way & West End Ave.) | 1 to 86th St. | 212-580-8923 | www.theparlour.com

There's "lots of room" to spread out at this "huge" double-decker Irish pub, a real "crowd-pleaser" where Upper Westsiders can watch a "soccer match" on TV or just "chill out" with friends; downstairs, a large private party space is used for dancing, karaoke and live bands.

☑ Pastis
24 | 22 | 18 | $13

Meatpacking | 9 Ninth Ave. (Little W. 12th St.) | A/C/E/L to 14th St./ 8th Ave. | 212-929-4844 | www.pastisny.com

The "volume is loud" and the vibe "Euro-worldly" at Keith McNally's "buzzy" Meatpacking bistro where "circus crowds" of "varying ages" convene in an "old-world Paris" setting; voted the Most Popular nightspot in this Survey, it's "always sociable", usually "cramped" and clearly "still happening" – just getting in "feels like an event" to many.

Patrick Conway's
▽ 18 | 13 | 21 | $8

E 40s | 40 E. 43rd St. (Madison Ave.) | 4/5/6/7/S to 42nd St./Grand Central | 212-286-1873 | www.patrickconways.com

This "quintessential pub" near Grand Central is an "absolutely Irish" enclave that attracts after-work suits ready to loosen their ties and bend their elbows before jumping on the train; "great bartenders" keep the pints flowing at the long wooden bar, while a free buffet of "typical" grub makes the happy hour even happier.

Patrick Kavanagh's
17 | 14 | 19 | $8

Murray Hill | 497 Third Ave. (bet. 33rd & 34th Sts.) | 6 to 33rd St. | 212-889-4304

A "regular" Irish pub in the middle of the "Murray Hill frat boy bar" wasteland, this local "standby" "isn't exactly a place to get down 'n' dirty", so "don't plan on hooking up"; instead, it's better for "grabbing beers with coworkers" and to simply "enjoy being out."

Patriot Saloon ⊅
14 | 8 | 17 | $5

TriBeCa | 110 Chambers St. (Church St.) | 1/2/3 to Chambers St. | 212-748-1162

For those "just-get-me-drunk" evenings, check out this "raunchy" honky-tonk with so "few redeeming qualities" that some call it "TriBeCa's best dive"; a rollicking "country juke" and super "cheap" swill offset the "ramshackle" decor and "rough-and-tumble" crowd.

Patroon
22 | 19 | 19 | $12

E 40s | 160 E. 46th St. (bet. Lexington & 3rd Aves.) | 4/5/6/7/S to 42nd St./ Grand Central | 212-883-7373 | www.patroonrestaurant.com

Come summer, there's "atmosphere" galore on the rooftop bar of this Midtown steakhouse where "pricey", "top-notch" cocktails and "finger food" draw "after-work suits and ties"; during cooler months, the downstairs bar exudes "old NY" appeal, but either way there's "no late-night fun" to be had, since they close fairly early (and they're also closed weekends).

☑ PDT
27 | 23 | 24 | $13

E Village | 113 St. Marks Pl. (bet. Ave. A & 1st Ave.) | 6 to Astor Pl. | 212-614-0386 | www.pdtnyc.com

Prove "how in-the-know you are" at this "sneaky" speakeasy accessed through a "Maxwell Smart phone booth" in the East Village's Crif Dogs, where "expert mixologists" whip up "imaginative concoctions" in compact, "taxidermy"-adorned digs; the "polite exclusivity" (the name's short for 'Please Don't Tell') is due to a no-standing rule, so reservations are essential – "someone must have told."

Peasant

23 24 19 $13

NoLita | 194 Elizabeth St., downstairs (bet. Prince & Spring Sts.) | 6 to Spring St. | 212-965-9511 | www.peasantnyc.com
In contrast to the "loud", "trendy" restaurant above it, this intimate NoLita wine bar nestled in a "hidden", "grottolike" basement has "romantic" interlude written all over it; its "attractive, relaxed" followers call it the "perfect neighborhood spot" and plead "don't tell anyone how great it is."

Peculier Pub ⊉

20 12 16 $7

G Village | 145 Bleecker St. (bet. La Guardia Pl. & Thompson St.) | 1 to Houston St. | 212-353-1327 | www.peculierpub.com
With one of the "most extensive beer menus in NY", this "inexpensive", cash-only Village pub is dead "serious" about suds, offering more than 600 brews "from around the world"; its "down-to-earth", "college-age crowd" doesn't mind its "divey", "rough-around-the-edges" look but warns that the scene may feel "played out if you're over 25."

Peggy O'Neill's

18 17 19 $10

Coney Island | KeySpan Park | 1904 Surf Ave. (19th St.) | Brooklyn | D/F/N/Q to Coney Island/Stillwell Ave. | 718-449-3200
"Everybody can (and will) know your name" at this "friendly" Irish pub in Coney Island; what with the "nice beers", "fun sports nights" and occasional karaoke, it's a "decent" enough destination, and the KeySpan Park location is "great after Cyclones games"; N.B. its Bay Ridge sibling has closed.

☑ Pegu Club

25 26 23 $14

SoHo | 77 W. Houston St., 2nd fl. (bet. W. B'way & Wooster St.) | B/D/F/V to B'way/Lafayette St. | 212-473-7348 | www.peguclub.com
"Chemical engineers are more relaxed about their work" than the "serious" mixologists at Audrey Saunder's "effortlessly hip" SoHo lounge catering to "cocktail connoisseurs" craving a "properly shaken, properly stirred drink" (with an "emphasis on gin"); the recipe for its success consists of "attentive" service, a "sexy", second-floor space that channels "Colonial India" and "expensive", "dangerously tasty" libations that are "tiny" but oh-so-"potent."

Pencil Factory ⊉

20 21 19 $8

Greenpoint | 142 Franklin St. (Greenpoint Ave.) | Brooklyn | G to Greenpoint Ave. | 718-609-5858
There's "room to breathe" at this "friendly" Greenpoint pub that began life as a dockworkers' social club (look across the street for the namesake factory); a varied selection of tap brews and a "good happy-hour special on Brooklyn beers" keep loyalists regular, though picky drinkers grumble it's just a "standard" watering hole.

Penthouse Executive Club

▽ 24 23 19 $16

W 40s | 603 W. 45th St. (11th Ave.) | A/C/E to 42nd St./Port Authority | 212-245-0002 | www.penthouseexecutiveclub.com
Ok, there may be "more plastic than a 1990 Ford Taurus" on display at this "hot" Hell's Kitchen "mammary mecca", but it still "shines above" many other "flash factories" since it showcases a "higher class of stripper"; too bad about the "lacking" service (the "hard sell can be a

little much"), but so long as you're carrying "lots of cash", you can count on a "great boys' night out."

Perdition

20 | 18 | 22 | $8

W 40s | 692 10th Ave. (bet. 48th & 49th Sts.) | C/E to 50th St. | 212-582-5660 | www.perditionnyc.com

An "out-of-the-way" location in Hell's Kitchen doesn't deter locals from this "laid-back" Irish "hideaway" known for its "frequent drink specials" and board game library; a "welcoming" staff, "hands-on owners" and "plenty of room to stretch out" make it a "solid" destination.

Perfect Pint

21 | 19 | 22 | $8

NEW E 40s | 203 E. 45th St. (bet. 2nd & 3rd Aves.) | 4/5/6/7/S to 42nd St./Grand Central | 212-867-8159
W 40s | 123 W. 45th St. (bet. B'way & 6th Ave.) | B/D/F/V to 47-50th Sts./ Rockefeller Ctr. | 212-354-1099
www.theperfectpintnyc.com

"Regular post-work stops", these "slightly upscale" crosstown Irish twins are set in "spacious", "multistory venues" (complete with "smoking balconies") where "no-pretense" tapmeisters draw an impressive "variety of beers"; while "nothing spectacular", they're perfectly "suitable" when you want to "loosen the tie", and "there's always a crowd."

NEW Perle

▽ 22 | 19 | 20 | $12

Financial District | 62 Pearl St.; downstairs (bet. Broad St. & Coenties Slip) | 4/5 to Bowling Green | 212-248-4848 | www.perle-nyc.com

Situated below a new French brasserie, this Financial District wine bar/lounge is a convenient retreat for "young" financiers trying to drink the lousy economy off their minds; the "dark", workmanlike decor may verge on the bare-bones, but at least the pricing is fair and the mood convivial.

Pershing Square/Buzz Bar

16 | 15 | 15 | $12

E 40s | 90 E. 42nd St. (Park Ave. S.) | 4/5/6/7/S to 42nd St./Grand Central | 212-286-9600 | www.pershingsquare.com

A "perfect commuter spot" given its across-from-Grand-Central address, this "convenient" bar/restaurant under the Park Avenue viaduct naturally boasts an active "after-work" scene, but as the night wears on, its "target audience is tourists"; while it "works in a pinch", the "nothing-special" vibe and "lackluster" service work against it.

Peter Dillon's Pub

▽ 16 | 12 | 17 | $6

E 40s | 130 E. 40th St. (bet. Lexington & 3rd Aves.) | 4/5/6/7/S to 42nd St./Grand Central | 212-213-3998

This "friendly" albeit "no-frills" Irish pub near Grand Central draws a steady "after-work" trade with a $3 Harp happy hour; "flat-screened" sports and a wood-lined room are part of a "standard" package that's sweetened by "reasonable" costs.

Peter McManus Cafe

19 | 12 | 18 | $6

Chelsea | 152 Seventh Ave. (19th St.) | 1 to 18th St. | 212-929-9691

Serving suds since 1936, this "old-old-school" Chelsea Irish pub is "still your grandfather's bar" dispensing cheap "cold ones" in "run-down" digs; its "across-the-board", all-ages appeal runs the gamut from "firefighters" to "FIT students", who all advise "eat, drink and be merry – for tomorrow joints like this will no longer exist."

| | APPEAL | DECOR | SERVICE | COST |

Peter's
17 | 13 | 16 | $9

W 60s | 182 Columbus Ave. (bet. 68th & 69th Sts.) | 1 to 66th St. | 212-877-4747

Lookswise, it may be "nothing special", but a "key" UWS location has kept this "solid" 27-year-old "always busy"; long renowned as a "pickup joint", it offers an "interesting mashup" of folks to choose from – "sports enthusiasts", "upscale media types" and "frat boys in their 30s" with one thing in common: they all "drink plenty."

Pete's Candy Store
23 | 17 | 20 | $7

Williamsburg | 709 Lorimer St. (bet. Frost & Richardson Sts.) | Brooklyn | G/L to Metropolitan Ave./Lorimer St. | 718-302-3770 | www.petescandystore.com

"Far enough from Manhattan" that it's "safe from the Manolo Blahnik"-wearers, this "quirky" Williamsburg magnet for the "thinking drunk" is a "delightfully neighborly" nexus with a "beat-up-to-perfection" ambiance; its "biggest draws" are its "game nights" (i.e. trivia quizzes, spelling bees) backed up by a "sweet backyard", "generous cocktails" and "loud art music" in a tiny adjacent performance space.

Pete's Tavern
21 | 17 | 18 | $9

Gramercy | 129 E. 18th St. (Irving Pl.) | 4/5/6/L/N/Q/R/W to 14th St./ Union Sq. | 212-473-7676

"Forever classic", this "cheery" Gramercy "legend" is arguably "NYC's oldest bar" (since 1864) and "still going strong" with locals, tourists and history buffs; ok, it's "grungy", "not fancy" and the staff is "sometimes gruff", but fans of "O. Henry" and anything "old-school" say "that's the charm" of it.

Petrarca Vino e Cucina
24 | 21 | 21 | $16

TriBeCa | 34 White St. (Church St.) | A/C/E to Canal St. | 212-625-2800 | www.petrarcatribeca.com

For a "touch of Italian flair", this "pricey but pretty" TriBeCa enoteca (spun off from nearby eatery Arqua) is "everything you'd expect", pouring an "extensive" vino selection in a "sleek", bottle-lined space with "sexy patrons" to match; its "neighborhood secret" status makes it a "good backup" for scenier spots.

Phebe's
16 | 11 | 16 | $7

E Village | 359 Bowery (4th St.) | B/D/F/V to B'way/Lafayette St. | 212-358-1902 | www.phebesnyc.com

"NYU students" are drawn to this "friendly", roomy Bowery pub, a longtimer that's undergone a number of personality changes in recent years; those who "liked it better when it was divey" say it's "lost its charm", but it still pleases "young" types with a "great happy hour", covered outdoor deck and a flurry of flat-screens showing "every conceivable sport."

Phoenix ☞
20 | 10 | 20 | $6

E Village | 447 E. 13th St. (bet. Ave. A & 1st Ave.) | L to 1st Ave. | 212-477-9979

The "clientele seems to be in a good mood" at this "all-inclusive", "utterly unpretentious" East Village gay bar, a "cozy dive" where the "down-to-earth" vibe extends to the "stellar jukebox", pool table and video games; since it's "jammed to the rafters" on weekends, you can usually count on "going home with something."

Pianos | 19 | 15 | 16 | $9 |

LES | 158 Ludlow St. (bet. Rivington & Stanton Sts.) | F/V to Lower East Side/ 2nd Ave. | 212-505-3733 | www.pianosnyc.com

"Indie rock band" heaven, this "high-energy" LES "old piano shop"-turned-performance venue features live acts in its back room as well as a "less crazy", DJ-d upstairs lounge; it "caters to all tastes", drawing everyone from "punk rockers" to "rowdy suburbanites", except on weekends when it tends to become "claustrophobically engulfed in hipsters."

Pieces ⊄ | ∇ 14 | 9 | 18 | $9 |

G Village | 8 Christopher St. (bet. Gay St. & Greenwich Ave.) | 1 to Christopher St. | 212-929-9291 | www.piecesbar.com

A Village gay bar "staple for God-knows-how-many years", this "fun" dive is famed for its popular Tuesday night karaoke, when "fierce queens" and the "tone-deaf" compete for the limelight; the just-folks crowd "runs the gamut of looks and ethnicities", but you might not want a piece of this action "if you're older than 25."

NEW Pierre Loti | ∇ 23 | 19 | 23 | $13 |

Gramercy | 53 Irving Pl. (bet. 17th & 18th Sts.) | 4/5/6/L/N/Q/R/W to 14th St./Union Sq. | 212-777-5684 | www.pierrelotiwinebar.com

Exuding an "authentic European vibe", this "quaint" Gramercy wine bar is a "cozy, candlelit" class act where the "knowledgeable" but "unpretentious" staff uncorks an "awesome" selection of Continental vintages ("each one better than the next"); it's dubbed the "perfect date spot" by a romantic lot who fervently "hope it doesn't get discovered."

Pinch Bar & Grill | 19 | 16 | 21 | $8 |

G Village | 237 Sullivan St. (W. 3rd St.) | A/B/C/D/E/F/V to W. 4th St. | 212-982-5222 | www.the-pinch-nyc.com

"Low-key" is the word for this "local" Villager where "flat-screens, dartboards and a chill vibe" are the lures; maybe "nothing stands out about it", but at least there's "nothing offensive" going on.

Pine Tree Lodge | 24 | 22 | 23 | $7 |
(aka Cabin Club)

Murray Hill | 326 E. 35th St. (bet. 1st & 2nd Aves.) | 6 to 33rd St. | 212-481-5490

"Novelty"-seekers like this "tucked-away", "lodge"-themed bar that "brings the Adirondacks" to Murray Hill and is a "great escape from the 34th Street frat-bar scene"; it also works for a "reunion with your summer camp buddies", what with the stuffed "dear heads", "flannel-covered cushions" and "cool garden patio" out back.

Pink Elephant | 24 | 22 | 20 | $15 |

Chelsea | 527 W. 27th St. (bet. 10th & 11th Aves.) | C/E to 23rd St. | 212-463-0000 | www.pinkelephantclub.com

"Well-hidden" underground on Chelsea's Bottle Service Row, this "exclusive" nightclub cranks up the smoke and "scent machines" for the amusement of its "attractive international" following; brace yourself for lots of "rich guys and anorexic girls", an "impossible" door manned by "uppity" bouncers and ultrahigh pricing.

Pink Pony ⇗ ▽ | 19 | 20 | 16 | $9

LES | 176 Ludlow St. (bet. Houston & Stanton Sts.) | F/V to Lower East Side/ 2nd Ave. | 212-253-1922 | www.pinkponynyc.com

"Read a book" at this literature-lined LES cafe where poetry readings and film screenings burnish the "eclectic" vibe; it's "nothing fancy" and service skews "slow", but it's a "cool" choice when "Pianos is too packed."

Pipa 21 | 24 | 17 | $12

Flatiron | 38 E. 19th St. (bet. B'way & Park Ave. S.) | 4/5/6/L/N/Q/R/W to 14th St./Union Sq. | 212-677-2233 | www.abchome.com

"Delicious small plates" and "massive pitchers of sangria" meet cute at this Flatiron tapas bar, a "haute hippie" den in ABC Carpet that's festooned with lots of "velvet" as well as "chandeliers with the tags still on" (most of which are "for sale"); it's just the ticket for a "fab girls' night out" – just beware that "Latin flare" extends to the "lothario bartenders."

P.J. Carney's 18 | 13 | 20 | $7

W 50s | 906 Seventh Ave. (bet. 57th & 58th Sts.) | N/Q/R/W to 57th St./ 7th Ave. | 212-664-0056 | www.pjcarneys.com

A "no-nonsense" tavern "where nobody knows your name", this Irish pub near Carnegie Hall is a "great place to watch the Mets" while eavesdropping on "colorful conversations"; sure, there's "nothing spectacular" going on, but "moderate prices" and a "hometown feel" compensate.

P.J. Clarke's 20 | 18 | 20 | $10

E 50s | 915 Third Ave. (55th St.) | 6/E/V to 51st-53rd Sts./Lexington Ave. | 212-317-1616

P.J. Clarke's at Lincoln Square

W 60s | 44 W. 63rd St. (Columbus Ave.) | 1 to 66th St. | 212-957-9700

P.J. Clarke's on the Hudson

Financial District | 4 World Financial Ctr. (Vesey St.) | 1/R/W to Rector St. | 212-285-1500

www.pjclarkes.com

"Unchanged by time" and nearly "as old as the planet", this circa-1884 Midtown Irish pub draws a mix of "after-work" suits, hard-core barflies and "tourists", all thirsting for "a taste of old New York"; the franchise is expanding with a World Financial Center outpost (complete with "Hudson River views" and replicas of the original's famed urinals), as well as a Lincoln Center satellite, which opened post-Survey.

P.J. Hanley's 18 | 19 | 19 | $9

Carroll Gardens | 449 Court St. (4th Pl.) | Brooklyn | F/G to Carroll St. | 718-834-8223

With "new management" and a "renovation", this circa-1874 Carroll Gardens pub shows an "improvement" and is now "more appealing" with its "large windows" and "old NY" marble bartop; some say its "regulars can be intimidating" to outsiders, but overall it's "decent all around."

Plan B 16 | 14 | 18 | $8

E Village | 339 E. 10th St. (bet. Aves. A & B) | L to 1st Ave. | 212-353-2303 | www.planbny.com

The "music is old-school" and the crowd "young hipsters" at this "always packed" East Village bar/lounge, a DJ-centric den where "people actually dance"; sure, it's "small" and "dark", but like "the name implies", it's a "decent" enough destination "if all else fails."

Playwright Tavern

18	16	19	$8

Garment District | 27 W. 35th St. (bet. 5th & 6th Aves.) | B/D/F/N/Q/R/V/W to 34th St./Herald Sq. | 212-268-8868

W 40s | 202 W. 49th St. (bet. B'way & 7th Ave.) | N/R/W to 49th St. | 212-262-9229

W 40s | 732 Eighth Ave. (bet. 45th & 46th Sts.) | A/C/E to 42nd St./Port Authority | 212-354-8404

www.playwrighttavern.com

"You won't go thirsty" at these Midtown Irish pubs where "union" guys "throw back Buds" and "corporate" dudes guzzle martinis; "reasonable" prices – not the "no-frills" decor – lend some "tourist" appeal.

Plaza Athénée Bar Seine

24	25	24	$17

E 60s | Plaza Athénée Hotel | 37 E. 64th St. (bet. Madison & Park Aves.) | 6 to 68th St. | 212-606-4647 | www.plaza-athenee.com

"Sedate" and "sophisticated" with Moroccan-themed decor and leather floors, this "very Upper East Side experience" in the Plaza Athénée is a good place to "take your parents" or "meet a spy"; "mature" types used to being "pampered" say there's "nowhere better for a quiet drink" – so long as "your boss from overseas is paying."

Plug Uglies

17	10	16	$6

Gramercy | 257 Third Ave. (21st St.) | 6 to 23rd St. | 212-780-1944

This "very social" Gramercy Irish "neighborhood dive" is best known for its "endlessly entertaining" free tabletop shuffleboard – "'nuff said"; after a few drinks, you might "hear sirens", but that's because it's also a popular "off-duty cop" hangout ("behave yourself").

☑ Plunge

25	23	16	$15

Meatpacking | Gansevoort Hotel | 18 Ninth Ave. (bet. Little W. 12th & 13th Sts.) | A/C/E/L to 14th St./8th Ave. | 212-206-6700 | www.chinagrillmgt.com

Dudes with dough and "Jersey girls trying to get their attention" collide at this "glam-all-the-way" Meatpacking rooftop/"pool lounge" known for its "incredible" views of Downtown Manhattan and the Hudson; though the pricing is equally "sky-high", the cocktails are the "size of an aquarium" and the staff's "attitude is free", so when you need a break from "navigating cobblestones in stilettos", this one's a "must."

NEW Pony Bar

-	-	-	I

W 40s | 637 10th Ave. (45th St.) | A/C/E to 42nd St./Port Authority | 212-586-2707 | www.theponybar.com

West Hell's Kitchen is home to this new suds specialist ponying up an all-American list of craft drafts (only Bud is available by the bottle); the name refers to the 'short beers' served in between races at the track, and it's already a hit out of the gate with serious hopsheads given the well-curated selections and palatable pricing.

Pop Burger

20	18	18	$11

E 50s | 14 E. 58th St. (bet. 5th & Madison Aves.) | N/R/W to 5th Ave./59th St. | 212-991-6644

Meatpacking | 58-60 Ninth Ave. (bet. 14th & 15th Sts.) | A/C/E/L to 14th St./8th Ave. | 212-414-8686

www.popburger.com

There are "burgers up front" and "plenty of meat in the back" of this "original" Meatpacking fast-food lounge where you can "grab some sliders" at the entrance, then settle back with martinis in the rear lounge; though the "crowd is mixed", the "drinks are strong" and there's a bonus pool table and "booths showing porn" for interactive types; N.B. a Midtown triplex, with grub on the ground floor and two lounges above, opened post-Survey.

Porky's

| 15 | 14 | 17 | $10 |

Flatiron | 55 W. 21st St. (bet. 5th & 6th Aves.) | F/V to 23rd St. | 212-675-8007 | www.porkysnyc.com

"College bar meets Cancún" at this "loud 'n' rowdy" Flatiron roadhouse, a roiling mix of "Jell-O shots", live bands, "fishbowls" and "frat boys" that's appropriately named after the raunchy '80s flick; while "beer-swillers" have a "good ol' time", party-poopers think the "downscale" "keg-party" mood is as "cheesy as can be."

Posh

| 20 | 15 | 17 | $8 |

W 50s | 405 W. 51st St. (bet. 9th & 10th Aves.) | C/E to 50th St. | 212-957-2222

This "typical", "no-fuss" gay watering hole in Hell's Kitchen (aka "Hellsea") has a distinct "neighborhood bar feel" that draws "older", "semi-cute" dudes; ok, the decor doesn't come close to the name and service can be a "crapshoot", but it's an "ok alternative" for a "last-resort hookup."

NEW Pranna

| - | - | - | E |

Murray Hill | 79 Madison Ave. (bet. 28th & 29th Sts.) | N/R/W to 28th St. | 212-696-5700 | www.prannarestaurant.com

Housed in the soaring, tri-level Murray Hill space that was once home to Scopa, this mammoth bar/lounge/Pan-Asian eatery lives up to its name ('breath of life' in Sanskrit) by bringing a glossy, Tao-ish vibe to the moribund lower Madison Avenue scene; party promoters, pretty people and premium pricing come with the territory.

☑ Pravda

| 24 | 23 | 19 | $13 |

NoLita | 281 Lafayette St. (bet. Houston & Prince Sts.) | 6 to Bleecker St. | 212-226-4944 | www.pravdany.com

Experience "Moscow on the Hudson" in NoLita at this "sexy subterranean" "oldie but goodie" where "Cold War" decor and house-infused vodkas ("served as cold as the blond waitresses") lure a "classy" crew; dissenters yawn "yesterday's news", but propagandists propound it's "better now that the masses have fled" – even if the "prices have gone up while the crowd has gone down."

Pressure

| 18 | 18 | 16 | $12 |

G Village | 110 University Pl., 5th fl. (bet. 12th & 13th Sts.) | 4/5/6/L/N/Q/R/W to 14th St./Union Sq. | 212-352-1161 | www.pressurenyc.com

"So much entertainment" awaits at this Village multimedia complex "above Bowlmor", a "warehouse-type" sprawl equipped with a "billiards lounge", "large movie screens" and a disco annex; it's a natural for "corporate events", though some see it as an "expensive wannabe club."

Prime

| 22 | 21 | 20 | $15 |

Chelsea | 511 W. 28th St. (bet. 10th & 11th Aves.) | A/C/E to 34th St./Penn Station | 212-268-5105 | www.primenightclub.com

Fusing the former Myst and Retox spaces into one "nice-size" megalounge, this West Chelsea dance palace houses a curvy bar, bottle-buyer-ready banquettes and plenty of floor space beneath the DJ's perch; it can get "pretty crowded", despite snipes at "overpriced" revelry that's "gone from trendy" to subprime.

NEW Prime Meats
-	-	-	M

Carroll Gardens | 465 Court St. (Luquer St.) | Brooklyn | F/G to Carroll St. | 718-254-0327 | www.frankspm.com

A few doors down from the original Frankies in Carroll Gardens, this new chip off the old block is quartered in an appealingly dark, old-school-looking corner nook barely big enough for its long bar and smattering of tables; most nights it mixes its retro-inspired craft cocktails – think Sazeracs, coolers, a daily punch – for a standing-room-only crowd, accompanied by a brief menu of German-accented nibbles.

Professor Thom's
19	16	18	$7

E Village | 219 Second Ave. (bet. 13th & 14th Sts.) | L to 3rd Ave. | 212-260-9480 | www.professorthoms.com

With flat-screens and "cheap drinks" aplenty, this sprawling East Village sports bar is naturally a "frat boy" magnet and a particular favorite of "Red Sox" rooters; the "high-ceilinged" ground-floor space may have a "shopping-mall look", so those seeking more "intimate" times head to the "dimly lit" upstairs lounge where the vibe's "cooler."

Prohibition
21	17	19	$10

W 80s | 503 Columbus Ave. (bet. 84th & 85th Sts.) | 1 to 86th St. | 212-579-3100 | www.prohibition.net

Nightly "live music at no cover" is the draw at this "festive" Upper Westsider that's somewhat "more upscale" than the competition and thus a "thirtysomething" hangout; "strong drinks", back-room billiards and a "melting pot" of a dance floor keep things "loud and fun."

Providence/Triumph Room
17	20	16	$10

W 50s | 311 W. 57th St. (bet. 8th & 9th Aves.) | 1/A/B/C/D to 59th St./Columbus Circle | 212-307-0062 | www.providencenyc.com

Given its "cool history" (originally a church, then a recording studio, then Le Bar Bat), there are high hopes for this "beautiful" but "sparsely furnished" triplex that includes a restaurant, lounge and "not-to-be-missed" weekend disco in the basement; still, its "downmarket" following, "pushy staff" and "random address" near Columbus Circle lead some to shrug "worth a look, but not much more."

PS 450
20	18	18	$10

Murray Hill | 450 Park Ave. S. (bet. 30th & 31st Sts.) | 6 to 28th St. | 212-532-7474 | www.ps450.com

"Young professionals" "get schooled in the art of nightlife" at this "huge", "no-attitude" bar that's become part of the Murray Hill "meat market circuit", populated by "types too cool to go out on Third Avenue"; sure, the "McLounge feel is a turnoff" for some, but it's "always busy", so evidently no one seems to mind much; P.S. insiders whisper the "semi-hidden back room is where it's at."

Public
24	26	22	$13

NoLita | 210 Elizabeth St. (bet. Prince & Spring Sts.) | 6 to Spring St. | 212-343-7011 | www.public-nyc.com

"Once the diners clear out", there's a "good scene at the bar" of this "chic" NoLita eatery that's been "beautifully designed" in an "old-time schoolhouse" vein; "original cocktails" and a "beauty convention crowd" make it a magnet for "real adults", and even if the pops are "pricey", they're "worth it" when poured by one of the "hottie bartenders."

NEW Public Assembly

APPEAL	DECOR	SERVICE	COST
20	18	20	$11

Williamsburg | 70 N. Sixth St. (bet. Kent & Wythe Aves.) | Brooklyn | L to Bedford Ave. | 718-384-4586 | www.publicassemblynyc.com

"Much like it was from its days as Galapagos", this sprawling Williamsburg bar/performance space still features a "reflecting pool" at the entrance and walls lined with votive candles; maybe the talent's more "inconsistent" than in the past, but its roster of local bands, cabaret, burlesque and art installations is still very much in keeping with its predecessor's arty vibe.

Public House

18	17	17	$10

E 40s | 140 E. 41st St. (bet. Lexington & 3rd Aves.) | 4/5/6/7/S to 42nd St./ Grand Central | 212-682-3710 | www.publichousenyc.com

Come quitting time, "Grand Central–area workers" drop by this "massive" Midtown outlet of a national chain, a "friendly" bar/restaurant festooned with "patriotic" decor; ok, it's "nothing special", but at least it's "not trying to be hip."

Puck Fair

18	16	19	$8

SoHo | 298 Lafayette St. (bet. Houston & Prince Sts.) | 6 to Bleecker St. | 212-431-1200 | www.puckfairbarnyc.com

A SoHo "mainstay", this "huge", "always buzzing" Irish pub attracts "fun-loving, drink-swigging" folk who like its "energy", "awesome beer selection" and "relatively cheap" tabs; even though it's equipped with a "long" bar, "upstairs alcoves" and "cozy nooks" in the cellar, there's often "no place to move" in the "jam-packed" space.

Pudding Stones

21	19	20	$14

E 80s | 1457 Third Ave. (bet. 82nd & 83rd Sts.) | 4/5/6 to 86th St. | 212-717-5797
W 90s | 635 Amsterdam Ave. (91st St.) | 1/2/3 to 96th St. | 212-787-0501
www.puddingstoneswinebar.com

"Stylish" but "not snooty", this "neighborhood" UES wine bar (and its "cozy" crosstown counterpart) is a "welcoming" place to sweeten up a "first date" with "quality" vinos and "yummy" bites; the "polished" interior, "helpful staff" and "relaxed vibe" provide a "nice alternative" to the sea of "sports bars and Irish pubs" hereabouts.

Puffy's Tavern

19	13	19	$8

TriBeCa | 81 Hudson St. (Harrison St.) | 1 to Franklin St. | 212-227-3912 | www.puffystavern.com

This "relaxed", circa-1945 TriBeCa "standby" has undergone considerable refurbishments that "haven't diminished its charm"; once dowdy, divey and down-home, the tavern's now subtly buffed up, though its original "no-frills" tin ceilings, wood bar and tile floors remain intact, ditto the "interesting characters" crowd.

Pussycat Lounge

18	10	13	$11

Financial District | 96 Greenwich St. (Rector St.) | 1/R/W to Rector St. | 212-349-4800 | www.pussycatlounge.com

Providing a "skanky" jolt to an area that's "otherwise dead by 8 PM", this "unique" Financial District strip club showcases a "sleazy" roster of "tired, bored" strippers dancing behind its "old-school" bar; hipsters like the "local bands" thrashing around in the "cool" upstairs lounge, but admit that a visit here is strictly a "hit-or-miss" proposition.

Pyramid Club ⊅   18 | 10 | 15 | $8

E Village | 101 Ave. A (bet. 6th & 7th Sts.) | L to 1st Ave. | 212-228-4888 | www.thepyramidclub.com

The "only place you can still dance to New Order without a remix", this East Village "oldie" has been around since the "beginning of time" and is best known for its "'80s-themed" parties that will make many "bop against their will"; what goes on the rest of the week, however, is more debatable: it's either "always fun" or "so over."

Raccoon Lodge   15 | 11 | 18 | $7

Financial District | 59 Warren St. (bet. Church St. & W. B'way) | 1/2/3 to Chambers St. | 212-227-9894

"Still alive after all these years", this "last of the lodges" holed up in the Financial District is a "genuine dive bar" with a "hills-of-West-Virginia" vibe; a pool table and "fairly hot" barmaids add to the "fun", though all the action takes place "after work" – it's "empty after happy hour."

Radegast Hall   ∇ 26 | 21 | 15 | $9

Williamsburg | 113 N. Third St. (Berry St.) | Brooklyn | L to Bedford Ave. | 718-963-3973 | www.radegasthall.com

Pound a few in "authentic German style" at this "rustic" Williamsburg beer hall that dispenses an "awesome variety" of Euro brews in either an "upscale" rathskeller or a skylit, "picnic-tabled" biergarten; it draws "big groups of hipsters" who find it especially *wunderbar* on "summer days."

⊠ Rainbow Grill   24 | 24 | 21 | $17

W 40s | 30 Rockefeller Plaza, 65th fl. (49th St.) | B/D/F/V to 47-50th Sts./ Rockefeller Ctr. | 212-632-5100 | www.rainbowroom.com

It's "all about the view" at this "impressive" bar/lounge set "high above the city" on the 65th floor of Rock Center's GE building, a former restaurant space that's now doing drinks only; sure, it's "beyond pricey" and more than "a little touristy", but at least all those bright lights might take your mind off the "dim economy."

⊠ NEW Raines Law Room   - | - | - | E

Flatiron | 48 W. 17th St., downstairs (bet. 5th & 6th Aves.) | 4/5/6/L/ N/Q/R/W to 14th St./Union Sq. | no phone

The faux speakeasy trend continues at this new subterranean Flatiron lounge with an obscure entrance marked only by a tiny plaque and a doorbell; inside, costly classic cocktails arrive in a plush, private-men's-club-like space that includes booths tented with gauzy curtains, pull chains to summon your server and racy wallpaper in the loo; fun fact: it's named after an ancient NYC blue law prohibiting drinking on Sundays.

Randolph, The   19 | 14 | 19 | $13

Little Italy | 349 Broome St. (bet. Bowery & Elizabeth St.) | 6 to Spring St. | 212-274-0667 | www.randolphnyc.com

Annexing the Little Italy duplex formerly known as M Bar, this unassuming watering hole draws a "too-cool-for-school" crowd with "high-end" classic cocktails (available by the glass "or the pitcher"); oddly enough, despite its claim to be the 'opposite' of its rather snooty neighbor, Gold Bar, there's a velvet rope out front manned by "obnoxious" clipboard-toters.

Rare View

| | 22 | 18 | 16 | $11 |

Murray Hill | Shelburne Murray Hill Hotel | 303 Lexington Ave., rooftop (37th St.) | 4/5/6/7/S to 42nd St./Grand Central | 212-481-8439 | www.rarebarandgrill.com

Like the name says, "beautiful" Midtown panoramas are the draw at this "relaxed" seasonal rooftop bar that's just the ticket on a "breezy summer night"; expect the usual "pricey drinks", long lines and "tightly packed elevators", so for best results "go early to avoid the craziness."

Rasputin

| | 21 | 23 | 18 | $15 |

Brighton Bch | 2670 Coney Island Ave. (Ave. X) | Brooklyn | B/Q to Sheepshead Bay | 718-332-8111 | www.rasputinny.com

Join the "crazy Russians drinking nonstop" at this Brighton Beach restaurant/cabaret where the decadent menu, "top-shelf" vodkas and pull-out-all-the-stops floor show add some bling to the borscht belt; it's "excellent" if you know what to expect, but a "difficult" location and "interesting" if rather "odd" entertainment means "once is usually enough."

Rathbones Pub

| | 18 | 13 | 21 | $7 |

E 80s | 1702 Second Ave. (88th St.) | 4/5/6 to 86th St. | 212-369-7361 | www.rathbonesnyc.com

This "long-lived" Upper Eastsider on "frat row" is home to a perpetual "recent college grad" scene, with "not a sober person" to be found at prime times; cynics call it "typically divey", but "addictive" burgers and a "friendly staff" make for a "decent" enough pit stop.

🆕 Ravel Rooftop

| | - | - | - | M |

LIC | Ravel Hotel | 8-08 Queens Plaza S. (Vernon Blvd.) | Brooklyn | 7/N/W to Queensboro Plaza | 718-289-6101 | www.ravelhotel.com

The rooftop craze comes to LIC via this new, 6,500-sq.-ft. deck atop a boutique hotel not far from Silvercup Studios; channeling Miami by way of Nikki Beach, it features dueling bars, breezy cabanas, a retractable roof and drop-dead views of Midtown Manhattan and the Queensboro Bridge.

Rawhide ⇗

| | 12 | 8 | 18 | $7 |

Chelsea | 212 Eighth Ave. (21st St.) | C/E to 23rd St. | 212-242-9332

Chelsea boys preferring "machismo over fashionismo" are all over this "trashy" gay "cruise bar" that's "older than your granny" and "hasn't changed" since it opened in 1979; its "easy", "aging" crowd is there for "sleazy pickups", lubricated by dirt-"cheap drinks", not the "scary" decor.

Rayuela

| | 26 | 27 | 23 | $14 |

LES | 165 Allen St. (bet. Rivington & Stanton Sts.) | F/V to Lower East Side/ 2nd Ave. | 212-253-8840 | www.rayuelanyc.com

This "beautiful" Latin bar/eatery rayses the LES "trendy" quotient, bringing some "Miami Beach" to the area with two floors of "sexy atmosphere" built around a "live olive tree" planted in the middle of the loungey downstairs; "creative cocktails" and a "great wine selection" are sure to "get the party started."

	APPEAL	DECOR	SERVICE	COST

R Bar
21 | 18 | 17 | $10

NoLita | 218 Bowery (bet. Prince & Spring Sts.) | 6 to Spring St. | 212-334-0484 | www.rbarnyc.com

Get some "R&R" on a "desolate part of the Bowery" at this "factory"-size bar, a red light–bathed space sporting rocker artwork and "stripper poles in back" for "gals in the mood"; it's "usually crowded" on weekends with "sloppy", "just-outta-college" kids, and despite the "annoying" bouncers and "trashy feel", it's on its way to becoming "birthday central."

NEW RDV
∇ 22 | 24 | 17 | $16

Meatpacking | 409 W. 13th St., downstairs (bet. 9th Ave. & Washington St.) | A/C/E/L to 14th St./8th Ave. | 212-255-1933

The initials are short for 'rendezvous', and this petite new Meatpacking District "secret" beneath the sceney restaurant Bagatelle kicks it up old-school style with a vaguely Victorian vibe, heavy on the velvet and the chandeliers, with some modern art thrown in for good measure; a super-tough door, ultrapricey pops and a "snobby", Eurocentric crowd come with the territory.

Rebar
21 | 21 | 20 | $12

Dumbo | 147 Front St. (bet. Jay & Pearl Sts.) | Brooklyn | F to York St. | 718-797-2322 | www.rebarnyc.com

There's "always something going on" at this "cavernous" Dumbo bar, a former factory space clad in "exposed brick" that hosts everything from eclectic live music to "gallery offerings" to "Monday night tango"; thanks to "premium beers" and "organic" wines, "selection is never a problem" at this "chill" local retreat.

Rebel
∇ 18 | 15 | 17 | $11

Garment District | 251 W. 30th St. (bet. 7th & 8th Aves.) | A/C/E to 34th St./Penn Station | 212-695-2747 | www.rebelnyc.com

Set in the former Downtime digs, this sprawling live music venue from the owners of Webster Hall sports three dance floors, three bars and a midsize performance stage; its "random" Garment District address may be off the beaten path, but proximity to MSG and Penn Station makes it a natural for commuters.

Red Bench
∇ 21 | 16 | 19 | $9

SoHo | 107 Sullivan St. (bet. Prince & Spring Sts.) | C/E to Spring St. | 212-274-9120

"Wind down with a nightcap" at this "dark" SoHo bar where a combination of candlelight and draped velvet can lead to "romantic" results; sure, it's "teeny-tiny", but the "intimate" dimensions make "making out" on the cushioned namesake bench all the easier.

Redemption
14 | 13 | 15 | $8

E 50s | 1003 Second Ave. (53rd St.) | E/V to Lexington Ave./53rd St. | 212-319-4545 | www.redemptionnyc.com

This Midtown happy-hour "pickup" spot is a "nice enough addition" to the Second Avenue "walk of happy hour" with the usual "blaring music" and "cheap drinks"; but the unredeemed say this "lame meat market" has an overpowering "college smell" and "investment wanker" crowd.

	APPEAL	DECOR	SERVICE	COST

Red Lion

G Village | 151 Bleecker St. (Thompson St.) | 6 to Bleecker St. | 212-260-9797 | www.redlionnyc.com

| | 19 | 13 | 16 | $8 |

Known for roarin' live music, this Village pub follows through with satellite sports that attract random "friends from across the pond"; many say it's among "the best bets on Bleecker", but weekend cover charges are bad news for the "cheap college kids" in the "fun crowd."

Red Sky

Murray Hill | 47 E. 29th St. (bet. Madison & Park Aves.) | 6 to 28th St. | 212-447-1820 | www.redskynyc.com

| | 17 | 15 | 18 | $10 |

"Three floors with different themes" (a bar, a "curtain-draped" lounge and a tiki-themed "outdoor deck") make this Murray Hill spot a "solid" enough destination; surveyors split on the vibe – "loads of fun" vs. "loud and crowded" – but most agree the "decor is pretty cheesy."

Regency Hotel Library Bar
(aka Loews Regency Hotel Library Bar)

E 60s | Loews Regency Hotel | 540 Park Ave. (61st St.) | 4/5/6/N/R/W to 59th St./Lexington Ave. | 212-339-4050 | www.loewshotels.com

| | 25 | 24 | 22 | $16 |

Don't be perplexed by the bookshelves and "great couches" of this "classic" Midtown East hotel bar: it's not your "grandfather's house", but rather a "refined" lounge inhabited by "tourists", "business travelers" and "savvy New Yorkers", mainly the "old and wealthy."

Rehab

E Village | 25 Ave. B (bet. 2nd & 3rd Sts.) | F/V to Lower East Side/2nd Ave. | 212-253-2595

| | ∇ 17 | 14 | 17 | $9 |

"Funky" and "fun", this bi-level East Village music bar features "good DJs upstairs" and a solid slate of local alterna-bands jamming in the basement; "punk rock/heavy metal karaoke" nights are another "redeeming quality" of this "decent enough" space.

Relish

Williamsburg | 225 Wythe Ave. (N. 3rd St.) | Brooklyn | L to Bedford Ave. | 718-963-4546 | www.relish.com

| | ∇ 18 | 15 | 15 | $11 |

Denizens of "hipsterville" relish the "retro chic" at this Williamsburg diner featuring a "classic" lunch counter, noirish rear bar and "great" outdoor area; other pluses include "reasonable" tabs and funky "people-watching", though service skews "apathetic" and "attitude abounds."

Reservoir Bar

G Village | 70 University Pl. (bet. 10th & 11th Sts.) | N/R/W to 8th St. | 212-475-0770

| | 17 | 13 | 19 | $8 |

Sports nuts and frat boys find "no frills" but "brilliant wings" at this "neighborhood" Village joint offering a "decent draft selection" and "great drink specials" in a "dingy old pub" setting; maybe it's "better when NYU is not in session", though it always does the job when you're in the mood for "two or seven cocktails."

Retreat

Flatiron | 37 W. 17th St. (bet. 5th & 6th Aves.) | 4/5/6/L/N/Q/R/W to 14th St./Union Sq. | 212-488-6600 | www.retreat-nyc.com

| | 17 | 19 | 15 | $13 |

Trying to keep the Flatiron "trendy", this "lodge-style" lounge is a "rustic" retreat with a lacquered log cabin look incorporating antler chandeliers and DJs spinning "mainly R&B and rap" from a treehouse-styled booth; still, some snipe the "irritating doormen", saying it's "not hot enough for the pretentiousness."

Revel

22 | 19 | 16 | $12

Meatpacking | 10 Little W. 12th St. (bet. 9th Ave. & Washington St.) | A/C/E/L to 14th St./8th Ave. | 212-645-5369 | www.revel-ny.com
Wayfarers in the "hectic Meatpacking District" feel lucky to stumble upon this "refreshing escape", a "tasteful" traditional bar with a "low-key feel", where the going's "a bit expensive but totally worth it"; despite its relative anonymity, it's "getting too popular", largely due to its "beautiful", all-seasons back garden.

Revival

19 | 13 | 18 | $9

Gramercy | 129 E. 15th St. (bet. Irving Pl. & 3rd Ave.) | 4/5/6/L/N/Q/R/W to 14th St./Union Sq. | 212-253-8061
Revive your spirits with a "low-key" quaff at this "collegial" Gramercy "standby", a "comfy", bi-level affair with a "narrow" bar, "spacious" upstairs lounge and an "outdoor terrace"; though "nothing to really dwell on", it's a "reliable" place to "unwind without spending a fortune."

NEW Richardson, The

- | - | - | M

Williamsburg | 451 Graham Ave. (Richardson St.) | Brooklyn | L to Graham Ave. | 718-389-0839 | www.therichardsonnyc.com
On an out-of-the-way corner near the BQE, this spacious new East Williamsburg bar sticks closely to the speakeasy-lite formula with classic cocktails and "attractive vintage decor" (think dim lighting, damask wallpaper, wooden banquettes); the "low-key hipsters" in attendance like the "friendly" barkeeps, not the verging-on-"expensive" pricing.

Rick's Cabaret

20 | 18 | 19 | $13

Garment District | 50 W. 33rd St. (bet. B'way & 5th Ave.) | B/D/F/N/Q/R/V/W to 34th St./Herald Sq. | 212-372-0850 | www.ricks.com
This "standard-issue gentlemen's club" in the Garment District is the flagship of the "upscale" Texas chain, and splayed out over three floors, offering good sightlines of "beautiful but typical strippers"; maybe the cocktails are "average", but let's face it honey, "one doesn't go there for the drinks"; P.S. there's no cover charge from 11 AM to 7 PM.

Rink Bar

24 | 19 | 16 | $12

W 50s | Rockefeller Plaza | 20 W. 50th St. (bet. 5th & 6th Aves.) | B/D/F/V to 47-50th Sts./Rockefeller Ctr. | 212-332-7620 | www.rapatina.com
"Elbow through the tourists" and the "Midtown corporate" types (they're busy "networking" anyway) to belly up to the bar of this ultra-"crowded" seasonal venue that doubles as Rock Center's ice-skating rink in the winter; it's on the "pricey" side, but "when the weather's beautiful", it's nothing short of "wonderful"; P.S. open May–September.

Riposo 46

20 | 18 | 21 | $13

W 40s | 667 Ninth Ave. (bet. 46th & 47th Sts.) | C/E to 50th St. | 212-247-8018

Riposo 72

W 70s | 50 W. 72nd St. (bet. Columbus Ave. & CPW) | 1/2/3 to 72nd St. | 212-799-4140
"Learn to love your neighbors" at this "minute" Hell's Kitchen wine bar, a "charming" nook to "squeeze" into and repose over a "fine selection"

of vinos paired with "tasty" apps; being "a bit pricey" doesn't dent its popularity, and a "welcome" UWS sibling offers an expanded bottle selection and twice the space.

Ritz, The
▽ | 20 | 21 | 19 | $13 |

W 40s | 369 W. 46th St. (bet. 8th & 9th Aves.) | C/E to 50th St. | 212-333-2554

Hell's Kitchen's mushrooming gay bar scene continues to swell with the arrival of this "classy" double-decker – on Restaurant Row, no less - offering cocktailing in two cozy bar areas or in two luxe lounges; a killer sound system, buff, "on-point" bartenders and sceney DJs are all part of the package.

❷ Ritz-Carlton Star Lounge
| 24 | 25 | 25 | $17 |

W 50s | Ritz-Carlton Central Park | 50 Central Park S. (bet. 5th & 6th Aves.) | N/R/W to 5th Ave./59th St. | 212-521-6125 | www.ritzcarlton.com

A "very classy bar in a very classy town", this "highfalutin joint" in the Ritz-Carlton across from Central Park mixes "strong" cocktails for "older" folks, "business travelers" and those in the mood for "romance"; it's definitely "pricey" ("bring your check book" *and* "your wallet"), but definitely worth it for "impeccable service", "lovely" digs and a "luxe-all-the-way" experience.

River Room
| 21 | 19 | 16 | $15 |

Harlem | Riverbank State Park | 750 W. 145th St. (Riverside Dr.) | 1 to 145th St. | 212-491-1500 | www.theriverroomofharlem.com

"Sweeping" views of the George Washington Bridge and the Palisades are all the "eye candy" you'll need at this "high-end" bar/restaurant set in a "glass atrium" in Harlem's Riverbank State Park; it's admittedly "out of the way", but live jazz on weekends makes it a destination for "change-of-pace" seekers.

Riviera Cafe
| 14 | 9 | 16 | $9 |

W Village | 225 W. Fourth St. (7th Ave. S.) | 1 to Christopher St. | 212-929-3250

Just off Sheridan Square, this veteran "New England sports bar" is "all about the Pats and the Red Sox" – and only for Yankee fans who "want some trouble"; sure, service is "slow" and the eats "below average", but then again the "crowd's fun" and there's "lots of room to spread out."

Rm. Fifty5
| 21 | 23 | 18 | $14 |

W 50s | Dream Hotel | 210 W. 55th St. (bet. B'way & 7th Ave.) | N/Q/R/W to 57th St./7th Ave. | 212-246-2211 | www.rmfifty5.com

An ornate eyeful in Midtown, this "sexy" hotel bar turns on the Provençal "allure" with rococo furniture and blue-glass chandeliers; the "definitely dreamlike" ambiance is "expensive but worth it" for "cocktails after work", even if the "random crowd" that comes with the "touristy" territory "brings you back to reality."

Rockwood Music Hall
| 23 | 16 | 19 | $8 |

LES | 196 Allen St. (bet. Houston & Stanton Sts.) | F/V to Lower East Side/2nd Ave. | 212-477-4155 | www.rockwoodmusichall.com

"Tight squeeze" is putting it mildly at this beyond-"cozy" LES concert space that gets "very cramped" very quickly ("are they kidding calling it a 'hall'?"); still, fans applaud its stellar acoustics, wide roster of "local acts" and a vibe that's slightly more "upscale" than its competitors.

	APPEAL	DECOR	SERVICE	COST

Rodeo Bar

20 | 17 | 17 | $8

Murray Hill | 375 Third Ave. (27th St.) | 6 to 28th St. | 212-683-6500 |
www.rodeobar.com

It's "more Manhattan, Kansas, than New York" at this "down 'n' dirty"
Murray Hill "honky-tonk" that ropes 'em in with "killer margaritas" and
live country music with "no cover"; its "rowdy", "college-age" crowd also
likes the "cheap" tabs, "converted camper back bar" and overall "high
energy" – plus "there are peanut shells on the floor, enough said."

Rogue

15 | 14 | 18 | $9

Chelsea | 757 Sixth Ave. (25th St.) | F/V to 23rd St. | 212-242-6434 |
www.roguenyc.com

There's "plenty of space to hang out" at this "casual" Chelsea sports
bar that's a "decent enough place to watch European football" along
with a "melting pot" crowd; too bad the lighting's "too bright" and the
place "thins out early", but at least there are "lots of TVs" and
the beer's "cheap."

☐ Room, The ⚗

26 | 22 | 21 | $9

SoHo | 144 Sullivan St. (bet. Houston & Prince Sts.) | C/E to Spring St. |
212-477-2102 | www.theroomsbeerandwine.com

"They like it quiet" at this "small" SoHo lounge, a "perfect date place"
stocked with enough "comfy couches" to make for a "very romantic"
mood; a "diverse wine" list and correspondingly "carefully selected"
suds (with an emphasis on Belgian brews) embellish the "relaxed" ambiance, except on weekends, when "sardinelike" conditions prevail.

Room Service

▽ 18 | 18 | 18 | $11

Flatiron | 35 E. 21st St. (bet. B'way & Park Ave. S.) | N/R/W to 23rd St. |
212-254-5709 | www.roomserviceny.com

Hotel hospitality and nightlife collide at this "dark" Flatiron club built
around nine "curtained-off" booths with mini-fridges, "plasma TVs"
and a personal "concierge"; critics hiss "too gimmicky", but fans say
it's "great if you're willing to plunk down the dough."

Rosa Mexicano

22 | 22 | 20 | $13

E 50s | 1063 First Ave. (58th St.) | 4/5/6/N/R/W to 59th St./Lexington Ave. |
212-753-7407

Flatiron | 9 E. 18th St. (bet. B'way & 5th Ave.) | 4/5/6/L/N/Q/R/W
to 14th St./Union Sq. | 212-533-3350

W 60s | 61 Columbus Ave. (62nd St.) | 1 to 66th St. | 212-977-7700
www.rosamexicano.com

"Signature" pomegranate margaritas and "*muy delicioso*" guacamole
made tableside are the calling cards of this Mexican trio also famed
for their "festive atmospheres" and "marathon table waits" for dinner;
voters single out the newest outpost on Union Square as "much roomier" than its Uptown cousins, with a "younger crowd" to boot.

Rose

▽ 21 | 20 | 19 | $11

Williamsburg | 345 Grand St. (bet. Havemeyer St. & Marcy Ave.) |
Brooklyn | L to Bedford Ave. | 718-599-0069 | www.liveatrose.com
World music is the thing at this Williamsburg performance venue set
on a happening stretch of Grand Street; though the retro nightclub
vibe works well for smart cocktails, its eclectic roster of artists (that
can usually be heard for no cover charge) is the real drawing card here.

☑ Rose Bar

23 | 26 | 21 | $18

Gramercy | Gramercy Park Hotel | 2 Lexington Ave. (21st St.) | 6 to 23rd St. | 212-920-3300 | www.gramercyparkhotel.com

More loungelike than the neighboring Jade Bar, this "beautiful" watering hole in Ian Schrager's revamped Gramercy Park Hotel is a vast, high-ceilinged thing dominated by a red-felt pool table and "amazing" artwork by Andy Warhol and Julian Schnabel (who also designed the room); expect "blow-your-budget" pricing and a tough door guarded by "snooty" "clipboard holders", with reservations required after 9 PM.

Rose Club

23 | 23 | 22 | $18

W 50s | Plaza Hotel | 768 Fifth Ave. (59th St.) | N/R/W to 5th Ave./ 59th St. | 212-759-3000 | www.theplaza.com

"Skilled bartenders", "lush decor" and a "sophisticated" crowd make for a "posh night out" at this "luxe" mezzanine lounge overlooking the lobby of the Plaza Hotel; true, the pricing may be "out of style for the current economy" and those "purple ceiling lights are great – *if* you like purple" – but ultimately it's one "sexy idea for a landmarked space."

☑ Roseland

19 | 13 | 14 | $13

W 50s | 239 W. 52nd St. (bet. B'way & 8th Ave.) | C/E to 50th St. | 212-247-0200 | www.roselandballroom.com

"Large and in charge" for over 50 years, this "so-cool" Theater District ballroom provides the opportunity for clubbers to see a concert or just "get up and dance" in "historic" digs; its varied roster includes everything from salsa spectaculars to "big acts that can't sell out the Garden or Radio City", and even though tickets can be "expensive", a visit to this "staple" is "a must."

Rouge Wine Bar

22 | 20 | 19 | $14

W Village | 99 Bank St., downstairs (Greenwich St.) | A/C/E/L to 14th St./ 8th Ave. | 212-929-0509 | www.pariscommune.net

Hidden behind a red velvet curtain, this "intimate" West Village wine bar beneath Paris Commune is perfect for "good conversation" in semi-"swanky" digs complete with a wraparound Toulouse-Lautrec–esque mural; a mirrored ceiling that feels like a skylight further embellishes the "cozy" scene.

Royale

▽ 21 | 19 | 20 | $7

Park Slope | 506 Fifth Ave. (bet. 12th & 13th Sts.) | Brooklyn | F/M/R to 4th Ave./9th St. | 718-840-0089 | www.royalebrooklyn.com

"Dark and bordellolike", this "laid-back" Park Slope watering hole is really "two bars in one", with a dim, red-lit front parlor backed up by a rear lounge exuding an "open-to-anything feel"; wallet-friendly pricing and DJ sets comprised of the "stuff hipsters eat up" make for some "first-rate" drinking here.

Royale ⌂

20 | 14 | 18 | $10

E Village | 157 Ave. C (bet. 9th & 10th Sts.) | L to 1st Ave. | 212-254-6600

"Cool locals" hold court at this affordable "neighborhood spot" that earns allegiance with its "excellent" house burger and "solid" suds selection; an off-the-grid Avenue C address keeps the mood "relaxed", and other attractions include a "friendly staff", classic rock on the juke and a sizable "outside area."

	APPEAL	DECOR	SERVICE	COST

Royal Oak ⚲

∇ **20** | **24** | **19** | **$8**

Williamsburg | 594 Union Ave. (N. 11th St.) | Brooklyn | L to Bedford Ave. | 718-388-3884 | www.sweetups.com

"Out of the way" in an "underserved" part of Williamsburg lies this "cavernous" taproom, a "wide-open", faintly retro space that recalls an Elks lodge with its abundance of tile and flocked wallpaper; it "jumps hard" on weekends, so on quieter school nights, regulars pretend it's their "private clubhouse."

Rudy's Bar

19 | **10** | **18** | **$6**

W 40s | 627 Ninth Ave. (bet. 44th & 45th Sts.) | A/C/E to 42nd St./ Port Authority | 212-974-9169 | www.rudysbarnyc.com/

A "free hot dog" with every drink provides a cheap thrill at this "rowdy" Hell's Kitchen barroom, a "no-pretenses" joint that's a "down-home" destination for a crowd that "runs the gamut from hookers to film crews to merchant marines"; good thing they "keep the lights low" – it helps disguise the "duct tape upholstery."

Rue B

22 | **22** | **21** | **$10**

E Village | 188 Ave. B (bet. 11th & 12th Sts.) | L to 1st Ave. | 212 358-1700

East Villagers say *"oui, oui!"* to this "faux French" bistro, a "home away from home" where "pleasant" barkeeps "mix a mean cocktail" to the tune of "unbeatable" live jazz; even better, one of the "happiest *heureuse* hours in town" offers two-for-one "froufrou" drinks.

Rum House

14 | **13** | **16** | **$10**

W 40s | Edison Hotel | 228 W. 47th St. (bet. B'way & 8th Ave.) | 1 to 50th St. | 212-869-3005

Half sports bar, half piano bar (with a touch of "pseudo-lounge" thrown in for good measure), this "casual" Theater District hangout is a "convenient" stop for "tourists and regulars" in need of a "quick drink" pre- or post-curtain; just don't look around too closely – the "dark" interior brings to mind an "old wooden ship" and "could use an update."

Rumours

17 | **15** | **17** | **$9**

W 50s | 933 Eighth Ave. (55th St.) | 1/A/B/C/D to 59th St./Columbus Circle | 212-757-2373 | www.rumoursbar.com

Hearsay has it that this "friendly", "sports-focused" Irish "local" in Hell's Kitchen is a "basic pub" that's "convenient" for "casual" quaffing in front of the flat-screens; a DJ "spinning tunes from a pulpit" is a stab at style, but it's "definitely not a scene."

Runway

16 | **17** | **13** | **$15**

Murray Hill | 4 E. 28th St. (bet. 5th & Madison Aves.) | N/R/W to 23rd St. | 347-604-2765 | www.runwaylounge.com

"Strut your stuff" on the catwalk at this Murray Hill club featuring "the usual" low lights and cushy, bottle service–ready banquettes; but once past the "rude door", critics of the "unimpressive" scenery maintain "despite the name", it's "not fashionable at all."

Rush

20 | **18** | **18** | **$14**

Chelsea | 579 Sixth Ave. (16th St.) | F/L/V to 14th St./6th Ave. | 212-243-6100

"Very young" revelers get a rush from this Chelsea gay club in the former Heaven space, a triple-tiered dance party where a "decent sound system" stirs up some "fun" grinding on the upstairs and downstairs floors; gawkers confirm the "lascivious" mood is "exactly what you'd expect."

Russian Samovar

20 | 16 | 22 | $11

W 50s | 256 W. 52nd St. (bet. B'way & 8th Ave.) | C/E to 50th St. | 212-757-0168 | www.russiansamovar.com

"Homemade" infused vodka – "and plenty of it" – supplies the "kick" at this Theater District "hoot" offering a "real Moscow" experience via authentic comrades in the crowd and a pianist conjuring up "Old Russia" on the keyboard; *da*, the "bar area's small" and the decor could stand an "overall update", but at least the pops are "potent" here.

Russian Vodka Room

21 | 16 | 18 | $10

W 50s | 265 W. 52nd St. (bet. B'way & 8th Ave.) | C/E to 50th St. | 212-307-5835 | www.russianvodkaroom.com

"Boris and Natasha types" gravitate to this "small, dark" Theater District boîte, a "tribute to the homeland" serving an "astonishing range" of "extraordinarily strong" infused vodkas; "short of going to Brooklyn", it feels particularly "authentic" thanks to the "heavily Russian crowd" ("half of whom sound exactly like Borat"), "all getting blasted."

☒ Rusty Knot

21 | 18 | 19 | $9

W Village | 425 West St. (W. 11th St.) | A/C/E/L to 14th St./8th Ave. | 212-645-5668

A "faux dive" with "ironic" decor that's half "nautical", half "1970s basement", this "low-priced", "way-the-hell-west" Villager vends "kitschy" rum drinks in "tiki glasses" along with "throwback" snacks (think pigs in a blanket, "pretzel dogs"); "sunset" views over the Hudson, "quick-on-the-draw" service and a "fantastic juke box" lures everyone from the "tragically hip" to "UES prepsters."

Ryan's Daughter

19 | 15 | 21 | $7

E 80s | 350 E. 85th St. (bet. 1st & 2nd Aves.) | 4/5/6 to 86th St. | 212-628-2613

The "same as it ever was", this 28-year-old Irish pub is an "all-around pleasant" UES hang with the usual pool, darts and video games, plus "free potato chips"; one thing's a bit different, though: the "old mix with the young" here, so be cool with the idea that the "people next to you are the same age as your parents."

Ryan's Irish Pub

17 | 16 | 20 | $7

E Village | 151 Second Ave. (bet. 9th & 10th Sts.) | 6 to Astor Pl. | 212-979-9511 | www.ryansnyc.com

A long-standing East Village "standby", this "small" Irish pub lures "young" folk with "fair" prices and "quick service"; its sidewalk seating with front-row views of the Second Avenue parade "can't be beat on a nice evening", but otherwise, it's "eh, just eh."

☒ Sakagura

27 | 24 | 24 | $14

E 40s | 211 E. 43rd St., downstairs (bet. 2nd & 3rd Aves.) | 4/5/6/7/S to 42nd St./Grand Central | 212-953-7253 | www.sakagura.com

A "deep lineup of top-notch sakes" lures fans to this "clandestine" Japanese bar/restaurant with a "strange location" in the basement of a "nondescript", Grand Central-area office building; nothing gets "lost in translation" here – the "refined service" is like being "back in Tokyo" – and adding to the "authenticity", it's as "expensive as hell."

Sake Hana

	APPEAL	DECOR	SERVICE	COST
	24	22	21	$11

E 70s | 265 E. 78th St. (bet. 2nd & 3rd Aves.) | 6 to 77th St. | 212-327-0582
"Sultry" and "sophisticated", this "tiny" UES Japanese lounge offers a variety of sake and "Asian-inspired drinks", plus a "nice, dark" vibe perfect for "intimacy or serious talk" – "definitely bring a date."

Sala

	23	21	22	$10

Flatiron | 35 W. 19th St. (bet. 5th & 6th Aves.) | N/R/W to 23rd St. | 212-229-2300
NoHo | 344 Bowery (Great Jones St.) | 6 to Bleecker St. | 212-979-6606
www.salanyc.com
This "classy Spanish taverna" in NoHo vends "potent sangria" and *muy bueno* tapas in "dimly lit", double-decker digs designed for those "who are a little older than 22"; its Flatiron sib may not be as sultry, but service is just as "friendly" and the happy-hour acoustics just as "loud."

Salon de Ning

	26	25	22	$18

W 50s | Peninsula Hotel | 700 Fifth Ave., 23rd fl. (55th St.) | E/V to 5th Ave./53rd St. | 212-903-3097 | www.salondening.com
Though "not much different" than its predecessor (the Pen-Top), this "very upscale" Midtown rooftop now incorporates the Sino-chic stylings of prewar Shanghai into its "sophisticated" glassed-in bar and daybed-equipped terrace; the "fantastic views" and "old-school service" appease the "masters of the universe" in the crowd, but "bring the platinum card" – or go when "someone else is paying."

Saloon

	17	15	18	$10

E 80s | 1584 York Ave. (bet. 83rd & 84th Sts.) | 4/5/6 to 86th St. | 212-570-5454 | www.saloonnyc.com
When you "want to feel like a freshman" again, it's "frat central" at this big but "not overpacked" UES bar/dance club that attracts a "just-out-of-college" crew; the DJs spin a "nice variety" of "'80s and hip-hop" tunes, and there's sideline "standing room" even when the floor fills up.

Salt Bar

	24	20	21	$10

LES | 29A Clinton St. (bet. Houston & Stanton Sts.) | F/J/M/Z to Delancey/Essex Sts. | 212-979-8471 | www.saltnyc.com
Lower Eastsiders find "pure romance" at this "cool little" bar/noshery that provides a "great evening" via "excellent" specialty cocktails, "delicious" wines and "yummy" small plates; the "intimate", "low-key" setting convinces many to settle in and "chill there all night."

Sample

	19	18	22	$8

Cobble Hill | 152 Smith St. (Bergen St.) | Brooklyn | F/G to Bergen St. | 718-643-6622
Though this "remarkably friendly" Smith Street wine bar has scant space and "no kitchen", it compensates with an ample lineup of "reasonably priced" vinos, "interesting cocktails" and globe-trotting "snacks straight out of a can"; there's also a sample-size "garden out back."

Ⓩ NEW Santos Party House

	21	13	17	$10

Chinatown | 96 Lafayette St. (bet. Walker & White Sts.) | A/C/E to Canal St. | 212-714-4646 | www.santospartyhouse.com
"Party you will" at this double-decker Chinatown dance club-cum-music venue (part-owned by dude gone wild Andrew W.K.) that deliv-

ers on its promise as live groups, the "finest DJs" and a "great sound system" are showcased on its black-walled, disco-balled ground floor or in the more bare-bones basement; fans feel it "fills a void" for "great energy" and "no-fuss" hedonism.

Sapphire Lounge
▽ 18 | 13 | 14 | $9

LES | 249 Eldridge St. (Houston St.) | F/V to Lower East Side/2nd Ave. | 212-777-5153 | www.sapphirenyc.com

"Low-key and friendly", this petite Lower East Side danceteria boasts "one of the best dance floors in the city" and attracts a "mix of people" in the mood to party without the "hassle of a megaclub"; alright, it "isn't glamorous" (some say it's "like dancing in a garage"), but it is "lots of fun" and the "music goes all night."

NEW Sapphire NY
21 | 18 | 21 | $15

E 60s | 333 E. 60th St. (bet. 1st & 2nd Aves.) | 4/5/6/N/R/W to 59th St./Lexington Ave. | 212-421-3600 | www.nysapphire.com

Fans of the Vegas original welcome this "upscale" stripteaser to Scores' old UES site, where "yummy" silicone sisters bare their essentials in a 10,000-sq.-ft., blue-hued space; maybe the tabs are a "total rip-off", but patrons with "headlights" in their eyes swear the talent will "satisfy even the most discerning."

Savalas
▽ 16 | 13 | 16 | $7

Williamsburg | 285 Bedford Ave. (bet. Grand & S. 1st Sts.) | Brooklyn | L to Bedford Ave. | 718-599-5565 | www.savalasnyc.com

An "eclectic crowd" turns up at this "solid" South Williamsburg barroom where the drinks are "cheap" and the mood is "relaxed" thanks to a cozy setting; even though it's away from the Bedford Avenue scene, "phenomenal DJs" make it a "destination" for true believers.

Schiller's
22 | 21 | 19 | $10

LES | 131 Rivington St. (Norfolk St.) | F/J/M/Z to Delancey/Essex Sts. | 212-260-4555 | www.schillersny.com

Aka "Pastis East", Keith McNally's LES "hipster haven" may be "more restaurant" than bar, but that doesn't keep thirsty "European socialites", "cool kids" and "wannabes" away from its "vintage" digs channeling a '20s Parisian cafe; brace yourself for a "loud", "electric" scene at prime times, and don't miss its "funky bathroom" complete with an amusing "unisex handwashing station."

Scratcher
20 | 16 | 19 | $7

E Village | 209 E. Fifth St., downstairs (bet. 2nd & 3rd Aves.) | 6 to Astor Pl. | 212-477-0030

The name is Irish slang for 'bed', but this "laid-back" East Village pub keeps "younger" patrons alert with "strong drinks", "cheap" tabs and a "convivial" vibe; the simple "picnic-bench" seating can accommodate "a pile of friends", though aesthetes fret it's "getting grungier."

Z SEA
25 | 27 | 19 | $11

NEW Meatpacking | 835 Washington St. (Little W. 12th St.) | A/C/E/L to 14th St./8th Ave. | 212-243-3339
Williamsburg | 114 N. Sixth St. (Berry St.) | Brooklyn | L to Bedford Ave. | 718-384-8850 | www.seathairestaurant.com

Even Manhattanites "make the trip" to Williamsburg for a gander at this over-the-top Thai bar/restaurant set in a "glamorous cavern" replete with club lighting, "suspended swings" and a reflecting pool; a "DJ spins groovy mixes" while "hipsters strain to out-hipster each other" over the din of the "loud", "crowded", "killer" scene; N.B. the new Meatpacking satellite opened post-Survey.

Secret

| | 20 | 20 | 18 | $11 |

Chelsea | 525 W. 29th St. (bet. 10th & 11th Aves.) | A/C/E to 34th St./Penn Station | 212-268-5580

The "best-kept secret" on a "dead block" in far West Chelsea, this "undercover" gay/straight-friendly lounge is set in an "old warehouse space" (think "G" but with "more space to breathe and mingle"); the "out-of-the-way" locale keeps "off hours" quiet, but a "decent" enough weekend crowd means you can "go with friends – or find new ones."

Sequoia

| | 22 | 18 | 20 | $15 |

Seaport | Pier 17 | 89 South St. (Fulton St.) | 2/3/4/5/A/C/J/M/Z to Fulton St./B'way/Nassau | 212-732-9090 | www.arkrestaurants.com

This "South Street Seaport staple" turns from seafood palace to boogiefest on summer Fridays with "party-all-night music" and "plenty of dancing"; the "million-dollar view of the East River" lures tourists and "suits" alike, all clamoring for the prime "outdoor seating."

Serafina

| | 20 | 19 | 19 | $13 |

E 50s | 38 E. 58th St. (bet. Madison & Park Aves.) | 4/5/6/N/R/W to 59th St./Lexington Ave. | 212-832-8888

E 60s | 29 E. 61st St. (bet. Madison & Park Aves.) | 4/5/6/N/R/W to 59th St./Lexington Ave. | 212-702-9898

E 70s | 1022 Madison Ave., 2nd fl. (79th St.) | 6 to 77th St. | 212-734-2676

W 40s | Time Hotel | 224. W. 49th St. (bet. B'way & 8th Ave.) | C/E to 50th St. | 212-247-1000

W 50s | Dream Hotel | 210 W. 55th St. (bet. B'way & 7th Ave.) | N/Q/R/W to 57th St./7th Ave. | 212-315-1700

www.serafinarestaurant.com

These "très chic" Italians "do the job" with "classy" surroundings and an "international" clientele of "good lookers" and "fashion victims"; each outpost has its own "trendy" decor and the potables are "consistent" if "costly", but you may need to "bring a bullhorn when they're crowded."

Session 73

| | 19 | 15 | 16 | $11 |

E 70s | 1359 First Ave. (73rd St.) | 6 to 77th St. | 212-517-4445 | www.session73.com

"Post-college" kids keep this "loud" Upper East Side music venue hopping to the sounds of live blues, jazz and funk, not to mention weekly "salsa lessons"; true, the decor's "generic", but it sure beats the long "trek Downtown" – and the "scene changes" from night to night, depending who's onstage.

7B

| | 19 | 13 | 17 | $6 |

(aka Horseshoe Bar)

E Village | 108 Ave. B (7th St.) | F/V to Lower East Side/2nd Ave. | 212-473-8840

This "dive bar from back in the day" is East Village "attitude personified" with its "seedy" surroundings, "cheap booze" and juke "cranked up to 11"; the tapsters behind the horseshoe counter may "ignore more than they pour", but it's "popular" with everyone from "hipsters to the anti-hip" – and even "yuppie" hoofbeats are sometimes heard.

	APPEAL	DECOR	SERVICE	COST

17 Murray

| | 14 | 13 | 18 | $11 |

Financial District | 17 Murray St. (bet. B'way & Church St.) | R/W to City Hall | 212-608-3900 | www.17murray.com

Pick up all the "political" poop at this Financial District "local", a "popular" caucus for "City Hall" and Centre Street denizens who elect to "defer going home at night"; maybe it's too "isolated" and "lacks atmosphere", but for certain constituencies its "low cost" is enough of a draw.

Shade

| | ▽ 26 | 23 | 23 | $11 |

G Village | 241 Sullivan St. (bet. Bleecker & W. 3rd Sts.) | A/B/C/D/E/F/V to W. 4th St. | 212-982-6275

Cozy up on "dark rainy nights" at this "tiny" Greenwich Village wine bar where "great crêpes" and an "eclectic iPod mix" work with the vino to make for a "mellow" mood; even better, the "friendly staff" guarantees an "unpretentious" experience.

Shalel Lounge

| | 24 | 24 | 16 | $10 |

W 70s | 65½ W. 70th St., downstairs (bet. Columbus Ave. & CPW) | B/C to 72nd St. | 212-873-2300

There's "no sign" on the street for this "sultry", "subterranean oasis" under an UWS Greek taverna, but the word is out, so the "nooks-and-crannies" setting fills up fast on weekends; "lots of candles", "grottoes" and a "waterfall" add to its "sexy" sheen, and most are so involved in "PDA" that they fail to notice the "poor service."

🆕 Shang Bar

| | - | - | - | E |

LES | Thompson LES Hotel | 187 Orchard St. (bet. Houston & Stanton Sts.) | F/V to Lower East Side/2nd Ave. | 212-260-7900 | www.shangnyc.com

The '90s live on in this slick cocktail lounge opposite the same-named eatery in the new Thompson LES hotel; dim lighting, ambient music and banquettes made from tufted black leather are catnip to its black-clad fashionista following who think nothing of shelling out big bucks for fancy-schmancy cocktails.

Shebeen

| | 22 | 19 | 19 | $11 |

NoLita | 202 Mott St. (bet. Kenmare & Spring Sts.) | 6 to Spring St. | 212-625-1105

When it comes to "mellow hipness", it's tough to top this "cool, down-low" NoLita bar that's notably "friendly" and "not overly crowded"; the "amazing martinis" (especially the "tasty lychee" variety) help blot out its "small" dimensions.

Sherwood Cafe ⊘

| | ▽ 23 | 20 | 19 | $9 |

Boerum Hill | 195 Smith St. (bet. Baltic & Warren Sts.) | Brooklyn | F/G to Bergen St. | 718-596-1609 | www.sherwoodcafe.com

Just like "hanging out in grandma's attic", this "antiques"-filled Smith Street bistro is full of "quirky" items, most of which are for sale; in addition to the "kitschy" atmospherics, expect a "cool fireplace", a "spectacular backyard" and service that's "good, if occasionally absent-minded."

Ship of Fools

| | 16 | 12 | 18 | $7 |

E 80s | 1590 Second Ave. (bet. 82nd & 83rd Sts.) | 4/5/6 to 86th St. | 212-570-2651 | www.shipoffoolsnyc.com

"Pub central" for athletic supporters, this "big" Upper East Side sports bar sports "TVs at every angle" plus an easily mopped-up tile floor that's a "handy companion to their pitcher specials"; sure, the mood is strictly "frat-house haze", but for "buckets of suds with your buds", it's a "decent" enough destination.

Shoolbred's

20 | 20 | 19 | $8

E Village | 197 Second Ave. (bet. 12th & 13th Sts.) | L to 1st Ave. | 212-529-0340 | www.shoolbreds.com

"Classier than your average" East Villager, this Scot-inspired "stop-by" transports you "out of Manhattan" with a "publike" bar fronting a "cozy", fireplace-equipped rear area; throw in tapsters serving up "eclectic" suds and single-malts, and it's a bonny "respite" bred with a bit "more character and charm" than the norm.

NEW SideBar

21 | 18 | 20 | $11

Gramercy | 120 E. 15th St. (Irving Pl.) | 4/5/6/L/N/Q/R/W to 14th St./ Union Sq. | 212-677-2900 | www.sidebarnyc.com

This "shiny" new Gramercy sports bar-cum-lounge finds "young professionals" sipping 'tinis side by side with "massive crowds" of "Penn State" alums and "Wrong Islanders" who make it a "post-game madhouse"; the candlelight, glass walls and plasma TVs may be a "weird mix", but cheerleaders contend it's "fair enough given the nearby alternatives."

Sidecar

20 | 19 | 20 | $11

Park Slope | 560 Fifth Ave. (bet. 15th & 16th Sts.) | Brooklyn | R to Prospect Ave. | 718-369-0077

South Slope "yuppies who are too lazy to travel" settle into this "excellent" venue, a "classic" railroad-style bar/restaurant with "professional" service and a "focus on the cocktail" that are "rare for the 'hood"; though "a little expensive", it's already "popular" since there's "nothing like it" on this side of the tracks.

Sidetracks

15 | 17 | 18 | $10

Sunnyside | 45-08 Queens Blvd. (bet. 45th & 46th Sts.) | Queens | 7 to 46th St. | 718-786-3570 | www.sidetracksny.com

"Party with middle-class" folks at this "casual" restaurant/bar in Sunnyside that's "nothing special" on school nights but more happening when it "turns into a nightclub on weekends"; service may be "slow" and the drinks "pricey", but a renovation has added more decor appeal.

Sidewalk

19 | 10 | 19 | $7

E Village | 94 Ave. A (6th St.) | L to 1st Ave. | 212-473-7373 | www.sidewalkmusic.net

Enabling East Village "brunching and cocktailing" for 25 years, this bar (with an adjacent restaurant) also hosts "live music" and "open-mike" performances; ok, the performers can be "hit-or-miss", but at least they are acts "you won't see anyplace else."

Simone

19 | 21 | 16 | $10

E Village | 134 First Ave. (St. Marks Pl.) | 6 to Astor Pl. | 212-982-6665 | www.simonemartinibar.com

"Elaborate", bordello-esque decor that "draws you in from the street" is the calling card of this "sultry", "retro-sexy" East Villager from the Yaffa Cafe folks; a "fun martini list" helps blot out the "strange" service, "tourist"-prone crowd and "not-cutting-edge" vibe.

Sing Sing Karaoke

21 | **13** | **17** | **$9**

E Village | 81 Ave. A (bet. 5th & 6th Sts.) | L to 1st Ave. | 212-674-0700
E Village | 9 St. Marks Pl., 2nd fl. (bet. 2nd & 3rd Aves.) | 6 to Astor Pl. | 212-387-7800
www.karaokesingsing.com

These East Village karaoke joints boast a "great array of songs" with which to "make a fool of yourself", but regulars take shelter in the "tiny" private rooms given the "drunken off-key" crooning going on in the public bar; an "unremarkable drink selection" means it's "best to be already soused before you walk through the door."

Sin Sin/Leopard Lounge

18 | **16** | **15** | **$9**

E Village | 248 E. Fifth St. (2nd Ave.) | 6 to Astor Pl. | 212-253-2222 | www.leopardloungenyc.com

Maybe there's "not much sinning going on" at this "average" bi-level East Villager, but its "cool hip-hop" beats and "velvety seats" come at a "low cover" for those "not in the mood for a big club"; the upstairs dance floor can get "packed and sweaty", but hey, "sometimes you need that."

Sip

18 | **17** | **18** | **$7**

W 100s | 998 Amsterdam Ave. (bet. 109th & 110th Sts.) | 1 to Cathedral Pkwy./110th St. | 212-316-2747 | www.sipbar.com

This "shoebox-size" Morningside Heights coffeehouse-cum-lounge-cum-"hipster vortex" is a welcome alternative to the area's "usual frat hangouts", and fans hope it's a portent of the "rejuvenation of Amsterdam Avenue"; while the "quirky decor" divides voters ("cool" vs. "tries too hard"), there's agreement on the "friendly staff", "excellent DJs" and "reasonable prices."

NEW 675 Bar

- | **-** | **-** | **M**

Meatpacking | 675 Hudson St., downstairs (enter on 13th St., bet. Hudson St. & 9th Ave.) | A/C/E/L to 14th St./8th Ave. | 212-699-2410 | www.675bar.com

The high-flying Meatpacking District goes downscale at this new rec room–ish basement, a reworking of the former Level V digs featuring flea-market furnishings and a foosball table instead of velvet ropes and bottle service; divided into five cozy chambers, the meandering space offers simple pleasures – arcade games, card tables, a library – to distract from uncertain economic times.

Sixth Ward

22 | **19** | **21** | **$12**

LES | 191 Orchard St. (bet. Houston & Stanton Sts.) | F/V to Lower East Side/2nd Ave. | 212-228-9888 | www.sixthwardnyc.com

Named for NYC's old Irish district, this Celtic pub is "getting some traction" as Lower Eastsiders belly up for a "fine selection" of beverages served by "entertaining" tapsters; expect a booth-lined room with "groovy" red lighting, a pool table and one of Downtown's most expansive backyards, and a mood that varies from "mellow" to "lively."

NEW 67 Orange Street

22 | **23** | **21** | **$15**

Harlem | 2082 Frederick Douglass Blvd. (bet. 112th & 113th Sts.) | B/C to 116th St. | 212-662-2030 | www.67orangestreet.com

The speakeasy comes to Harlem via this shadowy new watering hole, a "very small" duplex mixing "exotic" libations that are "redolent of the old days"; "nice" bartenders and "cozy" atmospherics compensate for tabs that may be too "pricey" for the neighborhood.

Skinny, The
16 | 11 | 18 | $7

LES | 174 Orchard St. (Stanton St.) | F/J/M/Z to Delancey/Essex Sts. | 212-228-3668 | www.theskinnybarlounge.com

"Good deals on the cheap stuff" lure "hipsters" and those in their thrall to this LES "dive", a "narrow" thing that gets way "crowded" on prime nights; decent DJs, a "tabletop Ms. Pac-Man" and rotating art on the walls help distract from the "sticky floors" and that "outrageous line for the single bathroom."

Sláinte
18 | 15 | 19 | $7

NoHo | 304 Bowery (bet. Bleecker & Houston Sts.) | B/D/F/V to B'way/ Lafayette St. | 212-253-7030 | www.slaintenyc.com

Set in a "huge" space with an "atmosphere conducive to mingling", this "modern Irish bar" on the Bowery is a "comfortable", "chill" pub with a "friendly staff", "diverse" crowd and "great pint selection"; sure, it gets "fratty on weekends" and some moan about the "Bennigan's"-style decor, but it's usually "quiet" enough to "have a conversation with friends."

Slane
17 | 16 | 18 | $7

G Village | 102 MacDougal St. (Bleecker St.) | A/B/C/D/E/F/V to W. 4th St. | 212-505-0079 | www.slanenyc.com

"If you yearn for college days", drop by this "cross between an Irish pub and a lounge" in the Village that owes its "student" appeal to "lotsa TVs" and "every-night beer specials"; dim lighting and a variety of "nooks and crannies" add to its "mellow" vibe.

Slate
21 | 21 | 19 | $10

Flatiron | 54 W. 21st St. (bet. 5th & 6th Aves.) | F/V to 23rd St. | 212-989-0096 | www.slate-ny.com

"Unlike traditional pool halls", this "different" Flatiron billiards parlor is set in a vast bi-level space with an "upscale" bar/lounge upstairs, an "unexpected" felt forum below and an "industrial-warehouse" feel throughout; though it's easy to "drop a pretty penny" here, supporters say the "fun games", "great cocktails" and "lively atmosphere" are worth the payout; P.S. it's got "multiple Ping-Pong" tables too.

Slaughtered Lamb Pub
17 | 18 | 18 | $9

G Village | 182 W. Fourth St. (Jones St.) | A/B/C/D/E/F/V to W. 4th St. | 212-627-5262 | www.slaughteredlambpub.com

A "must for Halloween", this "kitschy" (verging on "creepy") Village pub "feels like an homage to taxidermy" with its faux-werewolves-and-skeletons decor; the rest of the year, this longtime "standard" draws a mix of "frat boyz" and "B&T" types thanks to a "big beer menu", reasonable pricing and a "real working fireplace."

Slipper Room
∇ 20 | 19 | 16 | $8

LES | 167 Orchard St. (Stanton St.) | F/V to Lower East Side/2nd Ave. | 212-253-7246 | www.slipperroom.com

There's something "different every night" at this "blast" of a Lower East Side performance space that stages everything from "comedy shows" to "trivia spectaculars" to "hot burlesque"; ok, the "talent varies wildly" and the "acts can drag on", but few in the very "mixed" crowd care – most everyone's "smashed and silly by midnight."

	APPEAL	DECOR	SERVICE	COST

Smalls ⊄
24 | 14 | 16 | $9

W Village | 183 W. 10th St. (7th Ave. S.) | 1 to Christopher St. | 212-252-5091 | www.fatcatjazz.com

A "teeny club" with a "big heart", this cash-only West Village "treasure" – "completely redone with a bar" and "no longer BYO" – serves up "steamy jazz" till the "crack of dawn" to an "international" "cool-cat" crowd; just remember "if your conversation drowns out the band, you'll suffer the consequences."

☑ Smith & Mills ⊄
23 | 23 | 18 | $14

TriBeCa | 71 N. Moore St. (Greenwich St.) | 1 to Franklin St. | no phone | www.smithandmills.com

Drink in the "old-time charm" at this "unmarked" TriBeCan, a "bohemian" hideaway installed in an "insanely small" former horse stable where the "industrial" trappings belie the "perfectly mixed" drinks, "ultrahip crowd" and spendy tabs; an "awesome" bathroom built into an ancient elevator cab (and equipped with a fold-up train-car sink) is "worth the price of admission."

Smith's
22 | 21 | 21 | $11

G Village | 79 MacDougal St. (bet. Bleecker & Houston Sts.) | A/B/C/D/E/F/V to W. 4th St. | 212-260-0100 | www.smithsnyc.com

"Comfortable" and "quiet", the "bar tucked in back" of this chic Village eatery is a velvety sanctuary specializing in seasonal cocktails, wines by the glass and "unbeatable" service; sure, the barroom's "rather small" and the tabs "a bit pricey", but it's certainly "worth checking out" for the "hip, hot" crowd alone.

Smith's Bar
17 | 13 | 17 | $10

W 40s | 701 Eighth Ave. (44th St.) | A/C/E to 42nd St./Port Authority | 212-246-3268 | www.smithsbar.com

"No frills here" report the regulars of this "last of the Mohicans" Times Square "swill mill", a well-worn "standby" for "drunks, tourists" and thirsty "theatergoers"; a "basic drink selection" and "decent live music" distract from the "dingy" surroundings and "not-great crowd."

Smoke
22 | 18 | 20 | $10

W 100s | 2751 Broadway (bet. 105th & 106th Sts.) | 1 to 103rd St. | 212-864-6662 | www.smokejazz.com

"Greats, not-quites and stars-in-the-making" take the stage at this "little" UWS "jazz niche", a "red, velvety boîte" with a "perfect" "small-club atmosphere"; even though purists protest it's "not as good without the smoke" ("thanks to Bloomberg"), it's very popular with an "older", "upscale" crowd fond of "strong drinks" and "friendly" service.

S.O.B.'s
22 | 16 | 17 | $12

SoHo | 204 Varick St. (Houston St.) | 1 to Houston St. | 212-243-4940 | www.sobs.com

If you're "serious about dancing the night away" to "eclectic world music" ("bhangra, reggae, salsa – the list is endless"), this SoHo Latin club is "still tons of fun" and as much of a "total party" as ever; you can always count on it for "high energy", though there are "different crowds, depending on the night" at this "something-for-everyone" spot.

	APPEAL	DECOR	SERVICE	COST

Social

W 40s | 795 Eighth Ave. (bet. 48th & 49th Sts.) | C/E to 50th St. | 212-459-0643 | www.socialbarnyc.com

17 | 15 | 17 | $8

'Business casual' describes the dress code and the "corporate" types tippling at this "upscale" Theater District Irish pub that's always packed at "happy hour"; there's "plenty of space" to "get your drink on" (three "different floors with different vibes", plus an outdoor deck), while tons of flat-screens make it just the ticket when the "big game" is on.

Soda Bar

Prospect Heights | 629 Vanderbilt Ave. (bet. Prospect Pl. & St. Marks Ave.) | Brooklyn | 2/3 to Grand Army Plaza | 718-230-8393

20 | 17 | 19 | $7

This "cozy nook" of a "neighborhood bar" in Prospect Heights is "worth the subway ride" for its "excellent tap brew selection" and "yummy eats" (its "grunge" crowd is a bit more iffy); an expanded space, "lovely outdoor patio" and affordable pops keep things bubbling here.

Soft Spot ∌

Williamsburg | 128 Bedford Ave. (bet. N. 9th & 10th Sts.) | Brooklyn | L to Bedford Ave. | 718-384-7768

- | - | - | I

Williamsburg's one-and-only piano bar, this "cozy" spot brings laid-back imbibing to Bedford Avenue to the tune of a jazz pianist as well as occasional live karaoke; mood lighting, "great happy-hour specials" and a "nice patio" complete the picture.

Soho Billiards

NoHo | 56 E. Houston St. (Mott St.) | B/D/F/V to B'way/Lafayette St. | 212-925-3753

15 | 10 | 14 | $9

There's "always an open table" at this "no-frills" NoHo pool hall that's "never crowded", given the "nonexistent decor", "shady clientele" and overall "lame scene" ("you're clearly paying for the location"); no one minds much since the "tables are nicely spaced" and it's "perfect for a first date – if you want to lower their expectations."

Soho House

Meatpacking | 29-35 Ninth Ave. (14th St.) | A/C/E/L to 14th St./8th Ave. | 212-627-9800 | www.sohohouseny.com

24 | 23 | 19 | $16

"Home away from home for Brits" and "networking" "European media types", this "exclusive" Meatpacking hotel/"members-only club" exudes enough "too-cool-for-school sophistication" to be considered one of "NYC's finest see-and-be-seeners"; the "food's ok, the drinks are better" and the "rooftop pool can't be beat", but if you're not "rich or famous", "you will be ignored"; N.B. the grub should be better now that chef Neil Ferguson (ex Allen & Delancey, Gordon Ramsay) is on board.

SoHo Park

SoHo | 62 Prince St. (Lafayette St.) | N/R/W to Prince St. | 212-219-2129 | www.sohoparknyc.com

∇ 18 | 17 | 15 | $9

The mood's "fun" and so's the crowd at this indoor/outdoor SoHo spot, an "outdoorsy", glass-walled space that looks like a "retro gas station" furnished by Applebee's; the value-priced offerings include European-American street food (think designer hot dogs) paired with a limited list of beer and wine, all best enjoyed alfresco in its small biergarten.

	APPEAL	DECOR	SERVICE	COST

SoHo Room
▽ 14 | 15 | 15 | $11

SoHo | 203 Spring St. (Sullivan St.) | C/E to Spring St. | 212-334-3855
Formerly 203 Spring, this "nothing special" reincarnation of the long-time SoHo lounge is "trying to develop a new identity" with an Internet jukebox, though some sigh it's a "lost soul" that's "turning into a Midtown tavern"; still, it's good enough for a "quiet after-work drink."

Sol
18 | 18 | 18 | $13

Chelsea | 609 W. 29th St. (bet. 11th & 12th Aves.) | A/C/E to 34th St./Penn Station | 212-643-6464 | www.sol-nyc.com
"Still loud, still expensive", this West Chelsea hip-hop club retains the wide-open dimensions from its earlier days as Ruby Falls, bumped up by a souped-up sound system and light show – "music is a priority" here.

Solas
19 | 17 | 16 | $8

E Village | 232 E. Ninth St. (bet. 2nd & 3rd Aves.) | 6 to Astor Pl. | 212-375-0297
The "laid-back atmosphere" is the draw at this long-running East Villager broken into two parts: a mobbed downstairs bar and a more "comfy" mezzanine lounge; no matter where you end up, the crowd is "frat boy" and the mood meat market.

Solex
22 | 20 | 21 | $14

E Village | 103 First Ave. (bet. 6th & 7th Sts.) | F/V to Lower East Side/2nd Ave. | 212-777-6677
A "sleek" East Village nexus, this "fetching" French wine bar is a "digni-fied" yet "accessible oasis" where "knowledgeable" sommeliers pour a "lovely selection" of vins matched with "delectable finger foods"; the "narrow" setup bounded by "blond woods" and a wavy ceiling is either "claustrophobic" or "cozy", depending on who's talking.

Son Cubano
23 | 20 | 20 | $13

Meatpacking | 405 W. 14th St. (Washington St.) | A/C/E/L to 14th St./8th Ave. | 212-366-1640 | www.soncubanonyc.com
"Festive" teetering on "rambunctious", this "hot" Meatpacking District bar/restaurant "transports you to La Habana" with its *fabu-loso* mojitos, "fiery salsa" and live bands pumping out "Cuban beats"; what with one of the city's "longest bartops" and "plenty of Latin lov-ers on the prowl", it's a "jumping", albeit "deafening", experience – "if you're sitting down, you may be the only one."

Sophie's
22 | 15 | 20 | $11

E Village | 507 E. Fifth St. (bet. Aves. A & B) | F/V to Lower East Side/2nd Ave. | 212-228-5680
"As old-school East Village as you can get", this "lovable", sign-free "dive" is a bona fide "dump" complete with funky patrons, an authen-tic "smell" and iffy bathrooms; fans of honest hooch at "good prices" say they "never want to leave" – bars like this are "unfortunately be-coming a rarity" in NYC.

NEW Sorella
- | - | - | M

LES | 95 Allen St. (bet. Broome & Delancey Sts.) | F to Delancey/Essex Sts. | 212-274-9595 | www.sorellanyc.com
The latest arrival on up-and-coming Allen Street, this new LES wine bar specializes in Northern Italian labels accompanied by small plates

from Italy's Piedmont region; the narrow space features a long bar up front catering to sippers and nibblers, while a back room is reserved for full-out dining.

Southpaw

| 22 | 17 | 19 | $7 |

Park Slope | 125 Fifth Ave. (bet. Sterling & St. Johns Pls.) | Brooklyn | B/Q to 7th Ave. | 718-230-0236 | www.spsounds.com

"Not quite CBGB's", this "nice-size" Park Slope sound factory steps up to the plate with "top name" indie bands and a fine suds selection; its "cool", 5,000-sq.-ft. setting has been expanded to include Down South, a basement bar/lounge that hosts "great DJs" as well as live feeds of the action upstairs.

NEW Southside

| 18 | 15 | 16 | $13 |

Little Italy | 1 Cleveland Pl., downstairs (bet. Broome & Kenmare Sts.) | 6 to Spring St. | 212-680-5601 | www.nycsouthside.com

"It's a scene" at this subterranean "lair" under Little Italy's Bar Martignetti that now sports a "new look" ("palm-leaf wallpaper", a black-and-white checkerboard floor) but the "same" crowd of "Choate/Andover/Hotchkiss" alums; although the "strict door" relaxes when you have "pretty young things in tow", skeptics still see "nothing to write home about."

SouthWest NY

| 19 | 19 | 19 | $12 |

Financial District | 2 World Financial Ctr. (bet. Liberty St. & South End Ave.) | 1/2/3 to Chambers St. | 212-945-0528 | www.southwestny.com

"Summer is best" at this Battery Park City Southwesterner, when its outdoor patio overlooking the Hudson offers the opportunity to pair "beautiful sunsets" with frozen margaritas; a "lively" after-work scene for WFC suits, it's also "one of the few places in the Financial District active on weekends."

Z Spice Market

| 24 | 27 | 20 | $15 |

Meatpacking | 403 W. 13th St. (9th Ave.) | A/C/E/L to 14th St./8th Ave. | 212-675-2322 | www.jean-georges.com

There's "quite a scene" still in progress at Jean-Georges Vongerichten's "gorgeous" restaurant, an "anchor of the Meatpacking District" purveying Asian street food at tabs that "don't translate to street prices"; thirsty "beautiful" types make a beeline for its "exotic" downstairs lounge, a "nooks-and-crannies"-heavy space that's perfect for "after-dinner, before-sex drinks" since it looks like a cross between a "bordello" and an "opium den."

Spike Hill

| 22 | 18 | 23 | $8 |

Williamsburg | 184 Bedford Ave. (N. 7th St.) | Brooklyn | L to Bedford Ave. | 718-218-9737 | www.spikehill.com

An "impressive selection" of suds and "barrels of top-notch" single-malts make this Billyburg bar a "solid" choice for "grown-up" imbibing in wood-paneled digs with "little nook booths" in the rear; "big picture windows" offering "great Bedford Avenue people-watching" seal the deal.

Spirit Cruises

| 20 | 18 | 16 | $14 |

Chelsea | Chelsea Piers | Pier 62 (Hudson River & W. 23rd St.) | C/E to 23rd St. | 866-483-3866 | www.spiritcruises.com

"Stunning" skyline vistas of the "most breathtaking city" in the world make this dinner and dancing "booze cruise" an obvious choice for "tourists" and "prom-goers"; still, given the "erratic" service and "lackluster entertainment", it may be "one of those things you only need do once if you're a local"; N.B. a recent renovation is not yet reflected in the Decor score.

⮕ Spitzer's Corner

22	21	18	$10

LES | 101 Rivington St. (Ludlow St.) | F/J/M/Z to Delancey/Essex Sts. | 212-228-0027 | www.spitzerscorner.com

Proof that "hipsters and prepsters can coexist", this LES beer hall hooks hopsheads with a "compelling" selection of some 50 "hard-to-find" brews tapped in a "bare-bones" setting with "rustic benches", "communal tables" and walls "open to the street"; the "cool corner location" on happening Rivington Street means you should "be prepared for a packed house."

Splash ⊅

20	15	17	$10

Flatiron | 50 W. 17th St. (bet. 5th & 6th Aves.) | F/L/V to 14th St./6th Ave. | 212-691-0073 | www.splashbar.com

This bi-level Flatiron "mega-gay bar" lures "rainbow crowds" of "bridge-and-tunnel boys" with a great "big" dance floor, "changing theme nights" and "ample eye candy"; despite "expensive" pops and bartenders "hired for their muscles, not their service", it does the trick when you feel like "standing and posing" the night away.

Spotted Pig

23	20	17	$11

W Village | 314 W. 11th St. (Greenwich St.) | 1 to Christopher St. | 212-620-0393 | www.thespottedpig.com

Alright already, this "always crowded" West Villager is "more of a food than a drinks place" with a bartop that's "usually packed with dinner patrons" waiting for a table (it accepts "no reservations"); but regulars report the bar scene becomes more "happening" – and more "celeb"-heavy – late night, once the "elbow-to-elbow" eaters are gone.

Spring Lounge

19	13	19	$8

NoLita | 48 Spring St. (Mulberry St.) | 6 to Spring St. | 212-965-1774 | www.thespringlounge.com

"Keeping it real in NoLita", this "old-time" dive gives off an "unpretentious" air (i.e. "no whiney rich kids") that's no mean feat "considering the neighborhood"; too bad "frat rats" take it over on weekends, drawn by a "great jukebox" and an "ever-changing draft selection."

Sputnik

18	14	18	$8

Clinton Hill | 262 Taaffe Pl. (bet. DeKalb & Willoughby Aves.) | Brooklyn | G to Classon Ave. | 718-398-6666 | www.barsputnik.com

It may be a "little hard to find" and a tad "drab", but this "popular Pratt student hangout" in Clinton Hill has a "great vibe" and "plenty of space" to move around in; the ground-floor bar is nice and "chill", while things get more arty in the basement thanks to live bands and a gallery space.

Spuyten Duyvil

24	18	20	$8

Williamsburg | 359 Metropolitan Ave. (Havemeyer St.) | Brooklyn | L to Bedford Ave. | 718-963-4140 | www.spuytenduyvilnyc.com

One of the "best Belgian beer lists outside of Belgium" awaits at this Williamsburg brew palace, a "funky yet comfortable" space featuring "garage-sale decor" (with some of the "knickknacks for sale"); "patient", "knowledgeable" bartenders and a "fantastic, tree-lined patio" (that's recently doubled in size) keep the "local hipsters" coming.

NEW Stag's Head

| | - | - | - | M |

E 50s | 252 E. 51st St. (bet. 2nd & 3rd Aves.) | 6 to 51st St./Lexington Ave. | 212-888-2453 | www.thestagsheadnyc.com

This new East Midtown duplex has been around for years under different names (CB Six, Mica Bar) and has been reinvented as an unassuming British gastropub offering a well-curated variety of draft and bottled brews; a wood-lined downstairs taproom is topped by a loft-like dining room dominated by a large communal table.

NEW Standard Hotel Living Room

| | - | - | - | M |

Meatpacking | Standard Hotel | 848 Washington St. (13th St.) | A/C/E/L to 14th St./8th Ave. | 212-645-4646 | www.standardhotels.com

Set in the Meatpacking District's latest boutique hotel, this midsize lounge off the lobby sports a mod look, with plenty of room for spillover thanks to additional alfresco seating in the plaza out front; more nightlife options within the property are in the offing – given its proximity to an entrance to the High Line, traffic should be brisk throughout.

Standings

| | ∇ 25 | 17 | 26 | $7 |

E Village | 43 E. Seventh St. (bet. 2nd & 3rd Aves.) | F/V to Lower East Side/2nd Ave. | 212-420-0671 | www.standingsbar.com

Now standing in the former Brewsky's space, this East Villager looks much the same as before, from the "small", divey setup to the beer cellar shared with Burp Castle next door; it still boasts a "solid lineup of microbrews", though they've added more TVs to the mix as part of its makeover into a sports bar.

St. Andrews

| | 20 | 19 | 20 | $8 |

W 40s | 140 W. 46th St. (bet. 6th & 7th Aves.) | 1/2/3/7/N/Q/R/S/W to 42nd St./Times Sq. | 212-840-8413 | www.standrewsnyc.com

It's moved two blocks north, but this Theater District "homage to all things Scottish" still hosts a thriving "after-work" scene thanks to "lads in kilts" tending a bar stocked with "one of the city's best collections of single-malts"; the new incarnation is shinier and bigger, however, now spread out over a double-decker space.

Stand-Up NY Comedy Club

| | 18 | 10 | 16 | $14 |

W 70s | 236 W. 78th St. (bet. Amsterdam Ave. & B'way) | 1 to 79th St. | 212-595-0850 | www.standupny.com

"Pretty good" laughs lie ahead at this UWS "neighborhood" comedy club where the "overpriced" drinks and "cramped" seating aren't so funny; overall, it's "decent but nothing spectacular", except for nights when brand-name comics (like Chris Rock and Robin Williams) drop by.

Stan's

| | ∇ 12 | 7 | 12 | $6 |

Bronx | 836 River Ave. (opposite Yankee Stadium) | 4/B/D to Yankee Stadium | 718-993-5548

Either "mega-crowded or closed", this Bronx sports bar near Yankee Stadium only operates during home games, but when open, it's a "loud, fun" time; it could sure "use a face-lift" but the "cold" beers are "cheap" and the "sawdust on the floor brings you back to your childhood days."

	APPEAL	DECOR	SERVICE	COST

Stanton Public
| | 21 | 19 | 17 | $11 |

LES | 17 Stanton St. (bet. Bowery & Chrystie St.) | F/V to Lower East Side/ 2nd Ave. | 212-677-5555 | www.stantonpublic.com

This "solid" LES pub "holds firm to its local, divey feel" with a "great selection" of suds (some drawn straight from the cask with a beer engine) augmented by flat-screens, dartboards and an "awesome backyard"; its "mellow" mood is "much needed" in this "increasingly trendy area."

☑ Stanton Social
| | 25 | 25 | 20 | $12 |

LES | 99 Stanton St. (bet. Ludlow & Orchard Sts.) | F/V to Lower East Side/ 2nd Ave. | 212-995-0099 | www.thestantonsocial.com

An "upscale spot in a downscale 'hood", this "hip, hot" Lower Eastsider features a ground-floor dining room serving "creative" small plates topped by a "stylish" lounge where the "old-fashioned" cocktails work well with the pseudo-"antique" decor; given the "supertrendy", people-"on-top-of-each-other" scene, "you have to be social here"; P.S. don't forget "daddy's credit card."

Star Lounge
| | 19 | 18 | 17 | $15 |

Chelsea | Chelsea Hotel | 222 W. 23rd St. (bet. 7th & 8th Aves.) | C/E to 23rd St. | 212-255-4646 | www.starloungechelsea.com

There's a "hip party" going on in the Chelsea Hotel's subterranean lounge, now a "bohemian" satellite of the Hamptons hot spot that's "much improved since its days as Serena"; "young trendy" types cavort to "excellent DJs" in a warren of "low-ceilinged" rooms, yet those opposed to the "overly hyped" scene find "nothing über-cool" about it.

Stay
| | 19 | 19 | 15 | $9 |

E Village | 244 E. Houston St. (bet. Aves. A & B) | F/V to Lower East Side/ 2nd Ave. | 212-982-3532 | www.stay-nyc.com

This "serious pickup party place" on the East Village/Lower East Side border is a "small" club done up in '60s mod style; since there's usually "no cover", the "same faces" seem to "stay forever", in spite of the "bridge-and-tunnel" following and the sometimes "crowded" conditions.

St. Dymphna's
| | 20 | 18 | 18 | $8 |

E Village | 118 St. Marks Pl. (bet. Ave. A & 1st Ave.) | L to 1st Ave. | 212-254-6636

There's a "real Irish atmosphere" to be had at this "affordable" East Village pub named after the patron saint of the mentally disabled; "family-owned and -run", it's perfect for a "nice pint of Guinness" at "affordable" rates, with a swell back patio as a bonus.

Still
| | 15 | 12 | 18 | $8 |

Gramercy | 192 Third Ave. (bet. 17th & 18th Sts.) | 4/5/6/L/N/Q/R/W to 14th St./Union Sq. | 212-471-9807 | www.stillnyc.com

"Former frat boys pick up former sorority girls" or "reminisce about how great college was" at this "generic" Gramercy tavern; still, pennypinchers praise this "neighborhood staple" for its "cheap" tap brews.

Stillwater
| | 20 | 15 | 19 | $9 |

E Village | 78-80 E. Fourth St. (bet. Bowery & 2nd Ave.) | 6 to Astor Pl. | 212-253-2237

The name's been changed (from East 4th Street Bar), but otherwise things are much the same at this "strictly-for-locals" East Villager providing the usual amenities – pool, video games, "sports all the time" on the tube – spread out over two rooms; it's a "no-frills" kind of joint that draws the "overflow from the better places in the area."

Stir

| 19 | 21 | 18 | $11 |

E 70s | 1363 First Ave. (bet. 73rd & 74th Sts.) | 6 to 77th St. | 212-744-7190 | www.stirnyc.com

An extensive list of "creative martinis" is the hook at this UES lounge that's an "oasis" for "fresh-out-of-college" types in an "area where there isn't much to pick from"; too bad about the "overpriced drinks" and "variable crowd", though romeos report it's "perfect for a first date."

Stitch

| 17 | 16 | 17 | $9 |

Garment District | 247 W. 37th St. (bet. 7th & 8th Aves.) | 1/2/3 to 34th St./Penn Station | 212-852-4826 | www.stitchnyc.com

"Always packed" after work, this Garment District duplex is "great for the commuting crowd" given its location in the "boring" area between Penn Station and Port Authority; although some yawn "pretty ordinary", it's "big" and "airy" with a "nice upper balcony" area that's "conducive to groups."

STK

| 23 | 24 | 19 | $13 |

Meatpacking | 26 Little W. 12th St. (bet. 9th Ave. & Washington St.) | A/C/E/L to 14th St./8th Ave. | 646-624-2444 | www.stkhouse.com

A "fabulous hybrid of bar, lounge and restaurant", this "super-trendy" steakhouse is a "happening" nexus for "good-looking girls" and the "expense account"–toting guys who love them; appropriately set in the Meatpacking District, the dark, fireplace-equipped room has the requisite "sexy" vibe, though "crowded" conditions and not-so-hot service can make this "total scene" seem over-cooked.

St. Marks Ale House

| 17 | 13 | 19 | $7 |

E Village | 2 St. Marks Pl. (3rd Ave.) | 6 to Astor Pl. | 212-260-9762

"Lots of sports" on the "big screens" pretty much guarantee that this "generic" East Village bar will be "crowded" on game nights (and during "end of semester" frat-pack invasions); still, some bench-warmers find it "only good for one or two beers before moving on" to somewhere else.

St. Nick's Jazz Pub ⊄

| ▽ 20 | 12 | 19 | $8 |

Harlem | 773 St. Nicholas Ave. (149th St.) | 3 to 145th St. | 212-283-9728 | www.stnicksjazzpub.net

"Live modern jazz" is served up in a historic setting (fka Luckey's Rendezvous in the '30s) at this "no-frills" "hole-in-the-wall" in Harlem's Sugar Hill; today, there's "music almost every night" from "up-and-coming" talent, plus "normal" pricing and "low (or no) cover charges."

Stone Creek

| 19 | 17 | 22 | $8 |

Murray Hill | 140 E. 27th St. (bet. Lexington & 3rd Aves.) | 6 to 28th St. | 212-532-1037 | www.stonecreeknyc.com

Down an "off-the-beaten-track" Curry Hill side street lies this "relatively unknown" Murray Hill watering hole where a stone-walled front bar area leads to an airport lounge–like back room; its "comfortable" vibe works equally well for everything from "quiet dates" to "group outings."

Stoned Crow

	APPEAL	DECOR	SERVICE	COST
	19	15	20	$6

G Village | 85 Washington Pl. (bet. 6th Ave. & Washington Sq. W.) | F/L/V to 14th St./6th Ave. | 212-677-4022 | www.thestonedcrownyc.com

There's "not an ounce of pretension" in this NYU-area basement, a "dump with character" that's the most "real bar in the immediate neighborhood"; done up in "college dorm" style with "obscure" movie posters on the walls and "free popcorn" littering the floor, it's best known for its "very serious" pool table.

Z Stonehome Wine Bar

	27	24	24	$10

Fort Greene | 87 Lafayette Ave. (bet. Portland Ave. & S. Elliott Pl.) | Brooklyn | G to Fulton St. | 718-624-9443 | www.stonehomewinebar.com

This Fort Greene "neighborhood gem" supplies "everything you need for a romantic evening": "low lighting", "soft music" and a "charming" garden, all enhanced by a wine selection that's as "thoughtful" as it is vast; "friendly", "knowledgeable" service seals the deal, and now there's a full dinner menu too.

Stone Rose

	23	24	18	$15

W 60s | Time Warner Ctr. | 10 Columbus Circle, 4th fl. (60th St.) | 1/A/B/C/D to 59th St./Columbus Circle | 212-823-9769 | www.gerberbars.com

"Huge windows" framing "fantastic views" of Columbus Circle and Central Park make this Time Warner Center bar/lounge a "top-of-the-line" choice for the "corporate-card" carriers and "out-of-work models" who patronize it; ok, it's "insanely expensive" and the "gorgeous", "underdressed" waitresses "could use less attitude", but ultimately this "great retreat" is "worth it for the setting" alone.

Stonewall Inn

	20	15	18	$10

G Village | 53 Christopher St. (bet. 7th Ave. S. & Waverly Pl.) | 1 to Christopher St. | 212-488-2705 | www.thestonewallinnnyc.com

Following a "revamp", this Village "perennial" – the flashpoint of the "legendary" '69 riot that launched the "fight for gay rights" – is now "spiffed up" (or "at least not grungy") with an overhauled interior and a "cozy lounge" area; if the mix of "locals", "tourists" and "AARP members" is "not the trendiest", at least you can "respect the history."

Stout

	21	20	20	$8

Garment District | 133 W. 33rd St. (bet. 6th & 7th Aves.) | 1/2/3 to 34th St./Penn Station | 212-629-6191 | www.stoutnyc.com

Expect "lots of beer and lots of space" at this "modern" mega-Irish pub in the Garment District, a "stylish place" rife with "high ceilings", "huge flat-screens" and an "attractive" balcony made for lofty dining and drinking; it's usually "packed at rush hour and before MSG concerts", yet despite the "touristy location", there's "no touristy feel."

Strata

	19	19	17	$15

Flatiron | 915 Broadway (21st St.) | N/R/W to 23rd St. | 212-586-6000 | www.stratanyc.com

This two-tiered Flatiron event space "earns its stripes" as a weekends-only "party" site for "young wannabes" strutting their stuff on dual dance floors as DJs spin house and hip-hop; still, quibblers cite a too-"picky door" for a "run-of-the-mill" scene that's "old news by now."

	APPEAL	DECOR	SERVICE	COST

Studio B
▽ **24** | **15** | **16** | **$10**

Greenpoint | 259 Banker St. (bet. Calyer St. & Meserole Ave.) | Brooklyn | G to Greenpoint Ave. | 718-389-1880 | www.clubstudiob.com

"Escape oversaturated Manhattan" at this "best-kept secret" in Greenpoint, a "cavernous" club-cum-concert space featuring a "worthy" slate of indie-darling bands, "bangin'" DJs and an expansive dance floor; getting there may be "a chore", but the "upbeat" attitude is bound to "please."

NEW Stumble Inn
15 | **12** | **17** | **$7**

E 70s | 1454 Second Ave. (76th St.) | 6 to 77th St. | 212-650-0561 | www.nycbestbar.com

A "revamp of old favorite Mo's Caribbean", this UES "boozefest" has "dropped the Mexican food" but retained the "inexpensive drinks", "beer pong" tournaments and "zoo"-like, "totally fratty" vibe; it's a "default" for "cheap pitchers" and "Sunday football", but veterans say "Stumble Out" might be a more appropriate moniker.

SubMercer
24 | **23** | **22** | **$16**

SoHo | Mercer Hotel | 147 Mercer St. (Prince St.) | N/R/W to Prince St. | 212-966-6060

Beyond "impenetrable" bouncers, a freight elevator and a series of unmarked doors, this "clandestine" venue under SoHo's Mercer Hotel is a "chic" late-night lounge where "froufrou" types burrow "wall-to-wall" amid "exposed brick", crimson banquettes and a matching "stripper pole"; "getting in is no easy task", but once inside it "might be even harder to leave."

Subway Inn ⌖
17 | **7** | **16** | **$6**

E 60s | 143 E. 60th St. (Lexington Ave.) | 4/5/6/N/R/W to 59th St./Lexington Ave. | 212-223-8929

"Refreshingly skanky", this 1934 "time capsule" located opposite Bloomingdale's has "all the charm of the subway" with "ripped vinyl seats", a "stale smell" and one of the "worst toilets" in town; the mixed crowd propping up the bar - everyone from "hoodlums" and "bums" to "millionaires" - wonders how it's "survived at such a hot location" for so long, but still hope it "lasts forever."

Sugarcane
21 | **23** | **17** | **$12**

Flatiron | 243 Park Ave. S. (bet. 19th & 20th Sts.) | 4/5/6/L/N/Q/R/W to 14th St./Union Sq. | 212-475-9377 | www.sushisamba.com

This "ultracool" adjunct to the "ever-popular SushiSamba" ranks a "notch above" its competitors thanks to "high-concept mixed drinks" and a "dark", sexy setting; sure, pricing's "steep" and the ceilings "low", but it's a no-brainer "while waiting for a table" next door.

Suite
▽ **16** | **16** | **18** | **$8**

W 100s | 992 Amsterdam Ave. (109th St.) | 1 to Cathedral Pkwy./110th St. | 212-222-4600 | www.suitenyc.com

Columbia's "only real gay bar", this "endearing" Upper Westsider is a "worthy successor to Saints", its former incarnation; expect a "mixed-bag" crowd - everyone from "sugar daddies" and "Ivy Leaguers" to "drag queens singing 'I Will Survive'" - mingling in an Ikea-esque space.

	APPEAL	DECOR	SERVICE	COST

Suite
18 | 18 | 16 | $10

Bay Ridge | 437 88th St. (bet. 4th & 5th Aves.) | Brooklyn | R to 86th St. | 718-748-1002 | www.bayridgesuite.com

"Brooklynites unite" for sweet mirror-ball nostalgia at this Bay Ridge disco that "appeals to your basic" Tony Manero "wannabes" with a "good-size dance floor" and DJs spinning tracks "you can fist pump to"; just "throw on all your designer labels" and "get dolled up" to fit in.

Sullivan Hall
18 | 16 | 19 | $10

G Village | 214 Sullivan St. (bet. Bleecker & W. 3rd Sts.) | A/B/C/D/E/F/V to W. 4th St. | 212-477-2782 | www.sullivanhallnyc.com

A new sound and lighting system, spruced-up bar and larger stage signal the "much improved" vibe at this revamped music venue near NYU; "reasonable" prices offset the cover for the nightly multi-act roster.

Sullivan Room
∇ 18 | 16 | 17 | $11

G Village | 218 Sullivan St. (bet. Bleecker & W. 3rd Sts.) | A/B/C/D/E/F/V to W. 4th St. | 212-252-2151 | www.sullivanroom.com

"Underground" both literally and spiritually, this Village DJ lair offers prime audiophile downtime as "top-notch" deckmeisters drop "quality house" mixes; the sub-street level space is "too sketchy to be chichi", "too glam to be a dive" but just clubby enough for "a little naughtiness."

Sunny's ⊘
∇ 26 | 18 | 24 | $5

Red Hook | 253 Conover St. (bet. Beard & Reed Sts.) | Brooklyn | F/G to Carroll St. | 718-625-8211 | www.sunnysredhook.com

You can "smell the waterfront" at this "middle of nowhere" Red Hook "neighborhood bar" that's been dispensing spirits since the 1890s under different names and today is run by the great-grandson of the original owner; sure, it's a kitschy, "paraphernalia"-laden joint, but its hippie-artist-beatnik following finds it "nostalgic" and "beyond charming."

Superfine
24 | 21 | 19 | $8

Dumbo | 126 Front St. (bet. Jay & Pearl Sts.) | Brooklyn | F to York St. | 718-243-9005

Despite the "trendy" warehouse space, this "wonderful" Dumbo bar/restaurant exudes small-town charm; a "lively" following, free pool table and "cool art for sale" burnish the "interesting" vibe.

Supreme Trading
23 | 21 | 20 | $9

Williamsburg | 213 N. Eighth St. (bet. Driggs Ave. & Roebling St.) | Brooklyn | L to Bedford Ave. | 718-599-4224 | www.supremetradingny.com

Packing "lots of different environments" into one sprawling space, this "cool" Williamsburger offers bar, lounge and art exhibition options topped off by an "outside smoking patio"; sure, it's usually "filled with hipsters", but a "general sense of goodwill" pervades – "no one's too cool for school here"; N.B. it's in the midst of a complete renovation.

SushiSamba
22 | 22 | 18 | $13

Flatiron | 245 Park Ave. S. (bet. 19th & 20th Sts.) | 4/5/6/L/N/Q/R/W to 14th St./Union Sq. | 212-475-9377
G Village | 87 Seventh Ave. S. (Barrow St.) | 1 to Christopher St. | 212-691-7885
www.sushisamba.com

"Hot" crowds jam into these "happening" Brazilian/Japanese fusion specialists that still emit a "very *Sex and the City* vibe" with their "splashy" design, "yummy drinks" and "blow-a-lot-of-money" pricing; though both are "chic and hip", most "prefer the Village" satellite – and its "terrific roof deck" – over the Flatiron mother ship.

Sutra

18 | 19 | 16 | $9

E Village | 16 First Ave. (bet. 1st & 2nd Sts.) | F/V to Lower East Side/2nd Ave. | 212-677-9477 | www.sutranyc.com

There's "potential" in the air at this bi-level East Village lounge that's "bathed in red light" upstairs and features a funky underground lounge; still, foes fault the "loud music", "trying-too-hard" vibe and "long, narrow" setup with "no room to get your groove on."

Sutton Place

18 | 16 | 16 | $9

E 50s | 1015 Second Ave. (bet. 53rd & 54th Sts.) | E/V to Lexington Ave./53rd St. | 212-207-3777 | www.suttonplacenyc.com

Brace yourself for a "boisterous party" at this longtime Midtown triplex, a "male-dominated" scene that draws young "investment banker types" bent on "drowning their work sorrows" (on weekends, it morphs into a "total meat market" that wags tag "Slutton Place"); an "awesome" roof deck is the "main attraction on summer evenings", while the lower floors are pretty "generic" and "personality free."

Suzie Wong

20 | 21 | 19 | $14

Chelsea | 547 W. 27th St. (bet. 10th & 11th Aves.) | C/E to 23rd St. | 212-268-5105 | www.suziewongnyc.com

The Far East lands in West Chelsea at this "sexy" Chinese-style lounge, a "red"-lit sanctum with box lanterns, brocaded banquettes and a bottle-service list that includes top-shelf sakes; but despite a "tough door", some gong it as a "bridge-and-tunnel trap" populated by a "hit-or-miss" crowd.

Sway

25 | 22 | 17 | $11

SoHo | 305 Spring St. (bet. Greenwich & Hudson Sts.) | 1 to Houston St. | 212-620-5220 | www.swaylounge.com

"Is it back again?" – "after all these years", this West SoHo Moroccan-themer has "stayed hep" and "getting in is still an obstacle"; it's "best after 1:30", when the "über-cool" cats blow in – everyone from "incognito" frock stars to "heavily tattooed" hipsters, all "popping the champers" and shake-shake-"shaking their booties."

NEW Sweet & Lowdown

18 | 16 | 19 | $11

LES | 123 Allen St., downstairs (bet. Delancey & Rivington Sts.) | F/J/M/Z to Delancey/Essex Sts. | 212-228-7746 | www.sweetandlowdown.com

An all-American vino list is the hook at this new LES wine bar specializing in U.S. varietals, accompanied by the customary small-plates snacks; the "bland", candlelit setting takes a page out of the Ikea school of design, and if "never crowded", it's a natural for clandestine romancing.

Sweet & Vicious

17 | 16 | 16 | $9

NoLita | 5 Spring St. (bet. Bowery & Elizabeth St.) | 6 to Spring St. | 212-334-7915 | www.sweetandviciousnyc.com

Now in its 12th year, this "chill" NoLita bar keeps its twentysomething following "returning time and time again" thanks to a "fun" vibe, "excellent" DJs and that "really nice patio"; despite the "pouty service" and "nothing-special" looks ("you don't go here for the decor"), it's "always super-crowded" on weekends.

Sweet Paradise Lounge ⬎

APPEAL	DECOR	SERVICE	COST
▽ 22	20	15	$12

LES | 14 Orchard St. (bet. Canal & Hester Sts.) | F/J/M/Z to Delancey/Essex Sts. | 212-226-3612 | www.sweetparadiselounge.com

From the owner of Welcome to the Johnsons comes this Lower East Side "dive bar", a long, narrow thing with plenty of "hipster appeal"; in addition to alcohol, there's movie "concession stand candy" for sale (it was a sweet shop in a former life), but otherwise this dark, underpopulated den is primarily a destination for those who don't want to be seen.

Sweet Rhythm

21	19	20	$12

W Village | 88 Seventh Ave. S. (bet. Bleecker & Grove Sts.) | 1 to Christopher St. | 212-255-3626 | www.sweetrhythmny.com

Alright, it "ain't Sweet Basil" (the legendary jazz club that preceded it), but this West Village performance space does offer a variety of "top-notch" groups of all musical persuasions; despite its location on a "touristy" stretch of Seventh Avenue South, there's usually a "low turnout" audiencewise in contrast to the "high-grade talent" onstage.

Swift

22	17	21	$7

NoHo | 34 E. Fourth St. (bet. Bowery & Lafayette St.) | 6 to Astor Pl. | 212-227-9438 | www.swiftnycbar.com

A "local bar with international appeal", NoHo's "updated version of an Irish pub" is renowned for its "excellent draft and bottled beer lineup" and "welcoming" staff; on weekends, it can be "more crowded than the middle seat of a coach flight to Manchester."

Swig

16	14	18	$9

E 80s | 1629 Second Ave. (bet. 84th & 85th Sts.) | 4/5/6 to 86th St. | 212-628-2364 | www.swignyc.com

"Just hang out" and swig "a beer or two" at this "basic" Upper Eastsider, yet another "neighborhood" Irish pub catering to "frat dudes" and their post-grad peers; its plain-vanilla environs are "cleaner" and "quieter" than the norm, but otherwise expect "nothing special."

Swing 46 Jazz Club

21	17	18	$13

W 40s | 349 W. 46th St. (bet. 8th & 9th Aves.) | 1/2/3/7/N/Q/R/S/W to 42nd St./Times Sq. | 212-262-9554 | www.swing46.com

"Always a draw for swingers", this Restaurant Row supper club "stays true" to the "jazzy" tradition with "upbeat" live combos onstage and a hardwood floor where hoofers relive the "1940s" big-band era; it "welcomes beginners" with "quickie dance lessons", though cynics nix this "throwback" as strictly for "tourists" and the "40-plus" crowd.

▣ Tabla

24	26	24	$13

Flatiron | 11 Madison Ave. (24th St.) | 6 to 23rd St. | 212-889-0667 | www.tablany.com

"Interesting drinks" and "delectable" bar snacks draw a "fun work crowd" to this "super-duper" spot from restaurateur Danny Meyer that's naturally renowned for its "gracious service"; equally "outstanding" is the "exotic" deco Indian decor and "nice outdoor seating" overlooking Madison Square Park.

| | APPEAL | DECOR | SERVICE | COST |

Tailor
23 | 22 | 21 | $15

SoHo | 525 Broome St. (bet. Sullivan & Thompson Sts.) | C/E to Spring St. | 212-334-5182 | www.tailornyc.com

"Obvious creativity" is the hallmark of this "sultry" downstairs bar in a SoHo dessert specialist, where "expert mixologists" tailor "amazing cocktails" from "quirky" ingredients like kumquats and bubblegum cordial; a haven of dim lights, "funky wallpaper" and retro "cool", it's a "super" – if "expensive" – way to "wind down."

Taj II
20 | 22 | 17 | $12

Flatiron | 48 W. 21st St. (bet. 5th & 6th Aves.) | N/R/W to 23rd St. | 212-620-3033 | www.tajlounge.com

"Mostly twentysomethings" patronize this Indian-themed Flatiron lounge that "still exudes a sexy vibe", though some say it's "lost its golden touch"; sure, it can be "overrun by a bridge-and-tunnel element" and the staff may treat you like a "walking wallet", but at least there's "no hassle to get in" and they "play all the music you want to hear."

NEW Talay
19 | 21 | 18 | $12

Harlem | 701 W. 135th St. (12th Ave.) | 1 to 137th St./City College | 212-491-8300 | www.talayrestaurant.com

Bringing "yuppie street cred" to West Harlem, this bi-level Thai-Latin eatery is a "cool addition" for night crawlers given its expansive main-floor bar and smooth, Asian-themed upstairs lounge that kicks into "high-energy" mode on weekends; it's part of a burgeoning scene on a stretch of 12th Avenue informally dubbed 'ViVa' (i.e. 'Viaduct Valley').

☒ Tao
24 | 27 | 19 | $15

E 50s | 42 E. 58th St. (bet. Madison & Park Aves.) | 4/5/6/N/R/W to 59th St./Lexington Ave. | 212-888-2288 | www.taorestaurant.com

"Trendy to a T", this "buddhaful" Asian-themed Midtowner is a "real scene" but can also be a "real hassle" given the din from the "wall-to-wall" mobs "sucking down Cosmos like there's no work tomorrow" (brush up on your "sign language"); maybe it's "past its heyday" and "not on Page Six" as frequently as its Vegas spin-off, but it remains "visually amazing" and a magnet for "sugar daddies", "model types", "Eurotrash" and those who love them.

Tap a Keg
▽ 10 | 7 | 16 | $6

W 100s | 2731 Broadway (bet. 104th & 105th Sts.) | 1 to 103rd St. | 212-749-1734

The "close-to-Columbia" address gives this "old-time" Upper West Side "staple" a distinct "frat-boy" flavor even though there are also "lots of old people" in attendance; regulars try to "avoid it around closing time" when all the "bar leftovers are scrambling for their last sips."

Tapeo 29
24 | 22 | 22 | $10

LES | 29 Clinton St. (Stanton St.) | F/V to Lower East Side/2nd Ave. | 212-979-0002 | www.tapeo29.com

A "little place with big appeal", this Lower East Side wine bar offers an "excellent", Spanish-accented list poured in "casual", brick-lined digs with a distinct "European cafe" vibe; the "intimate" mood makes it a "solid addition to Clinton Street", and the "sangria is amazing."

	APPEAL	DECOR	SERVICE	COST

Tavern on Jane
21 | 17 | 22 | $8

W Village | 31 Eighth Ave. (Jane St.) | A/C/E/L to 14th St./8th Ave. |
212-675-2526 | www.tavernonjane.com

"Definitely a locals' joint", this Village "neighborhood tradition" is a "totally cozy" spot that appeals to "older" types since the mood is "relaxed" and the "music isn't too loud"; a "surprisingly broad food menu" (including a "great burger") leads some to dub it "Corner Bistro for adults."

Tavern on the Green
22 | 23 | 19 | $16

W 60s | Central Park W. (bet. 66th & 67th Sts.) | B/C to 72nd St. |
212-873-3200 | www.tavernonthegreen.com

It's "all about the ambiance" at this Manhattan "landmark" widely known for its "over-the-top" dining rooms with "Central Park greenery as the backdrop", though night owls reserve it for "outdoor dancing" in the summertime; sure, the drinks are "predictably overpriced" and the crowd "touristy" ("is anybody here from NY?"), but ultimately it remains "eternally popular" for a reason.

NEW t.b.d.
– | – | – | M

Greenpoint | 224 Franklin St. (Green St.) | Brooklyn | G to Greenpoint Ave. |
718-349-6727 | www.tbdbrooklyn.com

Something different for Greenpoint, this big bar/lounge carved out of a former warehouse is a minimalist, industrial-chic showplace furnished with low-slung couches, rotating artwork, a roll-up garage door and flat-screens broadcasting everything except sports; while the vibe is more art gallery than barroom, free WiFi, exotic tap brews and comfort-food snacks keep the locals satisfied.

Tea Lounge
20 | 16 | 19 | $6

Cobble Hill | 254 Court St. (bet. Butler & Kane Sts.) | Brooklyn | F/G to Bergen St. | 718-624-5683 ⊄
Park Slope | 837 Union St. (bet. 6th & 7th Aves.) | Brooklyn | M/R to Union St. | 718-789-2762
www.tealoungeny.com

"If your battle for a seat is successful, you can hang out forever" at these "cozy" Brooklyn coffeehouses that morph into beer-and-wine lounges after dark; the "hippie" vibe and "crunchy" music is made for "wooing that special friend" ("you know, the one with dreads") so long as you can abide the "ragtag furnishings."

Teddy's
∇ 23 | 20 | 23 | $7

Williamsburg | 96 Berry St. (N. 8th St.) | Brooklyn | L to Bedford Ave. |
718-384-9787

On the Williamsburg scene since 1887, this "real bar" is a piece of authentic olde NY with its vintage tile floor, tin ceiling and stained glass, and spices things up with a "superb Bloody Mary"; the low pricing – including a dollar tap-brew at happy hour – is old-fashioned too.

Telephone Bar
18 | 17 | 19 | $8

E Village | 149 Second Ave. (bet. 9th & 10th Sts.) | 6 to Astor Pl. |
212-529-5000 | www.telebar.com

"English phone booths" out front lure "NYU students" and "neighborhood locals" into this "fun Brit" bar/eatery that's "popular without being mobbed"; given the "moderate prices", it's a "good fallback", even if some shrug there's "nothing special" going on.

| | APPEAL | DECOR | SERVICE | COST |

Temple Bar

24 | 24 | 23 | $14

NoHo | 332 Lafayette St. (bet. Bleecker & Houston Sts.) | 6 to Bleecker St. | 212-925-4242 | www.templebarnyc.com

"Full of dark corners for dark deeds", this "seductive" NoHo bar is "not a substitute for foreplay, it's foreplay embodied", with a "low noise level", "astute service" and strong, "old-school" cocktails; in short, it works well for a "sexy assignation" with your "secretary" or when rendezvousing with a "double agent."

Ten Bells ⌀

23 | 21 | 20 | $11

LES | 247 Broome St. (bet. Ludlow & Orchard Sts.) | F/J/M/Z to Delancey/Essex Sts. | 212-228-4450 | www.thetenbells.com

"Just what a wine bar should be", this snug, tin-ceilinged Lower Eastsider vends a "wonderful" lineup of all-organic labels along with "tasty" nibbles and a "European" ambiance; though the name's lifted from the London pub favored by Jack the Ripper, its "low-key" intimacy rings "perfect for a date."

⚡ Tenjune

25 | 21 | 19 | $15

Meatpacking | 26 Little W. 12th St., downstairs (bet. 9th Ave. & Washington St.) | A/C/E/L to 14th St./8th Ave. | 646-624-2410 | www.tenjunenyc.com

A "tough door" policy and "no elbow room" collide at this subterranean Meatpacking club that's "totally hot" for the moment – "until the next one comes along"; brace yourself for an "ultratrendy" crowd where "everyone looks like a model" (or an "overly groomed gold digger"), all "dancing their butts off", "bumping into the who's who" of the nightlife world and wishing they could "afford bottle service."

Ten's

21 | 15 | 19 | $14

Flatiron | 35 E. 21st St. (bet. B'way & Park Ave. S.) | N/R/W to 23rd St. | 212-254-2444 | www.tensnewyork.com

"Hubba-hubba": "beautiful", "untouchable" gals "looking to lighten your wallet" shake their groove thangs at this "typical upscale" strip club in the Flatiron; like the rest of the genre, it's "expensive as all hell", but if "excellent drinks", flattering "mood lighting" and a "convenient" address are turn-ons, you've "come to the right place."

1020 Bar

16 | 11 | 15 | $8

W 100s | 1020 Amsterdam Ave. (110th St.) | 1 to 110th St. | 212-531-3468

Reminiscent of "your favorite college dive", this "Columbia hangout" is a shot of "extended adolescence", complete with a pool table where "tipsy undergrads attempt to show off their skills"; the "packed" room proves that everyone from "frat boys" to "pseudointellectuals" appreciates "beer this cheap."

Terminal 5

18 | 14 | 17 | $10

W 50s | 610 W. 56th St. (bet. 11th & 12th Aves.) | 1/A/B/C/D to 59th St./Columbus Circle | 212-665-3832 | www.terminal5nyc.com

A "fresh" music venue on Midtown's western fringe, this big hall presents midlevel rock acts in a "multitiered" "warehouse" setting outfitted with a "grand" stage and "several bars"; insiders advise "get there early" for a choice spot, since it's "terminally" "packed" and "acoustics can be a bit muddled."

	APPEAL	DECOR	SERVICE	COST

Terra Blues
| | 22 | 17 | 19 | $11 |

G Village | 149 Bleecker St., 2nd fl. (bet. La Guardia Pl. & Thompson St.) | A/B/C/D/E/F/V to W. 4th St. | 212-777-7776 | www.terrablues.com
Catch "reliably good music" at this "quintessential Village blues bar" that features a bevy of bourbons and single-malts served by "hot" bar-maids; given the reasonable cover charges, it's an economically sound choice if you're planning on "staying there all night."

Terroir
| | 22 | 19 | 22 | $13 |

E Village | 413 E. 12th St. (bet. Ave. A & 1st Ave.) | L to 1st Ave. | no phone | www.wineisterroir.com
If you're "lucky enough to get a seat", this "solid" East Village wine bar from "Hearth guy" Marco Canora pairs a "can't-go-wrong" lineup of international labels with "delicious light fare"; a "fun communal table" and a staff that's the "perfect amount of knowledgeable" make the "unassuming" space "inviting", but the quarters can be "close" so go "early."

T.G. Whitney's
| | 16 | 13 | 17 | $7 |

E 50s | 244 E. 53rd St. (bet. 2nd & 3rd Aves.) | E/V to Lexington Ave./ 53rd St. | 212-888-5772 | www.tgwhitneys.com
"Just-out-of-college" types "meet up with the gang after softball" at this "nondescript" Irish tavern that lures 'em in with nightly "drink specials"; ok, it's "very typical" for its East Midtown neighborhood, but an outdoor patio and "good karaoke" on weekends are further draws.

Therapy
| | 24 | 25 | 21 | $10 |

W 50s | 348 W. 52nd St. (bet. 8th & 9th Aves.) | C/E to 50th St. | 212-397-1700 | www.therapy-nyc.com
The "flagship of trendy gay hangouts", this Hell's Kitchen "hot spot" set in a split-level, "woodwork"-heavy setting boasts a "delectable", "tight-tank-topped" staff serving "pricey" drinks "strong enough to make the drag performers look good"; there's "lots to pick from" in the "cute" crowd, so pull up your socks, "suck in your cheeks" and get busy.

Third & Long
| | 14 | 11 | 18 | $7 |

Murray Hill | 523 Third Ave. (35th St.) | 6 to 33rd St. | 212-447-5711 | www.thirdandlong.ypguides.net
This Murray Hill booze bin is a sure bet "if you want to drink cheap" what with the "dollar beer nights" and "amazing happy-hour specials"; it draws a "sports-happy", "frat-boy" crew ("don't expect too many women") who report it's just "so-so", despite the "catchy name."

Thirsty Scholar
| | 17 | 14 | 18 | $7 |

E Village | 155 Second Ave. (bet. 9th & 10th Sts.) | 6 to Astor Pl. | 212-777-6514 | www.ryansnyc.com
Ok, the crowd at this East Village Irish bar may not be very scholarly but it's "definitely thirsty" for "good tap beers" on the "cheap"; known as an "NYU" hangout, it's certainly "low-key", though probably best to leave the schoolwork at home.

13
| | 15 | 13 | 16 | $10 |

G Village | 35 E. 13th St. (University Pl.) | 4/5/6/L/N/Q/R/W to 14th St./ Union Sq. | 212-979-6677 | www.bar13.com
A lucky number for all the "NYU party" peeps, this Village bar/lounge occupies "two floors" where a matriculated "mix" can "hang and

dance"; if the "dank" interior seems a tad too "funky", the "very cool" roof deck still works for "a summer night out."

Thom Bar
24 | 24 | 18 | $15

SoHo | 60 Thompson Hotel | 60 Thompson St., 2nd fl. (bet. Broome & Spring Sts.) | C/E to Spring St. | 212-219-3200 | www.thompsonhotels.com
"Attitude and high prices abound" at this "glitzy" SoHo boutique hotel bar where "interesting" cocktails are served by a "disinterested" staff to a crowd of "fashionistas", "Wall Streeters" and "out-of-town cougars"; P.S. its "gorgeous" seasonal rooftop, A60, formerly reserved only for members and hotel guests, is now more accessible.

THOR Lobby Bar
20 | 22 | 17 | $13

LES | The Hotel on Rivington | 107 Rivington St. (bet. Essex & Ludlow Sts.) | F/J/M/Z to Delancey/Essex Sts. | 212-475-2600 | www.hotelonrivington.com
The "Gisele Bundchen of hotel bars", this "chic" ground-floor lounge in THOR may be "far too swanky for the Lower East Side", given its "Eurotrashy" "scenester" crowd and "ultraposh" design, but it stays "ridiculously busy" despite "steep prices" and "waitresses on a permanent break"; P.S. the second-floor lounge is less crowded but not less expensive.

300 New York
19 | 15 | 15 | $11

Chelsea | Chelsea Piers | Pier 60 (Hudson River & W. 18th St.) | A/C/E/L to 14th St./8th Ave. | 212-835-2695 | www.3hundred.com
Keglers who spend their spare time at this "pricey" Chelsea Piers lane/lounge combo report "good clean fun" via "awesome disco bowling" ("current music", "nice glow-in-the-dark effects") that evokes "middle school, but with vodka"; there's a bonus too: "no waits" on weeknights due to its way-West locale.

Three of Cups Lounge
19 | 17 | 19 | $8

E Village | 83 First Ave. (5th St.) | F/V to Lower East Side/2nd Ave. | 212-388-0059 | www.threeofcupsnyc.com
"Uptown fur-wearers" and "tattooed East Villagers" converge at this "run-down" basement lounge beneath a pizza/pasta shop that's one of the "best little rock coves in town"; "small", "loud" and "always crowded", it's no good for groups: "there won't be any room."

3Steps
22 | 17 | 21 | $11

Gramercy | 322 Second Ave. (bet. 18th & 19th Sts.) | 6 to 23rd St. | 212-533-5336 | www.3stepsnyc.com
Located in a "nightlife no-man's-land", this "intimate" Gramercy Parker prides itself on "friendly service" and classy cocktails (check the "fantastic martini list"); the "subdued" atmosphere makes it a "cool" stepping stone "at the beginning or end of the evening."

Tillman's
22 | 22 | 20 | $14

Chelsea | 165 W. 26th St. (bet. 6th & 7th Aves.) | 1 to 28th St. | 212-627-8320 | www.tillmansnyc.com
For an "unexpected" dose of "neo-soul" in Chelsea, this "throwback" bar/lounge evokes "old-school Harlem" of the *Superfly* era with an amber-hued interior sporting vintage pix and curvy booths; as a "mixed hipster crowd" chills over "fabulous cocktails", the "wonderful sounds" of R&B and "killer jazz" maximize the "cool vibe."

	APPEAL	DECOR	SERVICE	COST

Tin Lizzie
13 | 11 | 15 | $7

E 80s | 1647 Second Ave. (bet. 85th & 86th Sts.) | 4/5/6 to 86th St. |
212-288-7983

"Lame guys throw lame lines" at this UES "meat market"; despite "slippery floors" and all that "touchy"-feeley action, it's nearly the "same crowd every night", "reaching for their frat-party glory days."

Tír na Nóg
20 | 18 | 19 | $8

Garment District | 5 Penn Plaza (8th Ave., bet. 33rd & 34th Sts.) | A/C/E to
34th St./Penn Station | 212-630-0249 | www.tirnanognyc.com

"Authentically Irish" – "right down to the hangover the next day" – this "lively" pub is one of the few "decent" bars "in the land of Penn Station"; rugby on the tube, "accents" on the staff and lots of "Guinness" on the taps add to the genuine vibe, and it's only "steps from MSG" to boot.

Tom & Jerry's ⊘
(aka 288)
21 | 15 | 21 | $7

NoHo | 288 Elizabeth St. (bet. Bleecker & Houston Sts.) | 6 to Bleecker St. |
212-260-5045

"Always comfortably buzzing", this "laid-back" NoHo neighborhood hang is "perfect for daytime weekend drinking", especially given the buy-one-get-one-free Bloody Mary deal; decorwise, it's on the "spare" side, save for the collection of Tom & Jerry crockery behind the bar.

Tonic
19 | 20 | 18 | $9

W 40s | 727 Seventh Ave. (bet. 48th & 49th Sts.) | 1 to 50th St. |
212-382-1059 | www.tonicbarnyc.com

The flat-screens are "gigantic" and the range of sporting events broadcast is "vast" at this "awesome" Times Square sports bar triplex that also "appeals to women" with its slick, shiny looks; sure, it's "touristy", given the location, but it's "good during happy hour" if you'd like to meet someone from Morgan Stanley, whose world headquarters are nearby.

Tonic East
20 | 18 | 15 | $9

Murray Hill | 411 Third Ave. (29th St.) | N/R/W to 28th St. | 212-683-7090 |
www.toniceast.com

"Huge" is the word for this "stylish" Murray Hill "mega-bar", with two "jam-packed" floors, wall-to-wall "flat-screens showing three games at once" and a "solid roof deck" complete with "Empire State Building" views; the crowd is "young", the decibels "loud" and it's already garnering a rep as a "Penn State football" shrine.

Top of the Tower
24 | 21 | 20 | $13

E 40s | Beekman Tower Hotel | 3 Mitchell Pl., 26th fl. (1st Ave. & 49th St.) | 6 to
51st St./Lexington Ave. | 212-980-4796 | www.thetopofthetower.com

"Feel like you're in a '30s movie" at this Midtown "art deco experience", where the wraparound "view, view, view" stirs "romantic" impulses, abetted by an airy terrace seating; it's a "classic" for "tourists and jaded New Yorkers alike", even though the "high prices match the setting."

Tortilla Flats
19 | 15 | 17 | $9

W Village | 767 Washington St. (12th St.) | A/C/E/L to 14th St./8th Ave. |
212-243-1053 | www.tortillaflatsnyc.com

"Free-flowing tequila" sets the "happy-go-lucky" mood at this Village Mexican "fiesta", a "loud, crowded, crazy" spot luring "young" folks with "bingo", "drunken hula-hoop" contests and cheap, "sugary drinks" that "you'll regret" in the morning; the "kitsch-tastic" room includes shrines to "Ernest Borgnine" and "Velvet Elvis", and hosts "every bachelorette and birthday party in town" nightly.

Total Wine Bar
25 | 22 | 25 | $11

Park Slope | 74 Fifth Ave. (bet. St. Marks Pl. & Warren St.) | Brooklyn | 2/3 to Bergen St. | 718-783-5166 | www.totalwinebar.com

"Brilliant wines" are decanted by "bantering bartenders" at this Park Slope "oenophile heaven", a "really sweet place" with the "perfect mix of appeal and decor"; "bon vivants" praising its "nice seasonal selection" and "friendly" staff have only one caveat: they "wish it were bigger."

Touch
25 | 25 | 19 | $15

W 50s | 240 W. 52nd St. (bet. B'way & 8th Ave.) | B/D/E to 7th Ave. | 212-489-7656 | www.touchnewyorkcity.com

The "most Downtown spot" in Midtown is the early word on this "exciting" megaclub, a "breath of fresh air" in a dead zone featuring an "amazing multilevel space" endowed with cushy perches, a "huge dance floor" and a futuristic, glows-on-contact bar; folks "tired of the Meatpacking District" scene say this one's "untouchable."

Townhouse ⌫
22 | 23 | 21 | $13

E 50s | 236 E. 58th St. (bet. 2nd & 3rd Aves.) | 4/5/6/N/R/W to 59th St./ Lexington Ave. | 212-754-4649 | www.townhouseny.com

Year after year, the "same patrons sing the same show tunes" at the piano bar of this longtime gay duplex near the Queensboro Bridge popular with "gray-haired daddies" and the "well-dressed younger men" out to nab them; it's a "mature" scene that's "as steady and reliable as the QE2", and let's face it, honey, "everyone comes here sooner or later."

Town Tavern
15 | 12 | 15 | $7

G Village | 134 W. Third St. (bet. MacDougal St. & 6th Ave.) | A/B/C/ D/E/F/V to W. 4th St. | 212-253-6955 | www.towntavernnyc.com

A "100% post-college pickup scene" is in swing at this "down-to-earth" Village double-decker exuding "high energy" in both its "friendly" ground-floor bar and fireplace-equipped upstairs lounge; it's "fun" and it's "young", but can get "too crowded" to move.

Trailer Park
19 | 20 | 18 | $9

Chelsea | 271 W. 23rd St. (bet. 7th & 8th Aves.) | C/E to 23rd St. | 212-463-8000 | www.trailerparklounge.com

"Mullets reign supreme" at this Chelsea salute to "white trash", where folks "get in touch with their inner redneck" in a "kitschy" setting that includes such "hillbilly" items as a "toilet seat ashtray" and an "actual trailer"; don't forget your "sense of humor", and although "tattoos aren't required", you'll "feel out of place without one."

Trash
▽ 18 | 13 | 18 | $7

Williamsburg | 256 Grand St. (bet. Driggs Ave. & Roebling St.) | Brooklyn | L to Bedford Ave. | 718-599-1000 | www.thetrashbar.com

This "wild" Williamsburg rock 'n' roll showcase features a no-cover "main bar in front" with "ongoing", cover-charging bands thrashing away in the back; the feel of a biker clubhouse littered with metalheads is pitch "perfect if that's what you're looking for."

Tribeca Grill

23	22	22	$14

TriBeCa | 375 Greenwich St. (Franklin St.) | 1 to Franklin St. | 212-941-3900 | www.tribecagrill.com

Locals and occasional "A-list" types collide at this longtime "TriBeCa tradition" that's best enjoyed on an "expense account"; while most show up to eat, a big "square" mahogany bar (salvaged from Maxwell's Plum, the legendary '60s restaurant) tantalizes tipplers.

Tribeca Tavern

18	12	19	$8

TriBeCa | 247 W. Broadway (bet. Walker & White Sts.) | A/C/E to Canal St. | 212-941-7671

A "good place to be anonymous", this "laid-back" tavern "doesn't attract a big crowd" despite nightly pitcher deals, a pool table and random video games; snobs say its "grubby" vibe is too "mediocre" for swinging TriBeCa - it's just a "regulars bar like you find in every neighborhood."

Trinity Place

21	25	18	$13

Financial District | 115 Broadway (enter on Cedar St., bet. B'way & Trinity Pl.) | 1/R/W to Rector St. | 212-964-0939 | www.trinityplacenyc.com

Master-of-the-universe types have a "cool" "after-work" destination in this "beautiful" Financial District bar/restaurant set in an "old bank vault" (with its original 35-ton doors intact); it's a "great change of pace from the bland Downtown scene" boasting a dark-wooded drinking area, but it "doesn't draw a crowd except for happy hour."

Trinity Pub

20	16	24	$7

E 80s | 229 E. 84th St. (bet. 2nd & 3rd Aves.) | 4/5/6 to 86th St. | 212-327-4450 | www.trinitypubnyc.com

"About as wide as a phone booth", this "pocket-size" UES tribute to the Emerald Isle is "more charming" than most pubs and "always packed on weekends"; the "authentic" Irish bartenders not only make you "feel like you're back in the old country", they "make the beer seem tastier" too.

Triple Crown

18	17	18	$11

Chelsea | 330 Seventh Ave. (bet. 28th & 29th Sts.) | 1 to 28th St. | 212-736-1575 | www.thetriplecrownalehouse.com

"Commuterish" sorts, "college" grinds and comics from nearby improv companies favor this "large", pony-themed "Irish sports bar" in Chelsea for its "decent-priced" suds and pub grub; though more "garden variety" than thoroughbred, it's a "viable option" before your Penn Station train or an event at MSG.

Trophy

▽ 19	17	19	$11

Williamsburg | 351 Broadway (bet. Keap & Rodney Sts.) | Brooklyn | J/M/Z to Marcy Ave. | 347-227-8515 | www.trophybar.com

The founders of Williamsburg's Stay Gold gallery put plenty of effort into this barroom parked under the J/M/Z line, with polished wood floors and subway tile-lined walls; a back garden, hot DJs and a vintage jukebox playing 45s are bonus draws for its young, style-conscious following.

Tropical 128 ⊅

▽ 19	18	19	$14

Little Italy | 128 Elizabeth St. (bet. Broome & Grand Sts.) | B/D to Grand St. | 212-925-8219 | www.tropical128.com

A kitschy tiki bar and a low-rent pool hall collide at this "fun" Little Italy venue (fka 128 Billiards), a sprawling space festooned with aquariums, flat-screens, Japanese lanterns, tropical foliage and Christmas tree lights; the crowd is "young" and it's usually underpopulated, thus it's a natural for clandestine tippling.

Turkey's Nest ⊘

▽ **16** | **11** | **15** | **$5**

Williamsburg | 94 Bedford Ave. (N. 12th St.) | Brooklyn | L to Bedford Ave. | 718-384-9774

"Cheap beer in Big Gulp–size" Styrofoam cups is the hook at this Billyburg "archetype of a dive" where "hip young folk" who "miss the decor and prices of their hometown bar" come to reclaim their "ironic blue-collar roots"; sure, the "lighting's harsh" and the mood "no-frills", but ultimately it's a "great place to get plowed."

Turks & Frogs

22 | **22** | **20** | **$12**

TriBeCa | 458 Greenwich St. (bet. Desbrosses & Watts Sts.) | 1 to Canal St. | 212-966-4774

W Village | 323 W. 11th St. (bet. Greenwich & Washington Sts.) | A/C/E/L to 14th St./8th Ave. | 212-691-8875
www.turksandfrogs.com

"Charming and intimate", this "tiny" West Village wine bar is "great for a romantic outing" with a vibe that's "conducive to conversation" and a "couldn't-be-more-friendly" staff; "delicious Turkish appetizers" designed to be paired with the vinos are also offered; P.S. the newer TriBeCa outpost is "totally a restaurant", with only a "tiny bar" area.

Turtle Bay

15 | **13** | **16** | **$9**

E 50s | 987 Second Ave. (bet. 52nd & 53rd Sts.) | E/V to Lexington Ave./53rd St. | 212-223-4224 | www.turtle-bay.com

"First stop for all new college grads in the city", this bi-level bar in the "general nowhereland of East Midtown" attracts everyone from "preppies" and "gold diggers" to "U.N. interns" with its "giant meat market" scene (not the "run-down" looks); just enjoy it while you can: "once you're out of school for more than two years, it loses its appeal."

Twelve
(aka XII)

16 | **16** | **18** | **$9**

Murray Hill | 206 E. 34th St. (3rd Ave.) | 6 to 33rd St. | 212-545-9912 | www.bar12.com

It's "all about sports" at this sprawling, "well-kept" barroom where "tons of flat-screens" – even "tiny TVs on the beer taps" – turn it into a total "sausagefest" when "big games" air; "live DJs keep the playlist fresh" on weekends, and even though it's "off the Third Avenue path", its "post-collegiate" following is "very Murray Hill."

12th Street Ale House

18 | **14** | **21** | **$10**

E Village | 192 Second Ave. (12th St.) | L to 1st Ave. | 212-253-2323
Keep a "low profile" at this East Villager, a "cookie-cutter" "local" with flat-screen sports and "conversational" barkeeps for those out to "grab a beer" or "begin an evening"; then again, the "beer pong table" suggests "fratty" times ahead.

ⓩ 21 Club

26 | **25** | **25** | **$17**

W 50s | 21 W. 52nd St. (bet. 5th & 6th Aves.) | B/D/F/V to 47-50th Sts./Rockefeller Ctr. | 212-582-7200 | www.21club.com

One "very smart spot", this ex-speakeasy "staple" in Midtown remains the "epitome" of "old-fashioned style" for "power" players planning to "discuss big things" over "sharp martinis" and "savvy" service; all that "exclusive appeal" can "hit you in the wallet", but it's "still happening" – so "dress for the occasion" (that's a jacket at dinner-time) and "go at least once."

2A
18 | 13 | 17 | $8

E Village | 25 Ave. A (2nd St.) | F/V to Lower East Side/2nd Ave. | 212-505-2466

East Villagers who need a "laid-back" refuge that's "not a big bridge-and-tunnel" magnet are glad this "grungily fab" veteran is "always there" with "decent cocktails", an "indie soundtrack" and "popcorn to boot"; in fact, the upstairs "perch" with its "comfortable" seating and "floor-to-ceiling windows" almost "feels like home."

NEW 249 Bar & Lounge
- | - | - | M

Park Slope | 249 Fourth Ave. (bet. Carroll & President Sts.) | Brooklyn | M/R to Union St. | 718-230-5740 | www.249barlounge.com

The limited lesbian bar scene gets a lift with the arrival of this new Park Sloper, a reworking of the former Cattyshack space; expect the same split-level setup, outdoor deck, pool table and hot grrls on the prowl.

200 Fifth
17 | 16 | 19 | $8

Park Slope | 200 Fifth Ave. (bet. Sackett & Union Sts.) | Brooklyn | M/R to Union St. | 718-638-2925 | www.200-fifth.com

An abundance of "flat-screens" "keeps you abreast" of the action at this Park Slope sports bar, a "straightforward" stop for a "beer with a bud"; the "tired" interior is "not for the romantic", but it's "been around" many a season and is still "packed on the weekends."

205 Club
20 | 13 | 16 | $12

LES | 205 Chrystie St. (Stanton St.) | B/D to Grand St. | 212-477-6688

"Trust fund hipsters" and "young professionals" frequent this "trendy" Lower Eastsider where the "Warholian upstairs" bar recalls the artist's notorious Silver Factory and the "kitschy", lower-level lounge is plastered with Craigslist personal ads; regulars say it "differs from night to night", with a particularly "excellent scene on Tuesdays."

212
18 | 19 | 17 | $13

E 60s | 133 E. 65th St. (bet. Lexington & Park Aves.) | 6 to 68th St. | 212-249-6565 | www.212restaurant.com

The "narrow" space suits the "size 0" clientele to a tee at this "very Euro" Upper East Side bar/restaurant, where flirty "30s" count on the "vodka selection" and the "banker-type guys" for a "convivial" pick-me-up; some say the reception is "as uppity as the prices", but for area "scenesters", this one has a "good ring to it."

Z 230 Fifth
25 | 23 | 16 | $13

Chelsea | 230 Fifth Ave., penthouse (bet. 26th & 27th Sts.) | N/R/W to 28th St. | 212-725-4300 | www.230-fifth.com

The latest "'it' roof bar", this "sprawling", vaguely "tropical" deck crowning a Chelsea office building is "swamped" with "suity" "mingling singles" marveling at the "awesome cityscape" vistas and disregarding the "snooty service" and "steep" tabs; the "bottlenecked elevators" let out on an indoor penthouse that channels a "cruise-ship disco", but upstairs the "top-of-the-world" scene is the "only place to be during the summer."

	APPEAL	DECOR	SERVICE	COST

Ty's ⌷

	▽ 18	14	18	$9

W Village | 114 Christopher St. (bet. Bedford & Bleecker Sts.) | 1 to Christopher St. | 212-741-9641

This gay bar "standby" on the "Christopher Street crawl" since '72 attracts "men who like real men", i.e. "older neighborhood" dudes along with some "bear spillover from the Dugout"; "frequently deserted", it "comes to life on Sunday afternoons" when the "same guys who came here when it opened" drop in to hoist a pint and "relive their youth."

Ultra

	▽ 18	20	21	$14

Chelsea | 37 W. 26th St. (bet. B'way & 6th Ave.) | F/V to 23rd St. | 212-725-3860 | www.theultranyc.com

This "cool" Chelsea "bottle-service club" rolls out all the bells and whistles of high-end, "high-tech" nightlife – soaring ceilings, leather seating, theatrical lighting – and ups the ante with aromatherapy technology, a snow-making machine and specialty mixers (mint lemonade, passion fruit soda); a rear mezzanine done up as an abstract take on a "tree house" is reserved for the inevitable VIPs.

⑤ Ulysses

	22	18	18	$9

Financial District | 95 Pearl St. (off Hanover Sq.) | 4/5 to Bowling Green | 212-482-0400 | www.ulyssesbarnyc.com

"One of the most popular after-work hangouts" in the Financial District, this "jumping" Irish pub offers the opportunity to fraternize with a "ridiculous number" of "bulls, bears" and sundry "market high rollers"; come warm weather, what seems like the "entire Wall Street work force" hits the "unrivaled" back patio set on a "historic" "cobblestoned" lane.

Uncle Charlie's

	21	19	22	$11

E 40s | 139 E. 45th St., 2nd fl. (bet. Lexington & 3rd Aves.) | 4/5/6/7/S to 42nd St./Grand Central | 212-661-9097 | www.unclecharliesnyc.com

Hidden in a second-floor perch off a nondescript, Grand Central–area block, this gay watering hole takes a something-for-everyone approach with a spacious barroom, plus a separate piano bar and outdoor terrace; brought to you by the owners of the now-shuttered Pegasus, it's drawing the same type of crowd, i.e. older dudes and the musically inclined.

Underbar

	21	20	16	$12

Union Sq | W Union Square Hotel | 201 Park Ave. S. (17th St.) | 4/5/6/L/N/Q/R/W to 14th St./Union Sq. | 212-358-1560 | www.gerberbars.com

A "sexy aura" (ramped up by a random bed and "curtained booths") keeps this "stylish" "underground lair" beneath the W Union Square Hotel ever popular with an "eye-candy" combination of underemployed "i-bankers", "trust fund" kids and "wannabes galore"; it's so "dark", you may as well "go there blindfolded", though the "home equity loan"–worthy pricing is certainly eye-opening.

Underground

	18	14	17	$12

Murray Hill | 613 Second Ave. (bet. 33rd & 34th Sts.) | 6 to 33rd St. | 212-683-3000 | www.undergroundny.com

Appropriately one small step down from the curb, this Murray Hill good ol' boys' haven is set in a meandering space that includes a barroom, mini-lounge and "nice" back patio; while it "won't win any contests for name originality", the low ceilings and no-decor decor suits its sports-watching, beer-slugging demographic just fine.

	APPEAL	DECOR	SERVICE	COST

Underground Lounge
∇ 18 | 17 | 17 | $7

W 100s | 955 West End Ave. (107th St.) | 1 to Cathedral Pkwy./110th St. | 212-531-4759 | www.theundergroundnyc.com

This subterranean "Columbia hangout" in Morningside Heights has expanded its hours, and now functions as a daytime coffeehouse that morphs into a "lively" watering hole after dark (credit a pool table and a variety of live performances); like most places, it "tends to be more fun the more you drink."

Under the Volcano
18 | 19 | 17 | $8

Murray Hill | 12 E. 36th St. (bet. 5th & Madison Aves.) | 6 to 33rd St. | 212-213-0093

When Murray Hill's "Ginger Man gets too boisterous", there's always this "best-kept secret" alternative across the street where you can "actually hold a conversation" with "would-be literati" types (it's named after the Malcolm Lowry novel); besides the "quiet atmosphere", a "great selection of tequila" is its claim to fame.

Union Bar
18 | 17 | 15 | $11

Union Sq | 204 Park Ave. S. (bet. 17th & 18th Sts.) | 4/5/6/L/N/Q/R/W to 14th St./Union Sq. | 212-674-2105 | www.union-bar.com

Now in its 12th year, this DJ-driven Union Square "hideaway" draws crowds of "twentysomethings" who report a "guaranteed run-in with a friend from the past"; the atmosphere is vaguely "trendy" but "lacking in real energy", starting with the "bemused bartenders" and stripped-down decor.

☑ Union Hall
24 | 25 | 20 | $8

Park Slope | 702 Union St. (bet. 5th & 6th Aves.) | Brooklyn | M/R to Union St. | 718-638-4400 | www.unionhallny.com

Bookworms, keglers and indie music mavens find common ground at this "consciously eccentric" Park Slope destination that features a "loungey library" area up front (complete with towering, tome-filled shelves and a fireplace), a big "bocce ball court in back" and a performance space downstairs; it's "easygoing" during the week, "too packed for comfort on a Saturday night" and pretty "fabulous" all the time.

Union Pool
20 | 16 | 16 | $6

Williamsburg | 484 Union Ave. (Meeker Ave.) | Brooklyn | G/L to Metropolitan Ave./Lorimer St. | 718-609-0484

"Vintage fashion"-wearers, "motorcyclistas" and "twentysomething hipsters" crowd into this Billyburg "hot spot" that's "shoulder-to-shoulder" on weekends due to a "great central location" in a former pool supply store; despite plenty of diversions – a "spacious patio", "outdoor fire pit", photo booth, darts and "cheap" PBR – the mood is "nonchalant."

☑ Union Square Cafe
24 | 22 | 24 | $14

Union Sq | 21 E. 16th St. (bet. 5th Ave. & Union Sq. W.) | 4/5/6/L/N/Q/R/W to 14th St./Union Sq. | 212-243-4020 | www.unionsquarecafe.com

"Unwind or impress" at Danny Meyer's Union Square "must", a "no-attitude" scene where the bar area is "usually crowded" with "mature" types either dining or trying to "wiggle in without a reservation"; sure, it offers "great cocktails" – and the "food ain't bad either" – but the most "top shelf" thing about it is a staff that treats patrons like "the ladies and gentlemen you wish you were."

| | APPEAL | DECOR | SERVICE | COST |

United Palace
▽ 19 | 22 | 12 | $9

Washington Heights | 4140 Broadway (175th St.) | A to 175th St. |
212-568-6700 | www.theunitedpalace.com

An unlikely arrival on the indie music scene, this mammoth 3,300 seater in Washington Heights has come out of the gate strong by hiring the former booker of the Beacon Theatre, who's already managed to draw the likes of Arcade Fire, Björk and Iggy Pop; it's worth a trip just to see the "fabulous art deco" setting, a vast, circa-1930 movie palace that's a rococo take on Radio City.

Uptown Lounge
23 | 22 | 20 | $10

E 80s | 1576 Third Ave. (bet. 88th & 89th Sts.) | 4/5/6 to 86th St. |
212-828-1388 | www.uptownloungenyc.com

Set in the "nosebleed section of the UES" that's "overrun by frat-boy bars", this "decently upscale" lounge is perfect for a "night out away from the younger crowds"; of course, you'll "pay for it", but fans say its "classy" vibe and "sleek" decor is a fair substitute "when you don't want to travel Downtown."

Urge, The
▽ 19 | 14 | 16 | $8

E Village | 33 Second Ave. (bet. 1st & 2nd Sts.) | F/V to Lower East Side/2nd Ave. | 212-533-5757

"Everyone seems to be having a good time" at this spacious East Village gay bar where "gay-for-pay go-go boys" compete with a "cute crowd" and two jumbo screens for your attention.

Valhalla
18 | 18 | 19 | $10

W 50s | 815 Ninth Ave. (54th St.) | C/E to 50th St. | 212-757-2747

Ever gentrifying Hell's Kitchen is home to this "spacious" if "unassuming" barroom named after nothing less than the hall of Odin in Norse mythology; an "extensive selection" of craft brews takes your mind off the "no-frills", spare-verging-on-spartan decor.

NEW Van Diemens
18 | 16 | 19 | $9

Murray Hill | 383 Third Ave. (bet. 27th & 28th Sts.) | 6 to 28th St. |
212-532-1123 | www.vandiemensnyc.com

Borrowing Tasmania's original name, this "upscale" Murray Hill newcomer brings a dash of "Down Under" to an "airy" space outfitted with "big TVs" and a mezzanine loft used for overflow and private parties; the "frat boy–turned–i-banker" clientele (and "the girls who love them") may be "typical" for the area, but even so, partisans posit it "has potential."

V Bar
▽ 26 | 25 | 19 | $12

G Village | 225 Sullivan St. (bet. Bleecker & W. 3rd Sts.) | A/B/C/D/E/F/V to W. 4th St. | 212-253-5740 | www.vbar.net

It's "easy to be casual" at this "cozy" Village wine bar where "overeducated NYU grad students" linger in a "living room"–like setting; "entertaining" staffers make it a pleasure during the week, though regulars report "sardine-can" conditions "when strangers invade" on weekends.

NEW Velour
▽ 20 | 19 | 18 | $12

Chelsea | 297 10th Ave. (27th St.) | C/E to 23rd St. | 212-279-9707 |
www.velournyc.com

The former Brite Bar - once a low-key alternative to West Chelsea's club row - has joined the pack and gone swanky in this latest incarnation, an artful mix of velvet, suede and exposed brick; seating is sparse (no more barstools), but there is a velvet-roped, bottle-service-only VIP area for those who still have money to burn.

Velvet Cigar Lounge

17 | 18 | 17 | $12

E Village | 80 E. Seventh St. (bet. 1st & 2nd Aves.) | 4/5/6/L/N/Q/R/W to 14th St./Union Sq. | 212-533-5582 | www.velvetcigars.com

Velvet Lounge

Williamsburg | 174 Broadway (bet. Bedford & Driggs Aves.) | Brooklyn | J/M/Z to Marcy Ave. | 718-302-4427 | www.velvetbrooklyn.com

"If you dig cigars", you'll like this "serious" East Village lounge, a "small", clubby 12-seater dedicated to stogie puffing, accompanied by a selection of wine and chocolate (cigarette smoking is verboten); the separately owned Williamsburg venue is larger and plusher, though if you want to smoke here, you'll have to do it outdoors on the sidewalk seats.

Verlaine

23 | 19 | 21 | $11

LES | 110 Rivington St. (bet. Essex & Ludlow Sts.) | F/J/M/Z to Delancey/Essex Sts. | 212-614-2494 | www.verlainenyc.com

Catering to "trendy" Lower East Side "arty" types, this "reliable", "semi-sleek" lounge is a chick magnet, though it's a perfectly "respectable place to take a date"; best known for its "kick-ass" lychee martinis, it also hosts a "long happy hour" that runs "till 10 PM, seven days a week."

Vero

24 | 21 | 23 | $11

NEW E 50s | 1004 Second Ave. (53rd St.) | E/V to Lexington Ave./53rd St. | 212-935-3530

E 70s | 1483 Second Ave. (bet. 77th & 78th Sts.) | 6 to 77th St. | 212-452-3354 | www.veronyc.com

For a "nice" Upper East Side "change of pace", check out this "cozy wine bar", a departure from the "typical frat bars that clog the area"; it may be a tad "tiny" and a "little expensive", but it's great for a date "when you want to stay local", especially when seated in the "sidewalk cafe"; N.B. the Midtown satellite opened post-Survey.

Vertigo

19 | 19 | 19 | $10

Murray Hill | 354 Third Ave. (26th St.) | 6 to 23rd St. | 212-696-1011

This Murray Hill spot is all about the "big glass walls" opening onto the street ("nice breeze"); otherwise, it's the usual "fratty" scene, with lots of "young business" types watching "lots of flat-screens", though some say things are more "social" during the "after-work happy hour."

View Bar ⌨

16 | 15 | 17 | $9

Chelsea | 232 Eighth Ave. (bet. 21st & 22nd Sts.) | C/E to 23rd St. | 212-929-2243 | www.viewbarnyc.com

"Drink specials rule" at this "unassuming" Chelsea gay bar that's "welcoming" if "nondescript" and oddly "underpopulated"; it's "best in warm weather" when its "modern", glass-fronted facade opens to the street, serving up a choice view of Eighth Avenue's "vibrant sidewalk culture."

View Lounge

24 | 22 | 18 | $15

W 40s | Marriott Marquis Hotel | 1535 Broadway, 48th fl. (bet. 45th & 46th Sts.) | 1/2/3/7/N/Q/R/S/W to 42nd St./Times Sq. | 212-704-8900 | www.nymarriottmarquis.com

A "civilized place above the chaos of Times Square", this "revolving" hotel bar boasts a one-of-a-kind "rotating panorama of Manhattan" from a 48th-floor vantage point; it's a natural for "first-time NYC tourists" and "worth every penny", even if locals yawn "dated."

Vig Bar
22 | 18 | 21 | $9

NoLita | 12 Spring St. (Elizabeth St.) | 6 to Spring St. | 212-625-0011 | www.vigbar.com

Fans of "high energy" hightail it over to this "upbeat" NoLita "go-to" bar, now in its 12th year thanks to a "cool" setting, "attractive" patrons and "amazing" DJs; when it gets "too crowded" on weekends, insiders retreat to the "cozy lounge in the back."

Vig 27
19 | 18 | 18 | $11

Murray Hill | 119 E. 27th St. (bet. Lexington Ave. & Park Ave. S.) | 6 to 28th St. | 212-686-5500 | www.vig27.com

Murray Hill's former Aubette space has been revamped into this "minimalist" lounge with "nothing on the walls" to distract you from the "total meat-market crowd"; regulars say it has "two personalities": "quiet and candlelit" during the week, "packed and loud" on weekends.

Village Lantern
▽ 19 | 14 | 19 | $8

G Village | 167 Bleecker St. (bet. Sullivan & Thompson Sts.) | A/B/C/D/E/F/V to W. 4th St. | 212-260-7993 | www.villagelantern.com

Different from the typical NYU haunts in the neighborhood, this Village bar/restaurant features "live music" and comedy routines upstairs; though critics detect "nothing inspiring" going on, regulars applaud the "great bartenders" who know how to "take care of you."

Village Pourhouse
18 | 13 | 18 | $8

E Village | 64 Third Ave. (11th St.) | 4/5/6/L/N/Q/R/W to 14th St./Union Sq. | 212-979-2337

NEW **W 100s** | 982 Amsterdam Ave. (bet. 108th & 109th Sts.) | 1 to Cathedral Pkwy./110th St. | 212-979-2337
www.pourhousenyc.com

"Bring your frat house buddies" and "chug a mug" at this "boisterous", "sprawling" duo with an "intimidating beer list" and HDTVs galore tuned to "college games"; with a "standing-room-only" crowd "getting rowdy on the cheap", they're "not the most relaxing" joints, but they're "definitely not pretentious"; N.B. the UWS branch will match the cost of your taxi ride over in a corresponding bar tab when you show your receipt.

Village Underground
18 | 13 | 16 | $10

G Village | 130 W. Third St., downstairs (bet. MacDougal St. & 6th Ave.) | A/B/C/D/E/F/V to W. 4th St. | 212-533-4790 | www.thevillageunderground.com

Formerly Rumor, this "long-standing" Villager shoehorned below the Fat Black Pussycat has reverted back to its original name, with its "slightly divey" atmosphere and "NYU"-heavy clientele intact; maybe "not as large as your typical club", it's still a "decent place to see a band and have a few beers" – if the "band rocks, this place rolls."

Village Vanguard ⌿
24 | 16 | 16 | $12

W Village | 178 Seventh Ave. S. (11th St.) | 1/2/3/L to 14th St./7th Ave. | 212-255-4037 | www.villagevanguard.com

"Beatniks still dwell" in this "Vatican of jazz" in the West Village, counting down since 1935 and arguably the "most storied jazz club in New York"; it's "mecca for big stars" (John Coltrane, Miles Davis and

Thelonious Monk have all graced its stage), and despite "expensive covers" and "tight seating", it's "must-see" material for serious hepcats.

NEW Vino
22	20	21	$14

E 60s | 1268 Second Ave. (bet. 66th & 67th Sts.) | 6 to 68th St. | 212-744-5370 | www.vinowinebarnyc.com

A "breath of fresh air" for Upper Eastsiders, this "neighborhood" enoteca from the Mediterraneo team offers a "super selection" of "all-Italian" vinos (plus lite bites) in "cozy", Tuscan-esque digs; "unpretentious" guidance from the staff adds to the "mellow" mood.

Vino di Vino
22	22	23	$12

Astoria | 29-21 Ditmars Blvd. (bet. 29th & 31st Sts.) | Queens | N/W to Astoria Blvd. | 718-721-3010 | www.vinodivinowinebar.com

This cavernous wine bar "attached to Trattoria L'Incontro" – one of the "best Italian restaurants in Astoria" – offers a "great" 300-bottle list to choose from as well as 50 by-the-glass selections; wall murals conjure up the old country (by way of Queens), and although it's meant to be a holding zone for folks waiting for a table, it's a bona fide destination in itself.

NEW Vino 313
22	21	20	$13

Murray Hill | 201 E. 31st St. (3rd Ave.) | 6 to 33rd St. | 212-725-8466 | www.vino313.com

"Older" types frequent this "intimate" new Murray Hill wine bar, a "casual", candlelit haven for "good" global vinos accompanied by small-plate nibbles; "chic" but "not too snooty", it's a "welcome change" from the neighborhood's typical "fraternity scene" on the Third Avenue runway.

Vino Vino
23	23	23	$14

TriBeCa | 211 W. Broadway (Franklin St.) | 1 to Franklin St. | 212-925-8510 | www.vinovino.net

A glass wall separates the wine store from the tasting room at this "beautiful", double-purpose TriBeCan that allows the option of sampling a glass from its "superb list" before shelling out for a bottle; minimal design and "rarely crowded" conditions can leave a chilly feeling, but the "knowledgeable" staff's passion for its product warms things up.

Vintage
▽ 25	20	21	$11

W 50s | 753 Ninth Ave. (bet. 50th & 51st Sts.) | C/E to 50th St. | 212-581-4655

With "more martinis than you can shake a stick at" ("you'll need a crane to pick up the list"), this "relaxed" Hell's Kitchen bar/eatery is a "great after-theater hangout" and occasionally offers the "chance to hobnob with Broadway stars"; sure, it may be on the "expensive" side, but is "well worth the price."

NEW Vintage Irving
21	19	20	$12

Gramercy | 118 E. 15th St. (Irving Pl.) | 4/5/6/L/N/Q/R/W to 14th St./Union Sq. | 212-677-6300 | www.vintageirvingnyc.com

"SideBar's next-door" sidekick, this new Gramercy wine bar caters to "all tastes" with a deserving lineup of vinos, microbrews and even an "absinthe list", all matched with "more-than-serviceable small plates"; lodged in "comfortable" quarters equipped with "high tables", it's a bit "pricey" but shows plenty of "potential."

	APPEAL	DECOR	SERVICE	COST

VIP Club

∇ **27** | **19** | **19** | **$13**

Flatiron | 20 W. 20th St. (bet. 5th & 6th Aves.) | N/R/W to 23rd St. | 212-633-1199 | www.thevipclubnyc.com

If you're "looking for naked chicks", this Flatiron stripteaser show-cases "actually attractive" dancers entertaining gents who "get exactly what they expect" so long as they flash a "stack of bills"; still, jugheads gripe "talent is scarce" and suggest you "go to Vegas" for the real deal; P.S. on Sundays, it morphs into Club 20, with go-go boys performing for the gay crowd.

Vlada

23 | **20** | **21** | **$9**

W 50s | 331 W. 51st St. (bet. 8th & 9th Aves.) | C/E to 50th St. | 212-974-8030 | www.vladabar.com

"Hot boys" and "icy cold drinks" meet cute at this "trendy" gay duplex that's one of "Hellsea's" "newer cruising grounds"; an "ice"-lined bar (to keep your drinks frosty) and a vlada "homemade" infused vodkas "set it apart" from its competitors, while "cool customers" in the crowd like the "posh" decor.

Vol de Nuit

25 | **18** | **18** | **$9**

G Village | 148 W. Fourth St. (bet. MacDougal St. & 6th Ave.) | A/B/C/D/E/F/V to W. 4th St. | 212-982-3388 | www.voldenuitbar.com

An "awesome Belgian brew selection" is the calling card of this bit of "Europe" in the Village that's "hard to find" given the "hidden entrance" accessed via a "beautiful courtyard" ("I walked past this place every day and still didn't know it existed"); inside, it's "so dark that decor is irrelevant", but its "NYU" following says it makes them "feel sexy."

Volstead, The

21 | **21** | **20** | **$12**

E 50s | 125 E. 54th St., downstairs (bet. Lexington & Park Aves.) | 4/6/E/V to 51st-53rd Sts./Lexington Ave. | 212-583-0411 | www.thevolstead.com

A "touch of old-school class", this Midtown bar/lounge is "a hit" with "after-work singles" seeking a "grown-up vibe"; named for the congressman who legislated Prohibition, its underground space is appropriately "speakeasy"-ish with mahogany paneling and other "snazzy" touches that justify the "pricey" tabs.

Von

26 | **19** | **20** | **$9**

NoHo | 3 Bleecker St. (bet. Bowery & Elizabeth St.) | 6 to Bleecker St. | 212-473-3039 | www.vonbar.com

"Dark and romantic", this candlelit NoHo den exudes a "cool, mellow" mood and is a "good place to chill" for "late 20s, early 30s" types; a "surprising wine selection" brings in the oenophiles, but there's a simpler reason for its success: "neither the bar nor its clientele try too hard to be hip"; N.B. they've just added a downstairs lounge.

Vudu Lounge

18 | **16** | **16** | **$15**

E 70s | 1487 First Ave. (bet. 77th & 78th Sts.) | 6 to 77th St. | 212-249-9540 | www.vudulounge.com

"Way Uptown meets the Upper East Side" at this long-running dance club attracting an "eclectic crowd" blinged out in "gold chains and diamonds"; despite "all the functional elements" needed for primo booty-shaking – a "good vibe", "off-the-meter music" – aficionados say it's "not the best" of the genre.

	APPEAL	DECOR	SERVICE	COST

Walker's
`21` `13` `20` `$8`

TriBeCa | 16 N. Moore St. (Varick St.) | 1 to Franklin St. | 212-941-0142
A "low-key alternative" in "trendy" TriBeCa, this timeworn tavern is home base for "neighborhood" types and those "pretending" they are ("nobody will point out that you actually live in Astoria"); while the "historic" front bar area has lots of "charm", it's generally a "hole-in-the-wall" and "not a place to impress a date."

Walter's Bar ⊘
`17` `13` `20` `$9`

Garment District | 389 Eighth Ave. (bet. 29th & 30th Sts.) | A/C/E to 34th St./Penn Station | 212-502-4023 | www.waltersbar.com
Join the "neighborhood characters" at this "true dive" in the "shadow of the Garden", a longtime "no-frills" spot to toss darts, "get hustled in a pool game" or bend your elbow at the "welcoming" bar; in the best "drinkers'-place" tradition, it's usually "more crowded in the daytime than at night."

Warsaw ⊘
▽ `19` `14` `18` `$8`

Greenpoint | 261 Driggs Ave. (Eckford St.) | Brooklyn | G/L to Metropolitan Ave./Lorimer St. | 718-387-0505 | www.warsawconcerts.com
Greenpoint is home to this "great concert venue" whose setting (a Polish community center) has an "Elk's Club feel" – but "that's a good thing"; there's "cheap" beer and pierogi in the front bar and a big ballroom performance space in back, and like most music halls, it's "only worth it if they've got a good band playing."

Waterfront Ale House
`20` `14` `20` `$8`

Murray Hill | 540 Second Ave. (30th St.) | 6 to 33rd St. | 212-696-4104
Brooklyn Heights | 155 Atlantic Ave. (bet. Clinton & Henry Sts.) | Brooklyn | 2/3/4/5/M/N/R/W to Borough Hall | 718-522-3794
www.waterfrontalehouse.com
"First-class tap lists" are the bait at these Kips Bay/Brooklyn Heights pubs known for their "constantly changing" brew selection and "generic" settings (with no water in sight); the Manhattan outpost's "slightly older" crowd is peppered with "doctors" given its "claim to fame": the "closest bar to Bellevue."

Watering Hole
`18` `15` `19` `$11`

Gramercy | 106 E. 19th St. (bet. Irving Pl. & Park Ave. S) | 4/5/6/L/N/Q/R/W to 14th St./Union Sq. | 212-674-5783 | www.wateringholenyc.com
Hole up and "get your drink on" at this "standard" Gramercy saloon, a "decent after-work" option that's notable for hosting "hilarious karaoke" Thursday–Saturday nights; maybe the brick-lined space is just "one step up from a dive", but it's also "friendly" and "not expensive" – a "rarity" in these parts.

Water Street Bar
`20` `18` `20` `$13`

Dumbo | 66 Water St. (bet. Dock & Main Sts.) | Brooklyn | A/C to High St. | 718-625-9352 | www.waterstreetrestaurant.com
Cavernous but "comfy", this overgrown Dumbo pub at water's edge is a "favorite hang" among locals who laud its "friendly" staff, 20-plus beers on tap and "good eats"; it also harbors a rugged performance space, and those willing to travel to the far-flung locale can count on "lots of seats."

	APPEAL	DECOR	SERVICE	COST

ⓩ Water Taxi Beach
22 | **15** | **14** | **$8**

NEW Seaport | South Street Seaport | Pier 17, northside (bet. Fulton & South Sts.) | 2/3 to Fulton St.
NEW Governors Island | Governors Island (catch ferry at 10 South St.) | 1 to South Ferry
LIC | Hunters Point Ferry Stop (Borden Ave. & 2nd St.) | Queens | 7 to Vernon Blvd./Jackson Ave.⌐
no phone | www.watertaxibeach.com

"Who needs the Hamptons?" when there's this seasonal "sandy beach" on the LIC shore of the East River known for its jaw-dropping view of the Midtown "NY skyline" (other outposts are in the works for Governors Island and the Seaport); despite no swimming, "long lines at the bar" and a "more family-oriented vibe than a true party-goer would like", it's at least "something different" for folks feeling "stuck in the city."

WCOU Radio ⌐
19 | **12** | **19** | **$8**
(aka Tile Bar)

E Village | 115 First Ave. (7th St.) | L to 1st Ave. | 212-254-4317
Ok, it's "clearly a dive", but this East Villager transmits plenty of "charm and charisma" via "colorful patrons" and a "great indie juke-box"; "cheap" prices seal the deal at this "solid neighborhood" spot.

ⓩ Weather Up
22 | **22** | **21** | **$13**

Prospect Heights | 589 Vanderbilt Ave. (bet. Bergen & Dean Sts.) | Brooklyn | C to Clinton/Washington Aves. | 718-788-1756
Brooklyn gets cocktails with a pedigree via this "upscale" Prospect Heights "home run" from the owner of East Side Company Bar, featuring bartenders schooled by Milk and Honey maestro Sasha Petraske; its "higher-priced-than-average" riffs on the classics are mixed in white-tiled, "speakeasy"-ish digs, complete with an "unmarked" exterior, but the "fantastic" back patio is the place to be during warm weather.

Webster Hall
19 | **16** | **14** | **$12**

E Village | 125 E. 11th St. (bet. 3rd & 4th Aves.) | 4/5/6/L/N/Q/R/W to 14th St./Union Sq. | 212-353-1600 | www.websterhall.com
"Multiple personality" types are drawn to this "huge" East Village dance hall–cum–concert venue since it provides "multirooms" on "multifloors" with music for every taste; still, those who say it's "not what it once was" cite "pricey drinks", a "played-out" vibe and a "sweaty B&T" crowd right out of a "Jerry Springer casting call."

Welcome to the Johnsons ⌐
18 | **16** | **17** | **$6**

LES | 123 Rivington St. (bet. Essex & Norfolk Sts.) | F/J/M/Z to Delancey/Essex Sts. | 212-420-9911
"Just like home" (if you live in an "RV park"), this Rivington Street "dive" is decorated like a "white trash living room" with "falling-apart couches", "clogged toilets" and an "old sweat socks smell"; economizers show up for the "ridiculously cheap PBRs", while nostalgists say it's an "old standby from the Lower East Side's pre-bourgeois days."

Westside Brewing Co.
17 | **14** | **18** | **$8**

W 70s | 340 Amsterdam Ave. (76th St.) | 1/2/3 to 72nd St. | 212-721-2161
"Come for burgers" and stay for suds at this UWS taproom that "would be more of a draw if they actually brewed the beer on-site"; otherwise, it's a "decent" "dive" with "outdoor seating" and "TVs for sports."

	APPEAL	DECOR	SERVICE	COST

Wet Bar
21 | 22 | 19 | $13

Murray Hill | W Court Hotel | 130 E. 39th St. (Lexington Ave.) | 4/5/6/7/S to 42nd St./Grand Central | 212-592-8844 | www.gerberbars.com
"Scantily clad", "part-time model" waitresses serve "lethal martinis" that "will cost you" to a "stand-around-and-look-pretty" crowd at this "dimly lit" Murray Hill lounge; jaded types yawn it's way "past its prime": "if you've been to one W Hotel bar, you've been to them all."

Wharf Bar & Grill
18 | 17 | 21 | $9

Murray Hill | 587 Third Ave. (bet. 38th & 39th Sts.) | 4/5/6/7/S to 42nd St./Grand Central | 212-490-7270
"You're not inundated with kids right out of college" at this Murray Hill duplex, a casual maritime themer with "decent" prices and a "cool terrace"; aye, it's "nothing special", but "it does the job."

Whiskey, The
20 | 19 | 19 | $13

W 40s | W Times Square Hotel | 1567 Broadway, downstairs (47th St.) | N/R/W to 49th St. | 212-930-7444 | www.gerberbars.com
Beautiful folk "get ugly on the dance floor" of this "high-end" club beneath the W Times Square Hotel, where the "multicolored" gel flooring evokes *Saturday Night Fever*; it may be "brimming with tourists", but there's compensation: "one-way mirrors" in the loos, so voyeurs can "watch pretty girls primping on the other side."

Whiskey Blue
23 | 23 | 18 | $13

E 40s | W New York Hotel | 541 Lexington Ave. (bet. 49th & 50th Sts.) | 6 to 51st St./Lexington Ave. | 212-407-2947 | www.gerberbars.com
"Another in the W Hotel bar tradition", this "trendy" Midtown lounge is "still going strong" with its trademark "dark" lighting and ridiculously "beautiful" waitresses clad in clinging, "low-cut" outfits; despite "second mortgage"–worthy tabs, "on-the-prowl" dudes set to "close the deal" note there are "hotel rooms just seconds away."

Whiskey Park
20 | 20 | 19 | $14

W 50s | 100 Central Park S. (6th Ave.) | N/R/W to 5th Ave./59th St. | 212-307-9222 | www.gerberbars.com
A bit "smaller" than the rest of Rande Gerber's "Whiskey empire", this "upscale" lounge "right across from Central Park" attracts the usual "young professional"/"trust-fund baby" following for "after-work schmoozing"; the ambiance is "slick", the lighting "low", the pops "pricey" and the waitresses poured into "short black cocktail dresses."

Whiskey River
18 | 15 | 18 | $8

Murray Hill | 575 Second Ave. (bet. 31st & 32nd Sts.) | 6 to 33rd St. | 212-679-6799 | www.whiskeyrivernyc.com
Once a "local secret" set on a "dead zone of Second Avenue", this now "crowded" Murray Hill "dive bar" is one part "Red Rock West", one part "Brother Jimmy's"; other secrets to its success include an "outdoor patio", "roaring fireplace", "fun bartenders" and "cheap" tabs.

NEW Whiskey Tavern
19 | 17 | 19 | $11

Chinatown | 79 Baxter St. (bet. Bayard & Walker Sts.) | 4/5/6/J/M/N/R/Q/W to Canal St. | 212-374-9119 | www.whiskeytavernnyc.com
"Da bomb" for the "whiskey aficionado", this new Whiskey Town sibling in Chinatown showcases an "awesome" selection of its namesake

spirit for the "real drinkers" gathered around its "cozy" bar; it's "not much to look at", but if you're pining for "good liquor and good times", it sure "scratches the itch."

Whiskey Town

APPEAL	DECOR	SERVICE	COST
20	18	20	$9

E Village | 29 E. Third St. (bet. Bowery & 2nd Ave.) | F/V to Lower East Side/2nd Ave. | 212-505-7344 | www.whiskeytownbar.com

A "straight-up bar with no frills", this East Village "local" flaunts a "totally rock 'n' roll" vibe, plying its "hipster" clientele with "canned beer" and 50 brands of the namesake likker; a "cool DJ" spinning "classic" radio hits cedes the floor to a jazz trio on Tuesdays and Wednesdays.

Whiskey Ward

19	12	21	$8

LES | 121 Essex St. (bet. Delancey & Rivington Sts.) | F/J/M/Z to Delancey/Essex Sts. | 212-477-2998 | www.thewhiskeyward.com

The "wide array" of whiskies and single-malts is the hook at this "saloon-type" LES "rock 'n' roll bar" where prices are "incredibly low" and the pool table and peanuts to "soak up the booze" are gratis; there's "no attitude" and it's "never too crowded", though picky drinkers shrug "nothing special."

Whistlin' Dixie's Texas Tavern

16	16	18	$9

W 50s | 714 11th Ave. (51st St.) | C/E to 50th St. | 212-349-4370 | www.dixiestexastavern.com

Settled in the "badlands" of Way West Midtown, this "rollicking" saloon exudes Lone Star kitsch with "frontier" decor, sports-tuned TVs and "accommodating" cowgirls in Stetsons and cutoffs hawking numerous "drink specials"; some sigh "honky-tonk wannabe", but rebels reckon it's "totally trashy fun."

☒ White Horse Tavern ⊘

20	15	17	$8

W Village | 567 Hudson St. (11th St.) | A/C/E/L to 14th St./8th Ave. | 212-243-9260

"Dumpy but historic", this "true West Village landmark" around since 1880 is famed as the site where "Dylan Thomas drank himself to death", but nowadays you're more likely to encounter a "just-out-of-college" crew "pretending that they're poets"; "outdoor picnic tables take it up a notch in nice weather", blotting out the "slow service" and only "edible food."

White Rabbit

18	18	20	$10

LES | 145 E. Houston St. (bet. Eldridge & Forsyth Sts.) | F/V to Lower East Side/2nd Ave. | 212-477-5005 | www.whiterabbitnyc.com

A "white-on-white" palette and "industrial" furnishings draw mixed impressions ("clean" vs. "cold") at this Lower East Side lounge; a "rockin'" DJ and movies projected on the wall add to the "cool" vibe, though like most clubs, it's "better during the week than on the bridge-and-tunnel weekends."

☒ NEW White Slab Palace

-	-	-	M

LES | 77 Delancey St. (Allen St.) | F/J/M/Z to Delancey/Essex Sts. | 212-334-0913

Parked on the rapidly gentrifying corner of Allen and Delancey Streets, this new barroom/Scandinavian eatery from the Good World folks looks like it's been there forever, with a saloonish vibe incorporating high barstools, weatherbeaten furniture and random

Menus, photos, voting and more – free at ZAGAT.com

taxidermy; two walls of floor-to-ceiling windows allow for amusing LES people-watching.

NEW White Star
20 | 17 | 18 | $12

LES | 21 Essex St. (bet. Canal & Hester Sts.) | F/J/M/Z to Delancey/Essex Sts. | 212-995-5464

Everything's "made with TLC" at mixology pasha Sasha Petraske's latest LES venture, originally conceived as a 'sipping spirits' bar focusing on absinthe and booze served neat, but now offering mixed cocktails as well; in keeping with the pared-down aesthetic, there's little decor in the tiny, "nondescript" space (fka KingSize) – and "slow service" from the "aloof" staff.

Wicked Monk
18 | 17 | 22 | $8

Bay Ridge | 8415 Fifth Ave. (85th St.) | Brooklyn | R to 86th St. | 718-921-0601

"Totally devoid of snootiness", this "real Brooklyn" Irish pub is an "old-school" Bay Ridge joint where "locals are all but assured of running into someone from their past"; darts, a pool table and "great live music" keep its "beer-guzzling, twentysomething" crowd content.

Wicked Willy's
18 | 14 | 16 | $10

G Village | 149 Bleecker St. (bet. LaGuardia Pl. & Thompson St.) | 6 to Bleecker St. | 212-254-8592

A "cheesy pirate motif" marks this Village "frat bar" that has the "NYU" crew on board nightly for "beer pong", bi-weekly karaoke and "live bands" on weekends; though these be wickedly "crowded" quarters with "beer-soaked floors", the "cheap drinks" will save you a few doubloons.

Wicker Park
18 | 16 | 18 | $9

E 80s | 1469 Third Ave. (83rd St.) | 4/5/6 to 86th St. | 212-734-5600 | www.wickerparknyc.com

"What used to be Martell's" has morphed into this UES pub that evokes the "same frat house" vibe as its predecessor albeit with a "better menu"; though it's the "perfect in-between place" – "not too trendy, not too divey" – some say it's "not as appealing anymore" given the "slow service" and a crowd right out of a "Young Republicans meeting."

NEW Wilfie & Nell
24 | 20 | 21 | $9

W Village | 228 W. Fourth St. (bet. 7th Ave. S & W. 10th St.) | 1 to Christopher St. | 212-242-2990 | www.wilfieandnell.com

A "new favorite" in the old Absolutely 4th digs, this "adorable" Village Irish bar draws crowds with its "excellent vibe", "surprisingly good bites" and shabby-chic setting that's "dark in all the right corners"; just remember to "arrive early" or "forget about" getting a seat.

Wine & Roses
21 | 21 | 19 | $13

W 70s | 286 Columbus Ave. (73rd St.) | 1/2/3 to 72nd St. | 212-579-9463 | www.wrbar.com

"Much needed" in the "lacking" Upper West Side scene, this "easy-going" wine bar is "one of the few adult places to have a drink" in a neighborhood "best known for college bars"; slightly "more spacious" than its archrival, Bin 71, it's already "packed most nights" despite being somewhat "overpriced."

Winebar

E Village | 65 Second Ave. (bet. 3rd & 4th Sts.) | F/V to Lower East Side/2nd Ave. | 212-777-1608 | www.winebarnyc.com

22 | 21 | 20 | $12

"Good taste" comes to the "bohemian East Village" via this "lovely" wine bar, a "warm" albeit "narrow" space where "conversations can actually be heard" and the "staff knows its stuff"; granted, the pours are on the "pricey" side, but the "bottle selection is impressive" and the "communal tables make it easy to meet new friends."

Wined Up

Flatiron | 913 Broadway, 2nd fl. (bet. 20th & 21st Sts.) | N/R/W to 23rd St. | 212-673-6333 | www.punchrestaurant.com

22 | 21 | 21 | $13

Oenophiles who "climb upstairs" from the Flatiron restaurant Punch wind up in this "sleek" wine bar, a "mellow place" to sample an "eclectic" selection; the "high-ceilinged" setting takes you "away from the bustle", and the "nonpretentious" mood makes for a "good date spot."

Winnie's ⇗

Chinatown | 104 Bayard St. (bet. Baxter & Mulberry Sts.) | A/C/E to Canal St. | 212-732-2384

18 | 14 | 16 | $10

"Let yourself go" with some "crazy karaoke" at this "rockin'" Chinatown dive, a "local fave" where a "hilarious mix" of patrons ranging from "bachelorettes" to "boys from the 'hood" carries on like "*American Idol* rejects" for a dollar a tune; ok, there's "zero ambiance", but it's "surprisingly fun" so long as you "make sure to get drunk."

Wogies

G Village | 39 Greenwich Ave. (Charles St.) | F/L/V to 14th St./6th Ave. | 212-229-2171 | www.wogies.com

21 | 14 | 25 | $7

"You couldn't ask for a friendlier staff" at this Village watering hole that caters to "Philadelphia expats", particularly adherents of "cheese steaks" and the Eagles; though it can be "too crowded" and "there's no decor" to speak of, the draft selection and "authentic" snacks rock.

Woody McHale's

W Village | 234 W. 14th St. (bet. 7th & 8th Aves.) | 1/2/3/L to 14th St./7th Ave. | 212-206-0430 | www.woodymchales.com

16 | 11 | 21 | $9

"Irish in name, country in music and American in fare", this subterranean West Village tavern is a good place for a beer and a burger; sure, the "log-cabin" decor may make it a better fit for "Brooklyn or Newark", but locals agree it has "plenty of potential."

World Bar

E 40s | Trump World Tower | 845 UN Plaza (1st Ave. & 47th St.) | 6 to 51st St./Lexington Ave. | 212-935-9361 | www.hospitalityholdings.com

23 | 25 | 20 | $14

"Drink with a diplomat" at this "fancy" lounge opposite the U.N., where an "older crowd" savors "superb", "pricey" potables; big spenders spring for its "signature" $50 'World Cocktail' – "topped with liquefied gold" – while gawkers are content to soak in the "quiet", "elegant" atmosphere.

World Yacht

W 40s | Pier 81 (Hudson River & W. 41st St.) | A/C/E to 42nd St./Port Authority | 212-630-8100 | www.worldyacht.com

▽ 23 | 18 | 21 | $16

The "best way to see the city" may be from the deck of this harbor cruise ship offering dinner, dancing and "breathtaking" views of

Gotham; the food's "not bad" and the dance band just "ok", but none-theless it's a "great treat" for out-of-towners – and even better if you "get aboard early to get a window seat."

W Times Square Living Room | 23 | 23 | 20 | $14 |

W 40s | W Times Square Hotel | 1567 Broadway, 7th fl. (47th St.) | N/R/W to 49th St. | 212-930-7447 | www.gerberbars.com

"Undeniably hip" and "oh-so-chic", this "sexy" Times Square lounge hid-den on the seventh floor of the W Hotel is an all-white, "minimalist" af-fair, tended to by a staff of "sirens" in little black dresses; the crowd's a blend of pre-theater types, "interesting out-of-towners" and "Botox" ad-dicts, but whether it's "expensive" or not "depends on who's paying."

☒ W Union Square Living Room | 22 | 22 | 18 | $14 |

Union Sq | W Union Square Hotel | 201 Park Ave. S. (17th St.) | 4/5/6/L/N/Q/R/W to 14th St./Union Sq. | 212-253-9119 | www.starwood.com

For a "bit of style in Union Square", glide by this "swank" hotel lounge where the crowd's "sophisticated, like the room" and the dress code "varies from smart casual to dressed up"; spoilers say this "triumph of marketing" "should be more impressive since they're charging $14 per drink", but fans counter it offers "people-watching galore" through those "huge picture windows."

WXOU Radio ⌐ | 21 | 11 | 18 | $8 |

W Village | 558 Hudson St. (bet. Perry & W. 11th Sts.) | A/C/E/L to 14th St./8th Ave. | 212-206-0381

A "locals-only hangout", this "unpretentious" West Villager is a "low-key", "conversation-friendly" joint with "no-nonsense appeal" and bo-nus "real-man eye candy"; too bad about the "cash-only" policy, but "good prices" and a "great jukebox" compensate.

Xai Xai Wine Bar | 23 | 22 | 20 | $14 |

W 50s | 369 W. 51st St. (bet. 8th & 9th Aves.) | C/E to 50th St. | 212-541-9241 | www.xaixaiwinebar.com

An "overdue" addition to Hell's Kitchen, this "fantastic" wine bar show-cases the "full span of South African" vintages in a woody, candlelit space recalling a chichi patch of the veldt; with its "large pours", "exotic lite menu" and "genuine hospitality", it's becoming "increasingly popu-lar" with "sophisticated" palates and accordingly "crowded."

xes lounge | 22 | 19 | 21 | $9 |

Chelsea | 157 W. 24th St. (bet. 6th & 7th Aves.) | 1 to 23rd St. | 212-604-0212 | www.xesnyc.com

Yes, the "name is 'sex' spelled backward" and fans say this "sassy" bar/lounge is a "hot" addition to the "gay-borhood", drawing an "approach-able" crowd sans the "typical Chelsea attitude"; emitting a slick vibe with "low-set" banquettes and buff "shirtless" bartenders, it's best known for its "cute" smoking patio, a "major plus in the right weather."

Xicala | 23 | 21 | 21 | $12 |

Little Italy | 151 Elizabeth St. (bet. Broome & Kenmare Sts.) | 6 to Spring St. | 212-219-0599 | www.xicala.net

"Thank goodness" they've expanded this wine bar "gem" hidden in Little Italy and offering a "great" list of mostly Spanish vinos along with "killer sangria" and "tasty tapas"; its "really hip" following digs the "warm service" and abides the "expensive-for-what-it-is" pricing.

	APPEAL	DECOR	SERVICE	COST

Xunta
19 | 13 | 16 | $8

E Village | 174 First Ave. (bet. 10th & 11th Sts.) | L to 1st Ave. | 212-614-0620 |
www.xuntatapasbar.com

"If you don't mind the sardine effect", this perpetually "crowded"
East Village tapas bar vends "knock-you-out" sangria and "tasty"
small plates at more than "affordable" tabs; "buzzkills" include
a "rude staff", "chintzy decor" and "uncomfortable seating"
on "back-breaking barrels", but the overall "fun vibe" keeps
the trade brisk.

Yankee Tavern
17 | 13 | 16 | $10

Bronx | 72 E. 161st St. (Gerard Ave.) | 4/B/D to Yankee Stadium |
718-292-6130 | www.yankeetavern.com

"Crowded all year round" with either "die-hard pinstripe fans" or
"court officers" (it's near both the stadium and the Bronx Supreme
Court building), this "old-time" tavern is festooned with plenty of
"Yankee memorabilia"; maybe there are "no surprises" in store, but at
least the staff's "friendly" and the beer's "cheap."

Zablozki's ⊘
22 | 20 | 22 | $6

Williamsburg | 107 N. Sixth St. (bet. Berry St. & Wythe Ave.) | Brooklyn |
L to Bedford Ave. | 718-384-1903

A "friendly place in hipsterville", this Williamsburg bar "bedecked
in dark wood and leather" is a "reliable mainstay" for "whiling
the night away" or while "waiting for your table at Sea" to open
up; "cheap" brew and a "classic rock" soundtrack add to the
"lovingly familiar" vibe.

Zampa
- | - | - | M

W Village | 306 W. 13th St. (bet. 8th Ave. & W. 4th St.) | A/C/E/L to
14th St./8th Ave. | 212-206-0601 | www.zampanyc.com

Nestled on a quiet West Village side street, this homey Italian wine
bar vends a well-parsed list of reds and whites accompanied by sand-
wiches and salads in cozy, no-frills digs; the rather obscure address
has made it a locals' haunt, and despite close proximity to the
Meatpacking District madness, it's refreshingly non-sceney.

Zanzibar
20 | 20 | 17 | $12

W 40s | 645 Ninth Ave. (45th St.) | A/C/E to 42nd St./Port Authority |
212-957-9197 | www.zanzibarnyc.com

"Spacious" and "stylish", this "surprisingly classy" Hell's Kitchen bar/
restaurant emits a "nice loungey vibe" with a "maze"-like setup ar-
ranged around a circular open-pit fireplace; it's usually "bustling" with
"Midtown after-work" types, even if a few snipe it "tries too hard" and
"thinks it's hipper than it really is."

Zarela
22 | 17 | 20 | $12

E 50s | 953 Second Ave. (bet. 50th & 51st Sts.) | 6 to 51st St./Lexington Ave. |
212-644-6740 | www.zarela.com

"Meaningful conversation" is futile after one of the "knock-
you-for-a-loop" margaritas at this Midtown cantina presided
over by super-chef "Zarela herself"; expect a "noisy" crowd "blowing off some steam after work", bring a "guide dog to get you
home" and if you "don't mind the loss of your hearing", you'll have
a "fun time."

	APPEAL	DECOR	SERVICE	COST

Zebulon

▽ 24 | 22 | 18 | $7

Williamsburg | 258 Wythe Ave. (bet. Metropolitan Ave. & N. 3rd St.) | Brooklyn | L to Bedford Ave. | 718-218-6934 | www.zebuloncafeconcert.com

One of Williamsburg's "best-kept secrets", this "unique" world music venue boasts an "incredibly cool" "1920s French cabaret vibe" for those seeking "a little *français* in Brooklyn"; while the musicians run the gamut from the "offbeat to the beat-less", you've got nothing to lose – there's "no cover."

Zinc Bar

22 | 20 | 19 | $13

G Village | 82 W. Third St., downstairs (bet. Sullivan & Thompson Sts.) | A/B/C/D/E/F/V to W. 4th St. | 212-477-9462 | www.zincbar.com

"Below ground" but "above average", this "intimate" Village jazz club has moved a few blocks away from its original Houston Street site and is "not as much of a dive" now (though "not a palace either"); still, its "diverse" crowd turns up to "hear the latest jazz currents" – as well as African, Latin and Brazilian music – and to enjoy a little "PDA" in the wee hours.

Zoë

20 | 19 | 21 | $13

SoHo | 90 Prince St. (bet. B'way & Mercer St.) | N/R/W to Prince St. | 212-966-6722 | www.zoerestaurant.com

This longtime SoHo "haunt" may have been "passed over for hipper spots" in recent years, but it's still a "relaxing respite" with an "open" feel, "tremendous" American wine list and "delicious" cocktails (mixology whiz "Dale DeGroff created them"); fans say it's a "fun" starting-off point, or at the very least, a "good place to take your mom."

Zombie Hut ⊅

21 | 21 | 19 | $7

Carroll Gardens | 273 Smith St. (Degraw St.) | Brooklyn | F/G to Carroll St. | 718-875-3433

"Tiki-a-go-go" comes to Smith Street via this "island oasis" located in a "cozy" lounge space done up in high "*Gilligan's Island*" style; though the "drop-dead beautiful" bartenders are appropriately "zombie"-like, they're forgotten in a haze of "potent" "umbrella drinks"; P.S. there's an "expansive" patio to boot.

Zum Schneider ⊅

23 | 17 | 20 | $8

E Village | 107 Ave. C (7th St.) | L to 1st Ave. | 212-598-1098 | www.zumschneider.com

Experience "Oktoberfest without a passport" at this "authentic" taste of "Bavaria on Avenue C" that's "low-key" in the afternoon and "crazy crowded" after dark; the "unparalleled" suds selection and "stomach-coating" grub are "*sehr gut*", even if the "beer-guzzling", "soccer"-watching scene becomes too "frat party"-ish for some.

INDEXES

LOCATION MAPS

Locations

Includes venue names and Appeal ratings.

Manhattan

CHELSEA

(26th to 30th Sts., west of 5th; 14th to 26th Sts., west of 6th)

Barracuda	19
Z Bar Veloce/Club	24
Bateaux NY	22
Billymark's West	15
Black Door	20
Blarney Stone	14
Bongo	18
Z Buddakan	24
Bungalow 8	25
Cabanas	22
Cafeteria	19
Z Cain Luxe	24
Chelsea Brewing	18
Comix	23
Del Posto	23
Dusk	21
Eagle	22
East of Eighth	19
El Quinto Pino	20
Flannery's	18
Flight 151	15
Z Frying Pan	-
g	20
NEW Gates	-
Glass	20
Gotham Comedy	19
Gstaad	17
Guest House	19
GYM Sportsbar	19
Half King	19
Highline Ballrm.	21
Hiro	22
Hog Pit	17
Home	21
Honey	19
Jake's Saloon	18
La Bottega	21
Le Zie 2000	22
Z Marquee	23
Merchants, NY	18
Moran's Chelsea	19
Morimoto	25
NEW Mr. West	20
Z NEW M2	20
Mustang Harry's	17

Mustang Sally's	17
Z 1 Oak	22
Park	21
Peter McManus	19
Pink Elephant	24
Prime	22
Rawhide	12
Rogue	15
Rush	20
Secret	20
Sol	18
Spirit Cruises	20
Star Lounge	19
Suzie Wong	20
300 New York	19
Tillman's	22
Trailer Park	19
Triple Crown	18
Z 230 Fifth	25
Ultra	18
NEW Velour	20
View Bar	16
xes lounge	22

CHINATOWN

(Canal to Pearl Sts., east of B'way)

Z NEW Apothéke	23
Z Bacaro	21
Z NEW Santos Party Hse.	21
NEW Whiskey Tavern	19
Winnie's	18

EAST 40s

Annie Moore's	16
NEW At Vermilion	-
Beer Bar/Centro	17
Blarney Stone	14
Bookmarks	24
Bull and Bear	21
Calico Jack's	15
Z Campbell Apt.	25
Connolly's	18
NEW La Fonda del Sol	-
Lea	19
LQ	21
NEW mad46	21
Maggie's	20
McFadden's	15
Michael Jordan's	20
925 Café & Cocktails	19

Overlook Lounge	17
Patrick Conway's	18
Patroon	22
Perfect Pint	21
Pershing Sq.	16
Peter Dillon's	16
Public House	18
☑ Sakagura	27
Top of the Tower	24
Uncle Charlie's	21
Whiskey Blue	23
World Bar	23

EAST 50s

NEW Beekman	23
Bill's Gay 90s	20
BlackFinn	17
Blackstone's	17
Bottega del Vino	22
Branch	17
Dos Caminos	22
NEW Evolve	22
☑ Four Seasons Bar	26
☑ Four Seasons Hotel Bar	25
Gilt	21
NEW Haven	18
Houston's	20
Jameson's	16
☑ King Cole Bar	28
Le Bateau Ivre	24
Le Cirque Wine	24
Le Colonial	21
Mantra	17
Metro 53	16
☑ Monkey Bar	-
Nikki Midtown	21
Opal	17
Opia	22
P.J. Clarke's	20
Pop Burger	20
Redemption	14
Rosa Mexicano	22
Serafina	20
NEW Stag's Head	-
Sutton Place	18
☑ Tao	24
T.G. Whitney's	16
Townhouse	22
Turtle Bay	15
Vero	24
Volstead	21
Zarela	22

EAST 60s

☑ Accademia di Vino	22
Baker Street	18

Becky's	18
Club Macanudo	24
Dangerfield's	16
☑ Daniel	27
Feinstein's at Loews	23
Felice	22
Geisha	22
Merchants, NY	18
O'Flanagan's	15
Plaza Athénée	24
Regency Library Bar	25
NEW Sapphire NY	21
Serafina	20
Subway Inn	17
212	18
NEW Vino	22

EAST 70s

American Trash	13
Baraonda	21
Bar Coastal	14
Bar Italia	20
☑ Bemelmans	27
☑ Boathouse	26
Bounce	19
☑ Brother Jimmy's	17
☑ Cafe Carlyle	26
Canyon Road	19
Citibar	18
David Copperfield	17
Doc Watson's	17
Finnegans Wake	15
Hi-Life	17
Iggy's	17
Lexington Bar & Books	21
Luke's B&G	19
Sake Hana	24
Serafina	20
Session 73	19
Stir	19
NEW Stumble Inn	15
Vero	24
Vudu Lounge	18

EAST 80s

Aces & Eights	15
Auction House	22
Back Page	18
NEW Balon	-
Bar @ Etats-Unis	23
BB&R	18
Brandy's	23
Cafe Notte	21
Cavatappo Grill/Wine	22
Comic Strip	17

Danny & Eddie's	14	Blue & Gold	18
Dorrian's	16	Blue Owl	23
East End Tav.	16	Boiler Room	17
Gaf Bar	22	Boucarou	20
Genesis	20	Bounce	19
Jack Russell's	19	Bourgeois Pig	24
Johnny Foxes	16	Bowery Electric	21
Mad River	14	☑ Bowery Hotel Bar	23
Metropolitan Mus. Roof	26	Bowery Wine Company	20
Molly Pitcher's	21	Boxcar Lounge	18
Mustang Grill	16	B-Side	17
Pudding Stones	21	Bua	21
Rathbones	18	Bull McCabe's	17
Ryan's Daughter	19	Burp Castle	18
Saloon	17	Butter	22
Ship of Fools	16	NEW Cabin Down Below	-
Swig	16	Cafe Deville	21
Tin Lizzie	13	Casimir	21
Trinity Pub	20	Central Bar	19
Uptown Lounge	23	Cheap Shots	19
Wicker Park	18	Cherry Tavern	14
		China 1	19

EAST 90s & 100s

(90th to 110th Sts.)

		Cloister Cafe	23
Bar East	13	Cock	18
Biddy's	22	Common Ground	19
Big Easy	13	Company	20
Blondies	19	Continental	16
☑ Brother Jimmy's	17	Coyote Ugly	13
Kinsale	20	Crocodile Lounge	19
		Croxley Ales	20

EAST VILLAGE

(14th to Houston Sts., east of B'way, excluding NoHo)

		☑ d.b.a.	22
		☑ Death & Co	25
		Decibel	24
Ace Bar	21	NEW Desnuda	23
Aces & Eights	15	Doc Holliday's	15
Against the Grain	22	Double Down	17
Alphabet Lounge	18	Drom	21
Amsterdam Billiards	17	Drop Off Service	20
Angels & Kings	19	NEW DTOX	18
☑ Angel's Share	26	Duke's	18
Anyway Cafe	20	Easternbloc	22
Arlo & Esme	21	NEW East Village Tavern	19
Babel Lounge	21	NEW EastVille Comedy	18
Back Forty	22	Edge	19
Banjo Jim's	21	11th St. Bar	21
Baraza	22	NEW Ella	21
Bar Carrera	23	NEW Elsa	21
Bar None	11	Finnerty's	10
Bar on A	17	Forbidden City	19
☑ Bar Veloce/Club	24	40c	18
Beauty Bar	19	Forum	18
Big Bar	19	Grape & Grain	26
Black & White	19	Grassroots	19
Blind Pig	19	Heathers	19

Hi-Fi	21
Holiday Cocktail	18
Hop Devil Grill	18
NEW Hose	-
Il Posto Accanto	24
Indochine	20
International Bar	-
In Vino	25
Jimmy's No. 43	22
Joe's Bar	20
Joe's Pub	25
Jules	23
Kabin	16
Karma	21
Keybar	23
KGB	21
King's Head	14
Klimat	18
Lakeside Lounge	19
La Linea	18
Lava Gina	23
Library	20
Lit	19
Louis 649	26
Luca Bar/Lounge	21
Lucy's	19
Lunasa	22
Mama's Bar	22
Manitoba's	21
Mars Bar	19
NEW Mayahuel	-
McSorley's	23
Nevada Smith's	16
Niagara/Lei Bar	19
No Malice Palace	19
Nowhere	18
Nublu	26
Nuyorican Poets	21
One & One	18
Otto's Shrunken	21
Z PDT	27
Phebe's	16
Phoenix	20
Plan B	16
Professor Thom's	19
Pyramid	18
Rehab	17
Royale	20
Rue B	22
Ryan's Irish Pub	17
Scratcher	20
7B	19
Shoolbred's	20
Sidewalk	19

Simone	19
Sing Sing	21
Sin Sin/Leopard	18
Solas	19
Solex	22
Sophie's	22
Standings	25
Stay	19
St. Dymphna's	20
Stillwater	20
St. Marks Ale	17
Sutra	18
Telephone	18
Terroir	22
Thirsty Scholar	17
Three of Cups	19
12th St. Ale	18
2A	18
Urge	19
Velvet	17
Village Pourhouse	18
WCOU	19
Webster Hall	19
Whiskey Town	20
Winebar	22
Xunta	19
Zum Schneider	23

FINANCIAL DISTRICT
(South of Murray St.)

Bayard's	19
Blarney Stone	14
Bridge Cafe	24
Dakota Roadhse.	15
Full Shilling	18
Jeremy's Ale	16
John Street B&G	16
Merchants, NY	18
NEW Perle	22
P.J. Clarke's	20
Pussycat Lounge	18
Raccoon Lodge	15
17 Murray	14
SouthWest NY	19
Trinity Place	21
Z Ulysses	22

FLATIRON DISTRICT
(14th to 26th Sts., 6th Ave. to Park Ave. S., excluding Union Sq.)

Aspen	21
Aura	20
NEW Catch-22	20
NEW Citrine	21
Dewey's Flatiron	14

Duvet	20
Eleven Madison Pk.	25
Z Flatiron Lounge	25
Flûte	22
40/40	21
Z Gramercy Tavern	26
NEW Imperial	18
Karaoke One 7	21
NEW Lillie's	-
Live Bait	15
Metropolitan Rm.	20
No Idea	17
Z Old Town Bar	21
Park Bar	21
Pipa	21
Porky's	15
ZNEW Raines Law Rm.	-
Rctreat	17
Room Service	18
Rosa Mexicano	22
Sala	23
Slate	21
Splash	20
Strata	19
Sugarcane	21
SushiSamba	22
Z Tabla	24
Taj II	20
Ten's	21
VIP Club	27
Wined Up	22

GARMENT DISTRICT

(30th to 40th Sts., west of 5th)

Australian	20
Blarney Stone	14
NEW Blue Ruin	-
Z Brother Jimmy's	17
Escuelita	17
NEW 508 Sports	-
Hammerstein	20
HeadQuarters	-
Heartland Brew.	16
HK Lounge	20
NEW Houndstooth	19
Katwalk	16
Keens Steak	21
Local	16
Metro Grill Roof	20
Mr. Black	20
Playwright	18
Rebel	18
Rick's Cabaret	20
Stitch	17
Stout	21

Tír na Nóg	20
Walter's Bar	17

GRAMERCY PARK

(14th to 23rd Sts., east of Park Ave. S.)

Barfly	16
Bar Jamón	24
Belmont	16
Black Bear	17
Bull's Head	18
Cibar	22
Duke's	18
Fillmore	22
NEW Globe	19
Jade Bar	25
Japonais	22
McSwiggan's	12
Molly's	22
119 Bar	16
Pete's Tavern	21
NEW Pierre Loti	23
Plug Uglies	17
Revival	19
Z Rose Bar	23
NEW SideBar	21
Still	15
3Steps	22
NEW Vintage Irving	21
Watering Hole	18

GREENWICH VILLAGE

(Houston to 14th Sts., west of B'way, east of 7th Ave. S.)

Alibi	17
Back Fence	17
Bar Carrera	23
NEW Bar 108	20
Barrow St. Ale	18
Bar 6	23
Bitter End	19
Z Blind Tiger	20
Z Blue Note	23
Blue Ribbon Bar	23
Bowlmor Lanes	22
Cafe Wha?	21
Caffe Dante	21
Caffe Reggio	20
Comedy Cellar	23
Cornelia St. Cafe	23
Daddy-O	21
Z Dove	24
Down the Hatch	16
Duplex	19
1849	17

8th St. Winecellar	23
Elettaria	24
Fat Black Pussycat	17
Fiddlesticks	18
55 Bar	22
Four-Faced Liar	18
Garage	21
🏆 Gotham B&G	25
Gottino	22
Grey Dog's	22
Half Pint	22
Jekyll & Hyde	17
Josie Wood's	14
Julius	12
Kenny's Castaways	14
Kettle of Fish	21
Kingswood	23
La Lanterna	25
NEW Le Poisson Rouge	22
Love	20
MacDougal St. Ale	18
Madame X	20
Monster	16
Mr. Dennehy's	20
Murphy & Gonzalez	17
99 Below	19
Off the Wagon	17
Oliver's B&G	17
One if by Land	26
124 Rabbit	24
Otto	25
Peculier Pub	20
Pieces	14
Pinch B&G	19
Pressure	18
Red Lion	19
Reservoir Bar	17
Shade	26
Slane	17
Slaughtered Lamb	17
Smith's	22
Stoned Crow	19
Stonewall Inn	20
Sullivan Hall	18
Sullivan Room	18
SushiSamba	22
Terra Blues	22
13	15
Town Tavern	15
V Bar	26
Village Lantern	19
Village Underground	18
Vol de Nuit	25
Wicked Willy's	18

Wogies	21
Zinc Bar	22

HARLEM/ EAST HARLEM

(110th to 157th Sts., excluding Columbia U. area)

NEW Body	22
NEW Covo	25
Den	21
NEW El Morocco	20
Harlem Lanes	20
🏆 Lenox Lounge	21
Minton's	23
NEW Nectar	23
River Room	21
NEW 67 Orange St.	22
St. Nick's Jazz Pub	20
NEW Talay	19

LITTLE ITALY

(Canal to Kenmare Sts., Bowery to Lafayette St.)

🏆 GoldBar	23
🏆 La Esquina	24
Lucky's Eleven	-
Moomia Lounge	18
Obivia	24
Onieal's Grand St.	20
Randolph	19
NEW Southside	18
Tropical 128	19
Xicala	23

LOWER EAST SIDE

(Houston to Canal Sts., east of Bowery)

NEW Above Allen	22
Allen & Delancey	25
Annex	22
Arlene's Grocery	20
Back Room	23
Barramundi	19
Barrio Chino	22
NEW BEast	21
Blue Seats	16
Bob	19
Boss Tweed's	17
Bowery Ballroom	24
🏆 Box	25
Café Charbon	23
Cake Shop	20
NEW Chloe	22
Clandestino	19
Crash Mansion	15
Dark Room	18

Delancey	20	
NEW Diamond's Wine	22	
NEW Donnybrook	19	
East Side Co.	24	
NEW Eldridge	22	
Element	22	
Epstein's Bar	14	
Essex	20	
Essex Ale House	20	
Fat Baby	19	
Fontana's	19	
Z Freemans	26	
GalleryBar	19	
Happy Ending	19	
Home Sweet Home	19	
Iggy's	17	
Z inoteca	24	
Jadis	22	
Katra	18	
Kush	22	
Label	17	
La Caverna	18	
Laugh Lounge	16	
Libation	18	
Living Room	22	
Local 138	19	
NEW Local 269	-	
Lolita	19	
Loreley	21	
Lucky Jack's	20	
Magician	16	
Marshall Stack	22	
Mason Dixon	17	
Max Fish	17	
Mehanata	19	
Mercury Lounge	20	
Z Milk & Honey	27	
Motor City	18	
National Underground	23	
Nurse Bettie	19	
151	21	
105 Riv	22	
169 Bar	22	
Parkside	18	
Pianos	19	
Pink Pony	19	
Rayuela	26	
Rockwood Music	23	
Salt Bar	24	
Sapphire	18	
Schiller's	22	
NEW Shang Bar	-	
Sixth Ward	22	
Skinny	16	

Slipper Room	20	
NEW Sorella	-	
Z Spitzer's Corner	22	
Stanton Public	21	
Z Stanton Social	25	
NEW Sweet & Lowdown	18	
Sweet Paradise	22	
Tapeo 29	24	
Ten Bells	23	
THOR Lobby Bar	20	
205 Club	20	
Verlaine	23	
Welcome/Johnsons	18	
Whiskey Ward	19	
White Rabbit	18	
Z NEW White Slab Palace	-	
NEW White Star	20	

MEATPACKING DISTRICT

(Gansevoort to 15th Sts., west of 9th Ave.)

APT	21	
Ara Wine Bar	22	
NEW Bijoux	23	
Brass Monkey	19	
Buddha Bar	24	
Cielo	23	
Diner	19	
5 Ninth	23	
Gaslight/G2	17	
NEW Griffin	-	
Hogs & Heifers	16	
Kiss & Fly	20	
Merkato 55	22	
One	22	
Ono	24	
Z Pastis	24	
Z Plunge	25	
Pop Burger	20	
NEW RDV	22	
Revel	22	
Z SEA	25	
NEW 675 Bar	-	
Soho House	24	
Son Cubano	23	
Z Spice Market	24	
NEW Standard Hotel	-	
STK	23	
Z Tenjune	25	

MURRAY HILL

(26th to 40th Sts., east of 5th; 23rd to 26th Sts., east of Park Ave. S.)

Arctica	18	
Z Asia de Cuba	24	
Bar 515	15	

Black Sheep	15
Blender Theater	19
Blue Smoke	21
Bogart's	14
☑ Brother Jimmy's	17
Cavatappo Grill/Wine	22
Chill Lounge	17
Choice	21
Country Champ. Lounge	25
Desmond's Tavern	11
Dos Caminos	22
Duke's	18
El Rio Grande	19
Failte	17
Fitzgerald's	16
Galway Hooker	18
☑ Ginger Man	22
Hairy Monk	17
NEW Hill	17
Hook & Ladder	13
Houston's	20
☑ 'inoteca	24
I Trulli Enoteca	24
☑ Jazz Standard	26
Joshua Tree	15
Maker's	13
Margarita Murphy's	17
McCormack's	19
Mercury Bar	16
Morgans Bar	22
New York Comedy	18
Paddy Reilly's	20
Patrick Kavanagh's	17
Pine Tree Lodge	24
NEW Pranna	-
PS 450	20
Rare View	22
Red Sky	17
Rodeo Bar	20
Runway	16
Stone Creek	19
Third & Long	14
Tonic East	20
Twelve	16
Underground	18
Under the Volcano	18
NEW Van Diemens	18
Vertigo	19
Vig 27	19
NEW Vino 313	22
Waterfront Ale Hse.	20
Wet Bar	21
Wharf Bar & Grill	18
Whiskey River	18

NOHO

(Houston to 4th Sts., Bowery to B'way)

Ace of Clubs	19
Agozar!	18
Antik	18
Aroma	25
B Bar	18
Bleecker St. Bar	18
Bond Street	24
Bowery Poetry Club	23
Chinatown Brasserie	23
Gonzalez y Gonzalez	18
Kings Cross	22
☑ NEW Madam Geneva	25
Mannahatta	18
Sala	23
Sláinte	18
Soho Billiards	15
Swift	22
Temple Bar	24
Tom & Jerry's	21
Von	26

NOLITA

(Houston to Kenmare Sts., Bowery to Lafayette St.)

Botanica	15
Cafe Gitane	22
Chibi's Sake Bar	23
Eight Mile Creek	23
Epistrophy	21
Firefly	19
Gatsby's	13
Monday Room	24
Peasant	23
☑ Pravda	24
Public	24
R Bar	21
Shebeen	22
Spring Lounge	19
Sweet & Vicious	17
☑ Bar Veloce/Club	24
Vig Bar	22

SOHO

(Canal to Houston Sts., west of Lafayette St.)

Anchor	18
Antarctica	17
☑ Balthazar	25
Bar 89	22
Blue Ribbon	25
Broome St. Bar	16
Cafe Noir	22
Cipriani Downtown	24
Circa Tabac	21

🆉NEW City Winery	23
Corio	18
Cub Room	19
Cupping Room	18
NEW Delicatessen	19
Don Hill's	20
Dos Caminos	22
Ear Inn	21
Fanelli's	18
Grand Bar	25
NEW Greenhouse	21
Ideya	23
I Tre Merli	20
L'Orange Bleue	21
Merc Bar	23
Mercer Bar	23
Milady's	13
Ñ	24
Naked Lunch	19
Novecento	21
🆉 Pegu Club	25
Puck Fair	18
Red Bench	21
🆉 Room	26
S.O.B.'s	22
SoHo Park	18
SoHo Room	14
SubMercer	24
Sway	25
Tailor	23
Thom Bar	24
Zoë	20

SOUTH STREET SEAPORT

Bin No. 220	21
Harbour Lights	21
Heartland Brew.	16
Paris	19
Sequoia	22
🆉 Water Taxi Beach	22

TRIBECA

(Canal to Murray Sts., west of B'way)

anotheroom	24
B Flat	22
🆉 Brandy Library	25
Bubble Lounge	22
Canal Room	20
Church Lounge	24
City Hall	23
Dylan Prime	23
Flor de Sol	23
Hideaway	22
🆉NEW Macao Trading	25
Megu	24

Mocca	21
M1-5 Bar	17
Nancy Whiskey	17
Odeon	20
Patriot Saloon	14
Petrarca Vino	24
Puffy's	19
🆉 Smith & Mills	23
Tribeca Grill	23
Tribeca Tavern	18
Turks & Frogs	22
Vino Vino	23
Walker's	21

UNION SQUARE

(14th to 17th Sts., 5th Ave. to Union Sq. E.)

🆉 Blue Water Grill	23
Coffee Shop	18
Heartland Brew.	16
Underbar	21
Union Bar	18
🆉 Union Sq. Cafe	24
🆉 W Union Sq.	22

WASHINGTON HTS./ INWOOD

(North of W. 157th St.)

Bleu Evolution	19
United Palace	19

WEST 40s

Algonquin	23
🆉 Bar Centrale	29
Bar 44	21
Bar 41	19
Barrage	20
B. B. King Blues	21
Birdland	23
Blarney Stone	14
Blue Fin	23
NEW Bourbon St. B&G	20
Bryant Park Grill	22
Carolines	21
Cellar Bar	22
Channel 4	13
Chez Josephine	22
Connolly's	18
Croton Reservoir	17
Daltons	16
Dave & Buster's	21
Don't Tell Mama	24
NEW Eden	19
ESPN Zone	18
Fashion 40	18

LOCATIONS

Valhalla	18
Vintage	25
Vlada	23
Whiskey Park	20
Whistlin' Dixie's	16
Xai Xai	23

WEST 60s

Barcibo Enoteca	22
Bar Masa	23
Café des Artistes	24
NEW Clo	22
Z Dizzy's Club	25
Empire Hotel Bar	19
Z NEW Empire Hotel Roof	24
MO Bar	23
O'Neals'	20
Peter's	17
P.J. Clarke's	20
Rosa Mexicano	22
Stone Rose	23
Tavern on the Green	22

WEST 70s

Beacon Theatre	23
Bin 71	22
Blondies	19
Z Boat Basin	24
Bourbon St.	15
Citrus B&G	20
Columbus 72	15
Dive 75	21
Dublin House	16
Malachy's	14
Riposo	20
Shalel Lounge	24
Stand-Up NY	18
Westside Brewing	17
Wine & Roses	21

WEST 80s

Blue Donkey Bar	18
Z Brother Jimmy's	17
Cafe Lalo	22
Z Calle Ocho	23
Dead Poet	20
Edgar's Cafe	21
Firehouse	16
420	15
George Keeley's	23
Gin Mill	16
Hi-Life	17
Jake's Dilemma	16
McAleer's Pub	15
Parlour	17
Prohibition	21

WEST 90s

Buceo 95	21
Cleopatra's Needle	18
Dive Bar	18
Pudding Stones	21

WEST 100s

(See also Harlem/East Harlem)

Abbey Pub	19
NEW Amsterdam 106	19
Broadway Dive	15
Ding Dong Lounge	18
Heights B&G	18
Lion's Head Tavern	15
O'Connell's	16
Sip	18
Smoke	22
Suite	16
Tap a Keg	10
1020 Bar	16
Underground Lounge	18
Village Pourhouse	18

WEST VILLAGE

(Houston to 14th Sts.,
west of 7th Ave. S., excluding
Meatpacking District)

Art Bar	20
Arthur's Tavern	22
Automatic Slim's	17
B&S NY	14
Bayard's Ale	17
Z Beatrice Inn	21
NEW Bleecker Heights	-
Z Bobo	22
NEW Casa La Femme	-
Centro Vinoteca	21
Chow Bar	18
Z Commerce	22
Corner Bistro	22
NEW Country Club	19
Cowgirl	18
Cubby Hole	20
Dublin 6	22
Dugout	16
Z Employees Only	24
EN Shochu Bar	22
Fat Cat	19
49 Grove	18
Greenwich Treehouse	19
Hangar Bar	13
Henrietta Hudson	18
Hudson Bar & Books	21
I Tre Merli	20

Johnny's Bar	20
Lederhosen	21
LelaBar	25
Le Royale	16
Lips	20
☑ Little Branch	26
Marie's Crisis	22
☑ Otheroom	27
Riviera	14
Rouge Wine Bar	22
☑ Rusty Knot	21
Smalls	24
Spotted Pig	23
Sweet Rhythm	21
Tavern on Jane	21
Tortilla Flats	19
Turks & Frogs	22
Ty's	18
Village Vanguard	24
☑ White Horse	20
NEW Wilfie & Nell	24
Woody McHale's	16
WXOU	21
Zampa	-

Bronx

An Béal Bocht	21
Hard Rock Cafe	16
Stan's	12
Yankee Tavern	17

Brooklyn

BAY RIDGE

Delia's	22
Suite	18
Wicked Monk	18

BOERUM HILL

Boat	20
Brazen Head	20
☑ Brooklyn Inn	27
NEW Building on Bond	-
Camp	21
Hank's	20
Pacific Standard	21
Sherwood	23

BRIGHTON BEACH

Rasputin	21

BROOKLYN HEIGHTS

Eamonn's	14
Floyd, NY	22

Jack the Horse	22
Waterfront Ale Hse.	20

CARROLL GARDENS

Abilene	20
Bar Great Harry	20
☑ Black Mtn. Wine	28
☑ Brooklyn Social	25
B61	24
NEW Chestnut Bar	22
Gowanus Yacht	23
☑ JakeWalk	21
miniBar	20
P.J. Hanley's	18
NEW Prime Meats	-
Zombie Hut	21

CLINTON HILL

Sputnik	18

COBBLE HILL

Angry Wade's	14
Apt. 138	19
Bar Tabac	22
NEW Char No. 4	24
☑ NEW Clover Club	25
Downtown B&G	18
Joya	23
Last Exit	20
Sample	19
Tea Lounge	20

CONEY ISLAND

NEW Beer Island	23
Peggy O'Neill's	18

DOWNTOWN

BAMcafé	21

DUMBO

☑ Galapagos	-
Rebar	21
Superfine	24
Water St. Bar	20

FORT GREENE

Five Spot	17
Frank's	19
Hideout	19
Moe's	22
☑ Stonehome	27

GOWANUS

☑ NEW Bell House	22
Draft Barn	-

GRAVESEND

Draft Barn	-

GREENPOINT

Alligator	20
Black Rabbit	-
Enid's	19
Europa	17
Gutter	24
Matchless	21
Pencil Factory	20
Studio B	24
NEW t.b.d.	-
Warsaw	19

MANHATTAN BEACH

Anyway Cafe	20

PARK SLOPE

Barbès	25
Bar 4	20
Beer Table	24
NEW Belleville Lounge	-
Blue Ribbon Bklyn.	23
NEW Brookvin	22
Buttermilk	23
NEW Cabana Bar	22
Cherry Tree	16
Commonwealth	19
Dram Shop	-
Excelsior	19
Fourth Ave. Pub	18
Gate	22
Ginger's	16
Great Lakes	22
Loki	17
Lucky 13	17
O'Connor's	22
Park Slope Ale	18
Royale	21
Sidecar	20
Southpaw	22
Tea Lounge	20
Total Wine	25
NEW 249 Bar	-
200 Fifth	17
Z Union Hall	24

PROSPECT HEIGHTS

Freddy's	18
NEW Manhattans	-
Soda Bar	20
Z Weather Up	22

RED HOOK

Moonshine	19
Sunny's	26

SHEEPSHEAD BAY

Anyway Cafe	20

SUNSET PARK

Living Rm. Lounge	22

WILLIAMSBURG

Abbey	21
Alligator	20
Barcade	24
Bembe	23
Black Betty	19
Brooklyn Ale	18
NEW Brooklyn Bowl	-
Brooklyn Brew.	23
Bushwick Country	18
Cornichon	21
Daddy's	19
Z d.b.a.	22
D.O.C. Wine	25
Duff's	19
East River	20
NEW Gibson	-
Harefield Rd.	20
Z Hotel Delmano	24
Huckleberry	22
Hugs	17
Iona	21
K & M Bar	-
Larry Lawrence	28
Levee	19
Lodge	18
Metropolitan	19
Monkey Town	21
NEW Mother's	19
Moto	24
Mug's Ale	25
Music Hall	22
Pete's Candy	23
NEW Public Assembly	20
Radegast	26
Relish	18
NEW Richardson	-
Rose	21
Royal Oak	20
Savalas	16
Z SEA	25
Soft Spot	-
Spike Hill	22
Spuyten Duyvil	24
Supreme Trading	23

Teddy's	23
Trash	18
Trophy	19
Turkey's Nest	16
Union Pool	20
Velvet	17
Zablozki's	22
Zebulon	24

Governors Island

| **Z** Water Taxi Beach | 22 |

Queens

ASTORIA

Athens Café	17
Bohemian Hall	25
Cafe Bar	22
Z Cávo	26
Central	19
Grand Café	21
Hell Gate Social	22
NEW Lavish Lounge	-
Vino di Vino	22

BAYSIDE

| Donovan's | 20 |
| First Edition | 15 |

FOREST HILLS

| Bartini's | 17 |

LONG ISLAND CITY

Creek & the Cave	19
Domaine Bar a Vins	21
NEW Dutch Kills	-
L.I.C. Bar	25
Lounge 47	20
NEW Ravel Rooftop	-
Z Water Taxi Beach	22

SUNNYSIDE

| Sidetracks | 15 |

WOODSIDE

| Donovan's | 20 |

Staten Island

Beer Garden	17
Big Nose Kate's	14
Cargo Café	20
Killmeyer's	23
L'Amour	17
Martini Red	19
Muddy Cup	17

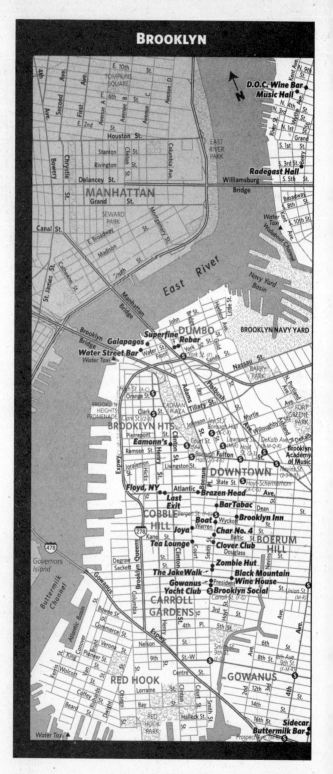

BROOKLYN

D.O.C. Wine Bar
Music Hall

Radegast Hall

EAST
RIVER
PARK

Williamsburg
Bridge

MANHATTAN

East River

Navy Yard
Basin

BROOKLYN NAVY YARD

DUMBO
Superfine
Rebar
Galapagos
Water Street Bar
Water Taxi

BARRY
PARK

BROOKLYN
HEIGHTS
PROMENADE

BROOKLYN HTS.
Eamonn's

FORT
GREENE
PARK

Brooklyn
Academy
of Music

DOWNTOWN

Floyd, NY
Brazen Head
Last
Exit
BarTabac
Brooklyn Inn
COBBLE
HILL
Boat
Char No. 4
Joya
Clover Club
Tea Lounge
Zombie Hut
The JakeWalk
Black Mountain
Gowanus
Wine House
Yacht Club
Brooklyn Social

BOERUM
HILL

Governors
Island

Buttermilk
Channel

CARROLL
GARDENS

RED HOOK

GOWANUS

Sidecar
Buttermilk Bar

Water Taxi

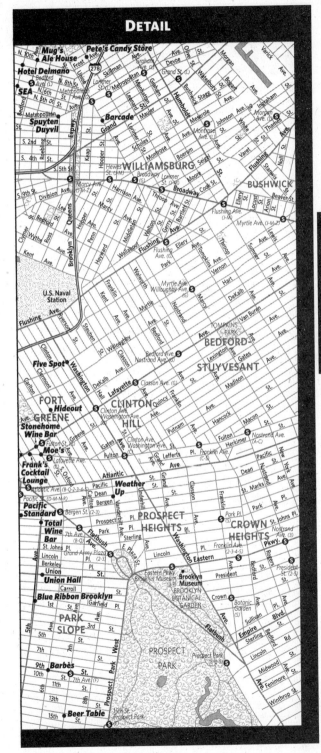

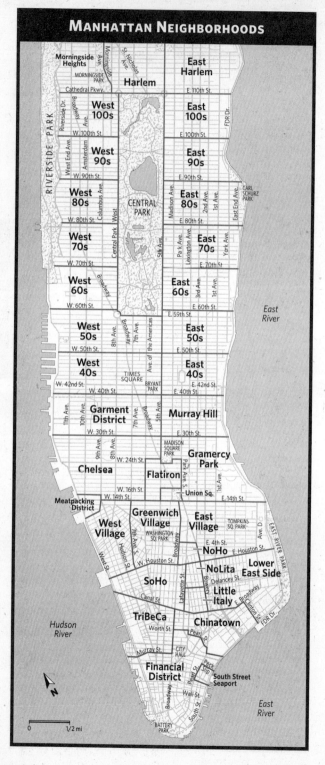

MANHATTAN NEIGHBORHOODS

Menus, photos, voting and more – free at ZAGAT.com

Special Appeals

Listings cover the best in each category and include venue names, locations and Appeal ratings. Multi-location nightspots' features may vary by branch.

AFTER WORK

Abilene	**Carroll Gdns**	20	Landmark Tav.	**W 40s**	21
Annie Moore's	**E 40s**	16	Le Colonial	**E 50s**	21
NEW At Vermilion	**E 40s**	-	Mad River	**E 80s**	14
Ava Lounge	**W 50s**	24	Maggie's	**E 40s**	20
Bar 515	**Murray Hill**	15	M Bar	**W 40s**	20
Bar Nine	**W 50s**	15	McFadden's	**E 40s**	15
Bayard's	**Financial**	19	McGee's	**W 50s**	15
Beer Bar/Centro	**E 40s**	17	Merchants, NY	**multi.**	18
Z Bemelmans	**E 70s**	27	Mercury Bar	**multi.**	16
Black Door	**Chelsea**	20	Metro 53	**E 50s**	16
Z Blue Water Grill	**Union Sq**	23	Moda Outdoors	**W 50s**	20
Z Boat Basin	**W 70s**	24	Mustang Harry's	**Chelsea**	17
Bogart's	**Murray Hill**	14	No Idea	**Flatiron**	17
Bookmarks	**E 40s**	24	**Z** Oak Bar	**W 50s**	24
Branch	**E 50s**	17	O'Flaherty's Ale	**W 40s**	18
Brasserie 8½	**W 50s**	21	**Z** Old Town Bar	**Flatiron**	21
Bryant Park Grill	**W 40s**	22	O'Lunney's	**W 40s**	21
Bull and Bear	**E 40s**	21	**NEW** 123 Burger	**W 50s**	20
Z Calle Ocho	**W 80s**	23	Opal	**E 50s**	17
Z Campbell Apt.	**E 40s**	25	Opia	**E 50s**	22
Church Lounge	**TriBeCa**	24	Palio Bar	**W 50s**	22
Cibar	**Gramercy**	22	Paramount	**W 40s**	23
Connolly's	**multi.**	18	Park Bar	**Flatiron**	21
Croton Reservoir	**W 40s**	17	Patrick Conway's	**E 40s**	18
Dewey's Flatiron	**Flatiron**	14	Pershing Sq.	**E 40s**	16
Divine Bar	**W 50s**	22	P.J. Carney's	**W 50s**	18
Eamonn's	**Bklyn Hts**	14	P.J. Clarke's	**E 50s**	20
El Rio Grande	**Murray Hill**	19	**NEW** Pony Bar	**W 40s**	-
Faces & Names	**W 50s**	18	PS 450	**Murray Hill**	20
Fashion 40	**W 40s**	18	Redemption	**E 50s**	14
Flûte	**W 50s**	22	Rink Bar	**W 50s**	24
Z Four Seasons Bar	**E 50s**	26	Rosa Mexicano	**multi.**	22
Full Shilling	**Financial**	18	Sequoia	**Seaport**	22
Gaf Bar	**W 40s**	22	Shalel Lounge	**W 70s**	24
NEW Gates	**Chelsea**	-	Social	**W 40s**	17
Z Ginger Man	**Murray Hill**	22	SouthWest NY	**Financial**	19
Heartland Brew.	**multi.**	16	Splash	**Flatiron**	20
Houston's	**E 50s**	20	St. Andrews	**W 40s**	20
Hudson Hotel	**W 50s**	24	Stitch	**Garment**	17
Iguana	**W 50s**	18	Sutton Place	**E 50s**	18
Jake's Saloon	**multi.**	18	**Z** Tao	**E 50s**	24
Jameson's	**E 50s**	16	Tír na Nóg	**Garment**	20
Jeremy's Ale	**Financial**	16	Turtle Bay	**E 50s**	15
John Street B&G	**Financial**	16	**Z** 21 Club	**W 50s**	26
Katwalk	**Garment**	16	**Z** 230 Fifth	**Chelsea**	25
Z King Cole Bar	**E 50s**	28	**Z** Ulysses	**Financial**	22
NEW La Fonda del Sol	**E 40s**	-	Under the Volcano	**Murray Hill**	18
La Linea	**E Vill**	18	Union Bar	**Union Sq**	18
			Walker's	**TriBeCa**	21

SPECIAL APPEALS

Wet Bar	Murray Hill	21
Whiskey	W 40s	20
Whiskey Blue	E 40s	23
Whiskey Park	W 50s	20
NEW Wilfie & Nell	W Vill	24

ART BARS

Bowery Poetry Club	NoHo	23
Z Box	LES	25
Creek & the Cave	LIC	19
Freddy's	Prospect Hts	18
Z Galapagos	Dumbo	-
GalleryBar	LES	19
Half King	Chelsea	19
KGB	E Vill	21
Monkey Town	W'burg	21
Nublu	E Vill	26
Nuyorican Poets	E Vill	21
NEW Public Assembly	W'burg	20
Sputnik	Clinton Hill	18
Supreme Trading	W'burg	23
NEW t.b.d.	Greenpt	-

BACHELOR PARTIES

Corio	SoHo	18
ESPN Zone	W 40s	18
Flashdancers	W 50s	18
40/40	Flatiron	21
HeadQuarters	Garment	-
Hogs & Heifers	Meatpacking	16
Hustler Club	W 50s	22
Johnny Utah's	W 50s	20
Penthse. Exec. Club	W 40s	24
Pussycat Lounge	Financial	18
Rick's Cabaret	Garment	20
NEW Sapphire NY	E 60s	21
Slipper Room	LES	20
Ten's	Flatiron	21
VIP Club	Flatiron	27

BACHELORETTE PARTIES

Automatic Slim's	W Vill	17
Cafe Wha?	G Vill	21
Hogs & Heifers	Meatpacking	16
Lips	W Vill	20
L'Orange Bleue	SoHo	21
Slipper Room	LES	20
Tortilla Flats	W Vill	19
Xunta	E Vill	19

BEAUTIFUL PEOPLE

NEW Above Allen	LES	22
Z Asia de Cuba	Murray Hill	24
Aspen	Flatiron	21
Ava Lounge	W 50s	24
Z Balthazar	SoHo	25
Z Beatrice Inn	W Vill	21
NEW Bijoux	Meatpacking	23
Blue Ribbon	SoHo	25
Bond Street	NoHo	24
Z Bowery Hotel Bar	E Vill	23
Z Box	LES	25
Brasserie 8½	W 50s	21
Z Buddakan	Chelsea	24
Bungalow 8	Chelsea	25
Cabanas	Chelsea	22
Cafeteria	Chelsea	19
Z Cain Luxe	Chelsea	24
Cellar Bar	W 40s	22
NEW Chloe	LES	22
Cielo	Meatpacking	23
Coffee Shop	Union Sq	18
NEW Delicatessen	SoHo	19
D'Or	W 50s	21
g	Chelsea	20
NEW Gates	Chelsea	-
Z GoldBar	L Italy	23
Grand Bar	SoHo	25
Hiro	Chelsea	22
Hudson Hotel	W 50s	24
Indochine	E Vill	20
La Bottega	Chelsea	21
Z La Esquina	L Italy	24
Z NEW Macao Trading	TriBeCa	25
Z NEW Madam Geneva	NoHo	25
Z Marquee	Chelsea	23
Mercer Bar	SoHo	23
Morgans Bar	Murray Hill	22
Morimoto	Chelsea	25
Nikki Midtown	E 50s	21
Odeon	TriBeCa	20
Z 1 Oak	Chelsea	22
Z Pastis	Meatpacking	24
Z Plunge	Meatpacking	25
NEW Pranna	Murray Hill	-
NEW RDV	Meatpacking	22
Room Service	Flatiron	18
Z Rose Bar	Gramercy	23
Z Rusty Knot	W Vill	21
Schiller's	LES	22
NEW Shang Bar	LES	-
Z Spice Market	Meatpacking	24
Spotted Pig	W Vill	23
Z Stanton Social	LES	25
Star Lounge	Chelsea	19
Stone Rose	W 60s	23
SubMercer	SoHo	24
SushiSamba	G Vill	22

Z Tao | **E 50s**	24
Z Tenjune | **Meatpacking**	25
Therapy | **W 50s**	24
Thom Bar | **SoHo**	24
THOR Lobby Bar | **LES**	20
Underbar | **Union Sq**	21
Wet Bar | **Murray Hill**	21
Whiskey | **W 40s**	20
Whiskey Blue | **E 40s**	23

BOTTLE SERVICE

(Bottle purchase sometimes required to secure a table)

Antik | **NoHo**	18
Z NEW Apothéke | **Chinatown**	23
Aspen | **Flatiron**	21
Aura | **Flatiron**	20
NEW Bijoux | **Meatpacking**	23
NEW Body | **Harlem**	22
Z Box | **LES**	25
Bungalow 8 | **Chelsea**	25
Butter | **E Vill**	22
Z Cain Luxe | **Chelsea**	24
Cielo | **Meatpacking**	23
NEW Citrine | **Flatiron**	21
NEW Country Club | **W Vill**	19
NEW Eldridge | **LES**	22
NEW El Morocco | **Harlem**	20
49 Grove | **W Vill**	18
NEW Gates | **Chelsea**	-
NEW Greenhouse | **SoHo**	21
NEW Griffin | **Meatpacking**	-
Guest House | **Chelsea**	19
Hiro | **Chelsea**	22
Home | **Chelsea**	21
Hustler Club | **W 50s**	22
Kiss & Fly | **Meatpacking**	20
LQ | **E 40s**	21
Z NEW Lucky Strike Lanes | **W 40s**	21
Z Marquee | **Chelsea**	23
NEW Mr. West | **Chelsea**	20
Z NEW M2 | **Chelsea**	20
Nikki Midtown | **E 50s**	21
Z 1 Oak | **Chelsea**	22
105 Riv | **LES**	22
Pacha | **W 40s**	20
Penthse. Exec. Club | **W 40s**	24
Pink Elephant | **Chelsea**	24
Z Plunge | **Meatpacking**	25
Prime | **Chelsea**	22
NEW RDV | **Meatpacking**	22
Room Service | **Flatiron**	18
Runway | **Murray Hill**	16
NEW Sapphire NY | **E 60s**	21
Sol | **Chelsea**	18

Stay | **E Vill**	19
Strata | **Flatiron**	19
SubMercer | **SoHo**	24
Suzie Wong | **Chelsea**	20
Sway | **SoHo**	25
Taj II | **Flatiron**	20
Z Tenjune | **Meatpacking**	25
Touch | **W 50s**	25
Z 230 Fifth | **Chelsea**	25
Ultra | **Chelsea**	18
NEW Velour | **Chelsea**	20

CABARET

Z Box | **LES**	25
Z Cafe Carlyle | **E 70s**	26
Don't Tell Mama | **W 40s**	24
Duplex | **G Vill**	19
Feinstein's at Loews | **E 60s**	23
Joe's Pub | **E Vill**	25
Lips | **W Vill**	20
Metropolitan Rm. | **Flatiron**	20
Z Oak Room | **W 40s**	25
Rasputin | **Brighton Bch**	21

CELEB-SIGHTINGS

Z Balthazar | **SoHo**	25
Z Bar Centrale | **W 40s**	29
Z Beatrice Inn | **W Vill**	21
Z Box | **LES**	25
Bungalow 8 | **Chelsea**	25
Butter | **E Vill**	22
Z Cain Luxe | **Chelsea**	24
NEW Chloe | **LES**	22
Cipriani Downtown | **SoHo**	24
40/40 | **Flatiron**	21
Z Freemans | **LES**	26
Z GoldBar | **L Italy**	23
Z Monkey Bar | **E 50s**	-
Pink Elephant | **Chelsea**	24
Z Rose Bar | **Gramercy**	23
Spotted Pig | **W Vill**	23
Z Tenjune | **Meatpacking**	25

CHEAP DRINKS

Abbey | **W'burg**	21
Aces & Eights | **E 80s**	15
Bar East | **E 90s**	13
Big Easy | **E 90s**	13
Billymark's West | **Chelsea**	15
Blue & Gold | **E Vill**	18
NEW Blue Ruin | **Garment**	-
Boat | **Boerum Hill**	20
Bohemian Hall | **Astoria**	25
Boxcar Lounge | **E Vill**	18
Brazen Head | **Boerum Hill**	20

Brooklyn Brew.	W'burg	23	Rudy's	W 40s	19
B61	Carroll Gdns	24	Ryan's Irish Pub	E Vill	17
Bull McCabe's	E Vill	17	Savalas	W'burg	16
Bushwick Country	W'burg	18	Skinny	LES	16
Cheap Shots	E Vill	19	Solas	E Vill	19
Cherry Tavern	E Vill	14	Sophie's	E Vill	22
Continental	E Vill	16	St. Marks Ale	E Vill	17
Corner Bistro	W Vill	22	Subway Inn	E 60s	17
Desmond's Tavern	Murray Hill	11	Tap a Keg	W 100s	10
Doc Holliday's	E Vill	15	Turkey's Nest	W'burg	16
Double Down	E Vill	17	12th St. Ale	E Vill	18
Down the Hatch	G Vill	16	Warsaw	Greenpt	19
Dublin House	W 70s	16	Welcome/Johnsons	LES	18
East River	W'burg	20		
Edge	E Vill	19		

COFFEEHOUSES

1849	G Vill	17	Arlo & Esme	E Vill	21
Enid's	Greenpt	19	Athens Café	Astoria	17
NEW 508 Sports	Garment	-	NEW Building on Bond	Boerum Hill	-
Flannery's	Chelsea	18		
Floyd, NY	Bklyn Hts	22	Cafe Gitane	NoLita	22
Fontana's	LES	19	Cafe Lalo	W 80s	22
Freddy's	Prospect Hts	18	Caffe Dante	G Vill	21
Gowanus Yacht	Carroll Gdns	23	Caffe Reggio	G Vill	20
Grassroots	E Vill	19	Cake Shop	LES	20
Gutter	Greenpt	24	Edgar's Cafe	W 80s	21
Holiday Cocktail	E Vill	18	Grey Dog's	G Vill	22
NEW Houndstooth	Garment	19	NEW Knave	W 50s	22
International Bar	E Vill	-	Mocca	TriBeCa	21
Iona	W'burg	21	Muddy Cup	SI	17
Jeremy's Ale	Financial	16	Sip	W 100s	18
Jimmy's Corner	W 40s	25	Tea Lounge	multi.	20
Johnny's Bar	W Vill	20	Underground Lounge	W 100s	18
NEW Local 269	LES	-		

COMEDY CLUBS

MacDougal St. Ale	G Vill	18	(Call ahead to check nights, times, performers and covers)	
Mad River	E 80s	14		
NEW Manhattans	Prospect Hts	-	Carolines	W 40s	21
Manitoba's	E Vill	21	Comedy Cellar	G Vill	23
Mars Bar	E Vill	19	Comic Strip	E 80s	17
McAleer's Pub	W 80s	15	Comix	Chelsea	23
McSorley's	E Vill	23	Dangerfield's	E 60s	16
Milady's	SoHo	13	NEW EastVille Comedy	E Vill	18
Moonshine	Red Hook	19	Gotham Comedy	Chelsea	19
Motor City	LES	18	Laugh Lounge	LES	16
Mug's Ale	W'burg	25	New York Comedy	Murray Hill	18
Nancy Whiskey	TriBeCa	17	Stand-Up NY	W 70s	18
National Underground	LES	23		
99 Below	G Vill	19		

COMMUTER OASES

O'Connor's	Park Slope	22	Grand Central	
Off the Wagon	G Vill	17	Annie Moore's	E 40s	16
NEW 123 Burger	W 50s	20	Beer Bar/Centro	E 40s	17
Pieces	G Vill	14	Blarney Stone	E 40s	14
Plug Uglies	Gramercy	17	Bookmarks	E 40s	24
NEW Pony Bar	W 40s	-	Z Campbell Apt.	E 40s	25
Redemption	E 50s	14	NEW La Fonda del Sol	E 40s	-

Lea | **E 40s**	19
Michael Jordan's | **E 40s**	20
Overlook Lounge | **E 40s**	17
Patrick Conway's | **E 40s**	18
Pershing Sq. | **E 40s**	16
Peter Dillon's | **E 40s**	16
Public House | **E 40s**	18

Penn Station

Blarney Stone | **multi.**	14
NEW Houndstooth | **Garment**	19
Local | **Garment**	16
Mustang Sally's | **Chelsea**	17
Playwright | **Garment**	18
Rick's Cabaret | **Garment**	20
Stitch | **Garment**	17
Stout | **Garment**	21
Tír na Nóg | **Garment**	20
Triple Crown | **Chelsea**	18
Walter's Bar | **Garment**	17

Port Authority

Bar 41 | **W 40s**	19
NEW Blue Ruin | **Garment**	-
Croton Reservoir | **W 40s**	17
Daltons | **W 40s**	16
Fashion 40 | **W 40s**	18
NEW 508 Sports | **Garment**	-
HK Lounge | **Garment**	20

COOL LOOS

Baraza | **E Vill**	22
Bar 89 | **SoHo**	22
Dusk | **Chelsea**	21
Duvet | **Flatiron**	20
ESPN Zone | **W 40s**	18
Glass | **Chelsea**	20
Grace Hotel Bar | **W 40s**	18
Jekyll & Hyde | **G Vill**	17
Monkey Town | **W'burg**	21
Morimoto | **Chelsea**	25
Ono | **Meatpacking**	24
P.J. Clarke's | **multi.**	20
Schiller's | **LES**	22
Z SEA | **W'burg**	25
Z Smith & Mills | **TriBeCa**	23
Splash | **Flatiron**	20
Z Tao | **E 50s**	24
Tropical 128 | **L Italy**	19

DANCE CLUBS

Aura | **Flatiron**	20
Branch | **E 50s**	17
Cielo | **Meatpacking**	23
Columbus 72 | **W 70s**	15
Element | **LES**	22
NEW El Morocco | **Harlem**	20

Escuelita | **Garment**	17
Europa | **Greenpt**	17
Gonzalez y Gonzalez | **NoHo**	18
NEW Greenhouse | **SoHo**	21
NEW Griffin | **Meatpacking**	-
NEW Imperial | **Flatiron**	18
Kiss & Fly | **Meatpacking**	20
Le Royale | **W Vill**	16
Love | **G Vill**	20
Monster | **G Vill**	16
Mr. Black | **Garment**	20
NEW Mr. West | **Chelsea**	20
Z NEW M2 | **Chelsea**	20
Pacha | **W 40s**	20
Prime | **Chelsea**	22
Providence/Triumph | **W 50s**	17
Pyramid | **E Vill**	18
Rebel | **Garment**	18
Rush | **Chelsea**	20
Saloon | **E 80s**	17
Z NEW Santos Party Hse. | **Chinatown**	21
Sapphire | **LES**	18
S.O.B.'s | **SoHo**	22
Sol | **Chelsea**	18
Studio B | **Greenpt**	24
Suite | **Bay Ridge**	18
Swing 46 | **W 40s**	21
Touch | **W 50s**	25
Vudu Lounge | **E 70s**	18
Webster Hall | **E Vill**	19

DINNER CRUISES

Bateaux NY | **Chelsea**	22
Spirit Cruises | **Chelsea**	20
World Yacht | **W 40s**	23

DIVES

Abbey Pub | **W 100s**	19
Ace of Clubs | **NoHo**	19
Alligator | **W'burg**	20
American Trash | **E 70s**	13
Antarctica | **SoHo**	17
Arlene's Grocery | **LES**	20
Back Fence | **G Vill**	17
Barfly | **Gramercy**	16
Bar Great Harry | **Carroll Gdns**	20
Bar None | **E Vill**	11
Billymark's West | **Chelsea**	15
Black & White | **E Vill**	19
Blarney Stone | **multi.**	14
Blue & Gold | **E Vill**	18
NEW Blue Ruin | **Garment**	-
Boiler Room | **E Vill**	17
Botanica | **NoLita**	15

Broadway Dive	W 100s	15	O'Flanagan's	E 60s	15
B-Side	E Vill	17	151	LES	21
Bull McCabe's	E Vill	17	119 Bar	Gramercy	16
Bull's Head	Gramercy	18	169 Bar	LES	22
Bushwick Country	W'burg	18	Otto's Shrunken	E Vill	21
Cheap Shots	E Vill	19	Parkside	LES	18
Cherry Tavern	E Vill	14	Patriot Saloon	TriBeCa	14
Cock	E Vill	18	Peculier Pub	G Vill	20
Continental	E Vill	16	Peter McManus	Chelsea	19
Coyote Ugly	E Vill	13	Phoenix	E Vill	20
Desmond's Tavern	Murray Hill	11	Pieces	G Vill	14
Ding Dong Lounge	W 100s	18	Plug Uglies	Gramercy	17
Dive Bar	W 90s	18	Pussycat Lounge	Financial	18
Doc Holliday's	E Vill	15	Pyramid	E Vill	18
Don Hill's	SoHo	20	Raccoon Lodge	Financial	15
Double Down	E Vill	17	Rathbones	E 80s	18
Down the Hatch	G Vill	16	Rawhide	Chelsea	12
Dublin House	W 70s	16	Red Lion	G Vill	19
Duke's	E Vill	18	Rudy's	W 40s	19
East River	W'burg	20	7B	E Vill	19
11th St. Bar	E Vill	21	Skinny	LES	16
55 Bar	G Vill	22	Sophie's	E Vill	22
NEW 508 Sports	Garment	–	Spring Lounge	NoLita	19
Freddy's	Prospect Hts	18	Stoned Crow	G Vill	19
Gin Mill	W 80s	16	Subway Inn	E 60s	17
Grassroots	E Vill	19	Tap a Keg	W 100s	10
Great Lakes	Park Slope	22	Trash	W'burg	18
Hangar Bar	W Vill	13	Turkey's Nest	W'burg	16
Hank's	Boerum Hill	20	Walter's Bar	Garment	17
Holiday Cocktail	E Vill	18	WCOU	E Vill	19
Iggy's	E 70s	17	Welcome/Johnsons	LES	18
International Bar	E Vill	–	Westside Brewing	W 70s	17
Jake's Dilemma	W 80s	16	Whiskey River	Murray Hill	18
Jeremy's Ale	Financial	16	Winnie's	Chinatown	18
Jimmy's Corner	W 40s	25		
Joe's Bar	E Vill	20	**DJs**	
Johnny's Bar	W Vill	20	Annex	LES	22
John Street B&G	Financial	16	APT	Meatpacking	21
Lakeside Lounge	E Vill	19	Aura	Flatiron	20
Live Bait	Flatiron	15	Bob	LES	19
NEW Local 269	LES	–	Branch	E 50s	17
Lucky 13	Park Slope	17	Buddha Bar	Meatpacking	24
Lucy's	E Vill	19	Z Cain Luxe	Chelsea	24
Malachy's	W 70s	14	Canal Room	TriBeCa	20
NEW Manhattans	Prospect Hts	–	Cielo	Meatpacking	23
Mars Bar	E Vill	19	Columbus 72	W 70s	15
McAleer's Pub	W 80s	15	Element	LES	22
McSwiggan's	Gramercy	12	NEW El Morocco	Harlem	20
Milady's	SoHo	13	Escuelita	Garment	17
Nancy Whiskey	TriBeCa	17	Europa	Greenpt	17
Nevada Smith's	E Vill	16	Gonzalez y Gonzalez	NoHo	18
Ninth Ave. Saloon	W 40s	20	Grand Bar	SoHo	25
No Idea	Flatiron	17	NEW Greenhouse	SoHo	21
O'Connor's	Park Slope	22	NEW Griffin	Meatpacking	–

Guest House | **Chelsea**	19
Hiro | **Chelsea**	22
NEW Imperial | **Flatiron**	18
Kiss & Fly | **Meatpacking**	20
Le Royale | **W Vill**	16
Lit | **E Vill**	19
Love | **G Vill**	20
Z Marquee | **Chelsea**	23
Monster | **G Vill**	16
Mr. Black | **Garment**	20
NEW Mr. West | **Chelsea**	20
Z NEW M2 | **Chelsea**	20
Nublu | **E Vill**	26
Pacha | **W 40s**	20
Park | **Chelsea**	21
Pianos | **LES**	19
Plan B | **E Vill**	16
Prime | **Chelsea**	22
Providence/Triumph | **W 50s**	17
Pyramid | **E Vill**	18
Rebel | **Garment**	18
Rush | **Chelsea**	20
Saloon | **E 80s**	17
Z NEW Santos Party Hse. | **Chinatown**	21
Sapphire | **LES**	18
Savalas | **W'burg**	16
S.O.B.'s | **SoHo**	22
Sol | **Chelsea**	18
Splash | **Flatiron**	20
Studio B | **Greenpt**	24
Suite | **Bay Ridge**	18
Sullivan Room | **G Vill**	18
Suzie Wong | **Chelsea**	20
Swing 46 | **W 40s**	21
Touch | **W 50s**	25
Vudu Lounge | **E 70s**	18
Webster Hall | **E Vill**	19

DRAG SHOWS

Barracuda | **Chelsea**	19
NEW Belleville Lounge | **Park Slope**	-
NEW DTOX | **E Vill**	18
Escuelita | **Garment**	17
Lips | **W Vill**	20
Monster | **G Vill**	16
Ninth Ave. Saloon | **W 40s**	20
Pieces | **G Vill**	14
Slipper Room | **LES**	20
Stonewall Inn | **G Vill**	20
Suite | **W 100s**	16
Urge | **E Vill**	19
Vlada | **W 50s**	23
xes lounge | **Chelsea**	22

DRINK SPECIALISTS

BEER
(* Microbrewery)

Against the Grain | **E Vill**	22
anotheroom | **TriBeCa**	24
Baker Street | **E 60s**	18
Barcade | **W'burg**	24
Bar Great Harry | **Carroll Gdns**	20
Barrow St. Ale | **G Vill**	18
Beer Bar/Centro | **E 40s**	17
Beer Table | **Park Slope**	24
Z Blind Tiger | **G Vill**	20
Blue Smoke | **Murray Hill**	21
Bohemian Hall | **Astoria**	25
Boxcar Lounge | **E Vill**	18
Brass Monkey | **Meatpacking**	19
Brazen Head | **Boerum Hill**	20
Brooklyn Ale | **W'burg**	18
Brooklyn Brew.* | **W'burg**	23
Burp Castle | **E Vill**	18
Chelsea Brewing* | **Chelsea**	18
Croxley Ales | **E Vill**	20
David Copperfield | **E 70s**	17
Z d.b.a. | **multi.**	22
Dewey's Flatiron | **Flatiron**	14
Downtown B&G | **Cobble Hill**	18
Draft Barn | **Gowanus**	-
NEW East Village Tavern | **E Vill**	19
Essex Ale House | **LES**	20
Fourth Ave. Pub | **Park Slope**	18
Gate | **Park Slope**	22
NEW Gibson | **W'burg**	-
Z Ginger Man | **Murray Hill**	22
Half Pint | **G Vill**	22
Harefield Rd. | **W'burg**	20
Heartland Brew.* | **multi.**	16
Hop Devil Grill | **E Vill**	18
House of Brews | **W 40s**	19
Iona | **W'burg**	21
Jake's Dilemma | **W 80s**	16
Jeremy's Ale | **Financial**	16
Jimmy's No. 43 | **E Vill**	22
K & M Bar | **W'burg**	-
Killmeyer's | **SI**	23
King's Head | **E Vill**	14
Kinsale | **E 90s**	20
Lederhosen | **W Vill**	21
NEW Lillie's | **Flatiron**	-
Loreley | **LES**	21
MacDougal St. Ale | **G Vill**	18
Matchless | **Greenpt**	21
McSorley's | **E Vill**	23
Moto | **W'burg**	24
Mug's Ale | **W'burg**	25

O'Flaherty's Ale	**W 40s**	18
124 Rabbit	**G Vill**	24
Z Otheroom	**W Vill**	27
Pacific Standard	**Boerum Hill**	21
Park Slope Ale	**Park Slope**	18
Peculier Pub	**G Vill**	20
NEW Pony Bar	**W 40s**	-
Puck Fair	**SoHo**	18
Radegast	**W'burg**	26
Z Room	**SoHo**	26
Sixth Ward	**LES**	22
Slaughtered Lamb	**G Vill**	17
Spike Hill	**W'burg**	22
Z Spitzer's Corner	**LES**	22
Spuyten Duyvil	**W'burg**	24
NEW Stag's Head	**E 50s**	-
Standings	**E Vill**	25
St. Andrews	**W 40s**	20
St. Marks Ale	**E Vill**	17
Stout	**Garment**	21
Swift	**NoHo**	22
Tír na Nóg	**Garment**	20
200 Fifth	**Park Slope**	17
Z Ulysses	**Financial**	22
Valhalla	**W 50s**	18
Village Pourhouse	**E Vill**	18
Vol de Nuit	**G Vill**	25
Waterfront Ale Hse.	**multi.**	20
Westside Brewing	**W 70s**	17
Zum Schneider	**E Vill**	23

CHAMPAGNE

Bubble Lounge	**TriBeCa**	22
Champagne Bar/Plaza	**W 50s**	25
Country Champ. Lounge	**Murray Hill**	25
Flûte	**multi.**	22
Morrell Wine Bar	**W 40s**	24

COCKTAILS

Z Angel's Share	**E Vill**	26
Z NEW Apothéke	**Chinatown**	23
Z Asia de Cuba	**Murray Hill**	24
Z Bemelmans	**E 70s**	27
B Flat	**TriBeCa**	22
Bond Street	**NoHo**	24
Z Brandy Library	**TriBeCa**	25
Z Brooklyn Social	**Carroll Gdns**	25
Church Lounge	**TriBeCa**	24
Cibar	**Gramercy**	22
City Hall	**TriBeCa**	23
Z NEW Clover Club	**Cobble Hill**	25
Z Death & Co	**E Vill**	25
Del Posto	**Chelsea**	23
NEW Dutch Kills	**LIC**	-

East Side Co.	**LES**	24
Elettaria	**G Vill**	24
Z Employees Only	**W Vill**	24
Z Flatiron Lounge	**Flatiron**	25
Flûte	**multi.**	22
Z Freemans	**LES**	26
Hideout	**Ft Greene**	19
Z Hotel Delmano	**W'burg**	24
Z JakeWalk	**Carroll Gdns**	21
Z King Cole Bar	**E 50s**	28
Le Colonial	**E 50s**	21
Z Little Branch	**W Vill**	26
Z NEW Macao Trading	**TriBeCa**	25
Z NEW Madam Geneva	**NoHo**	25
Z Milk & Honey	**LES**	27
Z Modern	**W 50s**	25
Z Monkey Bar	**E 50s**	-
Z PDT	**E Vill**	27
Z Pegu Club	**SoHo**	25
Z Pravda	**NoLita**	24
NEW Prime Meats	**Carroll Gdns**	-
Z NEW Raines Law Rm.	**Flatiron**	-
Z Rusty Knot	**W Vill**	21
Sidecar	**Park Slope**	20
Slipper Room	**LES**	20
Z Tabla	**Flatiron**	24
Tailor	**SoHo**	23
Z Tao	**E 50s**	24
Z 21 Club	**W 50s**	26
Verlaine	**LES**	23
Z Weather Up	**Prospect Hts**	22
NEW White Star	**LES**	20
World Bar	**E 40s**	23
Zoë	**SoHo**	20

MARTINIS

Z Angel's Share	**E Vill**	26
Z Asia de Cuba	**Murray Hill**	24
Z Balthazar	**SoHo**	25
Bar 89	**SoHo**	22
Bar 4	**Park Slope**	20
Bar Nine	**W 50s**	15
Bartini's	**Forest Hills**	17
Bayard's	**Financial**	19
Z Bemelmans	**E 70s**	27
Blue Ribbon Bklyn.	**Park Slope**	23
Carnegie Club	**W 50s**	24
Cellar Bar	**W 40s**	22
Cibar	**Gramercy**	22
Circa Tabac	**SoHo**	21
Delia's	**Bay Ridge**	22
Divine Bar	**W 50s**	22
Dylan Prime	**TriBeCa**	23
Z Four Seasons Bar	**E 50s**	26
Z King Cole Bar	**E 50s**	28

MO Bar | **W 60s**	23
Onieal's Grand St. | **L Italy**	20
Pink Elephant | **Chelsea**	24
Ƶ Pravda | **NoLita**	24
Rue B | **E Vill**	22
Shebeen | **NoLita**	22
SoHo Room | **SoHo**	14
Stir | **E 70s**	19
Temple Bar | **NoHo**	24
Tribeca Grill | **TriBeCa**	23
Ƶ 21 Club | **W 50s**	26
Vintage | **W 50s**	25

SAKE/SHOCHU/SOJU

Chibi's Sake Bar | **NoLita**	23
Decibel | **E Vill**	24
EN Shochu Bar | **W Vill**	22
Forbidden City | **E Vill**	19
Megu | **TriBeCa**	24
Morimoto | **Chelsea**	25
Nobu 57 | **W 50s**	25
Ono | **Meatpacking**	24
Ƶ Sakagura | **E 40s**	27
Sake Hana | **E 70s**	24
Sugarcane | **Flatiron**	21
SushiSamba | **multi.**	22
Suzie Wong | **Chelsea**	20

SCOTCH/SINGLE MALTS

Ƶ Brandy Library | **TriBeCa**	25
Brazen Head | **Boerum Hill**	20
Bridge Cafe | **Financial**	24
Bull and Bear | **E 40s**	21
Carnegie Club | **W 50s**	24
Club Macanudo | **E 60s**	24
Ƶ d.b.a. | **multi.**	22
Harefield Rd. | **W'burg**	20
Hudson Bar & Books | **W Vill**	21
Keens Steak | **Garment**	21
Landmark Tav. | **W 40s**	21
Lexington Bar & Books | **E 70s**	21
Spike Hill | **W'burg**	22
St. Andrews | **W 40s**	20
Swift | **NoHo**	22
Terra Blues | **G Vill**	22
Tír na Nóg | **Garment**	20
Whiskey Ward | **LES**	19

TEQUILA

Barrio Chino | **LES**	22
Citrus B&G | **W 70s**	20
Cowgirl | **W Vill**	18
Ƶ d.b.a. | **multi.**	22
Dos Caminos | **multi.**	22
Ƶ La Esquina | **L Italy**	24

NEW Mayahuel | **E Vill**	-
Mustang Grill | **E 80s**	16
Under the Volcano | **Murray Hill**	18
Whistlin' Dixie's | **W 50s**	16

VODKA

Anyway Cafe | **multi.**	20
Mama's Bar | **E Vill**	22
Ƶ Pravda | **NoLita**	24
Rasputin | **Brighton Bch**	21
Russian Samovar | **W 50s**	20
Russian Vodka Rm. | **W 50s**	21
Temple Bar | **NoHo**	24
212 | **E 60s**	18
Vlada | **W 50s**	23

WHISKEY

NEW Char No. 4 | **Cobble Hill**	24
Ƶ d.b.a. | **multi.**	22
JakeWalk | **Carroll Gdns**	21
NEW Lillie's | **Flatiron**	-
Moonshine | **Red Hook**	19
Whiskey Town | **E Vill**	20
Whiskey Ward | **LES**	19

WINE BARS

Ƶ Accademia di Vino | **E 60s**	22
Ara Wine Bar | **Meatpacking**	22
Aroma | **NoHo**	25
Ƶ Bacaro | **Chinatown**	21
NEW Balon | **E 80s**	-
Bar @ Etats-Unis | **E 80s**	23
Bar Carrera | **multi.**	23
Barcibo Enoteca | **W 60s**	22
Bar Italia | **E 70s**	20
Bar Jamón | **Gramercy**	24
Ƶ Bar Veloce/Club | **multi.**	24
Bin No. 220 | **Seaport**	21
Bin 71 | **W 70s**	22
Ƶ Black Mtn. Wine | **Carroll Gdns**	28
Blue Ribbon Bar | **G Vill**	23
Bottega del Vino | **E 50s**	22
Bowery Wine Company | **E Vill**	20
NEW Brookvin | **Park Slope**	22
Buceo 95 | **W 90s**	21
Cafe Notte | **E 80s**	21
Cavatappo Grill/Wine | **multi.**	22
Ƶ **NEW** City Winery | **SoHo**	23
NEW Clo | **W 60s**	22
Cornichon | **W'burg**	21
NEW Desnuda | **E Vill**	23
NEW Diamond's Wine | **LES**	22
Divine Bar | **W 50s**	22
D.O.C. Wine | **W'burg**	25
Domaine Bar a Vins | **LIC**	21

SPECIAL APPEALS

8th St. Winecellar | **G Vill**	23
Epistrophy | **NoLita**	21
Felice | **E 60s**	22
Flûte | **multi.**	22
Gallo Nero | **W 40s**	21
Gottino | **G Vill**	22
Grape & Grain | **E Vill**	26
Il Posto Accanto | **E Vill**	24
Z 'inoteca | **multi.**	24
In Vino | **E Vill**	25
I Trulli Enoteca | **Murray Hill**	24
Jadis | **LES**	22
Le Bateau Ivre | **E 50s**	24
LelaBar | **W Vill**	25
Michael Jordan's | **E 40s**	20
Monday Room | **NoLita**	24
Morrell Wine Bar | **W 40s**	24
NEW Nectar | **Harlem**	23
Peasant | **NoLita**	23
Petrarca Vino | **TriBeCa**	24
NEW Pierre Loti | **Gramercy**	23
Pudding Stones | **multi.**	21
Riposo | **multi.**	20
Rouge Wine Bar | **W Vill**	22
Sample | **Cobble Hill**	19
Shade | **G Vill**	26
Solex | **E Vill**	22
NEW Sorella | **LES**	-
Z Stonehome | **Ft Greene**	27
NEW Sweet & Lowdown | **LES**	18
Tapeo 29 | **LES**	24
Ten Bells | **LES**	23
Terroir | **E Vill**	22
Total Wine | **Park Slope**	25
Turks & Frogs | **W Vill**	22
V Bar | **G Vill**	26
Vero | **multi.**	24
NEW Vino | **E 60s**	22
Vino di Vino | **Astoria**	22
NEW Vino 313 | **Murray Hill**	22
Vino Vino | **TriBeCa**	23
NEW Vintage Irving | **Gramercy**	21
Von | **NoHo**	26
Wine & Roses | **W 70s**	21
Winebar | **E Vill**	22
Wined Up | **Flatiron**	22
Xai Xai | **W 50s**	23
Xicala | **L Italy**	23
Zampa | **W Vill**	-

WINE BY THE GLASS
(See also Wine Bars, above)

anotheroom | **TriBeCa**	24
Bar 6 | **G Vill**	23
Country Champ. Lounge | **Murray Hill**	25

Eleven Madison Pk. | **Flatiron**	25
Z Gotham B&G | **G Vill**	25
Z Gramercy Tavern | **Flatiron**	26
Iridium | **W 50s**	21
Le Cirque Wine | **E 50s**	24
Lexington Bar & Books | **E 70s**	21
Louis 649 | **E Vill**	26
Ñ | **SoHo**	24
Z Otheroom | **W Vill**	27
Otto | **G Vill**	25
Z Room | **SoHo**	26
Smoke | **W 100s**	22
Z Tabla | **Flatiron**	24
Tavern on the Green | **W 60s**	22
Tribeca Grill | **TriBeCa**	23
Z 21 Club | **W 50s**	26
Z Union Sq. Cafe | **Union Sq**	24
Z Bar Veloce/Club | **NoLita**	24
Zoë | **SoHo**	20

EURO

Z Asia de Cuba | **Murray Hill**	24
Z Balthazar | **SoHo**	25
Baraonda | **E 70s**	21
Bar 44 | **W 40s**	21
Bar 6 | **G Vill**	23
Z Bar Veloce/Club | **E Vill**	24
Bottega del Vino | **E 50s**	22
Bungalow 8 | **Chelsea**	25
Cafe Gitane | **NoLita**	22
Cafe Noir | **SoHo**	22
Z Cain Luxe | **Chelsea**	24
Casimir | **E Vill**	21
Cielo | **Meatpacking**	23
Cipriani Downtown | **SoHo**	24
Circa Tabac | **SoHo**	21
Coffee Shop | **Union Sq**	18
Flûte | **multi.**	22
Geisha | **E 60s**	22
Z GoldBar | **L Italy**	23
Grand Bar | **SoHo**	25
Hudson Hotel | **W 50s**	24
Indochine | **E Vill**	20
I Tre Merli | **SoHo**	20
Kiss & Fly | **Meatpacking**	20
Le Colonial | **E 50s**	21
L'Orange Bleue | **SoHo**	21
Mercer Bar | **SoHo**	23
Merkato 55 | **Meatpacking**	22
Novecento | **SoHo**	21
Opia | **E 50s**	22
Z Pastis | **Meatpacking**	24
NEW RDV | **Meatpacking**	22
Schiller's | **LES**	22

Soho House | **Meatpacking**	24
⚡ Tao | **E 50s**	24
Thom Bar | **SoHo**	24
THOR Lobby Bar | **LES**	20
212 | **E 60s**	18

EXPENSE-ACCOUNTERS

NEW Above Allen | **LES**	22
⚡ Asia de Cuba | **Murray Hill**	24
⚡ Balthazar | **SoHo**	25
Bar Masa | **W 60s**	23
Bateaux NY | **Chelsea**	22
Bayard's | **Financial**	19
⚡ Bemelmans | **E 70s**	27
Blue Fin | **W 40s**	23
⚡ Blue Note | **G Vill**	23
⚡ Blue Water Grill | **Union Sq**	23
Bond Street | **NoHo**	24
⚡ Brandy Library | **TriBeCa**	25
Brasserie 8½ | **W 50s**	21
Bubble Lounge | **TriBeCa**	22
⚡ Buddakan | **Chelsea**	24
Bull and Bear | **E 40s**	21
⚡ Cafe Carlyle | **E 70s**	26
Café des Artistes | **W 60s**	24
⚡ Campbell Apt. | **E 40s**	25
Carnegie Club | **W 50s**	24
Cellar Bar | **W 40s**	22
Champagne Bar/Plaza | **W 50s**	25
Church Lounge | **TriBeCa**	24
Club Macanudo | **E 60s**	24
⚡ Daniel | **E 60s**	27
Del Posto | **Chelsea**	23
Eleven Madison Pk. | **Flatiron**	25
Flûte | **multi.**	22
⚡ Four Seasons Bar | **E 50s**	26
Gilt | **E 50s**	21
⚡ GoldBar | **L Italy**	23
⚡ Gotham B&G | **G Vill**	25
⚡ Gramercy Tavern | **Flatiron**	26
Grand Bar | **SoHo**	25
Hudson Hotel | **W 50s**	24
Indochine | **E Vill**	20
I Trulli Enoteca | **Murray Hill**	24
Keens Steak | **Garment**	21
⚡ King Cole Bar | **E 50s**	28
Le Cirque Wine | **E 50s**	24
Le Colonial | **E 50s**	21
Megu | **TriBeCa**	24
Michael Jordan's | **E 40s**	20
MO Bar | **W 60s**	23
⚡ Modern | **W 50s**	25
⚡ Monkey Bar | **E 50s**	-
Morimoto | **Chelsea**	25

Morrell Wine Bar | **W 40s**	24
Nobu 57 | **W 50s**	25
⚡ Oak Bar | **W 50s**	24
⚡ Oak Room | **W 40s**	25
One if by Land | **G Vill**	26
Pink Elephant | **Chelsea**	24
Plaza Athénée | **E 60s**	24
NEW Pranna | **Murray Hill**	-
⚡ Rainbow Grill | **W 40s**	24
Regency Library Bar | **E 60s**	25
Rink Bar | **W 50s**	24
Rose Club | **W 50s**	23
⚡ Sakagura | **E 40s**	27
Salon de Ning | **W 50s**	26
NEW Sapphire NY | **E 60s**	21
NEW Shang Bar | **LES**	-
STK | **Meatpacking**	23
Stone Rose | **W 60s**	23
⚡ Tabla | **Flatiron**	24
⚡ Tao | **E 50s**	24
Tavern on the Green | **W 60s**	22
Tribeca Grill | **TriBeCa**	23
⚡ 21 Club | **W 50s**	26
212 | **E 60s**	18
Ultra | **Chelsea**	18
Underbar | **Union Sq**	21
⚡ Union Sq. Cafe | **Union Sq**	24
Whiskey | **W 40s**	20
Whiskey Blue | **E 40s**	23
Whiskey Park | **W 50s**	20
World Bar | **E 40s**	23

EYE-OPENERS

(Serves alcohol starting at 8 AM on most days)

⚡ Balthazar | **SoHo**	25
Billymark's West | **Chelsea**	15
Blarney Stone | **multi.**	14
Cafe Lalo | **W 80s**	22
Cafeteria | **Chelsea**	19
Dublin House | **W 70s**	16
Flannery's | **Chelsea**	18
Jeremy's Ale | **Financial**	16
Kinsale | **E 90s**	20
Rudy's | **W 40s**	19
Spring Lounge | **NoLita**	19

FINE FOOD TOO

Allen & Delancey | **LES**	25
⚡ Asia de Cuba | **Murray Hill**	24
NEW At Vermilion | **E 40s**	-
⚡ Balthazar | **SoHo**	25
Bar Masa | **W 60s**	23
NEW BEast | **LES**	21
Blue Fin | **W 40s**	23

SPECIAL APPEALS

Blue Ribbon	SoHo	25	Blackstone's	E 50s	17
Blue Ribbon Bklyn.	Park Slope	23	Boat	Boerum Hill	20
Blue Ribbon Sushi	W 50s	22	Bookmarks	E 40s	24
Z Blue Water Grill	Union Sq	23	Z Bowery Hotel Bar	E Vill	23
Z Bobo	W Vill	22	Z Brandy Library	TriBeCa	25
NEW Brooklyn Bowl	W'burg	-	Camp	Boerum Hill	21
Z Buddakan	Chelsea	24	Carnegie Club	W 50s	24
Café des Artistes	W 60s	24	NEW Casa La Femme	W Vill	-
Centro Vinoteca	W Vill	21	Central Bar	E Vill	19
Z Commerce	W Vill	22	Cherry Tree	Park Slope	16
Z Daniel	E 60s	27	Chill Lounge	Murray Hill	17
Del Posto	Chelsea	23	Cibar	Gramercy	22
Dos Caminos	Murray Hill	22	Z NEW Clover Club	Cobble Hill	25
Elettaria	G Vill	24	Cornelia St. Cafe	G Vill	23
Eleven Madison Pk.	Flatiron	25	Delancey	LES	20
5 Ninth	Meatpacking	23	Delia's	Bay Ridge	22
Z Four Seasons Bar	E 50s	26	Donovan's	Woodside	20
Gilt	E 50s	21	Dorrian's	E 80s	16
Z Gotham B&G	G Vill	25	Dublin 6	W Vill	22
Z Gramercy Tavern	Flatiron	26	Z NEW Empire Hotel Roof	W 60s	24
Le Colonial	E 50s	21	Z Employees Only	W Vill	24
Megu	TriBeCa	24	Faces & Names	W 50s	18
Mercer Bar	SoHo	24	Failte	Murray Hill	17
Merkato 55	Meatpacking	22	5 Ninth	Meatpacking	23
Michael Jordan's	E 40s	20	Garage	G Vill	21
Z Modern	W 50s	25	Gaslight/G2	Meatpacking	17
Morimoto	Chelsea	25	NEW Gates	Chelsea	-
Nobu 57	W 50s	25	Gin Mill	W 80s	16
Otto	G Vill	25	Harbour Lights	Seaport	21
NEW Pranna	Murray Hill	-	Hudson Hotel	W 50s	24
NEW Prime Meats	Carroll Gdns	-	Iguana	W 50s	18
Public	NoLita	24	Jack Russell's	E 80s	19
Rayuela	LES	26	Jekyll & Hyde	G Vill	17
NEW Shang Bar	LES	-	Josie Wood's	G Vill	14
Smith's	G Vill	22	Keens Steak	Garment	21
Z Spice Market	Meatpacking	24	Keybar	E Vill	23
Spotted Pig	W Vill	23	La Lanterna	G Vill	25
Z Tabla	Flatiron	24	Latitude	W 40s	17
Tailor	SoHo	23	Lexington Bar & Books	E 70s	21
Z 21 Club	W 50s	26	Lion's Head Tavern	W 100s	15
Z Union Sq. Cafe	Union Sq	24	Loki	Park Slope	17

FIREPLACES

			McGee's	W 50s	15
			Merchants, NY	multi.	18
Amsterdam Billiards	E Vill	17	Metropolitan	W'burg	19
Angry Wade's	Cobble Hill	14	Molly's	Gramercy	22
Arctica	Murray Hill	18	Moran's Chelsea	Chelsea	19
Art Bar	W Vill	20	Z NEW M2	Chelsea	20
Auction House	E 80s	22	O'Flaherty's Ale	W 40s	18
Back Room	LES	23	One if by Land	G Vill	26
Bar 44	W 40s	21	Park	Chelsea	21
Bayard's Ale	W Vill	17	P.J. Hanley's	Carroll Gdns	18
Black Bear	Gramercy	17	Playwright	W 40s	18
Z Black Mtn. Wine	Carroll Gdns	28	Raccoon Lodge	Financial	15
Black Rabbit	Greenpt	-	Retreat	Flatiron	17

Riviera | **W Vill**	14
☑ Rose Bar | **Gramercy**	23
☑ SEA | **Meatpacking**	25
Sherwood | **Boerum Hill**	23
Shoolbred's | **E Vill**	20
Slaughtered Lamb | **G Vill**	17
SouthWest NY | **Financial**	19
STK | **Meatpacking**	23
Sutton Place | **E 50s**	18
Tavern on Jane | **W Vill**	21
Teddy's | **W'burg**	23
Telephone | **E Vill**	18
T.G. Whitney's | **E 50s**	16
Tillman's | **Chelsea**	22
Town Tavern | **G Vill**	15
Turtle Bay | **E 50s**	15
☑ 21 Club | **W 50s**	26
☑ Union Hall | **Park Slope**	24
Velvet | **E Vill**	17
Vig 27 | **Murray Hill**	19
Westside Brewing | **W 70s**	17
Wet Bar | **Murray Hill**	21
Whiskey River | **Murray Hill**	18
Zanzibar | **W 40s**	20
Zombie Hut | **Carroll Gdns**	21

Flor de Sol | **TriBeCa**	23
Forbidden City | **E Vill**	19
Grape & Grain | **E Vill**	26
Hudson Hotel | **W 50s**	24
Il Posto Accanto | **E Vill**	24
I Trulli Enoteca | **Murray Hill**	24
☑ Jazz Standard | **Murray Hill**	26
Le Colonial | **E 50s**	21
Louis 649 | **E Vill**	26
MO Bar | **W 60s**	23
Morgans Bar | **Murray Hill**	22
Onieal's Grand St. | **L Italy**	20
☑ Otheroom | **W Vill**	27
Park Bar | **Flatiron**	21
Pipa | **Flatiron**	21
☑ NEW Raines Law Rm. | **Flatiron**	–
Red Bench | **SoHo**	21
☑ Room | **SoHo**	26
Sake Hana | **E 70s**	24
Sala | **multi.**	23
SoHo Room | **SoHo**	14
Stir | **E 70s**	19
Temple Bar | **NoHo**	24
Von | **NoHo**	26
Zanzibar | **W 40s**	20

FIRST DATE

☑ Angel's Share | **E Vill**	26
anotheroom | **TriBeCa**	24
Art Bar | **W Vill**	20
Bar 4 | **Park Slope**	20
Bar 6 | **G Vill**	23
☑ Bemelmans | **E 70s**	27
Black Door | **Chelsea**	20
Blue Smoke | **Murray Hill**	21
☑ Boat Basin | **W 70s**	24
☑ Boathouse | **E 70s**	26
Bongo | **Chelsea**	18
Bowlmor Lanes | **G Vill**	22
Bubble Lounge | **TriBeCa**	22
☑ Cafe Carlyle | **E 70s**	26
Caffe Reggio | **G Vill**	20
☑ Calle Ocho | **W 80s**	23
Canyon Road | **E 70s**	19
Casimir | **E Vill**	21
Cibar | **Gramercy**	22
Cub Room | **SoHo**	19
Delia's | **Bay Ridge**	22
☑ Dizzy's Club | **W 60s**	25
D.O.C. Wine | **W'burg**	25
Dylan Prime | **TriBeCa**	23
Edgar's Cafe | **W 80s**	21
Eight Mile Creek | **NoLita**	23
Eleven Madison Pk. | **Flatiron**	25

FOREIGN FEELING

ASIAN

Bar Masa | **W 60s**	23
☑ Buddakan | **Chelsea**	24
Buddha Bar | **Meatpacking**	24
Chibi's Sake Bar | **NoLita**	23
China 1 | **E Vill**	19
Chow Bar | **W Vill**	18
Decibel | **E Vill**	24
EN Shochu Bar | **W Vill**	22
Forbidden City | **E Vill**	19
Geisha | **E 60s**	22
Indochine | **E Vill**	20
Japonais | **Gramercy**	22
Joya | **Cobble Hill**	23
Le Colonial | **E 50s**	21
Megu | **TriBeCa**	24
Morimoto | **Chelsea**	25
Nobu 57 | **W 50s**	25
Ono | **Meatpacking**	24
NEW Pranna | **Murray Hill**	–
☑ Sakagura | **E 40s**	27
Sake Hana | **E 70s**	24
☑ SEA | **W'burg**	25
☑ Spice Market | **Meatpacking**	24
Sugarcane | **Flatiron**	21
SushiSamba | **multi.**	22

FRENCH

☑ Balthazar | **SoHo**	25
Barbès | **Park Slope**	25
Bar 6 | **G Vill**	23
Bar Tabac | **Cobble Hill**	22
NEW Belleville Lounge | **Park Slope**	–
Café Charbon | **LES**	23
Cafe Gitane | **NoLita**	22
Chez Josephine | **W 40s**	22
☑ Daniel | **E 60s**	27
Indochine | **E Vill**	20
Jules | **E Vill**	23
La Bottega | **Chelsea**	21
Le Bateau Ivre | **E 50s**	24
L'Orange Bleue | **SoHo**	21
☑ Pastis | **Meatpacking**	24
Rouge Wine Bar | **W Vill**	22
Rue B | **E Vill**	22
Schiller's | **LES**	22
Sherwood | **Boerum Hill**	23
Zebulon | **W'burg**	24

GERMAN

Bohemian Hall | **Astoria**	25
Killmeyer's | **SI**	23
Lederhosen | **W Vill**	21
Loreley | **LES**	21
Zum Schneider | **E Vill**	23

INDIAN

NEW At Vermilion | **E 40s**	–
K Lounge | **W 50s**	20
Sutra | **E Vill**	18
Taj II | **Flatiron**	20

IRISH

An Béal Bocht | **Bronx**	21
Annie Moore's | **E 40s**	16
Baker Street | **E 60s**	18
Bar East | **E 90s**	13
Biddy's | **E 90s**	22
Black Sheep | **Murray Hill**	15
Blackstone's | **E 50s**	17
Blarney Stone | **multi.**	14
Boss Tweed's | **LES**	17
Bua | **E Vill**	21
Bull McCabe's | **E Vill**	17
Central Bar | **E Vill**	19
Channel 4 | **W 40s**	13
Cherry Tree | **Park Slope**	16
Connolly's | **multi.**	18
Dead Poet | **W 80s**	20
Desmond's Tavern | **Murray Hill**	11
Doc Watson's | **E 70s**	17
Donovan's | **multi.**	20

Dorrian's | **E 80s**	16
Druids | **W 50s**	19
Dublin House | **W 70s**	16
Dublin 6 | **W Vill**	22
Eamonn's | **Bklyn Hts**	14
East End Tav. | **E 80s**	16
11th St. Bar | **E Vill**	21
Emmett O'Lunney's | **W 50s**	16
Failte | **Murray Hill**	17
Fiddlesticks | **G Vill**	18
Finnegans Wake | **E 70s**	15
Finnerty's | **E Vill**	10
Fitzgerald's | **Murray Hill**	16
Flannery's | **Chelsea**	18
Four-Faced Liar | **G Vill**	18
Full Shilling | **Financial**	18
Gaf Bar | **W 40s**	22
Galway Hooker | **Murray Hill**	18
Gatsby's | **NoLita**	13
Genesis | **E 80s**	20
George Keeley's | **W 80s**	23
NEW Globe | **Gramercy**	19
Hairy Monk | **Murray Hill**	17
Half King | **Chelsea**	19
Harefield Rd. | **W'burg**	20
Iggy's | **multi.**	17
Iona | **W'burg**	21
Irish Rogue | **W 40s**	19
Jake's Saloon | **multi.**	18
Jameson's | **E 50s**	16
Johnny Foxes | **E 80s**	16
Josie Wood's | **G Vill**	14
Kinsale | **E 90s**	20
Landmark Tav. | **W 40s**	21
Lansdowne Rd. | **W 40s**	21
NEW Lillie's | **Flatiron**	–
Local 138 | **LES**	19
Lucky Jack's | **LES**	20
Lunasa | **E Vill**	22
Maggie's | **E 40s**	20
Malachy's | **W 70s**	14
Margarita Murphy's | **Murray Hill**	17
McAleer's Pub | **W 80s**	15
McCormack's | **Murray Hill**	19
McFadden's | **E 40s**	15
McGee's | **W 50s**	15
McSorley's | **E Vill**	23
McSwiggan's | **Gramercy**	12
Molly Pitcher's | **E 80s**	21
Molly's | **Gramercy**	22
Moran's Chelsea | **Chelsea**	19
Mr. Dennehy's | **G Vill**	20
Mustang Harry's | **Chelsea**	17
Mustang Sally's | **Chelsea**	17

Menus, photos, voting and more – free at ZAGAT.com

O'Connell's	**W 100s**	16	LQ	**E 40s**	21
O'Connor's	**Park Slope**	22	Ñ	**SoHo**	24
O'Flaherty's Ale	**W 40s**	18	Novecento	**SoHo**	21
O'Flanagan's	**E 60s**	15	Nuyorican Poets	**E Vill**	21
O'Lunney's	**W 40s**	21	Pipa	**Flatiron**	21
O'Neals'	**W 60s**	20	Sala	**NoHo**	23
One & One	**E Vill**	18	S.O.B.'s	**SoHo**	22
Paddy Reilly's	**Murray Hill**	20	Son Cubano	**Meatpacking**	23
Paris	**Seaport**	19	Tapeo 29	**LES**	24
Parlour	**W 80s**	17	Xunta	**E Vill**	19
Patrick Conway's	**E 40s**	18	Zinc Bar	**G Vill**	22
Patrick Kavanagh's	**Murray Hill**	17		

MOROCCAN

Peggy O'Neill's	**Coney Is**	18	Babel Lounge	**E Vill**	21
Perdition	**W 40s**	20	Bar 6	**G Vill**	23
Perfect Pint	**multi.**	21	Black Betty	**W'burg**	19
Peter Dillon's	**E 40s**	16	Cafe Gitane	**NoLita**	22
Peter McManus	**Chelsea**	19	**NEW** Casa La Femme	**W Vill**	–
P.J. Carney's	**W 50s**	18	Casimir	**E Vill**	21
P.J. Clarke's	**multi.**	20	Karma	**E Vill**	21
Playwright	**multi.**	18	Katra	**LES**	18
Plug Uglies	**Gramercy**	17	Kemia Bar	**W 40s**	26
Puck Fair	**SoHo**	18	Kush	**LES**	22
Rumours	**W 50s**	17	L'Orange Bleue	**SoHo**	21
Ryan's Daughter	**E 80s**	19	Obivia	**L Italy**	24
Ryan's Irish Pub	**E Vill**	17	Plaza Athénée	**E 60s**	24
Scratcher	**E Vill**	20	Royale	**Park Slope**	21
Sixth Ward	**LES**	22	Shalel Lounge	**W 70s**	24
Sláinte	**NoHo**	18	Sway	**SoHo**	25
Slane	**G Vill**	17	Zinc Bar	**G Vill**	22
Social	**W 40s**	17		

RUSSIAN

St. Dymphna's	**E Vill**	20	Anyway Cafe	**multi.**	20
Stout	**Garment**	21	KGB	**E Vill**	21
Swift	**NoHo**	22	**Z** Pravda	**NoLita**	24
Swig	**E 80s**	16	Rasputin	**Brighton Bch**	21
T.G. Whitney's	**E 50s**	16	Russian Samovar	**W 50s**	20
Thirsty Scholar	**E Vill**	17	Russian Vodka Rm.	**W 50s**	21
Tír na Nóg	**Garment**	20		

FRAT HOUSE

Trinity Pub	**E 80s**	20	American Trash	**E 70s**	13
Triple Crown	**Chelsea**	18	Bar Coastal	**E 70s**	14
Z Ulysses	**Financial**	22	Bar East	**E 90s**	13
Water St. Bar	**Dumbo**	20	Bar 515	**Murray Hill**	15
Wicked Monk	**Bay Ridge**	18	Bar Great Harry	**Carroll Gdns**	20
NEW Wilfie & Nell	**W Vill**	24	Bar None	**E Vill**	11
	Barrow St. Ale	**G Vill**	18

LATIN

	BB&R	**E 80s**	18
Agozar!	**NoHo**	18	Big Easy	**E 90s**	13
Baraza	**E Vill**	22	Blackstone's	**E 50s**	17
Barrio Chino	**LES**	22	**NEW** Bleecker Heights	**W Vill**	–
Z Calle Ocho	**W 80s**	23	Bleecker St. Bar	**NoHo**	18
Citrus B&G	**W 70s**	20	Bounce	**multi.**	19
Coffee Shop	**Union Sq**	18	Bourbon St.	**W 70s**	15
Escuelita	**Garment**	17	**Z** Brother Jimmy's	**multi.**	17
Flor de Sol	**TriBeCa**	23		
Gonzalez y Gonzalez	**NoHo**	18		
Ideya	**SoHo**	23		

Bull's Head | **Gramercy**	18
Calico Jack's | **E 40s**	15
Dewey's Flatiron | **Flatiron**	14
Dive Bar | **W 90s**	18
Doc Watson's | **E 70s**	17
NEW Donnybrook | **LES**	19
Down the Hatch | **G Vill**	16
1849 | **G Vill**	17
Fat Black Pussycat | **G Vill**	17
Fiddlesticks | **G Vill**	18
Firehouse | **W 80s**	16
Genesis | **E 80s**	20
Gin Mill | **W 80s**	16
Half Pint | **G Vill**	22
NEW Hill | **Murray Hill**	17
Iggy's | **E 70s**	17
Jake's Dilemma | **W 80s**	16
Jeremy's Ale | **Financial**	16
Joshua Tree | **multi.**	15
Josie Wood's | **G Vill**	14
Kabin | **E Vill**	16
Loki | **Park Slope**	17
Lucky Jack's | **LES**	20
MacDougal St. Ale | **G Vill**	18
Mad River | **E 80s**	14
McFadden's | **E 40s**	15
Molly Pitcher's | **E 80s**	21
99 Below | **G Vill**	19
No Idea | **Flatiron**	17
Off the Wagon | **G Vill**	17
NEW 123 Burger | **W 50s**	20
Peculier Pub | **G Vill**	20
Porky's | **Flatiron**	15
Professor Thom's | **E Vill**	19
Raccoon Lodge | **Financial**	15
Rathbones | **E 80s**	18
Ryan's Daughter | **E 80s**	19
Saloon | **E 80s**	17
Ship of Fools | **E 80s**	16
Sláinte | **NoHo**	18
NEW Southside | **L Italy**	18
Still | **Gramercy**	15
Stout | **Garment**	21
NEW Stumble Inn | **E 70s**	15
Sutton Place | **E 50s**	18
Tap a Keg | **W 100s**	10
Third & Long | **Murray Hill**	14
Tin Lizzie | **E 80s**	13
Tonic East | **Murray Hill**	20
Tortilla Flats | **W Vill**	19
Town Tavern | **G Vill**	15
Turtle Bay | **E 50s**	15
12th St. Ale | **E Vill**	18
Underground | **Murray Hill**	18

Wicker Park | **E 80s**	18
Woody McHale's | **W Vill**	16

GAMES

BOARD GAMES

Abilene | **Carroll Gdns**	20
BB&R | **E 80s**	18
Belmont | **Gramercy**	16
Black Rabbit | **Greenpt**	-
Blue & Gold | **E Vill**	18
Broadway Dive | **W 100s**	15
🗹 Brooklyn Inn | **Boerum Hill**	27
Buttermilk | **Park Slope**	23
Camp | **Boerum Hill**	21
Cheap Shots | **E Vill**	19
Cherry Tree | **Park Slope**	16
Common Ground | **E Vill**	19
🗹 d.b.a. | **E Vill**	22
Dive 75 | **W 70s**	21
Dram Shop | **Park Slope**	-
Dublin 6 | **W Vill**	22
Emmett O'Lunney's | **W 50s**	16
Fat Cat | **W Vill**	19
Heathers | **E Vill**	19
Hog Pit | **Chelsea**	17
Huckleberry | **W'burg**	22
Levee | **W'burg**	19
Lion's Head Tavern | **W 100s**	15
Lounge 47 | **LIC**	20
miniBar | **Carroll Gdns**	20
Obivia | **L Italy**	24
Perdition | **W 40s**	20
Rebar | **Dumbo**	21
NEW 675 Bar | **Meatpacking**	-
Soho House | **Meatpacking**	24
Solas | **E Vill**	19
St. Dymphna's | **E Vill**	20
Tap a Keg | **W 100s**	10
Tea Lounge | **Park Slope**	20
Tom & Jerry's | **NoHo**	21
Total Wine | **Park Slope**	25
V Bar | **G Vill**	26
Wogies | **G Vill**	21
World Bar | **E 40s**	23
Zombie Hut | **Carroll Gdns**	21

BOCCE BALL

Floyd, NY | **Bklyn Hts**	22
🗹 Union Hall | **Park Slope**	24

BOWLING

Bowlmor Lanes | **G Vill**	22
NEW Brooklyn Bowl | **W'burg**	-
NEW Frames | **W 40s**	-

Gutter | **Greenpt**	24
Harlem Lanes | **Harlem**	20
☒ **NEW** Lucky Strike Lanes | **W 40s**	21
300 New York | **Chelsea**	19

DARTS

Ace Bar | **E Vill**	21
An Béal Bocht | **Bronx**	21
Angry Wade's | **Cobble Hill**	14
Back Page | **E 80s**	18
Barcelona Bar | **W 50s**	21
Bar Coastal | **E 70s**	14
Bar East | **E 90s**	13
Barfly | **Gramercy**	16
Barrow St. Ale | **G Vill**	18
Beer Garden | **SI**	17
Biddy's | **E 90s**	22
Billymark's West | **Chelsea**	15
Blackstone's | **E 50s**	17
Blarney Stone | **Chelsea**	14
Bleecker St. Bar | **NoHo**	18
Blondies | **E 90s**	19
Boss Tweed's | **LES**	17
Brazen Head | **Boerum Hill**	20
Broadway Dive | **W 100s**	15
Brooklyn Ale | **W'burg**	18
Bull McCabe's | **E Vill**	17
Bull's Head | **Gramercy**	18
Cheap Shots | **E Vill**	19
Cherry Tree | **Park Slope**	16
Coyote Ugly | **E Vill**	13
Dakota Roadhse. | **Financial**	15
Danny & Eddie's | **E 80s**	14
David Copperfield | **E 70s**	17
Desmond's Tavern | **Murray Hill**	11
Dive Bar | **W 90s**	18
Dram Shop | **Park Slope**	–
Duke's | **E Vill**	18
Eamonn's | **Bklyn Hts**	14
Edge | **E Vill**	19
Fat Black Pussycat | **G Vill**	17
Fiddlesticks | **G Vill**	18
Finnerty's | **E Vill**	10
Fitzgerald's | **Murray Hill**	16
Flannery's | **Chelsea**	18
Gaf Bar | **multi.**	22
Galway Hooker | **Murray Hill**	18
Gate | **Park Slope**	22
George Keeley's | **W 80s**	23
Grassroots | **E Vill**	19
GYM Sportsbar | **Chelsea**	19
Hook & Ladder | **Murray Hill**	13
John Street B&G | **Financial**	16
Josie Wood's | **G Vill**	14
Kettle of Fish | **G Vill**	21

Lansdowne Rd. | **W 40s**	21
Lion's Head Tavern | **W 100s**	15
Loki | **Park Slope**	17
MacDougal St. Ale | **G Vill**	18
McAleer's Pub | **W 80s**	15
McSwiggan's | **Gramercy**	12
Molly Pitcher's | **E 80s**	21
M1-5 Bar | **TriBeCa**	17
Moonshine | **Red Hook**	19
O'Connell's | **W 100s**	16
O'Flaherty's Ale | **W 40s**	18
169 Bar | **LES**	22
Overlook Lounge | **E 40s**	17
Pacific Standard | **Boerum Hill**	21
Paddy Reilly's | **Murray Hill**	20
Patriot Saloon | **TriBeCa**	14
Pinch B&G | **G Vill**	19
Puffy's | **TriBeCa**	19
Ryan's Daughter | **E 80s**	19
Ship of Fools | **E 80s**	16
Southpaw | **Park Slope**	22
Stanton Public | **LES**	21
Stout | **Garment**	21
Tap a Keg | **W 100s**	10
1020 Bar | **W 100s**	16
T.G. Whitney's | **E 50s**	16
Thirsty Scholar | **E Vill**	17
Turkey's Nest | **W'burg**	16
Underground Lounge | **W 100s**	18
Union Pool | **W'burg**	20
Walter's Bar | **Garment**	17
Wicked Monk | **Bay Ridge**	18
Zablozki's | **W'burg**	22

FOOSBALL

Apt. 138 | **Cobble Hill**	19
Back Page | **E 80s**	18
Bar East | **E 90s**	13
Bar 4 | **Park Slope**	20
B-Side | **E Vill**	17
Dakota Roadhse. | **Financial**	15
Down the Hatch | **G Vill**	16
East River | **W'burg**	20
Fat Cat | **W Vill**	19
Finnerty's | **E Vill**	10
Freddy's | **Prospect Hts**	18
Hog Pit | **Chelsea**	17
Hugs | **W'burg**	17
Jake's Dilemma | **W 80s**	16
Luca Bar/Lounge | **E Vill**	21
Matchless | **Greenpt**	21
M1-5 Bar | **TriBeCa**	17
Off the Wagon | **G Vill**	17
Parkside | **LES**	18
Royal Oak | **W'burg**	20

SPECIAL APPEALS

NEW 675 Bar | **Meatpacking**	–
Soho House | **Meatpacking**	24
Spike Hill | **W'burg**	22

PINBALL

Ace Bar | **E Vill**	21
Bar Carrera | **E Vill**	23
Boat | **Boerum Hill**	20
Boiler Room | **E Vill**	17
Buttermilk | **Park Slope**	23
Daddy's | **W'burg**	19
Double Down | **E Vill**	17
Dugout | **W Vill**	16
Easternbloc | **E Vill**	22
Enid's | **Greenpt**	19
Fontana's | **LES**	19
NEW Frames | **W 40s**	–
Hi-Fi | **E Vill**	21
Irish Rogue | **W 40s**	19
Kettle of Fish | **G Vill**	21
Levee | **W'burg**	19
Lucy's | **E Vill**	19
Max Fish | **LES**	17
Motor City | **LES**	18
Mug's Ale | **W'burg**	25
Otto's Shrunken | **E Vill**	21
Rawhide | **Chelsea**	12
Rehab | **E Vill**	17
7B | **E Vill**	19
Sherwood | **Boerum Hill**	23
Sixth Ward | **LES**	22
Southpaw | **Park Slope**	22
Spike Hill | **W'burg**	22
Supreme Trading | **W'burg**	23
Zablozki's | **W'burg**	22

PING-PONG

Fat Cat | **W Vill**	19
☑ Frying Pan | **Chelsea**	–
Iona | **W'burg**	21
Slate | **Flatiron**	21
☑ Water Taxi Beach | **Seaport**	22

POOL HALLS

Amsterdam Billiards | **E Vill**	17
Fat Cat | **W Vill**	19
Pressure | **G Vill**	18
Slate | **Flatiron**	21
Soho Billiards | **NoHo**	15
Tropical 128 | **L Italy**	19

POOL TABLES
(See also Pool Halls)

Abbey | **W'burg**	21
Ace Bar | **E Vill**	21
Aces & Eights | **E 80s**	15

Alligator | **W'burg**	20
American Trash | **E 70s**	13
Angry Wade's | **Cobble Hill**	14
Antarctica | **SoHo**	17
Apt. 138 | **Cobble Hill**	19
Arlo & Esme | **E Vill**	21
Back Page | **E 80s**	18
Barcade | **W'burg**	24
Bar East | **E 90s**	13
Barfly | **Gramercy**	16
Barracuda | **Chelsea**	19
Barrow St. Ale | **G Vill**	18
BB&R | **E 80s**	18
Billymark's West | **Chelsea**	15
Blackstone's | **E 50s**	17
NEW Bleecker Heights | **W Vill**	–
Bleecker St. Bar | **NoHo**	18
Blondies | **multi.**	19
Blue & Gold | **E Vill**	18
Blue Donkey Bar | **W 80s**	18
NEW Blue Ruin | **Garment**	–
Boiler Room | **E Vill**	17
Boss Tweed's | **LES**	17
Bourbon St. | **W 70s**	15
Brooklyn Ale | **W'burg**	18
☑ Brooklyn Inn | **Boerum Hill**	27
☑ Brooklyn Social | **Carroll Gdns**	25
B61 | **Carroll Gdns**	24
Bull McCabe's | **E Vill**	17
Bull's Head | **Gramercy**	18
Cargo Café | **SI**	20
Cherry Tavern | **E Vill**	14
Citibar | **E 70s**	18
Crash Mansion | **LES**	15
Creek & the Cave | **LIC**	19
Dakota Roadhse. | **Financial**	15
Danny & Eddie's | **E 80s**	14
Dewey's Flatiron | **Flatiron**	14
Dive Bar | **W 90s**	18
Doc Holliday's | **E Vill**	15
Doc Watson's | **E 70s**	17
Double Down | **E Vill**	17
Dram Shop | **Park Slope**	–
Dugout | **W Vill**	16
Duke's | **E Vill**	18
Dusk | **Chelsea**	21
Eagle | **Chelsea**	22
East End Tav. | **E 80s**	16
East River | **W'burg**	20
Edge | **E Vill**	19
1849 | **G Vill**	17
Europa | **Greenpt**	17
Failte | **Murray Hill**	17
Fat Black Pussycat | **G Vill**	17

Fiddlesticks	G Vill	18
Finnerty's	E Vill	10
NEW 508 Sports	Garment	-
Fontana's	LES	19
40c	E Vill	18
40/40	Flatiron	21
Galway Hooker	Murray Hill	18
Ginger's	Park Slope	16
GYM Sportsbar	Chelsea	19
Hangar Bar	W Vill	13
Hank's	Boerum Hill	20
Henrietta Hudson	W Vill	18
Hi-Fi	E Vill	21
Hogs & Heifers	Meatpacking	16
Hook & Ladder	Murray Hill	13
Hudson Hotel	W 50s	24
Irish Rogue	W 40s	19
Jack Russell's	E 80s	19
Jake's Dilemma	W 80s	16
Joe's Bar	E Vill	20
John Street B&G	Financial	16
Josie Wood's	G Vill	14
Kabin	E Vill	16
Lansdowne Rd.	W 40s	21
Latitude	W 40s	17
Levee	W'burg	19
Living Rm. Lounge	Sunset Pk	22
Loki	Park Slope	17
Lucky Jack's	LES	20
Z NEW Lucky Strike Lanes	W 40s	21
Lucy's	E Vill	19
MacDougal St. Ale	G Vill	18
Maker's	Murray Hill	13
Matchless	Greenpt	21
Max Fish	LES	17
McSwiggan's	Gramercy	12
Metropolitan	W'burg	19
Milady's	SoHo	13
M1-5 Bar	TriBeCa	17
Moonshine	Red Hook	19
No Idea	Flatiron	17
Nowhere	E Vill	18
O'Flaherty's Ale	W 40s	18
O'Flanagan's	E 60s	15
119 Bar	Gramercy	16
169 Bar	LES	22
Overlook Lounge	E 40s	17
Parkside	LES	18
Park Slope Ale	Park Slope	18
Patriot Saloon	TriBeCa	14
Peter Dillon's	E 40s	16
Phoenix	E Vill	20
Pieces	G Vill	14
Playwright	Garment	18

Plug Uglies	Gramercy	17
Pop Burger	Meatpacking	20
Prohibition	W 80s	21
Raccoon Lodge	Financial	15
Rawhide	Chelsea	12
Reservoir Bar	G Vill	17
Z Rose Bar	Gramercy	23
Z Rusty Knot	W Vill	21
Ryan's Daughter	E 80s	19
Ship of Fools	E 80s	16
NEW 675 Bar	Meatpacking	-
Sixth Ward	LES	22
Skinny	LES	16
Slaughtered Lamb	G Vill	17
Soho House	Meatpacking	24
Sophie's	E Vill	22
Southpaw	Park Slope	22
Stillwater	E Vill	20
Stoned Crow	G Vill	19
Stonewall Inn	G Vill	20
Stout	Garment	21
Superfine	Dumbo	24
Supreme Trading	W'burg	23
Tap a Keg	W 100s	10
1020 Bar	W 100s	16
THOR Lobby Bar	LES	20
Trash	W'burg	18
Tribeca Tavern	TriBeCa	18
Turkey's Nest	W'burg	16
Walter's Bar	Garment	17
Water St. Bar	Dumbo	20
Webster Hall	E Vill	19
Welcome/Johnsons	LES	18
Whiskey Park	W 50s	20
Whiskey Ward	LES	19
Wicked Monk	Bay Ridge	18
Wicked Willy's	G Vill	18
Zablozki's	W'burg	22

SKEE-BALL

Ace Bar	E Vill	21
Crocodile Lounge	E Vill	19
Dave & Buster's	W 40s	21
Hugs	W'burg	17

TRIVIA NIGHTS

Baker Street	E 60s	18
Black Rabbit	Greenpt	-
Cheap Shots	E Vill	19
Double Down	E Vill	17
Duke's	Murray Hill	18
Excelsior	Park Slope	19
Flight 151	Chelsea	15
Henrietta Hudson	W Vill	18
Iggy's	multi.	17

Johnny Foxes | **E 80s** 16
King's Head | **E Vill** 14
Last Exit | **Cobble Hill** 20
Minton's | **Harlem** 23
Otto's Shrunken | **E Vill** 21
Pete's Candy | **W'burg** 23
Professor Thom's | **E Vill** 19
Skinny | **LES** 16
Soft Spot | **W'burg** -
Stonewall Inn | **G Vill** 20
Tortilla Flats | **W Vill** 19
Twelve | **Murray Hill** 16

VIDEO GAMES

Abbey | **W'burg** 21
Ace Bar | **E Vill** 21
Ace of Clubs | **NoHo** 19
Aces & Eights | **E 80s** 15
Alligator | **W'burg** 20
American Trash | **E 70s** 13
Amsterdam Billiards | **E Vill** 17
Apt. 138 | **Cobble Hill** 19
Arlo & Esme | **E Vill** 21
Back Page | **E 80s** 18
Barcade | **W'burg** 24
Barcelona Bar | **W 50s** 21
Bar Coastal | **E 70s** 14
Bar East | **E 90s** 13
Barfly | **Gramercy** 16
Bar 4 | **Park Slope** 20
Bar None | **E Vill** 11
Barrow St. Ale | **G Vill** 18
BB&R | **E 80s** 18
Becky's | **E 60s** 18
Beer Garden | **SI** 17
Big Easy | **E 90s** 13
Big Nose Kate's | **SI** 14
Billymark's West | **Chelsea** 15
Black Bear | **Gramercy** 17
Blackstone's | **E 50s** 17
Blarney Stone | **Chelsea** 14
NEW Bleecker Heights | **W Vill** -
Bleecker St. Bar | **NoHo** 18
Blue Donkey Bar | **W 80s** 18
Boat | **Boerum Hill** 20
Bohemian Hall | **Astoria** 25
Boiler Room | **E Vill** 17
Boss Tweed's | **LES** 17
Bourbon St. | **W 70s** 15
Broadway Dive | **W 100s** 15
Z Brother Jimmy's | **E 70s** 17
Bull's Head | **Gramercy** 18
Bushwick Country | **W'burg** 18
Buttermilk | **Park Slope** 23
Cheap Shots | **E Vill** 19

Chelsea Brewing | **Chelsea** 18
Cherry Tavern | **E Vill** 14
Cherry Tree | **Park Slope** 16
Citibar | **E 70s** 18
Coyote Ugly | **E Vill** 13
Crash Mansion | **LES** 15
Crocodile Lounge | **E Vill** 19
Daddy's | **W'burg** 19
Dakota Roadhse. | **Financial** 15
Danny & Eddie's | **E 80s** 14
Dave & Buster's | **W 40s** 21
David Copperfield | **E 70s** 17
Z d.b.a. | **W'burg** 22
Dead Poet | **W 80s** 20
Desmond's Tavern | **Murray Hill** 11
Ding Dong Lounge | **W 100s** 18
Dive Bar | **W 90s** 18
Doc Holliday's | **E Vill** 15
Doc Watson's | **E 70s** 17
Donovan's | **Woodside** 20
Double Down | **E Vill** 17
Down the Hatch | **G Vill** 16
Dublin House | **W 70s** 16
Dugout | **W Vill** 16
Duke's | **E Vill** 18
Duplex | **G Vill** 19
Eagle | **Chelsea** 22
East End Tav. | **E 80s** 16
East River | **W'burg** 20
1849 | **G Vill** 17
Enid's | **Greenpt** 19
ESPN Zone | **W 40s** 18
Europa | **Greenpt** 17
Failte | **Murray Hill** 17
Fat Black Pussycat | **G Vill** 17
Firehouse | **W 80s** 16
First Edition | **Bayside** 15
Flight 151 | **Chelsea** 15
Fourth Ave. Pub | **Park Slope** 18
NEW Frames | **W 40s** -
Freddy's | **Prospect Hts** 18
Gaf Bar | **multi.** 22
George Keeley's | **W 80s** 23
Ginger's | **Park Slope** 16
Greenwich Treehouse | **W Vill** 19
GYM Sportsbar | **Chelsea** 19
Hangar Bar | **W Vill** 13
Hank's | **Boerum Hill** 20
Harlem Lanes | **Harlem** 20
Hi-Fi | **E Vill** 21
Hog Pit | **Chelsea** 17
Hogs & Heifers | **Meatpacking** 16
Home Sweet Home | **LES** 19
Hook & Ladder | **Murray Hill** 13

Hop Devil Grill | **E Vill**	18
Hugs | **W'burg**	17
Iggy's | **multi.**	17
Iona | **W'burg**	21
Jack Russell's | **E 80s**	19
Jake's Dilemma | **W 80s**	16
Jekyll & Hyde | **G Vill**	17
Jeremy's Ale | **Financial**	16
Jimmy's Corner | **W 40s**	25
Johnny Foxes | **E 80s**	16
Johnny's Bar | **W Vill**	20
John Street B&G | **Financial**	16
Josie Wood's | **G Vill**	14
Julius | **G Vill**	12
Kabin | **E Vill**	16
Kenny's Castaways | **G Vill**	14
Kettle of Fish | **G Vill**	21
Lakeside Lounge | **E Vill**	19
Levee | **W'burg**	19
Library | **E Vill**	20
Lion's Head Tavern | **W 100s**	15
Luca Bar/Lounge | **E Vill**	21
Lucy's | **E Vill**	19
Maker's | **Murray Hill**	13
McSwiggan's | **Gramercy**	12
Metropolitan | **W'burg**	19
Milady's | **SoHo**	13
Moe's | **Ft Greene**	22
M1-5 Bar | **TriBeCa**	17
Moonshine | **Red Hook**	19
Motor City | **LES**	18
Nevada Smith's | **E Vill**	16
Nowhere | **E Vill**	18
O'Connell's | **W 100s**	16
Otto's Shrunken | **E Vill**	21
Paris | **Seaport**	19
Parkside | **LES**	18
Patriot Saloon | **TriBeCa**	14
Peculier Pub | **G Vill**	20
Peggy O'Neill's | **Coney Is**	18
Peter McManus | **Chelsea**	19
Peter's | **W 60s**	17
Phoenix | **E Vill**	20
Pinch B&G | **G Vill**	19
Pine Tree Lodge | **Murray Hill**	24
Pussycat Lounge | **Financial**	18
Raccoon Lodge | **Financial**	15
Rathbones | **E 80s**	18
Rawhide | **Chelsea**	12
Reservoir Bar | **G Vill**	17
Rudy's | **W 40s**	19
Ryan's Daughter | **E 80s**	19
7B | **E Vill**	19
Ship of Fools | **E 80s**	16

Sidecar | **Park Slope**	20
NEW 675 Bar | **Meatpacking**	-
Skinny | **LES**	16
Slaughtered Lamb | **G Vill**	17
Sophie's | **E Vill**	22
Southpaw | **Park Slope**	22
Sputnik | **Clinton Hill**	18
Stillwater | **E Vill**	20
St. Marks Ale | **E Vill**	17
Stoned Crow | **G Vill**	19
NEW Stumble Inn | **E 70s**	15
Subway Inn | **E 60s**	17
Swig | **E 80s**	16
Tap a Keg | **W 100s**	10
Tea Lounge | **multi.**	20
T.G. Whitney's | **E 50s**	16
Tribeca Tavern | **TriBeCa**	18
Turkey's Nest | **W'burg**	16
Ty's | **W Vill**	18
Underground Lounge | **W 100s**	18
View Bar | **Chelsea**	16
Village Pourhouse | **W 100s**	18
Watering Hole | **Gramercy**	18
Water St. Bar | **Dumbo**	20
Welcome/Johnsons | **LES**	18
Wharf Bar & Grill | **Murray Hill**	18
Whiskey River | **Murray Hill**	18
Wicked Monk | **Bay Ridge**	18
Wicked Willy's | **G Vill**	18
Yankee Tavern | **Bronx**	17
Zablozki's | **W'burg**	22

GAY

(See also Lesbian; * certain nights only)

B&S NY | **W Vill**	14
Barracuda | **Chelsea**	19
Barrage | **W 40s**	20
B Bar* | **NoHo**	18
Boiler Room | **E Vill**	17
Cock | **E Vill**	18
NEW DTOX | **E Vill**	18
Dugout | **W Vill**	16
Eagle | **Chelsea**	22
Easternbloc | **E Vill**	22
Element* | **LES**	22
Escuelita | **Garment**	17
NEW Evolve | **E 50s**	22
Excelsior | **Park Slope**	19
g | **Chelsea**	20
GYM Sportsbar | **Chelsea**	19
Hangar Bar | **W Vill**	13
Hiro* | **Chelsea**	22
HK Lounge | **Garment**	20
NEW Hose | **E Vill**	-
Julius | **G Vill**	12

NEW Lavish Lounge | **Astoria**	–
Lips | **W Vill**	20
Marie's Crisis | **W Vill**	22
Metropolitan | **W'burg**	19
Monster | **G Vill**	16
Mr. Black | **Garment**	20
Ninth Ave. Saloon | **W 40s**	20
Nowhere | **E Vill**	18
Phoenix | **E Vill**	20
Pieces | **G Vill**	14
Posh | **W 50s**	20
Pyramid* | **E Vill**	18
Rawhide | **Chelsea**	12
Ritz | **W 40s**	20
Rush | **Chelsea**	20
Secret | **Chelsea**	20
Splash | **Flatiron**	20
Stonewall Inn | **G Vill**	20
Suite | **W 100s**	16
Therapy | **W 50s**	24
Townhouse | **E 50s**	22
Ty's | **W Vill**	18
Uncle Charlie's | **E 40s**	21
Urge | **E Vill**	19
View Bar | **Chelsea**	16
VIP Club* | **Flatiron**	27
Vlada | **W 50s**	23
xes lounge | **Chelsea**	22

HAPPY HOUR

Abilene | **Carroll Gdns**	20
Agozar! | **NoHo**	18
Angry Wade's | **Cobble Hill**	14
Back Page | **E 80s**	18
Baker Street | **E 60s**	18
Bar Coastal | **E 70s**	14
Bar None | **E Vill**	11
Barrage | **W 40s**	20
Barrow St. Ale | **G Vill**	18
Big Easy | **E 90s**	13
Bleecker St. Bar | **NoHo**	18
Blondies | **W 70s**	19
Bob | **LES**	19
Boss Tweed's | **LES**	17
Botanica | **NoLita**	15
Bounce | **E 70s**	19
Bourbon St. | **W 70s**	15
Boxcar Lounge | **E Vill**	18
Brazen Head | **Boerum Hill**	20
Z Brother Jimmy's | **multi.**	17
Bull McCabe's | **E Vill**	17
Bull's Head | **Gramercy**	18
Cafe Deville | **E Vill**	21
Calico Jack's | **E 40s**	15

Cloister Cafe | **E Vill**	23
Company | **E Vill**	20
Continental | **E Vill**	16
David Copperfield | **E 70s**	17
Dead Poet | **W 80s**	20
Doc Holliday's | **E Vill**	15
Down the Hatch | **G Vill**	16
Dugout | **W Vill**	16
Enid's | **Greenpt**	19
Epstein's Bar | **LES**	14
Fat Black Pussycat | **G Vill**	17
First Edition | **Bayside**	15
Five Spot | **Ft Greene**	17
Flight 151 | **Chelsea**	15
420 | **W 80s**	15
g | **Chelsea**	20
Gate | **Park Slope**	22
Gatsby's | **NoLita**	13
George Keeley's | **W 80s**	23
Gin Mill | **W 80s**	16
Hairy Monk | **Murray Hill**	17
Heights B&G | **W 100s**	18
Iggy's | **E 70s**	17
Jake's Dilemma | **W 80s**	16
Jameson's | **E 50s**	16
Johnny's Bar | **W Vill**	20
John Street B&G | **Financial**	16
Karma | **E Vill**	21
Kenny's Castaways | **G Vill**	14
Lakeside Lounge | **E Vill**	19
La Linea | **E Vill**	18
Lit | **E Vill**	19
Local 138 | **LES**	19
Lolita | **LES**	19
Mad River | **E 80s**	14
Manitoba's | **E Vill**	21
Metro 53 | **E 50s**	16
Metropolitan | **W'burg**	19
Nancy Whiskey | **TriBeCa**	17
Off the Wagon | **G Vill**	17
O'Flaherty's Ale | **W 40s**	18
Paddy Reilly's | **Murray Hill**	20
Parlour | **W 80s**	17
Pieces | **G Vill**	14
Plug Uglies | **Gramercy**	17
Posh | **W 50s**	20
Rawhide | **Chelsea**	12
Riviera | **W Vill**	14
Russian Vodka Rm. | **W 50s**	21
Sapphire | **LES**	18
7B | **E Vill**	19
Shade | **G Vill**	26
Ship of Fools | **E 80s**	16
Sidewalk | **E Vill**	19

Menus, photos, voting and more – free at ZAGAT.com

Sláinte | **NoHo**	18
Splash | **Flatiron**	20
St. Dymphna's | **E Vill**	20
St. Marks Ale | **E Vill**	17
Superfine | **Dumbo**	24
Tap a Keg | **W 100s**	10
T.G. Whitney's | **E 50s**	16
Thirsty Scholar | **E Vill**	17
Tortilla Flats | **W Vill**	19
Town Tavern | **G Vill**	15
Turtle Bay | **E 50s**	15
Vertigo | **Murray Hill**	19
View Bar | **Chelsea**	16
WCOU | **E Vill**	19
Welcome/Johnsons | **LES**	18
WXOU | **W Vill**	21
xes lounge | **Chelsea**	22

HOOKAHS

Babel Lounge | **E Vill**	21
Cloister Cafe | **E Vill**	23
Karma | **E Vill**	21
Katra | **LES**	18
Kush | **LES**	22
La Caverna | **LES**	18
Moomia Lounge | **L Italy**	18

HOTEL BARS

Algonquin Hotel	
Algonquin | **W 40s**	23
☑ Oak Room | **W 40s**	25
Beekman Tower Hotel	
Top of the Tower | **E 40s**	24
Bowery Hotel	
☑ Bowery Hotel Bar | **E Vill**	23
Bryant Park Hotel	
Cellar Bar | **W 40s**	22
Carlton Hotel	
Country Champ. Lounge | **Murray Hill**	25
Carlyle Hotel	
☑ Bemelmans | **E 70s**	27
☑ Cafe Carlyle | **E 70s**	26
Chelsea Hotel	
Star Lounge | **Chelsea**	19
Dream Hotel	
Ava Lounge | **W 50s**	24
D'Or | **W 50s**	21
Rm. Fifty5 | **W 50s**	21
Serafina | **W 50s**	20
Edison Hotel	
Rum House | **W 40s**	14
Elysée Hotel	
☑ Monkey Bar | **E 50s**	-

Empire Hotel	
Empire Hotel Bar | **W 60s**	19
☑ NEW Empire Hotel Roof | **W 60s**	24
Flatotel	
Moda Outdoors | **W 50s**	20
Four Seasons Hotel	
☑ Four Seasons Hotel Bar | **E 50s**	25
Gansevoort Hotel	
Ono | **Meatpacking**	24
☑ Plunge | **Meatpacking**	25
Grace Hotel	
Grace Hotel Bar | **W 40s**	18
Gramercy Park Hotel	
Jade Bar | **Gramercy**	25
☑ Rose Bar | **Gramercy**	23
Hotel 41 at Times Sq.	
Bar 41 | **W 40s**	19
Hotel on Rivington, The	
105 Riv | **LES**	22
THOR Lobby Bar | **LES**	20
Hudson Hotel	
Hudson Hotel | **W 50s**	24
Inn at Irving Pl.	
Cibar | **Gramercy**	22
Le Parker Meridien	
NEW Knave | **W 50s**	22
Library Hotel	
Bookmarks | **E 40s**	24
Loews Regency Hotel	
Feinstein's at Loews | **E 60s**	23
Regency Library Bar | **E 60s**	25
Mandarin Oriental Hotel	
MO Bar | **W 60s**	23
Mansfield Hotel	
M Bar | **W 40s**	20
Marcel Hotel	
☑ 'inoteca | **Murray Hill**	24
Maritime Hotel	
Cabanas | **Chelsea**	22
Hiro | **Chelsea**	22
La Bottega | **Chelsea**	21
Marriott Marquis Hotel	
View Lounge | **W 40s**	24
Mercer Hotel	
Mercer Bar | **SoHo**	23
SubMercer | **SoHo**	24
Metro Hotel	
Metro Grill Roof | **Garment**	20
Morgans Hotel	
☑ Asia de Cuba | **Murray Hill**	24
Morgans Bar | **Murray Hill**	22
Night Hotel	
Night Hotel Bar | **W 40s**	18

NY Palace Hotel		
Gilt	**E 50s**	21
Paramount Hotel		
Paramount	**W 40s**	23
Peninsula Hotel		
Salon de Ning	**W 50s**	26
Plaza Athénée Hotel		
Plaza Athénée	**E 60s**	24
Plaza Hotel		
Champagne Bar/Plaza	**W 50s**	25
☑ Oak Bar	**W 50s**	24
Rose Club	**W 50s**	23
Pod Hotel		
Le Bateau Ivre	**E 50s**	24
Radisson Lexington Hotel		
LQ	**E 40s**	21
Ravel Hotel		
NEW Ravel Rooftop	**LIC**	–
Renaissance Hotel 57		
Opia	**E 50s**	22
Ritz-Carlton Central Park		
☑ Ritz-Carlton Star	**W 50s**	24
Roosevelt Hotel		
NEW mad46	**E 40s**	21
Royalton Hotel		
Bar 44	**W 40s**	21
Shelburne Murray Hill Hotel		
Rare View	**Murray Hill**	22
6 Columbus Hotel		
Blue Ribbon Sushi	**W 50s**	22
60 Thompson Hotel		
Thom Bar	**SoHo**	24
SoHo Grand Hotel		
Grand Bar	**SoHo**	25
Standard Hotel		
NEW Standard Hotel	**Meatpacking**	–
Stay Hotel		
Aspen	**W 50s**	21
St. Regis Hotel		
☑ King Cole Bar	**E 50s**	28
Thompson LES Hotel		
NEW Above Allen	**LES**	22
NEW Shang Bar	**LES**	–
Time Hotel		
Inc	**W 40s**	22
Serafina	**W 40s**	20
Tribeca Grand Hotel		
Church Lounge	**TriBeCa**	24
Waldorf-Astoria		
Bull and Bear	**E 40s**	21
W Court Hotel		
Wet Bar	**Murray Hill**	21
W New York Hotel		
Whiskey Blue	**E 40s**	23
W Times Square Hotel		
Blue Fin	**W 40s**	23
Whiskey	**W 40s**	20
W Times Sq.	**W 40s**	23
W Union Square Hotel		
Underbar	**Union Sq**	21
☑ W Union Sq.	**Union Sq**	22

JAZZ CLUBS

Arthur's Tavern	**W Vill**	22
B. B. King Blues	**W 40s**	21
Birdland	**W 40s**	23
☑ Blue Note	**G Vill**	23
Cleopatra's Needle	**W 90s**	18
☑ Dizzy's Club	**W 60s**	25
Fat Cat	**W Vill**	19
55 Bar	**G Vill**	22
Iridium	**W 50s**	21
☑ Jazz Standard	**Murray Hill**	26
☑ Lenox Lounge	**Harlem**	21
Louis 649	**E Vill**	26
Minton's	**Harlem**	23
Smalls	**W Vill**	24
Smoke	**W 100s**	22
St. Nick's Jazz Pub	**Harlem**	20
Swing 46	**W 40s**	21
Village Vanguard	**W Vill**	24
Zinc Bar	**G Vill**	22

JUKEBOXES

Abbey	**W'burg**	21
Abbey Pub	**W 100s**	19
Ace Bar	**E Vill**	21
Aces & Eights	**multi.**	15
Alligator	**W'burg**	20
American Trash	**E 70s**	13
NEW Amsterdam 106	**W 100s**	19
Angels & Kings	**E Vill**	19
Angry Wade's	**Cobble Hill**	14
Antarctica	**SoHo**	17
Apt. 138	**Cobble Hill**	19
Arlene's Grocery	**LES**	20
Art Bar	**W Vill**	20
Australian	**Garment**	20
Back Page	**E 80s**	18
B&S NY	**W Vill**	14
Banjo Jim's	**E Vill**	21
Barcelona Bar	**W 50s**	21
Bar East	**E 90s**	13
Barfly	**Gramercy**	16
Bar None	**E Vill**	11
Barrow St. Ale	**G Vill**	18
Bayard's Ale	**W Vill**	17
Becky's	**E 60s**	18
Beer Garden	**SI**	17

Biddy's | **E 90s**	22
Big Nose Kate's | **SI**	14
Billymark's West | **Chelsea**	15
Black Bear | **Gramercy**	17
Black Sheep | **Murray Hill**	15
Blackstone's | **E 50s**	17
Blarney Stone | **multi.**	14
NEW Bleecker Heights | **W Vill**	-
Blondies | **W 70s**	19
Blue & Gold | **E Vill**	18
Blue Donkey Bar | **W 80s**	18
NEW Blue Ruin | **Garment**	-
Boat | **Boerum Hill**	20
Bohemian Hall | **Astoria**	25
Boiler Room | **E Vill**	17
Boss Tweed's | **LES**	17
Bowery Wine Company | **E Vill**	20
Broadway Dive | **W 100s**	15
Brooklyn Ale | **W'burg**	18
Z Brooklyn Inn | **Boerum Hill**	27
Z Brooklyn Social | **Carroll Gdns**	25
Broome St. Bar | **SoHo**	16
B-Side | **E Vill**	17
B61 | **Carroll Gdns**	24
Bull McCabe's | **E Vill**	17
Bull's Head | **Gramercy**	18
Bushwick Country | **W'burg**	18
Buttermilk | **Park Slope**	23
Cargo Café | **SI**	20
Cheap Shots | **E Vill**	19
Cherry Tavern | **E Vill**	14
Coffee Shop | **Union Sq**	18
Coliseum Bar | **W 50s**	11
Common Ground | **E Vill**	19
Commonwealth | **Park Slope**	19
Connolly's | **multi.**	18
Continental | **E Vill**	16
Corner Bistro | **W Vill**	22
Coyote Ugly | **E Vill**	13
Croton Reservoir | **W 40s**	17
Cubby Hole | **W Vill**	20
Daddy's | **W'burg**	19
Dakota Roadhse. | **Financial**	15
Danny & Eddie's | **E 80s**	14
Dark Room | **LES**	18
David Copperfield | **E 70s**	17
Dead Poet | **W 80s**	20
Desmond's Tavern | **Murray Hill**	11
Dive Bar | **W 90s**	18
Dive 75 | **W 70s**	21
Doc Holliday's | **E Vill**	15
Doc Watson's | **E 70s**	17
Donovan's | **multi.**	20
Dorrian's | **E 80s**	16

Double Down | **E Vill**	17
Dram Shop | **Park Slope**	-
Drop Off Service | **E Vill**	20
Druids | **W 50s**	19
Dublin House | **W 70s**	16
Duff's | **W'burg**	19
Dugout | **W Vill**	16
Duke's | **E Vill**	18
Dusk | **Chelsea**	21
Eamonn's | **Bklyn Hts**	14
East River | **W'burg**	20
Edge | **E Vill**	19
1849 | **G Vill**	17
Essex Ale House | **LES**	20
Excelsior | **Park Slope**	19
Fat Baby | **LES**	19
Fat Black Pussycat | **G Vill**	17
Fat Cat | **W Vill**	19
Finnerty's | **E Vill**	10
Firehouse | **W 80s**	16
First Edition | **Bayside**	15
Fitzgerald's | **Murray Hill**	16
Flannery's | **Chelsea**	18
Flight 151 | **Chelsea**	15
Floyd, NY | **Bklyn Hts**	22
Fontana's | **LES**	19
Four-Faced Liar | **G Vill**	18
Gaf Bar | **multi.**	22
Gate | **Park Slope**	22
Genesis | **E 80s**	20
George Keeley's | **W 80s**	23
Z Ginger Man | **Murray Hill**	22
Ginger's | **Park Slope**	16
Grassroots | **E Vill**	19
Great Lakes | **Park Slope**	22
Greenwich Treehouse | **W Vill**	19
Hank's | **Boerum Hill**	20
Hi-Fi | **E Vill**	21
Hog Pit | **Chelsea**	17
Hogs & Heifers | **Meatpacking**	16
Holiday Cocktail | **E Vill**	18
Home Sweet Home | **LES**	19
Hook & Ladder | **Murray Hill**	13
Hop Devil Grill | **E Vill**	18
Iggy's | **multi.**	17
International Bar | **E Vill**	-
Jack Russell's | **E 80s**	19
Jake's Saloon | **multi.**	18
Jameson's | **E 50s**	16
Jeremy's Ale | **Financial**	16
Jimmy's Corner | **W 40s**	25
Joe's Bar | **E Vill**	20
Johnny's Bar | **W Vill**	20
John Street B&G | **Financial**	16

Joshua Tree	**multi.**	15	Patriot Saloon	**TriBeCa**	14
Josie Wood's	**G Vill**	14	Peculier Pub	**G Vill**	20
Julius	**G Vill**	12	Peggy O'Neill's	**Coney Is**	18
Kenny's Castaways	**G Vill**	14	Peter Dillon's	**E 40s**	16
Kettle of Fish	**G Vill**	21	Peter McManus	**Chelsea**	19
King's Head	**E Vill**	14	Peter's	**W 60s**	17
Kinsale	**E 90s**	20	Pete's Tavern	**Gramercy**	21
La Bottega	**Chelsea**	21	Phoenix	**E Vill**	20
Lakeside Lounge	**E Vill**	19	Pine Tree Lodge	**Murray Hill**	24
Lansdowne Rd.	**W 40s**	21	Pink Pony	**LES**	19
Lederhosen	**W Vill**	21	P.J. Carney's	**W 50s**	18
☑ Lenox Lounge	**Harlem**	21	P.J. Clarke's	**multi.**	20
Levee	**W'burg**	19	Playwright	**W 40s**	18
Library	**E Vill**	20	Plug Uglies	**Gramercy**	17
Lion's Head Tavern	**W 100s**	15	Professor Thom's	**E Vill**	19
Living Rm. Lounge	**Sunset Pk**	22	Raccoon Lodge	**Financial**	15
Loki	**Park Slope**	17	Rawhide	**Chelsea**	12
Lucky 13	**Park Slope**	17	Red Sky	**Murray Hill**	17
Lucy's	**E Vill**	19	Reservoir Bar	**G Vill**	17
MacDougal St. Ale	**G Vill**	18	Riviera	**W Vill**	14
Magician	**LES**	16	Royale	**E Vill**	20
Maker's	**Murray Hill**	13	Rudy's	**W 40s**	19
Malachy's	**W 70s**	14	Rum House	**W 40s**	14
Mama's Bar	**E Vill**	22	☑ Rusty Knot	**W Vill**	21
Manitoba's	**E Vill**	21	Ryan's Daughter	**E 80s**	19
Mars Bar	**E Vill**	19	7B	**E Vill**	19
Marshall Stack	**LES**	22	Sherwood	**Boerum Hill**	23
Max Fish	**LES**	17	Ship of Fools	**E 80s**	16
McAleer's Pub	**W 80s**	15	Sidecar	**Park Slope**	20
McCormack's	**Murray Hill**	19	Skinny	**LES**	16
McCoy's Bar	**W 50s**	17	Soda Bar	**Prospect Hts**	20
McGee's	**W 50s**	15	SoHo Room	**SoHo**	14
McSwiggan's	**Gramercy**	12	Sophie's	**E Vill**	22
Mercury Bar	**multi.**	16	Spike Hill	**W'burg**	22
Metropolitan	**W'burg**	19	Spring Lounge	**NoLita**	19
Milady's	**SoHo**	13	Spuyten Duyvil	**W'burg**	24
Molly Pitcher's	**E 80s**	21	Stanton Public	**LES**	21
Molly's	**Gramercy**	22	Stitch	**Garment**	17
Moonshine	**Red Hook**	19	St. Nick's Jazz Pub	**Harlem**	20
Mug's Ale	**W'burg**	25	Stone Creek	**Murray Hill**	19
Murphy & Gonzalez	**G Vill**	17	Stoned Crow	**G Vill**	19
Ninth Ave. Saloon	**W 40s**	20	Subway Inn	**E 60s**	17
No Idea	**Flatiron**	17	Sweet & Vicious	**NoLita**	17
Nowhere	**E Vill**	18	Sweet Paradise	**LES**	22
O'Connell's	**W 100s**	16	Swig	**E 80s**	16
O'Connor's	**Park Slope**	22	Tap a Keg	**W 100s**	10
Off the Wagon	**G Vill**	17	Teddy's	**W'burg**	23
O'Flaherty's Ale	**W 40s**	18	300 New York	**Chelsea**	19
Oliver's B&G	**G Vill**	17	Tom & Jerry's	**NoHo**	21
Paddy Reilly's	**Murray Hill**	20	Tonic East	**Murray Hill**	20
Paris	**Seaport**	19	Town Tavern	**G Vill**	15
Parkside	**LES**	18	Trailer Park	**Chelsea**	19
Patrick Conway's	**E 40s**	18	Trash	**W'burg**	18
Patrick Kavanagh's	**Murray Hill**	17	Tribeca Tavern	**TriBeCa**	18

Trinity Pub | **E 80s**	20
Triple Crown | **Chelsea**	18
Trophy | **W'burg**	19
Turkey's Nest | **W'burg**	16
Twelve | **Murray Hill**	16
Underground | **Murray Hill**	18
Underground Lounge | **W 100s**	18
Z Union Hall | **Park Slope**	24
Valhalla | **W 50s**	18
NEW Vintage Irving | **Gramercy**	21
Walter's Bar | **Garment**	17
Watering Hole | **Gramercy**	18
WCOU | **E Vill**	19
Welcome/Johnsons | **LES**	18
Wharf Bar & Grill | **Murray Hill**	18
Whiskey River | **Murray Hill**	18
Whiskey Ward | **LES**	19
Z White Horse | **W Vill**	20
Wicked Monk | **Bay Ridge**	18
Wicker Park | **E 80s**	18
Woody McHale's | **W Vill**	16
WXOU | **W Vill**	21
Yankee Tavern | **Bronx**	17

JURY DUTY

(Near Manhattan courthouses)

City Hall | **TriBeCa**	23
Dakota Roadhse. | **Financial**	15
John Street B&G | **Financial**	16
Mocca | **TriBeCa**	21
Raccoon Lodge | **Financial**	15
17 Murray | **Financial**	14

KARAOKE BARS

(Call to check nights, times and prices)

Karaoke One 7 | **Flatiron**	21
Sing Sing | **E Vill**	21
Winnie's | **Chinatown**	18

LESBIAN

(* Certain nights only; call ahead)

Angels & Kings* | **E Vill**	19
Cubby Hole | **W Vill**	20
Ginger's | **Park Slope**	16
Henrietta Hudson | **W Vill**	18
Metropolitan* | **W'burg**	19
Nowhere* | **E Vill**	18
NEW 249 Bar | **Park Slope**	-

LIVE ENTERTAINMENT

(See also Cabaret, Comedy Clubs, Drag Shows, Jazz Clubs, Karaoke Bars, Music Clubs, Piano Bars, Spoken Word, Strip Clubs)

Agozar! | Latin | **NoHo**	18
Alphabet Lounge | bands | **E Vill**	18
American Trash | bands | **E 70s**	13

Anyway Cafe | bands | **E Vill**	20
Baker Street | guitar | **E 60s**	18
Bar Nine | rock | **W 50s**	15
Bar on A | blues | **E Vill**	17
Bateaux NY | jazz | **Chelsea**	22
Z Bemelmans | piano | **E 70s**	27
Big Easy | bands | **E 90s**	13
Big Nose Kate's | bands | **SI**	14
Black & White | spoken word | **E Vill**	19
Blue Fin | jazz | **W 40s**	23
Z Blue Water Grill | jazz | **Union Sq**	23
Bohemian Hall | bands | **Astoria**	25
Bubble Lounge | bands | **TriBeCa**	22
Bull's Head | bands | **Gramercy**	18
Z Campbell Apt. | jazz | **E 40s**	25
Carnegie Club | swing | **W 50s**	24
NEW Casa La Femme | belly dancers | **W Vill**	-
Central Bar | rock | **E Vill**	19
Chez Josephine | jazz | **W 40s**	22
Connolly's | bands | **W 40s**	18
Continental | rock | **E Vill**	16
Desmond's Tavern | bands | **Murray Hill**	11
Doc Watson's | Irish | **E 70s**	17
Dos Caminos | jazz | **Murray Hill**	22
Eight Mile Creek | bands | **NoLita**	23
Flannery's | rock | **Chelsea**	18
Flor de Sol | flamenco/jazz | **TriBeCa**	23
Flûte | jazz | **multi.**	22
Garage | jazz | **G Vill**	21
Gonzalez y Gonzalez | Latin | **NoHo**	18
Gowanus Yacht | jazz | **Carroll Gdns**	23
Great Lakes | bands | **Park Slope**	22
Hook & Ladder | folk | **Murray Hill**	13
Houston's | jazz | **E 50s**	20
Iggy's | bands/karaoke | **E 70s**	17
Joshua Tree | karaoke | **W 40s**	15
Jules | jazz | **E Vill**	23
King's Head | rock | **E Vill**	14
Lava Gina | belly dancer | **E Vill**	23
Le Bateau Ivre | jazz | **E 50s**	24
Lit | karaoke | **E Vill**	19
L'Orange Bleue | Mid. Eastern | **SoHo**	21
Manitoba's | bands | **E Vill**	21
Merchants, NY | jazz | **E 60s**	18
Mustang Grill | karaoke | **E 80s**	16
Ñ | flamenco | **SoHo**	24
Nevada Smith's | karaoke | **E Vill**	16
O'Flaherty's Ale | rock | **W 40s**	18
One if by Land | piano | **G Vill**	26
Opal | bands | **E 50s**	17

Paddy Reilly's | Irish | **Murray Hill**	20
Parkside | spoken word | **LES**	18
Parlour | comedy | **W 80s**	17
Prohibition | R&B/soul | **W 80s**	21
Rue B | jazz | **E Vill**	22
Russian Vodka Rm. | jazz/piano | **W 50s**	21
Sidewalk | open mike | **E Vill**	19
St. Andrews | Celtic | **W 40s**	20
Superfine | comedy/fashion | **Dumbo**	24
Swift | Irish | **NoHo**	22
Tavern on the Green | piano | **W 60s**	22
Teddy's | bands | **W'burg**	23
T.G. Whitney's | karaoke | **E 50s**	16
Tin Lizzie | rock | **E 80s**	13
Walker's | jazz | **TriBeCa**	21

MATURE CROWDS

Algonquin | **W 40s**	23
Bar Masa | **W 60s**	23
NEW Beekman | **E 50s**	23
☑ Bemelmans | **E 70s**	27
Brasserie 8½ | **W 50s**	21
Bull and Bear | **E 40s**	21
☑ Cafe Carlyle | **E 70s**	26
Café des Artistes | **W 60s**	24
☑ Campbell Apt. | **E 40s**	25
Carnegie Club | **W 50s**	24
Champagne Bar/Plaza | **W 50s**	25
☑ **NEW** City Winery | **SoHo**	23
Club Macanudo | **E 60s**	24
Country Champ. Lounge | **Murray Hill**	25
☑ Daniel | **E 60s**	27
Del Posto | **Chelsea**	23
☑ Dizzy's Club | **W 60s**	25
Eleven Madison Pk. | **Flatiron**	25
Feinstein's at Loews | **E 60s**	23
☑ Four Seasons Bar | **E 50s**	26
Geisha | **E 60s**	22
Gilt | **E 50s**	21
☑ Gotham B&G | **G Vill**	25
☑ King Cole Bar | **E 50s**	28
NEW Knave | **W 50s**	22
Le Colonial | **E 50s**	21
Lexington Bar & Books | **E 70s**	21
M Bar | **W 40s**	20
Metropolitan Rm. | **Flatiron**	20
Morrell Wine Bar | **W 40s**	24
Nobu 57 | **W 50s**	25
☑ Oak Bar | **W 50s**	24
☑ Oak Room | **W 40s**	25
Palio Bar | **W 50s**	22
P.J. Clarke's | **E 50s**	20
Plaza Athénée | **E 60s**	24

☑ Rainbow Grill | **W 40s**	24
Tavern on the Green | **W 60s**	22
Top of the Tower | **E 40s**	24
Townhouse | **E 50s**	22
☑ 21 Club | **W 50s**	26
☑ Union Sq. Cafe | **Union Sq**	24
Village Vanguard | **W Vill**	24
World Bar | **E 40s**	23

MEAT MARKETS

Aspen | **Flatiron**	21
Automatic Slim's | **W Vill**	17
Bar 89 | **SoHo**	22
Bar 515 | **Murray Hill**	15
Barrage | **W 40s**	20
Bar 6 | **G Vill**	23
B Bar | **NoHo**	18
Belmont | **Gramercy**	16
Big Easy | **E 90s**	13
NEW Bijoux | **Meatpacking**	23
Bogart's | **Murray Hill**	14
Bounce | **E 70s**	19
Bourbon St. | **W 70s**	15
Branch | **E 50s**	17
☑ Brother Jimmy's | **multi.**	17
Bryant Park Grill | **W 40s**	22
Butter | **E Vill**	22
Cafeteria | **Chelsea**	19
☑ Cain Luxe | **Chelsea**	24
NEW Catch-22 | **Flatiron**	20
Church Lounge | **TriBeCa**	24
Cock | **E Vill**	18
Coffee Shop | **Union Sq**	18
NEW Country Club | **W Vill**	19
NEW Delicatessen | **SoHo**	19
Divine Bar | **W 50s**	22
Dorrian's | **E 80s**	16
Dos Caminos | **Murray Hill**	22
Duvet | **Flatiron**	20
Eagle | **Chelsea**	22
NEW Eden | **W 40s**	19
Elettaria | **G Vill**	24
El Rio Grande | **Murray Hill**	19
Forum | **E Vill**	18
Grand Bar | **SoHo**	25
GYM Sportsbar | **Chelsea**	19
Home | **Chelsea**	21
NEW Hose | **E Vill**	-
Houston's | **multi.**	20
Hudson Hotel | **W 50s**	24
Iguana | **W 50s**	18
Joshua Tree | **multi.**	15
Kiss & Fly | **Meatpacking**	20
NEW Lavish Lounge | **Astoria**	-
Libation | **LES**	18

Mad River	**E 80s**	14
McFadden's	**E 40s**	15
Mercer Bar	**SoHo**	23
Mr. Black	**Garment**	20
☑ NEW M2	**Chelsea**	20
Naked Lunch	**SoHo**	19
Nikki Midtown	**E 50s**	21
925 Café & Cocktails	**E 40s**	19
105 Riv	**LES**	22
Opal	**E 50s**	17
Park	**Chelsea**	21
Parlour	**W 80s**	17
Pink Elephant	**Chelsea**	24
☑ Plunge	**Meatpacking**	25
PS 450	**Murray Hill**	20
Redemption	**E 50s**	14
Red Sky	**Murray Hill**	17
Revival	**Gramercy**	19
Saloon	**E 80s**	17
Sin Sin/Leopard	**E Vill**	18
SouthWest NY	**Financial**	19
Splash	**Flatiron**	20
Sutton Place	**E 50s**	18
☑ Tao	**E 50s**	24
Therapy	**W 50s**	24
13	**G Vill**	15
Tin Lizzie	**E 80s**	13
Tonic East	**Murray Hill**	20
Tortilla Flats	**W Vill**	19
Touch	**W 50s**	25
Townhouse	**E 50s**	22
Turtle Bay	**E 50s**	15
2A	**E Vill**	18
212	**E 60s**	18
☑ 230 Fifth	**Chelsea**	25
Underbar	**Union Sq**	21
Vertigo	**Murray Hill**	19
Vig 27	**Murray Hill**	19
Vlada	**W 50s**	23
Vudu Lounge	**E 70s**	18
Webster Hall	**E Vill**	19
Wet Bar	**Murray Hill**	21
Whiskey	**W 40s**	20
Whiskey Blue	**E 40s**	23
Whiskey Park	**W 50s**	20
Whistlin' Dixie's	**W 50s**	16
xes lounge	**Chelsea**	22

MUSIC CLUBS

(See also Jazz Clubs)

Arlene's Grocery	**LES**	20
Back Fence	**G Vill**	17
Banjo Jim's	**E Vill**	21
Beacon Theatre	**W 70s**	23
Blender Theater	**Murray Hill**	19

Bowery Ballroom	**LES**	24
NEW Brooklyn Bowl	**W'burg**	-
Cafe Wha?	**G Vill**	21
Cake Shop	**LES**	20
Canal Room	**TriBeCa**	20
☑ NEW City Winery	**SoHo**	23
Delancey	**LES**	20
Don Hill's	**SoHo**	20
Drom	**E Vill**	21
NEW El Morocco	**Harlem**	20
Europa	**Greenpt**	17
Fat Baby	**LES**	19
Fillmore	**Gramercy**	22
Fontana's	**LES**	19
☑ Galapagos	**Dumbo**	-
Hammerstein	**Garment**	20
Highline Ballrm.	**Chelsea**	21
Lakeside Lounge	**E Vill**	19
NEW Le Poisson Rouge	**G Vill**	22
Living Room	**LES**	22
Mercury Lounge	**LES**	20
Music Hall	**W'burg**	22
Nokia Theatre	**W 40s**	21
Otto's Shrunken	**E Vill**	21
Pianos	**LES**	19
NEW Public Assembly	**W'burg**	20
Rebel	**Garment**	18
Rodeo Bar	**Murray Hill**	20
Rose	**W'burg**	21
☑ Roseland	**W 50s**	19
☑ NEW Santos Party Hse.	**Chinatown**	21
Slipper Room	**LES**	20
S.O.B.'s	**SoHo**	22
Studio B	**Greenpt**	24
Sullivan Hall	**G Vill**	18
Terminal 5	**W 50s**	18
Trash	**W'burg**	18
☑ Union Hall	**Park Slope**	24
United Palace	**Wash. Hts**	19
Village Underground	**G Vill**	18
Warsaw	**Greenpt**	19
Zebulon	**W'burg**	24

NOTEWORTHY NEWCOMERS (111)

Above Allen	**LES**	22
Amsterdam 106	**W 100s**	19
☑ Apothéke	**Chinatown**	23
At Vermilion	**E 40s**	-
Balon	**E 80s**	-
Bar 108	**G Vill**	20
BEast	**LES**	21
Beekman	**E 50s**	23
Beer Island	**Coney Is**	23

Belleville Lounge | **Park Slope**	-
☑ **Bell House** | **Gowanus**	22
Bijoux | **Meatpacking**	23
Bleecker Heights | **W Vill**	-
Blue Ruin | **Garment**	-
Body | **Harlem**	22
Bourbon St. B&G | **W 40s**	20
Brooklyn Bowl | **W'burg**	-
Brookvin | **Park Slope**	22
Building on Bond | **Boerum Hill**	-
Cabana Bar | **Park Slope**	22
Cabin Down Below | **E Vill**	-
Casa La Femme | **W Vill**	-
Catch-22 | **Flatiron**	20
Char No. 4 | **Cobble Hill**	24
Chestnut Bar | **Carroll Gdns**	22
Chloe | **LES**	22
Citrine | **Flatiron**	21
☑ **City Winery** | **SoHo**	23
Clo | **W 60s**	22
☑ **Clover Club** | **Cobble Hill**	25
Country Club | **W Vill**	19
Covo | **Harlem**	25
Delicatessen | **SoHo**	19
Desnuda | **E Vill**	23
Diamond's Wine | **LES**	22
Donnybrook | **LES**	19
DTOX | **E Vill**	18
Dutch Kills | **LIC**	-
East Village Tavern | **E Vill**	19
EastVille Comedy | **E Vill**	18
Eden | **W 40s**	19
Eldridge | **LES**	22
Ella | **E Vill**	21
El Morocco | **Harlem**	20
Elsa | **E Vill**	21
☑ **Empire Hotel Roof** | **W 60s**	24
Evolve | **E 50s**	22
508 Sports | **Garment**	-
Frames | **W 40s**	-
Gates | **Chelsea**	-
Gibson | **W'burg**	-
Globe | **Gramercy**	19
Greenhouse | **SoHo**	21
Griffin | **Meatpacking**	-
Haven | **E 50s**	18
Hill | **Murray Hill**	17
Hose | **E Vill**	-
Houndstooth | **Garment**	19
Hudson Terrace | **W 40s**	23
Imperial | **Flatiron**	18
Knave | **W 50s**	22
La Fonda del Sol | **E 40s**	-
Lavish Lounge | **Astoria**	-
Le Poisson Rouge | **G Vill**	22
Lillie's | **Flatiron**	-
Local 269 | **LES**	-
☑ **Lucky Strike Lanes** | **W 40s**	21
☑ **Macao Trading** | **TriBeCa**	25
mad46 | **E 40s**	21
☑ **Madam Geneva** | **NoHo**	25
Manhattans | **Prospect Hts**	-
Mayahuel | **E Vill**	-
Mother's | **W'burg**	19
Mr. West | **Chelsea**	20
☑ **M2** | **Chelsea**	20
Nectar | **Harlem**	23
123 Burger | **W 50s**	20
Perle | **Financial**	22
Pierre Loti | **Gramercy**	23
Pony Bar | **W 40s**	-
Pranna | **Murray Hill**	-
Prime Meats | **Carroll Gdns**	-
Public Assembly | **W'burg**	20
☑ **Raines Law Rm.** | **Flatiron**	-
Ravel Rooftop | **LIC**	-
RDV | **Meatpacking**	22
Richardson | **W'burg**	-
☑ **Santos Party Hse.** | **Chinatown**	21
Sapphire NY | **E 60s**	21
Shang Bar | **LES**	-
SideBar | **Gramercy**	21
675 Bar | **Meatpacking**	-
67 Orange St. | **Harlem**	22
Sorella | **LES**	-
Southside | **L Italy**	18
Stag's Head | **E 50s**	-
Standard Hotel | **Meatpacking**	-
Stumble Inn | **E 70s**	15
Sweet & Lowdown | **LES**	18
Talay | **Harlem**	19
t.b.d. | **Greenpt**	-
249 Bar | **Park Slope**	-
Van Diemens | **Murray Hill**	18
Velour | **Chelsea**	20
Vino | **E 60s**	22
Vino 313 | **Murray Hill**	22
Vintage Irving | **Gramercy**	21
Whiskey Tavern | **Chinatown**	19
☑ **White Slab Palace** | **LES**	-
White Star | **LES**	20
Wilfie & Nell | **W Vill**	24

NOTEWORTHY CLOSINGS (66)

Azza

Baggot Inn

Bamn!

Menus, photos, voting and more – free at ZAGAT.com

Bar Milano
Bar Vespa
Cachaça
CB Six
Circus
Comedy Village
Cosmo
Cutting Room
Devin Tavern
Dip
Django
Donna da Vine
Door Lounge
Earth
G Spa & Lounge
Gibraltar
Gold St.
Grace
Grand
Grayz
Gypsy Tea
Hanger
Highline
Ice Bar
Island
Julep
Kanvas
KingSize
Laila Lounge
Le Figaro Cafe
Level V
Lollipop
Lotus
Luna Lounge
Luv 24-7
Madison
Mambi Lounge
Manor
Martignetti Downstairs
Mo's Caribbean
Nest
O.W.
Opus 22
Plumm
Red Rock West
Rififi
Rise
Rubyfruit
Scores
Shag
Socialista
Spotlight Live
Spy
Suba
Town

Tribe
Uncle Ming's
Vasmay Lounge
Vesta
Vintage New York Wine Bar
Waikiki Wally's
Why Not?
Zipper Tavern

NY STATE OF MIND

Algonquin	**W 40s**	23
Arlene's Grocery	**LES**	20
Arthur's Tavern	**W Vill**	22
☑ Bemelmans	**E 70s**	27
Bill's Gay 90s	**E 50s**	20
Bitter End	**G Vill**	19
Blue & Gold	**E Vill**	18
☑ Blue Note	**G Vill**	23
☑ Boathouse	**E 70s**	26
☑ Box	**LES**	25
Bridge Cafe	**Financial**	24
☑ Brooklyn Inn	**Boerum Hill**	27
☑ Brooklyn Social	**Carroll Gdns**	25
Café des Artistes	**W 60s**	24
Caffe Dante	**G Vill**	21
Caffe Reggio	**G Vill**	20
City Hall	**TriBeCa**	23
Corner Bistro	**W Vill**	22
Eagle	**Chelsea**	22
Ear Inn	**SoHo**	21
Fanelli's	**SoHo**	18
NEW Globe	**Gramercy**	19
☑ Gotham B&G	**G Vill**	25
Jeremy's Ale	**Financial**	16
K & M Bar	**W'burg**	-
Keens Steak	**Garment**	21
☑ King Cole Bar	**E 50s**	28
☑ Lenox Lounge	**Harlem**	21
MacDougal St. Ale	**G Vill**	18
Marie's Crisis	**W Vill**	22
McAleer's Pub	**W 80s**	15
McSorley's	**E Vill**	23
Metropolitan Mus. Roof	**E 80s**	26
Michael Jordan's	**E 40s**	20
Mickey Mantle's	**W 50s**	18
Moto	**W'burg**	24
Nuyorican Poets	**E Vill**	21
☑ Oak Bar	**W 50s**	24
Odeon	**TriBeCa**	20
☑ Old Town Bar	**Flatiron**	21
One if by Land	**G Vill**	26
Pete's Tavern	**Gramercy**	21
P.J. Clarke's	**E 50s**	20
☑ Rainbow Grill	**W 40s**	24
☑ Roseland	**W 50s**	19

Rudy's | **W 40s**	19
Schiller's | **LES**	22
Smalls | **W Vill**	24
Stan's | **Bronx**	12
St. Nick's Jazz Pub | **Harlem**	20
Tavern on the Green | **W 60s**	22
🆉 21 Club | **W 50s**	26
🆉 230 Fifth | **Chelsea**	25
Village Vanguard | **W Vill**	24
Webster Hall | **E Vill**	19
🆉 White Horse | **W Vill**	20

OLD NEW YORK

(50+ yrs.; Year opened; * building)

1784 | One if by Land* | **G Vill**	26
1794 | Bridge Cafe* | **Financial**	24
1800 | Sunny's | **Red Hook**	26
1804 | Pussycat Lounge* | **Financial**	18
1817 | Ear Inn* | **SoHo**	21
1826 | Bayard's Ale* | **W Vill**	17
1827 | Julius* | **G Vill**	12
1834 | Moran's Chelsea | **Chelsea**	19
1842 | Tavern on Jane* | **W Vill**	21
1847 | Fanelli's | **SoHo**	18
1851 | Bayard's* | **Financial**	19
1854 | McSorley's | **E Vill**	23
1860 | Brooklyn Inn* | **Boerum Hill**	27
1864 | Pete's Tavern | **Gramercy**	21
1873 | Paris | **Seaport**	19
1874 | P.J. Hanley's | **Carroll Gdns**	18
1880 | Globe* | **Gramercy**	19
1880 | White Horse | **W Vill**	20
1884 | P.J. Clarke's | **E 50s**	20
1885 | Keens Steak | **Garment**	21
1886 | Webster Hall* | **E Vill**	19
1887 | Teddy's | **W'burg**	23
1892 | Old Town Bar | **Flatiron**	21
1902 | Algonquin | **W 40s**	23
1903 | M Bar* | **W 40s**	20
1904 | Trinity Place* | **Financial**	21
1906 | Hammerstein | **Garment**	20
1910 | Bohemian Hall | **Astoria**	25
1911 | Commerce* | **W Vill**	22
1915 | Caffe Dante | **G Vill**	21
1917 | Café des Artistes* | **W 60s**	24
1919 | 55 Bar | **G Vill**	22
1919 | Roseland | **W 50s**	19
1920 | Barrow St. Ale* | **G Vill**	18
1920 | Garage* | **G Vill**	21
1920 | Milady's | **SoHo**	13
1920 | Standings* | **E Vill**	25
1923 | Campbell Apt.* | **E 40s**	25
1923 | Yankee Tavern | **Bronx**	17
1924 | Molly's | **Gramercy**	22

1926 | Bill's Gay 90s | **E 50s**	20
1927 | Caffe Reggio | **G Vill**	20
1927 | P.J. Carney's | **W 50s**	18
1928 | Beacon Theatre | **W 70s**	23
1929 | Marie's Crisis | **W Vill**	22
1929 | Top of the Tower* | **E 40s**	24
1929 | 21 Club | **W 50s**	26
1930 | Bemelmans | **E 70s**	27
1930 | O'Connor's | **Park Slope**	22
1934 | Moonshine* | **Red Hook**	19
1934 | Rudy's | **W 40s**	19
1934 | Smith's Bar | **W 40s**	17
1934 | Subway Inn | **E 60s**	17
1935 | 7B | **E Vill**	19
1935 | Village Vanguard | **W Vill**	24
1936 | Desmond's Tavern | **Murray Hill**	11
1936 | Peter McManus | **Chelsea**	19
1937 | Arthur's Tavern | **W Vill**	22
1938 | Bowlmor Lanes | **G Vill**	22
1939 | Lenox Lounge | **Harlem**	21
1940 | Sophie's | **E Vill**	22
1945 | Back Fence | **G Vill**	17
1945 | Holiday Cocktail | **E Vill**	18
1945 | Oak Bar | **W 50s**	24
1945 | Puffy's | **TriBeCa**	19
1948 | First Edition | **Bayside**	15
1949 | King Cole Bar | **E 50s**	28
1950 | Fat Black Pussycat* | **G Vill**	17
1950 | Kettle of Fish | **G Vill**	21
1952 | Boathouse | **E 70s**	26
1952 | Duplex | **G Vill**	19
1952 | Lucy's* | **E Vill**	19
1952 | Relish* | **W'burg**	18
1953 | McAleer's Pub | **W 80s**	15
1955 | Cafe Carlyle | **E 70s**	26
1955 | Parkside | **LES**	18
1958 | Blue & Gold | **E Vill**	18

OUTDOOR SPACES

GARDEN

Anyway Cafe | **multi.**	20
Apt. 138 | **Cobble Hill**	19
Back Forty | **E Vill**	22
NEW Balon | **E 80s**	-
Baraza | **E Vill**	22
Black Betty | **W'burg**	19
Bohemian Hall | **Astoria**	25
Boxcar Lounge | **E Vill**	18
Brazen Head | **Boerum Hill**	20
NEW Brookvin | **Park Slope**	22
Bryant Park Grill | **W 40s**	22
Bull McCabe's | **E Vill**	17
Casimir | **E Vill**	21

🅉 Cávo | **Astoria**	26
Central | **Astoria**	19
Cherry Tree | **Park Slope**	16
Cibar | **Gramercy**	22
Clandestino | **LES**	19
Cloister Cafe | **E Vill**	23
Commonwealth | **Park Slope**	19
Cornichon | **W'burg**	21
Croxley Ales | **E Vill**	20
Daddy's | **W'burg**	19
Danny & Eddie's | **E 80s**	14
🅉 d.b.a. | **multi.**	22
Den | **Harlem**	21
🅉 'disiac | **W 50s**	26
Doc Watson's | **E 70s**	17
Donovan's | **Bayside**	20
Draft Barn | **Gravesend**	-
Dram Shop | **Park Slope**	-
Druids | **W 50s**	19
East of Eighth | **Chelsea**	19
Eight Mile Creek | **NoLita**	23
🅉 Employees Only | **W Vill**	24
Excelsior | **Park Slope**	19
5 Ninth | **Meatpacking**	23
Fourth Ave. Pub | **Park Slope**	18
Ginger's | **Park Slope**	16
Gowanus Yacht | **Carroll Gdns**	23
Half King | **Chelsea**	19
Hell Gate Social | **Astoria**	22
Huckleberry | **W'burg**	22
International Bar | **E Vill**	-
Iona | **W'burg**	21
Joya | **Cobble Hill**	23
Killmeyer's | **SI**	23
Last Exit | **Cobble Hill**	20
L.I.C. Bar | **LIC**	25
Loki | **Park Slope**	17
Loreley | **LES**	21
Lounge 47 | **LIC**	20
Luca Bar/Lounge | **E Vill**	21
Lunasa | **E Vill**	22
Madame X | **G Vill**	20
Moonshine | **Red Hook**	19
Mug's Ale | **W'burg**	25
Mustang Grill | **E 80s**	16
No Malice Palace | **E Vill**	19
Nublu | **E Vill**	26
O'Flaherty's Ale | **W 40s**	18
Ono | **Meatpacking**	24
Park | **Chelsea**	21
Pete's Candy | **W'burg**	23
Radegast | **W'burg**	26
Revel | **Meatpacking**	22
Revival | **Gramercy**	19
Rose | **W'burg**	21
Royale | **E Vill**	20
Rudy's | **W 40s**	19
Rue B | **E Vill**	22
Sherwood | **Boerum Hill**	23
Sixth Ward | **LES**	22
Soda Bar | **Prospect Hts**	20
Soft Spot | **W'burg**	-
SoHo Park | **SoHo**	18
Spuyten Duyvil | **W'burg**	24
🅉 Stonehome | **Ft Greene**	27
Sweet & Vicious | **NoLita**	17
Tavern on the Green | **W 60s**	22
Trophy | **W'burg**	19
NEW Whiskey Tavern | **Chinatown**	19

PATIO/TERRACE

APT | **Meatpacking**	21
Arctica | **Murray Hill**	18
NEW At Vermilion | **E 40s**	-
Babel Lounge | **E Vill**	21
Barcade | **W'burg**	24
Bar 4 | **Park Slope**	20
Bar Tabac | **Cobble Hill**	22
B Bar | **NoHo**	18
Beer Bar/Centro | **E 40s**	17
NEW Beer Island | **Coney Is**	23
Belmont | **Gramercy**	16
Bin No. 220 | **Seaport**	21
Bleu Evolution | **Wash. Hts**	19
🅉 Blue Water Grill | **Union Sq**	23
🅉 Boat Basin | **W 70s**	24
🅉 Boathouse | **E 70s**	26
🅉 Bobo | **W Vill**	22
Boss Tweed's | **LES**	17
Boucarou | **E Vill**	20
NEW Bourbon St. B&G | **W 40s**	20
🅉 Brandy Library | **TriBeCa**	25
Bushwick Country | **W'burg**	18
NEW Cabana Bar | **Park Slope**	22
Cafe Deville | **E Vill**	21
Camp | **Boerum Hill**	21
Cargo Café | **SI**	20
🅉 Cávo | **Astoria**	26
NEW Char No. 4 | **Cobble Hill**	24
Chelsea Brewing | **Chelsea**	18
China 1 | **E Vill**	19
Choice | **Murray Hill**	21
Cielo | **Meatpacking**	23
City Hall | **TriBeCa**	23
Creek & the Cave | **LIC**	19
Crocodile Lounge | **E Vill**	19
🅉 d.b.a. | **E Vill**	22
Den | **Harlem**	21
Diner | **Meatpacking**	19

☑ 'disiac | **W 50s**	
Divine Bar | **W 50s**	22
Dos Caminos | **SoHo**	22
Double Down | **E Vill**	17
Druids | **W 50s**	19
Duff's | **W'burg**	19
Duke's | **Murray Hill**	18
Duke's | **E Vill**	18
East River | **W'burg**	20
El Rio Grande | **Murray Hill**	19
NEW Evolve | **E 50s**	22
Flor de Sol | **TriBeCa**	23
Frank's | **Ft Greene**	19
Gate | **Park Slope**	22
Ginger's | **Park Slope**	16
Glass | **Chelsea**	20
Gutter | **Greenpt**	24
GYM Sportsbar | **Chelsea**	19
Harbour Lights | **Seaport**	21
Harefield Rd. | **W'burg**	20
Heartland Brew. | **Seaport**	16
NEW Hill | **Murray Hill**	17
HK Lounge | **Garment**	20
Hook & Ladder | **Murray Hill**	13
Hooters | **W 50s**	15
House of Brews | **W 50s**	19
Hudson Hotel | **W 50s**	24
Hugs | **W'burg**	17
Jekyll & Hyde | **G Vill**	17
Kiss & Fly | **Meatpacking**	20
La Bottega | **Chelsea**	21
Larry Lawrence | **W'burg**	28
Local | **Garment**	16
Loki | **Park Slope**	17
Merchants, NY | **multi.**	18
Metropolitan | **W'burg**	19
Moda Outdoors | **W 50s**	20
Morrell Wine Bar | **W 40s**	24
NEW Mother's | **W'burg**	19
Night Hotel Bar | **W 40s**	18
Nublu | **E Vill**	26
Ono | **Meatpacking**	24
Opia | **E 50s**	22
Overlook Lounge | **E 40s**	17
Park Slope Ale | **Park Slope**	18
Patroon | **E 40s**	22
Peggy O'Neill's | **Coney Is**	18
Perfect Pint | **W 40s**	21
Phoenix | **E Vill**	20
NEW Pierre Loti | **Gramercy**	23
Pine Tree Lodge | **Murray Hill**	24
P.J. Clarke's | **Financial**	20
P.J. Hanley's | **Carroll Gdns**	18
Playwright | **W 40s**	18

Professor Thom's | **E Vill**	19
Rayuela | **LES**	26
Relish | **W'burg**	18
Rink Bar | **W 50s**	24
River Room | **Harlem**	21
Rosa Mexicano | **W 60s**	22
Sample | **Cobble Hill**	19
Sequoia | **Seaport**	22
Serafina | **multi.**	20
Social | **W 40s**	17
SouthWest NY | **Financial**	19
St. Dymphna's | **E Vill**	20
St. Nick's Jazz Pub | **Harlem**	20
Supreme Trading | **W'burg**	23
Swig | **E 80s**	16
Swing 46 | **W 40s**	21
☑ Tabla | **Flatiron**	24
T.G. Whitney's | **E 50s**	16
Top of the Tower | **E 40s**	24
Tribeca Grill | **TriBeCa**	23
Tribeca Tavern | **TriBeCa**	18
212 | **E 60s**	18
☑ Ulysses | **Financial**	22
Uncle Charlie's | **E 40s**	21
Underground | **Murray Hill**	18
Underground Lounge | **W 100s**	18
Union Pool | **W'burg**	20
Vintage | **W 50s**	25
Vol de Nuit | **G Vill**	25
☑ Weather Up | **Prospect Hts**	22
Wharf Bar & Grill | **Murray Hill**	18
Whiskey River | **Murray Hill**	18
xes lounge | **Chelsea**	22
Zombie Hut | **Carroll Gdns**	21

ROOFTOP

NEW Above Allen | **LES**	22
Ava Lounge | **W 50s**	24
Bookmarks | **E 40s**	24
Brass Monkey | **Meatpacking**	19
Cabanas | **Chelsea**	22
Delancey | **LES**	20
Eagle | **Chelsea**	22
NEW Eden | **W 40s**	19
☑ NEW Empire Hotel Roof | **W 60s**	24
Heights B&G | **W 100s**	18
Highbar | **W 40s**	21
HK Lounge | **Garment**	20
Hudson Hotel | **W 50s**	24
NEW Hudson Terrace | **W 40s**	23
Hustler Club | **W 50s**	22
Local | **Garment**	16
NEW mad46 | **E 40s**	21
Metro Grill Roof | **Garment**	20
Metropolitan Mus. Roof | **E 80s**	26

Park | **Chelsea** — 21
Patroon | **E 40s** — 22
Perfect Pint | **E 40s** — 21
🔁 Plunge | **Meatpacking** — 25
Rare View | **Murray Hill** — 22
NEW Ravel Rooftop | **LIC** — -
Red Sky | **Murray Hill** — 17
Salon de Ning | **W 50s** — 26
Soho House | **Meatpacking** — 24
Studio B | **Greenpt** — 24
SushiSamba | **G Vill** — 22
Sutton Place | **E 50s** — 18
13 | **G Vill** — 15
Thom Bar | **SoHo** — 24
Tonic East | **Murray Hill** — 20
NEW 249 Bar | **Park Slope** — -
🔁 230 Fifth | **Chelsea** — 25

SIDEWALK
Aroma | **NoHo** — 25
Athens Café | **Astoria** — 17
Bar Carrera | **G Vill** — 23
Barfly | **Gramercy** — 16
Bar Italia | **E 70s** — 20
Bar 6 | **G Vill** — 23
Bayard's Ale | **W Vill** — 17
Bin 71 | **W 70s** — 22
Blue Smoke | **Murray Hill** — 21
Bottega del Vino | **E 50s** — 22
Bowery Wine Company | **E Vill** — 20
Brass Monkey | **Meatpacking** — 19
Bua | **E Vill** — 21
Cafe Bar | **Astoria** — 22
Cafe Gitane | **NoLita** — 22
Cafeteria | **Chelsea** — 19
Caffe Dante | **G Vill** — 21
Caffe Reggio | **G Vill** — 20
Cavatappo Grill/Wine | **E 80s** — 22
Chinatown Brasserie | **NoHo** — 23
Chow Bar | **W Vill** — 18
Cipriani Downtown | **SoHo** — 24
Citrus B&G | **W 70s** — 20
Coffee Shop | **Union Sq** — 18
Cornelia St. Cafe | **G Vill** — 23
Cowgirl | **W Vill** — 18
Daltons | **W 40s** — 16
NEW Delicatessen | **SoHo** — 19
NEW Diamond's Wine | **LES** — 22
Dive Bar | **W 90s** — 18
Doc Watson's | **E 70s** — 17
D.O.C. Wine | **W'burg** — 25
Dos Caminos | **E 50s** — 22
Downtown B&G | **Cobble Hill** — 18
Dublin 6 | **W Vill** — 22
Duplex | **G Vill** — 19

Epstein's Bar | **LES** — 14
Felice | **E 60s** — 22
Fiddlesticks | **G Vill** — 18
Finnegans Wake | **E 70s** — 15
Firehouse | **W 80s** — 16
Four-Faced Liar | **G Vill** — 18
Gallo Nero | **W 40s** — 21
Garage | **G Vill** — 21
Genesis | **E 80s** — 20
Grand Café | **Astoria** — 21
Heartland Brew. | **multi.** — 16
Henrietta Hudson | **W Vill** — 18
Hideout | **Ft Greene** — 19
Hi-Life | **W 80s** — 17
Honey | **Chelsea** — 19
🔁 Hotel Delmano | **W'burg** — 24
Il Posto Accanto | **E Vill** — 24
Irish Rogue | **W 40s** — 19
Jack Russell's | **E 80s** — 19
Jake's Dilemma | **W 80s** — 16
Jake's Saloon | **W 50s** — 18
Johnny Foxes | **E 80s** — 16
Joshua Tree | **multi.** — 15
Jules | **E Vill** — 23
K & M Bar | **W'burg** — -
Le Zie 2000 | **Chelsea** — 22
Lodge | **W'burg** — 18
L'Orange Bleue | **SoHo** — 21
Luke's B&G | **E 70s** — 19
Mama's Bar | **E Vill** — 22
McAleer's Pub | **W 80s** — 15
Merchants, NY | **Financial** — 18
Merkato 55 | **Meatpacking** — 22
Mickey Mantle's | **W 50s** — 18
Moran's Chelsea | **Chelsea** — 19
Mustang Sally's | **Chelsea** — 17
Odeon | **TriBeCa** — 20
One | **Meatpacking** — 22
One & One | **E Vill** — 18
Opal | **E 50s** — 17
Park Blue | **W 50s** — 22
Park Slope Ale | **Park Slope** — 18
🔁 Pastis | **Meatpacking** — 24
Pencil Factory | **Greenpt** — 20
Pershing Sq. | **E 40s** — 16
Pete's Tavern | **Gramercy** — 21
Pinch B&G | **G Vill** — 19
Pipa | **Flatiron** — 21
Posh | **W 50s** — 20
Prohibition | **W 80s** — 21
Public | **NoLita** — 24
Pudding Stones | **W 90s** — 21
Redemption | **E 50s** — 14
Red Lion | **G Vill** — 19

Riviera | **W Vill**	14
Rogue | **Chelsea**	15
Ryan's Irish Pub | **E Vill**	17
Savalas | **W'burg**	16
Serafina | **W 50s**	20
Session 73 | **E 70s**	19
Shoolbred's | **E Vill**	20
Sidewalk | **E Vill**	19
Simone | **E Vill**	19
Slaughtered Lamb | **G Vill**	17
Smoke | **W 100s**	22
SoHo Room | **SoHo**	14
Son Cubano | **Meatpacking**	23
Z Spice Market | **Meatpacking**	24
NEW Stumble Inn | **E 70s**	15
SushiSamba | **G Vill**	22
Teddy's | **W'burg**	23
Telephone | **E VIII**	18
Three of Cups | **E Vill**	19
3Steps | **Gramercy**	22
Tortilla Flats | **W Vill**	19
Triple Crown | **Chelsea**	18
Turks & Frogs | **TriBeCa**	22
Twelve | **Murray Hill**	16
Uptown Lounge | **E 80s**	23
Vero | **multi.**	24
NEW Vino | **E 60s**	23
Vino Vino | **TriBeCa**	23
Vlada | **W 50s**	23
Westside Brewing | **W 70s**	17
Whistlin' Dixie's | **W 50s**	16
Z White Horse | **W Vill**	20
Wicker Park | **E 80s**	18
Winebar | **E Vill**	22
Wogies | **G Vill**	21
Xicala | **L Italy**	23
Zanzibar | **W 40s**	20
Zum Schneider | **E Vill**	23

WATERSIDE

Bateaux NY | **Chelsea**	22
Z Boat Basin | **W 70s**	24
Z Boathouse | **E 70s**	26
Chelsea Brewing | **Chelsea**	18
Z Frying Pan | **Chelsea**	-
Harbour Lights | **Seaport**	21
Heartland Brew. | **Seaport**	16
P.J. Clarke's | **Financial**	20
River Room | **Harlem**	21
Sequoia | **Seaport**	22
SouthWest NY | **Financial**	19
Spirit Cruises | **Chelsea**	20
Z Water Taxi Beach | **multi.**	22
World Yacht | **W 40s**	23

PHOTO BOOTHS

BB&R | **E 80s**	18
Bleecker St. Bar | **NoHo**	18
Bushwick Country | **W'burg**	18
Crash Mansion | **LES**	15
Crocodile Lounge | **E Vill**	19
Dave & Buster's | **W 40s**	21
GalleryBar | **LES**	19
Hugs | **W'burg**	17
Lakeside Lounge | **E Vill**	19
L.I.C. Bar | **LIC**	25
Living Room | **LES**	22
Niagara/Lei Bar | **E Vill**	19
Otto's Shrunken | **E Vill**	21
7B | **E Vill**	19
Southpaw | **Park Slope**	22
Trailer Park | **Chelsea**	19
Union Pool | **W'burg**	20

PIANO BARS

Bill's Gay 90s | **E 50s**	20
Brandy's | **E 80s**	23
Don't Tell Mama | **W 40s**	24
Duplex | **G Vill**	19
NEW Ella | **E Vill**	21
Marie's Crisis | **W Vill**	22
Monster | **G Vill**	16
Rum House | **W 40s**	14
Townhouse | **E 50s**	22
Uncle Charlie's | **E 40s**	21

PUNK BARS

Ding Dong Lounge | **W 100s**	18
Don Hill's | **SoHo**	20
Duff's | **W'burg**	19
L'Amour | **SI**	17
Lucky 13 | **Park Slope**	17
Manitoba's | **E VIII**	21
Mars Bar | **E Vill**	19
Trash | **W'burg**	18

QUIET CONVERSATION

Z Angel's Share | **E Vill**	26
anotheroom | **TriBeCa**	24
Ara Wine Bar | **Meatpacking**	22
Back Room | **LES**	23
Z Bemelmans | **E 70s**	27
Bin No. 220 | **Seaport**	21
Bin 71 | **W 70s**	22
Z Black Mtn. Wine | **Carroll Gdns**	28
Bleu Evolution | **Wash. Hts**	19
Blue Ribbon Bar | **G Vill**	23
Boxcar Lounge | **E Vill**	18
Z Brandy Library | **TriBeCa**	25
Burp Castle | **E Vill**	18

Café des Artistes | **W 60s**	24
Caffe Dante | **G Vill**	21
Caffe Reggio | **G Vill**	20
Champagne Bar/Plaza | **W 50s**	25
Cibar | **Gramercy**	22
Cloister Cafe | **E Vill**	23
Cupping Room | **SoHo**	18
Decibel | **E Vill**	24
NEW Dutch Kills | **LIC**	-
Epistrophy | **NoLita**	21
Flûte | **multi.**	22
Z Four Seasons Bar | **E 50s**	26
Gilt | **E 50s**	21
Hudson Bar & Books | **W Vill**	21
Il Posto Accanto | **E Vill**	24
I Trulli Enoteca | **Murray Hill**	24
Z King Cole Bar | **E 50s**	28
NEW Knave | **W 50s**	22
Z Little Branch | **W Vill**	26
M Bar | **W 40s**	20
Z Milk & Honey | **LES**	27
Onieal's Grand St. | **L Italy**	20
Z Otheroom | **W Vill**	27
Paramount | **W 40s**	23
Z PDT | **E Vill**	27
Plaza Athénée | **E 60s**	24
Pudding Stones | **E 80s**	21
Z Rainbow Grill | **W 40s**	24
Z NEW Raines Law Rm. | **Flatiron**	-
Regency Library Bar | **E 60s**	25
Rose Club | **W 50s**	23
NEW Sweet & Lowdown | **LES**	18
Tea Lounge | **Park Slope**	20
Temple Bar | **NoHo**	24
Top of the Tower | **E 40s**	24
Total Wine | **Park Slope**	25
Velvet | **E Vill**	17
NEW Vino | **E 60s**	22
Von | **NoHo**	26
NEW White Star | **LES**	20
World Bar | **E 40s**	23

ROADHOUSES

Aces & Eights | **E 80s**	15
American Trash | **E 70s**	13
Bar None | **E Vill**	11
Big Easy | **E 90s**	13
Billymark's West | **Chelsea**	15
Coyote Ugly | **E Vill**	13
Dakota Roadhse. | **Financial**	15
Doc Holliday's | **E Vill**	15
Duke's | **multi.**	18
Ear Inn | **SoHo**	21
Hogs & Heifers | **Meatpacking**	16
Live Bait | **Flatiron**	15

Porky's | **Flatiron**	15
Raccoon Lodge | **Financial**	15
Rodeo Bar | **Murray Hill**	20
Trailer Park | **Chelsea**	19
Whistlin' Dixie's | **W 50s**	16

ROMANTIC

Allen & Delancey | **LES**	25
Z Angel's Share | **E Vill**	26
Z NEW Apothéke | **Chinatown**	23
Aspen | **W 50s**	21
Auction House | **E 80s**	22
Z Balthazar | **SoHo**	25
Bateaux NY | **Chelsea**	22
Z Bemelmans | **E 70s**	27
Z Black Mtn. Wine | **Carroll Gdns**	28
Z Blue Water Grill | **Union Sq**	23
Z Boathouse | **E 70s**	26
Bookmarks | **E 40s**	24
Bubble Lounge | **TriBeCa**	22
Café des Artistes | **W 60s**	24
NEW Casa La Femme | **W Vill**	-
Casimir | **E Vill**	21
Cellar Bar | **W 40s**	22
Chez Josephine | **W 40s**	22
Cibar | **Gramercy**	22
Cloister Cafe | **E Vill**	23
Country Champ. Lounge | **Murray Hill**	25
Cub Room | **SoHo**	19
Z Daniel | **E 60s**	27
Decibel | **E Vill**	24
Delia's | **Bay Ridge**	22
Z Dove | **G Vill**	24
Dylan Prime | **TriBeCa**	23
NEW Ella | **E Vill**	21
Z Flatiron Lounge | **Flatiron**	25
Flor de Sol | **TriBeCa**	23
Flûte | **multi.**	22
Hudson Bar & Books | **W Vill**	21
Il Posto Accanto | **E Vill**	24
I Tre Merli | **SoHo**	20
I Trulli Enoteca | **Murray Hill**	24
Jules | **E Vill**	23
Z King Cole Bar | **E 50s**	28
K Lounge | **W 50s**	20
Kush | **LES**	22
La Lanterna | **G Vill**	25
Le Bateau Ivre | **E 50s**	24
Le Colonial | **E 50s**	21
Lexington Bar & Books | **E 70s**	21
Z Little Branch | **W Vill**	26
Madame X | **G Vill**	20
M Bar | **W 40s**	20
Metropolitan Mus. Roof | **E 80s**	26

🅩 Milk & Honey | **LES**	27
Morgans Bar | **Murray Hill**	22
🅩 Oak Room | **W 40s**	25
One if by Land | **G Vill**	26
Onieal's Grand St. | **L Italy**	20
Park Bar | **Flatiron**	21
Peasant | **NoLita**	23
🅩 Pegu Club | **SoHo**	25
🅩 Rainbow Grill | **W 40s**	24
Red Bench | **SoHo**	21
Regency Library Bar | **E 60s**	25
Rue B | **E Vill**	22
Shade | **G Vill**	26
Shalel Lounge | **W 70s**	24
🅩 Spice Market | **Meatpacking**	24
Spirit Cruises | **Chelsea**	20
Temple Bar | **NoHo**	24
Top of the Tower | **E 40s**	24
Von | **NoHo**	26
World Yacht | **W 40s**	23

SMOKING PERMITTED

NEW Beekman | **E 50s**	23
Carnegie Club | **W 50s**	24
Circa Tabac | **SoHo**	21
Club Macanudo | **E 60s**	24
Hudson Bar & Books | **W Vill**	21
Karma | **E Vill**	21
Lexington Bar & Books | **E 70s**	21
Merchants, NY | **E 60s**	18
Velvet | **E Vill**	17

SPEAKEASY-STYLE

(*real deal former speaks)

🅩 NEW Apothéke | **Chinatown**	23
Back Room | **LES**	23
🅩 Beatrice Inn* | **W Vill**	21
B Flat | **TriBeCa**	22
Bill's Gay 90s* | **E 50s**	20
Black Door | **Chelsea**	20
Blue Owl | **E Vill**	23
🅩 Brooklyn Social | **Carroll Gdns**	25
🅩 Commerce* | **W Vill**	22
🅩 Death & Co | **E Vill**	25
NEW Dutch Kills | **LIC**	-
East Side Co. | **LES**	24
🅩 Employees Only | **W Vill**	24
Flûte* | **W 50s**	22
🅩 Freemans | **LES**	26
Hideout | **Ft Greene**	19
🅩 Hotel Delmano | **W'burg**	24
🅩 JakeWalk | **Carroll Gdns**	21
🅩 La Esquina | **L Italy**	24
🅩 Little Branch | **W Vill**	26
🅩 Milk & Honey | **LES**	27

124 Rabbit | **G Vill**	24
Onieal's Grand St.* | **L Italy**	20
🅩 PDT | **E Vill**	27
NEW Prime Meats | **Carroll Gdns**	-
🅩 NEW Raines Law Rm. | **Flatiron**	-
NEW Richardson | **W'burg**	-
🅩 Smith & Mills | **TriBeCa**	23
🅩 21 Club* | **W 50s**	26
Volstead | **E 50s**	21
🅩 Weather Up | **Prospect Hts**	22
NEW White Star | **LES**	20

SPOKEN WORD

An Béal Bocht | **Bronx**	21
Back Fence | **G Vill**	17
BAMcafé | **Downtown Bklyn**	21
Barbès | **Park Slope**	25
NEW Belleville Lounge | **Park Slope**	-
Bowery Poetry Club | **NoHo**	23
Cornelia St. Cafe | **G Vill**	23
Ear Inn | **SoHo**	21
Four-Faced Liar | **G Vill**	18
Freddy's | **Prospect Hts**	18
Half King | **Chelsea**	19
Happy Ending | **LES**	19
Joe's Pub | **E Vill**	25
KGB | **E Vill**	21
NEW Le Poisson Rouge | **G Vill**	22
Love | **G Vill**	20
Nuyorican Poets | **E Vill**	21
Pacific Standard | **Boerum Hill**	21
Pete's Candy | **W'burg**	23
Pianos | **LES**	19
Pink Pony | **LES**	19
Rebar | **Dumbo**	21
Rose | **W'burg**	21
Stay | **E Vill**	19
Sunny's | **Red Hook**	26
Telephone | **E Vill**	18
13 | **G Vill**	15
Zinc Bar | **G Vill**	22

SPORTS BARS

Angry Wade's | **Cobble Hill**	14
Back Page | **E 80s**	18
Baker Street | **E 60s**	18
Bar Coastal | **E 70s**	14
Bar 515 | **Murray Hill**	15
Barfly | **Gramercy**	16
NEW Bar 108 | **G Vill**	20
BB&R | **E 80s**	18
Becky's | **E 60s**	18
Beer Garden | **SI**	17
BlackFinn | **E 50s**	17

Black Sheep | **Murray Hill**	15
Blackstone's | **E 50s**	17
NEW Bleecker Heights | **W Vill**	-
Blondies | **multi.**	19
Blue Seats | **LES**	16
Bounce | **multi.**	19
Bourbon St. | **W 70s**	15
Z Brother Jimmy's | **multi.**	17
Central Bar | **E Vill**	19
Croxley Ales | **E Vill**	20
Daltons | **W 40s**	16
Desmond's Tavern | **Murray Hill**	11
Down the Hatch | **G Vill**	16
Downtown B&G | **Cobble Hill**	18
ESPN Zone | **W 40s**	18
Firefly | **NoLita**	19
Firehouse | **W 80s**	16
First Edition | **Bayside**	15
Fitzgerald's | **Murray Hill**	16
NEW 508 Sports | **Garment**	-
40/40 | **Flatiron**	21
Genesis | **E 80s**	20
Gin Mill | **W 80s**	16
GYM Sportsbar | **Chelsea**	19
Harlem Lanes | **Harlem**	20
NEW Hill | **Murray Hill**	17
Irish Rogue | **W 40s**	19
Jack Russell's | **E 80s**	19
Jake's Dilemma | **W 80s**	16
John Street B&G | **Financial**	16
Joshua Tree | **multi.**	15
Katwalk | **Garment**	16
Kinsale | **E 90s**	20
Lansdowne Rd. | **W 40s**	21
Lion's Head Tavern | **W 100s**	15
MacDougal St. Ale | **G Vill**	18
Malachy's | **W 70s**	14
McAleer's Pub | **W 80s**	15
McCormack's | **Murray Hill**	19
McFadden's | **E 40s**	15
Mercury Bar | **multi.**	16
Mickey Mantle's | **W 50s**	18
Molly Pitcher's | **E 80s**	21
Nevada Smith's | **E Vill**	16
Off the Wagon | **G Vill**	17
O'Flanagan's | **E 60s**	15
NEW 123 Burger | **W 50s**	20
Overlook Lounge | **E 40s**	17
Peggy O'Neill's | **Coney Is**	18
Professor Thom's | **E Vill**	19
Rathbones | **E 80s**	18
Red Lion | **G Vill**	19
Reservoir Bar | **G Vill**	17
Riviera | **W Vill**	14

Rogue | **Chelsea**	15
Ship of Fools | **E 80s**	16
NEW SideBar | **Gramercy**	21
Slane | **G Vill**	17
Social | **W 40s**	17
Standings | **E Vill**	25
Stan's | **Bronx**	12
St. Marks Ale | **E Vill**	17
Sutton Place | **E 50s**	18
Third & Long | **Murray Hill**	14
Tonic | **W 40s**	19
Tonic East | **Murray Hill**	20
Triple Crown | **Chelsea**	18
Turtle Bay | **E 50s**	15
Twelve | **Murray Hill**	16
200 Fifth | **Park Slope**	17
Underground | **Murray Hill**	18
Village Pourhouse | **multi.**	18
Yankee Tavern | **Bronx**	17

STRIP CLUBS

Corio | **SoHo**	18
Flashdancers | **W 50s**	18
HeadQuarters | **Garment**	-
Hustler Club | **W 50s**	22
Penthse. Exec. Club | **W 40s**	24
Pussycat Lounge | **Financial**	18
Rick's Cabaret | **Garment**	20
NEW Sapphire NY | **E 60s**	21
Ten's | **Flatiron**	21
VIP Club | **Flatiron**	27

SUITS

Bar 41 | **W 40s**	19
Bayard's | **Financial**	19
Beer Bar/Centro | **E 40s**	17
Z Blue Water Grill | **Union Sq**	23
Bogart's | **Murray Hill**	14
Branch | **E 50s**	17
Z Brandy Library | **TriBeCa**	25
Bryant Park Grill | **W 40s**	22
Bull and Bear | **E 40s**	21
Z Campbell Apt. | **E 40s**	25
Carnegie Club | **W 50s**	24
Cellar Bar | **W 40s**	22
Church Lounge | **TriBeCa**	24
Club Macanudo | **E 60s**	24
Country Champ. Lounge | **Murray Hill**	25
Croton Reservoir | **W 40s**	17
Del Posto | **Chelsea**	23
Full Shilling | **Financial**	18
Geisha | **E 60s**	22
Gilt | **E 50s**	21
Z Ginger Man | **Murray Hill**	22

Heartland Brew. | **multi.**	16
Houston's | **multi.**	20
John Street B&G | **Financial**	16
Keens Steak | **Garment**	21
K Lounge | **W 50s**	20
Lea | **E 40s**	19
Le Colonial | **E 50s**	21
Michael Jordan's | **E 40s**	20
MO Bar | **W 60s**	23
Moda Outdoors | **W 50s**	20
Nikki Midtown | **E 50s**	21
Nobu 57 | **W 50s**	25
⚡ Oak Bar | **W 50s**	24
Opia | **E 50s**	22
Patroon | **E 40s**	22
P.J. Clarke's | **E 50s**	20
Rink Bar | **W 50s**	24
Sequoia | **Seaport**	22
SouthWest NY | **Financial**	19
Stone Rose | **W 60s**	23
Sutton Place | **E 50s**	18
⚡ Tao | **E 50s**	24
Top of the Tower | **E 40s**	24
Townhouse | **E 50s**	22
⚡ 21 Club | **W 50s**	26
⚡ Ulysses | **Financial**	22
Vig 27 | **Murray Hill**	19
Whiskey Blue | **E 40s**	23
World Bar | **E 40s**	23
W Times Sq. | **W 40s**	23

SWANKY

NEW Above Allen | **LES**	22
Allen & Delancey | **LES**	25
⚡ Asia de Cuba | **Murray Hill**	24
Ava Lounge | **W 50s**	24
⚡ Balthazar | **SoHo**	25
Bar 44 | **W 40s**	21
NEW Beekman | **E 50s**	23
NEW Bijoux | **Meatpacking**	23
⚡ Bowery Hotel Bar | **E Vill**	23
⚡ Brandy Library | **TriBeCa**	25
Brasserie 8½ | **W 50s**	21
Bubble Lounge | **TriBeCa**	22
⚡ Buddakan | **Chelsea**	24
Buddha Bar | **Meatpacking**	24
Bungalow 8 | **Chelsea**	25
Butter | **E Vill**	22
⚡ Cafe Carlyle | **E 70s**	26
⚡ Cain Luxe | **Chelsea**	24
⚡ Campbell Apt. | **E 40s**	25
Carnegie Club | **W 50s**	24
Cellar Bar | **W 40s**	22
Champagne Bar/Plaza | **W 50s**	25

Church Lounge | **TriBeCa**	24
Cibar | **Gramercy**	22
Club Macanudo | **E 60s**	24
⚡ Daniel | **E 60s**	27
Del Posto | **Chelsea**	23
D'Or | **W 50s**	21
NEW Eldridge | **LES**	22
NEW Ella | **E Vill**	21
Empire Hotel Bar | **W 60s**	19
Feinstein's at Loews | **E 60s**	23
Flûte | **multi.**	22
⚡ Four Seasons Bar | **E 50s**	26
NEW Gates | **Chelsea**	-
Geisha | **E 60s**	22
Gilt | **E 50s**	21
⚡ GoldBar | **L Italy**	23
Grand Bar | **SoHo**	25
Guest House | **Chelsea**	19
Highbar | **W 40s**	21
HK Lounge | **Garment**	20
Home | **Chelsea**	21
Hudson Hotel | **W 50s**	24
Jade Bar | **Gramercy**	25
Japonais | **Gramercy**	22
⚡ King Cole Bar | **E 50s**	28
K Lounge | **W 50s**	20
Le Cirque Wine | **E 50s**	24
Le Colonial | **E 50s**	21
⚡**NEW** Lucky Strike Lanes | **W 40s**	21
⚡ Marquee | **Chelsea**	23
M Bar | **W 40s**	20
MO Bar | **W 60s**	23
⚡ Modern | **W 50s**	25
⚡ Monkey Bar | **E 50s**	-
Morimoto | **Chelsea**	25
⚡**NEW** M2 | **Chelsea**	20
Nikki Midtown | **E 50s**	21
Nobu 57 | **W 50s**	25
One | **Meatpacking**	22
⚡ 1 Oak | **Chelsea**	22
105 Riv | **LES**	22
Paramount | **W 40s**	23
Park Blue | **W 50s**	22
⚡ Pegu Club | **SoHo**	25
Pink Elephant | **Chelsea**	24
⚡ Plunge | **Meatpacking**	25
NEW Pranna | **Murray Hill**	-
⚡ Rainbow Grill | **W 40s**	24
NEW RDV | **Meatpacking**	22
Rm. Fifty5 | **W 50s**	21
Room Service | **Flatiron**	18
⚡ Rose Bar | **Gramercy**	23
Rose Club | **W 50s**	23
Salon de Ning | **W 50s**	26

NEW Shang Bar	**LES**	-
Z Spice Market	**Meatpacking**	24
Star Lounge	**Chelsea**	19
Stone Rose	**W 60s**	23
Suzie Wong	**Chelsea**	20
Thom Bar	**SoHo**	24
THOR Lobby Bar	**LES**	20
Z 230 Fifth	**Chelsea**	25
Ultra	**Chelsea**	18
World Bar	**E 40s**	23

THEME BARS

Aces & Eights	**E 80s**	15
Barcade	**W'burg**	24
Beauty Bar	**E Vill**	19
Big Easy	**E 90s**	13
Big Nose Kate's	**SI**	14
Black Bear	**Gramercy**	17
Bourbon St.	**W 70s**	15
Cowgirl	**W Vill**	18
ESPN Zone	**W 40s**	18
Flight 151	**Chelsea**	15
Gstaad	**Chelsea**	17
Hard Rock	**W 40s**	16
Hooters	**W 50s**	15
Jekyll & Hyde	**G Vill**	17
Johnny Utah's	**W 50s**	20
KGB	**E Vill**	21
K Lounge	**W 50s**	20
Otto's Shrunken	**E Vill**	21
Pine Tree Lodge	**Murray Hill**	24
Rodeo Bar	**Murray Hill**	20
Slaughtered Lamb	**G Vill**	17
Trailer Park	**Chelsea**	19
Wicked Monk	**Bay Ridge**	18
Wicked Willy's	**G Vill**	18
Zombie Hut	**Carroll Gdns**	21

TOUGH DOORS

Z Beatrice Inn	**W Vill**	21
NEW Bijoux	**Meatpacking**	23
Z Box	**LES**	25
Bungalow 8	**Chelsea**	25
Z Cain Luxe	**Chelsea**	24
NEW Chloe	**LES**	22
Cipriani Downtown	**SoHo**	24
NEW Eldridge	**LES**	22
NEW Gates	**Chelsea**	-
Z GoldBar	**L Italy**	23
NEW Griffin	**Meatpacking**	-
Kiss & Fly	**Meatpacking**	20
Z Marquee	**Chelsea**	23
NEW Mr. West	**Chelsea**	20
Z 1 Oak	**Chelsea**	22
Pink Elephant	**Chelsea**	24

NEW RDV	**Meatpacking**	22
Z Rose Bar	**Gramercy**	23
SubMercer	**SoHo**	24
Z Tenjune	**Meatpacking**	25

TRENDY

NEW Above Allen	**LES**	22
Z NEW Apothéke	**Chinatown**	23
Z Bacaro	**Chinatown**	21
NEW BEast	**LES**	21
Z Beatrice Inn	**W Vill**	21
Z NEW Bell House	**Gowanus**	22
NEW Bijoux	**Meatpacking**	23
Z Bobo	**W Vill**	22
Z Bowery Hotel Bar	**E Vill**	23
Z Box	**LES**	25
Z Buddakan	**Chelsea**	24
NEW Cabin Down Below	**E Vill**	-
Z Cain Luxe	**Chelsea**	24
NEW Chloe	**LES**	22
NEW Citrine	**Flatiron**	21
Z NEW City Winery	**SoHo**	23
Z NEW Clover Club	**Cobble Hill**	25
Z Commerce	**W Vill**	22
NEW Delicatessen	**SoHo**	19
NEW Dutch Kills	**LIC**	-
NEW Eldridge	**LES**	22
Elettaria	**G Vill**	24
Z NEW Empire Hotel Roof	**W 60s**	24
Z Employees Only	**W Vill**	24
Z Freemans	**LES**	26
NEW Gates	**Chelsea**	-
Z GoldBar	**L Italy**	23
NEW Greenhouse	**SoHo**	21
NEW Griffin	**Meatpacking**	-
Highbar	**W 40s**	21
Z Hotel Delmano	**W'burg**	24
NEW Imperial	**Flatiron**	18
Kiss & Fly	**Meatpacking**	20
Z La Esquina	**L Italy**	24
NEW La Fonda del Sol	**E 40s**	-
Z NEW Lucky Strike Lanes	**W 40s**	21
Z NEW Macao Trading	**TriBeCa**	25
Z NEW Madam Geneva	**NoHo**	25
Z Marquee	**Chelsea**	23
Z Monkey Bar	**E 50s**	-
Mr. Black	**Garment**	20
NEW Mr. West	**Chelsea**	20
Z 1 Oak	**Chelsea**	22
Z PDT	**E Vill**	27
Z Pegu Club	**SoHo**	25
Pink Elephant	**Chelsea**	24
Z NEW Raines Law Rm.	**Flatiron**	-
NEW RDV	**Meatpacking**	22

Ritz | **W 40s**	20
🔲 Rusty Knot | **W Vill**	21
🔲**NEW** Santos Party Hse. | **Chinatown**	21
🔲 Smith & Mills | **TriBeCa**	23
NEW Southside | **L Italy**	18
🔲 Spice Market | **Meatpacking**	24
Spotted Pig | **W Vill**	23
🔲 Stanton Social | **LES**	25
SubMercer | **SoHo**	24
🔲 Tenjune | **Meatpacking**	25
🔲 230 Fifth | **Chelsea**	25
NEW White Star | **LES**	20
NEW Wilfie & Nell | **W Vill**	24

VIEWS

NEW Above Allen | **LES**	22
Ava Lounge | **W 50s**	24
Bateaux NY | **Chelsea**	22
🔲 Boat Basin | **W 70s**	24
Bookmarks | **E 40s**	24
Brass Monkey | **Meatpacking**	19
Bryant Park Grill | **W 40s**	22
B61 | **Carroll Gdns**	24
Cabanas | **Chelsea**	22
Chelsea Brewing | **Chelsea**	18
Delancey | **LES**	20
🔲 Dizzy's Club | **W 60s**	25
🔲**NEW** Empire Hotel Roof | **W 60s**	24
Harbour Lights | **Seaport**	21
Heartland Brew. | **Seaport**	16
Heights B&G | **W 100s**	18
Highbar | **W 40s**	21
Hudson Hotel | **W 50s**	24
NEW Hudson Terrace | **W 40s**	23
NEW mad46 | **E 40s**	21
Metropolitan Mus. Roof | **E 80s**	26
P.J. Clarke's | **Financial**	20
🔲 Plunge | **Meatpacking**	25
🔲 Rainbow Grill | **W 40s**	24
Rare View | **Murray Hill**	22
NEW Ravel Rooftop | **LIC**	-
River Room | **Harlem**	21
Salon de Ning | **W 50s**	26
Sequoia | **Seaport**	22
Soho House | **Meatpacking**	24
SouthWest NY | **Financial**	19
Spirit Cruises | **Chelsea**	20
Stone Rose | **W 60s**	23
Sutton Place | **E 50s**	18
Top of the Tower | **E 40s**	24
🔲 230 Fifth | **Chelsea**	25
View Lounge | **W 40s**	24
🔲 Water Taxi Beach | **multi.**	22
World Yacht | **W 40s**	23

WIFI ACCESS

Alligator | **W'burg**	20
NEW Amsterdam 106 | **W 100s**	19
Arctica | **Murray Hill**	18
Arlo & Esme | **E Vill**	21
Aroma | **NoHo**	25
Barcelona Bar | **W 50s**	21
NEW Bleecker Heights | **W Vill**	-
Brass Monkey | **Meatpacking**	19
Brooklyn Ale | **W'burg**	18
🔲 Brother Jimmy's | **Murray Hill**	17
Bryant Park Grill | **W 40s**	22
Bua | **E Vill**	21
Bubble Lounge | **TriBeCa**	22
Cafe Bar | **Astoria**	22
Cake Shop | **LES**	20
Centro Vinoteca | **W Vill**	21
Cheap Shots | **E Vill**	19
Cherry Tree | **Park Slope**	16
Coliseum Bar | **W 50s**	11
Corio | **SoHo**	18
NEW Covo | **Harlem**	25
Crash Mansion | **LES**	15
Dive Bar | **W 90s**	18
Dive 75 | **W 70s**	21
NEW Donnybrook | **LES**	19
Downtown B&G | **Cobble Hill**	18
Epistrophy | **NoLita**	21
Firefly | **NoLita**	19
NEW Gibson | **W'burg**	-
Grace Hotel Bar | **W 40s**	18
Grand Café | **Astoria**	21
Greenwich Treehouse | **W Vill**	19
Harefield Rd. | **W'burg**	20
Heathers | **E Vill**	19
Highbar | **W 40s**	21
Huckleberry | **W'burg**	22
Hudson Bar & Books | **W Vill**	21
Hudson Hotel | **W 50s**	24
Kiss & Fly | **Meatpacking**	20
NEW Knave | **W 50s**	22
La Bottega | **Chelsea**	21
Lakeside Lounge | **E Vill**	19
Landmark Tav. | **W 40s**	21
Lava Gina | **E Vill**	23
Lederhosen | **W Vill**	21
Lion's Head Tavern | **W 100s**	15
Lolita | **LES**	19
Loreley | **LES**	21
miniBar | **Carroll Gdns**	20
Molly Pitcher's | **E 80s**	21
Night Hotel Bar | **W 40s**	18
Park | **Chelsea**	21
Perdition | **W 40s**	20

Pete's Candy | **W'burg** 23
Z Plunge | **Meatpacking** 25
NEW Ravel Rooftop | **LIC** -
R Bar | **NoLita** 21
Rebar | **Dumbo** 21
Rodeo Bar | **Murray Hill** 20
Room Service | **Flatiron** 18
Rosa Mexicano | **E 50s** 22
Royale | **E Vill** 20
Schiller's | **LES** 22
Serafina | **W 50s** 20
NEW SideBar | **Gramercy** 21
Sip | **W 100s** 18
NEW 675 Bar | **Meatpacking** -
Soho House | **Meatpacking** 24
Solex | **E Vill** 22
Stay | **E Vill** 19
St. Dymphna's | **E Vill** 20
Sweet & Vicious | **NoLita** 17

Swift | **NoHo** 22
Tap a Keg | **W 100s** 10
NEW t.b.d. | **Greenpt** -
Tea Lounge | **multi.** 20
Teddy's | **W'burg** 23
Underground | **Murray Hill** 18
Underground Lounge | **W 100s** 18
Valhalla | **W 50s** 18
V Bar | **G Vill** 26
Village Pourhouse | **E Vill** 18
NEW Vintage Irving | **Gramercy** 21
Water St. Bar | **Dumbo** 20
White Rabbit | **LES** 18
NEW White Star | **LES** 20
NEW Wilfie & Nell | **W Vill** 24
Woody McHale's | **W Vill** 16
Xicala | **L Italy** 23
Zablozki's | **W'burg** 22
Zebulon | **W'burg** 24

Wine Vintage Chart

This chart, based on our 0 to 30 scale, is designed to help you select wine. The ratings (by **Howard Stravitz,** a law professor at the University of South Carolina) reflect the vintage quality and the wine's readiness to drink. We exclude the 1991–1993 vintages because they are not that good. A dash indicates the wine is either past its peak or too young to rate. Loire ratings are for dry white wines.

Whites	89	90	94	95	96	97	98	99	00	01	02	03	04	05	06	07
French:																
Alsace	24	25	24	23	23	22	25	23	25	26	22	21	24	25	24	-
Burgundy	23	22	-	27	26	23	21	25	25	24	27	23	26	27	25	23
Loire Valley	-	-	-	-	-	-	-	-	24	25	26	22	23	27	24	-
Champagne	26	29	-	26	27	24	23	24	24	22	26	21	-	-	-	-
Sauternes	25	28	-	21	23	25	23	24	24	29	25	24	21	26	23	27
California:																
Chardonnay	-	-	-	-	-	-	-	24	23	26	26	25	26	29	25	-
Sauvignon Blanc	-	-	-	-	-	-	-	-	-	-	-	26	27	26	27	26
Austrian:																
Grüner Velt./ Riesling	-	-	-	25	21	26	26	25	22	23	25	26	26	25	24	-
German:	26	27	24	23	26	25	26	23	21	29	27	24	26	28	24	-

Reds	89	90	94	95	96	97	98	99	00	01	02	03	04	05	06	07
French:																
Bordeaux	25	29	21	26	25	23	25	24	29	26	24	26	24	28	25	23
Burgundy	24	26	-	26	27	25	22	27	22	24	27	25	24	27	25	-
Rhône	28	28	23	26	22	24	27	26	27	26	-	26	24	27	25	-
Beaujolais	-	-	-	-	-	-	-	-	-	-	22	24	21	27	25	23
California:																
Cab./Merlot	-	28	29	27	25	28	23	26	-	27	26	25	24	26	23	-
Pinot Noir	-	-	-	-	-	-	-	24	23	25	28	26	27	25	24	-
Zinfandel	-	-	-	-	-	-	-	-	-	25	23	27	22	23	23	-
Oregon:																
Pinot Noir	-	-	-	-	-	-	-	-	-	-	27	25	26	27	26	-
Italian:																
Tuscany	-	25	23	24	20	29	24	27	24	27	-	25	27	25	24	-
Piedmont	27	27	-	-	26	27	26	25	28	27	-	24	23	26	25	24
Spanish:																
Rioja	-	-	26	26	24	25	-	25	24	27	-	24	25	26	24	-
Ribera del Duero/Priorat	-	-	26	26	27	24	25	24	24	27	20	24	27	26	24	-
Australian:																
Shiraz/Cab.	-	-	24	26	23	26	28	24	24	27	27	25	26	26	24	-
Chilean:	-	-	-	-	-	24	-	25	23	26	24	25	24	26	25	24

Menus, photos, voting and more – free at ZAGAT.com